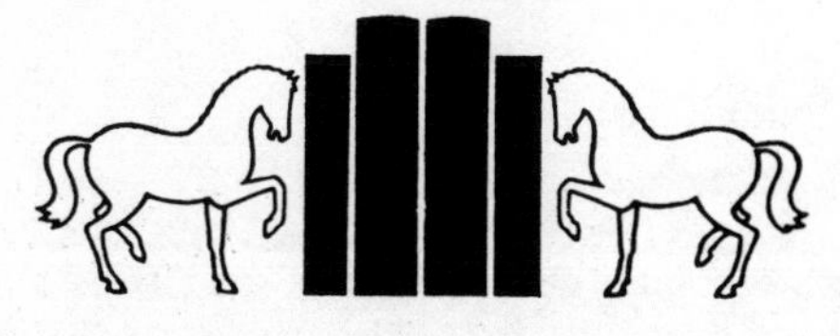

A BENN STUDY · LITERATURE

A Literary History of Ireland

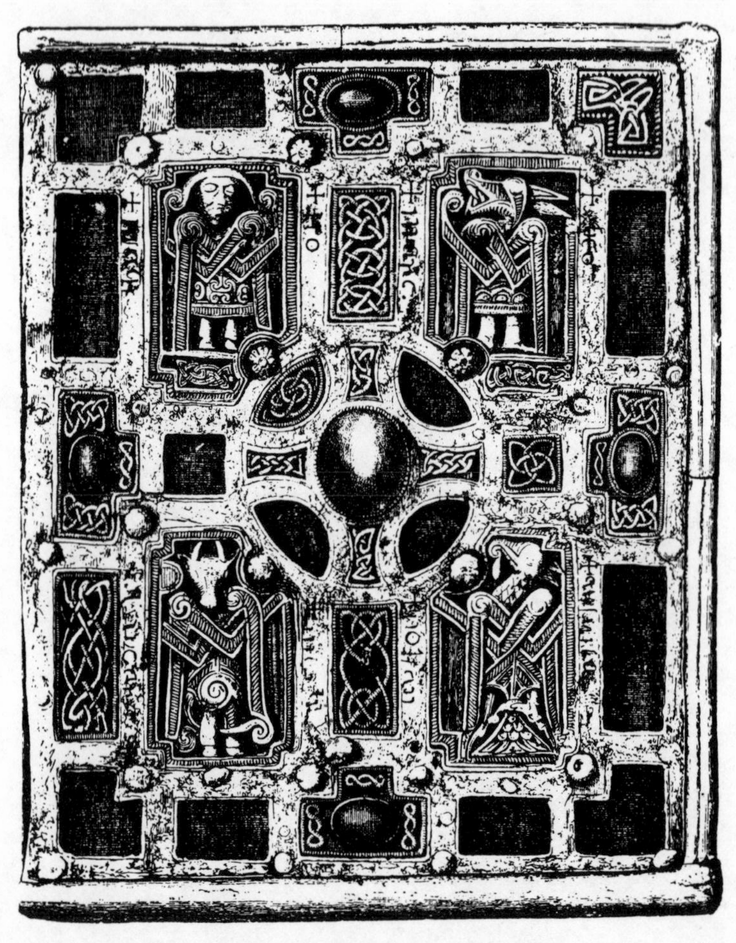

CASE OF MOLAISE'S GOSPELS

A LITERARY HISTORY OF IRELAND

FROM EARLIEST TIMES TO THE PRESENT DAY

BY DOUGLAS HYDE, LL.D., M.R.I.A.
(An Craoibhín Aoibhinn)

New Edition with Introduction by

BRIAN Ó CUÍV
Senior Professor, School of Celtic Studies
Dublin Institute for Advanced Studies

LONDON

ERNEST BENN LIMITED

First published by T. Fisher Unwin 1899

First edition in this form published 1967
by Ernest Benn Limited

25 New Street Square, Fleet Street, London, EC4A 3JA
and Sovereign Way, Tonbridge, Kent, TN9 1RW

Second impression 1980

Distributed in Canada by
The General Publishing Company Limited, Toronto

Reproduced from copy supplied
printed and bound in Great Britain
by Billing and Sons Limited
Guildford, London, Oxford, Worcester

British Library Cataloguing in Publication Data

Hyde, Douglas, *b.1860*
A literary history of Ireland.—New ed.
1. Irish literature—History and criticism
I. Title
891.6'2'09 PB1306

ISBN 0-510-31701-4

Dedication.

TO THE MEMBERS OF THE GAELIC LEAGUE,

THE ONLY BODY IN IRELAND WHICH APPEARS TO

REALISE THE FACT THAT IRELAND HAS A PAST, HAS A

HISTORY, HAS A LITERATURE, AND THE ONLY BODY IN

IRELAND WHICH SEEKS TO RENDER THE PRESENT A

RATIONAL CONTINUATION OF THE PAST,

I DEDICATE

THIS ATTEMPT AT A REVIEW OF THAT LITERATURE

WHICH DESPITE ITS PRESENT NEGLECTED POSITION

THEY FEEL AND KNOW TO BE A TRUE

POSSESSION OF NATIONAL

IMPORTANCE.

DO CHONNRADH NA GAEDHEILGE.

A Chonnradh chaoin, a Chonnradh chóir,
Rinn obair mhór gan ór gan cabhair,
Glacaidh an cíos a dlighim daoibh,
Guidhim, glacaidh go caoimh mo leabhar.

A cháirde cléibh is iomdha lá
D'oibrigheamar go breágh le chéile,
Gan clampar, agus fós gan éad,
'S dá mhéad ár dleas', gan puinn di-chéille.

Chuireabhar súil 'san bhfear bhi dall,
Thugabhar cluas don fhear bhi bodhar,
Glacaidh an cíos do bheirim daoibh,
—— Guidhim, glacaidh go caoimh mo leabhar.

INTRODUCTION

When the office of President of Ireland was created under the new Irish constitution in 1937 the suggestion was made in a leading article in *The Irish Times* that Douglas Hyde should be chosen to hold it for the first time. *The Irish Times* was never noted for its sympathy with Irish nationalist opinion, yet in this case it showed an appreciation of the connection between the political autonomy which had been achieved through the revolutionary movements of the preceding decades and the intellectual revolution which had been the forerunner of these. For there is no doubt that the founding of the Gaelic League in 1893 by Hyde and a handful of enthusiasts was one of the most important events in the history of modern Ireland. The League had come at a time when political activity was at a low ebb, in that period which Parnell's friend William O'Brien later described as 'years of hellish strife'. An era of intense political activity had come to an end with the Parnell split and the death of the 'Chief'. The subsequent squabbles among members of the Irish Parliamentary Party seemed degrading to many onlookers, and there was nation-wide despondency. It was at that time that the call went forth for action on the cultural front and the Gaelic League came into being. There were other national movements alongside it, some cultural, some economic, some industrial, but the League proved to be the most dynamic of them all, and from it derived much of the inspiration which filled the handful of men who marched out in Easter week of 1916 to challenge the might of an empire. Hyde was not one of these men, nor need we believe that his sympathies were with them. Yet there might well have been no '1916' but for him. This is in part the significance of his election as first President of Ireland. He had served the nation well in the past in developing in young Irish men and women an awareness of things of the spirit far removed from the material attitude to life which was so common about them. His election as President was not merely a recognition of the debt owed to him for that service. It also provided an opportunity for emphasising the continuity of national policy with regard to that language which Hyde held in such high esteem and for reaffirming that its restoration was a primary national aim. In this it was a fitting culmination of a life's work.

In order to appreciate fully the significance of this selection of Hyde as President of Ireland we must look back to the Ireland of the nineteenth century and see in what way he contributed to the development of the Ireland of our times. Gaelic Ireland, which to a large extent had held its own against English domination down to the end of the sixteenth century, was sadly reduced by the beginning of the nineteenth. The majority of the people, being Catholics, were held in subjection by a minority which had little concern for Ireland or its people but had an abject regard for the English 'connection' which had just recently been reinforced by the act of Union of Great Britain and

Ireland. Not only was the cultivation of Irish literature under the patronage of Irish-speaking rulers gone for good, but even the use of the Irish language had declined and this decline continued at a steadily-increasing rate throughout the century. The fact was that, as Hyde himself has shown in Chapter XLIV of his *Literary History,* the people of Ireland were themselves abandoning their native language and turning to English for a variety of reasons. This was something of which he himself became aware as a young boy when he observed in his native district the spiritless attitude of many of the people to their language and their disregard for the oral traditions which had survived along with it and which were part of a valuable cultural heritage. The fact that young Hyde appreciated this heritage or even understood the language with which it was associated might surprise us for, as son of a minister of the Church of Ireland, he might well have been expected to have learned in the course of his schooling that the Irish language and all that went with it were of little or no account.

As it happened, Douglas Hyde, son of the Reverend Arthur Hyde of Frenchpark, county Roscommon, and born on 17 January 1860, received little formal schooling. Most of his early education was acquired from his father who was apparently a good classical scholar, and he certainly does not seem to have shown any marked deficiencies in this respect in his subsequent academic career. He grew up keenly interested in outdoor pastimes, especially shooting and fishing, and thus he roamed the countryside about his home.

Irish had been the native language of the majority of the people of Roscommon down to about the middle of the nineteenth century, and even at the time when Hyde was born many of them, especially those around Frenchpark, still spoke it as their first language. According to the census returns for 1861, 5,735 persons in the barony of Frenchpark, representing 26 per cent of the population, spoke Irish and there were still some who spoke no English. The people of Roscommon were also preponderantly Catholic, less than one per cent of them being registered in 1861 as belonging to the Established Church. Thus the Hydes, as English-speaking Protestants of planter stock, were alien in more ways than one. Yet through his contact with the ordinary people around him young Douglas Hyde imbibed a love for the Irish language which proved to be the determining factor in his career, together with a sympathy with Catholic fellow-Irishmen which influenced him in his views on contemporary affairs and which was an immense asset in the work which he eventually set before himself. It was on the roads and in the fields and at cottage firesides in the west of Ireland that he heard for the first time the folk-tales, songs and prayers which caught his interest and prompted him to proceed further in the study of Ireland's native culture.

Hyde was only seventeen years old when the 'Society for the Preservation of the Irish Language' was founded, but he was soon an active member of it. He could speak, read and write Irish and before he was twenty he was contributing Irish verse compositions of his own to *The Irishman* and other periodicals. Between 1879 and 1884 over a hundred such items by him were published. As poetry they had not much merit, but they are interesting as revealing something of young

Hyde's views on the Ireland of his time. What seems to have been the first of them is a supposed lament by an Irishman who in his old age had been dispossessed of his property and had lost his wife and thirteen children. This was published under the pseudonym 'An Chraoibhín Aoibhinn' by which Hyde was to be so widely known in later years. The next item was a patriotic song beginning *Ólfamaid sláinte na tíré* in which Irish landlords were cursed for their treatment of their tenants. It ended:

Béidh cúitiughadh lá éigin go n-íocfaidh
An drong so a bh-fiacha go fóil,
'S béidh gach braon d'a bh-fuil ann a g-croidhthibh
Ro-bheag, as gach púnta d'á bh-feóil,

(There will be recompense yet one day when this crowd will pay their debts,
And every drop of blood in their hearts and every pound of their flesh will be insufficient).

Young Hyde made no secret of where his sympathies lay in national matters. In a poem composed a little later in honour of O'Donovan Rossa, the Fenian, he advised each of his fellow-countrymen to buy a rifle and a revolver, telling them that no bank would pay them so much interest as such an investment, for all that they might desire would come to them in a free Ireland, but that in order to attain a free Ireland they would have to abandon talk and return to 'the old fashion'.

It is not surprising, in view of these sentiments published by him when he was a young student in rooms in Trinity College, that Hyde regarded himself while there as an alien in a place where anti-Irish feeling prevailed. Yet not only did he pursue successfully his studies in German, French, Latin, English,

History and Celtic, gaining the B.A. in 1884 and the LL.D. in 1887, but he also won the Historical Society's Silver Medal for Oratory. His talents were considerable and his literary interests wide, but his great desire was to do something worthwhile to reinstate the Irish language. Indeed it might be said that, apart from a short period which he spent as Professor of Modern Languages in the University of New Brunswick in Canada in 1891, his life was devoted to this cause.

In the years before Hyde came to Dublin the writings on Irish literature and history by O'Donovan, O'Curry, O'Grady, Stokes and others had opened up new cultural vistas, thus adding to the inspiration which was drawn from the writers of the Young Ireland movement of the 'forties. In Dublin Hyde found himself associating with two groups. The first, represented by the 'Society for the Preservation of the Irish Language' and the 'Gaelic Union', was interested in the language, and Hyde not merely gave it his full support but also applied himself to the task of learning about the earlier literature. The second group consisted of litterateurs writing in English on Irish or 'Celtic' themes. It may have been through John O'Leary, the Fenian, who had settled in Ireland in 1885 and who was giving his support to various nationalist and Irish cultural movements of the time, that Hyde became so closely identified with the latter group. Certainly his connection with them was important to his future as a writer on Irish literary themes for it gave him valuable contacts, and it appears that through them he established connections with publishers such as David Nutt and T. Fisher Unwin which proved useful in the years ahead. Among this group of writers were Yeats, Rolleston and Katharine Tynan. Hyde gave his help willingly to others in their projects, and he was clearly held in high esteem by them. Thus in 1889 Yeats wrote of him: 'He is the best of all Irish folklorists and may do for us what Campbell did for Scotland'.[1]

Hyde had already shown an interest in earlier Irish tradition, for he had published a few traditional songs as far back as 1881. During the next seven or eight years he wrote down songs and prayers, stories and other items in many places in Connacht, and in 1889 came the first of many books in which this material was published. This was *Leabhar Sgeulaigheachta*,[2] a collection of short folk-tales which had been taken down from speakers in Roscommon, Leitrim, Galway and Donegal. What makes the book particularly interesting to us is that it contains a note 'On the reasons for keeping alive the Irish Language'. In this note Hyde repeated some views which he had already published elsewhere:

'Wherever Irish is the vernacular of the people there live enshrined in it memories and imaginations, deeds of daring, and tragic catastrophes, an heroic cycle of legend and poem, a vast and varied store of apothegms, sententious proverbs, and weighty sentences, which contain the very best and truest thoughts, not of the rude forefathers of the hamlet, but of the kings, sages, bards, and shanachies of bygone ages. Such a stream of collected thought as is everywhere found where the Irish language remains spoken must exercise an influence on those who come into contact with it, and such an influence must be an advantageous one . . . . I do not believe in resuscitating a great national language by twopenny-halfpenny bounties. If the Irish people are resolved to let the national language die, by all means let

[1] Alan Wade (ed.), *The Letters of W. B. Yeats*, London, 1954, p. 136.
[2] Dublin, 1889.

them. I believe the instinct of a nation is often juster than that of any individual. But this, at least, no one can deny, that hitherto the Irish nation has had no choice in the matter. What between the Anglo-Irish gentry, who came upon us in a flood after the confiscations of 1648, and again after 1691, whose great object it was to stamp out both the language and institutions of the nation, with their bards and shanachies, ollamhs and professors; what with the brutalized, sensual, unsympathetic gentry of the last century, the racing, blustering, drunken squireens, who usurped the places of the O'Connors, the O'Briens, the O'Donnells, the O'Cahans, the MacCarthys, our old and truly cultured nobility, who cherished hereditary poets and historians; what with the purblind, cringing pedagogues of the present century, whose habit it was to beat and threaten their pupils for talking Irish; what with the high-handed action of the authorities, who, with cool contempt of existing circumstances, continued to appoint English-speaking magistrates, petty-sessions clerks, and local officials among a people to whom they could not make themselves intelligible; what with the hostility of the Board of Education, who do not recognise the language of those baronies where no English is spoken, even to the extent of publishing school-books in it; what with this, and our long slavery as a nation, we assert that the Irish landguage (*sic*) has had no chance of showing its capabilities, or those who speak it of taking their own part, and making their voice heard.'[1]

In using such phrases as 'our living language' and 'our long slavery as a nation' Hyde had identified himself fully with Irish-speaking Ireland. He now reinforced his words with an appeal:

'I do not think there is much to add to what I have said here, except to observe that it is a national duty—I had almost said a moral one—for all those who speak Irish to speak it to their children also, and to take care that the growing generation shall know it as well as themselves: and in general, that it is the duty of all Irish-speakers to use their own language amongst themselves, and on all possible occasions, except where it *will not run*.

[1] pp. 215-18.

For, if we allow one of the finest and richest languages in Europe, which, fifty years ago, was spoken by nearly four millions of Irishmen, to die out without a struggle, it will be an everlasting disgrace and a blighting stigma upon our nationality.'[1]

In his next book, *Beside the Fire*,[2] which he published in 1890, Hyde was outspoken in his condemnation of 'the influential leaders of the race' from whom, he thought, a lead might have been expected:

'The inaction of the Parliamentarians, though perhaps dimly intelligible, appears, to me at least, both short-sighted and contradictory, for they are attempting to create a nationality with one hand and with the other destroying, or allowing to be destroyed, the very thing that would best differentiate and define that nationality. It is a making of bricks without straw. But the non-Parliamentarian Nationalists, in Ireland at least, appear to be thoroughly in harmony with them on this point.'[3]

It is clear from a further comment that in referring to 'non-Parliamentarian Nationalists' he had John O'Leary in mind. The fact that he was willing to criticise publicly a close friend shows how strongly he must have felt on the subject.

At this time Hyde's literary activity was considerable. In 1890 he began to publish in *The Nation* weekly articles on the songs of Connacht and these were continued later in *The Weekly Freeman*. From these there came in book form in 1893 the *Love Songs of Connacht* which brought home to many people for the first time what a literary treasure-store there was in Gaelic-speaking Ireland. In the meantime he had been in consultation with the publishing firm of Fisher Unwin which was contemplating issuing an 'Irish Saga Series'. Yeats referred to this in a letter in 1892 when he wrote:

[1] *ibid.*, p. 219 [2] London, 1890. [3] p. xlv *n.*

'It is to give standard translations by Hyde of the old Epic Tales and will consist of 8 or 9 volumes. Hyde is to send in a scheme for the first three or four in a couple of weeks. It will make the old stories accessible for the first time to everybody.'[1]

Here we see Hyde presented in the role of 'populariser' and there is little doubt that his writings did appeal to a wider public than they would have if they were more sophisticated or were invariably accompanied by the *apparatus criticus* of the professional scholar. Hyde could not have achieved what he did without a sound foundation of scholarship, but he did not parade his learning. In fact the 'Irish Saga Series' did not materialise although Fisher Unwin did publish in 1895 one volume of Hyde's containing the *Three Sorrows of Storytelling*. Perhaps the reason that Hyde abandoned the 'Sagas' was that he had undertaken to act as joint assistant, along with T. W. Rolleston, to Sir Charles Gavan Duffy who had been appointed to edit Fisher Unwin's series 'The New Irish Library'. Again it was Yeats who urged that Hyde should be brought into the scheme, and his judgment proved correct for Hyde produced for the new series *The Story of Early Gaelic Literature* which was published in 1895 and which was the forerunner of *A Literary History of Ireland*.

Through his association with writers such as Yeats, Rolleston and Sigerson, Hyde was drawn into various literary societies, and it was to one of these, 'The Irish National Literary Society', that he delivered in 1892 his now famous address on 'The necessity for de-Anglicising the Irish Nation', which contained a blistering attack on what he called 'west-Britonism'. Years later Hyde recalled that his appeal for de-

[2] Wade, op. cit, p. 201.

Anglicisation aroused no echo among his audience. Undaunted, he delivered another address in Cork in the same strain. Then came the fateful meeting on 31 July 1893, at which the Gaelic League was founded.

The history of the League and of Hyde's work for it in Ireland, Britain and America is well known. During the first fifteen years of its existence it pursued a policy of agitation which established it as a national force. It succeeded in focussing the attention of the Irish people on the fact that Irish was rapidly disappearing and it established the restoration of Irish as a prime national aim. But for many of its members it was more than a language movement. It was an active expression of Irish nationality. For this reason wider issues, social, economic and political, became inextricably associated with the language one, and in the long run it was these which became pre-eminent in the shaping of modern Ireland.

It was Eoin MacNeill who had taken the initiative which led to the founding of the Gaelic League, and it was he who did much of the work of organising in the early years. But it was Hyde who provided the inspiration. The fact that Hyde was a Protestant, an intellectual and a graduate of the University of Dublin gave the movement a standing which was invaluable. For more than twenty years he steered the League on a safe course, skilfully avoiding unnecessary contentious political matters while being uncompromising about those things which, according to his evaluation, were fundamental to the organisation. Thus when a 'Royal Commission on Intermediate Education' was set up as a result of the League's struggle with the Intermediate Board Hyde proved to be a tower of strength, and it is greatly to his credit that when the battle over Irish brought the League into conflict with the authorities of Trinity College, he did not stand aside. Instead, although he regretted the necessity for doing so, he gave Mahaffy and Atkinson and their colleagues more than they bargained for, and in doing so he established the claims of Irish scholarship and research to recognition in Ireland. Similarly when the proposal that Irish be made a required subject for matriculation in the newly-founded National University of Ireland brought the League into conflict with the Catholic Hierarchy and the leaders of the Irish Parliamentary Party Hyde stood his ground and the day was won for Irish.

In the long run it was on a political issue that Hyde retired from the leadership of the Gaelic League. From the outset he had endeavoured to keep any difference over religion or politics from entering into its organisation. He had even turned down an invitation from the Irish Parliamentary Party to stand in a 'safe' constituency for election to the British Parliament on the grounds that it would not be in the interests of the language movement for him to accept. However, in the national situation which developed after the founding of the Ulster Volunteers in 1913, some members of the League felt that it should make clear its position with regard to Irish political aspirations. Matters came to a head at the annual conference in 1915 when the League adopted a resolution which altered Rule 2 of its constitution to read:

> 'Connradh na Gaedhilge shall be strictly non-political and non-sectarian, and shall devote itself to realising the ideal of a free Gaelic-speaking Ireland.'

Hyde was convinced that a great disservice had been done to the League and he retired from its Presidency. Although his affection for the League and its individual members remained, the long association had ended.

Hyde had been appointed Professor of Modern Irish in University College, Dublin, in 1909 and after the break with the League he devoted himself particularly to his academic and literary work. His pioneering days were over, however, and it is for what he achieved before 1916 that he will be best remembered. After Saorstát Éireann was established he served for a short term in the Senate, but he was not re-elected. In 1938 he was nominated to a new Senate set up under the 1937 constitution and it was shortly after this that he was chosen as President of Ireland.

As far back as 1912 Patrick Pearse had described the Gaelic League as a spent force and he had called for a new national movement. He was not quite right in his judgment. What had happened was that he and others associated with him had adopted new priorities in their plans for Ireland. Their vision was justified by the events of the following years, but the aim which brought so many of them into public life still remains unfulfilled. Perhaps for this reason more than any other it was fitting that the first President of the Gaelic League should be unanimously elected first President of Ireland.

It would be impossible in a short introduction such as this to evaluate fully Hyde's literary work. Moreover, such an evaluation could be made only after an adequate consideration of all the circumstances in which the work was produced. However, some general observations may well be made to complete this brief account of Hyde and his work and to explain to some extent why a work first published in 1899 is now being re-issued.

In many ways Hyde as a literary man was among the pioneers. In 1882, when there was still among writers a strong bias towards imitating the literary Irish of earlier centuries, he advocated the use of the forms of the living language for literary purposes. His own Irish lacked the richness of idiom which characterised the language of the best speakers in the 'Gaeltacht' areas, but he was consistent in using it. Then again, Hyde started playwriting on its first faltering footsteps with such simple plays as *Casadh an tSugáin* and *An Tincéar agus an tSidheóg*.

However, it was in bringing Irish oral and literary tradition to the notice of a wide public that his achievement was greatest. Bibliographies of his published work show its extent and variety. It is not surprising that in the light of modern scholarship his editions of poetry and prose will not all stand the test of time textually. But, in fact, nobody has given us volumes to replace his *Love Songs of Connacht* or his editions of the poems of Raftery, and his *Religious Songs of Connacht* must still give pleasure to anyone fortunate enough to have a copy of the work. The same can also be said of *A Literary History of Ireland*.

This is a work which was designed to take its place beside similar works for India, America, Persia, Scotland, France, Russia, Rome and the Arabs. But what a difference there was between Hyde's task and that of other writers who could base their work on a wide printed literature. Here, because of our circumstances, the professional cultivation of literature in

Irish had all but come to an end in the seventeenth century and the study of the earlier literature was in its infancy when Hyde was born. In the previous generation O'Curry and O'Donovan had laid the foundations on which so much would be built, but it was only in Hyde's lifetime that any considerable advance had been made in the publication and study of the vast store of manuscript literature. And the proper organisation of the study at university level of Irish language and literature was something which still lay in the future. Indeed it may be said that it was with the establishment of the School of Irish Learning in Dublin in 1903 that the scientific training of Celtic scholars in Ireland began. So it is that when we look at Hyde's book we see the names of great continental scholars, such as Arbois de Jubainville, Zimmer, Windisch and Meyer, more frequently than those of Irishmen.

We need only look at the *Bibliography of Irish Philology and of Printed Irish Literature* compiled by R. I. Best to see how few were the works on Irish literature which might have served Hyde as a guide or have been a help to him in providing information or illustrative material. Outstanding among these were O'Curry's *Lectures on the Manuscript Materials of Ancient Irish History* (1861), another work which has not been superseded in the century since it was published, and his *On the Manners and Customs of the Ancient Irish* (1873). In addition we see O'Reilly's chronological list of Irish writers (1820), Arbois de Jubainville's *Introduction à l'étude de la littérature celtique* (1883), his *Essai d'un catalogue de la littérature épique de l'Irlande* (1883), his *Le cycle mythologique irlandais et la mythologie celtique* (1884), and his *L'épopée celtique en Irlande* (1892). There were, of course, other works, and especially articles of value which had been published in periodicals.

The labours of Stokes, O'Grady, Meyer, Windisch and others in the previous thirty years had added considerably to the amount of primary source material from manuscripts which was available in printed form, but there were important branches, especially of the later literature, which had been almost totally ignored. Moreover, because of the lack of printed catalogues of important collections of Irish manuscripts it was difficult to assess the extent, nature and value of unpublished material. It was in such circumstances that Hyde undertook the ambitious task of writing a literary history of Ireland 'from earliest times to the present day'.

We do not know what guide-lines, if any, the publishers gave him or what they expected of him. But we can see from even a superficial glance at the *Literary History* how wide is its scope. For Hyde's sense of the close relationship between the language and literature of a country on the one hand and the history of its people on the other impelled him to interweave them both throughout his work. In his earlier work *The Story of Early Gaelic Literature* he had not come beyond the period of the Vikings. Now he not only expanded his account of the earlier literature, adding greatly to his discussion and illustration of various branches, but he also continued the work to deal in Chapters XXXIII—XLIII with the late medieval and modern literature, finishing off with an account of Irish as a spoken language, which gave him an opportunity of reiterating his views on the attitude to Irish among those who had the power to affect the destinies of the nation.

It may be said that if the plan of Hyde's book is both original and ambitious, at least the basis for much of what it contains is to be found in the publications of other scholars. While that is true it must be pointed out, firstly, that the labour involved in collecting and co-ordinating such a mass of material must have been considerable and secondly, that a surprising amount of further matter in the book, ranging from *Táin Bó Cuailnge* to nineteenth-century poetry, is the result of Hyde's own reading of manuscripts. In this connection it is interesting to see him referring in specific terms to texts in manuscripts which are either still unpublished or which have been published only in quite recent years.

Few works are without blemish and Hyde's *Literary History* is no exception. Even his contemporaries could have found many linguistic mistakes in it, for Hyde was no expert philologist. There are obvious omissions and inconsistencies which could have been avoided. Thus Hyde overlooked the manuscript in the Bodleian Library in Oxford known as Rawlinson B 502 when he wrote 'The two oldest miscellaneous Irish MSS. which we have, are the Leabhar na h-Uidhre and the Book of Leinster' (p. 380). Two dates—985 (p. 380) and 975 (p. 429)—are given for the death of Cinaeth O Hartagain, and there is a similar slip in relation to Cormac mac Culenain. There are also, of course, many statements which could be corrected to-day in the light of more recent research. Some of Hyde's views may be rejected or at least questioned, for instance his conclusions on the reliability of historical and genealogical tradition for the early period including the pre-Christian centuries, and also his apparent acceptance of the supposed early date of certain Irish texts. However, neither the linguistic errors nor the various inconsistencies and mistakes nor the questionable views on historical and literary matters affect by and large the overall picture put before us by a scholar who was interested in people and in the more human aspects of the study of literature.

In the sixty years and more since the *Literary History* was published there has been a great deal of research on Irish. Scholars have tended to concentrate their energies on making available unpublished material, and in certain fields, such as early modern Irish poetry and prose, recent publications have added very much to our knowledge and understanding of Irish literary tradition. New material, such as the courtly love poetry of the period from the fourteenth century to the seventeenth, has come to light to show that our literature is even richer than Hyde thought. There has been considerable discussion of literature, but much of it has been restricted in scope, such as Thurneysen's great work on the heroic literature *Die irische Helden- und Königsage* (1921). The result is that very few works have been produced to find a place beside Hyde's as histories of Irish literature down to modern times. The books of Eleanor Hull, Aodh de Blacam and Caerwyn Williams listed in the bibliography are exceptions. Each has its merits but none of them has superseded the pioneer work which is now being made available once more.

Dublin, 1966 Brian Ó Cuív

NOTE TO 1980 EDITION

Since I wrote the introduction for the 1967 reprint a collection of diaries kept by Douglas Hyde in his early years has been made the basis of a book entitled *The Young Douglas Hyde.* I have included this in a revised bibliographical section in which I have also listed some other works relating to Hyde and his times.

Dublin, 1979 Brian Ó Cuív

BIBLIOGRAPHICAL

I

Some important works by Douglas Hyde

a) Literature and Folklore

Leabhar Sgeulaigheachta, Baile-ath-cliath, 1889.

Beside the Fire: A collection of Irish Gaelic Folk Stories, London, 1890.

[Another edition: (Dublin, 1892); reprint of first edition: Dublin, 1978]

Abhráin Grádh Chúige Connacht, or Love Songs of Connacht, London, Dublin, 1893.

[Other editions: Dundrum, 1904, Baile Átha Cliath, 1931; reprint edition, with an introduction by Mícheál Ó hAodha, Shannon, 1969]

The Last Three Centuries of Gaelic Literature, London, 1894.

The Story of Early Gaelic Literature, London, Dublin, New York, 1895.

The Three Sorrows of Story-telling and Ballads of St. Columkille, London, 1895.

An Sgeuluidhe Gaodhalach, I-III, Rennes, 1895-1901.
[Other editions: Lundún, Bail-Áth-Cliath, 1901, (Baile Átha Cliath), 1933]

Giolla an Fhiugha or, The Lad of the Ferule. Eachtra Cloinne Rígh na h-Ioruaidhe or, Adventures of the Children of the King of Norway (Irish Texts Society Vol. 1), London, 1899.

Filidheacht Ghaedhealach: Irish Poetry (MacTernan Prize Essays—II), Dublin, 1902.

Abhráin atá leagtha ar an Reachtúire, or Songs ascribed to Raftery, Dublin, 1903.
[Another edition: Baile Átha Cliath, 1933; reprint edition, with an introduction by Dominic Daly, Shannon, 1973]

Abhráin Diadha Chuige Connacht, or The Religious Songs of Connacht, I-II, London, Dublin, 1906.
[Reprint edition, with an introduction by Dominic Daly, Shannon, 1972]

Sgéaluidhe Fíor na Seachtmhaine, (Dublin), 1909.
[Another edition: Baile Átha Cliath, 1935]

Legends of Saints & Sinners, Dublin, (1914).
[A selection made from this work by Gerard O'Flaherty has been published under the title *The Stone of Truth and other Irish Folktales,* Dublin, 1979.]

Gabháltais Shearlais Mhóir: The Conquests of Charlemagne (Irish Texts Society Vol. 19), London, 1917.

Ocht Sgéalta ó Choillte Mághach, Baile Átha Cliath, 1936.

Sgéalta Thomáis Uí Chathasaigh (Irish Texts Society Vol. 36), Dublin, 1939.

b) Autobiographical

Mise agus an Connradh (go dtí 1905), Baile Átha Cliath, 1937.

Mo Thurus go h-Americe, Baile Átha Cliath, 1937.

II

Some works on Hyde and his times

Coffey, Diarmid, *Douglas Hyde: President of Ireland,* Dublin & Cork, 1938.

Daly, Dominic, *The Young Douglas Hyde,* Dublin, 1974.

Martin, F. X. (ed.), *Leaders and Men of the Easter Rising: Dublin, 1916,* London, Ithaca, N.Y., 1967.

Ní Mhuiríosa, Máirín, *Réamhchonraitheoirí,* Baile Atha Cliath, 1963.

Nowlan, Kevin B. (ed.), *The Making of 1916: Studies in the History of the Rising,* Dublin, 1969.

O'Brien, Conor Cruise (ed.), *The Shaping of Modern Ireland,* London, 1960.

Ó Tuama, Seán (ed.), *The Gaelic League Idea,* Cork and Dublin, 1972.

III

General

Readers will find comprehensive information on publications down to 1941 in *Bibliography of Irish Philology and of Printed Irish Literature* (Dublin, 1913) and *Bibliography of Irish Philology and Manuscript Literature: Publications 1913-1941* (Dublin, 1942), both compiled by R. I. Best. Works published in the thirty years after 1941 are dealt with in *Bibliography of Irish Linguistics and Literature, 1942-71,* compiled by Rolf Baumgarten, which is due to be published in 1980 by the Dublin Institute for Advanced Studies. For the convenience of readers a small selection of works is listed here, many of them being fairly recent publications. With the exception of Professor C. O'Rahilly's works on 'Táin Bó Cuailnge', editions of texts have not been included.

Bergin, Osborn, *Irish Bardic Poetry*, Dublin, 1970.

Binchy, D. A., *The Linguistic and Historical Value of the Irish Law Tracts* (British Academy Sir John Rhŷs Memorial Lecture), London, [1945].

(ed.) *Studies in Early Irish Law*, Dublin, 1936.

Brufurd, Alan, *Gaelic Folktales and Medieval Romances*, Dublin, 1969.

Carney, James, *Studies in Irish Literature and History*, Dublin, 1955 (reprinted with additions, Dublin, 1979).

The Irish Bardic Poet, Dublin, 1967.

(ed.) *Early Irish Poetry*, Cork, 1965.

Corkery, Daniel, *The Hidden Ireland*, Dublin, 1925.

The Fortunes of the Irish Language, Dublin, 1954.

de Blácam, Aodh, *Gaelic Literature Surveyed*, Dublin and Cork, 1933.

de Fréine, Seán, *The Great Silence*, Dublin, 1965.

de Paor, Liam, *Great Books of Ireland*, Dublin, 1967.

Delargy, J. H., *The Gaelic Story-teller* (British Academy Sir John Rhŷs Memorial Lecture), London, [1947].

Dillon, Myles, *The Cycles of the Kings*, London, New York, 1946.

Early Irish Literature, Chicago, 1948.

The Archaism of Irish Tradition (British Academy Sir John Rhŷs Memorial Lecture), London, [1948].

Celts and Aryans, Simla, 1975.

(transl.) *Gods and Heroes of the Celts* (from French of M. L. Sjoestedt), London, 1949.

(ed.) *Early Irish Society*, Dublin, 1954.

(ed.) *Irish Sagas*, Dublin, 1959.

Dillon, Myles, and Chadwick, Nora K., *The Celtic Realms*, London, 1967 (revised edition, London, 1972).

Flower, Robin, *The Irish Tradition*, Oxford, 1947.

Greene, David, *The Irish Language*, Dublin, 1966.

Henry, P. L., *Saoithiúlacht na Sean-Ghaeilge*, Baile Átha Cliath, 1978.

Hughes, Kathleen, *Early Christian Ireland: introduction to the sources,* London, 1972.

Hull, Eleanor, *A Text Book of Irish Literature,* I-II, Dublin, 1906-1908.

Jackson, Kenneth H., *Studies in Early Celtic Nature Poetry,* Cambridge, 1935.

The Oldest Irish Tradition: a Window on the Iron Age, Cambridge, 1964.

Kenney, J. F., *The Sources for the Early History of Ireland: Ecclesiastical,* New York, 1929 (reprinted with additions by Ludwig Bieler, New York, 1966).

Knott, Eleanor, *Irish Classical Poetry,* Dublin, 1960.

Mac Neill, Eoin, *Early Irish Laws and Institutions,* Dublin, n.d.

McNally, Robert (ed.), *Old Ireland,* Dublin, 1965.

McNamara, Martin, *The Apocrypha in the Irish Church,* Dublin, 1975.

Mercier, Vivian, *The Irish Comic Tradition,* Oxford, 1962.

Murphy, Gerard, *Duanaire Finn,* Part III (Irish Texts Society Vol. 53), Dublin, 1953.

Saga and Myth in Ancient Ireland, Dublin, 1955 (revised edition, Cork, 1971).

The Ossianic Lore and Romantic Tales of Medieval Ireland, Dublin, 1955 (revised edition, Cork, 1971).

Nicholls, Kenneth, *Gaelic and Gaelicised Ireland in the Middle Ages,* Dublin and London, 1972.

Ó Buachalla, Breandán, *I mBéal Feirste Cois Cuain,* Baile Átha Cliath, 1968.

Ó Cathasaigh, Tomás, *The Heroic Biography of Cormac mac Airt,* Dublin, 1977.

O'Connor, Frank, *The Backward Look: A Survey of Irish Literature,* London, 1967.

Ó Cuív, Brian, *Irish Dialects and Irish-speaking Districts,* Dublin, 1951.

Literary Creation and Irish Historical Tradition (British Academy Sir John Rhŷs Memorial Lecture), London, [1964].

The Linguistic Training of the Mediaeval Irish

Poet, Dublin, 1973.

The Irish Bardic Duanaire or 'Poem-Book', Dublin, (1974).

(ed.) *Seven Centuries of Irish Learning, 1000-1700,* Dublin, 1961.

(ed.) *A View of the Irish Language,* Dublin, 1969.

O'Rahilly, Cecile, *The Stowe Version of Táin Bó Cuailnge,* Dublin, 1961.

Táin Bó Cúalnge from the Book of Leinster, Dublin, 1967.

Táin Bó Cúailnge: Recension I, Dublin, 1976.

O'Rahilly, Thomas F., *Irish Dialects Past and Present,* Dublin, 1932 (reprinted with additions by Brian Ó Cuív, Dublin, 1972).

Early Irish History and Mythology, Dublin, 1946.

Ó Tuama, Seán, *An Grá in Amhráin na nDaoine,* Baile Atha Cliath, 1960.

Filí faoi Sceimhle: Seán Ó Ríordáin agus Aogán Ó Rathaille, Baile Átha Cliath, 1978.

Rees, Alwyn, and Rees, Brinley, *Celtic Heritage,* London, 1961.

Ryan, Desmond, *The Sword of Light,* London, 1939.

Walsh, Paul, *Irish Men of Learning,* Dublin, 1947.

Williams, J. E. Caerwyn, *Traddodiad Llenyddol Iwerddon,* Cardiff, 1958.

The Court Poet in Medieval Ireland (British Academy Sir John Rhŷs Memorial Lecture), London, [1972].

PREFACE

THE present volume has been styled—in order to make it a companion book to other of Mr. Unwin's publications—a "Literary History of Ireland," but a "Literary History of Irish Ireland" would be a more correct title, for I have abstained altogether from any analysis or even mention of the works of Anglicised Irishmen of the last two centuries. Their books, as those of Farquhar, of Swift, of Goldsmith, of Burke, find, and have always found, their true and natural place in every history of *English* literature that has been written, whether by Englishmen themselves or by foreigners.

My object in this volume has been to give a general view of the literature produced by the Irish-speaking Irish, and to reproduce by copious examples some of its more salient, or at least more characteristic features.

In studying the literature itself, both that of the past and that of the present, one of the things which has most forcibly struck me is the marked absence of the purely personal note, the absence of great predominating names, or of great predominating works; while just as striking is the almost universal diffusion of a traditional literary taste and a love of literature in the abstract amongst all classes of the native Irish. The whole history of Irish literature shows how warmly the efforts of all who assisted in its production were appreciated.

The greatest English bard of the Elizabethan age was allowed by his countrymen to perish of poverty in the streets of London, while the pettiest chief of the meanest clan would have been proud to lay his hearth and home and a share of his wealth at the disposal of any Irish "ollamh." The love for literature of a traditional type, in song, in poem, in saga, was, I think, more nearly universal in Ireland than in any country of western Europe, and hence that which appears to me to be of most value in ancient Irish literature is not that whose authorship is known, but rather the mass of traditional matter which seems to have grown up almost spontaneously, and slowly shaped itself into the literary possession of an entire nation. An almost universal acquaintance with a traditional literature was a leading trait amongst the Irish down to the last century, when every barony and almost every townland still possessed its poet and reciter, and song, recitation, music, and oratory were the recognised amusements of nearly the whole population. That population in consequence, so far as wit and readiness of language and power of expression went, had almost all attained a remarkably high level, without however producing any one of a commanding eminence. In collecting the floating literature of the present day also, the unknown traditional poems and the Ossianic ballads and the stories of unknown authorship are of greater value than the pieces of bards who are known and named. In both cases, that of the ancient and that of the modern Irish, all that is of most value as literature, was the property and in some sense the product of the people at large, and it exercised upon them a most striking and potent influence. And this influence may be traced amongst the Irish-speaking population even at the present day, who have, I may almost say, one and all, a remarkable command of language and a large store of traditional literature learned by heart, which strongly differentiates them from the Anglicised products of the "National Schools" to the bulk of whom poetry is an unknown term, and amongst whom there exists little or no trace of traditional Irish feelings, or indeed seldom of any feelings save those prompted by (when they read it) a weekly newspaper.

The exact extent of the Irish literature still remaining in manuscript has never been adequately determined. M. d'Arbois de Jubainville has noted 133 still existing manuscripts, all copied before the year 1600, and the whole number which he has found existing chiefly in public libraries on the Continent and in the British Isles amounts to 1,009. But many others have since been discovered, and great numbers must be scattered throughout the country in private libraries, and numbers more are perishing or have recently perished of neglect since the "National Schools" were established. Jubainville quotes a German as estimating that the literature produced by the Irish before the seventeenth century, and still existing, would fill a thousand octavo volumes. It is hard to say, however, how much of this could be called literature in a true sense of the word, since law, medicine, and science were probably included in the calculation. O'Curry, O'Longan, and O'Beirne Crowe catalogued something more than half the manuscripts in the Royal Irish Academy, and the catalogue of contents filled thirteen volumes containing 3,448 pages. To these an alphabetic index of the pieces contained was made in three volumes, and an index of the principal names, etc., in thirteen volumes more. From a rough calculation, based on an examination of these, I should place the number of different pieces catalogued by them at about ten thousand, ranging from single quatrains or even single sentences to long poems and epic sagas. But in the Academy alone, there are nearly as many more manuscripts which still remain uncatalogued.

It is probably owing to the extreme difficulty of arriving at any certain conclusions as to the real extent of Irish literature that no attempt at a consecutive history of it has ever previously been made. Despite this difficulty, there is no doubt that such a work would long ago have been attempted had it not been for the complete breakdown and destruction of Irish Ireland which followed the Great Famine, and the unexpected turn given to Anglo-Irish literature by the efforts of the Young Ireland School to compete with the English in their own style, their own language, and their own models.

For the many sins of omission and commission in this volume I must claim the reader's kind indulgence ; nobody can be better aware of its shortcomings than I myself, and the only excuse that I can plead is that over so much of the ground I have had to be my own pioneer. I confidently hope, however, that in the renewed interest now being taken in our native civilisation and native literature some scholar far more fully equipped for his task than I, may soon render this volume superfluous by an ampler, juster, and more artistic treatment of what is really a subject of great national importance.

National or important, however, it does not appear to be considered in these islands, where outside of the University of Oxford—which has given noble assistance to the cause of Celtic studies—sympathisers are both few and far between. Indeed, I fancy that anybody who has applied himself to the subject of Celtic literature would have a good deal to tell about the condescending contempt with which his studies have been regarded by his fellows. "I shall not easily forget," said Dr Petrie, addressing a meeting of the Royal Irish Academy upon that celebrated example of early Celtic workmanship the Tara Brooch, "that when in reference to the existence of a similar remain of ancient Irish art, I had first the honour to address myself to a meeting of this high institution, I had to encounter the incredulous astonishment of the illustrious Dr. Brinkley" [of Trinity College, President of the Academy] "which was implied in the following remark, 'Surely, sir, you do not mean to tell us that there exists the slightest evidence to prove that the Irish had any acquaintance with the arts of civilised life anterior to the arrival in Ireland of the English?' nor shall I forget that in the scepticism which this remark implied nearly all the members present very obviously participated." Exactly the same feeling which Dr. Petrie encountered was prevalent in my own *alma mater* in the eighties, where one of our most justly popular lecturers said—in gross ignorance but perfect good faith—that the sooner the Irish recognised that before the arrival of Cromwell they were utter savages, the better it would be for everybody concerned! Indeed, it was only the other day that one of our ablest and best known professors protested publicly in the *Contemporary Review* against the enormity of an Irish bishop signing so moderate, and I am sure so reasonable a document, as a petition asking to have Irish children who knew no English, taught through the medium of the language which they spoke. Last year, too, another most learned professor of Dublin University went out of his way to declare that "the mass of material preserved [in the Irish manuscripts] is out of all proportion to its value as 'literature,'" and to insist that "in the enormous mass of Irish MSS. preserved, there is absolutely nothing that in the faintest degree rivals the splendours of the vernacular literatures of the Middle Ages," that "their value as literature is but small," and that "for educational purposes save in this limited sense [of linguistic study] they are wholly unsuited," winding up with the extraordinary assertion that "there is no solid ground for supposing that the tales current at the time of our earliest MSS. were much more numerous than the tales of which fragments have come down to us." As to the civilisation of the early Irish upon which Petrie insisted, there is no longer room for the very shadow of a doubt; but whether the literature which they produced is so utterly valueless as this, and so utterly devoid of all interest as "literature," the reader of this volume must judge for himself. I should be glad also if he were to institute a comparison between "the splendours of the vernacular literatures" of Germany, England, Spain, and even Italy and France, prior to the year 1000, and that of the Irish, for I am very much mistaken if in their early development of rhyme, alone, in their masterly treatment of sound, and in their absolutely unique and marvellous system of verse-forms, the Irish will not be found to have created for themselves a place alone and apart in the history of European literatures.

I hardly know a sharper contrast in the history of human thought than the true traditional literary instinct which four years ago prompted fifty thousand poor hard-working Irishmen in the United States to contribute each a dollar towards the foundation of a Celtic chair in the Catholic University of Washington in the land of their adoption, choosing out a fit man and sending him to study under the great Celticists of Germany, in the hope that his scholarship might one day reflect credit upon the far-off country of their birth ; while in that very country, by far the richest college in the British Isles, one of the wealthiest universities in the world, allows its so-called "Irish professorship" to be an adjunct of its Divinity School, founded *and paid* by a society for—the conversion of Irish Roman Catholics through the medium of their own language !

This is the more to be regretted because had the unique manuscript treasures now shut up in cases in the underground room of Trinity College Library, been deposited in any other seat of learning in Europe, in Paris, Rome, Vienna, or Berlin, there would long ago have been trained up scholars to read them, a catalogue of them would have been published, and funds would have been found to edit them. At present the Celticists of Europe are placed under the great disadvantage of having to come over to Dublin University to do the work that it is not doing for itself.

It is fortunate however that the spread of education within the last few years (due perhaps partly to the establishment of the Royal University, partly to the effects of Intermediate Education, and partly to the numerous literary societies which working upon more or less national lines have spontaneously sprung up amongst the Irish people themselves) has, by taking the prestige of literary monopoly out of the hands of Dublin University, to a great extent undone the damage which had so long been caused to native scholarship by its attitude. It was the more necessary to do this, because the very fact that it had never taken the trouble to publish even a printed catalogue of its Irish manuscripts—as the British Museum authorities have done—was by many people interpreted, I believe, as a sort of declaration of their worthlessness.

In dealing with Irish proper names I have experienced the same difficulty as every one else who undertakes to treat of Irish history. Some native names, especially those with "mortified" or aspirated letters, look so unpronounceable as to prove highly disconcerting to an English reader. The system I have followed is to leave the Irish orthography untouched, but in cases where the true pronunciation differed appreciably from the sound which an English reader would give the letters, I have added a phonetic rendering of the Irish form in brackets, as "Muighmheadhon [Mwee-va-on], Lughaidh [Lewy]." There are a few names such as Ossian, Mève, Donough, Murrough and others, which have been almost adopted into English, and these forms I have generally retained —perhaps wrongly—but my desire has been to throw no unnecessary impediments in the way of an English reader ; I have always given the true Irish form at least once. Where the word "mac" is not part of a proper name, but really means "son of" as in Finn mac Cúmhail, I have printed it with a small "m" ; and in such names as "Cormac mac Art" I have usually not inflected the last word, but have written "Art" not "Airt," so as to avoid as far as possible confusing the English reader.

I very much regret that I have found it impossible, owing to the brief space of time between printing and publication, to submit the following chapters to any of my friends for their advice and criticism. I beg, however, to here express my best thanks to my friend Father Edmund Hogan, S.J., for the numerous memoranda which he was kind enough to give me towards the last chapter of this book, that on the history of Irish as a spoken language, and also to express my regret that the valuable critical edition of the Book of Hymns by Dr. Atkinson and Dr. Bernard, M. Bertrand's "Religion Gauloise," and Miss Hull's interesting volume on "Cuchullin Saga," which should be read in connection with my chapters on the Red Branch cycle, appeared too late for me to make use of.

RÁTH-TREAGH, OIDHCHE SAMHNA
MDCCCXCIX.

CONTENTS

A Literary History of Ireland

Literary History of Ireland

CHAPTER I

WHO WERE THE CELTS?

WHO were those Celts, of whose race the Irish are to-day perhaps the most striking representatives, and upon whose past the ancient literature of Ireland can best throw light?

Like the Greeks, like the Romans, like the English, this great people, which once ruled over a fourth of Europe, sprang from a small beginning and from narrow confines. The earliest home of the race from which they spread their conquering arms may be said, roughly speaking, to have lain along both banks of the upper Danube, and in that portion of Europe comprised to-day in the kingdoms of Bavaria and Würtemberg and the Grand Duchy of Baden, with the country drained by the river Main to the east of the Rhine basin. In other words, the Celtic race and the Celtic language sprang from the heart of what is to-day modern Germany, and issuing thence established for over two centuries a vast empire held together by the ties of political unity and a common language over all North-west and Central Europe.

The vast extent of the territory conquered and colonised by the Celts, and the unity of their speech, may be conjectured from an examination of the place-names of Celtic origin which either still exist or figure as having existed in European history.[1]

The Celts seem to have been first known to Greek—that is, to European history—under the semi-mythological name of the Hyperboreans,[2] an appellation which remained in force from the sixth to the fourth century before Christ. The name Celt or Kelt[3] first makes its appearance towards the year 500 B.C., in the geography of Hecatæus of Miletus, and is thereafter used successively by Herodotus, Xenophon, Plato, and Aristotle, and from that time forward it seems to have been employed by the Greek scholars and historians as a generic term whereby to designate the Celts of the Continent.

Soon afterwards the word Galatian came also into use,[4] and was used as a synonym for Celt. In the first century B.C., however, the discovery was made that the Germans and the Celts, who had been hitherto confounded in the popular estimation, were really two different peoples, a fact which Julius Cæsar was almost the first to point out. Diodorus Siculus,

[1] Take, for instance, the Celtic word *dúno-n*, Latinised *dunum*, which is the Irish *dún* "castle" or "fortress," so common in Irish topography, as in Dunmore, Dunsink, Shandun, &c. There are over a dozen instances of this word in France, nearly as many in Great Britain, more than half a dozen in Spain, eight or nine in Germany, three in Austria, a couple in the Balkan States, three more in Switzerland, one at least (Lug-dun, now Leyden) in the Low Countries, one in Portugal, one in Piedmont, one in South Russia.

Celtic was once spoken from Ireland to the Black Sea, although the population who can now speak Celtic dialects is not more than three or four millions. As for Celtic archæological remains "on les trouve tant dans nos musées nationaux (en particulier au Musée de Saint Germain) que dans les collections publiques de la Hongrie, de l'Autriche, de la Hesse, de la Bohême, du Würtemburg, du pays de Bade, de la Suisse, de l'Italie (Bertrand and Reinach, p. 3).

[2] Ὑπερβορείος.

[3] Κελτός. The Greeks, the Latins, and the Celts themselves pronounced Kelt, as do the modern Germans. It is against the genius of the French language to pronounce the *c* hard, but not against that of the English, who consequently had better say Kelt.

[4] Γαλατης.

accordingly, struck by this discovery, translates Cæsar's *Gallus* or Gaul by the word Celt, and his *Germanus* or German by the word Galatian, while the other Greek historian, Dion Cassius, does the exact opposite, calling the Celts "Galatians," and the Germans "Celts"! The examples thus set, however, were the result of ignorance and were never followed. Plutarch treats the two words as identical, as do Strabo, Pausanias and all other Greek writers.

The word Celt itself is probably of very ancient origin, and was, no doubt, in use 800 or 1,000 years before Christ.[1] It cannot, however, be proved that it is a generic Celtic name for the Celtic race, and none of the present Celtic-speaking races have preserved it in their dialects. Jubainville derives it, very doubtfully I should think, from a Celtic root found in the old Irish verb "ar-CHELL-aim" ("I plunder") and the old substantive to-CHELL ("victory"); while he derives Galatian from a Celtic substantive now represented by the Irish *gal*[2] ("bravery"). This latter word "Galatian" is one which the German peoples never adopted, and it appears to have only come into use subsequently to their revolt against their Celtic masters. After the break-up of the Celtic Empire it was employed to designate the eastern portion of the race, while the inhabitants of Gaul were called Celtæ and those of Spain Celtici or Celtiberi, but the Greeks called all indifferently by the common name of Galatians.

The Romans termed the Celts Galli, or Gauls, but they used the geographical term Gallia, or Gaul, in a restricted sense, first for the country inhabited by the Celts in North

[1] As is proved, according to Jubainville, by its having made its way into German before the so-called Laut-verschiebung took place, to the laws of which it submitted, for out of Celtis, the feminine form of it, they have made Childis, as in the Frank-Merovingian Bruni-Childis or Brunhild, and the old Scandinavian Hildr, the war-goddess.

[2] This was actually a living word as recently as ten years ago. I knew an old man who often used it in the sense of "spirit," "fire," "energy": he used to say *cuir gal ann*, meaning do it bravely, energetically. This was in the county Roscommon. I cannot say that I have heard the word elsewhere.

Italy upon their own side of the Alps, and after that for the Celtic territory conquered by Rome upon the other side of the Alps.

The Germans appear to have called the Celts Wolah, a name derived from the Celtic tribe the Volcæ, who were so long their neighbours, out of which appellation came the Anglo-Saxon Wealh and the modern English "Welsh."

There is one curious characteristic distinguishing, from its very earliest appearance, the Celtic language from its Indo-European sisters: this is the loss of the letter *p* both at the beginning of a word and when it is placed between two vowels.[1] This dropping of the letter *p* had already given to the Celtic language a special character of its own, at the time when breaking forth from their earliest home the Celts crossed the Rhine and proceeded, perhaps a thousand years before Christ, to establish themselves in the British Isles. The Celts who first colonised Ireland said, for instance, *atir* for *pater*, but they had not yet experienced, nor did they ever experience, that curious linguistic change which at a later time is assumed to have come over the Celts of the Continent and caused them to not only recover their faculty of pronouncing *p*, but to actually *change into a p* the Indo-European guttural *q*. Their descendants, the modern Irish, to this very day retain the primitive word-forms which had their origin a thousand years before Christ. So much so is this the case that the Welsh antiquary Lhuyd, writing in the last century, asserted, and with truth, that there were "scarce any words in the Irish besides what are borrowed from the Latin or some other language that begin with *p*, insomuch that in an ancient alphabetical vocabulary I have by me, that letter is omitted."[2] Even with the introduction of Christianity and

[1] Thus the Greek ὑπέρ, Latin s-uper, German über is *ver* in ancient Celtic (*for* in Old Irish, *ar* in the modern language), platanus becomes lĭtano-s (Irish leathan), παρά becomes *are*, and so on.

[2] Lhuyd's "Comparative Etymology," title i. p. 21. Out of over 700 pages in O'Reilly's Irish dictionary only twelve are occupied with the letter *p*.

the knowledge of Latin the ancient Irish persisted in their repugnance to this letter, and made of the Latin *Pasch-a* (Easter) the word *Cásg*, and of the Latin *purpur-a* the Irish *curcur*.

But meantime the Continental Celts had either—as Jubainville seems to think—recovered their faculty for pronouncing *p*, or else—as Rhys believes—been overrun by other semi-Celts who, owing to some strong non-Aryan intermixture, found *q* repugnant to them, and changed it into *p*. This appears to have taken place prior to the year 500 B.C., for it was at about this time that they, having established themselves round the Seine and Loire and north of the Garonne, overran Spain, carrying everywhere with them this comparatively newly adopted *p*, as we can see by their tribal and place-names. They appeared in Italy sometime about 400 B.C.,[1] founded their colony in Galatia about 279 B.C., and afterwards sent another swarm into Great Britain, and to all these places they bore with them this obtrusive letter in place of the primitive *q*, the Irish alone resisting it, for the Irish represented a first off-shoot from the cradle of the race, an off-shoot which had left it at a time when *q* represented *p*, and not *p q*. Hence it is that Welsh is so full of the *p* sound which the primitive Irish would never adopt, as a glance at some of the commonest words in both languages will show.

English :	Son	tree	head	person	worm	feather	everyone.
Welsh :	Ma*p*	*p*renn	*p*en	ne*p*	*p*ryv	*p*luv	*p*au*p*.
Irish :	Mac	*c*rann	*c*enn	'ne*ch*	cruiv[2]	cluv[2]	*các*h.

So that even the Irish St. Ciaran becomes Piaran in Wales.[3]

[1] Probably for the second time. MM. Bertrand and Reinach seem to have proved that the Cisalpine peoples of North Italy who were under the dominion of the Etruscans were Celtic in manners and costume, and probably in language also. *See* "Les Celtes dans les vallées du Pô et du Danube." Chapter on La Gaule Cisalpine.

[2] Rather "cruimh" and "clumh," the *mh* being pronounced *v*.

[3] In this matter of labialism Greek stands to some small extent with regard to Latin, as Welsh to Irish. Nor is Latin itself exempt from it; compare the labialised Latin *sept-em* with the more primitive Irish *secht*.

The Celts invaded Italy about the year 400 B.C., and stormed Rome a few years later. They were at this time at the height of their power. From about the year 500 to 300 B.C. they appear to have possessed a very high degree of political unity, to have been led by a single king,[1] and to have followed with signal success a wise and consistent external policy. The most important events in their history during this period were the three successful wars which they waged—first against the Carthaginians, out of whose hands they wrested the peninsula of Spain; secondly in Italy against the Etruscans, which ended in their making themselves masters of the north of that country; and thirdly against the Illyrians along the Danube. All of these wars were followed by large accessions of territory. One of the most striking features of their external policy during this period was their close alliance with the Greeks, whose commercial rivalry with the Phœnicians naturally brought them into relations with the Celtic enemies of Carthaginian power in Spain, relations from which they reaped much advantage, since the necessity of making head against the Celtic invaders of Spain must have seriously crippled the Carthaginian power, at the very time when, as ally of the Persians, she attacked the Greeks in Sicily, and lost the battle of Himera on the same day that the Persians lost that of Salamis. Greek writers of the fourth century speak of the Celts as practising justice, of having nearly the same manners and customs as the Greeks, and they notice their hospitality to Grecian strangers.[2] Their war with the Etruscans in North Italy completed the ruin of an hereditary enemy of

[1] See Livy's account of Ambicatus, who seems to have been a kind of Celtic Charlemagne, or more probably the equivalent of the Irish *ard-righ*. Livy probably exaggerates his importance.

[2] Cf. the remarkable verses quoted by d'Arbois de Jubainville of Scymnus of Chio, following Ephorus:

> "*Χρῶνται δὲ Κελτοὶ τοῖς ἔθεσιν Ἑλληνικοῖς*
> *ἔχοντες οἰκειότατα πρὸς τὴν Ἑλλάδα*
> *διὰ τὰς ὑποδοχὰς τῶν ἐπιξενουμένων.*"

the Greeks,[1] and their war with the Illyrians no doubt largely strengthened the hands of Philip, the father of Alexander the Great, and enabled him to throw off the tribute which the Illyrians had imposed upon Macedonia. Nor did Alexander himself embark upon his expedition into Asia without having first assured himself of the friendship of the Celts. He received their ambassadors with cordiality, called them his friends, and received from them a promise of alliance. "If we fulfil not our engagement," said they, "may the sky falling upon us crush us, may the earth opening swallow us up, may the sea overflowing its borders drown us," and we may well believe that these were the very words used by the Celtic chieftains when we find in an Irish saga committed to writing about the seventh century[2] the Ulster heroes swearing to their king when he wished to leave his wing of the battle to repel the attacks of a rival, and saying, "heaven is over us and earth is under us and sea is round about us, and unless the firmament fall with its star-showers upon the face of the earth, or unless the earth be destroyed by earthquake, or unless the ridgy, blue-bordered sea come over the expanse (?) of life, we shall not give one inch of ground."

While the ambassadors were drinking the young king asked them what was the thing they most feared, thinking, says the historian, that they would say himself, but their answer was quite different. "We fear no one," they said; "there is only one thing that we fear, which is, that the heavens may fall upon us; but the friendship of such a man as you we value more than everything," whereat the king, no doubt considerably astonished, remarked in a low voice to his courtiers what a vainglorious people these Celts were.[3]

[1] By this war the newly-arrived bands drove out the Etruscan aristocracy and took its place, ruling over a population of what were really their Celtic kinsmen.

[2] The Táin Bó Cuailnge.

[3] [Κελτοὺς] *ἀπέπεμψε, τοσοῦτον ὑπειπὼν ὅτι ἀλαζόνες* Κελτοί *εἰσιν* (Arrian, bk, i. chap. iv.).

All through the life of Alexander the Celts and Macedonians continued on good terms, and amongst the many envoys who came to Babylon to salute the youthful conqueror of Persia, appeared their representatives also. Some forty years later, however, this good understanding came to an end, and the Celts overthrew and slew in battle the Macedonian ruler Ptolemy Keraunos about 280 B.C.

With the Romans, as with the Greeks, the relations of the Celts were, during the fifth and fourth century B.C., upon the whole friendly, and their hostility to the Etruscans must have tended naturally to render them and the Romans mutual allies. The battle of Allia, fought on the 18th of July, 390 B.C., and the storming of Rome three days later, were a punishment inflicted on the Romans by the Celts in their exasperation at seeing the Roman ambassadors, contrary to the right of nations, assisting their enemies the Etruscans under the walls of Clusium, but these events appear to have been followed by a long peace.[1]

It is only in the third century B.C. that the hitherto victorious and widely-colonising Celts appear to have laid aside their internal political unity and to have lost their hitherto victorious tactics. The Germans, over whom they had for centuries domineered and whom they had deprived of their independence, rise against them about 300 B.C., and drive out their former conquerors from between the Rhine and

[1] *See* Livy, book v. chap. xxxvi.: "Ibi, jam urgentibus Romanam urbem fatis, legati contra jus gentium arma capiunt, nec id clam esse potuit, quum ante signa Etruscorum tres nobilissimi fortissimi-que Romanæ juventutis pugnarent. Tantum eminebat peregrina virtus. Quin etiam Q. Fabius erectus extra aciem equo, ducem Gallorum, ferociter in ipsa signa Etruscorum incursantem, per latus transfixum hastâ, occidit: spolia-que ejus legentem Galli agnovere, perque totem aciem Romanum legatum esse signum datum est. Omissâ inde in Clusinos irâ, receptui canunt minantes Romanis." It was the refusal of the Romans to give satisfaction for this outrage that first brought the Gauls upon them.

Jubainville rejects as fabulous the self-contradicting accounts of Livy about Roman wars with the Celts during the next forty years after the storming of Rome.

the Black Sea, from between the Elbe and the Main. The Celts fall out with the Romans and are beaten at Sentinum in 295 B.C.; they ally themselves with their former enemies the Etruscans, and are again beaten in 283 B.C. and lose territory. They cease their alliance with the Greeks, and are guilty of the shameful folly of pillaging the temple of Delphi, an act of brigandage from which no good results could come, and from which no acquisition of territory resulted. They established a colony in Asia Minor in 278 B.C., successfully indeed, but absolutely cut off from the rest of the Celtic Empire, and such as in any federation of the Celtic tribes could only be a source of weakness. Again, about the same time, we see Celts driving out and supplanting Celts in the districts between the Rhine, the Seine, and the Marne. In 262 B.C. we find a body of three or four thousand Celts assisting their former foes the Carthaginians at the siege of Agrigentum, where they perish. Many of the Celts now took foreign service. It was at their instigation that the war of mercenaries broke out, which at one time brought Carthage to the very verge of destruction.

Only two centuries and a half, as Jubainville remarks, had elapsed since the Celts had conquered Spain from the Phœnicians, and only a hundred and thirty years since they had taken Rome, but their victorious political unity had already begun to break up and crumble, and now Rome and Carthage commenced that deadly duel in which the victor was destined to impose his sway upon the ruins of the Celtic Empire as well as on that of Alexander—impose it, in fact, upon all the world then known to the Greeks, except only the extreme east.

One of the circumstances which must have helped most materially to break up the Celtic Empire was the successful revolt of the Germans against their former masters. The relation of the German to the Celtic tribes is very obscure and puzzling. The ancient Greek historians of the sixth, fifth, and fourth centuries B.C., who tell us so much about the

Celts, know absolutely nothing of the Germans. As early as the year 500 B.C. Hecatæus of Miletus is able to name three peoples and two cities of India. But of the Germans, who were so much nearer to Marseilles than the nearest point of India is to the most eastern Greek colony, he says not a word. Ephorus, in the fourth century, knows of only one people to the extreme west, and they are the Celts, and their immediate neighbours are the Scythians. He knows of no intermediate state or nation. Where, then, were the Germans?

The explanation lies, according to Jubainville, in this, that even before this period the German had been conquered by the Celt and become subordinated to him. The Greek historians knew of no independent state bordering upon the Scythians except the Celtic Empire alone, because none such existed. In the fifth and fourth centuries B.C., and perhaps as early as the seventh and sixth, the Germans had been subdued and had lost their independence. How and when this took place we can only conjecture, but we have philological reasons for believing that the two races had come into mutual contact at a very early date, probably as early as the eleventh century B.C. The early German name for the Rhine, for instance, *Rīno-s*, comes directly from the primitive Indo-European form *Reino-s* and not from the Celtic *Rēno-s*, which shows that the Germans had reached that river at a time when the Celts who lived along it still called it Reinos, not Rēnos. The Celts afterwards changed the primitive *ei* into *ē*, and from their carrying the form *réin*[1] with them into Ireland, they had probably done this as early as the ninth or tenth century B.C., for, as we have shown, the Celts who inhabited Ireland have preserved the very oldest forms of the Celtic speech.

On the other hand the Celts always called that Germanic tribe who accompanied the Cimbri by the name of Teutoni, thus showing that they first came in contact with them at a

[1] *Réin*=a primitive *rēni*. It occurs in the Amra Colum-cilli, meaning "of the sea."

date anterior to the phonetic law which introduced the so-called explosive consonants into German, and which caused the root Teutono (preserved intact by the Celts) to be turned into Theudono. From this it follows that the German and Celtic peoples were in touch with one another at a very remote period.

The long subordination of the German to the Celt has left its marks deeply behind it, for his "language had remained uncultivated during ages of slavery, had been reduced to the condition of a patois, and had forced the explosive consonants to submit to modifications of sound, the analogues of which appear in the Latin and Celtic languages during their decadence many centuries after those modifications of sound had deformed the language of the Germans."[1]

"In fine the Germanic has created for itself a place apart, amongst the other Indo-European languages, though the excessive poverty of its conjugation, which only knows three tenses—the present tense and two past tenses—and which has lost in particular the imperfect or secondary present, the future, and the sigmatic aorist, and which has not had strength to regain those losses by the aid of new composite tenses with the exception of its dental preterite. The Celtic has preserved the three tenses which the Germanic has lost."[2]

The Celtic language is in a manner allied to that of Italy, as is shown by its *grammar*, and out of all the circle of Indo-European languages the Latin comes nearest to it, and it and the Latin possess certain grammatical characteristics in common which are absent from the others.[3] To account for these we may

[1] D'Arbois de Jubainville's "Premiers Habitants de l'Europe," book iii. chap. iii. § 15.

[2] D'Arbois de Jubainville, *ibid.*

[3] "Some of the oldest and deepest morphological changes in Aryan speech are those which affect the Celto-Italic language. Such are the formation of a new passive, a new future, and a new perfect. Hence it is believed that the Celto-Italic languages may have separated from the rest while the other Aryan languages remained united." Taylor's "Origin of the Aryans," p. 257. Mr. Taylor is here alluding to the passive in *r* and the future in *bo*, but my friend, M. Georges Dottin, in his laborious and ample volume published last year, "Les désinences en R," has shown that the *r*-passives, at least, are, in Italic and Celtic, independent creations.

assume what may be called an Italo-Celtic period, prior, probably, to the establishment of the Italian races in Italy, perhaps some twelve hundred years before Christ.

On the other hand such mutual influence as Celtic and German have exercised upon each other is restricted merely to the *vocabularies* of the languages, for when these races came in contact with each other the two tongues had been already completely formed, and the grammar of the one could no longer be affected by that of the other.

That there existed a kind of Celto-Germanic civilisation is easily proved by the number of words common to each language which are not found in the other Indo-European tongues, or which if they occur in them, are found bearing a different meaning. The two peoples, the dominant Celts and the subject Germans, obeyed the same chiefs and fought in the same armies, and naturally a certain number of words became common to both. It is noticeable, however, that none of the terms relating to either gods or priests or religious ceremonies bear in either language the slightest resemblance to one another. It was probably this difference of religion which preserved the conquered people from being assimilated, and which was ultimately the cause of the successful uprising of the servile tribes.

The words which are common to the Germanic and the Celtic languages belong either to the art of government, political institutions, and law, or else to the art of war. These d'Arbois de Jubainville divides into two classes—those which can be phonetically proved to be of Celtic origin, and those which, though almost certainly of Celtic origin, yet cannot be proved to be so to actual demonstration. Such important German words[1] as *Reich* and *Amt* are beyond all doubt Celtic loan-

[1] These loan-words "can hardly be later than the time of the Gaulish Empire founded by Ambicatus in the sixth century B.C. We gather from them that at this or some earlier period the culture and political organisation of the Teutons was inferior to that of the Celts, and that the Teutons must have been subjected to Celtic rule. It would seem from the linguistic

words, as are probably such familiar vocables as *Bann*, *frei*, *Eid*, *Geisel*, *leihen*, *Erbe*, *Werth*,[1] all terms relating to law and government, imposed on or borrowed by the conquered Germans. From the Celts come also all such words concerning war and fighting as are common to both nations, such as *Held*, *Heer*, *Sieg*, *Beute*. From the Celts too come names of domiciles, as *Burg*, *Dorf*, *Zaun*, also of localities as *Land*, *Flur*, *Furt*, and the English *wood*, and of domestic aids as *Pferd*, *Beil*, and the Anglo-Saxon *Vîr* (a torque). They too seem to have been the first in Northern Europe to have practised the art of medicine, for from the Celtic comes the Gothic *lēkeis*—English *leech*.[2] Certain other domestic words, such as *Eisen*, *Loth*, and *Leder*, both races have in common.

Despite the long subjection of the Germans they never lost their language, nor were they assimilated by the conquering race, a fate from which they were probably preserved, as we have said, by the complete difference of their sacred customs. There is hardly one name in all the Teutonic theogony which even faintly resembles a Celtic one.[3] Their funeral rites were different,

evidence that the Teutons got from their Celtic and Lithuanian neighbours their first knowledge of agriculture and metals, of many weapons and articles of food and clothing, as well as the most elementary social, religious, and political conceptions, the words for nation, people, king, and magistrate being, for instance, loan-words from Celtic or Lithuanian."—Taylor's "Origin of the Aryans," p. 234.

[1] Also the Gothic word *magus* (" a slave"), old Irish *mug*, or *mogh*, *lugan* (" to swear "), Irish *luigh*, *dulgs* (a debt), Irish *dualgus*, &c.

[2] Irish *liaig*. The Finns again borrowed this word from the Germans. It is the root of the name Lee, in most Irish families of that surname, indicating that their ancestors practised leech-craft.

[3] Rhys indeed compares the great Teutonic sky-god Woden with the Welsh Gwydion and Thor with the Celtic Taranucus or Thunder-God, and is of opinion that a good deal of Teutonic mythology was drawn from Celtic sources—a theory which, when we consider how much the Germans are indebted to the Celts for their culture-terms, may well be true with regard to *later* mythological conceptions and mythological saga. However, it is now generally acknowledged that while all the nations of Aryan origin possess a common inheritance of language, any inheritance of a common mythology, if such exist at all, must be reduced to very small

the Germans burning, but the Celts burying their dead. Their systems of priesthood were absolutely different, that of the Celts being always an institution distinct from the kingship, while that of the Germans was for centuries vested in the head of the tribe or family. The priests of the Germans, even after the functions of priesthood had been severed from those of kingship, still exercised criminal jurisdiction, and even in the army a soldier could not be punished without their sanction. On the other hand the milder druids of the Celts appear to have never taken part in the judgment of delinquents against the State. Cæsar makes no mention of their ever acting as judges in criminal cases. The culprit guilty or treason was not put to death by them but by the citizens—*ab civitate.*[1]

It was about the year 300 B.C. that the German tribes, so long incorporated with the Celts, at last rose against their masters and broke their yoke from off their necks. They succeeded in dislodging the Celts from the country which lies between the Rhine and the North Sea, between the Elbe and the basin of the Main. It was in consequence of this blow that the Celtic Belgæ were obliged to withdraw from the right bank of the Rhine to the left, and to occupy the country between it, the Seine, and the Marne, whilst other tribes settled themselves along the Rhine, and others again marched upon Asia Minor and founded their famous colony of Galatia in the extreme east of Europe, to whom, over three centuries later, St. Paul addressed his epistle, and whose descendants were found by St. Jerome in the fourth century still speaking Celtic.[2]

proportions. The complete difference between the names of the Indian, Hellenic, Italic, Teutonic, and Celtic gods is very striking.

[1] "De Bello Gallico," book vii. chap. iv.

[2] Which he speaks of as a mark of folly, in just the same tone as an Anglicised Hibernian does of the Irish-speaking of the native Celts. His words are worth quoting :—"Antiquæ stultitiæ usque hodie manent vestigia. Unum est quod inferimus, et promissum in exordio reddimus, Galatas

It is no longer necessary to follow the fortunes of the Continental Celts, to trace the history of their Galatian colony, to tell how they lost Spain, to recount the exploits of Marius and Sylla, the wars of Cæsar, the heroic struggle of Vercingetorix, the division of Gaul by Octavius, the oppression of the Romans, and finally the inroads of the barbaric hordes of Visigoths, Burgundians, and Francs. It is sufficient to say that already in the third century of our era Gaul had lost every trace of its ancient Celtic organisation, and in its laws, habits, and civil administration had become purely Roman. The upper classes had, like the Irish upper classes of this and of the last century, thrown aside every vestige of Gaulish nationality, and piqued themselves upon the perfection with which they had Romanised themselves, as the Irish upper classes do upon the thoroughness with which they have become Anglicised. They threw aside their Gaulish names to adopt others more consonant to Latin ears, as the Irish are doing at this moment. Above all they prided themselves upon speaking only the language of their conquerors, and like so many of the Irish of to-day they derided their ancient language as *lingua rustica*. It, however, banished from the mouths of the nobles and officials, lived on in the villages and rural parts of Gaul, as it has to this day done in Ireland, until the sixth century, when it finally gave ground and retired into the mountains and wastes of Armorica, where it coalesced with the Welsh which the large colony of British brought in with them when flying from the Saxon, and where it, in the

excepto sermone Græco quo omnis Oriens loquitur propriam linguam eamdem pene habere quam Treviros, nec referre si aliqua exinde corrumperint, cum et Aphri Phœnicum linguam nonnullâ ex parte mutaverint, et ipsa Latinitas et regionibus quotidie mutetur et tempore." His insinuation that they spoke their own language badly is also thoroughly Anglo-Hibernian, reminding one very much of Sir William Petty and others. *See* Jerome's preface to his "Commentary on the Epistle to the Galatians," book vii. p. 429. Migne's edition. In another passage he is more complimentary, and calls them the Conquerors of the East and West—"Gallo-græcia [*i.e.*, Galatia] in qua consederunt Orientis Occidentisque victores." *See* his "Epistle to Rusticus," book i. p. 935. Migne.

Cymraeg form of it, is still spoken by a couple of million people.[1]

[1] Although Celtic has so long disappeared out of France with the exception of Armorica, it has left its traces deeply behind it upon the French language. This is also true even of linguistic sounds. "Tous les sons simples du français se retrouvent dans le breton, et tous ceux du breton à l'exception d'un seul (le *ch* on le χ) sont aussi dans notre langue : l'*u* et l'*e* très-ouvert, l'*e* muet si rare partout ailleurs, le *j* pur inconnu à toute l'Europe, les deux sons mouillés du *n* et du *l* (comme dans les mots bataille et dignité) sont communs à la langue française et aux idiomes celtiques," says Demogeot. Even in French customary law there are "distinct and numerous traces" of old Gaulish habits and legislation, as Laferrière has pointed out in his history of the civil law of Rome and France. Nor is this to be in the least wondered at, when we remember that nineteen-twentieths of the modern French blood is computed to be that of the aboriginal races—Aquitanians, Celts, and Belgæ; whilst out of the remaining twentieth "the descendants of the Teutonic invaders—Franks, Burgundians, Goths, and Normans doubtless contributed a more numerous element to the population than the Romans, who, though fewer in number than any of the others, imposed their language on the whole country" (*see* Taylor's "Origin of the Aryans," p. 204). The bulk of the French nation is probably pre-Celtic. The modern Frenchman does not at all resemble the Gallic type as described by the Greek and Roman writers.

CHAPTER II

EARLIEST ALLUSIONS TO IRELAND FROM FOREIGN SOURCES

Of all the tribes of the Celts, and indeed of all their neighbours in the west of Europe, the children of Milesius have been at once blessed and cursed beyond their fellows, for on the shores of their island alone did the Roman eagle check its victorious flight, and they alone of the nations of western Europe were neither moulded nor crushed into his own shape by the conqueror of Gaul and Britain.

Undisturbed by the Romans, unconquered though shattered by the Norsemen, unsubdued though sore-stricken by the Normans, and still struggling with the Saxons, the Irish Gael alone has preserved a record of his own past, and preserved it in a literature of his own, for a length of time and with a continuity which outside of Greece has no parallel in Europe.

His own account of himself is that his ancestors, the Milesians, or children of Miledh,[1] came to Ireland from Spain about the year 1000 B.C.,[2] and dispossessed the Tuatha De Danann who

[1] Milesius is the ordinary Latinised form of the Irish Miledh; the real name of Milesius was Golamh, but he was surnamed Miledh Easpáin, or the Champion of Spain. He himself never landed in Ireland.

[2] 1016 according to O'Flaherty, in the eighth century B.C. according to Charles O'Conor of Belanagare, but as far back as 1700 B.C. according to the chronology of the "Four Masters." Nennius, the Briton who wrote in

had come from the north of Europe, as these had previously dispossessed their kinsmen the Firbolg, who had arrived from Greece.

Such a suggestion, however, despite the continuity and volume of Irish tradition which has always supported it, appears open to more than one rationalistic objection, the chiefest being that the voyage from Spain to Ireland would be one of some six hundred miles, hardly to be attempted by the early Irish barks composed of wickerwork covered with hides, fragile crafts which could hardly hope to live through the rough waters of the Bay of Biscay and the Atlantic on a voyage from Spain, or through the Mediterranean and the Atlantic on a voyage from Greece.

On the other hand, if we assume that our ancestors passed over from Gaul into Britain and thence into Ireland, we shall find it fit in with many other facts. To begin with, the voyage from Gaul to Britain is one of only some two and twenty miles, and from Britain to Ireland, at its narrowest point, is hardly twelve. The splendid physique, too, of the Irish,[1] which is now alas! sadly degenerated through depression,

the time of Charlemagne, gives two different accounts of the landing of the Irish, one evidently representing the British tradition, and the other that of the Irish themselves, of which he says *sic mihi peritissimi Scotorum nunciaverunt.* Both these accounts make the Irish come from Spain, the first being that three sons of a certain Miles of Spain landed in Ireland from Spain at the third attempt. According to what the Irish told him they reached Ireland from Spain 1,002 years after flying from Egypt.

[1] Even Giraldus Cambrensis, that most bigoted of anti-Irishmen, could nevertheless write thus of the natives in the twelfth century. "In Ireland man retains all his majesty. Nature alone has moulded the Irish, and as if to show what she can do has given them countenances of exquisite colour, and bodies of great beauty, symmetry, and strength." This testimony agrees with what Cæsar says of the Celts of Gaul, whose large persons he compares with the short stature of the Romans, and admires their *mirifica corpora.* Strabo says of a Celtic tribe, the Coritavi, "to show how tall they are, I myself saw some of their young men at Rome, and they were taller by six inches than any one else in the city." The Belgic Gauls are uniformly described as tall, large-limbed, and fair, and Silius Italicus speaks of the huge limbs and golden locks of the Boii who gave their name

poverty, famine, and the rooting out of the best blood, but which has struck during the course of history such numerous foreign observers, seems certainly to connect the Irish by a family likeness with the Gauls, as these have been described to us by the Romans, and not with the Greeks or the swarthy, sunburnt Iberians. Tacitus also, writing less than a century after Christ, tells us that the Irish in disposition, temper, and habits, differ but little from the Britons, and we find in Britain, North Gaul, and Germany, tribes of the same nomenclature as several of those Irish tribes whose names are recorded by Ptolemy about the year 150.[1]

On the one hand, then, we have the ancient universal Irish traditions, backed up by all the authority of the bards, the annalists and the shanachies, that the Milesians—who are the ancestors of most of the present Irish—came to Ireland direct from Spain ; and, on the other hand, we have these rationalistic grounds for believing that Ireland was more probably peopled from Gaul and Britain. The question cannot here be carried further, except to remark that in an age ignorant of geography the term Spain may have been used very loosely, and may rather have implied some land oversea, rather than any particular land.[2]

to Bavaria (Boio-varia) and to Bohemia (Boio-haims). They were probably the ruling race in Gaul, but the type is now very rarely seen there, the aristocratic Celts having been largely wiped out by war, as in Ireland, and having when shorn of their power become amalgamated with the Ligurians and other pre-Celtic peoples.

[1] As the Brigantes, Menapii, and Cauci.

[2] Buchanan the Scotchman (1506–81), having urged some of these objections against the Irish tradition, is thus fairly answered by Keating, writing in Irish, about half a century after Buchanan's death : "The first of these reasons," says Keating (to prove that the Irish came from Gaul), "he deduces from the fact that Gaul was formerly so populous that the part of it called Gallia Lugdunensis would of itself furnish 300,000 fighting men, and that it was therefore likely that it had sent forth some such hordes to occupy Ireland, as were the tribes of the Gauls. My answer to that is that the author himself knew nothing of the specific time at which the Sons of Miledh arrived in Ireland, and that he was consequently perfectly ignorant as to whether France was populous or waste at that

If Ireland were not—thanks to her native annalists, her autochtonous traditions and her bardic histories—to a great extent independent of classical and foreign authors, she would have fared badly indeed, so far as history goes, lying as she does in so remote a corner of the world, and having been untrodden by the foot of recording Greek or masterful Roman. There are, however, some few allusions to the island to be found, of which, perhaps, the earliest is the quotation in Avienus, who writing about the year 380 mentions the account of the voyage of Himilco, a Phœnician,[1] to Ireland about the year 510 B.C., who said in his account that Erin was called "Sacra"[2] by the ancients, that its people navigated the vast sea in hide-covered barks, and that its land was populous and fertile. In the Argonautics of the pseudo-Orpheus, which may have been written about 500 B.C., the Iernian[3]—that is

epoch. And even though the country were as populous as he states, when the Sons of Miledh came to Ireland, it does not follow that we must necessarily understand that *it* was the country whence they emigrated ; for why should it be supposed to be more populous at that time than Spain, the country they really did come from ?"

[1] Aristotle, too, mentions the discovery by the Phœnicians, of an island supposed to be Ireland, rich in forest and river and fruit, which, however, this account would make out to have been uninhabited: *ἐν τῇ θαλάσσῃ τῇ ἔξω Ἡρακλείων στηλῶν φάσὶν ὑπό Καρχηδονίων νῆσον εὑρεθῆναι ἐρήμην, ἔχουσαν ὕλην τε παντοδαπῆ καὶ ποταμὸυς πλωτὸυς, καὶ τοῖς λοιποῖς καρποῖς θαυμαστὴν, ἀπέχουσαν δὲ πλειόνων ἡμερῶν*, etc. Ireland was splendidly wooded until after the Cromwellian wars, and not unfrequently we meet allusions in the old literature to the first clearances in different districts, associated with the names of those who cleared them.

[2] Sacra is apparently a translation of *Ἱερα* = Eiriu, old form of Eire now called Erin, which last is really an oblique case.

[3] *νήσοισιν Ἰερνίσιν*, and *νῆσον Ἰερνίδα*. The names by which Ireland and its inhabitants were known to the writers of antiquity are very various, as *Ἰουέρνια*, *Ἰουέρνοι*, Juverna, Juberna, Iverna, Hibernia, Hibernici, Hibernienses, Jouvernia, *Οὐερνία*, *Ἰουρνία*, and even Vernia and *Βερνία*. St. Patrick in his confessions calls the land Hyberione and speaks of Hibernæ Gentes and "filii Scotorum." There can be little doubt that Aristotle's *Ἰέρνη*, the *νῆσον Ἰερνίδα* of the Argonautics and Diodorus' *Ἶρις* represent the same country. Here are Keating's remarks on it: "An t-aonmhadh hainm déag Juvernia do réir Ptolomeus, no Juverna do réir Sholinuis, no Ierna do réir Claudianus, no Vernia do réir Eustatius ; measaim nach

apparently the Irish—Isle is mentioned. Aristotle knew about it too. Ierne, he says, is a very large island beyond the Celts. Strabo, writing soon after the birth of Christ, describes its position and shape, also calling it Ierne, but according to his account—which he acknowledges, however, that he does not make on good authority—it is barely habitable and its people are the most utter savages and cannibals.[1] Hibernia, says Julius Cæsar, is esteemed half the size of Britain and is as distant from it as Gaul is. Diodorus, some fifty years before Christ, calls it Iris, and says it was occupied by Britons.[2] Pomponius Mela, in the first century of our era, calls Ireland Iverna, and says that "so great was the luxuriance of grass there as to cause the cattle to burst"! Tacitus a little later, about the year 82, telling us how Agricola crossed the Clyde and posted troops in that part of the country which looked toward Ireland, says that Hibernia "in soil and climate, in the disposition, temper, and habits of its people, differed but little from Britain, and that its approaches and harbours were better known through traffic and merchants."[3]

bhfuil do cheill san deifir atá idir na h-ughdaraibh sin do leith an fhocail-se Hibernia, acht nár thuigeadar créad ó ttáinig an focal féin 7 dá réir sin go ttug gach aon fo leith amus uaidh féin air, agus is de sin tháinig an mhalairt úd ar an bhfocal." (*See* Haliday's "Keating," p. 119.)

[1] *'Ιέρνη περὶ ἧς οὐδὲν ἔχομεν λέγειν σαφὲς*, except that the inhabitants are *ἀνθρωποφάγοι* and *πολυφάγοι*! *Τούς τε πατέρας τελευτῆσαντας κατεσθίειν ἐν καλῷ τιθέμενοι.* He adds, however, *ταῦτα δ'οὕτω λέγομεν ὡς οὐκ ἔχοντες ἀξι πίστους μάρτυρας* (Book IV., ch. v.). In another passage he shows how utterly misinformed he must have been by saying that 'Ιερνη was *ἀθλίως δέ διὰ ψύχος οἰκουμένην ὥστε τὰ ἐπέκεινα νομίζειν ἀοίκητα* (II. 5). Elsewhere he calls the inhabitants *ἀγριώτεροι τῶν* Βρετανῶν.

[2] *τῶν* Βρεττανῶν, *τοὺς κατοικοῦντας την ὀνομαζομένην* Ἶριν.

[3] "Solum cœlumque et ingenia cultusque hominum haud multum a Britannia differunt; in melius aditus portusque per commercia et negociatores cogniti." This employment of *in* before *melius* is curious, and the passage, which Diefenbach in his Celtica malignly calls the "Lieblingsstelle der irischen Schriftsteller," is not universally accepted as meaning that the harbours of Ireland were better known than those of Great Britain; but when we consider the antiquarian evidence for ancient Irish civilisation, and that in artistic treatment, and fineness of manufacture

Ptolemy, writing about the year 150, unconsciously bears out to some extent what Tacitus had said of Ireland's harbours being better known than those of Britain, for he has left behind him a more accurate account of Ireland than of Britain, giving in all over fifty Irish names, about nine of which have been identified, and mentioning the names of two coast towns, seven inland towns, and seventeen tribes, some of which, as we have said, nearly resemble the names of tribes in Britain and North Gaul. Solinus, about A.D. 238, is the first to tell us that Hibernia has no snakes—observe this curious pre-Patrician evidence which robs our national saint of one of his laurels—saying, like Pomponius Mela, that it has luxurious pastures, and adding the curious intelligence that, "warlike beyond the rest of her sex, the Hibernian mother places the first morsel of food in her child's mouth with the point of the sword." Eumenius mentions the Hibernians about the year 306 in his panegyric on Constantine, saying that until now the Britons had been accustomed to fight only Pictish and Hibernian enemies. In 378 Ammianus Marcellinus mentions the Irish under the name of Scots, saying that the Scotti and Attacotti[1] commit dreadful depredations in Britain, and

Irish bronzes are fully equal to those of Great Britain, and her gold objects infinitely more numerous and every way superior, there seems no reason to doubt that the text of Tacitus must be translated as above, and not subjected to such forced interpretations as that the harbours and approaches of Ireland were better known *than the land itself!*

[1] "Picti Saxonesque et Scotti et Attacotti Britannos aerumnis vexavere continuis." These Attacotti appear to have been an Irish tribe. There is a great deal of controversy as to who they were. St. Jerome twice mentions them in connection with the Scots (*i.e.*, the Irish): *Scotorum et Atticotorum ritu*, they have their wives and children in common, as Plato recommends in his Republic! (Migne's edition, Book I., p. 735.) He says that he himself saw some of them when he was young, "*Ipse adolescens in Gallia viderim Attacottos, Scotorum* (one would expect *Attacotorum*) *natio uxores proprias non habet.* The name strongly resembles Cæsar's Aduatuci and Diodorus's Ατουατικοί and certainly appears to be same as the Gaelic Aitheach-Tuatha, so well known in Irish history, a name which O'Curry translates by "rent-paying tribes," probably of non-Milesian origin. These rose in the first century against their Milesian masters and massacred them. If as

Claudian a few years later speaks rather hyperbolically of the Irish invasion of Britain; "the Scot (*i.e.*, the Irishman)," he says, "moved all Ierne against us, and the Ocean foamed under his hostile oars—a Roman legion curbs the fierce Scot, through Stilicho's care I feared not the darts of the Scots—Icy Erin wails over the heaps of her Scots."[1] The Irish expeditions against both Gaul and Britain became more frequent towards the end of the fourth century, and at last the unfortunate Britons, driven to despair, and having in vain appealed to the now disorganised Romans to aid them, sooner than stand the fury of the Irish and Picts threw themselves into the arms of the Saxons.[2]

It is towards the middle or close of the fourth century that we come into much closer historical contact with the Irish, and indeed we know with some certainty a good deal about their internal history, manners, laws, language, and institutions from that time to the present. Of course if we can trust Irish sources we know a great deal about them for even seven or eight hundred years before this. The early Irish annalist, Tighearnach,[3] who died in 1088, and who had of course the

Thierry thinks the east and centre of Gaul were Gaelic speaking, they too may have had their Aitheach-Tuatha, which may have been a general name for certain non-Celtic tribes reduced by the Celts. According to the Itinerarium of Ricardus Corinensis quoted by Diefenbach, Book III., there were Attacotti along the banks of the Clyde: "*Clottæ ripas accolebant Attacotti, gens toti aliquando Britanniæ formidanda.*"

[1] "Scotorum cumulos flevit glacialis Ierne" ("glacialis," of course, only when looked at from a southern point of view. Strabo, as we have seen, said the island was scarcely habitable from cold).

"—Totam quum Scotus Iernen
Movit et infesto spumavit remige Tethys."

It is probably mere hyperbole of Claudian to say that the Roman chased the Irish out to sea,

"—nec falso nomine Pictos
Edomuit, Scotumque vago mucrone secutus
Fregit Hyperboreas velis audacibus undas."

[2] These appear in Britain in the middle of the fifth century, in 449 according to the Saxon Chronicle, which is probably *substantially* correct.

[3] Pronounced "Teear-nach."

records of the earliest Irish writers—so far as they had escaped extinction by the Danes—before his eyes when he wrote, and who quotes frequently and judiciously from Josephus, St. Jerome, Bede, and other authors, was of opinion, after weighing evidence and comparing Irish with foreign writers, that the *monumenta Scotorum*, or records of the Irish prior to Cimbaeth (*i.e.*, about 300 B.C.) were uncertain. This means that from that time forwards he at least considered that the substance of Irish history as handed down to us might, to say the least of it, be more or less relied upon. Cimbaeth was the founder of Emania, the capital of Ulster, the home of the Red Branch knights, which flourished for 600 years and which figures so conspicuously in the saga-cycle of Cuchulain.

What then—for we pass over for the present the colonies of Partholan, the Tuatha De Danann, and the Nemedians, leaving them to be dealt with among the myths—have our native bards and annalists to say of these six or seven centuries? As several of the best and greatest of Irish sagas deal with events within this period, we can—if bardic accounts, probably first committed to writing about the sixth or seventh century may at all be trusted—to some extent recall its leading features, or reconstruct them.

CHAPTER III

EARLY HISTORY DRAWN FROM NATIVE SOURCES

THE allusions to Ireland and the Irish from the third century before to the fourth century after Christ, are, as we have seen, both few and scanty, and throw little or no light upon the internal affairs or history of the island; for these we must go to native sources.

At the period when Emania was founded, that is, at the period when according to the learned native annalist Tighearnach, the records of the early Irish cease to be "uncertain," the throne of Ireland was occupied by a High-king called Ugony[1] the Great, and a certain body of saga, much of which is now lost, collected itself around his personality, and attached itself to his two sons, Cobhthach Caol-mBreagh and Leary[2] Lorc, and around Leary Lorc's grandson, Lowry[3] the mariner. It was this Ugony who attempted to substitute a new territorial division of Ireland in place of the five provinces into which it had been divided by the early Milesians. He exacted an oath by all the elements—the usual Pagan oath—from the men of Ireland that they would never oppose his children or his race, and then he divided the island into twenty-five parts,

[1] In Irish, Iugoine. [2] In Irish, Laoghaire.
[3] In Irish, Labhraidh Loingseach.

giving one to each of his children. He succeeded in this manner in destroying the ancient division of Ireland into provinces and in perpetuating his own, for several generations, when Eochaidh Féidhleach[1] once more reverted to the ancient system of the five provinces—Ulster, Connacht, Leinster, and the two Munsters. This Eochaidh Féidhleach came to the throne about 140 years before Christ, according to the "Four Masters,"[2] and it was his daughter who is the celebrated heroine Mève,[3] queen of Connacht, who reigned at Rathcroghan in Connacht, and who undertook the great Táin Bo or Cattle Raid into Ulster, that has been celebrated for nigh on 2,000 years in poem and annal among the children of the Gael; and her name introduces us to Conor[4] mac Nessa, king of Ulster, to the palace of Emania, to the Red Branch knights, to the tragedy of Déirdre and all the vivid associations of the Cuchulain cycle.

It was thirty-three years before Christ, according to the "Four Masters," that Conairé the Great, High-king of all Ireland, was slain, and he is the central figure of the famous and very ancient saga of the Bruidhean Da Derga.[5]

And now we come to the birth of Christ, which is thus recorded by the "Four Masters": "The first year of the age of Christ and the eighth of the reign of Crimhthan Niadhnair."[6] Crimhthan was no doubt one of the marauding Scots who plundered Britain, for it is recorded of him that "it was this Crimhthan who went on the famous expedition beyond the sea from which he brought home several extraordinary and costly

[1] Pronounced "Yo-hy Faylach."

[2] Less than 100 years before, according to Keating.

[3] In Irish, *Méadhbh*, pronounced Mève or Maev. In Connacht it is often strangely pronounced "Mow," rhyming with "cow." This name dropped out of uṣe about 150 years ago, being Anglicised into Maud.

[4] In Irish, Concobar, or Conchubhair, a name of which the English have made Conor, almost in accordance with the pronunciation.

[5] Pronounced "Breean Da Darga," *i.e.*, the Mansion Da Derga.

[6] Pronounced "Crivhan" or "Criffan Neeanār." Keating assigns the birth of Christ to the twelfth year of his reign.

treasures, among which were a gilt chariot and a golden chess-board, inlaid with three hundred transparent gems, a tunic of various colours and embroidered with gold, a shield embossed with pure silver," and many other valuables. Curiously enough O'Clery's Book of Invasions contains a poem of seventy-two lines ascribed to this king himself, in which he describes these articles. He was fabled to have been accompanied on this expedition by his "bain-leannán" or fairy sweetheart, one of an interesting race of beings of whom frequent mention is made in Irish legend and saga.

The next event of consequence after the birth of Christ is the celebrated revolt led by Cairbré Cinn-cait, of the Athach-Tuatha,[1] or unfree clans of Ireland, in other words the serfs or plebeians, against the free clans or nobility, whom they all but exterminated, three unborn children of noble line alone escaping.[2]

The people of Ireland were plagued—as though by heaven—with bad seasons and lack of fruit during the usurper Cairbré's reign. As the "Four Masters" graphically put it, "evil was the state of Ireland during his reign, fruitless her corn, for there used to be but one grain on the stalk; fishless

[1] The Athach (otherwise Aitheach) Tuatha Dr. O'Conor translates "giant-race," but it has probably no connection with the word [*f*]*athach*, "a giant." O'Curry and most authorities translate it "plebeian," or "rent-paying," and Keating expressly equates it with *daor-chlanna*, or "unfree clans." These were probably largely if not entirely composed of Firbolgs and other pre-Milesians or pre-Celtic tribes. *See* p. 22, note 1.

[2] These were Fearadach, from whom sprang all the race of Conn of the Hundred Battles, *i.e.*, most of the royal houses in Ulster and Connacht, Tibride Tireach, from whom the Dal Araide, the true Ulster princes, Magennises, etc., spring, and Corb Olum, from whom the kings of the Eoghanachts, that is, the royal families of Munster, come. O'Mahony, however, points out that this massacre could not have been anything like as universal as is here stated, for the ancestors of the Leinster royal families, of the Dál Fiatach of Ulster, the race of Conairé, that of the Ernaans of Munster, and several tribes throughout Ireland of the races of the Irians, Conall Cearnach, and Feargus Mac Róigh, were not involved in it.

her rivers; milkless her cattle; unplenty her fruit, for there used to be but one acorn on the oak." The belief that bad seasons were sent as a punishment of bad rulers was a very ancient and universal one in Ireland, and continued until very lately. The ode which the ollav or head-bard is said to have chanted in the ears of each newly-inaugurated prince, took care to recall it to his mind, and may be thus translated:—

"Seven witnesses there be
  Of the broken faith of kings.
First—to trample on the free,
  Next—to sully sacred things,
Next—to strain the law divine,
  (This defeat in battle brings).
Famine, slaughter, milkless kine,
  And disease on flying wings.
These the seven-fold vivid lights
  That light the perjury of kings!"[1]

According to the Book of Conquests the people of Ireland, plagued by famine and bad seasons, brought in, on the death of Cairbré, the old reigning families again, making Fearadach king, and the "Athach-Tuatha swore by the heaven and earth, sun, moon, and all the elements, that they would be obedient to them and their descendants, as long as the sea

[1] "Mos erat ut omni, qui in dignitatem elevatus fuerit, philosopho-poeta Oden caneret," etc. (*See* p. 10 of the "Institutio Principis" in the Transactions of the Gaelic Society, 1808, for O'Flanagan's Latin.) He does not give the original, nor have I ever met it. Consonant with this is a verse from Tadhg Mac Dairé's noble ode to Donogh O'Brien—

"Teirce, daoirse, díth ana,
Plágha, cogtha, conghala,
Díombuaidh catha, gairbh-shíon, goid,
Tre ain-bhfír flatha fásoid."

I.e., "Dearth, servitude, want of provisions, plagues, wars, conflicts, defeat in battle, rough weather, rapine, through the falsity of a prince they arise." I find a curious extension of this idea in a passage in the "Annals of Loch Cé" under the year 1568, which is recorded as "a cold stormy year of scarcity, and this is little wonder, for it was in it Mac Diarmada (Dermot) died"!

should surround Ireland." The land recovered its tranquillity with the reign of Fearadach. "Good was Ireland during his time. The seasons were right tranquil; the earth brought forth its fruit. Fishful its river mouths; milkful the kine; heavy-headed the woods."

There was a second uprising of the Athach-Tuatha later on,[1] when they massacred their masters on Moy Bolg. The lawful heir to the throne was yet unborn at the time of this massacre and so escaped. This was the celebrated Tuathal [Too-a-hal, now Toole], who ultimately succeeded to the throne and became one of the most famous of all the pre-Patrician kings. It was he who first established or cut out the province of Meath. The name Meath had always existed as the appellation of a small district near which the provinces of Ulster, Connacht, Leinster, and the two Munsters joined. Tuathal cut off from each of the four provinces the angles adjoining it, and out of these he constituted a new province[2] to be thenceforth the

[1] There is a rather suspicious parallelism between these two risings, which would make it appear as though part at least of the story had been reduplicated. First Cairbré Cinn-Cait, and the Athach-Tuatha, in the year 10, slay the nobles of Ireland, but Fearadach escapes in his mother's womb. His mother was daughter of the King of Alba. After five years of famine Cairbré dies and Fearadach comes back and reigns. Again, in the year 56, Fiachaidh, the legitimate king, is slain by the provincial kings at the instigation of the Athach-Tuatha, in the slaughter of Moy Bolg. His unborn son also escapes in the womb of his mother. This mother is also daughter of the King of Alba. Elim the usurper reigns, but God again takes vengeance, and during the time that Elim was in the sovereignty Ireland was "without corn, without milk, without fruit, without fish," etc. Again, on the death of Elim the legitimate son comes to the throne, and the seasons right themselves. Keating's account agrees with this except that he misplaces Cairbré's reign. There probably were two uprisings of the servile tribes against their Celtic masters, but some of the events connected with the one may have been reduplicated by the annalists. O'Donovan, in his fine edition of the "Four Masters," does not notice this parallelism.

[2] This would appear to have left six provinces in Ireland, but the distinction between the two Munsters became obsolete in time, though about a century and a half later we find Cormac levying war on Munster and demanding a double tribute from it as it was a double province! So late

special estate, demesne, and inheritance of the High-kings of Ireland. He built, or rebuilt, four palaces in the four quarters of the district he had thus annexed, all of them celebrated in after times—of which more later on. It was he also who, under evil auspices and in an evil hour, extorted from Leinster the first Borumha,[1] or Boru tribute,—*nomen infaustum*—a step which contributed so powerfully to mould upon lines of division and misery the history of our unhappy country from that day until the present, by estranging the province of Leinster, throwing it into the arms of foreigners, and causing it to put itself into opposition to the rest of Ireland. This unhappy tribute, of which we shall hear more later on, was imposed during the reigns of forty kings.

Thirteen years after the death of Tuathal, Cáthaoir [Cauheer], celebrated for his Will or Testament,[2] reigned; he was of pure Leinster blood, and the men of that province have always felicitated themselves upon having given at least this

as the fourteenth century O'Dugan, in his poem on the kings of the line of Eber, refers to the *two* provinces of Munster.

> "Dá thír is áille i n-Éirinn
> Dá chúige an Chláir léibhinn,
> Tír fhóid-sheang áird-mhin na ngleann
> Cóigeadh í d'Áird-righ Eireann"—

i.e., the two most beauteous lands in Ireland, the two provinces of the delightful plain, the slender-sodded, high-smooth land of the valleys, a province is she for the High-king of Ireland.

[1] There is a town in Clare called Bórúmha [*gen.* "Bóirbhe," according to O'Brien] from which it is said Brian Boru derived his name. But the usual belief is that he derived it from having imposed the *bóroimhe* tribute again on Leinster. Bórúmha is pronounced Bo-roo-a, hence the popular Boru[a] Boroimhe is pronounced Bo-rŭvă. It is also said that the town of Borumha in Clare got its name from having the Boroimhe tribute driven into it. The spelling Boroimhe [= Borŭvă] instead of Borumha [Boru-a] has been a great crux to English speakers, and I noticed the following skit, in a little Trinity College paper, the other day—

> "Says the warrior Brian Boroimhe,
> I'm blest if I know what to doimhe—
> My favourite duck
> In the chimney is stuck,
> And the smoke will not go up the floimhe!"

[2] *See* "The Book of Rights," p. 172.

one great king to Ireland. It is from him that the great Leinster families—the O'Tooles, O'Byrnes, Mac Morroughs or Murphys, O'Conor Falys, O'Gormans, and others—descend. He was slain, A.D. 123, by Conn of the Hundred Battles.[1]

There are few kings during the three hundred years preceding and following the birth of Christ more famous than this Conn, and there is a very large body of saga collected round him and his rival Eoghan [Owen], the king of Munster who succeeded in wresting half the sovereignty from him. As the result of their conflicts that part of Ireland which lies north of the Escir Riada,[2] or, roughly speaking, that lies north of a line drawn from Dublin to Galway, has from that day to this been known as Conn's Half, and that south of the same line as Owen's Half. Owen was at last slain by him of the hundred battles at the fight of Moy Léana.

Owen, as we have seen, was never King of Ireland, but he left behind him a famous son, Oilioll[3] Olum, who was married to Sadhbh,[4] the daughter of his rival and vanquisher, Conn of the Hundred Battles, and it is to this stem that nearly all the ruling families of Munster trace themselves. From his eldest

[1] It was O'Beirne Crowe, I think, who first translated this name by "Conn the Hundred-Fighter," "égal-à-cent-guerriers," as Jubainville has it, a translation which, since him, every one seems to have adopted. This translation makes the Irish adjective *céadcathach* exactly equivalent to the Greek ἑκατοντάμαχος, but it is certainly not correct, for Keating says distinctly that Conn was called *céadcathach*, or of the hundred battles, "from the hundreds of battles which he fought against the pentarchs or provincial kings of Ireland," quoting a verse from a bard by way of illustration

[2] Pronounced "Eskkir Reeada."

[3] Pronounced "Ell-yull."

[4] Pronounced "Sive," but as *Méadhbh* is curiously pronounced like "Mow" in Connacht, so is *Sadhbh* pronounced "sow," rhyming to "cow." I heard a Galway woman in America, the mother of Miss Conway, of the *Boston Pilot* quote these lines, which she said she had often heard in her youth—

"*Sow*, *Mow* [*i.e.*, Sive and Mève], Sorcha, Síghle,
Anmneacha cat agus madah na tíre."

I.e., "Sive, Mève, Sorcha and Sheela are the names of all the cats and dogs in the country," and hence by implication unsuited for human beings. This was part of the process of Anglicisation.

son, Owen Mór, come the Mac Carthys, O'Sullivans, O'Keefes, O'Callaghans, etc.; from his second son come the Mac Namaras and Clancys; and from his third son, Cian,[1] come the so-called tribes of the Cianachts, the O'Carrolls, O'Meaghers, O'Haras, O'Garas, Caseys, the southern O'Conors, and others. There is a considerable body of romance gathered around this Oilioll and his sons and wife, chiefly connected with the kingship of Munster.

Conn's son, Art the Lonely—so-called because he survived after the slaughter of his brothers—was slain by Mac Con, Sive's son by her first husband, and the slayer ruled in his place, being the third king of the line of the Ithians, of whom we shall read later on, who came to the throne.

He, however, was himself killed at the instigation of Cormac, son of Art, or Cormac mac Art, as he is usually designated. This Cormac is a central figure of the large cycle of stories connected with Finn and the Fenians. He was at last slain in the battle of Moy Mochruime. His advice to a prince, addressed to his son Cairbré of the Liffey, will be noticed later on, and, so far as it may be genuine, bears witness to his reputed wisdom, "as do the many other praiseworthy institutes named from him that are still to be found among the books of the Brehon Laws."[2] This Cormac it was who built the first mill in Ireland, and who made a banqueting-place of the great hall of Mi-Cuarta,[3] at Tara, which was one hundred yards long, forty-five feet high, one hundred feet broad, and which was entered by fourteen doors. The site is still to be seen, but no vestige of the building, which, like all early Irish structures, was of wood.

Cairbré of the Liffey succeeded his father Cormac, and it was he who fought the battle of Gabhra (Gowra) with the Fenians, in which he himself was slain, but in which he broke, and for ever, the power of that unruly body of warriors.

About the year 331 the great Ulster city and palace of

[1] Pronounced "Keean."

[2] Keating.

[3] *I.e.*, the hall of "the circulation of mead."

Emania, which had been the home of Conor and the Red Branch knights, and the capital of Ulster for six hundred years, was taken and burnt to the ground by the Three Collas, who thus become the ancestors of a number of the tribes of modern Ulster. From one of them descend the Mac Mahons, the ruling family of Monaghan; the Maguires, barons of Fermanagh; and the O'Hanlons, chiefs of Orior; while another was the ancestor of the Mac Donalds of Antrim and the Isles, of the Mac Dugalds, and the Mac Rories. The old nobility of Ulster, whose capital had been Emania, were thrust aside into the north-east corner of Ulster, whence most of them were expelled by the planters of James I.

We now come to Eochaidh [Yohee] Muigh-mheadhoin [Mwee-va-on] who was father of the celebrated Niall of the Nine Hostages. From one of his sons, Brian, come the Ui [Ee] Briain, that is, the collection of families composed of the seed of Brian—the O'Conors, kings of Connacht; the Mac Dermots, princes of Moylurg, afterwards of Coolavin; the O'Rorkes, princes of Breffny; the O'Reillys, O'Flaherties, and Mac Donaghs. From another son of his, Fiachrach, come the Ui Fiachrach, who were for ages the rivals of the Ui Briain in contesting the sovereignty of Connacht—the O'Shaughnesies were one of the principal families representing this sept.[1]

Eochaidh Muigh-mheadhoin was succeeded in 366[2] by Crimhthan [Crivhan], who was one of those militant Scots at whose hands the unhappy Britons suffered so sorely. He "gained victories," say the annals, "and extended his sway over Alba, Britain, and Gaul," which probably means that he raided all three, and possibly made settlements in South-west Britain. He was poisoned by his sister in the hope that the sovereignty would fall to her favourite son Brian. In this, however, she was disappointed, and it is a noticeable fact in

[1] Also the O'Dowdas of Mayo, the O'Heynes, O'Clearys, and Kilkellies.

[2] In 360 according to Keating.

Irish history that none of the Ui Briain, or great Connacht families, ever sat upon the throne of Ireland, with the exception of Turlough O'Conor, third last king of Ireland, ancestor of the present O'Conor Doñ, and Roderick O'Conor, the last of all the High-kings of the island.

Brian being set aside, Niall of the Nine Hostages ascended the throne in 379. It was he who first assisted the Dál Riada clans to gain supremacy over the Picts of Scotland. These Dál Riada were descended from a grandson, on the mother's side, of Conn of the Hundred Battles. There were two septs of these Dál Riada, one settled in Ulster and the other in Alba [Scotland]. It was from the conquests[1] achieved by the Scots [*i.e.* Milesians] of Ireland that Alba was called Lesser Scotia. In course of ages the inconvenient distinction of the countries into Lesser and Greater Scotia died away, but the name Scotia, or Scotland, without any qualifying adjective, clung to the lesser country to the frightful confusion of historians, while the greater remained known to foreigners as Erin, or Hibernia.[2] This Niall was surnamed "of the Nine Hostages," from his having extorted hostages from nine minor kings. He mercilessly plundered Britain and Gaul. The Picts and Irish

[1] One branch of the Dál Riada settled in Scotland in the third century, and their kinsfolk from Ulster kept constantly crossing over and assisting them in their struggles with the Picts. They were recruited also by some other minor emigrations of Irish Picts and Milesians. Their complete supremacy over the Picts was not obtained till the beginning of the sixth century. It was about the year 502 that Fergus the Great, leading a fresh and powerful army of the Dál Riada into Scotland, first assumed for himself Royal authority which his descendants retained for 783 years, down to the reign of Malcolm IV., slain in 1285. It was not, however, till about the year 844 that the Picts, who were almost certainly a non-Aryan race, were finally subdued by King Keneth Mac Alpin, who completely Gaelicised them.

[2] The name of Scotia was used for Ireland as late as the fifteenth century upon the Continent, in one or two instances at least, and "kommt noch am 15 Jahrhundert in einer Unkunde des Kaisers Sigismund vor, und der Name Schottenklöster setzt das Andenken an diese ursprüngliche Bezeichnung Irlands noch in mehreren Städten Deutschlands (Regensburg, Wurtzburg, Cöln, &c.), Belgien, Frankreich und der Schweiz fort" (Rodenberg's "Insel der Heiligen." Berlin, 1860, vol. i. p. 321).

Gaels combined had at one time penetrated as far as London and Kent, when Theodosius drove them back.[1] It was probably against Niall that Stilicho gained those successes so magniloquently eulogised by Claudian, "when the Scot moved all Ierne against us and the sea foamed under his hostile oars." Niall had eight sons, from whom the famous Ui [Ee] Neill are all descended. One branch of these, the branch descended from his son Owen, took the name of O'Neill in the eleventh century, not from him of the Nine Hostages, but from King Niall of the Black Knee, a less remote ancestor, of whom more later on. This was the great family of the Tyrone O'Neills. So solidly did the posterity of Niall establish itself, and upon so firm a basis was his power perpetuated, that almost all the following kings of Ireland were descended from him, besides multitudes of illustrious families, "nearly three hundred of his descendants, eminent for their learning and the sanctity of their lives," says O'Flaherty, "have been enrolled in the catalogue of the saints."[2] He it was who, while plundering in Britain or Armorica, led back amongst other captives the youth, then sixteen years old, who was destined, under the title of the Holy Patrick, to revolutionise Ireland.

St. Patrick's own "Confession" and his Epistle to Coroticus

[1] Bede describes the bitter complaints of the unfortunate Britons. "Repellunt," they said, "Barbari ad mare, repellit mare ad Barbaros. Inter hæc duo genera funerum oriuntur, aut jugulamur aut mergimur."

[2] The Northern and Southern Ui Neill [*i.e.*, the septs descended from Niall] are so inextricably connected with all Irish history that it may be as well to state here that four of his sons settled in Meath, and that their descendants are called the Southern Ui Neill. The so-called Four Tribes of Tara—O'Hart, O'Regan, O'Kelly of Bregia, and O'Conolly—with many more subsepts, belong to them. The other four sons are the ancestors of the Northern Ui Neill of Ulster, the O'Neills, O'Donnells, and their numerous co-relatives. The Ui Neill remained to the last the ablest and most powerful clan in Ireland, only rivalled—if rivalled at all—by the O'Briens of Thomond, and later by the Geraldines, who were of Italian lineage according to most authorities. "Giraldini qui amplissimos et potentissimos habeunt ditiones in Austro et Oriente, proxime quidem ex Britanniâ huc venerunt, origine verò sunt Itali nempè vetustissimi et nobilissimi Florentini sive Amerini" (Peter Lombard, "De Regno Hiberniæ." Louvain, 1632, p. 4).

have come down to us—the former preserved in the Book ot Armagh, a manuscript copied by a scribe named Ferdomnach in 807 (or 812 according to a truer chronology), apparently from St. Patrick's own copy, for at the end of the Confession the scribe adds this note: "Thus far the volume which Patrick wrote with his own hand."[1] In this ancient manuscript (itself only a copy of older ones so damaged as to be almost illegible[2] to the scribe who copied them in 807, a little more than three hundred years after St. Patrick's death), we find nearly a dozen mentions of Niall of the Nine Hostages, of his son Laeghaire [Leary], and several more who lived before St. Patrick's arrival, and so find ourselves for the first time upon tolerably solid historical ground, which from this out never deserts us. St. Columcille, the evangeliser of the Picts and the founder of Iona, was the great-great-grandson of this Niall, and the great-grandson of Conall Gulban, so celebrated even to this day in Irish romance and history.[3]

Ascertainable authenticated Irish history, then, begins with Niall and with Patrick, but in this chapter we have gone

[1] "Hucusque volumen quod Patricius manu conscripsit suá. Septima decima martii die translatus est Patricius ad cœlos."

[2] See Father Hogan's preface to his admirable edition of St. Patrick's life from the Book of Armagh edited by him for the Bolandists, where he says of the MS. that though beautifully coloured it is "tamen difficilis lectu, tum quod quaedam voces aut etiam paginæ plus minus injuria temporum deletæ sunt, tum quod ipsum exemplar unde exscriptus est jam videtur talem injuriam passum: quod indicant rursus notæ subinde ad marginem appositæ, præsertim vero signum *h* (vel *in* i.e. *incertum ?*) et *Z* (ζήτει) quæ dubitationem circa aliquot vocum scriptionem prodere videntur." The words *incertus liber hic*, "the book is not clear here," occur twice, and the zeta of inquiry eight times. *See* Dr. Reèves' paper, "Proceedings of the Royal Irish Academy." August, 1891.

[3] Heaven itself was believed to have reverenced this magnificent genealogy, for in his life, in the Book of Lecan, we read how "each man of the bishops used to grind a quern in turn, howbeit an angel from heaven used to grind on behalf of Columcille. This was the honour which the Lord used to render him because of the eminent nobleness of his race"! *See* Stokes' "Lives of the Saints, from the Book of Lecan," p. 173.

behind it to see what may be learned from native sources—rather traditional than historical—of Irish life and history, from the founding of Emania three hundred years before Christ down to the coming of St. Patrick. But for all the things which we have recounted we have no independent external testimony, nor have we now any manuscripts remaining of which we could say, "We have here documentary evidence fifteen or twenty centuries old attesting the truth of these things." No; we are entirely dependent for all that pre-Patrician history upon native evidence alone, and that evidence has come down to us chiefly but not entirely in manuscripts copied in the twelfth and in later centuries.

CHAPTER IV

HOW FAR CAN NATIVE SOURCES BE RELIED ON?

It must next be considered what amount of reliance can be placed upon the Irish annals and annalists, who have preserved to us our early history. If, in those few cases where we happen to have some credible external evidences of early events, we find our native annalists notoriously at variance with such evidences, our faith in them must of necessity be shaken. If, on the other hand, we find them to coincide fairly well with these other accounts taken from foreign sources, we shall be inclined to place all the more reliance on their accuracy when they record events upon which no such sidelights can be thrown.

Now, from the nature of the case, it is exceedingly difficult, considering how isolated Ireland was while evolving her own civilisation, and considering how little in early ages her internal affairs clashed with those of Europe, to find any specific events of which we have early external evidence. We can, for instance, apart from our own annals and poems, procure no corroborative evidence of the division of Ireland between Conn and Owen, of the destruction of Emania by the Three Collas, or of the battle of Gabhra. But despite the silence upon Irish affairs of ancient foreign writers, we have luckily another class of proof of the highest possible value, brought to light by the discoveries of modern science, and powerfully strengthening the credibility of our annals. This is nothing less than the record of natural phenomena. If we find, on calculating backwards, as modern science has enabled us to do, that such events as the appearance of comets or the occurrence of eclipses are recorded to the day and hour by the annalists, we can know with something like certainty that these phenomena *were recorded at the time of their appearance by writers who observed them*, whose writings must have been actually consulted and seen by those later annalists, whose books we now possess. Nobody could think of saying of natural phenomena thus accurately recorded, as they might of mere historical narratives, that they were handed down by tradition only, and reduced to writing for the first time many centuries later. Now it so happens that the Annals of Ulster, annals which treat of Ireland and Irish history from about the year 444, but of which the written copy dates only from the fifteenth century, contain from the year 496 to 884, as many as 18 records of eclipses and comets which agree exactly even to the day and hour with the calculations of modern astronomers. How impossible it is to keep such records unless written memoranda are made of them by eye-witnesses, is shown by the fact that Bede, born himself in 675, in recording the great solar eclipse which took place only eleven years before his own birth is yet two days astray in his date ; while, on the other hand, the Ulster annals give not only the correct day but the correct hour—thus showing that Cathal Maguire, their compiler, had access either to the original or to a copy of the original account of an eye-witness.[1]

Again, we occasionally find the early records of the two great

[1] Nor is this mere conjecture ; it is fully borne out by the annals themselves, which actually give us their sources of information. Thus under the year 439, we read that "Chronicon magnum (*i.e.*, The Senchas Mór) scriptum est"; at 467 and 468, the compiler quotes "Sic in Libro Cuanach inveni"; at 482, "Ut Cuana scripsit"; in 507, "Secundum librum Mochod"; in 628, "Sicut in libro Dubhdaleithe narratur," &c.

branches of the Celtic race, the Gaelic and the Cymric, throwing a mutual light upon each other. There exists, for instance, an ancient Irish saga, of which several versions have come down to us, a saga well known in Irish literature under the title of the Expulsion of the Dési,[1] which, according to Zimmer—than whom there can be no better authority—was, judging from its linguistic forms, committed to writing in the eighth century. The Dési were a tribe settled in Bregia, in Meath, and the Annals[2] tell us that the great Cormac mac Art defeated them in seven battles, forcing them to emigrate and seek new homes. This composition describes their wanderings in detail. Some of the tribe we are told migrated to Munster, whilst another portion crossed the Irish Sea and settled down in that part of South Wales called Dyfed, under the leadership of one Eochaidh [Yohy], thence called "from-over-sea." There Eochaidh with his sons and grand-children lived and died, and propagated themselves to the time of the writer, who states that they were then—at the time he wrote—ruled over by one Teudor mac Regin, king of Dyfed, who was then alive, and whose pedigree is traced in fourteen generations up to the father of that Eochaidh who had led them over in Cormac mac Art's time. Taking a generation as 33 years, and starting with the year 270, about the time of the expulsion of the Dési, we find that Teudor Mac Regin should have reigned about the year 730, and the Irish saga must have been written at this time, which agrees with Zimmer's reckoning, although his computation is based on purely linguistic grounds. That school of interpreters who decry all ancient Irish history as a mixture of mythology and fiction, and who can see in Cormac mac Art only a sun-god, would probably ascribe the expulsion of the Dési and other records of a similar nature to the creative imagination of the later Irish, who, they hold, invented their genealogies as they did their history. But in this case it happens by the merest accident that we *have* collateral evidence of these

[1] "Indarba inna nDési." [2] *See* "Four Masters," A.D. 265.

events, for in a Welsh pedigree of Ellen, mother of Owen, son of Howel Dda, preserved in a manuscript of the eleventh century, this same Teudor is mentioned, and his genealogy traced back by the Welsh scribe ; the names of eleven of his ancestors, corresponding—except for inconsiderable orthographical differences—with those preserved in the ancient Irish text.

> "When we consider," says Dr. Kuno Meyer, "that these Welsh names passed through the hands of who knows how many Irish scribes, one must marvel that they have preserved their forms so well;" and he adds, "in the light of this evidence alone, I have no hesitation in saying that the settlement of an Irish tribe in Dyfed during the latter half of the third century must be considered a well-authenticated fact." [1]

Dr. Reeves cites another remarkable case of undesigned coincidence which strongly testifies to the accuracy of the Irish annalists. In the Antiphonary of Bangor, an ancient service book still preserved on the Continent, we find the names of fifteen abbots of the celebrated monastery of Bangor—at which the heresiarch Pelagius was probably educated — and these fifteen abbots are recorded by the same names and in the same order as in the Annals; "and this undesigned coincidence," says Reeves, "is the more interesting because the testimonies are perfectly independent, the one being afforded by Irish records which never left the kingdom, and the other by a Latin composition which has been a thousand years absent from the country where it was written."

Another incidental proof of the accuracy of early Irish literary records is afforded by the fact that on the few occasions where the Saxon Bede, when making mention of some Scot, *i.e.*, Irishman, gives also the name of his father, this name coincides with that given by the annals.

We may, then, take it, without any credulity on our part,

[1] See Kuno Meyer's paper on the "Early Relations between the Gael and Brython," read before the Hon. Society of Cymmrodorion, May 28, 1896.

that Irish history as drawn from native sources may be very well relied upon from about the middle of the fourth century. Beyond that date, going backwards, we have no means at our disposal for checking its accuracy or inaccuracy, no means of determining the truth of such events as the struggle between Conn and Owen, between the Fenian bands and the High-king, between Ulster under Conor and Connacht under Mève, no means of determining the actual existence of Conairé the Great, or of Cuchulain, or of the heroes of the Red Branch, or of Finn mac Cumhail [Cool] and his son Ossian and his grandson Oscar. Is there any solid ground for treating these things as objective history?

It has been urged that it is unphilosophic of us and was unphilosophic of the annalist Tighearnach to fix the reign of Cimbaeth[1] [Kimbæ], who built Emania, the capital of Ulster, some three hundred years before Christ, as a terminus from which we may begin to place some confidence in Irish accounts, seeing that the Annals carry back the list of Irish kings with apparently equal certainty for centuries past him, and back even to the coming of the Milesians, which took place at the lowest computation some six or seven hundred years before. All that can be said in answer to this, is to point out that there must have been hundreds of documents existing at the timé when Tighearnach wrote, "the countless hosts of the illuminated books of the men of Erin," as his contemporary Angus called them—records of the past which he was able to examine and consult, but which we are not.

[1] To start with Cimbaeth as Tighearnach does "is just as uncritical as to take the whole tale of kings from the very beginning," says Dr. Atkinson, in his preface to the Contents of the facsimile Book of Leinster; and he adds, "if the kings who are supposed to have lived about fifteen centuries before Christ are mere figments, which is tolerably certain, there is little more reason for believing in the kings who reigned after Christ prior to the introduction of writing with Christianity (*sic*) into the island,"—an unconvincing *sorites!* One hundred and thirty-six pagan and six Christian kings in all reigned at Tara according to the fictions of the Bards.

Tighearnach was a professed annalist, "a modern but cautious chronicler,"[1] and for his age a very well-instructed man, and it seems evident that he would not have placed the founding of Emania as a terminus *a quo* if he had not inferred rightly or wrongly that native accounts could be fairly trusted from that forward. It certainly creates some feeling of confidence to find him pushing aside as uncertain and unproven the arid roll of kings so confidently carried back for hundreds of years before his starting-point. The historic sense was well developed in Tighearnach, and he no doubt discredited these far-reaching claims either because he could not find sufficiently early documentary evidence to corroborate them, or more likely because such accounts as he had access to, began to contradict one another and were unable to stand any scrutiny from this time backwards. With him it was probably largely a question of documents. But this brings us at once to the question, when did the Irish learn the use of letters and begin to write, to which we shall turn our attention in a future chapter.

[1] Dr. Whitley Stokes' "Tripartite Life of St. Patrick," vol. i. p. cxxix. "That Tighearnach had access to some library or libraries furnished with books of every description is manifest from his numerous references; and the correctness of his citations from foreign authors, with whose works we are acquainted may be taken as a surety for the genuineness of his extracts from the writings of our own native authors now lost." For the non-Irish portions of his annals Tighearnach used, as Stokes has shown, St. Jerome's "Interpretatio Chronicæ Eusebii Pamphili," the seven books of the history of Paulus Orosius, "The Chronicon, or Account of the Six Ages of the World," in Bede's Works, "The Vulgate," "The Etymologarium," "Libri XX of Isodorus Hispalensis," Josephus' "Antiquities of the Jews," probably in a Latin translation, and perhaps the lost Chronicon of Julius Africanus.

CHAPTER V

THE PRE-MILESIAN FABLE AND EARLY PANTHEON

In investigating the very early history of Ireland we are met with a mass of pseudo-historic narrative and myth, woven together into an apparently homogeneous whole, and all now posing as real history. This is backed up, and eked out, by a most elaborate system of genealogy closely interwoven with it, which, together with a good share of the topographical nomenclature of the island, is there to add its entire influence to that of historian and annalist in apparently attesting the truth of what these latter have recorded.

If in seeking for a path through this maze we grasp the skirt of the genealogist and follow his steps for a clue, we shall find ourselves, in tracing into the past the ancestry of any Milesian chief, invariably landed at the foot of some one of four persons, three of them, Ir, Eber, Eremon,[1] being sons of that Milesius who made the Milesian conquest, and the fourth being Lughaidh [Lewy], son of Ith, who was a nephew of the same. On one or other of these four does the genealogy of every chief and prince abut, so that all end ultimately in Milesius.

Milesius' own genealogy and the wanderings of his ancestors

[1] In modern times spelt Eíbhear [Ævir] and Eireamhóin [Æra-vone].

are also recounted for many generations before they land in Ireland, but during this pre-Milesian period there are no side-genealogies, the ancestors of Milesius himself alone are given, traced through twenty-two apparently Gaelic names and thirteen Hebrew ones, passing through Japhet and ending in Adam. It is only with the landing of the three sons and the nephew of Milesius that the ramifications of Irish genealogies begin, and they are backed up by the whole weight of the Irish topographical system which is shot through and through with places named after personages and events of the early Milesian period, and of the period of the Tuatha De Danann.

It will be well to give here a brief *résumé* of the accounts of the Milesians' wanderings before they arrived in Ireland. Briefly then the Gaels are traced back all the way to Fenius Farsa, a king of Scythia, who is then easily traced up to Adam. But beginning with this Fenius Farsa we find that he started a great school for learning languages. His son was Niul, who also taught languages, and his son again was Gaedhal, from whom the Gaels are so called. This Niul went into Egypt and married Scota, daughter of Pharaoh. This is a post-Christian invention, which is not satisfied without bringing Niul into contact with Aaron, whom he befriended, in return for which Moses healed his son Gaedhal from the bite of a serpent. Since then says an ancient verse—

> "No serpent nor vile venomed thing
> Can live upon the Gaelic soil,
> No bard nor stranger since has found
> A cold repulse from a son of Gaedhal."

Gaedhal's son was Esru, whose son was Sru, and when the Egyptians oppressed them he and his people emigrated to Crete. His son was Eber Scot, from whom some say the Gaels were called Scots, but most of the Irish antiquarians maintain that they are called Scots because they once came from Scythia,[1] to which cradle of the race Eber Scot led the nation back again. Expelled from Scythia a couple of generations later the race plant themselves in the country of Gaethluighe, where they were ruled over by one called Eber of the White Knee. The eighth in descent from him emigrated with four ships to Spain. His son was Breogan, who built Brigantia. His grandson was Golamh, called Miledh Easpáin, *i.e.*, Warrior of Spain,[2] whose name has been universally, but badly, Latinised Milesius, and it was his three sons and his nephew who landed in Ireland and who planted there the Milesian people. Milesius himself never put foot in Ireland, but he seems in his own person to have epitomised the wanderings of his race, for we find him returning to Scythia, making his way thence into Egypt, marrying Scota, a daughter of Pharaoh, and finally returning to Spain.

Much or all of this pre-Milesian account of the race must be unhesitatingly set down to the influence of Christianity, and to the invention of early Christian bards who felt a desire to trace their kings back to Japhet.[3] The native unchristianised

[1] It is just as likely that, as the only name of any people known to the early Irish antiquaries which bore some resemblance to their own was Scythia, they said that the Scoti came from thence.

[2] "The race of the warrior of Spain" continued until recent times to be a favourite bardic synonym for the Milesians. There is a noble war ode by one of the O'Dalys which I found preserved in the so-called "Book of the O'Byrnes," in Trinity College Library, in which he celebrates a victory of the O'Byrnes of Wicklow over the English about the year 1580 in these words:—

> "*Sgeul tásgmhar do ráinig fá chrióchaibh Fáil*
> *Dá táinig lán-tuile i nGaoidhiltigh* (?) *Chláir.*
> *Do chloinn âird áithiosaigh Mhile Easpáin*
> *Toisg airmioch* (?), *ar lár an laoi ghil bháin.*"

It is to be observed that of the four great Irish stocks the descendants of Ith are often called the Clanna Breógain.

[3] Nennius, in the time of Charlemagne, quotes the Annals of the Scots, and the narrative of the *peritissimi Scotorum* as his authorities for deducing the Scots, *i.e.* Irish, from a family of Scythia, who fled out of Egypt with the children of Israel, which shows that the original narrative had assumed this Christian form in the eighth century. In the Book of

genealogies all converge in the sons and nephew of Milesius. The legends of their exploits and those of their successors are the real race-heritage of the Gael, unmixed with the fanciful Christian allusions and Hebraic adulterations of the pre-Milesian story, which was the last to be invented.

The genuine and early combination of Irish myth and history centres not on foreign but on Irish soil, in the accounts of the Nemedians, the Firbolg, the Tuatha De Danann, and the early Milesians, accounts which have been handed down to us in short stories and more lengthy sagas, as well as in the bold brief chronicles of the annalists. No doubt the stories of the landing of his race on Irish soil, and the exploits of his first chieftains were familiar in the early days to every Gael. They became, as it were, part and parcel of his own life and being, and were preserved with something approaching a religious veneration. His belief in them entered into his whole political and social system, the holding of his tribe-lands was bound up with it, and a highly-paid and influential class of bardic historians was subsidised with the express purpose of propagating these traditions and maintaining them unaltered.

Everything around him recalled to the early Gael the traditional history of his own past. The two hills of Slieve Luachra in Kerry he called the paps of Dana,[1] and he knew that Dana was the mother of the gods Brian, Iuchar, and Iucharba, the story of whose sufferings, at the hands of Lugh

Invasions—the earliest MS. of which is of the twelfth century— the Christian invention has made considerable strides, and we start from Magog, Japhet, and Noah, and from the Tower of Babel pass into Egypt. Nel or Niul is called from the Plain of Senaar to the Court of Pharaoh, and marries his daughter Scota, and their son is named Gaedhal. They have their own exodus, and arrive in Scythia after many adventures ; thence into Spain, where Breogan built the tower from whose top Ireland was seen. It would seem from this that the later writer of the Book of Invasions enhanced the simpler account which the Irish had given Nennius three or four centuries before. Zimmer, however, thinks that Nennius quoted from a preceding Book of Invasions now lost.

[1] Ḍá chích Danainne.

the Long-handed, has in later times so often drawn tears from its auditors. When he beheld the mighty barrows piled upon the banks of the Boyne,[1] he knew that it was over the Dagda—an Irish Jupiter—and over his three sons [2] that they were heaped; and one of these, Angus of the Boyne, was, down to the present century, reverenced as the presiding genius of the spot. The mighty monuments of Knock Áine in Limerick, and Knock Gréine, as well as those of Knowth, Dowth, and New Grange, were all connected with his legendary past. It was Lugh of the Tuatha De Danann, he knew, who had first established the great fair of Tailltin,[3] to which he and his friends went from year to year to meet each other, and contract alliances for their grown children. The great funeral mound, round which the games were held, was sacred to Talti, the foster-mother of Lugh, who had there been buried, and in whose honour the games in which he participated were held upon the day which he called—and still calls, though he has now forgotten why—Lughnasa or Lugh's gathering.[4] His own country he called—and still calls—by the various names of Eire, Fódhla [Fola], and Banba, and they, as he knew, were three queens [5] of the Tuatha De Danann. The Gael of Connacht knew that Moycullen, near Galway, was so named from Uillin, a grandson of the Tuatha De Danann king Nuada; and Loch Corrib from Orbsen, the other name of the sea-god Manannán, slain there by this Uillin, and each of the provinces was studded with such memorials.

The early Milesian invaders left their names just as closely

[1] Sidh an Bhrogha [Shee in Vrow-a].

[2] Aengus, Aedh, and Cermad.

[3] Now monstrously called Telltown by the Ordnance Survey people, as though to make it as like an English word as possible, quite heedless of the remonstrance of the great topographer O'Donavan, and of the fact that they are demolishing a great national landmark.

[4] Or perhaps "Lugh's Memorial." Lúghnas is the 1st of August, and the month has received its name in Irish from Lugh's gathering.

[5] The Irish translation of Nennius ascribed to Giolla Caoimhghin [Gilla Keevin], who died in 1012, calls them goddesses, "*tri bandé Folla Banba ocus Eirc.*"

imprinted upon our topography as did their predecessors the Tuatha De Danann. The great plain of Bregia in Meath was so called from Brega, son of that Breogan who built Brigantia. Slieve Cualann in Wicklow—now hideously and absurdly called the Great Sugar Loaf!—is named from Cuala, another son of Breogan ; Slieve Bladhma, or Bloom, is called from another son of the same ; and from yet another is named the Plain of Muirthemni, where was fought the great battle in which fell Cuchulain "fortissimus heros Scotorum." The south of Munster is called Corca Luighe from Lughaidh, son of Ith, nephew of Milesius. The harbour of Drogheda was called Inver Colpa, from Colpa of the sword, another son of Milesius, who was there drowned when trying to effect a landing. The Carlingford Mountains were called Slieve Cualgni, and a well-known mountain in Armagh Slieve Fuad, from two more sons of Breogan of Brigantia, slain after the second battle with the Tuatha De Danann, while they followed up the chase. The sandhills in the west of Munster, where Donn, the eldest son of Milesius, was shipwrecked and lost his life—as did his whole crew consisting as is said of twenty-four warriors, five chiefs, twelve women, four servants, eight rowers, and fifty youths-in-training—is called Donn's House. So vivid is this tradition even still, that we find a Munster poet as late as the last century addressing a poem to this Donn as the tutelary divinity of the place, and asking him to take him into his sidh [shee] or fairy mound and become his patron. This poem is remarkable, as showing that in popular opinion the early Milesians shared the character of sub-gods, fairies, or beings of supernatural power, in common with the Tuatha De Danann themselves, for the poet treats him as still living and reigning in state, as peer of Angus of the Boyne, and cousin of Cliona, queen of the Munster fairies.[1] Wherever he

[1] It is worth while to quote some of these hitherto unpublished verses from a copy in my possession. The author, Andrew Mac Curtin, a good scholar and poet of Munster, knew of course perfectly well that Donn

turned the Gael was thus confronted with scenes from his own past, or with customs—like the August games at Tailltin—deliberately established to perpetuate them.

In process of time, partly perhaps through the rationalising influences of a growing civilisation, but chiefly through the direct action of Christianity, with which he came into active contact in perhaps the fourth, or certainly in the fifth century, the remembrance of the old Gaelic theogony, and the old Gaelic deities and his religious belief in them became blunted, and although no small quantity of matter that is purely pagan, and an immense amount of matter, but slightly tinged with Christianity, has been handed down to us, yet gods, heroes,

was a Milesian, yet he, embodying in his poem the popular opinion on the subject, treats him as a god or superior being, calls him brother or cousin of Áine and Aoife [Eefi] and "of the great son of Lear [*i.e.* Manannán], who used to walk the smooth sea," and relates him to Angus Óg, and Lugh the Long-handed, says that he witnessed the tragedy of the sons of Usnach, the feats of Finn mac Cool, and the battle of Clontarf, and treats him as still living and powerful. The poem begins, *Beannughadh doimhin duit a Dhoinn na Dáibhche.* It goes on to say—

"Nach tu bráthair Áine as Aoife
A's mic an Deaghadh do b' árd-fhlaith ar tíorthaibh,
A's móir-mhic Lir do ritheadh an mhín-mhuir
Dhoinn Chnuic-na-ndos agus Dhoinn Chnuic Fírinn' ?
Nach tu gan doirbhe do h-oileadh 'san ríogh-bhrogh
Ag Aongus óg na Bóinne caoimhe,
Do bhi tu ag Lugha ad' chongnamh i gcaoinsgir [cath]
Ag claoidh Balair a dhanar 's a dhraoithe.
Do bhi tu ag maidhm anaghaidh mic Mhiledh
Ag teacht asteach thar neart na gaoithe :
'S na dhiaigh sin i gciantaibh ag Naoise ;
Do bhi tu ag Conall 'san gcosgar do bh' aoirde
Ag ceann de'n ghad de cheannaibh righteadh :
Budh thaoiseach treasa i gcathaibh Chuinn thu."

The allusion in the last line but one is to the heads that Conall Cearnach strung upon the gad or rod, to avenge the death of Cuchulain, for which see later on.

Curtin finally asks Donn to let him into his fairy mansion, if not as a poet to enliven his feasts, then at least as a horse-boy to groom his horses.

"Munar bhodhar thu o throm ghuth na taoide
No mur bhfuarais bás mar chách a Dhoinn ghil," &c.

I.e., "unless thou hast grown deaf by the constant voice of the tide, or unless, O bright Donn, thou hast died like everybody else!"

and men have been so far brought to a common level, that it is next to impossible at first sight to disentangle them or to say which is which.

Very probably there was, even before the introduction of Christianity, no sharply-defined line of demarcation drawn between gods and heroes, that, in the words of Pindar, ἓν ἀνδρῶν ἓν Θεῶν γένος, "one was the race of gods and men," and when in after times the early mythical history of Ireland came to be committed to parchment, its historians saw in the Irish pantheon nothing but a collection of human beings. It is thus, no doubt, that we find the Fomorians and the Tuatha De Danann posing as real people, whilst in reality it is more than likely that they figured in the scheme of Gaelic mythology as races of beneficent gods and of evil deities, or at least as races of superhuman power.

The early Irish writers who redacted the mythical history of the country were no doubt imbued with the spirit of the so-called Greek "logographers," who, when collecting the Grecian myths from the poets, desired, while not eliminating the miraculous, yet to smooth away all startling discrepancies and present them in a readable and, as it were, a historical series.[1] Others no doubt wished to rationalise the early myths so far as they conveniently could, as even Herodotus shows an inclination to do with regard to the Greek marvels; and the later annalists and poets of the Irish went as far as ever went Euhemerus, reducing gods and heroes alike to the level of common men.

We find Keating, who composed in Irish his Forus Feasa or History, in the first half of the seventeenth century, and who only re-writes or abbreviates what he found before him in the ancient books of the Gaels now lost, distracted between his desire to euhemerise—in other words, to make mere men of the gods and heroes—and his unflinching fidelity

[1] Hellanikus, one of the best known of these, went so far as to give the very year, and even the very day of the capture of Troy.

to his ancient texts. Thus he professes to give the names of "the most famous and *noble persons* of the Tuatha De Danann," and amongst them he mentions "the six sons of Delbaeth, son of Ogma, namely, Fiacadh, Ollamh, Indaei, *Brian*, *Iuchar*, and *Iucharba*,"[1] but in another place he quotes this verse from some of his ancient sources—

"Brian Iucharba and the great Iuchar,
The *three gods* of the sacred race of Dana,
Fell at Mana on the resistless sea
By the hand of Lughaidh, son of Ethlenn."

These whom the ancient verse distinctly designates as gods, Keating makes merely "noble persons," but at the very same time in treating of the De Danann he interpolates amongst his list of their notable men and women this curious sentence:[2]

[1] Mac Firbis, in his great MS. book of genealogies, marks the mythical character of these personages still more clearly, for in his short chapter on the Tuatha De Danann he describes them as of light yellow hair, etc. [*monga finbuidhe orra*], and gives the names of their three Druids and their three distributors, who were called Enough, Plenty, Filling [*Sáith, Leór, Línad*]; their three gillies, three horses, three hounds, three musicians; Music Sweet and Sweetstring [Ceól Bind Tetbind], and so on, all evidently allegorical. *See* facsimile of the Book of Leinster, p. 30, col. 4, l. 40, and p. 187, col. 3, l. 55, for the oldest form of this.

[2] The following is the whole quotation from O'Mahony's Keating (for an account of this book see below, p. 556): "Here follows an enumeration of the most famous and noble persons of the Tuatha Da Danann, viz., Eochaidh the Ollamh called the Dagda, Ogma, Alloid, Bres, and Delbaeth, the five sons of Elathan, son of Niad, and Manannán, son of Alloid, son of Delbaeth. The six sons of Delbaeth, son of Ogma, namely, Fiachadh, Ollamh, Indaei, Brian, Iuchar, and Iucharba. Aengus Aedh Kermad and Virdir, the four sons of the Dagda. Lughaidh, son of Cian, son of Diancécht, sons of Esary, son of Niad, son of Indaei. Gobnenn the smith, Credni the artist, Diancécht the physician, Luchtan the mason, and Carbni the poet, son of Tura, son of Turell. Begneo, son of Carbni, Catcenn, son of Tabarn, Fiachadh, son of Delbaeth, with his son Ollamh, Caicer and Nechtan, the two sons of Namath. Eochaidh the rough, son of Duach Dall. Sidomel, the son of Carbri Crom, son of Elcmar, son of Delbaeth. Eri Fodhla and Banba, the three daughters of Fiachadh, son of Delbaeth, son of Ogma, and Ernin, daughter of Edarlamh, the mother of these women. The following are the names of their three goddesses, viz., Badhbh, Macha, and Morighan. Béchoil and Danaan were their two Ban-tuathachs, or chief ladies, Brighid was their poetess. Fé and Men

"The following are the names of three of their goddesses, viz., Badhbh [Bive], Macha, and Morighan." [1]

There are many allusions to the old Irish pantheon in Cormac's Glossary, which is a compilation of the ninth or tenth century explanatory of expressions which had even at that early date become obscure or obsolete, and many of these are evidently of pagan origin. Cormac describes Ana as *mater deorum hibernensium*, the mother of the Irish gods, and he adds, "Well used she to nourish the gods, it is from her name is said 'anæ,' *i.e.*, abundance, and from her name is called the two paps of Ana." Buanann, says Cormac, was the "nurse of heroes," as "Anu was mother of the gods, so Buanann was mother of the 'Fiann.'" Etán was nurse of the poets. Brigit, of which we have now made a kind of national Christian name, was in pagan times a female poet, daughter of the Dagda. Her divinity is evident from what Cormac says of her, namely, that "she was a goddess whom poets worshipped, for very great and very noble was her superintendence, therefore call they her goddess of poets by this name, whose sisters were Brigit, woman of smith-work, and Brigit, woman of healing, namely, goddesses—from whose names Brigit [2] was with all Irishmen called a goddess," *i.e.*, the terms "Brigit" and "goddess" were synonymous (?) The name itself he derives fancifully from the words *breo-shaighit*, "fiery arrow," as though the inspirations

were the ladies or ban-tuathachs of their two king-bards, and from them Magh Femen in Munster has its name. Of them also was Triathri Torc, from whom Tretherni in Munster is called. Cridinbhél, Brunni, and Casmael were their three satirists."

[1] O'Curry, who, like his great compeer O'Donovan, naturally took the De Danann to be a real race of men, comically calls these goddesses "three of the noble non-professional druidesses of the Tuatha De Danann." ("M. and C.," vol. ii. p. 187). We have seen how the Irish Nennius calls the three queens of the De Danann goddesses also.

[2] The "g" of Brigit was pronounced in Old Irish so that the word rhymed to English *spiggit*. In later times the "g" became aspirated and silent, the "t" turned into "d," and the word is now pronounced "B'reed," and in English very often "Bride," which is an improvement on the hideous Brid-get.

of a poet pierced like fiery arrows. Diancécht Cormac calls "the sage of the leech-craft of Ireland," but in the next line we read that he was so called because he was "Dia na cécht," *i.e.*, Deus salutis, or god of health. Zeuss quotes an incantation to this god from a manuscript which is, he says, at least a thousand years old. His daughter was Etán, an artificer, one of whose sayings is quoted by Cormac. Néith was the god of battle among the Irish pagans, Nemon was his wife. The euhemerising tendency comes out strongly in Cormac's account of Manannán, a kind of Irish Proteus and Neptune combined, who according to him was "a renowned trader who dwelt in the Isle of Man, he was the best pilot in the West of Europe; through acquaintance with the sky he knew the quarter in which would be fair weather and foul weather, and when each of these two seasons would change. Hence the Scots and Britons called him a god of the sea. Thence, too, they said he was the sea's son—Mac Lir, *i.e.*, son of the sea."

Another ancient Irish gloss [1] alludes to the mysterious Mór-rígan or war-goddess, of whom we shall hear more later on; and to Machæ, another war-goddess, "of whom is said Machæ's mast-feeding," meaning thereby, "the heads of men that have been slaughtered."

From all that we have said it clearly appears that carefully as the Christianised Irish strove to euhemerise their pantheon, they were unable to succeed. If, as Keating acknowledges, Brian, Iuchar, and Iucharba were gods, then *à fortiori* much more so must have been the more famous Lugh, who compassed their death, and the Dagda, and Angus Óg. Keating himself, in giving us a list of the famous Tuatha De Danann has probably given us also the names of a large number of primitive Celtic deities—not that these were at all confined to the De Danann tribes.

It is remarkable that there is no mention of temples nor of

[1] H. 2, 16, col. 119. Quoted by Stokes, "Old Irish Glossaries," p. xxxv.

churches dedicated to these Irish gods, nor do we find any of those inscriptions to them which are so common in Gaul, Belgium, Switzerland, and even Britain, but they appear from passages in Cormac's Glossary[1] to have had altars and images dedicated to them.

We are forced, then, to come to the conclusion that the pagan Irish once possessed a large pantheon, probably as highly organised as that of the Scandinavians, but owing to their earlier and completer conversion to Christianity only traces of it now remain.

[1] See the word "Hindelba" in the Glossary which is thus explained, "*i.e.*, the names of the altars or of those idols from the thing which they used to make (?) on them, namely, the *delba* or images of everything which they used to worship or of the beings which they used to adore, as, for instance, the form or figure of the sun on the altar." Again, the word "Hidoss" is explained as coming from "the Greek εῖδος which is found in Latin, from which the word *idolum*, namely, the shapes or images [*arrachta*] of the idols [or elements] which the Pagans used formerly to make."

CHAPTER VI

EVIDENCE OF TOPOGRAPHY AND GENEALOGY

THE ramifications of early Irish literary history and its claims to antiquity are so multiple, intricate, and inter-connected, that it is difficult for any one who has not made a close study of it to form a conception of the extent it covers and the various districts it embraces. The early literature of Ireland is so bound up with the early history, and the history so bound up and associated with tribal names, memorial sites, patronymics, and topographical nomenclature, that it presents a kind of heterogeneous whole, that which is recognised history running into and resting upon suspected or often even evident myth, while tribal patronymics and national genealogies abut upon both, and the whole is propped and supported by legions of place-names still there to testify, as it were, to the truth of all.

We have already glanced at some of the marks left by the mysterious De Danann race upon our nomenclature. Mounds, raths, and tumuli, called after them, dot all Ireland. It is the same with the early Milesians. It is the same with the men of the great pseudo-historic cycle of story-telling, that of Cuchulain and the Red Branch, not to speak of minor cycles. There is never a camping-ground of Mève's army on their march a century B.C. from Rathcroghan in

Roscommon to the plain of Mochruime in Louth, and never a skirmish fought by them that has not given its name to some plain or camping-ground or ford. Passing from the heroes of the Red Branch to the history of Finn mac Cool and the Fenians, we find the same thing. Finn's seat, the Hill of the Fenians, Diarmuid and Gráinne's bed, and many other names derived from them or incidents connected with them, are equally widely scattered.

The question now arises, does the undoubted existence of these place-names, many of them mentioned in the very oldest manuscripts we have—these manuscripts being only copies of still more ancient ones now lost—mentioned, too, in connection with the celebrated events which are there said to have given them their names, do these and the universally received genealogies of historic tribes which trace themselves back to some ancestor who figured at the time when these place-names were imposed, form credible witnesses to their substantial truth? In other words, are such names as Creeveroe[1] (Red Branch) given to the spot where the Red Branch heroes have been always represented as residing; or Ardee[2] (Ferdia's Ford) where Cuchulain fought his great single fight with that champion—are these to be accepted as collateral evidence of the Red Branch heroes of Ferdia and of Cuchulain? Are Seefinn[2] (Finn's seat) or Rath Coole[2] (Cool's rath) to be accepted as proving the existence of Finn and his father Cool?

In my opinion no stress, or very little, can be laid upon the argument from topography, which weighed so heavily with Keating, O'Donovan, and O'Curry, for if it is admitted at all it proves too much. If it proves the objective existence of Finn

[1] Craobh-ruadh.

[2] *I.e.*, Ath-Fhirdia, Suidhe Fhinn, Rath Chúmhail. There are See-finns or See-inns, *i.e.*, Finn's seats in Cavan, Armagh, Down, King's County, Galway, Mayo, Sligo, Tyrone, and perhaps elsewhere, and there are many forts, flats, woods, rivers, bushes, and heaps, which derive their name from the Fenians.

and of Cuchulain, so does it that of Dana, "the mother of the gods," and of divinities by the score. Besides the Gaels brought their topographical nomenclature with them to Alba, and places named from Finn and the Fenians, are nearly as plentiful there as in Ireland. Wherever the early Gaels went they took with them their heroic legends, and wherever they settled place-names relating to their legends which were so much a part of their intellectual life, grew up round them too. Something of the same kind may be seen in Greece—a land which presents so many and so striking analogies to that of the Gael; for wherever a Grecian colony settled, east or west, it was full of memorials of the legendary past, and Jasonia, or temples of Jason, and other memorials of the voyage of the Argonauts, are to be found from Abdêra to Thrace, eastward along the coast of the Euxine and in the heart of Armenia and Media, just as memorials of the flight of Diarmuid and of Gráinne from before Finn mac Cool may be found wherever the Gael are settled in Ireland, in Scotland, or the Isles.

Having come to the conclusion that Irish topography is useless for proving the genuineness of past history, let us look at Irish genealogy. When the Mac Carthys, descendants of Mac Carthy Mór, trace themselves through Oilioll Olum, king of Ireland in the second century, to Eber Finn, son of Milesius; when the O'Briens of Thomond trace themselves to the same through Oilioll Olum's second son; when the O'Carrolls of Ely trace themselves to the same through Cian, the third son; when the O'Neills trace themselves back through Niall of the Nine Hostages, and Conn of the Hundred Battles to Eremon, son of Milesius; when the O'Driscolls trace themselves to Ith, who was uncle of Milesius; when the Magennises trace themselves through Conall Cearnach, the Red Branch hero, back to Ir, the son of Milesius; and when every sept and name and family and clan in Ireland fit in, and even in our oldest manuscripts have always fitted in, each in its own place, with universally mutual acknowledgment and unanimity, each man carefully counting his ancestors through their hundredfold ramifications, and tracing them back first to him from whom they get their surname, and next to him from whom they get their tribe name, and from thence to the founder of their house, who in his turn grafts on to one of the great stems (Eremonian, Eberian, Irian, or Ithian)[1]; and when not only political friendships and alliances, but the very holding of tribal lands, depended upon the strict registration and observance of these things—we ask again do such facts throw any light upon the credibility of early Irish history and early Irish records?

The whole intricate system of Irish genealogy, jealously preserved from the very first, as all Irish literature goes to show,[2] played so important a part in Irish national history and in Irish social life, and is at the same time so intimately bound up with the people's traditions and literature, and throws so much light upon the past, that it will be well to try to get a grip of this curious and intricate subject, so important for all who would attempt to arrive at any knowledge of the life and feelings of the Irish and Scottish Gael, and upon which so much formerly depended in the history and alliances of both races.

All Milesian families trace themselves, as I have said, to one or other of the three sons of Milesius, who were Eremon, Eber, and Ir, or to his uncle Ith, who landed in Ireland at any time between

[1] As the various Teutonic races of Germany traced themselves up to one of the three main stems, Ingævones, Iscævones, and Herminones, who sprang from the sons of Mannus, whose father was the god Tuisco.

[2] A large part of the Books of Leinster, Ballymote, and Lecan, is occupied with these genealogies, continued up to date in each book. The MSS. H. 3. 18 and H. 2. 4 in Trinity College, Dublin, are great genealogical compilations. Well-known works were the Book of the genealogies of the Eugenians, the Book of Meath, the Book of the Connellians (*i.e.*, of Tirconnell), the genealogy of Brian, son of Eochaidh's descendants (see above, p. 33), the Book of Oriel, the Genealogies of the descendants of the Three Collas (see above, p. 33) in Erin and Scotland, the Book of the Maineach (men of O'Kelly's country), the Leinster Book of Genealogies, the Ulster Book, the Munster Book, and others.

1700 and 800 years before Christ according to Irish computation.[1] But while they all trace themselves back to this point, it is to be observed that long before they reach it, in each of the four branches, some place in the long row of ancestors is arrived at, some name occurs, in which all or most of the various genealogies meet, and upon which all the branch lines converge. Thus in the Eberian families it is found that they all spring from the three sons of Oilioll [Ul-yul] Olum, who according to all the annals lived in the second century—in this Oilioll all the Eberian families converge.

Again all, or nearly all, the Irians trace themselves to either Conall Cearnach or Fergus Mac Roy, the great Red Branch champions who lived in the North shortly before the birth of Christ.

The tribes of the Ithians, the least numerous and least important of the four, seem to meet in Mac Con, king of Ireland, who lived in the second century, and who is the hero of the saga called the Battle of Moy Mochruime, where Art, son of Conn of the Hundred Battles, was slain.

In the line of Eremon only, the greatest of the four, do we find two pedigrees which meet at points *considerably antecedent* to the birth of Christ, for the Dál Riada of Scotland join the same stem as the O'Neills as much as 390 years before Christ, and the O'Cavanaghs at a still more remote period, in the reign of Ugony Mór. But setting aside these two families we find that all the other great reigning houses, as the Mac Donnells of Antrim, Maguires of Fermanagh, O'Kellys of Connacht, and others, either meet in the third century in Cairbré of the Liffey, son of King Cormac mac Art, and grandson of Conn of the Hundred Battles; or else like the O'Neills of Tyrone, O'Donnells of Tirconnell, O'Dogherties of Inishowen, O'Conors of Connacht, O'Flaherties of Galway, they meet in a still later progenitor—the father of Niall of the Nine Hostages.

[1] See above, p. 17, note 2.

It will be best to examine here some typical Irish pedigree that we may more readily understand the system in its simplest form, and see how families branch from clans, and clans from stems. Let us take, then, the first pedigree of those given at the end of the Forus Feasa, that of Mac Carthy Mór, and study it as a type.

This pedigree begins with Donal, who was the first of the Mac Carthys to be created Earl of Clancare, or Clancarthy, in 1565. Starting from him the names of all his ancestors are traced back to Eber, son of Milesius. Passing over his five immediate ancestors, we come to the sixth. It was he who built the monastery of Irriallach on the Lake of Killarney. The seventh ancestor was Donal, from whose brother Donagh come the families of Ard Canachta and Croc Ornachta. The tenth was Donal Roe, from whom come the Clan Donal Roe, and from whose brother, Dermot of Tralee, come the family of Mac Finneens. The eleventh was Cormac Finn, from whom come also the Mac Carthys of Duhallow and the kings of Desmond; while from his brother Donal come the Mac Carthys Riabhach, or Grey Mac Carthys. The thirteenth was Dermot of Kill Baghani, from whom come the Clan Teig Roe na Sgarti. The fourteenth was Cormac of Moy Tamhnaigh, from whose brother Teig come the Mac Auliffes of Cork. The fifteenth was Muireadach, who was the first of the line to assume the surname of Mac Carthy, which he did from his father Carthach, from whom all the Síol Carthaigh [Sheeol Caurhy], or Seed of Carthach, including the Mac Fineens, Mac Auliffes, etc., are descended. The seventeenth was Saerbhrethach, from whose brother Murrough spring the sept of the O'Callaghans. The nineteenth was Callaghan of Cashel, king of Munster, celebrated in Irish romance for his warfare with the Danes. The twenty-third was Snedgus, who had a brother named Fogartach, from whose son Finguini sprang the Muinntir Finguini, or Finguini's People. The twenty-eighth was Falbi Flann, who was king of Munster from 622 to 633, from whose brother

Finghin sprang the sept of the O'Sullivans. The thirty-second was Angus, from one son of whom Eochaidh [Yohy] Finn are descended the O'Keefes; while from another son Enna, spring the O'Dalys of Munster—he was the first king of Munster who became a Christian, and he was slain in 484. The thirty-fourth was Arc, king of Munster, from whose son Cas, spring the following septs: The O'Donoghue Mór—from whom branched off the O'Donoghue of the Glen—O'Mahony Finn and O'Mahony Roe, *i.e.*, the White and Red O'Mahonys, and O'Mahony of Ui Floinn Laei, and O'Mahony of Carbery, also O'Mullane [1] and O'Cronin; while from his other son, "Cairbré the Pict," sprang the O'Moriarties, and from Cairbré's grandson came the O'Garvans. The thirty-sixth ancestor was Olild Flann Beg, king of Munster, who had a son from whom are descended the sept of O'Donovan, and the O'Coiléains, or Collinses. And a grandson from whom spring the O'Meehans, O'Hehirs, and the Mac Davids of Thomond. The thirty-seventh, Fiachaidh, was well known in Irish romance; the thirty-eighth was Eoghan, or Owen Mór, from whom all the septs of the Eoghanachts, or Eugenians of Munster come, who embrace every family and sept hitherto mentioned, and many more. They are carefully to be distinguished from the Dalcassians, who are descended from Owen's second son Cas. It was the Dalcassians who, with Brian Boru at their head, preserved Ireland from the Danes and won Clontarf. For many centuries the history of Munster is largely composed of the struggles between these two septs for the kingship. The thirty-ninth is the celebrated Oilioll [Ulyul] Olum, king of Munster, whose wail of grief over his son Owen is a stock piece in Irish MSS. He is a son of the great Owen, better known as Mogh Nuadhat, or Owen the Splendid, who wrested half the

[1] The great Daniel O'Connell's mother belonged to this sept of the O'Mullanes, and the so-called typical Hibernian physiognomy of the Liberator was derived from her people, whom he nearly resembled, and not from the O'Connells.

kingdom from Conn of the Hundred Battles, so that to this very day Connacht and Ulster together are called in Irish Conn's Half, and Munster and Leinster Owen's Half. The forty-third ancestor is Dergthini, who is known in Irish history as one of the three heirs of the royal houses in Ireland, whom I have mentioned before as having been saved from massacre when the Free Clans or Nobility were cut to pieces by the Unfree or Rent-paying tribes at Moy Cro—an event which is nearly contemporaneous with the birth of Christ. Hitherto there have been nine kings of Munster in this line, but not a single king of Ireland, but the forty-ninth ancestor, Duach Dalta Degadh, also called Duach Donn, attains this high honour, and takes his place among the Reges Hiberniæ about 172 years before Christ, according to the "Four Masters." After this a rather bald catalogue of thirty-six more ancestors are reckoned, no fewer than twenty-four being counted among the kings of Ireland, and at last, at the eighty-sixth ancestor from the Earl of Clancarthy, the genealogy finds its long-delayed goal in Eber, son of Milesius.

It will be seen from this typical pedigree of the Mac Carthys—any other great family would have answered our purpose just as well—how families spring from clans and clans from septs—to use an English word—and septs from a common stem ; and how the nearness or remoteness of some common ancestor bound a number of clans in nearer or remoter alliance to one another. Thus all septs of the great Eberian stem had some slight and faint tie of common ancestry connecting them, which comes out most strongly in their jealousy of the Eremonian or northern stem, but was not sufficient to produce a political alliance amongst themselves. Of a much stronger nature was the tie which bound those families descended from Eoghan Mór, the thirty-eighth ancestor from the first earl. These went under the name of the Eoghanachts, and held fairly together, always opposing the Dalcassians, descended from Cas. But when it came to the adoption of a surname, as it did in the eleventh century, those who descended from the ancestor who gave them their name, were bound to one another by the common ties of a nearer kinship and a common surname.

It will be seen at a glance from the above pedigree, how, taking the Mac Carthys as a stem, and starting from the first earl, the Mac Finneens join that stem at the eleventh ancestor from the earl, the Mac Auliffes at the fifteenth, the O'Callaghans at the eighteenth, the O'Sullivans at the twenty-ninth, the O'Keefes at the thirty-second, the O'Dalys[1] of Munster at the thirty-second, the O'Donoghues, O'Mahonys, O'Mullanes, O'Cronins, O'Garvans, and Moriartys at the thirty-fourth, the O'Donovans, Collinses, O'Meehans, O'Hehirs, and Mac Davids at the thirty-sixth.

Now each of these had his own genealogy equally carefully kept by his own ancestral bardic historian. If, for instance, the Mac Carthys could boast of nine kings of Munster amongst them, the O'Keefes could boast of ten; and an O'Keefe reckoning from Donal Óg, who was slain at the battle of Aughrim, would say that the Mac Carthys joined *his* line at the thirty-sixth ancestor from Donal.

All the Gaels of Ireland of the free tribes trace back their ancestry, as we have seen, to one or other of the four great stocks of Erimon, Eber, Ir, and Ith. Of these the EREMONIANS were by far the greatest, the EBERIANS coming next. The O'Neills, O'Donnells, O'Conors, O'Cavanaghs, and almost all the leading families of the north, the west, and the east were Erimonian; the O'Briens, Mac Carthys, and most of the leading tribes of the south were Eberians.[2] It was

[1] Not to be confounded with the Síol nDálaigh, who were the great northern family of the O'Donnells, who had also an ancestor called Dálach, from whom they derived, not their surname, but their race-patronymic.

[2] Strange to say Daniel O'Connell was not an Eberian but an Erimonian. The history of his tribe is very curious. It was descended from the celebrated Ernaan, or Degadian tribe to which the hero Curigh Mac Daire slain by Cuchulain belonged, who trace their genealogy back to Aengus Tuirmeach, High-king of Ireland about 388 B.C. These tribes were of Erimonian descent, but settled in the south. They were quite conquered

nearly always a member of one or the other of these two stems who held the high-kingship of Ireland, but so much more powerful were the Eremonians within historical times, that the Southern Eberians, although well able to maintain themselves in the south, yet found themselves absolutely unable to place more than one or two [1] high-kings upon the throne of All-Ireland, from the coming of Patrick, until the great Brian Boru once more broke the spell and wrested the monarchy from the Erimonians. The Irians gave few kings to Ireland, and the Ithians still less—only three or four, and these in very early, perhaps mythic, times.

If now we trace the O'Neill pedigree back as we did that of the Mac Carthys, we find the great Shane O'Neill who fought Elizabeth, traced back step by step to the perfectly historical character Niall of the Nine Hostages, son of Eochaidh Muigh-mheadhoin [Mwee-va-on], who was grandson of Fiachaidh Sreabhtine [Sravtinna], son of Cairbré of the Liffey, son of the great Cormac Mac Art, and grandson or Conn of the Hundred Battles, all of whom are celebrated in history and endless romance; and thence through a list containing in all forty-four High-kings of Ireland back to EREMON, son of Milesius, brother of that Eber from whom the Mac Carthys spring, and from whom he is the eighty-eighth in descent. The O'Donnells join his line at the thirty-sixth ancestor, the O'Gallaghers at the thirty-second, the O'Conor Doñ and O'Conor Roe and the O'Flaherty at the thirty-seventh. We find too, on examining these pedigrees, the most curious inter-mixtures and crossing of families. Thus, for instance, the two families of O'Crowley

by the descendants of Oilioll Olum—*i.e.*, the Eberians, who owned nearly all the south—yet they continued to exist in the extreme west of Munster. The O'Connells, from whom came Daniel O'Connell, the O'Falveys and the O'Sheas were their chief families, but none of them were powerful.

[1] The Munster annals of Innisfallen themselves claim only five, but the claims of some of them are untenable. Moore will not admit that any Eberian was monarch of Ireland from the coming of St. Patrick to the "usurpation" of Brian Boru.

in Munster spring from the Mac Dermot Roe of Connacht, who, with the Mac Donogh, sprang from Mac Dermot of Moylurg in Roscommon, ancestor of the prince of Coolavin; while the O'Gara, former lord of Coolavin in the same county, to whom the "Four Masters" dedicated their annals, was of southern Eberian stock.

The great warriors of the Red Branch, the men of the original kingdom of Uladh [Ulla, *i.e.*, Ulster], were of the third great stock, the IRIANS or race of Ir,[1] but they are perhaps better known as the Clanna Rudhraighe [Rury] or Rudricians, so named from Rudhraighe, a great monarch of Ireland who lived nearly three hundred years before Christ, or as Ulidians because they represented the ancient province of Uladh. But the Three Collas, grandsons of Cairbré of the Liffey, who was himself great-grandson of Conn of the Hundred Battles, and of course of the Eremonian stock, overthrew the Irians in the year 332, and burned their capital, Emania. The Irians were thus driven out by the Eremonians, and forced back into the present counties of Down and Antrim, where they continued to maintain their independence. So bitterly, however, did they resent the treatment they had received at the hands of the Eremonians, and so deeply did the burning of Emania continue to rankle in their hearts, that after a period of nearly 900 years they are said to have stood sullenly aloof from the other Irish, and to have refused to make common cause with them against the Normans at the battle of Downpatrick in 1260, where the prince of the O'Neills was slain.[2] So powerful, on the other hand, did the idea of race-connection remain, that we find one of the bards so late as the sixteenth

[1] Their greatest families were in later times the Magennises, now Guinnesses, O'Mores, O'Farrells, and O'Connor Kerrys, with their correlatives.

[2] O'Donovan says that Brian O'Neill was not assisted by any of the Ulidians at this battle, but of course they had more recent wrongs than the burning of Emania to complain of, for battles between them and the invading Eremonian tribes continued for long to be recorded in the annals. *See* p. 180, "Miscellany of the Celtic Society."

century urging a political combination and alliance between the descendants of the Three Collas who had burned Emania over twelve hundred years before, and who were then represented by the Maguires of Fermanagh, the Mac Mahons of Oriel [1] and the far-off O'Kellys of Ui Máine [2] [Ee maana].

As for the fourth great stock, the ITHIANS,[3] they were gradually pushed aside by the Eberians of the south, as the Irians had been by the Eremonians of the north, and driven into the islands and coasts of West Munster. Yet curiously enough the northern Dukes of Argyle and the Campbells and MacAllans of Scotland spring from them. Their chief tribes in Ireland were known as the Corca Laidhi [Corka-lee]; these were the pirate O'Driscolls and their correlatives, but they were pushed so hard by the Mac Carthys, O'Mahonys, and other Eberians, that in the year 1615 their territory was confined to a few parishes, and twenty years later even these are found paying tribute to the Mac Carthy Reagh. There is one very remarkable peculiarity about their genealogies, which is, that, though they trace themselves with great apparent, and no doubt real, accuracy back to Mac Con, monarch of Ireland and contemporary with Oilioll Olum in the end of the second century, yet from that point back to Milesius a great number of generations (some twenty or so) are missing, and no genealogist, so far as I know, in any of the books of pedigrees which I have consulted, has attempted to supply them by filling them up with a barren list of names, as has been done in the other three stems.[4]

[1] *I.e.* Monaghan. [2] Parts of the counties Galway and Roscommon.

[3] In later times their chief families were the O'Driscolls, the Clancys [Mac Fhlanchadhas] of the county Leitrim, the Mac Allans of Scotland, the Coffeys and the O'Learys of Roscarberry, etc. They were commonly called the Clanna Breogain, or Irish Brigantes, from Breogan, father of Ith.

[4] From Mac Con, son of Maicniad, king of Ireland, to the end of the second century, Mac Firbis's great book of genealogies only reckons twelve generations of Breogan, but in the smaller handwriting at the foot of the page twenty-two generations are counted up. See under the heading, "Do genealach Dairfhine agus shíl Luighdheach mic Iotha Mac Breoghain," at p. 670 of O'Curry's MS. transcript. Michael O'Clery's great book of

Let us now consider how far these genealogies tend to establish the authenticity of our early history, saga, and literature. The first plain and obvious objection to them is this—that genealogies which trace themselves back to Adam must be untrue inventions.

We grant it.

But all Gaelic genealogies meet, as we have shown in Milesius or his uncle, Ith. Strike off all that long tale of pre-Milesian names connecting him with Adam, and count them as a late excrescence—a mixture of pagan myth and Christian invention added to the rest for show. This leaves us only the four stems to deal with.

The next objection is that pedigrees which trace themselves back to the landing of the Milesians—a date in the computation of which Irish annalists themselves differ by a few hundred years—must also be untrue, especially as their own annalist, Tighearnach, has expressly said that all their history prior to about 300 B.C. is uncertain.

We grant this also.

What, then, remains?

This remains—namely the points in each of the four great race stems, in which all or the most of the leading tribes and families belonging to that stem converge, and, as we have seen, all of these with a few exceptions take place within reach of the historical period. In the lines of EBER and of ITH, this point is at the close of the second century; in the race of IR it is about the time of Christ's birth,[1] and in the fourth and

genealogies counts twenty-three generations from Maic Niad to Ith, both included, see p. 223 of O'Clery's MS. Keating's pedigree, as given in the body of his history, gives twenty-three generations also, but only seventeen in the special genealogy attached to it. There are no such curious discrepancies in the other three stems. I can only account for it by the impoverished and oppressed condition of the Ithians, which in later times may have made them lose their records.

[1] The chief exceptions being, as we have seen, the Scottish Dál Riada and the Leinster O'Cavanaghs, who do not join the Eremonian line, one till the fourth and the other till the seventh century before Christ.

perhaps most important stem, that of EREMON, the two main points of convergence are in the historical Niall of the Nine Hostages, who came to the throne in 356, and in Cairbré of the Liffey, who became High-king in 267.[1]

[1] Conall Cearnach, from whom, along with his friend Fergus mac Roigh or Roy, the Irians claim descent, was first cousin of Cuchulain, and Tighearnach records Cuchulain's death as occurring in the second year after the birth of Christ, the "Chronicon Scotorum" having this curious entry at the year 432, "a morte Concculaind herois usque ad hunc annum 431, a morte Concupair [Conor] mic Nessa 412 anni sunt." It is worth noting that none of the Gaelic families trace their pedigree, so far as I know, to either Cuchulain himself, or to his over-lord, King Conor mac Nessa. Cuchulain was himself not of Ithian but of Eremonian blood, although so closely connected with Emania, the Red Branch, and the Clanna Rury. If Irish pedigrees had been like modern ones for sale, or could in any way have been tampered with, every one would have preferred Cuchulain for an ancestor. That no one has got him is a strong presumption in favour of the genuineness of Irish genealogies.

CHAPTER VII

DOCUMENTARY EVIDENCE

We must now consider whether Irish genealogies were really traced or not to those points which I have mentioned. Is there any documentary evidence in support of such an assertion?

There is certainly some such evidence, and we shall proceed to examine it.

In the Leabhar na h-Uidhre [Lowar na Heera], or Book of the Dun Cow, the existing manuscript of which was transcribed about the year 1100, in the Book of Leinster, transcribed about fifty years later, in the Book of Ballymote and in the Book of Lecan, frequent reference is made to an ancient book now lost called the Cin or Codex of Drom-sneachta. This book, or a copy of it, existed down to the beginning of the seventeenth century, for Keating quotes from it in his history, and remarks at the same time, "and it was before the coming of Patrick to Ireland the author of that book existed."[1] This evidence of Keating might be brushed aside as an exaggeration did it stand alone, but it does not, for in a partially effaced memorandum in the Book of Leinster, transcribed from older books about the year 1150, we read: "[Ernin, son of]

[1] *See* Haliday's "Keating," p. 215.

Duach,[1] son of the king of Connacht, an ollav and a prophet and a professor in history and a professor in wisdom; it was he that collected the genealogies and histories of the men of Erin into one, and that is the Cin Droma-sneachta." Now there were only two Duachs according to our annals, one of these was great-grandson of Niall of the Nine Hostages, and of course a pagan, who died in 379; the other, who was an ancestor of the O'Flaherties, died one hundred and twenty years later. It was Duach the pagan, whose second son was Ernin; the other had only one son, whose name was Senach. If O'Curry has read the half-effaced word correctly, then the book may have been, as Keating says it was, written before St. Patrick's coming, and it contained, as the various references to it show, a *repertoire* of genealogies collected by the son of a man who died in 379; this man, too, being great-grandson of that Niall of the Nine Hostages in whose son so large a number of the Eremonian genealogies converge.[2]

There are many considerations which lead me to believe that Irish genealogical books were kept from the earliest introduction of the art of writing, and kept with greater accuracy, perhaps, than any other records of the past whatsoever. The chiefest of these is the well-known fact that, under the tribal system, no one possessed lawfully any portion of the soil inhabited by his tribe if he were not of the same race with his chief. Consequently even those of lowest rank in the tribe traced and recorded their pedigree with as much care as did the highest, for "it was from his own genealogy each man of the tribe, poor as well as rich, held the charter of his civil state, his right of property in the cantred in which he was

[1] See p. 15 of O'Curry's MS. Materials. There was some doubt in his mind about the words in brackets, but as the sheets of his book were passing through the press he took out the MS. for another look on a particularly bright day, the result of which left him no doubt that he had read the name correctly.

[2] For a typical citation of this book see p. 28 of O'Donovan's "Genealogy of the Corca Laidh," in the "Miscellany of the Celtic Society."

born." [1] All these genealogies were entered in the local books of each tribe and were preserved in the verses of the hereditary poets. There was no incentive to action among the early Irish so stimulative as a remembrance of their pedigree. It was the same among the Welsh, and probably among all tribes of Celtic blood. We find the witty but unscrupulous Giraldus, in the twelfth century, saying of his Welsh countrymen that every one of them, even of the common people, observes the genealogy of his race, and not only knows by heart his grandfathers and great-grandfathers, but knows all his ancestors up to the sixth or seventh generation,[2] or even still further, and promptly repeats his genealogy as Rhys, son of Griffith, son of Rhys, son of Teudor, etc.[3]

The poet, Cuan O'Lochain, who died in the year 1024, gives a long account of the Saltair of Tara now lost, the compilation of which he ascribes to Cormac mac Art, who came to the throne in 227,[4] and in which he says the synchronisms and chronology of all the kings were written. The Book of Ballymote too quotes from an ancient book, now lost, called the Book of the Uachongbhail, to the effect that "the synchronisms and genealogies and succession of their kings and monarchs, their battles, their contests, and their antiquities

[1] *See* "Celtic Miscellany," p. 144, O'Donovan's tract on Corca Laidh.

[2] "Generositatem vero et generis nobilitatem præ rebus omnibus magis appetunt. Unde et generosa conjugia plus longe capiunt quam sumptuosa vel opima. Genealogiam quoque generis sui etiam de populo quilibet observat, et non solum, avos, atavos, sed usque ad sextam vel septimam et ultra procul generationem, memoriter et prompte genus enarrat in hunc modum Resus filius Griffini filii Resi filii Theodori, filii Aeneæ, filii Hoeli filii Cadelli filii Roderici magni et sic deinceps.

"Genus itaque super omnia diligunt, et damna sanguinis atque dedecoris ulciscuntur. Vindicis enim animi sunt et iræ cruentæ nec solum novas et recentes injurias verum etiam veteres et antiquas velut instanter vindicare parati" ("Cambriæ Descriptio," Cap. XVII.).

[3] O'Donovan says—I forget where—that he had tested in every part of Ireland how far the popular memory could carry back its ancestors, and found that it did not reach beyond the seventh generation.

[4] According to the "Four Masters"; in 213, according to Keating.

from the world's beginning down to that time were written in it, and this is the Saltair of Tara, which is the origin and fountain of the historians of Erin from that period down to this time." This may not be convincing proof that Cormac mac Art wrote the Saltair, but it is convincing proof that what were counted as the very earliest books were filled with genealogies.

The subject of tribal genealogy upon which the whole social fabric depended was far too important to be left without a check in the hands of tribal historians, however well-intentioned. And this check was afforded by the great convention or Féis, which took place triennially at Tara,[1] whither the historians had to bring their books that under the scrutiny of the jealous eyes of rivals they might be purged of whatever could not be substantiated, "and neither law nor usage nor historic record was ever held as genuine until it had received such approval, and nothing that disagreed with the Roll of Tara could be respected as truth."[2]

"It was," says Duald Mac Firbis[3]—himself the author of probably the greatest book of genealogies ever written, speaking about the chief tribal historians of Ireland, "obligatory on every one of them who followed it to purify the profession"; and he adds very significantly, "Along with these [historians] the judges of Banba [Ireland] used to be in like manner preserving the history, *for a man could not be a judge without being a historian*, and he is not a historian who is not a judge in the BRETHADH NIMHEDH,[4] that is the last book in the study of the Shanachies and of the judges themselves."

[1] But see O'Donovan's introduction to "The Book of Rights," where he adduces some reasons for believing that it may have been a septennial not a triennial convocation.

[2] *See* Keating's History under the reign of Tuathal Teachtmhar.

[3] In the seventeenth century. His book on genealogies would, O'Curry computed, fill 1,300 pages of the size of O'Donovan's "Four Masters."

[4] This was a very ancient law book, which is quoted at least a dozen times in Cormac's Glossary, made in the ninth or tenth century.

The poets and historians "were obliged to be free from theft, and killing, and satirising, and adultery, and everything that would be a reproach to their learning." Mac Firbis, who was the last working historian of a great professional family, puts the matter nobly and well.

> "Any Shanachie," he says, "whether an ollav or the next in rank, or belonging to the order at all, who did not preserve these rules, lost half his income and his dignity according to law, and was subject to heavy penalties besides, so that it is not to be supposed that there is in the world a person who would not prefer to tell the truth, if he had no other reason than the fear of God and the loss of his dignity and his income: and it is not becoming to charge partiality upon these elected historians [of the nation]. However, if unworthy people did write falsehood, and attributed it to a historian, it might become a reproach to the order of historians if they were not on their guard, and did not look to see whether it was out of their prime books of authority that those writers obtained their knowledge. And that is what should be done by every one, both by the lay scholar and the professional historian—everything of which they have a suspicion, to look for it, and if they do not find it confirmed in good books, to note down its doubtfulness,[1] along with it, as I myself do to certain races hereafter in this book, and it is thus that the historians are freed from the errors of others, should these errors be attributed to *them*, which God forbid."

I consider it next to impossible for any Gaelic pedigree to have been materially tampered with from the introduction of the art of writing, because tribal jealousies alone would have prevented it, and because each stem of the four races was connected at some point with every other stem, the whole clan system being inextricably intertwined, and it was necessary for all the various tribal genealogies to agree, in order that each branch, sub-branch, and family might fit, each in its own place.

I have little doubt that the genealogy of O'Neill, for instance, which traces him back to the father of Niall of the

[1] Thus quaintly expressed in the original, for which see O'Curry's MS. Materials, p. 576: "muna ffaghuid dearbhtha iar ndeghleabhraibh é, a chuntabhairt fén do chur re a chois."

Nine Hostages who came to the throne in 356 is substantially correct. Niall, it must be remembered, was father of Laoghaire [Leary], who was king when St. Patrick arrived, by which time, if not before, the art of writing was known in Ireland. *À fortiori*, then, we may trust the pedigrees of the O'Donnells and the rest who join that stem a little later on.

If this be acknowledged we may make a cautious step or two backwards. No one, so far as I know, has much hesitation in acknowledging the historic character of that King Laoghaire whom St. Patrick confronted, nor of his father Niall of the Nine Hostages. But if we go so far, it wants very little to bring us in among the Fenians themselves, and the scenes connected with them and with Conn of the Hundred Battles; for Niall's great-grandfather was that Fiachaidh who was slain by the Three Collas—those who burnt Emania and destroyed the Red Branch—and his father is Cairbré of the Liffey, who overthrew the Fenians, and his father again is the great Cormac son of Art, son of Conn of the Hundred Battles who divided the kingdom with Owen Mór. But it is from the three grandsons of this Owen Mór the Eberians come, and from their half-brother come the Ithians, so that up to this point I think Irish genealogies may be in the main accepted. Even the O'Kavanaghs and their other correlations, who do not join the stem of Eremon till between 500 or 600 years before Christ, yet pass through Enna Cennsalach, king of Leinster, a perfectly historical character mentioned several times in the Book of Armagh,[1] who slew the father of Niall of the Nine Hostages; and I believe that, however we may account for the strange fact that these septs join the Eremonian stem so many hundreds of years before the O'Neills and the others, that up to this point their genealogy too may be trusted.

[1] *See* pp. 102, 113 of Father Hogan's "Documenta de S. Patricio ex Libro Armachano," where he is called Endae. He persecuted Cuthbad's three sons, "fosocart endae cennsalach fubîthin creitme riacâch," but Patrick is said to have baptized his son, "Luid iarsuidiu cucrimthan maccnêndi ceinnselich et ipse creditit."

If this is the case, and if it is true that every Gael belonging to the Free Clans of Ireland could trace his pedigree with accuracy back to the fourth, third, or even second century, it affords a strong support to Irish history, and in my opinion considerably heightens the credibility of our early annals, and renders the probability that Finn mac Cool and the Red Branch heroes were real flesh and blood, enormously greater than before. It will also put us on our guard against quite accepting such sweeping generalisations as those of Skene, when he says that the entire legendary history of Ireland prior to the establishment of Christianity in the fifth century partakes largely of a purely artificial character. We must not forget that while no Irish genealogy is traced to the De Danann tribes, who were undoubtedly gods, yet the ancestor of the Dalcassians—Cormac Cas, Oilioll Olum's son—is said to have married Ossian's daughter.

CHAPTER VIII

CONFUSION BETWEEN GODS AND MEN

Of that part of every Irish pedigree which runs back from the first century to Milesius nothing can be laid down with certainty, nor indeed can there be any *absolute certainty* in affirming that Irish pedigrees from the eleventh to the third century are reliable—we have only an amount of cumulative evidence from which we may draw such a deduction with considerable confidence. The mere fact that these pedigrees are traced back a thousand years further through Irish kings and heroes, and end in a son of Milesius, need not in the least affect—as in popular estimation it too often does—the credibility of the last seventeen hundred years, which stands upon its own merits.

On the contrary, such a continuation is just what we should expect. In the Irish genealogies the sons of Milesius occupy the place that in other early genealogies is held by the gods. And the sons of Milesius were possibly the tutelary gods of the Gael. We have seen how one of them was so, at least in folk belief, and was addressed in semi-seriousness as still living and reigning even in the last century.

All the Germanic races looked upon themselves as descended from gods. The Saxon, Anglian, Danish, Norwegian, and

Swedish kings were traced back either to Woden or to some of his companions or sons.[1] It was the same with the Greeks, to whom the Celts bear so close a similitude. Their Herakleids, Asklepiads, Æakids, Neleids, and Daedalids, are a close counterpart to our Eremonians, Eberians, Ithians, and Irians, and in each case all the importance was attached to the primitive eponymous hero or god from whom they sprang. Without him the whole pedigree became uninteresting, unfinished, headless. These beliefs exercised full power even upon the ablest and most cultured Greeks. Aristotle and Hippocratês, for instance, considered themselves descended from Asklêpius, Thucidydes from Æakus, and Socrates from Daedalus; just as O'Neill and O'Donnell did from Eremon, O'Brien from Eber, and Magennis from Ir. It was to the divine or heroic fountain heads of the race, not so much as to the long and mostly barren list of names which led up to it, that the real importance was attached. It is not in Ireland alone that we see mythology condensing into a dated genealogy. The same thing has happened in Persian history, and the history of Denmark by Saxo Grammaticus affords many such instances. In Greece the Neleid family of Pylus traced their origin to Neptune, the Lacedæmonian kings traced theirs to Cadmus and Danaüs, and Hekatæus of Miletus was the fifteenth descendant of a god.

Again we meet with in Teutonic and Hellenic mythology the same difficulty that meets us in our own—that of distinguishing gods from heroes and heroes from men. The legends of the Dagda and of Angus of the Boyne and the Tuatha De Danann, of Tighearnmas and the Fomorians, of Lugh the Long-handed and the children of Tuireann—all evidently mythologic—were treated in the same manner, recited by the same tongues, and regarded with the same unwavering belief, as the history of Conor mac Nessa and Déirdre, of Cuchulain

[1] These genealogies were in later times, like the Irish ones, extended to Noah.

and Mève, or that of Conn of the Hundred Battles, Owen Mór, Finn mac Cool, and the Fenians. The early Greek, in the same way, treated the stories of Apollo and Artemis, of Arês and Aphroditê, just as he did those of Diomede and Helen, Meleager and Althæa, Achilles, or the voyage of the *Argo*. All were in a primitive and uncritical age received with the same unsuspicious credulity, and there was no hard-and-fast line drawn between gods and men. Just as the Mór-rígan, the war-goddess, has her eye dashed out by Cuchulain, so do we find in Homer gods wounded by heroes. Thus, too, Apollo is condemned to serve Admetus, and Hercules is sold as a slave to Omphalê. Herodotus himself confesses that he is unable to determine whether a certain Thracian god Zalmoxis, was a god or a man,[1] and he finds the same difficulty regarding Dionysus and Pan; while Plutarch refuses to determine whether Janus was a god or a king;[2] and Herakleitus the philosopher, confronted by the same difficulty, made the admirable *mot* that men were "mortal gods," gods were "immortal men."[3]

In our literature, although the fact does not always appear distinctly, the Dagda, Angus Óg, Lugh the Long-handed, Ogma, and their fellows are the equivalents of the immortal gods, while certainly Cuchulain and Conor and probably Curigh Mac Daire, Conall Cearnach, and the other famous Red Branch chiefs, whatever they may have been in reality, are the equivalent of the Homeric heroes, that is to say, believed to have been epigoni of the gods, and therefore greater

[1] Herod. iv. 94–96. [2] Numa, ch. xix.

[3] "Θεοὶ θνητοί," "ἄνθρωποι ἀθάνατοι." It is most curious to find this so academic question dragged into the hard light of day and subjected to the scrutiny of so prosaic a person as the Roman tax-collector. Under the Roman Empire all lands in Greece belonging to the immortal gods were exempted from tribute, and the Roman tax-collector refused to recognise as immortal gods any deities who had once been men. The confusion arising from such questions offered an admirable target to Lucian for his keenest shafts of ridicule.

than ordinary human beings; while just as in Greek story there are the cycles of the war round Thebes, the voyage of the *Argo*, the fate of Œdipus, etc., so we have in Irish numerous smaller groups of epic stories—now unfortunately mostly lost or preserved in digests—which, leaving out the Cuchulain and Fenian cycles, centre round such minor characters as Macha, who founded Emania, Leary Lorc, Labhraidh [Lowry] the Mariner, and others.

That the Irish gods die in both saga and annals like so many human beings, in no wise militates against the supposition of their godhead. Even the Greek did not always consider his gods as eternal. A study of comparative mythology teaches that gods are in their original essence magnified men, and subject to all men's changes and chances. They are begotten and born like men. They eat, sleep, feel sickness, sorrow, pain, like men. "Like men," says Grimm, "they speak a language, feel passions, transact affairs, are clothed and armed, possess dwellings and utensils." Being man-like in these things, they are also man-like in their deaths. They are only on a greater scale than we. "This appears to me," says Grimm,[1] "a fundamental feature in the faith of the heathen, that they allowed to their gods not an unlimited and unconditional duration, but only a term of life far exceeding that of man." As their shape is like the shape of man only vaster, so are their lives like the lives of men only indefinitely longer. "With our ancestors [the Teutons]," said Grimm, "the thought of the gods being immortal retires into the background. The Edda never calls them 'eylifir' or 'ôdauðligir,' and their death is spoken of without disguise." So is it with us also. The Dagda dies, slain in the battle of North Moytura; the three "gods of the De Danann" die at the instigation of Lugh; and the great Lugh himself, from whom Lugdunum, now Lyons, takes its name, and to whom early Celtic inscriptions are found, shares the same fate. Manannán is

[1] "Deutsche Mythologie," article on the Condition of the Gods.

slain, so is Ogma, and so are many more. And yet though recorded as slain they do not wholly disappear. Manannán came back to Bran riding in his chariot across the Ocean,[1] and Lugh makes his frequent appearances amongst the living.

[1] "Voyage of Bran mac Febail," Nutt and Kuno Meyer, vol. i. p. 16.

CHAPTER IX

DRUIDISM

ALTHOUGH Irish literature is full of allusions to the druids it is extremely difficult to know with any exactness what they were. They are mentioned from the earliest times. The pre-Milesian races, the Nemedians and Fomorians, had their druids, who worked mutual spells against each other. The Tuatha De Danann had innumerable druids amongst them, who used magic. The invading Milesians had three druids with them in their ships, Amergin the poet and two others. In fact, druids are mentioned in connection with all early Irish fiction and history, from the first colonising of Ireland down to the time of the saints. It seems very doubtful, however, whether there existed in Ireland as definitely established an order of druids as in Britain and on the Continent.[1]

[1] Cæsar's words are worth repeating. He says that there were two sorts of men in Gaul both numerous and honoured—the knights and the Druids, "equites et druides," because the people counted for nothing and took the initiative in nothing. As for the Druids, he says: "Rebus divinis intersunt, sacrificia publica et privata procurant, religiones interpretantur. . . . nam fere de omnibus controversiis publicis privatisque constituunt, et si quod est admissum facinus, si cœdes facta, si de hereditate, de finibus controversia est iidem decernunt præmia, pœnasque constituunt." All this seems very like the duties of the Irish Druids, but not what follows: "si qui, aut privatus aut populus eorum decreto non stetit, sacrificiis inter-

They are frequently mentioned in Irish literature as ambassadors, spokesmen, teachers, and tutors. Kings were sometimes druids, so were poets. It is a word which seems to me to have been, perhaps from the first, used with great laxity and great latitude. The druids, so far as we can ascertain, do not seem to be connected with any positive rites or worship ; still less do they appear to have been a regular priesthood, and there is not a shadow of evidence to connect them with any special worship as that of the sun or of fire. In the oldest saga-cycle the druid appears as a man of the highest rank and related to kings. King Conor's father was according to some—probably the oldest—accounts a druid ; so was Finn mac Cool's grandfather.

Before the coming of St. Patrick there certainly existed images, or, as they are called by the ancient authorities, "idols" in Ireland, at which or to which sacrifice used to be offered, probably with a view to propitiating the earth-gods, possibly the Tuatha De Danann, and securing good harvests and abundant kine. From sacrificial rites spring, almost of necessity, a sacrificial caste, and this caste—the druids—had arrived at a high state of organisation in Gaul and Britain when observed by Cæsar, and did not hesitate to sacrifice whole hecatombs of human beings. "They think," said Cæsar, "that unless a man's life is rendered up for a man's life, the will of the immortal God cannot be satisfied, and they have sacrifices of this kind as a national institution."

There appears nothing, however, that I am aware of, to connect the druids in Ireland with human sacrifice, although such sacrifice appears to have been offered. The druids, however, appear to have had private idols of their own. We find a very minute account in the tenth-century glossary of King Cormac as to how a poet performed incantations with his

dicunt. Hæc pœna apud eos est gravissima." Nor do the Irish appear to have had the over-Druid whom Cæsar talks of. (*See* "De Bello Gallico," book vi. chaps. 13, 14).

idols. The word "poet" is here apparently equivalent to druid, as the word "druid" like the Latin *vates* is frequently a synonym for "poet." Here is how the glossary explains the incantation called *Imbas Forosnai*:—

"This," says the ancient lexicographer, "describes to the poet whatsoever thing he wishes to discover,[1] and this is the manner in which it is performed. The poet chews a bit of the raw red flesh of a pig, a dog, or a cat, and then retires with it to his own bed behind the door,[2] where he pronounces an oration over it and offers it to his *idol gods*. He then *invokes the idols*, and if he has not received the illumination before the next day, he pronounces incantations upon his two palms and takes his idol gods unto him [into his bed] in order that he may not be interrupted in his sleep. He then places his two hands upon his two cheeks and falls asleep. He is then watched so that he be not stirred nor interrupted by any one until everything that he seeks be revealed to him at the end of a *nomad*,[3] or two or three, or as long as he continues at his offering, and hence it is that this ceremony is called Imbas, that is, the two hands upon him crosswise, that is, a hand over and a hand hither upon his cheeks. And St. Patrick prohibited this ceremony, because it is a species of Teinm Laeghdha,[4] that is, he declared that any one who performed it should have no place in heaven or on earth."

These were apparently the private images of the druid himself which are spoken of, but there certainly existed public idols in pagan Ireland before the evangelisation of the island. St. Patrick himself, in his "Confession," asserts that before his coming the Irish worshipped idols—*idola et immunda*—and we have preserved to us more than one account of the great gold-covered image which was set up in Moy Slaught[5] [*i.e.*, the

[1] "Cach raet bid maith lasin filid agus bud adla(i)c dó do fhaillsiugad."

[2] Thus O'Curry ("Miscellany of the Celtic Society," vol. ii. p. 208); but Stokes translates, "he puts it then on the flagstone behind the door." See the original in Cormac's Glossary under "Himbas." I have not O'Donovan's translation by me.

[3] O'Curry translates this by "day." It is at present curiously used, I suppose by a kind of confusion with the English "moment," in the sense of a minute or other short measure of time. At least I have often heard it so used.

[4] Another species of incantation mentioned in the glossary.

[5] In Irish Magh Sleacht.

Plain of Adoration], believed to be in the present county of Cavan. It stood there surrounded by twelve lesser idols ornamented with brass, and may possibly have been regarded as a sun-god ruling over the twelve seasons. It was called the Crom Cruach or Cenn Cruach,[1] and certain Irish tribes considered it their special tutelary deity. The Dinnseanchas, or explanation of the name of Moy Slaught, calls it "the King Idol of Erin," "and around him were twelve idols made of stones, but he was of gold. Until Patrick's advent he was the god of every folk that colonised Ireland. To him they used to offer the firstlings of every issue and the chief scions of every clan;" and the ancient poem in the Book of Leinster declares that it was "a high idol with many fights, which was named the Cromm Cruaich."[2]

The poem tells us that "the brave Gaels used to worship it, and would never ask from it satisfaction as to their portion of the hard world without paying it tribute."

[1] In O'Donovan's fragmentary manuscript catalogue of the Irish MSS., in Trinity College, Dublin, he writes *apropos* of the life of St. Maedhog or Mogue, contained in H. 2, 6: "I searched the two Brefneys for the situation of Moy Sleacht on which stood the chief pagan Irish idol Crom Cruach, but have failed, being misled by Lanigan, who had been misled by Seward, who had been blinded by the impostor Beauford, who placed this plain in the county of Leitrim. It can, however, be proved from this life of St. Mogue that Magh Sleacht was that level part of the Barony of Tullaghan (in the county of Cavan) in which the island of Inis Breaghweė (now Mogue's Island), the church of Templeport, and the little village of Ballymagauran are situated." I have been told that O'Donovan afterwards found reason to doubt the correctness of this identification.

[2] M. de Jubainville connects the name with *cru* (Latin, *cruor*), "blood," translating Cenn Cruach by *tête sanglante* and Crom Cruach by *Courbe sanglante*, or *Croissant ensanglanté;* but Rhys connects it with Cruach, "a reek" or "mound," as in Croagh-Patrick, St. Patrick's Reek. Cenn Cruach is evidently the same name as the Roman station Penno-Crucium, in the present county of Stafford, the Irish "c" being as usual the equivalent of the British "p." This would make it appear that Cromm was no local idol. Rhys thinks it got its name Crom Cruach, "the stooped one of the mound," from its bent attitude in the days of its decadence.

"He was their God,[1]
The withered Cromm with many mists,
The people whom he shook over every harbour,
The everlasting kingdom they shall not have.

To him without glory
Would they kill their piteous wailing offspring,
With much wailing and peril
To pour their blood around Cromm Cruaich.

Milk and corn
They would ask from him speedily
In return for one-third of their healthy issue,
Great was the horror and scare of him.

To him
Noble Gaels would prostrate themselves,
From the worship of him, with many manslaughters
The Plain is called Moy Sleacht.

. . . .

In their ranks (stood)
Four times three stone idols
To bitterly beguile the hosts,
The figure of Cromm was made of gold.

Since the rule
Of Heremon,[2] the noble man of grace,
There was worshipping of stones
Until the coming of good Patrick of Macha [Ardmagh]."

There is not the slightest reason to distrust this evidence as far as the existence of Crom Cruach goes.

[1] Observe the exquisite and complicated metre of this in the original, a proof, I think, that the lines are not very ancient. It has been edited from the Book of Leinster, Book of Ballymote, Book of Lecan, and Rennes MS., at vol. i. p. 301 of Mr. Nutt's "Voyage of Bran," by Dr. Kuno Meyer—

"Ba hé a *nDia*
In Cromm Crín co n-immud *cia*
In lucht ro Craith ós cach *Cúan*
In flaithius *Búan* nochos *Bía*."

[2] *I.e.*, Eremon or Erimon, Son of Milesius, see above, p. 59.

"This particular tradition," says Mr. Nutt, "like the majority of those contained in it [the Dinnseanchas] must be of pre-Christian origin. It would have been quite impossible for a Christian monk to have invented such a story, and we may accept it as a perfectly genuine bit of information respecting the ritual side of insular Celtic religion."[1]

St. Patrick overthrew this idol, according both to the poem in the Book of Leinster and the early lives of the saint. The life says that when St. Patrick cursed Crom the ground opened and swallowed up the twelve lesser idols as far as their heads, which, as Rhys acutely observes, shows that when the early Irish lives of the saint were written the pagan sanctuary had so fallen into decay, that only the heads of the lesser idols remained above ground, while he thinks that it was at this time from its bent attitude and decayed appearance the idol was called Crom, "the Stooper."[2] There is, however, no

[1] The details of this idol, and, above all, the connection in which it stands to the mythic culture-king Tighearnmas, could not, as Mr. Nutt well remarks, have been invented by a Christian monk; but nothing is more likely, it appears to me, than that such a one, familiar with the idol rites of Judæa from the Old Testament, may have added the embellishing trait of the sacrifice of "the firstlings of every issue."

[2] Sir Samuel Ferguson's admirable poem upon the death of Cormac refers to the *priests* of the idol, but there is no recorded evidence of any such priesthood—

"Crom Cruach and his sub-gods twelve,
 Saith Cormac, are but carven treene,
The axe that made them haft or helve,
 Had worthier of your worship been.

But he who made the tree to grow,
 And hid in earth the iron stone,
And made the man with mind to know
 The axe's use is God alone.

Anon *to priests of Crom were brought*—
 Where girded in their service dread,
They ministered in red Moy Slaught—
 Word of the words King Cormac said.

They loosed their curse against the king,
 They cursed him in his flesh and bones,
And daily in their mystic ring
 They turned the maledictive stones."

apparent or recorded connection between this idol and the druids, nor do the druids appear to have fulfilled the functions of a public priesthood in Ireland, and the Introduction to the Seanchas Mór, or ancient Book of the Brehon Laws, distinctly says that, "until Patrick came only three classes of persons were permitted to speak in public in Erin, a chronicler to relate events and to tell stories, a poet to eulogise and to satirise, and a Brehon to pass sentence from precedents and commentaries," thus noticeably omitting all mention of the druids as a public body.

The idol Crom with his twelve subordinates may very well have represented the sun, upon whom both season and crops and consequently the life both of man and beast depend. The gods to whom the early Irish seem to have sacrificed, were no doubt, as I think Mr. Nutt has shown, agricultural powers, the lords of life and growth, and with these the sun, who is at the root of all growth, was intimately connected, "the object of that worship was to promote increase, the theory of worship was —life for life."[1] That the Irish swore by the sun and the moon and the elements is certain; the oath is quoted in many places,[2]

D'Arcy McGee also refers to Crom Cruach in terms almost equally poetic, but equally unauthorised:—

> "Their ocean-god was Manannán Mac Lir,
> Whose angry lips
> In their white foam full often would inter
> Whole fleets of ships.
> Crom *was their day-god and their thunderer*,
> Made morning and eclipse;
> Bride was their queen of song, and unto her
> They prayed with fire-touched lips!"

[1] Nutt's "Voyage of Bran," vol. ii. p. 250.

[2] The elements are recorded as having slain King Laoghaire because he broke the oath he had made by them. In the Lament for Patrick Sarsfield as late as the seventeenth century, the unknown poet cries:

> "Go mbeannaigh' an ghealach gheal 's an ghrian duit,
> Ó thug tu an lá as láimh Righ 'Liam leat."

I.e., May the white Moon and the Sun bless you, since thou hast taken the Day out of the hand of King William.

and St. Patrick appears to allude to sun-worship in that passage of his "Confession," where he says, "that sun which we see rising daily at His bidding for our sake, it will never reign, and its splendour will not last for ever, but those who adore it will perish miserably for all eternity:" this is also borne out by the passage in Cormac's Glossary of the images the pagans used to adore, "as, for instance, the form or figure of the sun on the altar."[1]

Another phase of the druidic character seems to have been that he was looked upon as an intermediary between man and the invisible powers. In the story which tells us how Midir the De Danann, carries off the king's wife, we are informed that the druid's counsel is sought as to how to recover her, which he at last is enabled to do "through his keys of science and Ogam," after a year's searching.

The druids are represented as carrying wands of yew, but there is nothing in Irish literature, so far as I am aware of, about their connection with the oak, from the Greek for which, δρῦς,[2] they are popularly supposed to derive their name. They used to be consulted as soothsayers upon the probable success of expeditions, as by Cormac mac Art, when he was thinking about extorting a double tribute from Munster,[3] and by Dáthi, the last pagan king of Ireland, when

And a little later we find the harper Carolan swearing "by the light of the sun."

> "Molann gach aon an té bhíos cráibhtheach cóir,
> Agus molann gach aon an té bhíos páirteach leó,
> *Dar solas na gréine* sé mo rádh go deó
> Go molfad gan spéis gan bhréig an t-áth mar geóbhad."

[1] See above, p. 55, note.

[2] The genitive of *drai*, the modern *draoi* (*dhree*) is *druad*, from whence no doubt the Latin *druidis*. It was Pliny who first derived the name from δρῦς. The word with a somewhat altered meaning was in use till recently. The wise men from the East are called druids (*draoithe*) in O'Donnell's translation of the New Testament. The modern word for enchantment (*draoidheacht*) is literally "druidism," but an enchanter is usually *draoidheadóir*, a derivation from *draoi*.

[3] See above, p. 29, note 2.

setting out upon his expedition abroad; they took auguries by birds, they could cause magic showers and fires, they observed stars and clouds, they told lucky days,[1] they had ordeals of their own,[2] but, above all, they appear to have been tutors or teachers.

Another druidic practice which is mentioned in Cormac's Glossary is more fully treated of by Keating, in his account of the great pagan convention at Uisneach, a hill in Meath, "where the men of Ireland were wont to exchange their goods and their wares and other jewels." This convention was held in the month of May,

> "And at it they were wont to make a sacrifice to the arch-god, whom they adored, whose name was Bél. It was likewise their usage to light two fires to Bél in every district in Ireland at this season, and to drive a pair of each herd of cattle that the district contained between these two fires, as a preservative, to guard them against all the diseases of that year. It is from that fire thus made that the day on which the noble feast of the apostles Peter and James is held has been called Bealtaine [in Scotch Beltane]. *i.e.*, Bél's fire."

Cormac, however, says nothing about a god named Bél—who, indeed, is only once mentioned elsewhere, so far as I know[3]—but explains the name as if it were Bil-tene, "goodly fire," from the fires which the druids made on that day through which to drive the cattle.[4]

[1] Cathbad, Conor mac Nessa's Druid, foretold that any one who took arms—the Irish equivalent for knighthood—upon a certain day, would become famous for ever, but would enjoy only a brief life. It was Cuchulain who assumed arms upon that day.

[2] O'Curry quotes a druidic ordeal from the MS. marked H. 3. 17 in Trinity College, Dublin. A woman to clear her character has to rub her tongue to a red-hot adze of bronze, which had been heated in a fire of blackthorn or rowan-tree.

[3] "Revue Celt.," vol. ii. p. 443. Is Bel to be equated with what Rhys calls in one place "the chthonian divinity Beli the Great," of the Britons, and in another "Beli the Great, the god of death and darkness"? (*See* "Hibbert Lectures," pp. 168 and 274.)

[4] The Christian priests, apparently unable to abolish these cattle ceremonies, took the harm out of them by transferring them to St. John's

Post-Christian accounts of the druids as a whole, and of individual druids differ widely. The notes on St. Patrick, in the Book of Armagh, present them in the worst possible light as wicked wizards and augurs and people of incantations,[1] and the Latin lives of the Saints nearly always call them "magi." Yet they are admitted to have been able to prophecy. King Laoghaire's [Leary's] druids prophesied to him three years before the arrival of Patrick that "adze-heads would come over a furious sea,

> "Their mantles hole-headed,
> Their staves crook-headed,
> Their tables in the east of their houses."[2]

In the lives of the early saints we find some of them on fair terms with the druids. Columcille's first teacher was a druid, whom his mother consulted about him. It is true that in the Lismore text he is called not a druid but a *fáidh*, *i.e.*, *vates* or prophet, but this only confirms the close connection between druid, prophet, and teacher, for his proceedings are distinctly druidical, the account runs: "Now when the time for reading came to him the cleric went to a certain prophet

Eve, the 24th of June, where they are still observed in most districts of Ireland, and large fires built with bones in them, and occasionally cattle are driven through them or people leap over them. The cattle were probably driven through the fire as a kind of substitute for their sacrifice, and the bones burnt in the fire are probably a substitute for the bones of the cattle that should have been offered up. Hence the fires are called "teine cnámh" (bone-fire) in Irish, and bōne-fire (not bŏnfire) in English.

[1] St. Patrick is there stated to have found around the king "scivos et magos et auruspices, incantatores et omnis malæ artis inventores."

[2] This means tonsured men, with cowls, with pastoral staves, with altars in the east end of the churches. The ancient Irish rann is very curious :—

> "Ticcat Tailcinn
> Tar muir meirceann,
> A mbruit toillceann.
> A crainn croimceann.
> A miasa n-airrter tige
> Friscerat uile amen."

who abode in the land to ask him when the boy ought to begin. When the prophet had scanned the sky, he said 'Write an alphabet for him now.' The alphabet was written on a cake, and Columcille consumed the cake in this wise, half to the east of a water, and half to the west of a water. Said the prophet through grace of prophecy, 'So shall this child's territory be, half to the east of the sea, and half to the west of the sea.'"[1] Columcille himself is said to have composed a poem beginning, "My Druid is the son of God." Another druid prophesies of St. Brigit before she was born,[2] and other instances connecting the early saints with druids are to be found in their lives, which at least show that there existed a sufficient number of persons in early Christian Ireland who did not consider the druids wholly bad, but believed that they could prophecy, at least in the interests of the saints.

From what we have said, it is evident that there were always druids in Ireland, and that they were personages of great importance. But it is not clear that they were an organised body like the druids of Gaul,[3] or like the Bardic body in later times in Ireland, nor is it clear what their exact functions were, but they seem to have been teachers above everything else. It is clear, too, that the ancient Irish—at least in some cases—possessed and worshipped images. That they sacrificed to them, and even offered up human beings, is by no means so certain, the evidence for this resting upon the single passage in the Dinnseanchas, and the poem (in a modern style of metre) in the Book of Leinster, which we have just given, and which though it is evidence for the existence of the idol Crom Cruach, known to us already from other sources, may possibly have had the trait of human sacrifice added as a heightening touch by a Christian chronicler familiar with the

[1] *I.e.*, one half in Ireland, the other in Scotland, alluding to his work at Iona and among the Picts.

[2] Stokes, "Lives of the Saints, from the Book of Lismore," p. 183.

[3] Who were, according to Ammianus Marcellinus, quoting the Greek historian, Timagenes, "sodaliciis adstricti consortiis."

accounts of Moloch and Ashtarôth. The complete silence which, outside of these passages,[1] exists in all Irish literature as to a proceeding so terrifying to the popular imagination, seems to me a proof that if human sacrifice was ever resorted to at all, it had fallen into abeyance before the landing of the Christian missionaries.

[1] There is one other instance of human sacrifice mentioned in the Book of Ballymote, but this is recorded in connection with funeral games, and appears to have been an isolated piece of barbarity performed "that it might be a reproach to the Momonians for ever, and that it might be a trophy over them." Fiachra, a brother of Niall of the Nine Hostages, in the fourth century, carried off fifty hostages from Munster, and dying of his wounds, the hostages were buried alive with him, round his grave: "ro hadnaicead na geill tucadh a neass ocus siad beo im fheart Fiachra comba hail for Mumain do gres, ocus comba comrama forra." For another allusion to "human sacrifice" see O'Curry's "Manners and Customs," vol. i. p. dcxli and cccxxxiii. The "Dinnseanchas," quoted from above, is a topographical work explaining the origin of Irish place-names, and attributed to Amergin mac Amhalgaidh, poet to King Diarmuid mac Cearbaill, who lived in the sixth century. "There seems no reason," says Dr. Atkinson, in his preface to the facsimile Book of Leinster, "for disputing his claims to be regarded as the original compiler of a work of a similar character—the original nucleus is not now determinable." The oldest copy is the Book of Leinster and treats of nearly two hundred places and contains eighty-eight poems. The copy in the Book of Ballymote contains one hundred and thirty-nine, and that in the Book of Lecan even more. The total number of all the poems contained in the different copies is close on one hundred and seventy. The copy in the Bodleian Library was published by Whitley Stokes in "Folk-lore," December, 1892, and that in the Advocates Library, in Edinburgh, in "Folk-lore," December, 1893. The prose tales, from a copy at Rennes, he published in the "Revue Celtique," vols. xv. and xvi. An edition of the oldest copy in the Book of Leinster is still a desideratum. The whole work is full of interesting pagan allusions, but the different copies, in the case of many names, vary greatly and even contradict each other.

CHAPTER X

THE IRISH ELYSIUM AND BELIEF IN REBIRTH

Cæsar, writing some fifty years before Christ about the Gauls and their Druids, tells his countrymen that one of the prime articles which they taught was that men's souls do not die—*non interire animas*—"but passed over after death from one into another," and their opinion is, adds Cæsar, that this doctrine "greatly tends to the arousing of valour, all fear of death being despised." [1] A few years later Diodorus Siculus wrote that one of their doctrines was "that the souls of men are undying, and that after finishing their term of existence they pass into another body," adding that at burials of the dead some actually cast letters addressed to their departed relatives upon the funeral pile, under the belief that the dead would read them in the next world. Timagenes, a Greek who wrote a history of Gaul now lost, Strabo, Valerius Maximus, Pomponius Mela, and Lucan [2] in his "Pharsalia," all have passages upon this vivid belief of the Gauls that the soul lived again. This doctrine must also have been current in Britain, where the Druidic teaching was, to use Cæsar's phrase,

[1] "De Bello Gallico," vi. 14.

[2] See "Voyage of Bran," vol. ii. pp. 107–111, where all these passages have been lucidly collected by Mr. Nutt.

"discovered, and thence brought into Gaul," and it would have been curious indeed if Ireland did not share in it.

There is, moreover, abundant evidence to show that the doctrine of metempsychosis was perfectly familiar to the pagan Irish, as may be seen in the stories of the births of Cuchulain, Etain, the Two Swineherds, Conall Cearnach, Tuan Mac Cairill, and Aedh Sláne.[1] But there is not, in our existing literature, any evidence that the belief was ever elevated into a philosophical doctrine of general acceptance, applicable to every one, still less that there was ever any ethical stress laid upon the belief in rebirth. It is only the mythological element in the belief in metempsychosis which has come down to us, and from which we ascertain that the pagan Irish believed that supernatural beings could become clothed in flesh and blood, could enter into women and be born again, could take different shapes and pass through different stages of existence, as fowls, animals, or men. What the actual doctrinal form of the familiar idea was, or how far it influenced the popular mind, we have no means of knowing. But as Mr. Nutt well remarks, "early Irish religion must have possessed some ritual, and what in default of an apter term must be styled philosophical as well as mythological elements. Practically the latter alone have come down to us, and that in a romantic rather than in a strictly mythical form. Could we judge Greek religion aright if fragments of Apollodorus or the 'Metamorphoses' were all that survived of the literature it inspired?"[2] The most that can be said upon the subject, then, is that the doctrine of rebirth was actually taught with a deliberate ethical purpose—that of making men brave, since on being slain in this life they passed into a new one—amongst the Celts of Gaul, that it must have been familiar to the Britons between whose Druids and those of Gaul so close a resemblance subsisted, and that the idea of rebirth which

[1] All of these have been studied by Mr. Nutt, chap. xiv.

[2] Vol. ii. p. 121.

forms part of half-a-dozen existing Irish sagas, was perfectly familiar to the Irish Gael, although we have no evidence that it was connected with any ritual or taught as a deliberate doctrine.

In reconstructing from our existing literature the beliefs and religion ot our ancestors, we can only do so incompletely, and with difficulty, from passages in the oldest sagas and other antique fragments, mostly of pagan origin, from allusions in very early poems, from scanty notices in the annals, and from the lives of early saints. The relatively rapid conversion of the island to Christianity in the fifth century, and the enthusiasm with which the new religion was received, militated against any full transmission of pagan belief or custom. We cannot now tell whether all the ancient Irish were imbued with the same religious beliefs, or whether these varied—as they probably did—from tribe to tribe. Probably all the Celtic races, even in their most backward state, believed—so far as they had any persuasion on the subject at all—in the immortality of the soul. Where the souls of the dead went to, when they were not re-incarnated, is not so clear. They certainly believed in a happy Other-World, peopled by a happy race, whither people were sometimes carried whilst still alive, and to gain which they either traversed the sea to the north-west, or else entered one of the Sidh [Shee] mounds, or else again dived beneath the water.[1] In all cases, however, whatever the mode of access, the result is much the same. A beautiful country is discovered

[1] In a large collection of nearly sixty folk-lore stories taken down in Irish from the lips of the peasantry, I find about five contain allusions to the belief in another world full of life under water, and about four in a life in the inside of the hills. The Hy Brasil type—that of finding the dead living again on an ocean island—is, so far as I have yet collected, quite unrepresented amongst them. An old Irish expression for dying is going "to the army of the dead," used by Déirdre in her lament, and I find a variant of it so late as the beginning of this century, in a poem by Raftery, a blind musician of the county Mayo, who tells his countrymen to remember that they must go "to the meadow of the dead." *See* Raftery's "Aithreachas," in my "Religious Songs of Connacht," p. 266.

where a happy race free from care, sickness, and death, spend the smiling hours in simple, sensuous pleasures.

There is a graphic description of this Elysium in the "Voyage of Bran," a poem evidently pagan,[1] and embodying purely pagan conceptions. A mysterious female, an emissary from the lovely land, appears in Bran's household one day, when the doors were closed and the house full of chiefs and princes, and no one knew whence she came, and she chanted to them twenty-eight quatrains describing the delights of the pleasant country.

"There is a distant isle
Around which sea-horses glisten,
A fair course against the white-swelling surge,
Four feet uphold it.[2]

Feet of white bronze under it,
Glittering through beautiful ages.
Lovely land throughout the world's age
On which the many blossoms drop.

An ancient tree there is with blossoms
On which birds call to the Hours.
'Tis in harmony, it is their wont
To call together every Hour.

. . . . .

[1] Admirably translated by Kuno Meyer, who says "there are a large number of [word] forms in the 'Voyage of Bran,' as old as any to be found in the Wurzburg Glosses," and these Professor Thurneysen ascribes unhesitatingly to the seventh century. Zimmer also agrees that the piece is not later than the seventh century, that is, was first written down in the seventh century, but this is no criterion of the date of the original composition.

[2] I give Kuno Meyer's translation: in the original—

"Fil inis i n-eterchéin
Immataitnet gabra rein
Rith find fris tóibgel tondat
Ceitheóir cossa foslongat."

In modern Irish the first two lines would run

"[Go] bhfuil inis i n-idir-chéin
Um a dtaithnigeann gabhra réin."

Réin being the genitive of *rian*, "the sea," which, according to M. d'Arbois, the Gaels brought with them as a reminiscence of the Rhine, see above p. 10.

Unknown is wailing or treachery
In the familiar cultivated land,
There is nothing rough or harsh,
But sweet music striking on the ear.

Without grief, without sorrow, without death,
Without any sickness, without debility,
That is the sign of Emain,
Uncommon, an equal marvel.

A beauty of a wondrous land
Whose aspects are lovely,
Whose view is a fair country,
Incomparable in its haze.

. . . . . .

The sea washes the wave against the land,
Hair of crystal drops from its mane.

Wealth, treasures of every hue,
Are in the gentle land, a beauty of freshness,
Listening to sweet music,
Drinking the best of wine.

Golden chariots on the sea plain
Rising with the tide to the sun,
Chariots of silver in the plain of sports
And of unblemished bronze.

. . . . . .

At sunrise there will come
A fair man illumining level lands,
He rides upon the fair sea-washed plain,
He stirs the ocean till it is blood.

. . . . . .

Then they row to the conspicuous stone
From which arise a hundred strains.

It sings a strain unto the host
Through long ages, it is not sad,
Its music swells with choruses of hundreds
They look for neither decay nor death.

There will come happiness with health
To the land against which laughter peals.
Into Imchiuin [the very calm place] at every season,
Will come everlasting joy.

It is a day of lasting weather
That showers [down] silver on the land,
A pure-white cliff in the verge of the sea
Which from the sun receives its heat."

Manannán, the Irish Neptune, driving in a chariot across the sea, which to him was a flowery plain, meets Bran thereafter, and chants to him twenty-eight more verses about the lovely land of Moy Mell, "the Pleasant Plain," which the unknown lady had described, and they are couched in the same strain.

"Though [but] one rider is seen
In Moy Mell of many powers,
There are many steeds on its surface
Although thou seest them not.

. . . . . .

A beautiful game, most delightful
They play [sitting] at the luxurious wine,
Men and gentle women under a bush
Without sin, without crime.

. . . . . .

A wood with blossom and fruit,
On which is the vine's veritable fragrance ;
A wood without decay, without defect,
On which are leaves of golden hue."

Then, prophesying of the death of Mongan, he sang—

"He will drink a drink from Loch Ló,
While he looks at the stream of blood ;
The white hosts will take him under a wheel of clouds,
To the gathering where there is no sorrow."

I know of few things in literature comparable to this lovely description, at once so mystic and so sensuous, of the joys of the other world. To my mind it breathes the very essence of Celtic glamour, and is shot through and through with the Celtic love of form, beauty, landscape, company, and the society of woman. How exquisite the idea of being transported from this world to an isle around which sea-horses glisten, where from trees covered with blossoms the birds call in harmony to the Hours, a land whose haze is incomparable! What a touch! Where hair of crystal drops from the mane of the wave as it washes against the land; where the chariots of silver and of bronze assemble on the plain of sports, in the country against which laughter peals, and the day of lasting weather showers silver on the land. And then to play sitting at the luxurious wine—

> "Men and gentle women under a bush
> Without sin, without crime!"

I verily believe there is no Gael alive even now who would not in his heart of hearts let drift by him the Elysiums of Virgil, Dante, and Milton to grasp at the Moy Mell of the unknown Irish pagan.

In another perhaps equally ancient story, that of the elopement of Connla, son of Conn of the Hundred Battles,[1] with a lady who is a denizen of this mysterious land, we find the unknown visitor giving nearly the same account of it as that given to Bran.

"Whence hast thou come, O Lady?" said the Druid.

"I have come," said she, "from the lands of the living in which there is neither death, nor sin, nor strife;[2] we enjoy perpetual feasts without anxiety, and benevolence without contention. A large Sidh [*Shee*, "fairy-mound"] is where we

[1] Preserved in the Leabhar na h-Uidhre, a MS. compiled from older ones about the year 1100. See for this story "Gaelic Journal," vol. ii. p. 306.

[2] "*Dodeochadsa for in ben a tirib beó áit inna bi bás na peccad na imorbus, i.e.* [go], ndeachas-sa ar san bhean ó tíribh na mbeó, áit ann nach mbionn bás ná peacadh ná immarbhádh."

dwell, so that it is hence we are called the Sidh [Shee] people."

The Druids appear, as I have already remarked, to have acted as intermediaries between the inhabitants of the other world and of this, and in the story of Connla one of them chants against the lady so that her voice was not heard, and he drives her away through his incantation. She comes back, however, at the end of a month, and again summons the prince.

"'Tis no lofty seat," she chanted, "upon which sits Connla amid short-lived mortals awaiting fearful death; the ever-living ones invite thee to be the ruler over the men of Tethra."

Conn of the Hundred Battles, who had overheard her speech, cried, "Call me the Druid; I see her tongue has been allowed her to-day [again]."

But she invisible to all save the prince replied to him—

"O Conn of the Hundred Battles, druidism is not loved, for little has it progressed to honour on the great Righteous Strand, with its numerous, wondrous, various families."

After that she again invites the prince to follow her, saying—

"There is another land which it were well to seek.
I see the bright sun is descending, though far off we shall reach it ere night.
'Tis the land that cheers the mind of every one that turns to me.
There is no race in it save only women and maidens."

The prince is overcome with longing. He leaps into her well-balanced, gleaming boat of pearl. Those who were left behind upon the strand "saw them dimly, as far as the sight of their eyes could reach. They sailed the sea away from them, and from that day to this have not been seen, and it is unknown where they went to."

In the fine story of Cuchulain's sick-bed,[1] in which though

[1] Also contained in the Leabhar na h-Uidhre, a MS. transcribed about the year 1100.

the language of the text is not so ancient, the conceptions are equally pagan, the deserted wife of Manannán, the Irish Neptune, falls in love with the human warrior, and invites him to the other-world to herself, through the medium of an ambassadress. Cuchulain sends his charioteer Laeg along with this mysterious ambassadress, that he may bring him word again, to what kind of land he is invited. Laeg, when he returns, repeats a glowing account of its beauty, which coincides closely with those given by the ladies who summoned Bran and Connla.

"There are at the western door,
In the place where the sun goes down,
A stud of steeds of the best of breeds
Of the grey and the golden brown.

There wave by the eastern door
Three crystal-crimson trees,
Whence the warbling bird all day is heard
On the wings of the perfumed breeze.

And before the central door
Is another, of gifts untold.
All silvern-bright in the warm sunlight,
Its branches gleam like gold."[1]

. . . . . .

In the saga of the Wooing of Etain we meet with what is substantially the same description. She is the wife of one of the Tuatha De Danann, is reborn as a mortal, and weds the king of Ireland. Her former husband, Midir, still loves her, follows her, and tries to win her back. She is unwilling, and he chants to her this description of the land to which he would lure her.

[1] Literally: "There are at the western door, in the place where the sun goes down, a stud of steeds with grey-speckled manes and another crimson brown. There are at the eastern door three ancient trees of crimson crystal, from which incessantly sing soft-toned birds. There is a tree in front of the court, it cannot be matched in harmony, a tree of silver against which the sun shines, like unto gold is its great sheen."

"Come back to me, lady, to love and to shine
In the land that was thine in the long-ago,
Where of primrose hue is the golden hair
And the limbs are as fair as the wreathed snow.

To the lakes of delight that no storm may curl,
Where the teeth are as pearl, the eyes as sloes,
Which alight, whenever they choose to seek,
On the bloom of a cheek where the foxglove glows.

Each brake is alive with the flowers of spring,
Whence the merles sing in their shy retreat ;
Though sweet be the meadows of Innisfail,
Our beautiful vale is far more sweet.

Though pleasant the mead be of Innisfail,
More pleasant the ale of that land of mine,
A land of beauty, a land of truth,
Where youth shall never grow old or pine.

Fair rivers brighten the vale divine,—
There are choicest of wine and of mead therein,
And heroes handsome and women fair
Are in dalliance there without stain or sin.

From thence we see, though we be not seen,
We know what has been and shall be again,
And the cloud that was raised by the first man's fall,
Has concealed us all from the eyes of men.

Then come with me, lady, to joys untold,
And a circlet of gold on thy head shall be,
Banquets of milk and of wine most rare,
Thou shalt share, O lady, and share with me." [1]

[1] A Befind in raga lim / I tír n-ingnad hifil rind / Is barr sobairche folt and / Is dath snechtu chorp coind. Literally : "O lady fair wouldst thou come with me to the wondrous land that is ours, where the hair is as the blossom of the primrose, where the tender body is as fair as snow. There shall be no grief there nor sorrow ; white are the teeth there, black are the eyebrows, a delight to the eye is the number of our host, and on every cheek is the hue of the foxglove.

"The crimson of the foxglove is in every brake, delightful to the eye [there] the blackbird's eggs. Although pleasant to behold are the plains of Innisfail, after frequenting the Great Plain rarely wouldst thou [remember them]. Though heady to thee the ale of Innisfail, headier the ale of the

The casual Christian allusion in the penultimate verse need not lead us astray, nor does it detract from the essentially pagan character of the rest, for throughout almost the whole of Irish literature the more distinctly or ferociously pagan any piece is, the more certain it is to have a Christian allusion added at the end as a make-weight. There is great ingenuity displayed in thus turning the pagan legend into a Christian homily by the addition of two lines suggesting that if men were not sinful, this beautiful pagan world and the beautiful forms that inhabited it would be visible to the human ken. This was sufficient to disarm any hostility to the legend on the part of the Church.

From what we have said it is evident that the ancient Irish pagans believed in the possibility of rebirth, and founded many of their mythical sagas on the doctrine of metempsychosis, and that they had a highly ornate and fully-developed belief in a happy other-world or Elysium, to which living beings were sometimes carried off without going through the forms of death. But it is impossible to say whether rebirth with life in another world, for those whom the gods favoured, was taught as a doctrine or had any ethical significance attached to it by the druids of Ireland, as it most undoubtedly had by their cousins the druids of Gaul.

great land, a beauty of a land, the land I speak of. Youth never grows there into old age. Warm, sweet streams traverse the country with choicest mead and choicest wine, handsome persons [are there], without blemish, conception without sin, without stain.

"We see every one on every side, and no one seeth us; the cloud of Adam's wrong-doing has concealed us from being numbered. O lady, if thou comest to my brave land, it is a crown of gold shall be upon thy head, fresh flesh of swine, banquets of new milk and ale shalt thou have with me then, fair lady."

Apropos of the Irish liking for swine's flesh, Stanihurst tells a good story: "'No meat,' says he, 'they fansie so much as porke, and the fatter the better. One of John O'Nel's [Shane O'Neill's] household demanded of his fellow whether beefe were better than porke. 'That,' quoth the other, 'is as intricate a question as to ask whether thou art better than O'Nell.'"

CHAPTER XI

EARLY USE OF LETTERS, OGAM AND ROMAN

WE now come to the question, When and where did the Irish get their alphabet, and at what time did they begin to practise the art of writing? The present alphabet of the Irish, which they have used in all their books from the seventh century down, and probably for three hundred years before that, is only a modification—and a peculiarly beautiful one—of the Roman letters. This alphabet they no doubt borrowed from their neighbours, the Romanised Britons, within whose territory they had established themselves, and with whom—now in peace, now in war—they carried on a vigorous and constant intercourse.[1] The *general* use of letters in Ireland is, however, to be attributed to the early Christian missionaries.

But there is no reason to believe that it was St. Patrick, or indeed any missionary, who first introduced them. There probably were in Ireland many persons in the fourth century, or perhaps even earlier, who were acquainted with the art of

[1] Dr. Jones, the Bishop of St. Davids, in his interesting book, "Vestiges of the Gael in Gwynedd" (North Wales) has come to the conclusion that the Irish occupied the whole of Anglesey, Carnarvon, Merioneth, and Cardiganshire, with at least portions of Denbighshire, Montgomery, and Radnor. Their occupation of part of the south and south-west of England is attested by the area of Ogam finds.

writing. Already, at the beginning of the third century at least, says Zimmer in his "Keltische Studien," British missionaries were at work in the south of Ireland. Bede, in his history, says distinctly that Palladius was sent from Rome in the year 431 to the Irish "who believed in Christ"—"ad Scottos in Christum credentes." Already, at the close of the third century, there was an organised British episcopate, and three British bishops attended the Council of Arles held in 314. It is quite impossible that the numerous Irish colonies settled in the south of England and in Wales could have failed to come into contact with this organised Church, and even to have been influenced by it. The account in the Acta Sanctorum, of Declan, Bishop of Waterford, said to have been born in 347, and of Ailbe, another southern bishop, who met St. Patrick, may be looked upon as perfectly true in so far as it relates to the actual existence of these pre-Patrician bishops. St. Chrysostom, writing in the year 387, mentions that already churches and altars had been erected in the British Isles. Pelagius, the subtle and persuasive heresiarch who taught with such success at Rome about the year 400, and acquired great influence there, was of Irish descent—"habet progeniem Scotticæ gentis de Brittanorum vicinia," said St. Jerome. As St. Augustine and Prosper of Aquitaine call him "Briton" and "British scribe," he probably belonged to one of the Irish colonies settled in Wales or the South-west of England. His success at Rome is a proof that some Irish families at least were within reach of literary education in the fourth century. His friend and teacher, Celestius, has also been claimed as an Irishman, but Dr. Healy has shown that this claim is perhaps founded upon a misconception.[1]

"The influence of the ancient Irish on the Continent," says Dr. Sigerson, "began in the works of Sedulius, whose 'Carmen Paschale,' published in the fifth century,

[1] "Ireland's Ancient Schools and Scholars," p. 39. I find Migne, in his note on Pelagius, apparently confounding Scotia with Great Britain.

is the first great Christian epic worthy of the name." Sedulius, the Virgil of theological poetry, flourished in the first half of the fifth century, and seems to have studied in Gaul, passed into Italy, and finally resided in Achaia in Greece, which he seems to have made his home. There are at least eight Irish Siadals (in Latin Sedulius, in English Shiel) commemorated by Colgan. The strongest evidence of Sedulius's Irish nationality is that the Irish geographer Dicuil, in the eighth century, quoting some of his lines, calls him *noster Sedulius*. John of Tritenheim, towards the close of the fifteenth century, distinctly calls him an Irishman *natione Scotus*, but attributes to him the verses of a later Sedulius. Dr. Sigerson, by a clever analysis of his verse-peculiarities confirms this opinion.[1]

In the "Tripartite Life of St. Patrick" we read that the druids at the king's court, when St. Patrick arrived there, possessed books, and when, at a later date, St. Patrick determined upon revising the Brehon law code, the books in which it was written down were laid before him. That there has come down to our time no written record earlier than the seventh or eighth century[2] is chiefly due to the enormous destruction of books by the Danes and English. The same causes produced a like effect in Britain, for the oldest surviving British MSS. are not even as old as ours, although the art of writing must have been known and practised there since the Roman occupation.

The Irish had, however, another system of writing which

[1] See for Dr. Sigerson's ingenious argument "Bards of the Gael and Gaul," Introduction, p. 30.

[2] Except perhaps on stone. There is an inscription on a stone in Galway, "Lie Luguaedon Macc Lmenueh," for a facsimile of which see O'Donovan's grammar, p. 411. O'Donovan says it was set up over a nephew of St. Patrick's. Mr. Macalister reads it no doubt correctly, "Lie Luguaedon macci Menueh." This is probably the oldest extant inscription in Roman letters, and it shows that the old Ogam form *maqui* had already changed into mac[c]i. The "c" in place of "q" is only found on the later Ogam stones, and only one stone is found to read "maic."

they themselves invented. This was the celebrated Ogam script, consisting of a number of short lines, straight or slanting,[1] and drawn either below, above, or through one long stem-line, which stem-line is generally the angle between two sides of a long upright rectangular stone. These lines represented letters; and over two hundred stones have been found inscribed with Ogam writing. It is a remarkable fact that rude as this device for writing is, it has been applied with considerable skill, and is framed with much ingenuity. For in every case it is found that those letters which, like the vowels, are most easily pronounced, are also in Ogam the easiest to inscribe, and the simpler sounds are represented by simpler characters than those that are more complex. To account for the philosophical character of this alphabet[2] "than which no

[1] Thus four cuts to the right of or below the long line stand for S, above it they mean C, passing through the long line half on one side and half on the other they mean E. These straight lines, being easily cut on stone with a chisel, continued long in use. The long line, with reference to which all the letters are drawn, is usually the right angle or corner of the upright stone between the two sides. The inscription usually begins at the left-hand corner of the stone facing the reader and is read upwards, and is sometimes continued down on the right-hand angular line as well. The vowels are very small cuts on the angle of the stone, but much larger than points. There is no existing book written in Ogam, but various alphabets of it have been preserved in the Book of Ballymote, and some small metal articles have been found inscribed with it, showing that its use was not peculiar to pillar stones.

[2] See a curious monograph by Dr. Ernst Rethwisch entitled, "Die Inschrift von Killeen Cormac und der Úrsprung der Sprache," 1886. "Einfachere Schriftzeichen als das keltische Alphabet sind nicht denkbar . . . die Vocale haben die einfachsten Symbole und unter den Vocalen haben wieder die am bequemsten auszusprechenden bequemer zu machende Zeichen wie die Andern. Unter den Consonanten, hat die Klasse die am schwierigsten gelingt . . . die am wenigsten leicht einzuritzenden Zeichen : die Gaumenlaute." He is greatly struck by "der so verständig und sachgemäss erscheinende Trieb dem einfachsten Laut das einfachste Symbol zu widmen." "Eine Erklärung [of the rational simplicity of the Ogam script] ist nur möglich wenn man annimmt dass die natürliche Begabung der Kelten, der praktische auf Einfachheit und Beobachtungsgabe beruhende Sinn viel früher zu einer gewissen Reife gediehen sind, als bei den Indogermanischen Verwandten" (p. 29).

simpler method of writing is imaginable," a German, Dr. Rethwisch, who examined it from this side, concluded that "the natural gifts of the Celts and their practical genius for simplicity and observation ripened up to a certain stage far earlier than those of their Indo-European relations." This statement, however, rests upon the as yet unproved assumption that Ogam writing is pre-Christian and pagan. What is of more interest is that the author of it supposed that with one or two changes it would make the simplest conceivable universal-alphabet or international code of writing. It is very strange that nearly all the Irish Ogam stones are found in the south-west, chiefly in the counties of Cork and Kerry, with a few scattered over the rest of the country—but one in West Connacht, and but one or two at the most in Ulster. Between twenty and thirty more have been found in Wales and Devonshire, and one or two even farther east, thus bearing witness to the colonies planted by the Irish marauders in early Britain, for Ogam writing is peculiar to the Irish Gael and only found where he had settled. Ten stones more have been found in Scotland, probably the latest in date of any, for some of these, unlike the Irish stones, bear Christian symbols. Many Ogams have been easily read, thanks to the key contained in the Book of Ballymote; thanks also to the fact that one or two Ogams have been found with duplicates inscribed in Latin letters. But many still defy all attempts at deciphering them, though numerous efforts have been made, treating them as though they were cryptic ciphers, which they were long believed to be. That Ogam was, as some assert, an early cryptic alphabet, and one intended to be read only by the initiated, is both in face of the numbers of such inscriptions already deciphered and in the face of the many instances recorded in our oldest sagas of its employment, an absurd hypothesis. It is nearly always treated in them as an ordinary script which any one could read. It may, however, have been occasionally used in later times in a cryptic sense, names being written backwards or syllables transposed, but this was certainly not the original invention. Some of the latest Ogam pillars are gravestones of people who died so late as the year 600, but what proportion of them, if any, date from before the Christian era it is as yet impossible to tell. Certain it is that the grammatical forms of the language inscribed upon most of them are vastly older than those of the very oldest manuscripts,[1] and agree with those of the old Gaulish linguistic monuments.

Cormac's Glossary—a work of the ninth or tenth century—the ancient sagas, and many allusions in the older literature, would seem to show that Ogam writing was used by the pagan Irish. Cormac, explaining the word *fé*, says that "it was a wooden rod used by the Gael for measuring corpses and graves, and that this rod used always to be kept in the burial-places of the heathen, and it was a horror to every one even to take it in his hand, and whatever was abominable to them they (the pagans) used to inscribe on it in Ogam."[2] The sagas also are full of allusions to Ogam writing. In the "Táin Bó Cuailnge," which probably assumed substantially its present shape in the seventh century, we are told how when Cuchulain, after assuming arms, drove into Leinster with

[1] As *Curci* and *maqi* for the genitives of Corc and mac. In later times the genitive ending i, became incorporated in the body of the word, making *Cuirc* and *maic* in the MSS., which latter subsequently became attenuated still further into the modern *mic*. Another very common and important form is *avi*, which has been explained as from a nominative *avios [for (*p)avios], Old Irish *auc*, modern *ua* or *o*. Another extraordinary feature is the suffix **gnos* = *cnos*, the regular patronymic formative of the Gaulish inscriptions. Another important word is *muco*, genitive *mucoi*, meaning "descendant," but in some cases apparently "chief." The word *anm* or even *ancm*, which often precedes the genitive of the proper noun, as *anm meddugini*, has not yet been explained or accounted for. All these examples help to show the great age of the linguistic monuments preserved in Ogam.

[2] "Ocus no bid in flesc sin dogres irelcib nangente ocus bafuath la cach a gabail inalaim ocus cach ni ba hadetchi leo dobertis [lege nobentis] tria Ogam innti, *i.e.* Agus do bhíodh an fleasg sin do ghnáth i reiligibh na ngente, agus budh fuath, le cách a gabháil ann a láimh, agus gach nidh budh ghránna leó do bhainidis [ghearradaois] tre Ogham innti."

his charioteer and came to the dún or fort of the three sons of Nechtan, he found on the lawn before the court a stone pillar, around which was written in Ogam that every hero who passed thereby was bound to issue a challenge. This was clearly no cryptic writing but the ordinary script, meant to be read by every one who passed.[1] Cuchulain in the same saga frequently cuts Ogam on wands, which he leaves in the way of Mève's army. These are always brought to his friend Fergus to read. Perhaps the next oldest allusion to Ogam writing is in the thoroughly pagan "Voyage of Bran," which both Zimmer and Kuno Meyer consider to have been committed to writing in the seventh century. We are there told that Bran wrote the fifty or sixty quatrains of the poem in Ogam. Again, in Cormac's Glossary[2] we find a story of how Lomna Finn mac Cool's fool (drúth) made an Ogam and put it in Finn's way to tell him how his wife had been unfaithful to him. A more curious case is the story in the Book of Leinster of Corc's flying to the Court of King Feradach in Scotland. Not knowing how he might be received he hid in a wood near by. The King's poet, however, meets him and recognises him, having seen him before that in Ireland. The poet notices an Ogam on the prince's shield, and asks him, "Who was it that befriended you with that Ogam, for it was not good luck which he designed for you?" "Why," asked the prince, "what does it contain?" "What it contains," said the poet, "is this—that if by day you arrive at the Court of Feradach the king, your head shall be struck off before night; if it be at night you arrive your head shall be struck off before morning."[3] This Ogam was

[1] See Zimmer's "Summary of the Táin Bó Cuailnge," *Zeit. f. vgl., Sprachforschung*, 1887, p. 448.

[2] Under the word *orc tréith*.

[3] The classical reader need hardly be reminded of the striking resemblance between this and the *σήματα λυγρὰ* which, according to Homer, Prœtus gave the unsuspecting Bellerophon to bring to the King of Lycia, *γράψας ἐν πίνακι πτυκτῷ θυμοφθόρα πολλά*.

apparently readable only by the initiated, for the prince did not himself know what he was bearing on his shield.

All ancient Irish literature, then, is unanimous in attributing a knowledge of Ogam to the pre-Christian Irish. M. d'Arbois de Jubainville seems also to believe in its pagan antiquity, for when discussing the story of St. Patrick's setting a Latin alphabet before Fiach, and of the youth's learning to read the Psalms within the following four-and-twenty hours, he remarks that the story is just possible since Fiach should have known the Ogam alphabet, and except for the form of the letters it and the Latin alphabet were the same.[1]

St. Patrick, too, tells us in his "Confession" how after his flight from Ireland he saw a man coming as it were from that country with innumerable letters, a dream that would scarcely have visited him had he known that there was no one in Ireland who could write letters.[2]

The Ogam alphabet, however, is based upon the Roman. Of this there can be no doubt, for it contains letters which,

[1] The "alphabet" laid before Fiacc, however, was not a list of letters, but a kind of brief catechism, in Latin "Elementa." St. Patrick is said to have written a number of these "alphabets" with his own hand.

[2] The "Confession" and Epistles attributed to St. Patrick are, by Whitley Stokes, Todd, Ussher, and almost all other authorities, considered genuine. Recently J. V. Pflugk-Harttung, in an article in the "Neuer Heidelberger Jahrbuch," Jahrgang iii., Heft. 1., 1893, has tried to show by internal evidence that the "Confession" and Epistle, especially the former, are a little later than St. Patrick's time, and he relies strongly on this passage, saying that it is difficult to imagine how St. Patrick came by the idea that a man could bring him "innumerable letters from the heathen Ireland of that time, where, except for Ogams and inscribed stones (*ausser Oghams und Skulpturzeichen*), the art of writing was as yet unknown." But seeing that Christian missionaries were almost certainly at work in Munster as early as the third century this contention is ridiculous. It is noteworthy, however, that even this critic seems to believe in the antiquity of the Ogam characters. As to his main contention that the "Confession" is not the work of Patrick, Jubainville writes, "Il ne m'a pas convaincu" (*Revue Celtique*, vol. xiv. p. 215), and M. L. Duchesne, commenting on Zimmer's view of St. Patrick's nebulousness, writes, "Contestir l'authenticité de la Confession et de la lettre à Coroticus me semble très aventuré" (Ibid., vol. xv. p. 188), and Thurneysen also entirely refuses his credence.

according to the key, represents Q (made by five upright strokes above the stem line), Z, and Y, none of which letters are used in even the oldest MSS., and two of which at least must have been borrowed from the Romans. The most, then, that can at present be said with absolute certainty is, as Dr. Whitley Stokes cautiously puts it, that these Ogam inscriptions and the language in which they are couched are "enough to show that some of the Celts of these islands wrote their language before the fifth century, the time at which Christianity is supposed to have been introduced into Ireland."[1] The presence of these Roman letters never used by the Irish on vellum, and the absence of any aspirated letters (which abound even in the oldest vellum MSS.) are additional proofs of the antiquity of the Ogam alphabet.

The Irish themselves ascribed the invention of Ogam to [the god] Ogma, one of the leading Tuatha De Danann,[2] and although it may be, as Rhys points out, philologically unsound to derive Ogam from Ogma, yet there appears to be an intimate connection between the two words, and Ogma may well be derived from Ogam, which in its early stage may have meant fluency or learning rather than letters. Certainly there cannot be any doubt that Ogma, the Tuatha De Danann, was the same as the Gaulish god Ogmïos of whom Lucian, that pleasantest of Hellenes, gives us an account so delightfully graphic that it is worth repeating in its entirety as another proof of what I shall have more to speak about later on, the solidarity—to use a useful Gallicism—of the Irish and the Continental Gauls.

[1] Preface to "Three Old Irish Glossaries," p. lv. Zeuss had already commented on the Ogams found in the St. Gall codex of Priscian, and written thus of them, "Figuræ ergo vel potius liniæ ogamicæ non diversæ ab his quæ notantur a grammaticis hibernicis, in usu jam in hoc vetusto codice, quidni etiam inde a longinquis temporibus?" There are eight Ogam sentences in a St. Gall MS. of the ninth century which have been published by Nigra in his "Manoscritto irlandese di S. Gallo."

[2] See above, p. 52, note. See O'Donovan's Grammar, p. xxviii, for the original of the passage from the Book of Ballymote.

"The Celts,"[1] says Lucian, "call Heracles in the language of their country Ogmios, and they make very strange representations of the god. With them he is an extremely old man with a bald forehead and his few remaining hairs quite grey; his skin is wrinkled and embrowned by the sun to that degree of swarthiness which is characteristic of men who have grown old in a seafaring life; in fact, you would fancy him rather to be a Charon or Japetus, one of the dwellers in Tartarus, or anybody rather than Heracles. But although he is of this description he is nevertheless attired like Heracles, for he has on him the lion's skin, and he has a club in the right hand; he is duly equipped with a quiver, and his left hand displays a bow stretched out, in these respects he is quite Heracles.[2] It struck me then that the Celts took such liberties with the appearance of Heracles in order to insult the gods of the Greeks and avenge themselves on him in their painting, because he once made a raid on their territory, when in search of the herds of Geryon he harassed most of the Western peoples. I have not yet, however, mentioned the most whimsical part of the picture, for this old man Heracles draws after him a great number of men bound by their ears, and the bonds are slender cords wrought of gold and amber, like necklaces of the most beautiful make; and although they are dragged on by such weak ties they never try to run away, though they could easily do it, nor do they at all resist or struggle against them, planting their feet in the ground and throwing their weight back in the direction contrary to that in which they are being led. Quite the reverse, they follow with joyful countenance in a merry mood, and praising him who leads them, pressing on, one and all, and slackening their chains in their eagerness to proceed; in fact, they look like men who would be grieved should they be set free. But that which seemed to me the most absurd thing of all I will not hesitate also to tell you: the painter, you see, had nowhere to fix the ends of the cords since the right hand of the god held the club and his left the

---

[1] Translated by Rhys in his "Hibbert Lectures," from Bekker's edition, No. 7, and Dindorf's, No. 55.

[2] The Gauls assimilated their pantheon to those of the Greeks and Romans in so far as they could, and as the Greek gods are by no means always the equivalents of the Roman gods with whom popular opinion equated them, still less were of course the Gaulish; and this is a good case in point, for Ogmios has evidently nothing of a Hercules about him, though the Gauls tried to make him the equivalent of Hercules by giving him the classical club and lion's skin, yet his attributes are perfectly different.

bow; so he pierced the tip of his tongue and represented the people as drawn on from it, and the god turns a smiling countenance towards those whom he is leading. Now I stood a long time looking at these things and wondered, perplexed and indignant. But a certain Celt standing by, who knew something about our ways, as he showed by speaking good Greek—a man who was quite a philosopher I take it in local matters—said to me: 'Stranger, I will tell you the secret of the painting, for you seem very much troubled about it. We Celts do not consider the power of speech to be Hermes as you Greeks do, but we represent it by means of Heracles, because he is much stronger than Hermes. Nor should you wonder at his being represented as an old man, for the power of words is wont to show its perfection in the aged; for your poets are, no doubt, right when they say that the thoughts of young men turn with every wind, and that age has something wiser to tell us than youth. And so it is that honey pours from the tongue of that Nestor of yours, and the Trojan orators speak with a voice of the delicacy of the lily, a voice well covered, so to say, with bloom, for the bloom of flowers, if my memory does not fail me, has the term lilies applied to it. So if this old man Heracles (the power of speech) draws men after him, tied to his tongue by their ears, you have no reason to wonder; as you must be aware of the close connection between the ears and the tongue. Nor is there any injury done him by the latter being pierced; for I remember, said he, learning, while among you, some comic iambics to the effect that all chattering fellows have the tongue bored at the tip. In a word, we Celts are of opinion that Heracles himself performed everything by the power of words, as he was a wise fellow, and that most of his compulsion was effected by persuasion. His weapons, I take it, were his utterances, which are sharp and well-aimed, swift to pierce the mind, and you too say that words have wings.' Thus far the Celt."

We see, then, that the Irish legend that it was Ogma (who is also said to have been skilled in dialects and poetry) who invented the Ogam alphabet, so useful as a medium through which to convey language, is quite borne out by the account given to Lucian of the Gaulish god Ogmios, the eloquent old man whose language was endowed with so great a charm that he took his hearers captive. He turns, says Lucian, towards his willing captives with a smiling face, and the Irish Ogma, too, is called Ogma "of the shining countenance."[1] Nor does the Gaul in dressing Ogma as a Hercules appear to have acted altogether whimsically, because not only is Ogma skilled in poetry and dialects and the inventor of Ogam, but he is also all through the battle of Moytura actually depicted as the *strong man* of the De Danann, strong enough to push a stone which eighty pair of oxen could not have moved.

The modern Irish names for books, reading, writing, letters, pens, and vellum, are all derived from the Latin.[2] But there seem to have been other names in use to designate the early writing materials of the Irish. These were the Taibhli Fileadh, "poets' tablets," and Tamhlorg Fileadh, which is translated by O'Curry as poets' "headless staves." This latter word, whatever may be the exact meaning of it, is at least pure Gaelic. We read in the "Colloquy of the Ancients" that St. Patrick began to feel a little uneasy at the delight with which he listened to the stories of the ancient Fenians, and in his over-scrupulous sanctity he feared it might be wrong to extract such pleasure from merely mundane narrations. Accordingly he consulted his two guardian angels on the matter, but received an emphatic response from both of them, not only to the effect that there was no harm in listening to the stories themselves, but actually desiring him to get them written down "in poets' *támhlorgs* and in the words of ollavs, for it will be a rejoicing to numbers and to the good people to the end of time, to listen to those stories."[3] An

[1] Grian-aineach, or "of the sunny countenance." See O'Curry MS. Mat., p. 249. Ogma was, according to some accounts, brother of Breas, who held the regency amongst the Tuatha De Danann for seven years, while Nuada was getting his silver hand.

[2] Leabhra, léigheadh, sgríobhadh, litreacha, pinn, meamram.

[3] "A anam a naem-chleirigh ni mó iná trian a scél innisit na senlaeich út, or dáig dermait ocus dichhuimne. Ocus sgribthar let-sa i támlorgaibh filed ocus i mbriathraib ollamhan, or bud gairdiugad do dronguibh ocus do degdáinib deirid aimsire eisdecht fris na scelaib sin" ("Agallamh," p. 101. Silva Gadelica," vol. ii.) O'Grady has here translated it by "tabular staffs." *Táibhli* is evidently a Latin loan word, *tabella*. The thing to be remembered is that Ogam writing on staves appears to be alluded to.

ancient passage from the Brehon Laws prescribes that a poet may carry a *tâbhall-lorg* or tablet-staff, and O'Curry acutely suggests that these so-called tablet-staves were of the nature of a fan which could be closed up in the shape of a square stick, upon the lines and angles of which the poet wrote in Ogam. We can well imagine the almost superstitious reverence which in rude times must have attached itself, and which as we know did attach itself, to the man who could carry about in his hand the whole history and genealogy of his race, and probably the catchwords of innumerable poems and the skeletons of highly-prized narratives. It was probably through these means that the genealogies of which I have spoken were so accurately transmitted and kept from the third or fourth century, and possibly from a still earlier period.

Amongst many other accounts of pre-Christian writing there is one so curious that it is worth giving here *in extenso.*[1]

THE STORY OF BAILE MAC BUAIN, THE SWEET-SPOKEN.

"Buain's only son was Baile.[2] He was specially beloved by Aillinn,[2] the daughter of Lewy,[3] son of Fergus Fairgé—but some say she was the daughter of Owen, son of Dathi—and he was specially beloved not of her only, but of every one who ever heard or saw him, on account of his delightful stories.

"Now Baile and Aillinn made an appointment to meet at Rosnaree, on the banks of the Boyne in Bregia. And he came from Emania in the north to meet her, passing over Slieve Fuad and Muirthuimhne to Tráigh mBaile (Dundalk), and here he and his troops unyoked their chariots, sent their horses out to pasture, and gave themselves up to pleasure and happiness.

"And while they were there they saw a horrible spectral personage coming towards them from the South. Vehement were his steps and his rapid progress. The way he sped over the earth might be com-

[1] O'Curry found this piece in the MS. marked H. 3. 18 in Trinity College, Dublin, and has printed it at page 472 of his MS. Materials. Kuno Meyer has also edited it from a MS. in the British Museum, full of curious word-equivalents or Kennings. (*See* "Revue Celtique," vol. xiii. p. 221. See also a fragment of the same story in Kuno Meyer's "Hibernica Minora," p. 84.)

[2] Pronounced "Bal-a," and "Al-yinn."

[3] In Irish, *Lughaidh.*

pared to the darting of a hawk down a cliff or to wind from off the green sea, and his left was towards the land [*i.e.*, he came from the south along the shore].

"'Go meet him,' said Baile, 'and ask him where he goes, or whence he comes, or what is the cause of his haste.'

"'From Mount Leinster I come, and I go back now to the North, to the mouth of the river Bann; and I have no news but of the daughter of Lewy, son of Fergus, who had fallen in love with Baile mac Buain, and was coming to meet him. But the youths of Leinster overtook her, and she died from being forcibly detained, as Druids and fair prophets had prophesied, for they foretold that they would never meet in life, but that they would meet after death, and not part for ever. There is my news,' and he darted away from them like a blast of wind over the green sea, and they were not able to detain him.

"When Baile heard this he fell dead without life, and his tomb and his rath were raised, and his stone set up, and his funeral games were performed by the Ultonians.

"And a yew grew up through his grâve, and the form and shape of Baile's head was visible on the top of it—whence the place is called Baile's Strand [now Dundalk].

"Afterwards the same man went to the South to where the maiden Aillinn was, and went into her grianan or sunny chamber.

"'Whence comes the man whom we do not know?' said the maiden.

"'From the northern half of Erin, from the mouth of the Bann I come, and I go past this to Mount Leinster.'

"'You have news?' said the maiden.

"'I have no news worth mentioning now, only I saw the Ultonians performing the funeral games and digging the rath, and setting up the stone, and writing the name of Baile mac Buain, the royal heir of Ulster, by the side of the strand of Baile, who died while on his way to meet a sweetheart and a beloved woman to whom he had given affection, for it was not fated for them to meet in life, or for one of them to see the other living,' and he darted out after telling the evil news.

"And Aillinn fell dead without life, and her tomb was raised, etc. And an apple tree grew through her grave and became a great tree at the end of seven years, and the shape of Aillinn's head was upon its top.

"Now at the end of seven years poets and prophets and visioners cut down the yew which was over the grave of Baile, and they made a *poet's tablet* of it, and they wrote the visions and the espousals and the loves and the courtships of Ulster in it. [The apple tree which grew over the grave of Aillinn was also cut down] and in like manner the courtships of Leinster were written in it.

"There came a November eve long afterwards, and a festival was made to celebrate it by Art, the son of Conn [of the Hundred Battles, High-king of Ireland], and the professors of every science came to that feast as was their custom, and they brought their tablets with them. And these tablets also came there, and Art saw them, and when he saw them he asked for them; and the two tablets were brought and he held them in his hands face to face. Suddenly the one tablet of them sprang upon the other, and they became united the same as a woodbine round a twig, and it was not possible to separate them. And they were preserved like every other jewel in the treasury at Tara until it was burned by Dúnlang, son of Enna, at the time he burnt the Princesses at Tara, as has been said

'The apple tree of noble Aillinn,
The yew of Baile—small inheritance—
Though they are introduced into poems
Unlearned people do not understand them.'

and Ailbhé, daughter of Cormac, grandson of Conn [of the Hundred Battles] said too

'What I liken Lumluine to
Is to the Yew of Baile's rath,
What I liken the other to
Is to the Apple Tree of Aillinn.'"

So far this strange tale. But poetic as it is, it yields—unlike most—its chief value when rationalised, for as O'Curry remarks, it was apparently invented to account for some inscribed tablets in the reign of King Art in the second century, which had—as we ourselves have seen in the case of so many leaves of very old manuscripts at this day—become fastened to each other, so that they clung inextricably together and could not be separated.

Now the massacre of the Princesses at Tara happened, according to the "Four Masters," in the year 241, when the tablets were burnt. Hence one of two things must be the case; the story must either have originated *before* that date to account for the sticking together of the tablets, or else some one must have invented it long afterwards, that is, must, without any apparent cause, have invented a story out of his own head, as to how there were *once on a time* two tablets made of trees which *once* grew on two tombs which were *once* fastened together before Art, son of Conn, and which were soon afterwards unfortunately burnt. A supposition which, considering there were then, *ex hypothesi*, no adhering tablets to prompt the invention, appears at first sight improbable.

Brash, who made personal examination of almost every Ogam known to exist, and whose standard work on the subject reproduces most of the inscriptions discovered up to the date of writing, was of opinion that no Ogam monument had anything Christian about it, and that if any Christian symbol were discovered on an Ogam stone, it must be of later date than the Ogam writing. Dr. Graves, however, has since shown that Ogam was in some few cases at least used over the graves of Christians; and he believes that all Ogam writing is really post-Christian, despite the absence of Christian emblems on the stones, and that it belongs to a comparatively modern period—"in fact, for the most part, to a time between the fifth and seventh century."[1] Brash's great work was supplemented by Sir Samuel Ferguson's, and since that time Professor Rhys[2] and Dr. Whitley Stokes have thrown upon the inscriptions themselves all the light that the highest critical acumen equipped with the completest philological training could do, and have, to quote Mr. Macalister, "between them reduced to order the confusion which almost seemed to warrant the cryptical theories, and have thereby raised Ogam inscriptions from the position of being mere learned playthings to a place of the highest philological importance, not only in Celtic but in Indo-European epigraphy."

[1] "Proceedings of the Royal Irish Academy," May, 1894.

[2] See "Proceedings of the Society of Antiquaries of Scotland," vol. xxvi. p. 263.

He himself—the latest to deal with the subject—waves for the present as "difficult—perhaps in some measure insoluble"—all "questions of the time, place, and manner of the development of the Ogham script."[1] Rhys has traced in certain of the inscriptions the influence exercised on the spoken language of the Celtic people by an agglutinating pre-Celtic tongue.[2] This gives us a glimpse at the pre-Aryan languages of the British Isles, which is in the highest degree interesting.

To me it seems probable that the Irish discovered the use ot letters either through trade with the Continent or through the Romanised Britons, at any time from the first or second century onward. But how or why they invented the Ogam alphabet, instead of using Roman letters, or else Greek ones like the Gauls, is a profound mystery. One thing is certain, namely, that the Ogam alphabet—at whatever time invented—is a possession peculiar to the Irish Gael, and only to be found where he made his settlements.

[1] "Studies in Irish Epigraphy," London, 1897, part i., by R. A. Stewart Macalister, who gives a most lucid study of the Ogam inscriptions in the Barony of Corcaguiney and of a few more, with a clear and interesting preface on the Ogam words and case-endings.

[2] It is thus he explains such Ogam forms as "Erc maqi maqi-Ercias," *i.e.*, [the stone] of Erc, son of, etc. But "Erc" is nominative, "maqi" is genitive, hence "Erc maqi" must be looked upon as one word, agglutinated as it were, in which the genitive ending of the "maqi" answers for both. As a rule, however, the name of the interred is in the genitive case in apposition to "maqi."

CHAPTER XII

EARLY IRISH CIVILISATION

It has been frequently assumed, especially by English writers, that the pre-historic Irish, because of their remoteness from the Continent, must have been ruder, wilder, and more uncivilised than the inhabitants of Great Britain. But such an assumption is—to say nothing of our literary remains—in no way borne out by the results of archæological research. The contrary rather appears to be the case, that in point of wealth, artistic feeling, and workmanship, the Irish of the Bronze Age surpassed the inhabitants of Great Britain.

When we read such accounts as that, for example, in the Book of Ballymote, of Cormac mac Art, taking his seat at the assembly in Tara, all covered with gold and jewels, we must not set it down to the perfervid imagination of the chronicler without first consulting what Irish archæology has to say upon the point. The appearance of Cormac (king of Ireland in the third century, and perhaps greatest of pre-Christian monarchs), is thus described. "Beautiful," says the writer, quoting probably from ancient accounts now lost, "was the appearance of Cormac in that assembly, flowing and slightly curling was his golden hair. A red buckler with stars and animals of gold and fastenings of silver upon him. A crimson cloak in wide descending folds around him, fastened at his neck with precious stones. A torque of gold around his neck. A white shirt with a full collar, and intertwined with red gold thread upon him. A girdle of gold, inlaid with precious stones, was around him. Two wonderful shoes of gold, with golden loops upon his feet. Two spears with golden sockets in his hands, with many rivets of red bronze. And he was himself, besides, symmetrical and beautiful of form, without blemish or reproach." The abundance of gold ornament which Cormac is here represented as wearing, is no mere imagination of the writer's. It is founded upon the undoubted fact that of all countries in the West of Europe Ireland was pre-eminent for its wealth in gold. How much wealthier was Ireland than Great Britain may be imagined from the fact that while the collection in the British Museum of pre-historic gold from England, Scotland, and Wales together amounted a couple of years ago to some three dozen ounces, that in the Royal Irish Academy in Dublin weighs five hundred and seventy ounces. And yet the collection in the Academy contains only a small part of the gold-finds made in Ireland, for before 1861, when the new law about treasure-trove came into force, great numbers of gold objects are known to have been sold to the goldsmiths and melted down. The wealth of Ireland in gold—some of it found and smelted in the Wicklow mountains[1]—must have at an early period deter-

[1] In the Irish Annals gold is said to have been first smelted in Leinster. As late as the last century native gold was discovered on the confines of Wicklow and Wexford, and nuggets of 22, 18, 9, and 7 ounces are recorded as having been found there. Mr. Coffey quotes a most interesting account by a Mr. Weaver, director of the works established there by the Irish Government before the Union to look for gold. "The discovery of native gold in Ballinvally stream, at Croghan Kinshella," says Mr. Weaver, "was at first kept secret, but being divulged, almost the whole population of the immediate neighbourhood flocked in to gather so rich a harvest, actually neglecting at the time the produce of their own fields. This happened about the autumn of the year 1796, when several hundreds of people might be seen daily assembled digging and searching for gold in the banks and bed of the stream. Considerable quantities were thus collected; this being as

mined continental trade in its direction, and we have seen that Tacitus reported its harbours as being better known through trade than those of Great Britain, or, on the most unfavourable reading of the passage, as being "known by commerce and merchants."[1] This is also borne out by archæologists. Professor Montelius, who has traced a close connection in pre-historic times between Scandinavia and the West of Europe,[2] regards much of the pre-historic gold found in the northern countries as Irish. Speaking of certain gold ornaments found in Fünen, which show, according to him, marked Irish influence, he writes: "Gold ornaments like these have not been discovered elsewhere in Scandinavia, while a great number of similar ornaments have been found in the British Isles, especially in Ireland, whose wealth of gold in the Bronze Age is amazing." Again he writes, "As certain of the gold

it subsequently proved the most productive spot; and the populace remained in undisturbed possession of the place for nearly six weeks, when Government determined to commence active operations. . . . Regular stream works were soon established, and up to the unhappy time of the rebellion in May, 1798, when the works were destroyed, Government had been fully reimbursed its advances; the produce of the undertaking having defrayed its own expenses and left a surplus in hand." The total amount of gold collected from this place in the last hundred years is valued at about £30,000. This particular spot had been probably overlooked, as Mr. Coffey remarks, by the searchers of earlier days, but no doubt other auriferous streams in the Wicklow mountains had given up their gold long since in pre-historic times to the ancient workers. (*See* Coffey's "Origins of Pre-historic Ornament in Ireland," p. 40.) Dr. Frazer, on the other hand, does not believe that any great part of the gold found in Ireland is indigenous, and talks of Spain and South Russia, and gold plundered from Britain. But if this be the case, what an enormous pre-historic trade Ireland must have carried on, or what a powerful invader she must have been to come by such quantities of gold! (*See* Dr. Frazer's paper in R. I. A. Proceedings, May, 1896). He has since supplemented this by another in the Journal of the Royal Society of Antiquaries in which he leans to the opinion that the Roman *aurei*, the coins plundered from the Britons, were the real source of Irish gold.

[1] See above, p. 21, note 3.

[2] "Verbindungen zwischen Skandinavien und dem westlichen Europa vor Christi Geburt" ("Archiv für Anthropologie," vol. xix., quoted by Mr. George Coffey in his "Origins of Pre-historic Ornament in Ireland," p. 63).

objects found in Denmark have been introduced demonstrably from the British Islands, probably from Ireland, the thought is obvious—is not a great part of the other gold objects found in Southern Scandinavia also of Irish origin, and of the Bronze Age there? . . . for this island [Ireland] was, during the Bronze Age, one of the lands of Europe richest in gold." "No other country in Europe possesses so much manufactured gold belonging to early and mediæval times," writes Mr. Ernest Smith.[1]

It is true that the Irish Celts, despite their mineral wealth, never minted coin, a want which has been adduced to prove a lack of civilisation on their part. But, as Mr. Coffey points out, coinage is a comparatively late invention; the Egyptians —for all their civilisation—never possessed a native coinage, and even such ancient trading cities as Carthage and Gades did not strike coins until a late period. "A little reflection," says Professor Ridgeway, "shows us that it has been quite possible for peoples to attain a high degree of civilisation without feeling any need of what are properly termed coins." "The absence of coinage," adds Mr. Coffey, "does not necessarily imply the absence of a currency system, and Professor Ridgeway has shown that the ancient Irish possessed a system of of currency or values, and a standard of weights."

A most interesting paper by Mr. Johnson, a Dublin jeweller, recently read before the Royal Irish Academy,[2] has

[1] "Notes on the Composition of Ancient Irish Gold and Silver Ornaments," by Ernest A. Smith, Assoc. R.S.M., F.C.S, Royal School of Mines, London, R. I. A. Transactions, May, 1896.

[2] "Proceedings of the Royal Irish Academy," May, 1896. The tools and appliances necessary for producing the fine gold fibulæ of a private collector, which Mr. Johnson examined, would be, he says, "a furnace, charcoal, crucible, mould for ingot, flux, bellows, several hammers, anvil, swage anvil, swages, chisels for ornament, sectional tool for producing concentric rings." On one of them, he says, "there is a thickened edge and a beautiful moulded ornament on the outer side only, which quite puzzles one as to how it was produced without suggesting what are considered to be modern tools."

shown with the authority due to an expert, the marvellous skill with which the pre-historic Irish worked their gold, and the wealth of proper appliances which they must have possessed in order to turn out such unique and admirable results.[1]

The workmanship of Irish bronze articles is also very fine, and fully equal to that of Britain, while Greenwell considers their clay urns and food-vessels superior to the British. In Ireland he says the urns, "and especially the food vessels, are of better workmanship, and more elaborately and tastefully ornamented than in most parts of Britain. Many of the food vessels found in Argyleshire, and in other districts in the South-west of Scotland, as might be perhaps expected, are very Irish in character, and may claim to be equally fine in taste and delicate in workmanship with those of Ireland." [2]

The brilliant appearance of Cormac mac Art when presiding over the assembly at Tara, covered with gold and jewels, receives enhanced credibility from the proofs of early Irish wealth and culture that I have just adduced. Let us glance at Tara itself, as it existed in the time of Cormac, and see whether archæology can throw any light upon the ancient accounts of that royal hill. It was round this hill that the great Féis, or assemblage of the men of all Ireland, took place triennially,[3] with a threefold purpose—to promulgate laws universally binding upon all Ireland; to test, purge, and

[1] A splendid find of gold ornaments made last year near the estuary of the Foyle river, of a golden model of a boat, evidently a votive offering, fitted with seat, mast, oars, and punting poles, an exquisitely-wrought gold collar, decorated in relief with the most beautiful embossed work, torques, neckchains, etc., has been dated from internal evidences as work of the second century, the neck-chains being clearly provincial Roman work of that date. It is to be regretted that these exquisite articles have found their way to the British Museum, where they will be practically lost, instead of being added to the unique Irish collection in Dublin, to which hey properly belong.

[2] Greenwell's "British Barrows," p. 62, quoted by Coffey.

[3] O'Donovan, in his preface to "The Book of Rights," gives some reasons for believing that it may have been held only septennially.

sanction the annals and genealogies of Ireland, in the presence of all men, so that no untruth or flaw might creep in ; and, finally, to register the same in the great national record, in later times called the Saltair of Tara, so that cases of disputed succession might be peacefully settled by reference to this central authoritative volume. The session of the men of Ireland thus convened took place on the third day before Samhain—November day—and ended the third day after it. We are told that Cormac, who presided over these assemblies,[1] had ten persons in constant waiting upon his person, who hardly ever left him. These were a prince of noble blood, a druid, a physician, a brehon, a bard, a historian, a musician, and three stewards. And Keating tells us that the very same arrangement was observed from Cormac's time—in the third century—to the death of Brian Boru in the eleventh, the only alteration being that a Christian priest was substituted for the druid.

To accommodate the chiefs and princes who came to the great Féis, Cormac built the renowned Teach Míodhchuarta [Toch Mee-coo-ar-ta] which was able to accommodate a thousand persons, and which was used at once for a house of assembly, a banqueting hall, and a sleeping abode. We have two accounts of this hall and of the other monuments of Tara, written, the one in poetry, the other in verse, some nine hundred years ago. The prose of the Dinnseanchus describes accurately the lie of the building, "to the north-west of the eastern mound." "The ruins of this house"—it lay in ruins then as now—"are thus situated : the lower part to the north and the higher part to the south ; and walls are raised about it to the east and to the west. The northern side of it is enclosed and small, the lie of it is north and south. It is in the form of a long house with twelve doors upon it, or fourteen, seven to the west and seven to the east. This was the great house of a thousand soldiers."[2] Keating, follow-

[1] *See* the Forus Feasa, p. 354 of O'Mahony's translation.

[2] *See* Petrie's "Antiquities of Tara Hill," p. 129.

ing his ancient authorities, graphically describes the Tara assembly.

"The nobles," he writes, "both territorial lords and captains of bands of warriors, were each man of them, always attended by his own proper shield-bearer. Again their banquet-halls were arranged in the following manner, to wit, they were long narrow buildings with tables arranged along both the opposite walls of the hall; then along these side walls there was placed a beam, in which were fixed numerous hooks (one over the seat destined for each of the nobles), and between every two of them there was but the breadth of one shield. Upon these hooks the shanachy hung up the shields of the nobles previously to their sitting down to the banquet, at which they all, both lords and captains, sat each beneath his own shield. However, the most honoured side of the house was occupied by the territorial lords, whilst the captains of warriors[1] were seated opposite to them at the other. The upper end of the hall was the place of the ollavs, while the lower end was assigned to the attendants and the officers in waiting. It was also prescribed that no man should be placed opposite another at the same table, but that all, both territorial lords and captains, should sit with their backs towards the wall, beneath their own shields. Again, they never admitted females into their banquet-halls; these had a hall of their own in which they were separately served. It was likewise the prescribed usage to clear out the banquet-hall previous to serving the assembled nobles therein. And no one was allowed to remain in the building but three, namely, a Shanachy and a *bolsgaire* [marshal or herald], and a trumpeter, the duty of which latter officer was to summon all the guests to the banquet-hall by the sound of his trumpet-horn. He had to sound his horn three times. At the first blast the shield-bearers of the territorial chieftains assembled round the door of the hall, where the marshal received from them the shields of their lords, which he then, according to the directions of the shanachy, hung up each in its assigned place. The trumpeter then sounded his trumpet a second time, and the shield-bearers of the chieftains of the military bands assembled round the door of the banquet-hall, where the marshal received their lords' shields from them also, and hung them up at the other side of the hall according to the orders of the shanachy, and over the table of the warriors. The trumpeter sounded his trumpet the third time, and thereupon

[1] This seems a plain allusion to the Fenians, believed in Ireland to have been Cormac's militia.

both the nobles and the warrior chiefs entered the banquet-hall, and then each man sat down beneath his own shield, and thus were all contests for precedency avoided amongst them."

These accounts of the Dinnseanchus and of Keating, taken from authorities now lost, will be likely to receive additional credit when we know that the statements made nine hundred years ago, when Tara had even then lain in ruins for four centuries, have been verified in every essential particular by the officers of the Ordnance Survey. The statement in the Dinnseanchus made nearly nine hundred years ago that there were either six or seven doors on each side, shows the condition into which Tara had then fallen, one on each side being so obliterated that now, also, it is difficult to say whether it was a door or not. The length of the hall, according to Petrie's accurate measurements, was *seven hundred and sixty feet*, and its breadth was nearly ninety. There was a double row of benches on each side, running the entire length of the hall, which would give four rows of men if we remember that the guests were all seated on the same side of the tables, and allowing the ample room of three feet to each man, this would just give accommodation to a thousand. In the middle of the hall, running down all the way between the benches, there was a row of fires, and just above each fire was a spit descending from the roof, at which the joints were roasted. There is a ground plan of the building, in the Book of Leinster, and the figure of a cook is rudely drawn with his mouth open, and a ladle in his hand to baste the joint. The king sat at the southern end of the hall, and the servants and retainers occupied the northern.

The banqueting-hall and all the other buildings at Tara were of wood, nor is the absence of stone buildings in itself a proof of low civilisation, since, in a country like Ireland, abounding in timber, wood could be made to answer every purpose—as in point of fact it does at this day over the greater part of America, and in all northern countries where forests are numerous.[1] All or most Irish houses, down to the period of the Danish invasions, were constructed of wood, or of wood and clay mixed, or of clay and unmortared stones, and their strongholds were of wooden pallisades planted upon clay earthworks. This is the reason why so few remains of pre-historic buildings have come down to us, but it is no reason for believing that, as in Cormac's banquet-hall, rude palatial effects were not often produced. An interesting poem in the Dialogue of the Sages, from the Book of Lismore, describes the house of the Lady Credé, said to have been a contemporary of Finn mac Cúmhail in the third century.[2] Though the poem may not itself be very old, it no doubt embodies many ancient truths, and is worth quoting from. A poet comes to woo the lady, and brings this poem with him. Finn accompanies him. When they reached her fortress "girls, yellow-haired, of marriageable age, showed on the balconies of her bowers." The poet sang to her—

"Happy is the house in which she is
Between men and children and women,
Between druids and musical performers,
Between cupbearers and doorkeepers.[3]

[1] Bede mentions, if I remember rightly—I forget where—a church built in the north of Britain, *more Scotorum, robore secto,* "of cleft oak, in the Irish fashion." The Columban churches were also of wood and wattles, contemporaneous with which were the beehive cells of uncemented stone, probably less warm and less comfortable than the thatched houses. "Ce que nous savons des anciens édifices irlandais," says M. Jubainville, "donne le droit d'affirmer que la plupart des constructions élevées a Emain macha [*i.e.*, Emania, the capital of Ulster, and of the Red Branch heroes, two miles west of Armagh] pendant le période épique de l'histoire d'Irlande, ont dû être en bois ; cependant il y avait été employé au moins quelques pierres." Angus the Culdee has a noble verse relating to the stones of Emania, the finest, perhaps, in the whole Saltair na rann, "Emania's palace has vanished, yet its stones still remain, but the Rome of the western world is now Glendaloch of the gatherings," "is Ruam iarthair beatha Gleann dalach dá locha."

[2] *See* "Silva Gadelica," p. 111, and O'Curry's MS. Materials, p. 595.

[3] Aibhinn in tech in atá,
Idir fira is maca is mná,
Idir dhruidh ocus aes ceóil,
Idir dhailiumh is dhoirseoir,

Between equerries without fear,
And distributors who divide [the fare],
And, over all these, the command belongs
To Credé of the yellow hair.

. . . . . .

The colour [of her house] is like the colour of lime,
Within it are couches and green rushes (?)
Within it are silks and blue mantles,
Within it are red, gold, and crystal cups.

Of its many chambers the corner stones,
Are all of silver and yellow gold,
In faultless stripes its thatch is spread,
Of wings of brown, and of crimson red.

Two door posts of green I see,
Door not devoid of beauty,
Of carved silver, long has it been renowned,
In the lintel that is over the door.

Credé's chair is on your left hand,
The pleasantest of the pleasant it is,
All over, a blaze [1] of Alpine gold
At the foot of her beautiful couch.

A splendid couch in full array
Stands directly above the chair ;
It was made by *Tuile* in the East,
Of yellow gold and precious stones.

There is another bed on your right hand
Of gold and silver without defect,
With curtains with soft [pillows],
With graceful rods of golden-bronze.

An hundred feet spans Credé's house
From one angle to the other,
And twenty feet are fully measured
In the breadth of its noble door.

Its portico is covered, too,
With wings of birds, both yellow and blue,
Its lawn in front and its well
Of crystal and of Carmogel."

[1] Thus O'Curry translates *casair* as if he had taken it to be *lasair*. O'Grady translates "an overlay of Elpa's gold."

The houses of the ancient Irish were either like Cormac's banqueting-hall and Credé's house, built quadrilaterally of felled trees or split planks planted upright in the earth, and thatched overhead, or else, as was most usually the case, they were cylindrical and made of wickerwork, with a cup-shaped roof, plastered with clay and whitewashed. The magnificent dimensions of Cormac's palace, verified as they are by the careful measurements of the Ordnance Survey—a palace certainly erected in pagan times, since Tara was deserted for ever about the year 550—bear evidence, like our wealth of beautifully-wrought gold ornaments, and the superior workmanship of our surviving articles of bronze and clay, to a high degree of civilisation and culture amongst the pre-Christian Irish; I have here adduced them as bearing indirect evidence in favour of the probability that a people so civilised would have been likely to have seized on the invention of writing when they first came in contact with it, and would have kept their annals and genealogies all the more accurately from the very fact that they were evidently so advanced in other matters.

CHAPTER XIII

ST. PATRICK AND THE EARLY MISSIONARIES

EVEN supposing the Ogam alphabet to have been used in pre-Christian times, though it may have been employed by ollavs and poets to perpetuate tribal names and genealogies, still it was much too cumbrous and clumsy an invention to produce anything deserving the name of real literature. It is, so far as we know, only with the coming of Patrick that Ireland may be said to have become, properly speaking, a literary country. The churches and monasteries established by him soon became so many nuclei of learning, and from the end of the fifth century a knowledge of letters seems to have entirely permeated the island. So suddenly does this appear to have taken place, and so rapidly does Ireland seem to have produced a flourishing literature of laws, poems, and sagas, that it is very hard to believe that the inhabitants had not, before his coming, arrived at a high state of indigenous culture. This aspect of the case has been recently strongly put by Dr. Sigerson. "I assert," said he, speaking of the early Brehon laws, at the revision of which in a Christian sense St. Patrick is said to have assisted, "that, speaking biologically, such laws could not emanate from any race whose brains have not been subject to the quickening influence of education for many generations."[1]

The usual date assigned for St. Patrick's landing in Ireland in the character of a missionary is 432, and his work among the Irish is said to have lasted for sixty years, during which time he broke down the idol Crom Cruach, burnt the books of the druids at Tara, ordained numerous missionaries and bishops, and succeeded in winning over to Christianity a great number of the chiefs and sub-kings, who were in their turn followed by their tribesmen.

St. Patrick did not work alone, nor did he come to Ireland as a solitary pioneer of a new religion; he was accompanied, as we learn from his life in the Book of Armagh, by a multitude of bishops, priests, deacons, readers, and others,[2] who had crossed over along with him for the service. Several were his own blood relations, one was his sister's son. Many likely youths whom he met on his missionary travels he converted to Christianity, taught to read, tonsured, and afterwards ordained. These new priests thus appointed worked in all directions, establishing churches and getting together congregations from amongst the neighbouring heathen. Unable to give proper attention to the teaching of the youths whom he elected as his helpers, so long as he himself was engaged in journeying through Ireland from point to point, he, after about twenty years of peripatetic teaching, established at Armagh about the year 450 the first Christian school ever founded in Ireland, the progenitor of that long line of colleges which made Ireland famous throughout Europe, and to which, two hundred years later, her Anglo-Saxon neighbours flocked in thousands.[3]

[1] "Contemporary Review."

[2] So Tirechan, in Book of Armagh, fol. 9. "Et secum fuit multitudo episcoporum sanctorum et presbiterorum, et diaconorum, ac exorcistarum, hostiarium, lectorumque, necnon filiorum quos ordinavit."

[3] So many English were attracted to Armagh in the seventh century that the city was divided into three wards, or thirds, one of which was called the Saxon Third.

The equipments of these newly-made priests was of the scantiest. Each, as he was sent forth, received an alphabet-of-the-faith or elementary-explanation of the Christian doctrine, frequently written by Patrick himself, a "Liber ordinis," or "Mass Book," a written form for the administration of the sacraments, a psaltery, and, if it could be spared, a copy of the Gospels.[1] A good-sized retinue followed Patrick in all his journeyings, ready to supply with their own hands all things necessary for the new churches established by the saint, as well as to minister to his own wants. He travelled with his episcopal coadjutor, his psalm-singer, his assistant priest, his judge—originally a Brehon by profession, whom he found most useful in adjudicating on disputed questions—a personal champion to protect him from sudden attack and to carry him through floods and other obstacles, an attendant on himself, a bellringer, a cook, a brewer, a chaplain at the table, two waiters, and others who provided food and accommodation for himself and his household. He had in his company three smiths, three artificers, and three ladies who embroidered. His smiths and artificers made altars, book-covers, bells, and helped to erect his wooden churches; the ladies, one of them his own sister, made vestments and altar linens.[2]

St. Patrick was essentially a man of work and not of letters, and yet it so happens that he is the earliest Irish writer of whom we can say with confidence that what is ascribed to him is really his. And here it is as well to say something about the genuineness of St. Patrick's personality and the authenticity of his writings, for the opinion started by Ledwich has gone abroad, and has somehow become prevalent, that St. Patrick's personality is nearly as nebulous as that of King Arthur or of Finn mac Cúmhail, and at the best is made up of a number of little Patricks lumped into one great one. That

[1] See Dr. Healy's "Ireland's Ancient Schools and Scholars," p. 64.

[2] There is a curious poem on St. Patrick's family of artificers quoted in the "Four Masters" under A.D. 278.

there was more than one Patrick[1] is certain,[2] and that the great Saint Patrick who wrote the "Confession" may have got credit in the early Latin and later Irish lives for the acts of others, is perfectly possible, but that most of the essential features of his life are true, is beyond all doubt, and we have a manuscript 1091 years old, apparently copied from his own handwriting, and containing his own confession and apologia.

How this exquisite manuscript, consisting of 216 vellum leaves, written in double columns, has happily been preserved to us, we shall not lose time in inquiring; but how its exact date has been ascertained through what Dr. Reeves has characterised as "one of the most elegant and recondite demonstrations

[1] There were no less than twenty-two saints of the name of Colum, yet that does not detract one iota from the genuineness of the life of the great Colum, called Columcille. There were fourteen St. Brendans, there were twenty-five St. Ciarans, and fifteen St. Brigits.

How Ledwich—who, however, as O'Donovan remarks, looks at everything Irish with a jaundiced eye—could have written down St. Patrick as a myth is inconceivable, in the face of the fact that he was already recognised in the sixth century as a great saint. The earliest mention of him is probably St. Columba's subscription to the Book of Durrow, in the sixth century, which runs: "Rogo beatitudinem tuam Sancte Presbyter Patrici, ut quicumque hunc libellum manu tenuerit Columbæ Scriptoris, qui hoc scripsi . . . met evangelium per xii. dierum spatium." Here we see a prayer already addressed to him as a national saint.

[2] This is clearly shown by the 56th chap. of Tirechan's life fol. 16aa of the Book of Armagh, where he makes the following statement: "XIII. Anno Teothosii imperatoris a Celestino episcopo papa Romæ Patricius episcopus ad doctrinam Scottorum mittitur. Qui Celestinus XLVII episcopus fuit a Petro apostolo in urbe Roma. Paladius episcopus primus mittitur [in the year 430, according to Bede] qui Patricius alio nomine appellabatur, qui martirium passus est apud Scottos, ut tradunt sancti antiqui. Deinde Patricius secundus ab anguelo Dei, Victor nomine, et a Celestino papa mittitur, cui Hibernia tota credidit, qui eam pene totam bab[titzavit]." Also it is to be observed that St. Patrick's life according to the usual computations, covers 120 years, which seems an improbably long period. According to the Brussels Codex of Muirchu Maccu Machteni's life, he died *a passione Domini nostri* 436; the author, no doubt, imagined the passion to have taken place in A.D. 34; this would fix Patrick's death as in 470. See p. 20 of Father Hogan's "Documenta ex Libro Armachano," and with this Tirechan also agrees, saying

which any learned society has on record, is worth mentioning." The Rev. Charles Graves, the present Bishop of Limerick, made a thorough examination of the whole codex when, after many vicissitudes and hair-breadth escapes from destruction, it had been temporarily deposited in the Royal Irish Academy. Knowing, as O'Curry pointed out, that it was the custom for Irish scribes to sign their own names, with usually some particulars about their writing, at the end of each piece they copied, he made a careful search and discovered that this had actually been done in the Book of Armagh, and in no less than eight places, but that on every spot where it occurred it had been erased for some apparently inscrutable reason, with the greatest pains. In the last place but one,

"A passione autem christi colleguntur anni ccccxxxvi. usque ad mortem Patricii." Tirechan curiously contradicts himself in saying, "Duobus autem vel v annis regnavit Loiguire post mortem Patricii, omnis autem regni illius tempus xxxvi. ut putamus," in chap. ii., and in chap. liii. he says that Patrick taught (*i.e.*, in Ireland) for 72 years! He evidently compiled badly from two different documents.

The only cogent reason for doubting about the reality of St. Patrick is that he is not mentioned in the Chronicon of Prosper, which comes down to the year 455, and which ascribes the conversion of Ireland to Palladius, as does Bede afterwards. It is the silence of Prosper and Bede about any one of the name of Patrick which has cast doubt upon his existence. A most ingenious theory has been propounded by Father E. O'Brien in the "Irish Ecclesiastical Record" to explain this. According to him Patrick *is* the Palladius of Prosper and Bede. The earliest lives, and the scholiast on Fiacc's hymn, tell us that Patrick had four names; one of these was Succat "*qui est deus belli*," but Palladius is the Latin of Patrick's name (succat). The *Deus belli* could only be rendered into Latin by the words Arius Martius or Palladius, these being the only names drawn from war-gods, and of these Palladius was the commonest. It seems not unlikely that the Patrick who wrote the "Confession" and converted Ireland is the Palladius of Bede and Prosper, who also converted Ireland. The Paladius of Tirechan who failed to convert Ireland is evidently another person altogether.

It is to be remarked that although Bede never mentions Patrick in his "Ecclesiastical History," nevertheless in the "Martyrology"—found by Mabillon at Rheims, and attributed to Bede, Patrick is distinctly commemorated—

"Patricius Domini servus conscendit ad aulam,
Cuthbertus ternas tenuit denasque Kalendas."

however, where the colophon occurred, the process of erasure had been less thorough than in the others, and after long consideration, and treatment of the erasure with gallic acid and spirits of wine, Dr. Graves discovered that the words so carefully rubbed out were *Pro Ferdomnacho ores*, "Pray for Ferdomnach." Turning to the other places, he found that the erased words in at least one other place were evidently the same. This settled the name of the scribe; he was Ferdomnach. The next step was to search the "Four Masters," who record the existence of two scribes of that name who died at Armagh, one in 726 and the other in 844. One of these it must have been who wrote the Book of Armagh,—but which? This also Dr. Graves discovered, with the greatest ingenuity. At the foot of Fols. 52–6 he was, with extreme difficulty, able to decipher the words . . . *ach hunc* . . . *e dictante* . . . *ach herede Patricii scripsit*. From these stray syllables he surmised that Ferdomnach had written the book at the bidding of some Archbishop of Armagh whose name ended in *ach*. For this the Psalter of Cashel, Leabhar Breac, and "Four Masters," were consulted, and it was found that one Archbishop Senaach died in 609; it could not then have been by his commands the book was written by the first Ferdomnach; then came, after a long interval, Faoindealach, who died in 794, Connmach, who died in 806, and Torbach, who held the primacy for one year after him. On examining the hiatus it was found that the letter which preceded the fragment *ach* could not have been either an *l* or an *m*, but might have been a *b*, thus putting out of the question the names of Connmach and Faoindealach. Besides the vacant space before the *ach* was just sufficient to admit of the letters *Tor*, but not *Conn*, much less *Faoindea*. The conclusion was obvious: the passage ran, *Ferdomnach hunc librum e dictante Torbach herede Patricii scripsit*, "Ferdomnach wrote this book at the dictation (or command) of Torbach, Patrick's heir (successor)." Torbach, as we have seen, became Archbishop in 806 and died in 807. The date was in this way recovered.[1]

I have been thus particular in tracing the steps by which the age of this manuscript came to light, because it contains the earliest piece of certain Irish literature we have, the "Confession of St. Patrick." Now the usually accepted date of St. Patrick's death, as given in the Annals of Ulster, is 492, about three hundred years before that, and Ferdomnach, the scribe, after copying it, added these words: "*Huc usque volumen quod patricius manu conscripsit sua. Septimadecima martii die translatus est patricius ad cælos, i.e.*, "thus far the volume which Patrick wrote with his own hand. On the seventeenth day of March was Patrick translated to the heavens." It would appear highly probable from this that Ferdomnach actually copied from St. Patrick's autograph,[2] which had become so defaced or faded during the three previous centuries, that the scribe has written in many places *incertus liber hic*, "the book is uncertain here," or else put a note [3] of

[1] For the full particulars of this acute discovery, which sets the date of the codex beyond doubt or cavil, see Dr. Graves' paper read before the Royal Irish Academy, vol. iii. pp. 316–324, and a supplementary paper giving other cogent reasons, vol. iii. p. 358. According to O'Donovan, the "Four Masters" antedate here by five years. It is worth remarking that Torbach, who caused this copy to be made, was himself a noted scribe. His death in 807 is recorded in the "Four Masters" and in the "Annals of Ulster," we read "Torbach, son of Gorman, scribe, lector, and Abbot of Armagh, died."

[2] There are several passages omitted in the Book of Armagh, which are found in an ancient Brussels MS. of the eleventh century. These were probably omitted from the Book of Armagh because they were undecipherable. The Brussels MS. and others contain nearly as much again as it, and there are many proofs that this extra matter is not of later or spurious origin; thus Tirechan refers to Patrick's own records, "*ut in scriptione sua affirmat*," for evidence of a fact not mentioned in the "Confession" as given in the Book of Armagh, but which is supplied by the other MSS., namely, that Patrick paid the price of fifteen "souls of men," or slaves, for protection on his missionary journey across Ireland. The frequent occurrence of *deest, et cetera, et reliqua*, show that the Armagh copy of the "Confession" is nothing like a full one. The Brussels MS. formerly belonged to the Irish monastery of Würzburg.

[3] *See* p. 36, note 2.

interrogation to indicate that he was not sure whether he had copied the text correctly. It will be seen from this that there was not the slightest trace of any concealment on the part of the scribe as to who he himself was, or what he was copying; there was no attempt to antedate his own writing, or to suggest that his copy was an original. But long after the scribe's generation had passed away and the origin of his work been forgotten, the volume which at first had been regarded only as a fine transcript of early documents, became known as "Canon Phádraig," or Patrick's Testament, and popular opinion, relying on the colophon "thus far the book which Patrick wrote with his own hand," set down the work as the saint's autograph. The belief that the volume was St. Patrick's own autograph of course enhanced enormously its value, and with it the dignity of its possessors, and the unscrupulous plan was resolved on of erasing the signature of the actual scribe. The veneration of the public was thus secured by interested persons at the cost of truth, and the deception probably lasted so long as the possession of such a volume brought with it either credit or dignity. This same volume [1] has another interest attaching to it, so that we cannot but felicitate ourselves that out of the wreck of so many thousands of volumes, it has been spared to us—it was brought to Brian Boru, when in the year 1004 he went upon his royal progress through Ireland, the first man of the race of Eber who had attained the proud position of monarch or Ard-righ for many centuries, and he, by the hand of his secretary, made an entry which may still be seen to-day, confirming the primacy of Armagh, and re-granting to it

[1] The other contents of the Book of Armagh, besides the Patrician documents, are a copy of the New Testament, enriched with concordance tables and illustrative matter from Jerome, Hilary, and Pelagius. It includes the Epistle to the Laodiceans attributed to St. Paul, but it is mentioned that Jerome denied its authenticity. There are some pieces relating to St. Martin of Tours, and the Patrician pieces—the Life, the Collectanea, the Book of the Angel, and the "Confession."

the episcopal supremacy of Ireland which it had always enjoyed.[1]

It is now time to glance at St. Patrick's "Confession," as it is usually called, though in reality it is much more of the nature of an apologia *pro vita sua*. The evidence in favour of its authenticity is overwhelming, and is accepted by such cautious scholars as Stokes,[2] Todd, and Reeves, no first-rate critic, with perhaps one exception, having so far as I know ever ventured to question its genuineness. It is impossible to assign any motive for a forgery, and casual references to Decuriones, Slave-traffic, and to the "Brittaniæ," or Britains, bear testimony to its antiquity. Again, the Latin in which it is written is barbarous in the extreme, the periods are rude, sometimes ungrammatical, often nearly unintelligible. He begins by telling us that his object in writing this confession in his old age was to defend himself from the charge of presumptuousness in undertaking the work he tried to perform amongst the Irish. He tells us that he had many toils and perils to surmount, and much to endure while engaged upon it. He never received one farthing for all his preaching and teaching. The people indeed were generous, and offered many gifts, and cast precious things upon the altar, but he would not receive them lest he might afford the unrighteous an occasion to cavil. He was still encompassed about with dangers, but he heeded them not, looking to the success which had attended his efforts, how "the sons of the Scots and the

[1] "Sanctus Patricus iens ad cœlum mandavit totum fructum laboris sui tam baptismi tam causarum quam elẹmoisinarum deferendum esse apostolicæ urbi quae scotice nominatur ardd-macha. Sic reperi in Bibliothics Scotorum. Ego scripsi, id est Caluus Perennis, in conspectu Briain imperatoris Scotorum, et quod scripsi finituit pro omnibus regibus Maceriae [*i.e.*, Cashel]." "Calvus Perennis" is the Latin translation of Mael-ṣuthain, Brian's scribe and secretary. For a curious story about this Mael-suthain, *see* p. 779 O'Curry's MS. Materials.

[2] See above p. 112, note 2. It has been printed in Haddan and Stubb's, "Councils," etc., vol. ii. p. 296, and also admirably in Gilbert's facsimiles of National MSS.

daughters of their princes became monks and virgins of Christ," and "the number of holy widows and of continent maidens was countless." It would be tedious were he to recount even a portion of what he had gone through. Twelve times had his life been endangered, but God had rescued him, and brought him safe from all plots and ambuscades and rewarded him for leaving his parents, and friends, and country, heeding neither their prayers nor their tears, that he might preach the gospel in Ireland. He appeals to all he had converted, and to all who knew him, to say whether he had not refused all gifts—nay, it was he himself who gave the gifts, to the kings and to their sons, and oftentimes was he robbed and plundered of everything, and once had he been bound in fetters of iron for fourteen days until God had delivered him, and even still while writing this confession he was living in poverty and misery, expecting death or slavery, or other evil. He prays earnestly for one thing only, that he may persevere, and not lose the people whom God has given to him at the very extremity of the world.

Unhappily this "Confession" is a most unsatisfying composition, for it omits to mention almost everything of most interest relating to the saint himself and to his mission. What floods of light might it have thrown upon a score of vexed questions, how it might have set at rest for ever theories on druidism, kingship, social life, his own birthplace, his mission from Rome,[1] his captors. Even of himself he tells us next to nothing, except that his father's name was Calpornus,[2] the son of

[1] It has often been said that the life of the saint in the Book of Armagh ignores the Roman Mission. But while the life of Muirchu Maccu Machteni does ignore it, Tirechan's his contemporary's, life, in the same book, distinctly acknowledges it, in these words, "deinde Patricius secundus ab anguelo dei, Victor nomine, *et a Celestino papa* mittitur cui Hibernia tota credidit, qui eam pene totam bap[titzavit]." (*See* chap. 56 of Tirechan's life.)

[2] In Irish he is usually called Son of Alprann or Alplann, the C of Calpornus being evidently taken as belonging to the Mac, thus Mac Calprainn became Mac Alprainn. In the Brussels Codex of Muirchu Maccu

Potitus, the son of Odissus, a priest, and that he dwelt in the *vicus* or township of Benaven Taberniæ ; he had also a small villa not far off, where he tells us he was made captive at the age of about sixteen years. Because his Christian training was bad, and he was not obedient to the priests when they admonished him to seek for salvation, therefore God punished him, and brought him into captivity in a strange land at the end of the world. When he was brought to Ireland he tells us that his daily task was to feed cattle, and then the love of God entered into his heart, and he used to rise before the sun and pray in the woods and mountains, in the rain, the hail, and the snow. Then there came to him one night a voice in his sleep saying to him "Your ship is ready," and he departed and went for two hundred miles, until he reached a port where he knew no one. This was after six years' captivity. The master of the ship would not take him on board, but afterwards he relented just as Patrick was about to return to the cottage where he had got lodging. He succeeded at last in reaching the home of his parents *in Britannis* [*i.e.*, in some part of Britain, including Scotland], and his parents besought him, now that he had returned from so many perils, to remain with them always. But the angel Victor came in the guise of a man from Ireland, and gave him a letter, in which the voice of the Irish called him away, and the voices of those who dwelt near the wood of Focluth called him to walk amongst them, and the spirit of God, too, urged him to return.[1]

Machteni's life, however, he is called *Alforni filius*, and the place of his birth is called *Ban navem thabur indecha*, supposed to be Killpatrick, near Dumbarton, in Scotland, which is evidently a corruption of his own Bannaven Taberniæ, which seems to mean River-head Tavern ; it may be from the two words *navem thabur* that St. Fiacc's hymn says that he was born in *nemthur*. Patrick himself only gives us two generations of his ancestry, and it is very significant of Irish ways to find Flann of Monasterboice, running it up to fourteen !

[1] It is worth while to transcribe this passage as a fair specimen of St. Patrick's style and latinity. "Et ibi scilicet in sinu noctis virum venientem quasi de Hiberione cui nomen Victoricus, cum æpistulis innumerabilibus

He says nothing of his training, or his ordination, or his long sojourn in Gaul, or of St. Germanus, with whom he studied according to the "Lives," but he alludes incidentally to his wish to see his parents and his native Britain, and to revisit the brethren in Gaul, and to see the face of God's saints there; but though he desired all this, he would not leave his beloved converts, but would spend the rest of his life amongst them.[1]

From this brief *résumé* of the celebrated "Confession" it will be seen that it is the perfervid outpouring of a zealous early Christian, anxious only to clear himself from the charges of worldliness or carelessness, and absolutely devoid of those appeals to general interest which we meet with in most of such memoirs, but there is a vein of warm piety running through the whole, and an abundance of scriptural quotations—all, of course, from the ante-Hieronymian or pre-Vulgate version, another proof of antiquity—which has caused it to be remarked that a forger might, perhaps, write equally bad Latin, but could hardly "forge the spirit that breathes in the language which is the manifest outpourings of a heart like unto the heart of St. Paul."[2]

There are two other pieces of literature assigned to St. Patrick, as well as the "Confession"; these are the "Epistle to Coroticus" in Latin, and the "Deer's Cry" in Irish. The

vidi; et dedit mihi unam ex his et legi principium æpistolæ continentem 'Uox Hiberionacum.' Et dum recitabam principium æpistolæ, putabam enim ipse in mente audire vocem ipsorum qui erant juxta silvam Focluti [in the county Mayo] quæ est prope mare occidentale. Et sic exclamaverunt: 'Rogamus te sancte puer ut venias et adhuc ambulas inter nos.' Et valde compunctus sum corde, et amplius non potui legere. Et sic expertus [*i.e.* experrectus] sum. Deo gratias quia post plurimos annos præstitit illis Dominus secundum clamorum illorum" (Folio 23, 66, Book of Armagh, p. 126 of Father Hogan's Bollandist edition).

[1] The "Confession" ends with a certain rough eloquence: "Christus Dominus pauper fuit pro nobis; ego vero miser et infelix, et si opes voluero jam non habeo; neque me ipsum judico quia quotidie spero aut internicionem aut circumveniri, aut redigi in servitatem, sive occassio cujus-libet. . . Et hæc est confessio mea antequam moriar."

[2] Dr. Healy's "Ireland's Ancient Schools and Scholars," p. 68.

Epistle is not found in the Book of Armagh, but it is found in other MSS. as old as the tenth or eleventh century, and bears such close resemblance in style and language to the "Confession," whole phrases actually occurring in both, that it also has generally been regarded as genuine.[1] There is some doubt as to who Coroticus was, but he seems to have been a semi-Christian king of Dumbarton who, along with some Scots, *i.e.*, Irish, and the Southern Picts who had fallen away from Christianity, raided the eastern shores of Ireland and carried off a number of St. Patrick's newly-converted Christians, leaving the white garments of the neophytes stained with blood, and hurrying into captivity numbers upon whose foreheads the holy oil of confirmation was still glistening. The first letter was to ask Coroticus to restore the captives, and when this request was derided the next was sent, excommunicating him and all his aiders and abettors, calling upon all Christians neither to eat nor drink in their company until they had made expiation for their crimes. Patrick himself had, he here explains, preached the gospel to the Irish nation for the sake of God, though they had made him a captive and destroyed the men-servants and maids of his father's house. He had been born a freedman and a noble, the son of a decurio or prefect, but he had sold his nobility for others and regretted it not. His lament over the loss of his converts is touching: "Oh! my most beautiful and most loving brothers and children whom in countless numbers I have begotten in Christ, what shall I do for you? Am I so unworthy before God and men that I cannot help you? Is it a crime to have been born in Ireland?[2] And have we not the same God as they have? I sorrow for you, yet I rejoice, for if ye are taken from the world ye are believers through me, and are gone to Paradise."

[1] It is printed by Haddan and Stubbs, "Councils," etc., vol. ii. p. 314.

[2] This is certainly the first time on record that this question—so often repeated since in so many different forms—was asked.

The "Cry of the Deer," or "Lorica," as it is also called, is in Irish. The saint is said to have made it when on his way to visit King Laoghaire [Leary] at Tara, and the assassins who had been planted by the king to slay him and his companions thought as he chanted this hymn that it was a herd of deer that passed them by, and thus they escaped. The metre of the original is a kind of unrhymed or half-rhymed rhapsody, called in Irish a *Rosg*, and is perfectly unadorned. The language, however, though very old, has of course been modified in the process of transcription. Patrick calls upon the Trinity to protect him that day at Tara, and to bind to him the power of the elements.

I bind me to-day [1]
God's might to direct me,
God's power to protect me,
God's wisdom for learning,
God's eye for discerning,
God's ear for my hearing,
God's word for my clearing,
God's hand for my cover,
God's path to pass over,
God's buckler to guard me,
God's army to ward me,
Against snares of the devils,
Against vices, temptations,

[1] See the original in Windsch's "Irische Texte," I. p. 53, and Todd's "Liber Hymnorum"—

"Atomrigh indiu niurt Dé dom luamaracht
Cumachta Dé dom chumgabail
Ciall Dé domm imthús
Rosc Dé dom reimcíse,
Cluas Dé dom éstecht
Briathar Dé dom erlabrai,
Lám De domm imdegail
Intech Dé dom remthechtas.
Sciath Dé dom dítin
Sochraite Dé domm anucul
Ar intledaib demna
Ar aslaigthib dualche
Ar cech nduine míduthrastar dam,
ícéin *ocus* i n-ocus
i n-uathed *ocus* hi sochaide," etc.

Against wrong inclinations,
Against men who plot evils
To hurt me anew,
Anear or afar with many or few.

. . . .

Christ near, Christ here,
Christ be with me,
Christ beneath me,
Christ within me,
Christ behind me,
Christ be o'er me,
Christ before me,
Christ in the left and the right,
Christ hither and thither,
Christ in the sight,
Of each eye that shall seek me,"[1] etc.

In the Book ot Armagh, in the last chapter of Tirechan's life, St. Patrick is declared to be entitled to four honours in every church and monastery of the island. One of these honours was that the hymn written by St. Seachnall, his nephew, in praise of himself, was to be sung in the churches during the days when his festival was being celebrated, and another was that "his Irish canticle" was to be always sung,[2] apparently all the year through, in the liturgy, but perhaps only during the week of his festival. The Irish canticle is evidently

[1] Thus translated almost literally by Dr. Sigerson, "Bards of the Gael and Gall," p. 138. This is not the only poem attributed to St. Patrick, several others are ascribed to him in the "Tripartite Life," and a MS. in the Bibliothèque Royale contains three others. Eight lines of one of them is found in the Vatican Codex of Marianus Scotus and are given by Zeuss in his "Grammatica Celtica," p. 961, second edition. The lines there given refer to St. Brigit. There is also a rann attributed to St. Patrick quoted by the "Four Masters," and the "Chronicon Scotorum" attributes to him a rann on Bishop Erc.

[2] "Canticum ejus scotticum semper canere," which a marginal note in the book explains as *Ymnus Comanulo,* which Father Hogan interprets as *protectio Clamoris,* adding "ac proinde synonyma voci Faith Fiada," which has been interpreted *clamor custodis* or "The Guardsman's Cry" by Stokes. The poem, then, was extant in the seventh century, was attributed to St. Patrick, and was sung in the churches—a strong argument for its authenticity.

this "Lorica," which was, as we see from this notice in the Book of Armagh, believed to be his in the seventh century, and it has been sung under that belief from that day almost to our own.[1]

The other hymn, the singing of which at his festival is alluded to as one of St. Patrick's "honours," was composed by Seachnall [Shaughnal],[2] a nephew of St. Patrick's, in laudation of the saint himself. It is a very interesting piece of rough latinity, and is generally regarded as genuine. The occasion of its composition deserves to be told, for it casts a ray of light on the prudential and self-restrained side of St. Patrick's character, which no doubt contributed largely to his success when working in the midst of his wavering converts. Seachnall said that Patrick's preaching would be perfect if he only insisted a little more on the necessity of giving, for then more property and land would be at the disposal of the Church for pious uses. This remark of his nephew was repeated to St. Patrick, who was very much annoyed at it, and said beautifully, that "for the sake of charity he forbore to preach charity," and intimated that the holy men who should come after him might benefit by the offerings of the faithful which he had left untouched. Then Seachnall, grieved at having thus pained his uncle, and anxious to win his regard again,

[1] "Even to this day," says Dr. Healy, in "Ireland's Ancient Schools and Scholars," p. 77, "the original is chanted by the peasantry of the south and west in the ancestral tongue, and it is regarded as a strong shield against all dangers natural or supernatural." I, myself, however, in collecting the "Religious Songs of Connacht," have found no trace of this, and I am not sure that the learned Bishop of Clonfert, led astray by Petrie, is not here confounding it with the "Marainn Phadraig," which mysterious piece is implicitly believed to be the work of St. Patrick, and is still recited all over the west, with the belief that there is a peculiar virtue attached to it. I have even known money to have been paid for its recital in the west of Galway, as a preventive of evil. For this curious piece, which is to me at least more than half unintelligible, see my 'Religious Songs of Connacht." It appears to have been founded upon an incident similar to that recorded by Muirchu Maccu Machteni, book . chap. 26.

[2] Of Dunshaughlin *recté* Dunsaughnil (Domhnach Seachnaill) in Meath.

composed a poem of twenty-two stanzas each beginning with a different letter, with four lines of fifteen syllables in each verse.[1] When he had done this he asked permission of Patrick to recite to him a poem which he had composed in praise of a holy man, and when Patrick said that he would gladly hear the praises of any of God's household, the poet adroitly suppressing Patrick's name which occurs in the first verse, recited it for him. Patrick was pleased, but interupted the poet at one stanza when he said that the subject of his laudations was *maximus in regno cælorum*,[2] "the greatest in the kingdom of heaven," asking how could that be said of any

[1] As this was probably the first poem in Latin ever composed in Ireland, it deserves some consideration. It is a sort of trochaic tetrameter catalectic, of the very rudest type. The *ictus*, or stress of the voice, which is supposed to fall on the first syllable of the first, third, fifth, and seventh feet, seldom corresponds with the accent. The elision of "m" before a vowel is disregarded, no quantities are observed, and the solitary rule of prosody kept is that the second syllable of the seventh foot is always short, with the exception of one word, *indutus*, which the poet probably pronounced as *indŭtus*. The third verse runs thus, with an evident effort at vowel rhyme ("Liber Hymnorum," vol. i. p. 11).

> "Beati Christi custodit mandata in omnibus
> Cujus opera refulgent clara inter homines."

Muratori printed this hymn, from the so-called Antiphonary of Bangor, a MS. of the eight century preserved in the Ambrosian Library. The rude metre is that employed by Hilary in his hymn beginning—

> "Ymnum dicat turba fratrum, ymnum cantus personet,"

which, as Stokes points out, is the same as that of the Roman soldiers, preserved in Suetonius,

> "Cæsar Gallias subégit, Nicomedes Cæsarem."

The internal evidence of the antiquity of this hymn is "strong," says Stokes, "first, the use of the present tense in describing the saint's actions; secondly, the absence of all reference to the miracles with which the Tripartite and other lives are crowded; and, thirdly, the absence of all allusion to the Roman mission on which many later writers from Tirechan downwards insist with much persistency." We may then, I think, receive this hymn as authentic.

[2] "Maximus namque in regno cælorum vocabitur,
Qui quod verbis docet sacris factis adimplet bonis;
Bono procedit exemplo formamque fidelium
Mundoque in corde habet ad Deum fiduciam."

man. *Maximus*, ingeniously replied Seachnall, does not here mean "greatest," but only "very great." He then disclosed to his uncle that he himself was the object of the poem, and asked—like all bards—for the reward for it, whereupon Patrick promised that to all who recited the hymn piously morning and evening, God in His mercy might give the glory of heaven. "I am content with that award," said the poet, "but as the hymn is long and difficult to be remembered I wish you would obtain the same reward for whosoever recites even a part of it." Whereupon St. Patrick promised that the recitation of the last three verses would be sufficient, and his nephew was satisfied, having proved himself the first poet of Christian Ireland, and having obtained such a reward for his verses as neither bard nor ollav had ever obtained before him. It was probably this same Seachnall who was the author of the much finer hymn of eleven verses which used to be sung in the old Irish churches at communion—

"Sancti venite
  Christi corpus sumite,
  Sanctum bibentes
  Quo redempti sanguinem.

Salvati Christi
  Corpore et sanguine,
  A quo refecti
  Laudes dicamus Deo.

Hoc sacramento
  Corporis et sanguinis
  Omnes exuti
  Ab inferni faucibus," etc.

The legend in the Leabhar Breac has it that this hymn was first chanted during the holy communion by the angels in his church, on the reconciliation between himself and Saint Patrick, whence the origin of chanting it during the communion service.

The Book of Armagh contains the two earliest lives of the national saint that we have, probably the two earliest biographies of any size ever composed in Ireland. They are written in rude Latin, with a good deal of Irish place-names and Irish words intermixed, the first by one Muirchu Maccu Machteni,[1] who tells us that he wrote at the instigation of Aed, bishop of Sletty, who, as we know from the "Four Masters," died about 698, and the second by Tirechan, who says he received his knowledge of the saint from the lips and writings of Bishop Ultan,[2] his tutor, who died in 656, and who, supposing him to have been seventy or eighty years old at the time of his death, must have been born only eighty or ninety years after the death of St. Patrick himself. Both of these writers appear to have had older memoirs to draw on, for Muirchu says that many had before them endeavoured to write the history of St. Patrick from what their fathers and those who were ministers of the Word from the beginning had told them, though none had ever succeeded in producing a proper biography,[3] and in Tirechan's life of him in the Book of Armagh—an evident patchwork—we read that all his godly doings had been brought together[4] and collected by the

[1] In the "Martyrology of Tallaght" this curious name is written Mac hui Machteni, *i.e.*, the son of the grandson of Machtenus, or Muirchu, *i.e.*, Murrough, descendant of Machtenus, and the Leabhar Breac has this note at the name of Muirchu: "*civitas ejus in uib Foelan, i.e., mac hui Mathcene,*" thereby giving us to understand that he was a native of what is the present county of Waterford. Maccumachteni is not a surname, for these were not introduced into Ireland for three centuries later.

[2] "Omnia quæ scripsi a principio libri hujus scitis quia in vestris regionibus gesta sunt, nizi de eis pauca inveni in utilitatem laboris mei a senioribus multis, ac ab illo Ultano episcopo Conchubernensi qui nutrivit me, retulit sermo!"

[3] "Multos jam conatos esse ordinare narrationem istam secundum quod patres eorum et qui ministri ab initio fuerunt sermonis tradiderunt illis; sed propter difficillimum narrationis opus diversasque opiniones et plurimorum plurimas suspiciones nunquam ad unum certumque historiae tramitem pervenisse."

[4] "Omnia in Deo gesta ab antiquis peritissimis adunata atque collecta sunt;" and again: "Post exitum Patricii alumpni sui valde ejusdem libros conscripserunt;" but this may mean that they made copies of the books left behind him.

most skilful of the ancients. The first of these lives consists of two books containing twenty-eight and thirteen short chapters, respectively, the second, Tirechan's, of one book containing fifty-seven chapters, in addition to which there are a number of minor notes referring to St. Patrick in Latin and in Irish, which Ferdomnach, who transcribed the book in 807, appears to have taken from other old lives or memoirs of the saint. The Irish portions of these notes are of peculiar interest, as showing what the Irish language was, as written about the year 800.[1]

If it is genuine the earliest life of Patrick ever written would probably be the brief metrical life ascribed to Fiacc of Sletty, the sixth or seventh in descent from Cáthaoir [Cauheer] Mór, who was king of Leinster at the close of the second century.[2] His mother was a sister of Dubhthach's [Duv-hach], the chief poet and Brehon of Ireland, who, we are told, helped St. Patrick to review and revise the Brehon Laws. Fiacc was a youthful poet in Dubhthach's train at Tara. Afterwards he was tonsured by St. Patrick, became Bishop of Sletty, and on Patrick's death is said to have written his life, and not forgetful of his former training, to have written it in elaborate verse.[3] So famous a critic as Zimmer believed half the poem to be genuine, but Thurneysen rejects

[1] Here is a specimen: "Dulluid pâtricc othemuir hicrîch Laigen conrâncatar ocus dubthach mucculugir uccdomnuch mâr criathar la auu censelich. Áliss pâtricc dubthach imdamnae .n. epscuip diadesciplib dilaignib idôn fer soêr socheniûil cenon cenainim nadip ru becc nadipromar bedasommae, toisclimm fer ôinsêtche dunarructhae actoentuistiu," which would run some way thus in the modern language: "Do luid (*i.e.*, Chuaidh) Pádraic ó Theamhair i gcrích Laighean go râncadar [fein] agus Dubhthach Mac Lugair ag Domhnach Mór Criathair le uibh Ceinnsealaigh. Ailis (*i.e.*, fiafruighis) Pádraic Dubhthach um damhna (*i.e.*, ádhbhar) easboig d' á dheiscioblaibh, eadhoin fear saor sói-chineáil, gan on gan ainimh (*i.e.*, truailiughadh), nâr 'bh ro bheag [agus] nár 'bh rómhór, a shaidhbhreas (?). Toisg [riachtanus] liom fear aon seitche [mná] d'á nach rugadh acht aon tuistui (gein)," etc.

[2] For Cáthaoir Mór, *see* p. 30.

[3] The metre was called *Cetal nothi*, Thurneysen's "Mittelirische Verslehren," p. 63. It scarcely differs in most parts from Little Rannaigheacht.

it because it does not fall in with his theories of Irish metre.[1]

But the longest and most important life of St. Patrick is that known as the Tripartite, or Triply-divided Life, which is really a series of three semi-historical homilies, or discourses, which were probably delivered in honour of the saint on the three festival days devoted to his memory, that is, the Vigil, the Feast itself, on March 17th, and the day after, or else the Octave. This Tripartite life, which is a fairly complete one, is written in ancient Irish, with many passages of Latin interspersed. The monk Jocelin, who wrote a life of the saint in the twelfth century, tells us that St. Evin[2] —from whom Monasterevin, in Queen's County, is called, a saint of the early sixth century—wrote a life of Patrick partly in Latin and partly in Gaelic, and Colgan, the learned Franciscan who translated the Tripartite in his "Trias Thaumaturga,"[3] believed that this was the very life which St. Evin wrote. Colgan found the Tripartite life in three very ancient Gaelic MSS., procured for him, no doubt, by the unwearied research of Brother Michael O'Clery in the early part of the seventeenth century, which he collated one with the other, and of which he gives the following noteworthy account :—

"The first thing to be observed is that it has been written by its first author and in the aforesaid manuscript, partly in Latin, partly

[1] *See* "Keltische Studien," Heft ii., and the "Revue Celtique." The first verses run thus :—

> "Genair Patraicc in Nemthur
> Is ed atfet hi scélaib
> Maccan se mbliadan déac
> In tan dobreth fo deraib.
>
> Succat a ainm itubrad
> Ced a athair ba fissi
> Mac Calpairn *maic* Otide
> Hoa deochain Odissi."

[2] He was tenth in descent from that Owen Môr who wrested half the sovereignty of Ireland from Conn of the Hundred Battles.

[3] *I.e.*, "The wonder-working Three," containing the lives of Patrick, Brigit, and Columcille, translated by Colgan from Irish into Latin.

in Gaelic, and this in very ancient language, almost impenetrable by reason of its very great antiquity, exhibiting not only in the same chapter, but also in the same line, alternate phrases now in the Latin, now in the Gaelic tongue. In the second place, it is to be noticed that this life, on account of the very great antiquity of its style, which was held in much regard, used to be read in the schools of our antiquarians in the presence of their pupils, being elucidated and expounded by the glosses of the masters, and by interpretations of and observations on the more abstruse words; so that hence it is not to be wondered at that some words—which certainly did happen—gradually crept from these glosses into the texts, and thus brought a certain colour of newness into this most ancient and faithful author, some things being turned from Latin into Gaelic, some abbreviated by the scribes, and some altogether omitted."

Colgan further tells us that, "of the three MSS. above mentioned, the first and chief is from very ancient vellums of the O'Clerys, antiquarians in Ulster; the second from the O'Deorans, of Leinster; the third taken from I know not what codex; and they differ from each other in some respects; one relating more diffusely what is more close in the others, and one relating in Latin what in the others was told in Gaelic; but we have followed the authority of that which relates the occurrences more diffusely and in Latin." O'Curry discovered in the British Museum a copy of this life, made in the fifteenth century, and it has since been admirably edited by Dr. Whitley Stokes, who, however, does not believe for philological and other reasons, that it could have been written before the middle of the tenth century. If so it is no doubt a compilation of all the pre-existing lives of the saint, and it mentions distinctly that six different writers, not counting Fiacc the poet, had collected the events of St. Patrick's life and his miracles, amongst whom were St. Columcille, who died in 592, and St. Ultan, who died in 656.[1] It is hardly

[1] Also St. Aileran the Wise, whose "Fragments" are published by Migne; St. Adamnan, the author of the "Life of Columcille"; St. Ciaran of Belach-Duin; and St. Colman. Jocelyn says that Benignus, who died in 468, wrote another life of Patrick, but of it nothing is known.

necessary, however, to say that in the matter of all anonymous Gaelic writings like the present, it is difficult to decide with any certainty as to age or date. The occurrence, indeed, of very old forms, shows that the sentences containing those old forms were first written at an early period; the occurrence of more modern forms, however, is no proof that the passages containing them were first written in modern times, for the words may have been altered by later transcribers into the language they spoke themselves; nor are allusions to events which we know were later than the date of an alleged writer, *always* conclusive proofs that the work which contains them cannot be his work, for such allusions constantly creep into the margin of books at the hands of copyists, especially if those books were—as Colgan says the Tripartite life was—annotated and explained in schools. In cases of this kind there is always considerable latitude to be allowed to destructive and constructive criticism, and at the end matters must still remain doubtful.[1]

So much for the more important lives of St. Patrick, the first known *littérateur* of Ireland.

[1] Here is a short passage from the Tripartite, which will show the language in which it is written: "Fecht ann occ tuidhecht do Patraic do Chlochur antuaith da fuarcaib a thren-fher dar doraid and, *i.e.*, Epscop mac Cairthind. Issed adrubart iar turcbail Patraic: uch uch. Mu Debroth, ol Patraic ni bu gnath in foculsin do rad duitsiu. Am senoir ocus am lobur ol Epscop Mac Cairthind," which would run some way thus in the modern language: "Feacht [uair] do bhi ann, ag tigheacht do Phádraig go Clochar (i gcondae, Tir-Eóghain) ón tuaidh, d' iomchair a threán-fhear é thar sruth do bhi ann, eadhoin Easbog Mac Cairthind. Is eadh adubhairt tar éis Padraig do thogbháil "Uch, uch!" Mo Dhebhroth [focal do bhi ag Padraig, ionnann agus "dar mo láimh" no mar sin], níor ghnáth an focal sin do rádh duit-se. Táim im sheanoir agus im lobhar ar Easbog Mac Cairthind. *See* O'Curry MS. Materials, p. 598.

CHAPTER XIV

ST. BRIGIT

St. Brigit was—after St. Patrick himself—probably the most noted figure amongst Irish Christians in the fifth century. She must have attained her extraordinary influence through sheer ability and intellectuality, for she appears to have been the daughter of a slave-woman,[1] employed in the mansion of a chief called Dubhthach [Duv-hach, or Duffach], who was himself tenth in descent from Felimidh, the lawgiver monarch of Ireland in the second century. The king's wife, jealous of her husband's liking for his slave, threatened him with these words, "Unless thou sellest yon bondmaid in distant lands I will exact my dowry from thee and I will leave thee," and so had her driven from the place and sold to a druid, in whose house her daughter, Dubhthach's offspring, soon afterwards saw the light. She was thus born into slavery, though not quite a slave; for Dubhthach, in selling the mother into slavery, expressly reserved for himself her offspring, whatever it might be. She must have been, at least, early inured to hardship, as St. Patrick had been. The druid, however, did

[1] Cogitosus, who probably wrote in the beginning of the eighth century, makes no allusion to her slave-parentage, but this was to be expected.

not prevent her from being baptized. She grew up to be a girl of exceeding beauty, and many suitors sought her in marriage. She returned to her father's house, but refused all offers of matrimony. She aroused the jealousy of her father's wife, as her mother had done before her, and Dubhthach, indignant at her unbounded generosity with his goods, decided upon selling her to the king of North Leinster. Her father's abortive attempt to get rid of her on this occasion is thus quaintly described in her Irish life in the Leabhar Breac.

"Thereafter," says the life, "Dubhthach and his consort were minded to sell the holy Brigit into bondage, for Dubhthach liked not his cattle and his wealth to be dealt out to the poor, and that is what Brigit used to do. So Dubhthach fared in his chariot and Brigit along with him.

"Said Dubhthach to Brigit, 'Not for honour or reverence to thee art thou carried in a chariot, but to take thee, to sell thee to grind the quern for Dunlang mac Enda, King of Leinster.'

"When they came to the King's fortress Dubhthach went in to the king, and Brigit remained in her chariot at the fortress door. Dubhthach had left his sword in the chariot near Brigit. A leper came to Brigit to ask an alms. She gave him Dubhthach's sword.

"Said Dubhthach to the King, 'Wilt thou buy a bondmaid, namely, my daughter?' says he.

"Said Dunlang, 'Why sellest thou thine own daughter?'

"Said Dubhthach, 'She stayeth not from selling my wealth and from giving it to the poor.'

"Said the King, 'Let the maiden come into the fortress.'

"Dubhthach went to Brigit, and was enraged against her because she had given his sword to the poor man.

"When Brigit came into the King's presence the King said to her, 'Since it is thy father's wealth that thou takest, much more wilt thou take *my* wealth and my cattle and give them to the poor.'

"Said Brigit, 'The Son of the Virgin knoweth if I had thy might, with all Leinster, and with all thy wealth, I would give them to the Lord of the Elements.'

"Said the King to Dubhthach, 'Thou art not fit on either hand to bargain about this maiden, for her merit is higher before God than before men,' and the King gave Dubhthach an ivory-hilted sword (*Claideb dét*), et sic liberata est sancta Virgo Brigita a captivititate.[1]"

[1] *See* Stokes, "Three Middle Irish Homilies."

She at length succeeded in assuming the veil of a nun at the hands of a bishop called Mucaille, along with seven virgin companions. With these she eventually retired into her father's territory and founded a church at Kildare, beside an ancient oak-tree, which existed till the tenth century, and which gives its name to the spot.[1] Even at this early period Kildare seems to have been a racecourse, and St. Brigit is described in the ancient lives as driving across it in her chariot.

It is remarkable that there is scarcely any mention of St. Brigit in the lives of St. Patrick, although, according to the usual chronology they were partly contemporaries, St. Brigit having become a nun about the year 467, and St. Patrick having lived until 492. About the only mention of her in the saint's life is that which tells how she once listened to Patrick preaching for three nights and days, and fell asleep, and as she dreamt she saw first white oxen in white corn-fields, and then darker ones took their place, and lastly black oxen. And thereafter, she beheld sheep and swine, and dogs and wolves quarrelling with each other, and upon her waking up, St. Patrick explained her dream as being symbolical of the history of the Irish Church present and future. The life of Brigit herself in the Book of Lismore tells the vision somewhat differently:

> " 'I beheld,' said she, to Patrick, when he asked her why she had fallen asleep, 'four ploughs in the north-east which ploughed the whole island, and before the sowing was finished the harvest was ripened, and clear well-springs and shiny streams came out of the furrows. White garments were on the sowers and ploughmen. I beheld four other ploughs in the north which ploughed the island athwart and turned the harvest again, and the oats which they had sown grew up at once and were ripe, and black streams came out of the furrows, and there were black garments on the sowers and on the ploughmen.' "

---

[1] Cill-dara, the "Church of the Oak-tree," now Kildare.

This vision Patrick explained to her, saying—

"'The first four ploughs which thou beheldest, those are I and thou, who sow the four books of the gospel with a sowing of faith and belief and piety. The harvest which thou beheldest are they who come unto that faith and belief through our teaching. The four ploughs which thou beheldest in the north are the false teachers and the liars which will overturn the teaching which we have sown.'"

St. Brigit's small oratory at Kildare, under the shadow of her branching oak, soon grew into a great institution, and within her own lifetime two considerable religious establishments sprang up there, one for women and the other for men. She herself selected a bishop to assist her in governing them, and another to instruct herself and her nuns. Long before her death, which occurred about the year 525, a regular city and a great school rivalling the fame of Armagh itself, had risen round her oak-tree. Cogitosus, himself one of the Kildare monks, who wrote a Latin life of St. Brigit at the desire of the community, gives us a fine description of the great church of Kildare in his own day, which was evidently some time prior to the Danish invasion at the close of the eighth century,[1] but how long before is doubtful. He tells us that the church was both large and lofty, with many pictures and hangings, and with ornamental doorways, and that a partition ran across the breadth of the church near the chancel or sanctuary :

"At one of its extremities there was a door which admitted the bishop and his clergy to the sanctuary and to the altar ; and at the

[1] He himself says, "Et quis sermone explicare potest maximum decorem hujus ecclesiæ et innumera illius civitatis quî dicemus miracula . . . [hic] nullus carnalis adversarius nec concursus timetur hostium, sed civitas est refugii tutissima . . . et quis ennumerare potest diversas turbas et innumerabiles populos de omnibus provinciis affluentes, alii ad epularum abundantiam, alii languidi propter sanitates, alii ad spectaculum turbarum, alii cum magnis donis venientes ad solemnitatem Nativitatis S. Brigitæ quæ in die Calendarum est," etc. These are the evident outcome of the piping times of peace which Ireland enjoyed in the seventh and eighth centuries. It would have been impossible to have written in this way after the close of the eighth century. See chap. 36 of Cogitosus's life, "Trias Thaumaturga," p. 524 of the Louvain edition.

other extremity on the opposite side there was a similar door by which Brigit and her virgins and widows used to enter to enjoy the banquet of the Body and Blood of Christ. Then a central partition ran down the nave, dividing the men from the women, the men being on the right and the women on the left, and each division having its own lateral entrance. These partitions did not rise to the roof of the church, but only so high as to serve their purpose. The partition at the sanctuary or chancel was formed with boards of wood decorated with pictures and covered with linen hangings which might, it seems, be drawn aside at the consecration, to give the people in the nave a better view of the holy mysteries."[1]

The two institutions—nuns and monks—planted by St. Brigit continued long to flourish side by side, and Kildare is the only religious establishment in Ireland, says Dr. Healy, which down to a comparatively recent period preserved the double line of succession, of abbot-bishops and of abbesses. The annalists always took care to record the names of the abbesses with the same accuracy as those of the abbots, and to the last the abbesses as successors of St. Brigit, were credited with, in public opinion, and probably enjoyed in fact, a certain supremacy over the bishops of Kildare themselves.

Amongst other occupations the monks and scholars of Kildare seem to have given themselves up to decorative art, and a school of metal work under the supervision of Brigit's first bishop soon sprang into existence, producing all kinds of artistically decorated chalices, bells, patens, and shrines ; and the impulse given thus early to artistic work and to beautiful creations seems to have long propagated itself in Kildare, as the description of the church by Cogitosus shows, and as we may still conjecture from the exquisite round tower with its unusually ornamented doorway and its great height of over 130 feet, the loftiest tower of the kind in Ireland.

[1] Thus well summarised by Dr. Healy from the more diffuse Latin of Cogitosus. His description of the church is as follows: It was "solo spatiosa et in altum minaci proceritate porrecta ac decorata pictis tabulis, tria intrinsecus habens oratoria ampla, et divisa parietibus tabulatis." One of the walls was "decoratus, et imaginibus depictus, ac linteaminibus tectus."

No doubt several attributes of the pagan Brigit,[1] who, as we have seen, was accounted by the ancient Irish to have been the goddess of poets, passed over to her Christian namesake, who was also credited with being the patroness of men of learning. On this, her life in the Book of Lismore contains the following significant and rather obscure passage :

"Brigit was once with her sheep on the Curragh, and she saw running past her a son of reading,[2] to wit Nindid the scholar was he.

"'What makes thee unsedate, O son of reading?' saith Brigit, 'and what seekest thou in that wise?'

"'O nun,' saith the scholar, 'I am going to heaven.'

"'The Virgin's son knoweth,' said Brigit, 'happy is he that goeth that journey, and for God's sake make prayer with me that it may be easy for me to go.'

"'O nun,' said the scholar, 'I have no leisure, for the gates of heaven are open now and I fear they may be shut against me. Or, if thou art hindering me pray the Lord that it may be easy for me to go to heaven, and I will pray the Lord for thee, that it may be easy for thee, and that thou mayest bring many thousands with thee, into heaven.'

---

[1] This has not escaped Windisch. "Während," he writes, "Patrick nur der christlichen Hagiologie angehört, scheint Brigit zugleich die Erbin einer alten heidnischen Gottheit zu sein. Ihr Wesen enthält Züge die mehr als eine heilig gesprochen Nonne hinter ihr vermuthen lassen." Windisch bases this chiefly upon the expressions in Broccan's hymn, which calls her the mother of Christ, and calls Christ her son, and equates her with Mary. The passage which I have adduced from the Irish life is even more remarkable :

"Brigit," writes Whitley Stokes "(cp. Skr. *bhargas*) was born at sunrise neither within nor without a house, was bathed in milk, her breath revives the dead, a house in which she is staying flames up to heaven, cow-dung blazes before her, oil is poured on her head ; she is fed from the milk of a white red-eared cow ; a fiery pillar rises over her head ; sun rays support her wet cloak ; she remains a virgin ; and she was one of the two mothers of Christ the Anointed. She has, according to Giraldus Cambrensis, a perpetual ashless fire watched by twenty nuns, of whom herself was one, blown by fans or bellows only, and surrounded by a hedge within which no male could enter" ("Top. Hib." chaps. 34, 35 and 36), from all which Stokes declares that one may without much rashness pick out certain of her life-incidents as having "originally belonged to the myth or the ritual of some goddess of fire." (*See* preface to "Three Middle Irish Homilies.")

[2] "Mac-léighinn," which is to this day a usual Irish term for student.

"Brigit recited a paternoster with him. And he was pious thenceforward, and it is he that gave her communion and sacrifice when she was dying. *Wherefore thence it came to pass that the comradeship of the world's sons of reading is with Brigit, and the Lord gives them through Brigit every perfect good they ask.*"[1]

As St. Patrick is pre-eminently the patron saint of Ireland, so is Brigit its patroness, and with the Irish people no Christian name is more common for their boys than Patrick, or for their girls than Brigit.[2] She was universally known as the "Mary of the Gael," and reverenced with a certain chivalric feeling which seems to have been always present with the Gaelic nation in the case of women, for, says her Irish life, her desire "was to satisfy the poor, to expel every hardship, to spare every miserable man. . . . It is she that helpeth every one who is in a strait or a danger; it is she that abateth the pestilences; it is she that quelleth the anger and the storm of the sea. She is the prophetess of Christ: she is the queen of the south: *She is the Mary of the Gael.*" The writer closes thus in a burst of eloquence:

[1] Thus translated by Dr. Whitley Stokes in his "Lives of the Saints from the Book of Lismore," p. 194. In the original: "Conid assein dorala cumthanus mac leighinn in domuin re Brigit, co tabair in coimdhi doibh tria atach Brigte gach maith fhoirbhthi chuinghid."

[2] Or to speak more accurately no names *were* more common, but owing to the action of various influences, particularly of the National Board, with unsympathetic persons at its head, and of the men who direct the modern education of the Irish, the people who are not allowed by the National Board to learn history, and who are taught to despise the Irish language, are gradually being made ashamed of any names that are not English, and Patrick and Brigit almost bid fair to follow the way of Cormac, Conn, Felim, Art, Donough, Fergus, Diarmuid, and a score of other Christian names of men in common use a century ago, but now almost wholly extinct, and of Mève, Sive, Eefi, Sheela, Nuala, and as many more female names now nearly or completely obsolete. A woman of some education said to me lately, "God forbid I should handicap my daughter in life by calling her Brigit;" and a Catholic bishop said the other day that too often when an Irish parent abroad did pluck up courage to christen his son "Patrick," he put it in, in a shamefaced whisper, at the end of several other names. This is the direct result of the teaching given by the National Board.

"Her relics are on earth, with honour and dignity and primacy, with miracles and marvels. Her soul is like a sun in the heavenly kingdom, among the choir of angels and archangels. And though great be her honour here at present, greater by far will it be when she shall arise like a shining lamp, in completeness of body and soul at the great Assembly of Doomsday, in union with cherubim and seraphim, in union with the Son of Mary the Virgin, in the union that is nobler than every union, in the union of the Holy Trinity, Father, Son, and Holy Spirit."

As of St. Patrick, so of his great co-evangeliser St. Brigit, there exist quite a number of various lives; the most ancient being probably a metrical life in Irish contained in the Book of Hymns, of which there still exists an eleventh century MS. It consists of fifty-three stanzas of four lines each, and is ascribed to St. Broccan or Brogan Cloen, who seems to have lived at the beginning of the seventh century.[1] This life does little more than expatiate upon Brigit's miracles and virtues. The next life of importance is that already mentioned, by Cogitosus, the Kildare monk, whose date is uncertain, but is clearly prior to the Danish invasions. This life, which is in very creditable Latin, and four others, were printed by Colgan. The first of these four is—probably falsely—attributed to St. Ultan, who died in the middle of the seventh century; the next is by a monk who is called Animosus, but of whom

[1] He is said to have written this hymn at the instigation of Ultan, who died in 653, but, as Windisch remarks, mention is probably made of Ultan only because he is said to have been the first to collect the miracles of Brigit—"die Sprache," adds Windisch, "ist alterthümlich; besonders beachtenswerth sind die ziemlich zahlreichen Perfectformen." It is remarkable that the miracles attributed to Brigit are given in the same order in this hymn and in Cogitosus' life of her. The metre is irregular.

"Ni bu Sanct Brigit suanach
Ni bu húarach im seirc Dé,
Sech ni chiuir ni cossena
Ind nóeb dibad bethath che."

The life by Cogitosus is evidently pre-Danish, and it is more likely to be an extension of the short metrical one, than that the metrical one should be a *résumé* of it. If this is so it bespeaks a considerable antiquity for the Irish verses.

nothing is known, though, as St. Donatus, who became bishop of Fiesole in 824, alludes to his works, he must have been an early author; the third is a twelfth-century work, by Laurence of Durham, an Englishman; and the last is in Latin verse, taken from a MS. which the unwearied Colgan procured from Monte Cassino, and which is attributed to Coelan, a monk of Iniscaltra, who probably lived in the eighth century, while a prologue to this life is prefixed by a later writer, the celebrated Irish bishop of Fiesole, Donatus, who, in the early part of the ninth century, worked with great success in Italy. There is something touching in the language with which this great and successful child of the Gael reverts in his prologue to the home of his childhood:—

> "Far in the west they tell of a matchless land,[1] which goes in ancient books by the name of Scotia [*i.e.*, Ireland]; rich in resources this land, having silver, precious stones, vestures and gold, well suited to earth-born creatures as regards its climate, its sun, and its arable soil; that Scotia of lovely fields that flow with milk and honey, hath skill in husbandry, and raiments, and arms, and arts, and fruits. There are no fierce bears there, nor ever has the land of Scotia brought forth savage broods of lions. No poisons hurt, no serpent creeps through the grass, nor does the babbling frog croak and complain by the lake. In this land the Scottish race are worthy to dwell, a renowned race of men in war, in peace, in fidelity."

Whitley Stokes has published the Irish lives of St. Brigit from the Leabhar Breac and the Book of Lismore, and Donatus alludes to other lives by St. Ultan[2] and St. Eleran,

[1] There is a fragment in the Irish MS. Rawlinson, B. 512, quoted somewhere by Kuno Meyer, which reminds one of this passage. It begins: "Now the island of Ireland, Inis Herenn, has been set in the west. As Adam's Paradise stands at the sunrise, so Ireland stands at the sunset, and they are alike in the nature of their soil," etc.

[2] St. Ultan wrote a beautiful Irish hymn and also a Latin hymn to her—at least they are attributed to him—beginning—

"Christus in nostra insola
Que vocatur hibernia
Ostensus est hominibus
Maximis mirabilibus.

so that Brigit has not lacked biographers. She herself is said to have written a rule for her nuns and some other things, and O'Curry prints one Irish poem ascribed to her—in which she prays for the family of heaven to be present at her feast: "I should like the men of heaven in my own house, I should like rivers of peace to be at their disposal," etc.—which appears to be alluded to in the preface to the Litany of Angus the Culdee, as the "great feast which St. Brigit made for Jesus in her heart." [1]

> Que perfecit per felicem
> Celestis vite virginem
> Precellentem pro merito
> Magno in mundi circulo."

See Todd's "Liber Hymnorum," vol. ii. p. 58. The Latin orthography of the Irish is seldom quite perfect.

[1] This poem begins:

> "Ropadh maith lem corm-lind mór
> Do righ na righ
> Ropadh maith lem muinnter nimhe
> Acca hol tre bithe shír."

I.e., "I would like a great lake of ale for the King of the kings, I would like the people of heaven to be drinking it through eternal ages," which sounds curious, but Brigit probably meant it allegorically.

CHAPTER XV

COLUMCILLE

THE third great patron Saint of Ireland, the man who stands out almost as conspicuously as St. Patrick himself in the religious history of the Gael, the most renowned missionary, scribe, scholar, poet, statesman, anchorite, and school-founder of the sixth century is St. Columcille.[1] Everything about this remarkable man has conspired to fix upon him the imagination of the Irish race. He was not, like St. Patrick, of alien, nor like St. Brigit, of semi-servile birth, but was sprung from the highest and bluest blood of the Irish, being son of Felemidh, son of Fergus, son of Conall Gulban—renowned to this day in saga and romance—son of Niall of the Nine Hostages, that great monarch of Ireland who ravaged Britain and exacted tributes far and wide from his conquered enemies.

He was born on the 7th of December, 521,[2] twenty-nine years after the reputed death of St. Patrick, and four years

[1] Also often called St. Columba, to be strictly distinguished from Columbanus, who laboured on the Continent. The name is written sometimes Colomb Cille and Colum Kille or Columkille. It is pronounced in Irish Cullum-killă, and means literally the "Dove of the Church," but in English the name is generally pronounced Columkill.

[2] As calculated by Dr. Reeves, who coincides with the "Four Masters" and Dr. Lanigan. The other Annals waver between 518 and 523.

before that of St. Brigit, at Gartan [1] in Donegal, a wild but beautiful district of which his father was the prince. The reigning monarch of Ireland was his half-uncle, while his mother Ethne was the direct descendant of the royal line of Cáthaoir [Cauheer] Mór, the regnant family of Leinster, and he himself would have had some chance of the reversion of the monarchy had he been minded to press his claims. Reared at Kilmacrenan, near Gartan, the place where the O'Donnells were afterwards inaugurated, he received his first teaching at the hands of St. Finnén or Finnian in his famous school at Moville, for already since Patrick's death Ireland had become dotted with such small colleges. It was here at this early age that his school-fellows christened him Colum-cille, or Colum of the Church, on account of the assiduity with which he sought the holy building. At this period the Christian clergy and the bardic order were the only two educational powers in Ireland, and after leaving St. Finnian, Columcille travelled south into Leinster to a bard called Gemmán [2] with whom he took lessons. From him he went to St. Finnén or Finnian of Clonard. While studying at Clonard it was the custom for each of the students to grind corn in his turn at a quern, but Columcille's Irish life in the Book of Lismore tells us naïvely, in true old Irish spirit, "howbeit an angel from heaven used to grind on behalf of Columcille; that was the honour which the Lord used to render him because of the eminent nobleness of his race." St. Ciaran [Keeran] was at this time a fellow-student with him, and Finnian, says the Irish life, saw one night a vision, "to wit, two moons arose from Clonard, a golden moon and a silver moon. The golden moon went into the north

[1] See the lines in O'Donnell's life of the saint, ascribed to St. Mura:

"Rugadh i nGartan da dheóin / S do h-oileadh i gCill mhic Neóin
'S do baisteadh mac na maise / A dTulaigh De Dubhghlaise."

[2] He is called "Germán the Master" in the Book of Lismore life. In the life of Finnian of Clonard he is called *Carminator nomine gemanus*, who brings to St. Finnian "quoddam carmen magnificum."

of the island, and Ireland and Scotland gleamed under it. The silver moon went on until it stayed by the Shannon, and Ireland at her centre gleamed." That, says the author, signified "Columcille with the grace of his noble kin and his wisdom, and Ciaran with the refulgence of his virtues and his good deeds."

Leaving Clonard behind him, Columcille passed on to yet another school—this time to that of Mobhí at Glasnevin, near Dublin, where there were as many as fifty students at work, living in huts or cells grouped round an oratory, some of whom were famous men in after-time, for they included Cainnech and Comgall and Ciaran. A curious incident is recorded of these three and of Columcille in the Irish life in the Book of Lismore.

Columcille was driven from Glasnevin by the approach of the great plague which ravaged the country, and of which his teacher Mobhí died.

"Once on a time," says the author, "a great church was built by Mobhí. The clerics were considering what each of them would like to have in the church. 'I should like,' said Ciaran, 'its full of church children to attend the canonical hours.' 'I should like,' said Cainnech, 'to have its full of books to serve the sons of life.' 'I should like,' said Comgall, 'its full of affliction and disease to be in my own body: to subdue me and repress me.' Then Columcille chose its full of gold and silver to cover relics and shrines withal. Mobhí said it should not be so, but that Columcille's community would be wealthier than any community, whether in Ireland or in Scotland."[1]

[1] A similar story of Cummain the Tall, of Guaire the Connacht king who still gives his name to the town of Gort, which is Gort Inse-Guaire, and of Cáimine of Inisceltra, is told in the Leabhar na h-Uidhre, and printed by Whitley Stokes in a note at p. 304 of his "Lives from the Book of Lismore." Each of the three got as he had desired, for, says the chronicler, "all their musings were made true. The earth was given to Guaire. Wisdom was given to Cummain. Diseases and sicknesses were inflicted on Cáimine, so that no bone of him joined together in the earth, but melted and decayed with the anguish of every disease and of every tribulation, so that they all went to heaven according to their musings." (See for the same story the Yellow Book of Lecan, p. 132, of facsimile.)

Betaking himself northward with a growing reputation, he was offered by his cousin, then Prince of Aileach, near Derry, and afterwards monarch of Ireland, the site of a monastery on the so-called island of Derry, a rising ground of oval shape, covering some two hundred acres, along the slopes of which flourished a splendid forest of oak-trees, which gave to the oasis its name of Derry or the oak grove. Columcille, like all Gaels—and indeed all Celts—was full of love for everything beautiful in nature, both animate and inanimate, and so careful was he of his beloved oaks that, contrary to all custom, he would not build his church with its chancel towards the east, for in that case some of the oaks would have had to be felled to make room for it. He laid strict injunctions upon all his successors to spare the lovely grove, and enjoined that if any of the trees should be blown down some of them should go for fuel to their own guest-house, and the rest be given to the people.

This was Columcille's first religious institution, and, like every man's firstling, it remained dear to him to the last. Years afterwards, when the thought of it came back to him on the barren shores of Iona, he expressed himself in passionate Irish poetry.

"For oh! were the tributes of Alba mine
  From shore unto centre, from centre to sea,
The site of one house, to be marked by a line
  In the midst of fair Derry were dearer to me.

That spot is the dearest on Erin's ground,
  For the treasures that peace and that purity lend,
For the hosts of bright angels that circle it round,
  Protecting its borders from end to end.

The dearest of any on Erin's ground
  For its peace and its beauty I gave it my love,
Each leaf of the oaks around Derry is found
  To be crowded with angels from heaven above.

My Derry! my Derry! my little oak grove,
My dwelling, my home, and my own little cell,
May God the Eternal in Heaven above
Send death to thy foes and defend thee well."[1]

Columcille was yet a young man, only twenty-five years of age, when he founded Derry, but both his own genius, and more especially his great friends and kinsfolk, had conspired to make him famous. For the next seventeen years he laboured in Ireland, and during this time founded the still more celebrated schools of Durrow in the present King's County, and of Kells in Meath, both of which became most famous in after years. Durrow,[2] which, like Derry, was named from

[1] Literally, "Were the tribute of all Alba mine, from its centre to its border, I would prefer the site of one house in the middle of Derry. The reason I love Derry is for its quietness, for its purity, and for the crowds of white angels from the one end to the other. The reason why I love Derry is for its quietness, for its purity, crowded full of heaven's angels in every leaf of the oaks of Derry. My Derry, my little oak grove, my dwelling and my little cell, O Eternal God in heaven above, woe be to him who violates it."

"Is aire, caraim Doire
Ar a reidhe, ar a ghloine,
's ar iomatt a aingel find
On chind go soich aroile."

This poem is taken from a Brussels MS., copied by Michael O'Clery for Father Colgan, and by him accepted apparently as genuine. Some of it may very well be so, only, as usual, it has been greatly altered and modified in transcription, as may be seen from the above verse. (*See* p. 288 of Reeves' "Adamnan.") Some of the verses are evidently interpelations, but the Irish life in the Book of Lismore distinctly attributes to him the verse which I have here given, going out of its way to quote it in full, but the third line is a little different as quoted in the life: "ár is lomlan aingeal bhfinn."

[2] In Irish Dair-magh, "oak-plain." Columcille seems to have been particularly fond of the oak, for his Irish life tells us that it was under a great oak-tree that he resided while at Kells also. The writer adds, "and it"—the great oak-tree—"remained till these latter times, when it fell through the crash of a mighty wind. And a certain man took somewhat of its bark to tan his shoes with. Now, when he did on the shoes, he was smitten with leprosy from his sole to his crown." It is well known to this day that it is unlucky, or worse, to touch a saint's tree. I have been observing one that was, when in the last stage of decrepitude, blown down

the beautiful groves of oak which were scattered along the slope of Druim-caín, or "the pleasant hill," seems to have retained to the last a hold upon the affections of Columcille second only to that of Derry. When its abbot, Cormac the voyager, visited him long years afterwards in Iona, and expressed his unwillingness to return to his monastery again, because, being a Momonian of the race of Eber, the southern Ui Neill were jealous of him, and made his abbacy unpleasant or impossible, Columcille reproached him in pathetic terms for abandoning so lovely an abode—

> "With its books and its learning,
> A devout city with a hundred crosses."

"O Cormac," he exclaimed—

> "I pledge thee mine unerring word
> Which it is not possible to impugn,
> Death is better in reproachless Erin
> Than perpetual life in Alba [Scotland].[1]

---

a few years ago at the well of St. Aracht or Atracta, a female saint of Connacht in the plains of Boyle; yet, though the people around are nearly famished for want of fuel, not one twig of it has yet been touched. In the Edinburgh MS. of Columcille's life we read how on another occasion he made a hymn to arrest a fire that was consuming the oak-wood, "and it is sung against every fire and against every thunder from that time to this." (*See* Skene's "Celtic Scotland," vol. ii. pp. 468–507.)

[1] "*Is sí mo cubhus gan col*
's nocha conagar m' eilughadh
Ferr écc ind Ëirind cen ail
Ina sir beatha ind Alpuin."

For the whole of this poem, in the form of a dialogue between Cormac and Columcille, see p. 264 of Reeves' "Adamnan." It is very hard to say how much or how little of these poems is really Columcille's. Colgan was inclined to think them genuine. Of course, as we now have them, the language is greatly modernised; but I am inclined to agree with Dr. Healy, who judges them rather from internal than from linguistic evidence; and while granting, of course, that they have been retouched by later bards, adds, "but in our opinion they represent substantially poems that were really written by the saint. They breathe his pious spirit, his ardent love for nature, and his undying affection for his native

And on another occasion, when it strikes him how happy the son of Dima, *i.e.*, Cormac, must be at the approach ot summer along the green hillside of Rosgrencha—another name for Durrow—amid its fair slopes, waving woods, and singing birds, compared with himself exiled to the barren shores of rugged Iona, he bursts forth into the tenderest song—

> " How happy the son is of Dima ! no sorrow
> For him is designed,
> He is having, this hour, round his own cell in Durrow
> The wish of his mind :
>
> The sound of the wind in the elms, like the strings of
> A harp being played,
> The note of the blackbird that claps with the wings of
> Delight in the glade.
>
> With him in Rosgrencha the cattle are lowing
> At earliest dawn,
> On the brink of the summer the pigeons are cooing
> And doves on his lawn," etc.[1]

Columcille continued his labours in Ireland, founding churches and monasteries and schools, until he was forty-two

land. Although retouched, perhaps, by a later hand, they savour so strongly of the true Columbian spirit that we are disposed to reckon them amongst the genuine compositions of the saint." (" Ireland's Schools and Scholars," p. 329.) "The older pieces here preserved," says Dr. Robert Atkinson in his preface to the contents of the *facsimile* of the Book of Leinster, " *and of whose genuineness and authenticity there seems no room for doubt, ex. gr., the Poems of Colum Cille*, bear with them the marks of the action of successive transcribers, whose desire to render them intelligible has obscured the linguistic proofs of their age."

[1] Literally, " How happy the son of Dima of the devout church, when he hears in Durrow the desire of his mind, the sound of the wind against the elms when 'tis played, the blackbird's joyous note when he claps his wings ; to listen at early dawn in Rosgrencha to the cattle, the cooing of the cuckoo from the tree on the brink of summer," etc. (*See* Reeves' " Adamnan," p. 274).

> " Fuaim na goithi ris in leman ardos peti
> Longaire luin duibh conati ar mben a eti."

years of age. He was at this time at the height of his physical and mental powers, a man of a masterful but of a too passionate character, of fine physique, and enjoying a reputation second to that of none in Erin. The commentator in the Féilire of Angus describes his appearance as that of "a man well-formed, with powerful frame; his skin was white, his face was broad and fair and radiant, lit up with large, grey,[1] luminous eyes; his large and well-shaped head was crowned, except where he wore his frontal tonsure, with close and curling hair. His voice was clear and resonant, so that he could be heard at the distance of 1,500 paces,[2] yet sweet with more than the sweetness of the bards." His activity was incessant. "Not a single hour of the day," says Adamnan, "did he leave unoccupied without engaging either in prayer, or in reading, or in writing, or in some other work;" and he laboured with his hands as well as with his head, cooking or looking after his ploughmen, or engaged in ecclesiastical or secular matters. All accounts go to show that he was of a hot and passionate temperament, and endowed with both the virtues and the faults that spring from such a character. Indeed this was, no doubt, why in the "famous vision"[3]

[1] He himself refers to his "grey eye looking back to Erin" in one of his best-known poems.

[2] In token of which is the Irish quatrain quoted in his life—

"Son a ghotha Coluim cille,
mór a binne os gach cléir
go ceann cúig ceád déag céimeann,
Aídhbhle réimeann, eadh ba réill.

[3] "So then Baithine related to him the famous vision, to wit, three chairs seen by him in heaven, even a chair of gold and a chair of silver and a chair of glass. Columcille explained the vision. Ciaran the Great, the carpenter's son, is the chair of gold for the greatness of his charity and his mercy. Molaisse is the chair of silver because of his wisdom and his piety. I myself am the chair of glass because of my affection, for I prefer the Gaels to the men of the world, and Kinel Conall [his own tribe] to the [other] Gaels, and the kindred of Lughid to the Kinel Conall." (Leabhar Breac, quoted by Stokes, "Irish Lives," p. 303; but the reason here given for being seated on a chair of glass is, as Stokes remarks, unmeaning.)

which Baithin saw concerning him, he was seated only on a chair of glass; while Ciaran was on a chair of gold, and Molaisse upon a chair of silver. The commentator on the Féilire of Angus boldly states that, "though his devotion was delightful, he was carnal and often frail even as glass is fragile." Aware of this, he wore himself out with fastings and vigils,[1] and no doubt—

> "Lenior et melior fit accedente senectu,"

for Adamnan describes him, from the recollections of the monks who knew him, as being angelic in aspect[2] and bright in conversation, and despite his great labours yet "dear to all, displaying his holy countenance always cheerful." A curious story is told in the Leabhar Breac, of the stratagems to which his people resorted to checkmate his self-imposed penance; for having one day seen an old woman living upon pottage of nettles, while she was waiting for her one cow to calve and give her milk, the notion came to him that he too would thenceforward live upon the same, for if she could do so, much more could he, and it would be profitable to his soul in gaining the kingdom of heaven. So, said the writer, he called his servant—

"'Pottage,' saith he, 'from thee every night, and bring not the milk with it.'

"'It shall be done,' said the cook.

"He (the cook) bores the mixing-stick of the pottage, so that it became a pipe, and he used to pour the meat juice into the pipe, down, so that it was mixed through the pottage. That preserves the cleric's (Columcille's) appearance. The monks perceived the

[1] "Jejunationum quoque et vigiliarum indefessis laboribus sine ulla intermissione, die noctu-que ita occupatus ut supra humanam possibilitatem uniuscujusque pondus specialis videretur operis," says Adamnan in the preface to his first book.

[2] "Erat enim aspectu angelicus, sermone nitidus, opere sanctus, ingenio optimus, consilio magnus. . . et inter hæc omnibus carus, hilarem semper faciem ostendens sanctam, spiritus sancti gaudio intimis lætificabatur præcordiis."

cleric's good appearance, and they talked among themselves. That is revealed to Columcille, so he said, 'May your successors be always murmuring.'

"'Well now,' said Columcille, said he, to his servant, 'what dost thou give me every day?'

"'Thou art witness,' said the cook, 'unless it come out of the iron of the pot, or out of the stick wherewith the pottage is mixed, I know nought else in it save pottage!'"

It was now, however, that events occurred which had the result of driving Columcille abroad and launching him upon a more stormy and more dangerous career, as the apostle of Scotland and the Picts. St. Finnian of Moville, with whom he studied in former days, had brought back with him from Rome a copy of the Psalms, probably the first copy of St. Jerome's translation, or Vulgate, that had appeared in Ireland, which he highly valued, and which he did not wish Columcille to copy. Columcille however, who was a dexterous and rapid scribe, found opportunity, by sitting up during several nights, to make a copy of the book secretly,[1] but Finnian learning it claimed

[1] This copy made by Columcille is popularly believed to be the celebrated codex known as the Cathach or "Battler," which was an heirloom of the saint's descendants, the O'Donnells. It was always carried three times round their army when they went to battle, on the breast of a cleric, who, if he were free from mortal sin, was sure to bring them victory. The Mac Robartaighs were the ancestral custodians of the holy relic, and Cathbar O'Donnell, the chief of the race at the close of the eleventh century, constructed an elaborately splendid shrine or cover for it. This precious heirloom remained with the O'Donnells until Donal O'Donnell, exiled in the cause of James II., brought it with him to the Continent and fixed a new rim upon the casket with his name and date. It was recovered from the Continent in 1802 by Sir Neal O'Donnell, and was opened by Sir William Betham soon after. This would in the previous century have been considered a deadly crime, for "it was not lawful" to open the Cathach; as it was, Sir Neal's widow brought an action in the Court of Chancery against Sir William Betham for daring to open it. There turned out to be a decayed wooden box inside the casket, and inside this again was a mass of vellum stuck together and hardened into a single lump. By long steeping in water however, and other treatment, the various leaves came asunder, and it was found that what it contained was really a Psalter, written in Latin, in a "neat but hurried hand." Fifty-eight leaves remained, containing from the 31st to the 106th Psalm, and an examination of

the copy. Columcille refused it, and the matter was referred to King Diarmuid at Tara. The monarch, to whom books and their surroundings were probably something new, as a matter for legal dispute, could find in the Brehon law no nearer analogy to adjudicate the case by, than the since celebrated sentence *le gach boin a boinín*, "with every cow her calf," in which terms he, not altogether unnaturally, decided in favour of St. Finnian, saying, "with every book its son-book, as with every cow her calf."[1] This alone might not have brought about the crisis, but unfortunately the son of the king of Connacht, who had been present at the great Convention or Féis of Tara, in utter violation of the law of sanctuary which alone rendered this great meeting possible, slew the son of the king's steward, and knowing that the penalty was certain death, he fled to the lodging of the northern princes Fergus and Domhnall [Donall] who immediately placed him under the protection of St. Columcille. This however did not avail him, for King Diarmuid, who was no respecter of persons, had him promptly seized and put to death in atonement for his crime. This, combined with his unfortunate judgment about the book, enraged the imperious Columcille to the last degree. He made his way northward and appealed to his kinsmen to avenge him. A great army was collected, led by Fergus and Domhnall, two first cousins of Columcille, and by the king of Connacht, whose son had been put to death. The High-king marched to meet this formidable combination with all the troops he could gather. Pushing his way across the island he met their combined forces in the present county of Sligo,

the text has shown that it really does contain a copy of the second revision of the Psalter by St. Jerome, which helps to strengthen the belief that this may have been the very book for which three thousand warriors fought and fell in the Battle of Cooldrevna.

[1] Keating says that this account of the affair was preserved in the Black Book of Molaga, one of his ancient authorities now lost. The king decided, says Keating, "*gorab leis gach leabhar a mhaic-leabhar, mar is le gach boinn a boinín*."

between Benbulbin and the sea. A furious battle was delivered in which he was defeated with the loss of three thousand men.

It was soon after this battle that Columcille decided to leave Ireland. There is a great deal of evidence that he did so as a kind of penance, either self-imposed or enjoined upon him by St. Molaíse [Moleesha], as Keating says, or by the "synod of the Irish saints," as O'Donnell has it. He had helped to fill all Ireland with arms and bloodshed, and three thousand men had fallen in one battle largely on account of him, and it was not the only appeal to arms which lay upon his conscience.[1] He set sail from his beloved Derry in the year 593, determined, according to popular tradition, to convert as many souls to Christ as had fallen in the battle of Cooldrevna. Amongst the dozen monks of his own order who accompanied him were his two first cousins and his uncle.

It was death and breaking of heart for him to leave the land of Erin, and he pathetically expresses his sorrow in his own Irish verses.

"Too swiftly my coracle flies on her way,
From Derry I mournfully turned her prow,
I grieve at the errand which drives me to-day
To the Land of the Ravens, to Alba, now.

. . . . . .

How swiftly we travel! there is a grey eye
Looks back upon Erin, but it no more
Shall see while the stars shall endure in the sky
Her women, her men, or her stainless shore.

[1] "These were," says the commentator on St. Columcille's hymn, the "Altus," "the three battles which he had caused in Erin, viz., the battle of Cúl-Rathain, between him and Comgall, contending for a church, viz., Ross Torathair; and the battle of Bealach-fheda of the weir of Clonard; and the battle of Cúl Dremhne [Cooldrevna] in Connacht, and it was against Diarmait Mac Cerball [the High-king], he fought them both." Keating's account also agrees with this, but Reeves has shown that the two later battles in which he was implicated probably took place after his exile.

From the plank of the oak where in sorrow I lie,
I am straining my sight through the water and wind,
And large is the tear of the soft grey eye
Looking back on the land that it leaves behind.

To Erin alone is my memory given,
To Meath and to Munster my wild thoughts flow,
To the shores of Moy-linny, the slopes of Loch Leven,
And the beautiful land the Ultonians know."

He refers distinctly to the penance imposed upon him by St. Moleesha.

"To the nobles that gem the bright isle of the Gael
Carry this benediction over the sea,
And bid them not credit Moleesha's tale,
And bid them not credit his words of me.

Were it not for the word of Moleesha's mouth
At the cross of Ahamlish that sorrowful day,
I now should be warding from north and from south
Disease and distemper from Erin away."

His mind reverts to former scenes of delight—

"How dear to my heart in yon western land
Is the thought of Loch Foyle where the cool waves pour,
And the bay of Drumcliff on Cúlcinnê's strand,
How grand was the slope of its curving shore!

. . . .

O bear me my blessing afar to the West,
For the heart in my bosom is broken; I fail.
Should death of a sudden now pierce my breast
I should die of the love that I bear the Gael!"[1]

[1] Literally: "How rapid the speed of my coracle and its stern turned towards Derry. I grieve at the errand over the proud sea, travelling to Alba of the Ravens. There is a grey eye that looks back upon Erin: it shall not see during life the men of Erin nor their wives. My vision o'er the brine I stretch from the ample oaken planks; large is the tear from my soft grey eye when I look back upon Erin. Upon Erin is my attention fixed, upon Loch Leven [Lough Lene in West Meath], upon Linè [Moy-linny, near

Columcille is the first example in the saddened page of Irish history of the exiled Gael grieving for his native land and refusing to be comforted, and as such he has become the very type and embodiment of Irish fate and Irish character. The flag in bleak Gartan, upon which he was born, is worn thin and bare by the hands and feet of pious pilgrims, and "the poor emigrants who are about to quit Donegal for ever, come and sleep on that flag the night before their departure from Derry. Columcille himself was an exile, and they fondly hope that sleeping on the spot where he was born will help them to bear with lighter heart the heavy burden of the exile's sorrows."[1] He is the prototype of the millions of Irish exiles in after ages—

"Ruined exiles, restless, roaming,
Longing for their fatherland,"[2]

and the extraordinary deep roots which his life and poetry have struck into the soil of the North was strikingly evidenced this

Antrim], upon the land the Ultonians own, upon smooth Munster, upon Meath. . . . Carry my benediction over the sea to the nobles of the Island of the Gael, let them not credit Moleesha's words nor his threatened persecution. Were it not for Moleesha's words at the Cross of Ahamlish, I should not permit during my life disease or distemper in Ireland. . . . Beloved to my heart also in the west is Drumcliff at Cúlcinne's strand : to behold the fair Loch Foyle, the form of its shores is delightful. . . . Take my blessing with thee to the west, broken is my heart in my breast, should sudden death overtake me it is for my great love of the Gael."

[1] Dr. Healy's "Ireland's Schools and Scholars," p. 293. A fact which is also confirmed by Dr. Reeves, p. lxviii of his "Adamnan," where he says: "The country people believe that whoever sleeps a night on this stone will be free from home-sickness when he goes abroad, and for this reason it has been much resorted to by emigrants on the eve of their departure." I cannot say whether the breaking up of old ties produced by the National Board—which has elsewhere so skilfully robbed the people of their birthright—may not have put an end to this custom within the last few years.

[2] "Deoraidhe gan sgith gan sos,
Mianaid a dtír 's a ndúthchas."

This verse was either composed or quoted by John O'Mahony, the Fenian Head-centre, when in America.

very year (1898) by the wonderful celebration of his centenary at Gartan, at which many thousands of people, who had travelled all night over the surrounding mountains, were present, and where it was felt to be so incongruous that the life of such a great Irish patriot, prince, and poet, in the diocese, too, of an O'Donnell, should be celebrated in English, that—probably for the first time in this century—Irish poems were read and Irish speeches made, even by the Cardinal-Primate and the Bishop of the diocese.

Of Columcille's life on the craggy little island or Iona, of his splendid labours in converting the Picts, and of the monastery which he established, and which, occupied by Irish monks, virtually rendered Iona an Irish island for the next six hundred years, there is no need to speak here, for these things belong rather to ecclesiastical than to literary history.

Columcille himself was an unwearied scribe, and delighted in poetry. Ample provision was made for the multiplication of books in all the monasteries which he founded, and his Irish life tells us that he himself wrote "three hundred gifted, lasting, illuminated, noble books." The life in the Book of Lismore tells us that he once went to Clonmacnois with a hymn he had made for St. Ciaran, 'for he made abundant praises for God's household, as said the poet,

> "Noble, thrice fifty, nobler than every apostle,
> The number of miracles [of poems] are as grass,
> Some in Latin, which was beguiling,
> Others in Gaelic, fair the tale."'

Of these only three in Latin are now known to exist, whilst of the great number of Irish poems attributed to him only a few—half a dozen at the most—are likely to be even partly genuine. His best known hymn is the "Altus," so called from its opening word ; it was first printed by Colgan,[1] and

[1] Also in the "Liber Hymnorum," vol. ii. ; and again in 1882 with a prose paraphrase and notes by the Marquis of Bute, who says : "the intrinsic

its genuineness is generally admitted. It is a long and rudely-constructed poem, of twenty-two stanzas, preserved in the Book of Hymns, a MS. probably of the eleventh century. Each stanza consists of six lines,[1] and each line of sixteen syllables. There is a pause after the eighth syllable, and a kind of rhyme between every two lines. The first verses run thus with an utter disregard of quantity.

> "Altus prosător, vetustus dierum et ingenitus,
> Erat absque origine primordii et crepidine,
> Est et erit in sæcula sæculorum infinitus,
> Cui est unigenitus Christus et Spiritus Sanctus," etc.

The second Latin hymn is a supplement to this one, composed in praise of the Trinity, because Pope Gregory who, as the legend states, perceived the angels listening when the "Altus" was recited to him, was yet of opinion that the first stanza of the original poem, despite its additional line, was insufficient to express a competent laudation of the mystery, consequently Columcille added, it was said, fifteen rude-rhyming couplets of the same character as the "Altus," but it is very doubtful whether they are genuine. The third hymn, the "Noli Pater," is still shorter, consisting of only seven rhyming couplets with sixteen syllables in each line. It was in ancient times considered an efficient safeguard against fire and lightning. Some of his reputed Irish poems we have already glanced at; three that Colgan considered genuine were printed by Dr. Reeves in his "Adamnan;" and another, the touching "Farewell to Ara," is contained in the "Gaelic Miscellany" of 1808; and another on his escape from

merits of the composition are undoubtedly very great, especially in the latter *capitula* [*i.e.*, stanzas], some of which the editor thinks would not suffer by comparison with the *Dies Iræ*." Dr. Dowden, Bishop of Edinburgh, has printed, in his pleasant little volume on the "Celtic Church in Scotland," p. 323, a most admirable translation of it into English verse by the Rev. Anthony Mitchell.

[1] Except the first stanza, which being in honour of the Holy Trinity has seven lines.

King Diarmuid, when the king of Connacht's son was put to death for violating the Féis at Tara, is printed in the "Miscellany" of the Irish Archæological Society.[1] There are three verses, composed by him as a prayer at the battle of Cooldrevna, ascribed to him in the "Chronicon Scotorum;" and there is a collection of fifteen poems attributed to him in the O'Clery MSS. at Brussels, and nearly a hundred more—mostly evident forgeries—in the Bodleian at Oxford.[2] He does not seem to have ever written any work in prose.

There are six lives of Columcille still extant, the greatest of them all being that in Latin by Adamnan,[3] who was one of his successors in the abbacy of Iona, and who was born only twenty-seven years after Columcille's death. This admirable work, written in flowing and very fair Latin, was derived, as Adamnan himself tells us, partly from oral and partly from written sources. A memoir of Columcille had already been written by Cuimine Finn or Cummeneus Albus,[4] as Adamnan calls him, the last Abbot of Iona but one before himself, and that memoir he almost entirely embodied in his third book. He had also some other written accounts before him, and the Irish poems, both of the saint himself and of other bards, amongst them Baithine Mór, who had enjoyed his personal friendship, and St. Mura, who was a little his junior—poems

[1] This poem begins—

"M'œnuran dam is in sliab,
A rig grian rop sorad sed,
Nocha n-eaglaigi dam ní,
Na du mbeind tri ficit céd."

I find other verses attributed to him in the MS marked H I. II. in Trinity College, Dublin.

[2] Laud, 615.

[3] Edited in 1857 for the Irish Archæological Society by Dr. Reeves, afterwards Bishop of Down, with all the perfection which the most accurate scholarship and painstaking research could accomplish. It is not too much to say that his name is likely to remain in the future associated with those of Adamnan and Columcille.

[4] Book iii., chapter 5 of Adamnan's "Life of Columcille."

now lost. He had also constant opportunities of conversing with those who had seen the great saint and had been familiar with him in life, and he was writing on the spot and amidst the associations and surroundings wherein his last thirty years had been spent, and which were inseparably connected with his memory. The result was that he produced a work, which although not ostensibly a history, and dealing only with the life of a single man, and that rather from the transcendental than from the practical side, is nevertheless of the utmost value to the historian on account not only of the general picture of manners and customs, but still more on account of its incidental references to contemporary history. "It is," says Pinkerton, who, as Dr. Reeves remarks, was a writer not over-given to eulogy, "the most complete piece of such biography that all Europe can boast of, not only at so early a period but even through the whole Middle Ages." Adamnan's other great work on Sacred Places is mentioned by his contemporary, the Venerable Bede, but he is silent as to Columcille's life. There is, however, abundant internal evidence of its authenticity. This evidence, however it might satisfy the minds of mere Irish students like Colgan and Stephen White, proved insufficient, however, to meet the exacting claims of certain British scholars. "I cannot agree," said Sir James Dalrymple, in the last century, "that the authority of Adamnanus is equal, far less preferable to that of Bede, since it was agreed on all hands to be a fabulous history lately published in his name, and that he was remarkable for nothing, but that he was the first abbot of that monastery who quit the *Scottish* institution, and became fond of the *English Romish* Rites." [1] Dr. Giles, too, who thought of editing it, tells us in his translation of Bede's "Ecclesiastical History," that he had "strong doubts of

[1] Alluding to the fact that Adamnan tried to persuade his countrymen to change their mode of calculating Easter, and to adopt the Roman tonsure. Sir James Dalrymple is here engaged in defending the Presbyterian view of church government.

Adamnan's having written it."[1] And, finally, Schoell, a German, professed to have convinced himself that Adamnan's preface could not have been written by the same hand which wrote the life, so different did the style of the two appear to him, and wholly rejected it as a work of the seventh century written at Iona.

But it so happened that shortly before the year 1851, when Schoell was impugning the genuineness of this work, the ancient manuscript from which it had been copied by the Irish Jesuit, Stephen White—and, from his copy, printed by Colgan—actually came to light again, discovered by Dr. Ferdinand Keller at the bottom of an old book-shelf in the public library of Schaffhausen, into which it had been turned with some other old manuscripts and books. A close examination of this remarkable text written in a heavy round Irish hand, in nearly the same type of script as the Books of Kells and Durrow, and of a more archaic character than that of the Book of Armagh (written in 807), rendered it certain that here was a codex of great value and antiquity. Nor was the usual colophon containing the scribe's name and asking a prayer for him missing. That name was Dorbene, a most rare one, of which only two instances are known, both connected with Iona, the first of which records the death of Faelcu, son of Dorbene, in 729, but as we know that Faelcu died in his eighty-second year his father could hardly have been the scribe. The other Dorbene was elected abbot of Iona in 713 and died the same year, so that it may be regarded as almost certain that this book was written by him and that this copy is in his handwriting. We have in this codex, then, the actual handwriting[2] of a contemporary of Adamnan himself, the handi-

[1] "It is to be hoped," Dr. Reeves caustically remarked, "that the doubts originated in a different style of research from that which made Bede's *Columcilli* an island, and Dearmach [Durrow] the same as Derry!"

[2] "It may be objected," says Dr. Reeves, "that it was written by another person of this name, or copied by a later hand from the autograph of this Dorbene. The former exception is not probable, the name being almost

work of the generation which succeeded Columcille, a volume a hundred years older than even the Book of Armagh, a volume which had been carried over to some of the numerous Irish institutions on the Continent after the break-up of Iona by the Northmen. There are several corrections of the orthography in a different and later hand, the date of which is fixed by Dr. Keller at 800–820, and these are evidently the work of a German monk, who was displeased with the peculiar orthography of the Irish school, and who made these emendations after the MS. had been brought from Iona to the Continent. The following passage describing the last hours of Columcille will both serve as a specimen of Adamnan's style and also afford a minutely particular account of the end of this great man. Its accuracy can hardly be impugned as it is written by one who had every minute particular from eye-witnesses, and as the actual manuscript from which it is printed was copied from the author's own, either during his life or within less than ten years after his death.[1]

Adamnan first tells us of several premonitions which the saint had of his approaching end, how he, "now an old man, wearied with age," was borne in his waggon to view his monks labouring in the fields on the western slope of the island, and intimated to them that his end was not far off, but that lest

unique, and found so pointedly connected with the Columbian society; the latter is less probable, as the colophon in Irish MSS. is always peculiar to the actual scribe and likely to be omitted in transcription, as is the case of later MSS. of the same recension preserved in the British Museum." "Hoc ipsum MS. credi posset authographum Dorbbenei," says Van der Meer, a learned monk, "subscriptio enim illa in rubro vix ab alio descriptore addita fuisset; characteres quoque antiquitatem sapiunt sæculi octavi."

[1] He died in 704, and Dorbene the scribe in 713. It is necessary to be thus particular, even at the risk of being tedious, to correct the unlearned assertions of people who can write that in treating of the "lives of St. Patrick and St. Columba, one's faith is tried to the uttermost, leading not a few to deny the very existence of the two missionaries" ("Irish Druids and Religions," Borwick, p. 304); or the biassed dicta of men like Ledwich who says that all Irish MSS. "savour of modern forgery."

their Easter should be one of grief, he would not be taken from them until it was over. Later on in the year he went out with his servant Diarmuid to inspect the granary, and was pleased at the two large heaps of grain which were lying there, and remarked that though he should be taken from his dear monks, yet he was glad to see that they had a supply for the year.

"And," says Aḋamnan, "when Diarmuid his servant heard this he began to be sad, and said, 'Father, at this time of year you sadden us too often, because you speak frequently about your decease.' When the saint thus answered, 'I have a secret word to tell you, which, if you promise me faithfully not to make it known to any before my death, I shall be able to let you know more clearly about my departure.' And when his servant, on bended knees, had finished making this promise, the venerable man thus continued, 'This day is called in the sacred volumes the Sabbath, which is interpreted Rest. And this day is indeed to me a sabbath, because it is my last of this present laborious life, in which, after the trouble of my toil, I take my rest; for in the middle of this coming sacred Sunday night, I shall to use the Scripture phrase, tread the way of my fathers; for now my Lord Jesus Christ deigns to invite me, to whom, I say, at the middle of this night, on His own invitation, I shall pass over; for it was thus revealed to me by the Lord Himself.' His servant, hearing these sad words, begins to weep bitterly: whom the saint endeavoured to console as much as he was able.

"After this the saint goes forth from the barn, and returning to the monastery sits down on the way, at the place where afterwards a cross let into a millstone, and to-day standing there, may be perceived on the brink of the road. And while the saint, wearied with old age, as I said before, sitting in that place was taking a rest, lo! the white horse, the obedient servant who used to carry the milk-vessels between the monastery and the byre, meets him. It, wonderful to relate, approached the saint and placing its head in his bosom, by the inspiration of God, as I believe, for whom every animal is wise with the measure of sense which his Creator has bidden, knowing that his master was about to immediately depart from him, and that he would see him no more, begins to lament and abundantly to pour forth tears, like a human being, into the saint's lap, and with beslavered mouth to make moan. Which when the servant saw, he proceeds to drive away the tearful mourner, but the saint stopped him, saying, 'Allow him, allow him who loves me, to pour his flood of bitterest tears into this my bosom. See, you, though you are a man and have a rational mind, could have in no way known about my departure if I had not myself lately disclosed it to you, but to this brute and irrational animal the Creator Himself, in His own way, has clearly revealed that his master is about to depart from him.' And saying this he blessed the sorrowful horse [the monastery's] servant, as it turned away from him.

"And going forth from thence and ascending a small hill, which rose over the monastery, he stood for a little upon its summit, and as he stood, elevating both his palms, he blessed his community and said, 'Upon this place however narrow and mean, not only shall the kings of the Scots [*i.e.*, Irish] with their peoples, but also the rulers of foreign and barbarous nations with the people subject to them, confer great and no ordinary honour. By the saints of other churches also, shall no common respect be accorded it.'

"After these words, going down from the little hill and returning to the monastery, he sat in his cell writing a copy of the Psalms, and on reaching that verse of the thirty-third Psalm where it is written, 'But they that seek the Lord shall lack no thing that is good;' 'Here,' said he, 'we may close at the end of the page; let Baithin write what follows.' Well appropriate for the parting saint was the last verse which he had written, for to him shall good things eternal be never lacking, while to the father who succeeded him [Baithin], the teacher of his spiritual sons, the following [words] were particularly apposite, 'Come, my sons, hearken unto me. I shall teach you the fear of the Lord,' since as the departing one desired, he was his successor not only in teaching but also in writing.[1]

"After writing the above verse and finishing the page, the saint enters the church for the vesper office preceding the Sunday; which finished, he returned to his little room, and rested for the night on his couch, where for mattress he had a bare flag, and for pillow a stone, which at this day stands as a kind of commemorative

[1] "Post hæc verba de illo descendens monticellulo, et ad monasterium revertens, sedebat in tugurio Psalterium scribens; et ad illum tricesimi tertii psalmi versiculum perveniens ubi scribitur, Inquirentes autem Dominum non deficient omni bono, Hic, ait, in fine cessandum est paginæ; quæ vero sequuntur Baitheneus scribat. Sancto convenienter congruit decessori novissimus versiculus quem scripserat, cui numquam bona deficient æterna: succesori vero sequens patri, spiritalium doctori filiorum, Venite filii, audite me, timorem Domini docebo vos, congruenter convenit; qui, sicut decessor commendavit, non solo ei docendo sed etiam scribendo successit."

monument beside his tomb.[1] And there, sitting, he gives his last mandates to the brethren, in the hearing of his servant only, saying, 'These last words of mine I commend to you, O little children, that ye preserve a mutual charity with peace, and a charity not feigned amongst yourselves; and if ye observe to do this according to the example of the holy fathers, God, the comforter of the good, shall help you, and I, remaining with Him, shall make intercession for you, and not only the necessaries of this present life shall be sufficiently supplied you by Him, but also the reward of eternal good, prepared for the observers of things Divine, shall be rendered you.' Up to this point the last words of our venerable patron [when now] passing as it were from this wearisome pilgrimage to his heavenly country, have been briefly narrated.

"After which, his joyful last hour gradually approaching, the saint was silent. Then soon after, when the struck bell resounded in the middle of the night,[2] quickly rising he goes to the church, and, hastening more quickly than the others he entered alone, and with bent knees inclines beside the altar in prayer. His servant, Diarmuid, following more slowly, at the same moment beholds, from a distance, the whole church inside filled with angelic light round the saint; but as he approached the door this same light, which he had seen, swiftly vanished; which light a few others of the brethren, also standing at a distance, had seen. Diarmuid then entering the church, calls aloud with a voice choked with tears, 'Where art thou, Father?' And the lamps of the brethren not yet being brought, groping in the dark, he found the saint recumbent before the altar: raising him up a little, and sitting beside him, he placed the sacred head in his own bosom. And while this was happening a crowd of monks running up with lights, and seeing their father dying, begin to lament. And as we have learned from some who were there present, the saint, his soul not yet departing, with eyes upraised, looked round on each side, with a countenance of wondrous joy and gladness, as though beholding the holy angels coming to meet him. Diarmuid then raises up the saint's right hand to bless the band of monks. But the venerable father himself, too, in so far as he was

[1] It is still shown at the east end of the Cathedral in Iona, surrounded by an iron cage to keep off tourists.

[2] "The saint had previously attended at the *vespertinalis Dominicæ noctis missa*, an office equivalent to the nocturnal vigil, and now at the turn of midnight the bell rings for matins, which were celebrated according to ancient custom a little before daybreak."—*Reeves.* The early bells were struck like gongs, not rung, hence the modern Irish for "ring the beal" is *bain an clog*, "strike the bell."

able, was moving his hand at the same time, so that he might appear to bless the brethren with the motion of his hand, what he could not do with his voice, during his soul's departure. And after thus signifying his sacred benediction, he straightway breathed forth his life. When it had gone forth from the tabernacle of his body, the countenance remained so long glowing and gladdened in a wonderful manner by the angelic vision, that it appeared not that of a dead man but of a living one sleeping. In the meantime the whole church resounded with sorrowful lamentations."[1]

Besides the lives of Columcille, written by Adamnan and Cummene, at least four more exist; an anonymous life in Latin, printed by Colgan and erroneously supposed by him to be that of Cummene; a life by John of Tinmouth, chiefly compiled from Adamnan, which is also printed by Colgan; the old Irish life contained in four Irish MSS., namely, in the Leabhar Breac, in the Book of Lismore, in a vellum MS. in Edinburgh, and in an Irish parchment volume found by the Revolutionary Commissioners, during the Republic, in a private house in Paris, and by them presented to the Royal Library of that city—

"Quæ regio in terris nostri non plena laboris!"

This life has been printed from the Book of Lismore by Dr. Whitley Stokes. The last and most copious life is a compilation of all existing documents and poems both in Latin and Old Irish, and was made by order of O'Donnell in 1532.

"Be it known," says the preface, "to the readers of this Life that it was Manus, son of Hugh, son of Hugh Roe, son of Niall Garv, son of Turlough of the wise O'Donnell, who ordered the part of this Life which was in Latin to be put into Gaelic; and who ordered the part that was in difficult Gaelic to be modified, so that it might be clear and comprehensible to every one; and who gathered and put together the parts of it that were scattered through the old

[1] This scene took place, as Dr. Reeves has shown, "just after midnight between Saturday the 8th and Sunday the 9th of June, in the year 597."

Books of Erin; and who dictated it out of his own mouth with great labour and a great expenditure of time in studying how he should arrange all its parts in their proper places, as they are left here in writing by us; and in love and friendship for his illustrious saint, relative, and patron, to whom he was devoutly attached. It was in the Castle of Port-na-tri-námhad [Lifford] that his Life was indited, when were fulfilled 12 years and 20 and 500 and 1000 of the age of the Lord."

This life, written in a large vellum folio, is preserved in the Bodleian Library at Oxford and has never yet been printed.[1]

The remains of Columcille, which after a three days' wake were interred in Iona, were left undisturbed for close upon a hundred years. They were afterwards disinterred and placed within a splendid shrine of gold and silver, which, in due time, became the prey of the marauding Norsemen. The belief is very general that his remains found their last resting-place in Downpatrick, along with those of St. Patrick and St. Brigit. The present appearance of the spot where they are supposed to lie, may be gathered from the indignant verses[2] of a member of a now defunct literary body, to which I had the honour of belonging some years ago, one of those numerous Irish literary societies which produce verses as thick as leaves in Vallombrosa.

"I stood at a grave by the outer wall
    Of the Strangers' Church in Down,
All lorn and lost in neglect, and crossed
    By the Church of the Strangers' frown.
All lorn and waste, and with footsteps crossed
    The grave of our Patrons Three,
Not a leaf to wave o'er that lonely grave
    That seemed not a grave to me!

[1] It is to be hoped that it may soon see the light as one of the volumes whose publication is contemplated by the new Irish Texts Society. The copy of it used by Colgan is now back in the Franciscans' Library in Dublin, a beautiful vellum written for Niall óg O'Neill.

[2] P. 50 of a little volume called "Lays and Lyrics of the Pan-Celtic Society," long out of print, by P. O'C. MacLaughlin.

But a trench where some traitor was flung of yore—
'Twas "a sight for a foeman's eye"!
Where Patrick still and Saint Columbkille
And the Dove [1] of the Oak Tree lie.

. . . .

Those men who spoke bravely of rending chains
(And never a fetter broke!)
Those men who adored the flashing sword
(When never a tocsin spoke!)
Those little men, who are very great
In marble and bronze, are still
The city's pride, whilst that trench holds Bride
And Patrick and Columbkille!"

[1] Evidently alluding to the passage in her Irish life which says, "Her type among created things is as the Dove among birds, the vine among trees, and the sun above stars." There is a Latin distich on this grave in Downpatrick which I have seen somewhere,

In burgo Duno tumulo tumulantur in uno
Brigida Patricius atque Columba pius.

CHAPTER XVI

THE FIRST SCHOOLS OF CHRISTIAN IRELAND

St. Patrick and the early Christians of the fifth century spent much of their time and labour in the conversion of pagans and the building of churches. Columcille and the leading churchmen of the sixth century, on the other hand, gave themselves up more to the foundation of monastic institutions and the conduct of schools. They belonged to what is well known in Irish ecclesiastical history as the second Order of Saints. The first Order was composed of Patrick and his associates, bishops filled with piety, founders of churches, three hundred and fifty in number, mostly Franks, Romans, and Britons, but with some Scots [*i.e.* Irish] also amongst them. These worshipped, says the ancient "Catalogue of the Saints," one head—Christ, and followed one leader—Patrick. They had one tonsure, one celebration of the Mass, and one Easter. They mixed freely in the society of women, because they feared not the wind of temptation, and this first Order of Saints, as it is called, is reckoned by the Irish to have lasted during four reigns.

The next Order of Saints had few bishops but many priests, this was the order to which Columcille belonged, and most of the saints who founded the great schools of Ireland which in the following century became so flourishing and spread their fame throughout Europe, as those of Ciaran and Finnian and Brendan, and a score of others. This Order shunned all association with women, and would not have them in their monasteries.[1] These saints whilst worshipping God as their head, and celebrating one Easter and having one tonsure, yet had different rites for celebrating, and different rules for living. The rite with which they celebrated Mass they are said to have secured from the British saints, St. David, St. Gildas, and others. They also lasted for four reigns, or, roughly speaking, during the last three quarters of the sixth century.

After these came what is called the third Order of Saints who appear in their time to have been pre-eminent amongst the other Christians, and to have been mostly anchorites, who lived on herbs and supported themselves by such alms as they were given, despising all things earthly and all things fleshly. They observed Easter differently, they had different tonsures, they had different rules of life, and different rites for celebrating Mass. They are said to have numbered about a hundred and to have lasted down to the time of the great plague in 664.

This third Order, says the writer of the "Catalogue of Saints," who gives their names, was holy, the second holier, but the first Order was most holy. "The first glowed like the sun in the fervour of their charity, the second cast a pale radiance like the moon, the third shone like the aurora. These three Orders the blessed Patrick foreknew, enlightened by heavenly wisdom, when in prophetic vision he saw at first all Ireland ablaze, and afterwards only the mountains on fire, and at last saw lamps lit in the valleys."

By the middle of the sixth century Ireland had been honeycombed from shore to shore with schools, monasteries, colleges,

[1] It is a common tradition that Columcille would not allow a cow on Iona, because, said he, "where there is a cow there will be a woman"! This tradition is entirely contradicted, however, by Adamnan's life.

and foundations of all kinds belonging to the Christian community, and books had multiplied to a marvellous extent. At the same time the professional bards flourished in such numbers that Keating says that "nearly a third of the men of Ireland belonged, about that period, to the poetic order." Omitting for the present the consideration of the bards and the non-Christian literature of poem and saga—mostly anonymous—which they produced, we must take a rapid survey of some of the most important of the Christian schools, whose pious professors, whose number, and whose learning, secured for Ireland the title of the Island of Saints. We have already seen how the three patron saints of Ireland established their schools in Armagh, Kildare, and Iona, and their example was followed by hundreds.

St. Enda, the son of a king of Oriel, after having studied at some school in Great Britain (probably with St. Ninian—who is said to have been himself an Irishman—at his noble monastery of Candida Casa in Galloway, built about the year 400), and after travelling through various parts of Ireland, settled down finally about the year 483 in the rocky and inaccessible island of Aran Mór, and was the first of those holy men who have won for it the appellation of Aran of the Saints. "One hundred and twenty-seven saints sleep in the little square yard around Killeany Church"[1] alone, and we are told that the countless numbers of saints who have mingled their clay with the holy soil of Aran will never be known until the day of Judgment. Here most of the saints of the second Order repaired sooner or later, to be instructed by, or to hold converse with St. Enda; amongst them Brendan the Voyager, whose wanderings, under the title of *Navigatio Brendani*, became so well known in later ages to all mediæval Europe. To him also came St. Finnian of Clonard, who was himself celebrated in later days as the "Tutor of the Saints of Erin." From the remote north came

[1] Dr. Healy's "Ireland's Schools and Scholars," p. 169.

Finnian of Moville, Columcille's first teacher, and Ciaran, the carpenter's son, the illustrious founder of Clonmacnois. St. Jarlath of Tuam was there too, with St. Carthach the elder, of Lismore, and with St. Keevin of Glendalough. St. Columcille[1] himself was amongst Enda's visitors, and tore himself away with the utmost difficulty, solacing himself by recourse to the Irish muse as was his wont—

"Farewell from me to Ara's Isle,
  Her smile is at my heart no more,
No more to me the boon is given
  With hosts of heaven to walk her shore.

How far, alas ! how far, alas !
  Have I to pass from Ara's view,
To mix with men from Mona's fen,
  With men from Alba's mountains blue.

Bright orb of Ara, Ara's sun,
  Ah ! softly run through Ara's sky,
To rest beneath thy beam were sweeter
  Than lie where Paul and Peter lie.

O Ara, darling of the West,
  Ne'er be he blest who loves not thee,
O God, cut short her foeman's breath,
  Let Hell and Death his portion be.

O Ara, darling of the West,
  Ne'er be he blest who loves not thee,
Herdless and childless may he go
  In endless woe his doom is dree.

O Ara, darling of the West,
  Ne'er be he blest who loves thee not,
When angels wing from heaven on high
  And leave the sky for this dear spot."[2]

[1] There is a story of Columcille when in Aran discovering the grave of an "abbot of Jerusalem" who had come to see Enda, and died there, printed by Kuno Meyer from Rawlinson B. 512 in the "Gaelic Journal," vol. iv. p. 162.

[2] Literally : "Farewell from me to Ara, it is it anguishes my heart not to be in the west among her waves, amid groups of the saints of heaven. It is far, alas ! it is far, alas ! I have been sent from Ara West, out towards

Another early school was that founded by St. Finnian at Cluain Eraird, better known under its corrupt form Clonard, a spot hard by the river Boyne, to which students from both north and south resorted in great numbers. Finnian, who was of the Clanna Rury, or Irian race, had been baptized by Bishop Fortchern, who—so quickly did the Christian cause progress—was a grandson of King Laeghaire, who withstood St. Patrick. This Fortchern, too, like Brigit's favourite bishop, was a skilled artificer in bronze and metal, a calling to which many of the early saints evinced a strong bias. Clonard even during Finnian's lifetime became a great school, and three thousand students are said to have been gathered round it, amongst them the so-called Twelve Apostles of Erin. These are Ciaran of Clonmacnois and Ciaran of Saigher, who is patron saint of Ossory; Brendan of Birr, the "prophet," and Brendan of Clonfert, the "navigator"; Columba of Tir-da-glass and Columcille; Mobhí of Glasnevin and—*infaustum nomen!*—Rodan of Lothra or Lorrha; Senanus of Iniscathy, whose name is known to the lovers of the poet Moore; Ninnidh of Loch Erne; Lasserian, and St. Cainnech of Kilkenny, known in Scotland as Kenneth, and second in that country only to St. Columcille and St. Brigit in popularity. The school of Clonard was founded about the year 520, when, to quote the rather jingling hymn from St. Finnian's office—

> "Reversus in Clonardiam
> Ad cathedram lecturæ
> Opponit diligentiam
> Ad studium scripturæ."

the population of Mona to visit the Albanachs. Ara sun, oh Ara sun, my affection lies buried in her in the west, it is the same to be beneath her pure soil as to be beneath the soil of Paul and Peter. Ara blessed, O Ara blessed, woe to him who is hostile to her, may he be given for it shortness of life and hell. Ara blessed, O Ara blessed, woe to him who is hostile to her, may their cattle decay and their children, and be he himself on the other side (of this life) in evil plight. O Ara blessed, O Ara blessed, woe to him who is hostile to her," etc.

The numbers who attended his teaching are given in another verse—

> "Trium virorum millium
> Sorte fit doctor humilis,
> Verbi his fudit fluvium
> Ut fons emanans rivulis."

Like all the other early Irish foundations which attained to wealth and dignity before the ninth century, Clonard suffered in proportion to its fame. It was after that date plundered and destroyed twelve times, and was fourteen times burnt down either wholly or in part. That being so, it is not much to be wondered at that there only remains a single surviving literary work of this school, which is the "Mystical Interpretation of the Ancestry of our Lord Jesus Christ," by St. Aileran the Wise, one of Finnian's successors, who died of the great plague in 664. This piece, like so many others, was found in the Swiss monastery of St. Gall, whither it had been brought by some monks from Ireland. The editors who printed it for the Benedictines in the seventeenth century say that, although the writer did not belong to their Order, they publish it because he "unfolded the meaning of sacred scripture with so much learning and ingenuity that every student of the sacred volume, and especially preachers of the Divine Word, will regard the publication as most acceptable." The learned editors could have hardly paid the Irish writer a higher compliment. "A Short Moral Explanation of the Sacred Names" is another still existing fragment of Aileran's, and "whether we consider the style of the latinity, the learning, or the ingenuity of the writer," says Dr. Healy, "it is equally marvellous and equally honourable to the school of Clonard." Aileran is said to have also written lives of St. Patrick, St. Brigit, and St. Fechin of Fore, and to be the original author of a litany, part Irish, part Latin, preserved in the Yellow Book of Lecan.

Another great Irish college was Clonfert on the Shannon,

founded about the year 556 by Brendan the Navigator, who, like Finnian, came of the Irian race, being descended from Fergus mac Roy.[1] He was born towards the close of the fifth century, and his school, too, became very famous, having, it is said, produced as many as three thousand monks. The influence of the *Navigatio Brendani*, by whomsoever written, was immense, and was felt through all Europe, so that in many of the great continental libraries good MS. copies of it, sometimes very ancient, may be found.[2] But perhaps Brendan's grand-nephew and pupil may have indirectly influenced European literature in a still more important manner. This was Fursa, afterwards St. Fursa, whose visions were known all over Ireland, Great Britain, and France. There can be no doubt about the substantial accuracy of St. Fursa's lite, for Bede himself, who dedicates a good deal of space to Fursa's visions,[3] refers to it. It must have been written within ten or fifteen years after his death, because it refers to the plague and the great eclipse of the sun which *happened last year*, that is 664. Now Dante was acquainted with Bede's writings, for he expressly mentions him, and Bede's account of Fursa and Fursa's own life may have been familiar to him, and furnished him with the groundwork of part of the Divine Comedy of which it seems a kind of prototype.[4]

[1] See p. 69, note.

[2] It has been edited both by a Frenchman, M. Jubinal, and a German, Karl Schroeder, from eleventh, twelfth, and thirteenth century MSS. preserved in Paris, Leipsic, and Wolfenbuttel, and by Cardinal Moran from, I believe, a ninth-century one in the Vatican. Giraldus Cambrensis alludes to it as well known in his time, "Hæc autem si quis audire gestierit qui de vita Brendani scriptus est libellum legat" ("Top. Hib.," II. ch. 43). There is a copy of Brendan's acts in the so-called Book of Kilkenny in Marsh's Library, Dublin, a MS. of probably the fourteenth century.

[3] "Eccles. Hist.," lib. iii. c. 19. He calls him "Furseus, verbo et actibus clarus sed et egregiis insignis virtutibus," and dedicates five pages of Mayer and Lumby's edition to an account of him and his visions.

[4] Father O'Hanlon, in his great work on the Irish saints, has pointed out a large number of close parallels between Fursa's vision and Dante's poem which seem altogether too striking to be fortuitous. (*See* vol. i.

Brendan's own adventures and his view of hell, which he was shown by the devil, may also have been known to Dante. Brendan prepared three vessels with thirty men in each, some clerics, some laymen, and with these, says his Irish life in the Book of Lismore, he sailed to seek the Promised Land, which, evidently influenced by the old pagan traditions of Moy Mell [1] and Hy Brassil, he expected to find as an island in the Western Sea, and so says his Irish life poetically—

"Brendan, son of Finnlug, sailed over the wave-voice of the strong-maned sea, and over the storm of the green-sided waves, and over the mouths of the marvellous awful bitter ocean, where they saw the multitude of the furious red-mouthed monsters with abundance of the great sea-whales. And they found beautiful marvellous islands, yet they tarried not therein."

Like Sindbad in the Arabian tales,[2] they land upon the back of a great whale as if it had been solid land. There they celebrated Easter. They endured much peril from the sea. "On a certain day, as they were on the marvellous ocean"—this adjective is strongly indicative of the spirit in which the Celt regards the works of nature—"they beheld the deep bitter streams and the vast black whirlpools of the strong-maned sea, and in them their vessels were being constrained to founder because of the greatness of the storm." Brendan, however, cried to the sea, "It is enough for thee, O mighty sea, to drown me alone, but let this folk escape thee," and on hearing

pp. 115–120.) There are a poem and a litany attributed to St. Fursa in the MS. H. I. 11. in Trinity College, Dublin. The visions of Purgatory seen by Dryhthelm, a monk of Melrose, as recorded by Bede, which are later than St. Fursa's vision, are conceived very much in the same style, only are much more doctrinal in their purgatorial teaching. "Tracing the course of thought upwards," says Sir Francis Palgrave ("History of Normandy and England"), "we have no difficulty in deducing the poetic genealogy of Dante's 'Inferno' to the Milesian Fursæus."

[1] *See* above, p. 97.

[2] The same story, as Whitley Stokes points out, is told in two ninth-century lives of St. Machut, so that a tenth-century version of Sindbad's first voyage cannot have been the origin of it.

his cry the sea grew calm. It was after this that Brendan got a view of hell.

"On a certain day," says the Irish Life, "that they were on the sea, the devil came in a form old, awful, hideous, foul, hellish, and sat on the rail of the vessel before Brendan, and none of them saw him save Brendan alone. Brendan asked him why he had come before his proper time, that is, before the time of the great resurrection. 'For this have I come,' said the devil, 'to seek my punishment in the deep closes of this black, dark sea.' Brendan inquired of him, 'What is this, where is that infernal place?' 'Sad is that,' said the devil; 'no one can see it and remain alive afterwards.' Howbeit the devil there revealed the gate of hell to Brendan, and Brendan beheld that rough, hot prison full of stench, full of flame, full of filth, full of the camps of the poisonous demons, full of wailing and screaming and hurt and sad cries and great lamentations and moaning and handsmiting of the sinful folks, and a gloomy, mournful life in hearts of pain, in igneous prisons, in streams of the rows of eternal fire, in the cup of eternal sorrow and death, without limit, without end; in black, dark swamps, in fonts of heavy flame, in abundance of woe and death and torments, and fetters, and feeble wearying combats, with the awful shouting of the poisonous demons, in a night ever-dark, ever-cold, ever-stinking, ever-foul, ever-misty, ever-harsh, ever-long, ever-stifling, deadly, destructive, gloomy, fiery-haired, of the loathsome bottom of hell. On sides of mountains of eternal fire, without rest, without stay, were hosts of demons dragging the sinners into prisons . . . black demons; stinking fires; streams of poison; cats scratching; hounds rending; dogs baying; demons yelling; stinking lakes; great swamps; dark pits; deep glens; high mountains; hard crags; . . . winds bitter, wintry; snow frozen, ever-dropping; flakes red, fiery; faces base, darkened; demons swift, greedy; tortures vast, various."[1]

This is one of the earliest attempts in literature at the pourtrayal of an Inferno.

[1] This is evidently the passage upon which Keating's description of hell in the "Three Shafts of Death," Leabh. III. allt. ix., x., xi., is modelled. He quite outdoes his predecessor in declamation and exuberance of alliterative adjectives. Compare also the description in the vision of Adamnan of the infernal regions as it is elaborated in the copy in the Leabhar Breac, in contradistinction to the more sober colouring of the older Leabhar na h-Uidhre.

After a seven-years' voyage Brendan returned home to his own country without having found his Earthly Paradise, and his people and his folk at home "brought him," says the Irish Life, "treasures and gifts as if they were giving them to God"!

His foster-mother St. Ita now advised him not to put forth in search of that glorious land in those dead stained skins which formed his currachs, for it was a holy land he sought, and he should look for it in wooden vessels. Then Brendan built himself "a great marvellous vessel, distinguished and huge." He first sailed to Aran to consort with St. Enda, but after a month he heaved anchor and sailed once more into the West.

He reaches the Isle of Paradise after many adventures, and is invited on shore by an old man "without any human raiment, but all his body full of bright white feathers like a dove or a sea-mew, and it was almost the speech of an angel that he had." "O ye toilsome men," he said, "O hallowed pilgrims, O folk that entreat the heavenly rewards, O ever-weary life expecting this land, stay a little now from your labour." The land is described in terms that forcibly record the delights of the pagan Elysium of Moy Mell, and prove how intimately the Brendan legend is bound up with primitive pre-Christian mythological beliefs. "The delightful fields of the land" are described as "radiant, famous, lovable,"—"a land odorous, flower-smooth, blessed, a land many-melodied, musical, shouting-for-joy, unmournful." "Happy," said the old man, "shall he be with well-deservingness and with good deeds, whom Brandan, son of Finnlug, shall call into union with him on that side to inhabit for ever and ever the island whereon we stand."

But better known—at least in ecclesiastical history—than even St. Brendan, is St. Cummian, surnamed "fada" or the Long, who was one of his successors in the school of Clonfert, and who perished in or a little before the great plague of 664.

There are two hymns, one by himself in Latin,[1] and one in Irish by his tutor, Colman Ua Cluasaigh [Clooasy] of Cork, preserved in the "Liber Hymnorum." But his great achievement was his celebrated letter on the Paschal question addressed to his friend Segienus, the abbot of Iona. The question of when to celebrate Easter day was one which long sundered the British and Irish Churches from the rest of Europe, and has, as students of ecclesiastical history know, given rise to all sorts of conjectures as to the independence of these churches. The charge against the Irish was that they celebrated Easter on any day from the fourteenth to the twentieth day of the moon, even on the fourteenth if it should happen to be Sunday, but the fourteenth was a Jewish festival and the Council of Nice had, in 325, declared it to be unlawful to celebrate the Christian Easter on a Jewish festival.[2] The Irish had obtained their own doctrine of Easter from the East, through Gaul, which was largely open to Eastern influence; also the Irish used the old Roman cycle of 84 years, not the newer and more correct Alexandrian one of 19 years. The consequence was the scandal of having different Churches of Christendom celebrating Easter on different days, and some mourning when others were

[1] Beginning:—

"Celebra Juda festa Christi gaudia
Apostulorum exultans memoria.
Claviculari Petri primi pastoris
Piscium rete evangelii corporis
Alleluia."

This hymn, says Dr. Todd, "bears evident marks of the high antiquity claimed for it, and there seem no reasonable grounds for doubting its authenticity."

[2] "The correct system lays down three principles. First, Easter day must be always a Sunday, never on but *next after* the fourteenth day of the moon; secondly, that fourteenth day of the full moon should be that on or next after the vernal equinox; and thirdly, the equinox itself was invariably assigned to the 21st of March" (Dr. Healy's "Ireland's Schools and Scholars," p. 234). At Rome the 18th had been regarded as the equinox; St. Patrick, however, rightly laid it down that the equinox took place on the 21st.

feasting, a scandal which the Epistle of Cummian was designed to put an end to.

"I call this letter," says Professor G. Stokes,[1] "a marvellous composition because of the vastness of its learning; it quotes besides the Scriptures and Latin authors, Greek writers like Origen, and Cyril, Pachomius the head and reformer of Egyptian monasticism, and Damascius the last of the celebrated neo-Platonic philosophers of Athens, who lived about the year 500, and wrote all his works in Greek. Cummian discusses the calendars of the Macedonians, Hebrews, and Copts, giving us the Hebrew, Greek, and Egyptian names of months and cycles, and tells us that he had been sent as one of a deputation of learned men a few years before to ascertain the practice of the Church of Rome. When they came to Rome they lodged in one hospital with a Greek and a Hebrew, an Egyptian, and a Scythian, who told them that the whole world celebrated the Roman and not the Irish Easter."

Cummian throughout this letter displays the true spirit of a scholar, he humbly apologises for his presumption in addressing such holy men, and calls God to witness that he is actuated by no spirit of pride or contempt for others. When the new cycle of 532 years was first introduced into Ireland he did not at once accept it, but held his peace and took no side in the matter, because he did not think himself wiser than the Hebrews, Greeks, and Latins, nor did he venture to disdain the food he had not yet tasted. So he retired for a whole year into the study of the question, to examine for himself the facts of history, the nature of the various cycles in use, and the testimony of Scripture.

There is another book, "De Mensura Pœnitentiarum," ascribed to Cummian and printed in Migne; and there is a poem on his death by his tutor, St. Colman, who was carried off by the same plague a short time after him.[2]

[1] Late professor of Ecclesiastical History in Dublin University. See "Proceedings of the Royal Irish Academy," May, 1892, p. 195.

[2] The first verse runs thus :—

"Ni beir Luimneach for a druim
Di sil Muimhneach i Leth Cuinn
Marbán in noi bu fiú do
Do Cuimmine mac Fiachno"—

The great institution presided over by St. Cummian was flourishing in full vigour at the time of the first incursions of the Northmen. It is frequently mentioned in the Irish Annals as a place of note and learning. Turgesius the Dane, attracted by so fair a booty, promptly plundered and burnt it to the ground. Again and again it was rebuilt, and again and again the same fate befell it. The monastery and the school survived, however, until the coming of the Normans, and the "Four Masters" under the year 1170 record the death of one of its teachers, Cormac O'Lumlini, whom they pathetically designate "the remnant of the sages of Erin," for by this time Clonfert had been six times burnt and four times plundered.

Even a greater school, however, than Clonfert, was that founded by St. Ciaran [Keeran], the carpenter's son, beside a curve in the Shannon, at Clonmacnois, not far from Athlone, about the year 544. He had himself been educated by St. Finnian of Clonard, and he died at the early age of thirty-three, immediately after laying the foundations of what was destined to become the greatest Christian college in Ireland.[1]

The monastery and cells of St. Ciaran rapidly grew into a city, to which students flocked from far and near. In one sense the College of Clonmacnois had an advantage over all its rivals, for it belonged to no one race or clan. Its abbots and teachers were drawn from many different tribes, and situated as it was, in almost the centre of the island, all the great races, Erimonians, Eberians, Irians, and Ithians, resorted to it impartially, and it became a real university. There the O'Conors, kings of Connacht, had their own separate church; there the Southern Ui Neill reared apart their own cathedral; there the MacDermots, princes of Moylurg, and the

"The lower Shannon bears not upon its surface, of Munster race in Leath Cuinn, any corpse in boat, equal to him, to Cuimin, son of Fiachna." His corpse was apparently brought home by water.

[1] There is a verse ascribed to Ciaran in the "Chronicon Scotorum," beginning "Darerca mo mháthair-si," and a poem ascribed to him in H. I. 11. Trinity College, Dublin.

O'Kellys, kings of Hy Mainy, had each their own mortuary chapels; there the Southerns built one round tower, the O'Rorkes another; and there too the Mac Carthys of Munster had a burial-place. Who, even at this day, has not heard of the glories of Clonmacnois, of its ruins, its graves, its crosses; of its churchyard, which possesses a greater variety of sculptured and decorated stones than perhaps all the rest of Ireland put together, and of which the Irish poet beautifully sang so long ago—

"In a quiet watered land, a land of roses,
  Stands St. Ciaran's city fair,
And the warriors of Erin in their famous generations,
  Slumber there.

There beneath the dewy hill-side sleep the noblest
  Of the clan of Conn,
Each below his stone, with name in branching Ogham,
  And the sacred knot thereon.

There they laid to rest the seven kings of Tara,
  There the sons of Cairbré sleep,
Battle-banners of the Gael that in Ciaran's Plain of Crosses,
  Now their final hosting keep.

And in Clonmacnois they laid the men of Teffia,
  And right many a lord of Breagh.
Deep the sod above Clan Creidé and Clan Conaill,
  Kind in hall and fierce in fray.

Many and many a son of Conn the Hundred-Fighter
  In the red earth lies at rest,
Many a blue eye of Clan Colman the turf covers,
  Many a swan-white breast." [1]

[1] Thus admirably translated by my friend Mr. Rolleston in "Poems and Ballads of Young Ireland," Dublin, 1888, a little volume which seems to have been the precursor of a considerable literary movement in Ireland. Literally: "The city of Ciaran of Clonmacnois, a dewy-bright red-rose town, of its royal seed, of lasting fame, the hosts in the pure-streamed peaceful town. The nobles of the clan of Conn are in the flag-laid brown-sloped churchyard, a knot or a branch above each body and a fair correct name in Ogam. The sons of Cairbré over the seven territories, the seven great princes from Tara, many a sheltering standard on a field of battle is

Some of the most distinguished scholars of Ireland, if not of Europe, were educated at Clonmacnois, including Alcuin, the most learned man at the French court, who remembered his alma mater so affectionately that he extracted from King Charles of France a gift of fifty shekels of silver, to which he added fifty more of his own, and sent them to the brotherhood of Clonmacnois as a gift, with a quantity of olive oil for the Irish bishops. His affectionate letter to "his blessed master and pious father" Colgan, chief professor at Clonmacnois, is still extant.

This Colgu, or Colgan, himself wrote a book in Irish, called "The Besom of Devotion," which appears to be now lost. A litany of his still remains. The great eleventh-century annalist, Tighearnach, was an alumnus of Clonmacnois. So, too, was the reputed author of the "Chronicon Scotorum," O'Malone, in 1123. The Annals of Clonmacnois was one of the books in the hands of the "Four Masters," but it is now lost, and a different book called by the same name (the original

with the people of Ciaran's Plain of Crosses. The men of Teffia, the tribes of Breagh were buried beneath the clay of Cluain[macnois]. The valiant and hospitable are yonder beneath the sod, the race of Creidé and the Clan Conaill. Numerous are the sons of Conn of the Battles, with red clay and turf covering them, many a blue eye and white limb under the earth of Clan Colman's tomb." The first verses run in modern spelling thus:

"Cáthair Chiaráin Chluain-mic-Nóis
Baile drucht-solas, dearg-rois.
Da shíl rioghraidh is buan bládh
Sluaigh fá'n sith-bhaile sruth-ghlan.

Atáid uaisle cloinne Chuinn
Fa'n reilig leacaigh learg-dhuinn
Snaoidhm no Craobh os gach cholain
Agus ainm caomh ceart Oghaim."

The clan of Conn here mentioned are principally the Ui Neill and their correlatives. Teffia is something equivalent to Longford, and Breagh to Meath. Clan Creidé are the O'Conors of Connacht, and the Clan Colman principally means the O'Melaughlins and their kin. "Colman mor, a quo Clann Cholmáin ie Maoileachlain cona fflaithibh" (Mac Firbis MS. Book of Genealogies, p. 161 of O'Curry's transcript). Colman was the brother of King Diarmuid, who was slain in 552.

of which has also perished) was translated into English by Macgeoghegan in 1627.[1] The celebrated Leabhar na h-Uidhre [Lowar na Heera] or "Book of the Dun Cow," compiled about the year 1100, emanated from this centre of learning. Like Clonfert, and every other home of Irish civilisation, the city of Clonmacnois fell a prey to the barbarians. The Northmen plundered it or burnt it, or both, on ten separate occasions. Turgesius, their leader, set up his wife Ota as a kind of priestess to deliver oracles from its high altar;[2] and some of the Irish themselves, reduced to a state of barbarism by the horrors of the period, laid their sacrilegious hands upon its holy places; and afterwards the English of Athlone stepped in and completed its destruction. It now remains only a ruin and a name.

Another very celebrated school was that of Bangor, on Belfast Loch, founded by Comgall, the friend of Columcille, between 550 and 560. It soon became crowded with scholars, and next to Armagh it was certainly the greatest school of the northern province, and produced men of the highest eminence at home and abroad. Its fame reached far across the sea. St. Bernard called it "a noble institution, which was inhabited by many thousands of monks;" and Joceline of Furness, in the twelfth century, called it "a fruitful vine breathing the odour of salvation, whose offshoots extended not only over all Ireland, but far beyond the seas into foreign countries, and filled many lands with its abounding fruitfulness."

The most distinguished of Bangor's sons of learning were Columbanus, the evangeliser of portions of Burgundy and Lombardy; St. Gall, the evangeliser of Switzerland; Dungal, the astronomer; and later on, in the twelfth century, Malachy

[1] Published a couple of years ago by the late Father Murphy, S.J., for the Royal Antiquarian Society of Ireland.

[2] "Airgid cealla ardnaomh Ereann uile ocus as ar altoir Cluana mac Nois do bhereadh Otta bean Tuirghes uirigheall do gach ae[n]" (Mac Firbis MS. of Genealogies, p. 768 in O'Curry's transcript). Also "Gael and Gall," p. 13.

O'Morgair, who, though not known as an author, distinguished himself in the province of Church discipline.

The lives of St. Columbanus and of St. Gall belong rather to foreign than to Irish history, but we may glance at them again in another place. Dungal, poet, astronomer, and theologian, was also like them, for a time, an exile. His identity is uncertain; the "Four Masters" mention twenty-two persons of the same name between the years 744 and 1015, but his Irish nationality is certain, and he calls himself "Hibernicus exul" in his poem addressed to his patron Charlemagne. He appears to have died in the Irish monastery at Bobbio, in North Italy, to which he left his library, and amongst other books the celebrated Antiphonary of Bangor, his possession of which seems to warrant us in supposing that Bangor was his original college. He appears to have been a close friend of Charlemagne's, and in 811 he wrote him his celebrated letter, explanatory of the two solar eclipses which had taken place the year before. The emperor could apparently find at his court no other astronomer of sufficient learning to explain the phenomena. Later on we find Dungal, at the request of Lothaire, Charlemagne's grandson, opening a school at Pavia to civilise the Lombards, to which institution great numbers of students flocked from every quarter. Dungal may, in fact, be regarded as the founder of the University of Pavia. His greatest effort whilst in Pavia was his work against the Iconoclasts. Dungal's attack upon the cultured Spanish bishop, Claudius, who championed them, as it was the first, so it appears to have been the ablest blow struck; and Western iconoclasm seemed to have for the time received a mortal wound from his hand.[1] Besides his long eulogy on his friend and patron Charlemagne, several other smaller

[1] Claudius was Bishop of Turin, and a man of much culture and ability; so disgusted was he with the congregation of ignorant Italian bishops—culture was then at the lowest ebb in Italy—before whom he argued his case that he called them a *congregatio asinorum*, and says Zimmer, "Ein Ire, Dungal, musste für sie die Vertheidigung des Bilderdienstes übernehmen."

poems of his survive, showing him to have been—like almost all Irishmen of that date—no mere pedant and student.

Like almost all the more famous and attractive of the Irish colleges, Bangor suffered fearfully from the attacks of the northern pirates, who, according to St. Bernard, slew there as many as nine hundred monks. "Not a cross, not even a stone," says Dr. Healy, "now remains to mark the site of the famous monastery, whose crowded cloisters for a thousand years overlooked the pleasant islets and broad waters of Inver Becne." It has shared the fate of its compeers :

etiam periere ruinæ.

It would prove too tedious to enumerate the other Irish colleges which dotted the island in the sixth and seventh centuries. The most remarkable of them besides those that I have mentioned were Moville, at the head of Loch Cuan or Strangford Lough, in the County Down, founded by St. Finnian, who was born before 500, and who is often wrongly identified with Frigidian, Bishop of Lucca, in Italy. Colman, whose hymn is preserved in the "Liber Hymnorum," and Marianus Scotus, the Chronicler, were *alumni* of Moville.

Cluain Eidnech, or Clonenagh, the "Ivy Meadow," was founded by St. Fintan, near Maryborough, in the present Queen's County. Angus the Culdee, who with its Abbot Maelruain is said to have composed the Martyrology of Tallaght prior to 792, was its greatest ornament. Of his Irish works we shall have more to say later on. Clonenagh suffered so much from the Northmen, that its great foundation had already in the twelfth century dwindled to a parochial church ; in the nineteenth it is a green mound.

Glendalough, founded by the celebrated St. Kevin,[1] became also a college of much note. St. Moling, to whom a great

[1] Pronounced "Keevin," not "Kĕvin." The Irish form is Caoimh- [=keev, "aoi" being in Irish always pronounced like *ce*, and "mh" like *v*] ghinn, the "g" being aspirated is scarcely pronounced.

number of Irish poems [1] are ascribed, was one of his successors in the seventh century, and his life seems to have taken peculiar hold upon the imagination of the populace, for he has more poems—many of them evident forgeries—attributed to him than we find ascribed to any of the saints except to Columcille; and he has a place amongst the four great prophets of Erin.[2] It was he who procured the remission of

[1] The celebrated Evangelistarium, or Book of Moling, was, with its case or cover, deposited in Trinity College, Dublin, in the last century by the Kavanaghs of Borris. Giraldus Cambrensis classes Moling as a prophet with Merlin, and as a saint with Patrick and Columba. One of the prophecies assigned to him is given by O'Curry, MS. Mat., p. 427. The oldest copy of any of Moling's poems is in the monastery of St. Paul in Carinthia, contained in a MS. originally brought from Augia Dives, or Reichenau. It is in the most perfect metre, and runs :—

> " Is en immo niada sás
> Is nau tholl diant eslinn guas,
> Is lestar fás, is crann crín
> Nach digni toil ind rig tuas."

> (" He is a bird round which a trap closes,
> He is a leaky bark in weakness of peril,
> He is an empty vessel, he is a withered tree
> Who doth not do the will of the King above.")

I.e., " Is eán um a n-iadhann sás / is nau (long) thollta darb' éislinn guais. Is leastar fas (folamh) " is crann críon, [an te] nach ndeanann toil an righ shuas."

The poem is also given in the Book of Leinster, and contains eight verses. One would perhaps have expected the third line to run, " is crann crín is lestar fás." The St. Paul MS., which is of the eighth century, contains two of Molling's poems, and they scarcely differ in wording or orthography from copies in MSS. six hundred years later.

[2] Patrick, Columcille, and Berchan of Clonsast, are the others. Even the English settlers had heard of their fame. Baron Finglas, writing in Henry VIII.'s reign, says, " The four saints, St. Patrick, St. Columb, St. Braghane [*i.e.*, Berchan], and St. Moling, which many hundred years agone made prophecy that Englishmen should have conquered Ireland, and said that the said Englishmen should keep their owne laws, and as soon as they should leave, and fall to Irish order, then they should decay, the experience whereof is proved true." (From Ryan's " History and Antiquities of the co. Carlow," p. 93.) A still more curious allusion to the four Irish prophets is one in the Book of Howth, a small vellum folio of the sixteenth century, written in thirteen different hands, published in the Calendar of State Papers. " Men say," recounts the anonymous writer, 'that the Irishmen had four prophets in their time, Patrick, Marten [*sic*],

the Boru tribute from King Finnachta about the year 693. Glendalough was plundered and destroyed by the Danes five times over, within a period of thirty years, yet it to some extent recovered itself, and the great St. Laurence O'Toole, who was Archbishop of Dublin at the coming of the Normans, had been there educated.

Lismore, the great college of the south-east, was founded by St. Carthach in the beginning of the seventh century, who left behind him, according to O'Curry, a monastic rule of 580 lines of Irish verse.[1] Cathal, or Cathaldus, born in the beginning of the seventh century, who afterwards became bishop and patron saint of Tarentum, in Italy, was a student, and perhaps professor in this college. The office of St. Cathaldus states that Gauls, Angles, Irish, and Teutons, and very many people of neighbouring nations came to hear his lectures at Lismore, and Morini's life of him expresses in poetic terms the tradition of Lismore's greatness.[2] St. Cuanna, another member of Lismore, was probably the author of the Book or

Brahen [*i.e.*, Berchan], and Collumkill. Whosoever hath books in Irish written every of them speak of the fight of this conquest, and saith that long strife and oft fighting shall be for this land, and the land shall be harried and stained with great slaughter of men, but the Englishmen fully shall have the mastery a little before doomsday, and that land shall be from sea to sea i-castled ana fully won, but the Englishmen shall be after that well feeble in the land and disdained ; so Barcan [Berchan] saith : that through a king shall come out of the wild mountains of St. Patrick's, that much people shall slew and afterwards break a castle in the wooden of Affayle, with that the Englishmen of Ireland shall be destroyed by that." The prophecy that the Englishmen fully shall have the mastery a little before Doomsday is amusingly equivocal !

[1] Described in O'Curry's MS. Materials, p. 375, but I do not know where the original is.

[2] Quoted in O'Halloran's "History of Ireland," bk. ix. chap. 4. "Celeres vastissima Rheni / jam vada Teutonici, jam deseruere Sicambri ; / Mittit ab extremo gelidos Aquilone Boemos / Albis et Arvenni cöeunt, Batavi-que frequentes, / Et quicunque colunt alta sub rupe Gebennas. / . . . Certatim hi properunt diverso tramite ad urbem / Lesmoriam [Lismore] juvenis primos ubi transigit annos." *See* also corroborative proof of the numbers of Gauls, Teutons, Swiss, and Italians visiting Lismore about the year 700 in Ussher's "Antiquities," Works, vi., p. 303.

Cuanach, now lost, but often quoted in the Annals of Ulster. He died in 650, and the book is not quoted after the year 628, which makes it more than probable that he was the author. Lismore was burnt down by the Danes, but recovered itself in the general revival of native institutions that took place prior to the conquest of the Anglo-Normans. However, when these latter came upon the Irish stage it fared ill with Lismore. Strongbow, indeed, was bought off from burning its churches in 1173 by a great sum of money, but in the following year his son, in spite of this, plundered the place. Four years later the English forces again attacked it, plundered it, and set it on fire. In 1207 the whole town and all about it was finally consumed, so that at the present day not a vestige remains behind of its schools, its cloisters, or its twenty churches.

Cork college was founded by St. Finnbarr towards the end of the sixth century. One of its professors, Colman O'Cluasaigh, who died in 664, wrote the curious Irish hymn or prayer mixed with Latin, preserved in the Book of Hymns.[1] The place was burned four times between 822 and 840, but in the twelfth century the ancient monastery which had fallen into decay was rebuilt by Cormac Mac Carthy, king

[1] Reprinted by Windisch in his "Irische Texte," Heft I., p. 5. The first verse runs—

> "Sén De don fe for don te
> Mac maire ron feladar!
> For a fhoessam dún anocht
> Cia tiasam, cain temadar,"

which is in no wise easy to translate! There are fifty-six verses not all in the same metre. Another acknowledges St. Patrick as a patron saint, it would run thus, in modernised orthography—

> "Beannacht ar erlám [pátrún] Pádraig
> Go naomhaib Eireann uime
> Beannacht ar an gcáthair-se
> Agus ar chách bhfuil innti!

A three-quarter Latin verse runs thus—

> "Regem regum rogamus/ in nostris sermonibus
> Anacht Noe a luchtlach/ diluvi temporibus."

of Munster, and builder of the celebrated Cormac's Chapel at Cashel.

The school of Ross was founded by St. Fachtna for the Ithian tribes[1] of Corca Laidhi [Cor-ka-lee] in South-west Munster. Ross is frequently referred to in the Annals up to the tenth century. There is extant an interesting geographical poem in Irish, of 136 lines, written by one of the teachers there in the tenth century, and apparently intended as a kind of simple text to be learned by heart by the students.[2] Ross was plundered by the Danes in 840, but appears to have been flourishing until North-west Munster was laid waste by the Anglo-Normans under FitzStephen, after which no more is heard of its schools or colleges.

Innisfallen was founded upon an exquisite site on the lower lake of Killarney by St. Finan.[3] The well-known "Annals of Innisfallen," preserved in the Bodleian Library, were probably written by Maelsuthain [Calvus Perennis] O'Carroll, the "soul-friend" of Brian Boru, who inserted the famous entry in the Book of Armagh.[4] It is probable that Brian himself was also educated there. This monastery, owing to its secure retreat in the Kerry mountains, appears to have remained unplundered by the Norsemen, and to have been accounted "a paradise and a secure sanctuary."

Iniscaltra is a beautiful island in the south-west angle of Loch Derg, between Galway and Clare, still famous for its splendid round tower. It was here Columba of Terryglass, who died in 552, established a school and monastery which became so famous that in the life of St. Senan seven ships are mentioned as arriving at the mouth of the Shannon crowded with students for Iniscaltra. It was this Columba who, when asked by one of his disciples why the birds that frequented the island were not afraid of him, made the somewhat dramatic answer,

[1] *See* p. 67. [2] *See* "Proceedings of R. I. Academy for 1884."

[3] Whose name is preserved in O'Connell's residence, "Derrynane," which is really "Derry-finan" (Doire-Fhionáin). [4] *See* p. 140 and 141 note

"Why should they fear me? am I not a bird myself, for my soul always flies to heaven as they fly through the sky." Columba had a celebrated successor called Caimin, who died in 653. Ussher, who calls him St. Caminus, tells us that part of his Psalter was extant in his own time, and that he had himself seen it "having a collation of the Hebrew text placed on the upper part of each page, and with brief scholia added on the exterior margin."[1]

A great number of lesser monastic institutions and schools seem to have existed alongside of these more famous ones, and it is hardly too much to say that during the sixth, seventh, eighth, and perhaps ninth centuries Ireland had caught and held aloft the torch of learning in the lampadia of mankind, and procured for herself the honourable title of the island of saints and scholars.

[1] "Habebatur psalterium, cujus unicum tantum quaternionem mihi videre contigit, obelis et asteriscis diligentissime distinctum; collatione cum veritate Hebraica in superiore parte cujusque paginæ posita, et brevibus scholiis ad exteriorem marginem adjectis." (*See* "Works," vol. vi. p. 544. Quoted by Professor G. Stokes, "Proceedings R. I. Academy," May, 1892.)

CHAPTER XVII

THEIR FAME AND TEACHING

It is very difficult to say what was exactly the curriculum of the early Irish colleges, and how far they were patronised by laymen. Without doubt their original design was to propagate a more perfect knowledge of the Scriptures and of theological learning in general, but it is equally certain that they must have, almost from the very first, taught the heathen classics and the Irish language side by side with the Scriptures and theology. There is no other possible way of accounting for the admirable scholarship of the men whom they turned out, and for their skill in Latin and often also in Irish poetry. Virgil, Ovid, Terence, and most of the Latin poets must have been widely taught and read. "It is sufficient," says M. d'Arbois de Jubainville, talking of Columbanus who was born in 543, and who was educated at Bangor, on Belfast Loch, "to glance at his writings, immediately to recognise his marvellous superiority over Gregory of Tours and the Gallo-Romans of his time. He lived in close converse with the classical authors, as later on did the learned men of the sixteenth century, whose equal he certainly is not, but of whom he seems a sort of precursor." From the sixth to the sixteenth century is a long leap, and no higher eulogium could be passed upon the scholarship of Columbanus and the training given by his Irish college.[1] All the studies of the time appear to have been taught in them through the medium of the Irish language, not merely theology but arithmetic, rhetoric, poetry, hagiography, natural science as then understood, grammar, chronology, astronomy, Greek, and even Hebrew.

"The classic tradition," sums up M. Darmesteter, "to all appearances dead in Europe, burst out into full flower in the Isle of Saints, and the Renaissance began in Ireland 700 years before it was known in Italy. During three centuries Ireland was the asylum of the higher learning which took sanctuary there from the uncultured states of Europe. At one time Armagh, the religious capital of Christian Ireland, was the metropolis of civilisation."

[1] Here are a few lines from the well-known Adonic poem which he, at the age of 68, addressed to his friend Fedolius—

"*Extitit ingens*
Causa malorum
Aurea pellis,
Corruit auri
Munere parvo
Cœna Deorum.
Ac tribus illis
Maxima lis est
Orta Deabus.
Hinc populavit
Trogugenarum
Ditia regna
Dorica pubes.
Juraque legum
Fasque fides que
Rumpitur aure.

Impia quippe
Pygmalionis
Regis ob aurum
Gesta leguntur.

. . .

Fœmina sæpe
Perdit ob aurum
Casta pudorem.
Non Jovis auri
Fluxit in imbre
Sed quod adulter
Obtulit aurum
Aureus ille
Fingitur imber."

Dr. Sigerson in "Bards of the Gael and Gaul," p. 407, prints as Jubainville also does, the whole of this noted poem, and points out that it is shot through and through with Irish assonance. "Not less important than its assonance," writes Dr. Sigerson, "is the fact that it introduces into Latin verse the use of returning words, or burthens with variations, which supply the vital germs of the rondeau and the ballad." I am not myself convinced of what Dr. Sigerson considers marks of *intentional* assonance in almost *every* line.

His chief remaining works are a Monastic Rule in ten chapters; a book on the daily penances of the monks; seventeen sermons; a book on the measure of penances; a treatise on the eight principal vices; five epistles written to Gregory the Great and others; and a good many Latin verses. His life is written by the Abbot Jonas, a contemporary of his own.

"Ireland," says Babington in his "Fallacies of Race Theories,"[1] "had been admitted into Christendom and to some measure of culture only in the fifth century. At that time Gaul and Italy enjoyed to the full all the knowledge of the age. In the next century the old culture-lands had to turn for some little light and teaching to that remote and lately barbarous land."

When we remember that the darkness of the Middle Ages had already set in over the struggles, agony, and confusion of feudal Europe, and that all knowledge of Greek may be said to have died out upon the Continent—"had elsewhere absolutely vanished," says M. Darmesteter—when we remember that even such a man as Gregory the Great was completely ignorant of it, it will appear extraordinary to find it taught in Ireland alone, out of all the countries of Western Europe.[2] Yet this is capable of complete and manifold proof. Columbanus for instance, shows in his letter to Pope Boniface that he knows something of both Greek and Hebrew.[3] Aileran, who died of the plague in 664, gives evidence of the same in his book on our Lord's genealogy. Cummian's letter to the Abbot of Iona has been referred to before, and, as Professor G. Stokes puts it, "proves the fact to demonstration that in the first half of the seventh century there was a wide range of Greek learning, not ecclesiastical merely, but chronological, astronomical, and philosophical, away at Durrow in the very centre of the Bog of Allen." Augustine, an un-identified Irish monk of the second half of the seventh century, gives many proofs of Greek and Oriental learning and quotes the Chronicles of Eusebius. The later Sedulius, the versatile abbot of Kildare, about the year 820 "makes parade of his Greek knowledge," to quote a French writer in the "Revue Celtique," "employs Greek words

[1] P. 122.

[2] "Grössere oder geringere Kenntniss klassischen Alterthums, vor allem Kenntniss des Griechischen ist daher in jener Zeit ein Mazstab sowohl für die Bildung einer einzelnen Persönlichkeit als auch für den Culturgrad eines ganzen Zeitalters" (Zimmer, "Preussische Jahrbûcher," January, 1887).

[3] He plays on his own name Columba, "a dove," and turns it into Greek and Hebrew, περιστερά and יונה

without necessity, and translates into Greek a part of the definition of the pronoun."[1] St. Caimins's Psalter, seen by Bishop Ussher with the Hebrew text collated, convinced Dr. Reeves that Hebrew as well as Greek was studied in Ireland about the year 600. Nor did this Greek learning tend to die out. In the middle of the ninth century John Scotus Erigena, summoned from Ireland to France by Charles the Bald, was the only person to be found able to translate the Greek works of the pseudo-Dionysius,[2] thanks to the training he had received in his Irish school. The Book of Armagh contains the Lord's Prayer written in Greek letters, and there is a Greek MS. of the Psalter, written in Sedulius' own hand, now preserved in Paris. Many more Greek texts, at least a dozen, written by Irish monks, are preserved elsewhere in Europe. "These eighth and ninth century Greek MSS.," remarks Professor Stokes, "covered with Irish glosses and Irish poems and Irish notes, have engaged the attention of palæographers and students of the Greek texts of the New Testament during the last two centuries." They are indeed a proof that—as Dr. Reeves puts it—the Irish School "was unquestionably the most advanced of its day in sacred literature."

This remarkable knowledge of Greek was evidently derived from an early and direct commerce with Gaul, where Greek had been spoken for four or five centuries, first alongside of Celtic, and in later times of Latin also.[3] The knowledge

[1] Dr. Sigerson prints an admirably graceful poem either by this or another Sedulius of the ninth century at p. 411 of his "Bards of the Gael and Gaul." It shows how far from being pedants the Irish monks were. This poem is a dispute between the rose and lily.

[2] This translation which Charles sent to the Pope threw Anastasius, the Librarian of the Roman Church, into the deepest astonishment. "Mirandum est," he writes in his letter of reply, dated 865, "quomodo vir ille barbarus in finibus mundi positus, talia intellectu capere in aliamque linguam transferre valuerit" (*See* Prof. Stokes, "R. I. Academy Proceedings," May, 1892).

[3] St. Jerome tells us that the people of Marseilles were in his day trilingual, "Massiliam Phocæi condiderunt quos ait Varro trilingues esse, quod et Græce loquantur, et Latine et Gallice" (Migne's edition, vol. vii. p. 425).

of Hebrew may have been derived from the Egyptian monks who passed over from Gaul into Ireland. Egypt and the East were more or less in close communication with Gaul in the fifth century, and the Irish Litany, ascribed to Angus the Culdee, commemorates seven Egyptian monks amongst many other Gauls, Germans, and Italians who resided in Ireland. The close and constant intercommunication between Greek-speaking Gaul and Ireland accounts for the planting and cultivation of the Greek language in the Irish schools, and once planted there it continued to flourish more or less for some centuries. There is ample evidence to prove the connection between Gaul and Ireland from the fifth to the ninth century. We find Gaulish merchants in the middle of Ireland at Clonmacnois, who had no doubt sailed up the Shannon in the way of commerce, selling wine to Ciaran in the sixth century. We find Columbanus, a little later on, inquiring at Nantes for a vessel engaged in the Irish trade—*quæ vexerat commercium cum Hibernia.* In Adamnan's Life of Columcille we find mention of Gaulish sailors arriving at Cantire. Adamnan's own treatise on Holy Places was written from the verbal account of a Gaul. In the Old Irish poem on the Fair of Carman in Wexford—a pagan institution which lived on in Christian times—we find mention of the

> "Great market of the foreign Greeks,
> Where gold and noble clothes were wont to be;"[1]

the foreign Greeks being no doubt the Greek-speaking Gaulish merchants. Alcuin sends his gifts of money and oil and his letters direct from Charlemagne's court to his friends in Clonmacnois, probably by a vessel engaged in the direct Irish trade, for, as he himself tells us, the sea-route between England and France was then closed. If more proof of the

[1] *See* appendix to O'Curry's "Manners and Customs," vol. iii. p. 547—

> "Margaid mor na n-gall ngregach
> I mbid or is ard étach."

close communication between Ireland and Gaul were wanted, the fact that Dagobert II., king of France in the seventh century, was educated at Slane,[1] in Ireland, and also that certain Merovingian and French coins have been found here, should be sufficient.

The fame of these early Irish schools attracted students in the seventh, eighth, and ninth centuries from all quarters to Ireland, which had now become a veritable land of schools and scholars. The Venerable Bede tells us of the crowds of Anglo-Saxons who flocked over into Ireland during the plague, about the year 664, and says that they were all warmly welcomed by the Irish, who took care that they should be provided with food every day, without payment on their part; that they should have books to read, and that they should receive gratuitous instruction from Irish masters.[2] Books must have already multiplied considerably when the swarms of Anglo-Saxons could thus be supplied with them gratis. This noble tradition of free education to strangers lasted down to the establishment of the so-called "National" schools in Ireland, for down to that time "poor scholars" were freely supported by the people and helped in their studies. The number of scribes whose deaths have been considered worth recording by the annalists is very great, and books consequently must have been very numerous. This plentifulness of books probably added to the renown of the Irish schools. An English prince as well as a French one was educated by them in the seventh century; this was Aldfrid, king of Northumbria, who

[1] He is said to have spent eighteen or twenty years there and to have acquired all the wisdom of the Scots. The reason why he was sent to Slane, as Dr. Healy well observes, was, not because it was the most celebrated school of the time, but because it was in Meath where the High-kings mostly dwelt, and it was only natural to bring the boy to some place near the Royal Court. ("Ireland's Schools and Scholars," p. 590.)

[2] "Quos omnes Scotti libentissime suscipientes victum eis quotidianum sine pretio, libros quoque ad legendum, et magisterium gratuitum, præbere curabant" ("Ecc. Hist.," book iii. chap. 27). Amongst these were the celebrated Egbert, of whom Bede tells us so much, and St. Chad.

was trained in all the learning of Erin, and who always aided and abetted the Irish in England, in opposition to Wilfrid, who opposed them. That the king got a good education in Ireland may be conjectured from the fact that Aldhelm, abbot of Malmesbury, dedicated to him a poetic epistle on Latin metric and prosody, in which, says Dr. Healy, "he congratulates the king on his good fortune in having been educated in Ireland." Aldhelm's own master was also an Irishman, Mael-dubh, and his abbacy of Malmesbury is only a corruption of this Irishman's name Maeldubh's-bury.[1] In another place Aldhelm tells us that while the great English school at Canterbury was by no means overcrowded, the English swarmed to the Irish schools like bees. Aldfrid himself, when leaving Ireland, composed a poem of sixty lines in the Irish language and metre, which he must have learned from the bards, in which he compliments each of the provinces severally, as though he meant to thank the whole nation for their hospitality.[2]

> "I found in Inisfail the fair
> In Ireland, while in exile there,
> Women of worth, both grave and gay men,
> Learned clerics, heroic laymen.

[1] He is called Mailduf by Bede, and Malmesbury Maildufi urbem, which shows that the aspirated "b" in *dubh* had twelve hundred years ago the sound of "f" as it has to-day in Connacht.

[2] O'Reilly states that the poem consisted of ninety-six lines, but Hardiman, in his "Irish Minstrelsy," vol. ii. p. 372, gives only sixty. Hardiman has written on the margin of O'Reilly's "Irish Writers" in my possession, "I have a copy, the character is ancient and very obscure." Aldfrid may well have written such a poem, of which the copy printed by Hardiman may be a somewhat modernised version. It begins—

> "Ro dheat an inis finn Fáil
> In Eirinn re imarbháidh,
> Iomad ban, ni baoth an breas,
> Iomad laoch, iomad cleireach."

It was admirably and fairly literally translated by Mangan for Montgomery. His fourth line, however, runs, "Many clerics and many laymen," which conveys no meaning save that of populousness. I have altered this line to make it suit the Irish "many a hero, many a cleric."

"I travelled its fruitful provinces round,
And in every one of the five I found,
Alike in church and in palace hall,
Abundant apparel and food for all."

St. Willibrord, a Saxon noble educated in Ireland about the same time with King Aldfrid, went out thence and ultimately became Archbishop of Utrecht. Another noted scholar of the same period was Agilbert, a Frank by birth, who spent a long time in Ireland for the purpose of study and afterwards became Bishop of Paris.[1] We have seen how the Office of St. Cathaldus states that the school of Lismore was visited by Gauls, Angles, Scotti, Teutons, and scholars from other neighbouring nations. The same was more or less the case with Clonmacnois, Bangor, and some others of the most noted of the Irish schools.

It was not in Greek attainments, nor in ecclesiastical studies, nor in Latin verses alone, that the Irish excelled; they also produced astronomers like Dungal and geographers like Dicuil. Dungal's attainments we have glanced at, but Dicuil's book—*de mensura orbis terrarum*—written about the year 825, is more interesting, although nothing is known about the author's own life, nor do we know even the particular Irish school to which he belonged.[2] His book was published by a Frenchman because he found Dicuil's descriptions of the measurements of the Pyramids a thousand years ago tallied with his own.

"Antioch," writes Professor G. Stokes, "about A.D. 600, was the centre of Greek culture and Greek erudition, and the chronicle of Malalas, as embodied in Niebuhr's series of Byzantine historians, is a mine of information on many questions; but compare it with the Irish work of Dicuil and its mistakes are laughable."

[1] "Natione quidem Gallus," says Bede, "sed tunc legendarum gratiâ scripturarum in Hibernia non parvo tempore demoratus."

[2] Probably Clonmacnois. *See* Stokes, "Celtic Church," p. 214, and Dr. Healy's "Ireland's Schools and Scholars," p. 283.

A great deal of his work is founded of course upon Pliny, Solinus, and Priscian, but he shows a highly-developed critical sense in comparing and collating various MSS. which he had inspected to ensure accuracy. What he tells us at first-hand, however, is by far the most interesting. In speaking of the Nile he says that :—

"Although we never read in any book that any branch of the Nile flows into the Red Sea, yet Brother Fidelis told in my presence to my master Suibhne [Sweeny]—to whom under God I owe whatever knowledge I possess—that certain clerics and laymen from Ireland who went to Jerusalem on pilgrimage sailed up the Nile a long way."

They sailed thence by a canal into the Red Sea, and this statement proves the accuracy of Dicuil, for this canal really existed and continued in use until 767, when it was closed to hinder the people of Mecca and Medina getting supplies from Egypt. The account of the Pyramids is particularly interesting. "The aforesaid Brother Fidelis measured one of them and found that the square face was 400 feet in length." The same brother wished to examine the exact point where Moses had entered the Red Sea in order to try if he could find any traces of the chariots of Pharaoh or the wheel tracks, but the sailors were in a hurry and would not allow him to go on this excursion. The breadth of the sea appeared to him at this point to be about six miles. Dicuil describes Iceland long before it was discovered by the Danes.

"It is now thirty years," said he, writing in 825, "since I was told by some Irish ecclesiastics, who had dwelt in that island from the 1st of February to the 1st of August, that the sun scarcely sets there in summer, but always leaves, even at midnight, light enough to do one's ordinary business—*vel pediculos de camisia abstrahere*"!

Those writers are greatly mistaken, he says, who describe the Icelandic sea as always frozen, and who say that there is day there from spring to autumn and from autumn to spring, for the Irish monks sailed thither through the open sea in a month of great natural cold, and yet found alternate day and night, except about the period of the summer solstice. He also describes the Faroe Isles:—

> "A certain trustworthy monk told me that he reached one of them by sailing for two summer days and one night in a vessel with two benches of rowers. . . . In these islands for almost a hundred years there dwelt hermits who sailed there from our own Ireland [nostra Scottia], but now they are once more deserted as they were at the beginning, on account of the ravages of the Norman pirates."

This is proof positive that the Irish discovered and inhabited Iceland and the Faroe Islands half a century or a century before the Northmen. Dicuil was distinguished as a grammarian, metrician, and astronomer,[1] but his geographical treatise, written in his old age, is the most interesting and valuable of his achievements.

Fergil, or Virgilius, as he is usually called, was another great Irish geometer, who eventually became Archbishop of Salzburg and died in 785. He taught the sphericity of the earth and the doctrine of the Antipodes, a truth which seems also to have been familiar to Dicuil. St. Boniface, afterwards Archbishop of Mentz, evidently distorting his doctrine, accused him to the Pope of heresy in teaching that there was another world and other men under the earth, and another sun and moon. "Concerning this charge of false doctrine, if it shall be established," said the Pope, "that Virgil taught this perverse and wicked doctrine against God and his own soul, do you then convoke a council, degrade him from the priesthood, and drive him from the Church." Virgil, however, seems to have satisfactorily explained his position, for nothing was done against him.

These instances help to throw some light upon a most difficult subject—the training given in the early Irish Christian schools, and the cause of their undoubted popularity for three centuries and more amongst the scholars of Western Europe.

[1] His astronomical work, written in 814–16, remains as yet unpublished.

CHAPTER XVIII

CONFLICTS WITH THE CIVIL POWER

THE extraordinary and abnormal receptivity of the Irish of the fifth century, and the still more wonderful and unprecedented activity of their descendants in the sixth and following ones had almost bid fair to turn the nation into a land of apostles. This outburst of religious zeal, glorious and enduring as it was, carried with it, like all sudden and powerful movements, an element of danger. It was unfortunately destined in its headlong course to overflow its legitimate barriers and to come into rude contact with the civil power which had been established upon lines more ancient and not wholly sympathetic.

A striking passage in one of Renan's books dwells upon the obvious religious inferiority of the Greeks and Romans to the Jews, while it notes at the same time their immense political and intellectual superiority over the Semitic nation. The inferiority of the Jew in matters political and intellectual the French writer seems inclined to attribute to his abnormally developed religious sense, which, absorbed in itself, took all too little heed of the civic side of life and of the necessities of the state. Nor can it, I think, be denied that primitive Christianity in some cases took over from the Hebrews a certain amount of this spirit of self-absorption and of disregard for the civil side of life and social polity. "Quand on prend les choses humaines par ce côté," remarks Renan, "on fonde de grands prosélytismes universels, on a des apôtres courant le monde d'un bout à l'autre, et le convertissant ; mais on ne fonde pas des institutions politiques, une indépendance nationale, une dynastie, un code, un peuple."

We have already seen how the exaggerated pretensions of St. Columcille had come almost at once into opposition with the established law of the land, the law which enjoined death as the penalty for homicide at Tara, and how the priest unjustifiably took upon himself to override the civil magistrate in the person of the king.

Of precisely such a nature—only with far worse and far more enduring consequences—was the cursing of Tara by St. Ruadhan of Lothra. The great palace where, according to general belief, a hundred and thirty-six pagan and six Christian kings had ruled uninterruptedly, the most august spot in all Ireland, where a "truce of God" had always reigned during the great triennial assemblies, was now to be given up and deserted at the curse of a tonsured monk. The great Assembly or Féis of Tara, which accustomed the people to the idea of a centre of government and a ruling power, could no more be convened, and a thousand associations and memories which hallowed the office of the High-king were snapped in a moment. It was a blow from which the monarchy of Ireland never recovered, a blow which, by putting an end to the great triennial or septennial conventions of the whole Irish race, weakened the prestige of the central ruler, increased the power of the provincial chieftains, segregated the clans of Ireland from one another, and opened a new road for faction and dissension throughout the entire island.

There is a considerable amount of mystery attached to this whole transaction, and all the great Irish annalists, the "Four

Masters," the "Chronicon Scotorum," the Annals of Ulster, Tighearnach, and Keating, are absolutely silent upon the matter.[1] The "Four Masters," indeed, under the year 554 record "the last Féis of Tara,"[2] as does Tighearnach also; but why it was the last, or why Tara was deserted, they do not say. Yet so great a national event was infinitely too important to have been passed over in silence except for some special reason, and I cannot help thinking that it was not alluded to because the annalists did not care to recall it. The authorities for the cursing of Tara are the lost "Annals of Clonmacnois," which were translated into English by Connell Mac Geoghegan in 1627, and which give a very long and full account of the matter;[3] an Irish MS. in Trinity College, Dublin;[4] the Life of St. Ruadhan himself, in the fourteenth century (?) codex the Book of Kilkenny, now in Marsh's Library; and his life as published by the Bollandists; the ancient scholiast on Fiach's hymn on the Life of St. Patrick; a fifteenth century vellum in the British Museum, which professes to copy from the lost Book of Sligo; the Book of Rights,[5] and the Book of Lismore, which last, though it turns the story into an *úrsgeul*, or romance, yet agrees closely in essentials with the lost "Annals of Clonmacnois." The story, as told in this manuscript, is worth producing as a specimen of how the Irish loved to turn every great historical event into an *úrsgeul*, seasoned with a good spice of the marvellous, and dressed up dramatically. How much of such pseudo-histories is true, how much invented for the occasion, and how much may be stock-in-trade of the

[1] The silence of Keating seems to me particularly strange, for he devotes a good deal of space to King Diarmuid's reign, yet he must have been perfectly well aware of the stories then current and the many allusions in vellum MSS. to the cursing of Tara.

[2] "Féis dedheanach Teamhra do deanamh la Diarmaitt righ Ereann." Tighearnach calls it "Cena postrema."

[3] Printed for the Royal Society of Antiquaries by the late Denis Murphy, S.J., Dublin, 1896. *See* p. 85.

[4] H., I. 15.

[5] Pp. 53–57.

story-teller, is never easily determined. The story runs as follows :—

King Diarmuid's steward and spear-bearer had been ill and wasting away for a year. On his recovery he goes to the King, and asks him whether "the order of his discipline and peace" had been observed during the time of his illness. The King answered that he had noticed no breach or diminution of it. The spear-bearer said he would make sure of the King's peace by travelling round Ireland with his spear held transversely, and he would see whether the door of every liss and fortress would be opened wide enough to let the spear pass—such on the approach of the King's spear seems to have been the law—and "so shall the regimen and peace of Ireland," said he "be ascertained."

"From Tara, therefore, goes forth the spear-bearer,[1] and with him the King of Ireland's herald, to proclaim Ireland's peace, and he arrived in the province of Connacht, and made his way to the mansion of Aedh [Æ] Guairè of Kinelfechin. And he at that time had round his rath a stockade of red oak, and had a new house too, that was but just built [no doubt inside the rath] with a view to his marriage feast. Now, a week before the spear-bearer's arrival the other had heard that he was on his way to him, and had given orders to make an opening before him in the palisade [but not in the dwelling].

"The spear-bearer came accordingly, and Aedh Guairè bade him welcome. The spear-bearer said that the house must be hewn [open to the right width] before him.

"'Give thine own orders as to how it may please thee to have it hewn,' said Aedh Guairè, but, even as he spake it, he gave a stroke of his sword to the spear-bearer, so that he took his head from off him.

"Now at this time the discipline of Ireland was such that whosoever killed a man void of offence, neither cattle nor other valuable consideration might be taken in lieu of the slain, but the slayer must be killed, unless it were that the King should order or permit the acceptance of a cattle-price.

---

[1] He is called Aedh Baclamh here, "Bacc Lonim" in the "Life." Baclamh apparently indicates some office. I have here called him only the spear-bearer.

"When King Diarmuid heard of the killing he sent his young men and his executive to waste and to spoil Aedh Guairè. And he flees to Bishop Senan, for one mother they had both, and Senan the bishop goes with him to Ruadhan of Lothra, for it was two sisters of Lothra that nursed Bishop Senan, Cael and Ruadhnait were their names. But Aedh Guairè found no protection with Ruadhan, but was banished away into Britain for a year, and Diarmuid's people came to seek for him in Britain, so he was again sent back to Ruadhan. And Diarmuid himself comes to Ruadhan to look for him, but he had been put into a hole in the ground by Ruadhan, which is to-day called 'Ruadhan's Hole.' Diarmuid sent his man to look in Ruadhan's kitchen whether Aedh Guiarè were there. But on the man's going into the kitchen his eyes were at once struck blind. When Diarmuid saw this, he went into the kitchen himself, but he did not find Aedh Guiarè there. And he asked Ruadhan where he was, for he was sure he would tell him no lie.

"'I know not where he is,' said Ruadhan, 'if he be not under yon thatch.'

"After that Diarmuid departs to his house, but he remembered the cleric's word and returns to the recluse's cell, and he sees the candle being brought to the spot where Aedh Guairè was. And he sends a confidential servant to bring him forth—Donnán Donn was his name—and he dug down in the hiding place, but the arm he stretched out to take Aedh withered to the shoulder. And he makes obeisance to Ruadhan after that, and the two servants remained with Ruadhan after that in Poll Ruadhain. After this Diarmuid [himself] carries off Aedh Guairè to Tara."

Upon this, we are told, Ruadhan made his way to Brendan of Birr, and thence to the so-called twelve apostles of Ireland,[1] and they all followed the King and came to Tara, and they fast upon the King that night, and he, "relying on his kingly quality and on the justice of his cause, fasts upon them."[2]

"In such fashion, and to the end of a year they continued before Tara under Ruadhan's tent exposed to weather and to wet, and they were every other night without food, Diarmuid and the clergy, fasting on each other."

After this the story goes on that Brendan the Navigator had in the meantime landed from his foreign expeditions, and

[1] *See* above, p. 196.

[2] "A niurt a fhlatha ocus a fhírinne."

hearing that the other saints of Ireland were fasting before Tara, he also proceeds thither. But King Diarmuid, learning of his coming, was terrified, and consented to give up Aedh Guairè for "fifty horses, blue-eyed with golden bridles." Brendan the Voyager, fresh from his triumphs on the ocean, summons fifty seals and makes them look like horses, and guaranteeing them for a year and a quarter, hands them over to the King and receives Aedh Guairè. But when the time guaranteed was out, they became seals again, and brought their riders with them into the sea. And Diarmuid was very wroth at the deception, "and shut the seven lisses of Tara to the end that the clergy should not enter into Tara, lest they should leave behind malevolence and evil bequests."

It appears that the clerics still continued fasting upon the King, and he fasting upon them,

"And people were assigned [by the King] to wait upon them and to keep watch and ward over them until the clergy should have accomplished the act of eating and consuming food in their presence. But on this night Brendan gave them this advice—their cowls to be about their heads and they to let their meat and ale pass by their mouths into their bosoms and down to the ground, and this they did. Word was brought to the King that the clergy were consuming meat and ale, so Diarmuid ate meat that night, but the clerics on the other hand fasted on him through stratagem.

"Now Diarmuid's wife—Mughain was his wife—saw a dream, which dream was this, that upon the green of Tara was a vast and wide-foliaged tree, and eleven slaves hewing at it, but every chip which they knocked from it would return into its place again and adhere to it [as before], till at last there came one man that dealt the tree but a stroke, and with that single cut laid it low, as the poet spoke the lay—

"'An evil dream did she behold
The wife of the King of Tara of the heavy torques,
Although it brought to her grief and woe
She could not keep from telling it.
A powerful stout tree did she behold,
That might shelter the birds of Ireland,
Upon the hill-side, smitten with axes,
And champions hewing together at it, etc.

(48 lines more.)

As for Diarmuid, son of Cerbhall [the King], after that dream he arose early, so that he heard the clergy chant their psalms, and he entered into the house in which they were.

"'Alas!' he said, 'for the iniquitous contest which ye have waged against me, seeing that it is Ireland's good that I pursue, and to preserve her discipline and royal right, but 'tis Ireland's unpeace and murderousness which ye endeavour after. For God Himself it is who on such or such a one confers the orders of prince, of righteous ruler, and of equitable judgment, to the end that he may maintain his truthfulness, his princely quality, and his governance. Now that to which a king is bound is to have mercy coupled with stringency of law, and peace maintained in the sub-districts, and hostages in fetters; to succour the wretched, but to overwhelm enemies, and to banish falsehood, for unless on this hither side one do the King of Heaven's will, no excuse is accepted by him on the other. And thou, Ruadhan,' said Diarmuid, 'through thee it is that injury and rending of my mercy and of mine integrity to Godward is come about, and I pray God that thy diocese be the first in Ireland that shall be renounced, and thy Church lands the first that shall be impugned.'

"But Ruadhan said, 'Rather may thy dynasty come to nought, and none that is son or grandson to thee establish himself in Tara for ever!'

"Diarmuid said, 'Be thy Church desolate continually.'

"Ruadhan said, 'Desolate be Tara for ever and for ever.

"Diarmuid said, 'May a limb of thy limbs be wanting to thee, and come not with thee under ground, and mayest thou lack an eye!'

"'Have thou before death an evil countenance in sight of all; may thine enemies prevail over thee mightily, and the thigh that thou liftedst not before me to stand up, be the same mangled into pieces.'

"Said Diarmuid, 'The thing [*i.e.*, the man] about which is our dispute, take him with you, but in thy church, Ruadhan, may the alarm cry sound at nones always, and even though all Ireland be at peace be thy church's precinct a scene of war continuously.'

"And from that time to this the same is fulfilled." [1]

There follows a poem of 88 lines uttered by the King.

The same story in all its essential details is told in the MS.

[1] There is a poem ascribed to Ruadhan in the MS. marked H. 4. in Trinity College. O'Clery's Féilire na Naomh has a curious note on Ruadhan which runs thus: Ruadhan of Lothra, "he was of the race of Owen Mór, son of Oilioll Olum. A very old ancient book (sein leabhar ró aosta) as we have mentioned at Brigit, 1st of February, states that Ruadhan of Lothra was in manners and life like Matthew the Apostle."

Egerton 1782, a vellum of the fifteenth century, which professes to follow the lost Book of Sligo. It is quite as unbiassed and outspoken about the result of the clerics' action as the Book of Lismore. It makes Diarmuid address the clerics thus—

"'Evil is that which ye have worked O clerics, my kingdom's ruination. For in the latter times Ireland shall not be better off than she is at this present. But, however it fall out,' said he, 'may bad chiefs, their heirs-apparent, and their men of war, quarter themselves in your churches, and may it be their [*read* your ?] own selves that in your houses shall pull off such peoples' brogues for them, ye being the while powerless to rid yourselves of them.'"

This codex sympathises so strongly with the king that it states that one of Ruadhan's eyes burst in his head when the king cursed him. Beg mac De, the celebrated Christian prophet, is made to prophecy thus, when the king asks him in what fashion his kingdom should be after his death,

"'An evil world,' said the prophet, 'is now at hand, in which men shall be in bondage, woman free; mast wanting; woods smooth; blossom bad; winds many; wet summer; green corn; much cattle; scant milk; dependants burdensome in every country, hogs lean, chiefs wicked; bad faith; *chronic killing; a world withered, raths in number.*'"

King Diarmuid died in 558, according to the "Four Masters;" it is certain he never retreated a foot from Tara, but it was probably his next successor who, intimidated at the clerics' curse and the ringing of their bells—for they circled Tara ringing their bells against it—deserted the royal hill for ever.[1]

The palace of Cletty, not far from Tara, was also cursed by St. Cairneach at the request of the queen of the celebrated Muircheartach Mór mac Earca, and deserted in consequence.[2]

[1] After this the High-kings of Ireland belonging to the northern Ui Neill resided in their own ancient palace of Aileach near Derry, and the High-kings of the southern Ui Neill families resided at the Rath near Castlepollard, or at Dún-na-sgiath ("the Fortress of the Shields") on the brink of Loch Ennell, near Mullingar. Brian Boru resided at Kincora in Clare.

[2] See O'Donovan's letter from Navan on Brugh na Bóinne.

Another, but probably more justifiable, instance of the clergy fasting upon a lay ruler and cursing him, was that of the notorious Raghallach (Reilly), king of Connacht, who made his queen jealous by his infidelity, and committed other crimes. The story is thus recorded by Keating—

> "The scandal of that evil deed soon spread throughout all the land and the saints of Ireland were sorrowful by reason thereof. St. Fechin of Fobar [Fore is West Meath] came in person to Raghallach to reprehend him, and many saints came in his company to aid him in inducing the prince to discontinue his criminal amour. But Raghallach despised their exhortations. Thereupon they fasted against him, and as there were many other evil-minded persons besides him in the land, they made an especial prayer to God that for the sake of an example he should not live out the month of May, then next to come on, and that he should fall by the hands of villains, by vile instruments, and in a filthy place; and all these things happened to him,"

as Keating goes on to relate, for he was killed by turf-cutters.

Sometimes the saints are found on opposite sides, as at the Battle of Cooldrevna where Columcille prayed against the High-king's arms, and Finian prayed for them; or as in the well-known case of the expulsion of poor old St. Mochuda [1] and his monks in 631 from the monastery at Rathain, where his piety and success had aroused the jealousy of the clerics of the Ui Neill, who ejected him by force, despite his malediction. It was then he returned to his own province and founded Lismore, which soon became famous.[2]

Led away by our admiration of the magnificent outburst or learning and the innumerable examples of undoubted devotion displayed by Irishmen from the sixth to the ninth century, we are very liable to overlook the actual state of society, and to read into a still primitive social constitution the thoughts and ideas of later ages, forgetting the real spirit of those early times. We must remember that St. Patrick had made no change in the social constitution of the people, and that the new religion

[1] Also called Carthach.

[2] See above, p. 211.

in no way affected their external institutions, and as a natural consequence even saints and clerics took the side of their own kings and people, and fought in battle with as much gusto as any of the clansmen. Women fought side by side with men, and were only exempted from military service in 590, through the influence of Columcille at the synod of Druimceat—of which synod more hereafter, and Adamnan had to get the law renewed over a hundred years later, for it had become inoperative. The monks were of course as liable as any other of the tribesmen to perform military duty to their lords, and were only exempted [1] from it in the year 804. The clergy fought with Cormac mac Culenain as late as 908 at the battle where he fell, and a great number of them were killed.[2] The clergy often quarrelled among themselves also. In 673 the monks of Clonmacnois and Durrow fought one another, and the men of Clonmacnois slew two hundred of their opponents. In 816 four hundred men were slain in a fight between rival monasteries. The clan system, in fact, applied down to the eighth or ninth century almost as much to the clergy as to the laity, and with the abandonment of Tara and the weakening of the High-kingship, the only power which bid fair to override feud and faction was got rid of, and every man drank for himself the intoxicating draught of irresponsibility, and each princeling became a Cæsar in his own community.

The saints with their long-accredited exercises of semi-miraculous powers, formed an admirable ingredient wherewith to spice a historic romance, such as the soul of the Irish story-tellers loved, and they were not slow to avail themselves of it.

A passage in the celebrated history of the Boru tribute, preserved in the twelfth-century Book of Leinster, turns both Columcille and his biographer Adamnan to account in this way, by introducing dialogues between them and their con-

[1] By Fothadh called "na Canóine" who persuaded Aedh Oirnide to release them from this duty.

[2] *See* "Fragments of Irish Annals" by O'Donovan, p. 210, and his note

temporary kings of Ireland, which are worth giving here, as they preserve some primitive traits, but more especially as an example of how the later mediævalists conceived their own early saints. Aedh [Ae], the High-king of Ireland, had asked Columcille how many kings of all whom he himself had come in contact with, or had cognisance of, would win, or had won, to heaven; and Columcille answered:

"'Certainly I know of only three, Daimín King of Oriel, and Ailill King of Connacht, and Feradach of Corkalee, King of Ossory.

"'And what good did they do,' said Aedh, 'beyond all other kings?'

"'That's easy told,' said Columcille, 'as for Daimín no cleric ever departed from him having met with a refusal, and he never reviled a cleric, nor spoiled church nor sanctuary, and greatly did he bestow upon the Lord. Afterwards he went to heaven, on account of his mild dealing with the Lord's people; and the clerics still chant his litany.

"'As for Ailill, moreover, this is how he found the Lord's clemency; he fought the battle of Cúl Conairé with the Clan Fiacrach, and they defeated him in that battle, and he said to his charioteer, "Look behind for us, and see whether the slaying is great, and are the slayers near us?"

"'The charioteer looked behind him, and 'twas what he said:

"'"The slaying with which your people are slain," said he, "is unendurable."

"'"It is not their own guilt that falls on them, but the guilt of my pride and my untruthfulness," said he; "and turn the chariot for us against [the enemy]," said he, "for if I be slain amidst them (?) it will be the saving of a multitude.'

"'Thereupon the chariot was turned round against the enemy, and thereafter did Ailill earnestly repent, and fell by his enemies. So that man got the Lord's clemency,' said Columcille.

"'As for Feradach,[1] the King of Ossory, moreover, he was a covetous man without a conscience, and if he were to hear that a man in his territory had only one scruple of gold or silver, he would take it to himself by force, and put it in the covers of goblets and crannogues and swords and chessmen. Thereafter there came upon him an unendurable sickness. They collect round him all his treasures, so that he had them in his bed. His enemies came, the Clan Connla, after that, to seize the house on him. His sons,

[1] This story is also told in the "Three Fragments of Irish Annals," p. 9.

too, came to him to carry away the jewels with them [to save them for him].

"'" Do not take them away, my sons," said he, "for I harried many for those treasures, and I desire to harry myself on this side the tomb for them, and that my enemies may bring them away of my good will, so that the Deity may not harry me on the other side."

"'After that his sons departed from him, and he himself made earnest repentance, and died at the hands of his enemies, and gains the clemency of the Lord.'

"'Now as for me myself,' said Aedh, 'shall I gain the Lord's clemency?'

"'Thou shalt not gain it on any account,' said Columcille.

"'Well, then, cleric,' said he, 'procure for me from the Deity that the Leinster men [at least] may not overthrow me.'

"'Well, now, that is difficult for me,' said Columcille, 'for my mother was one of them, and the Leinstermen came to me to Durrow,[1] and made as though they would fast upon me, till I should grant them a sister's son's request, and what they asked of me was that no outside king should ever overthrow them; and I promised them that too, but here is my cowl for thee, and thou shalt not be slain while it is about thee.'"

Less clement is Adamnan depicted in his interview, over a century later, with King Finnachta, who had just been persuaded by St. Molling[2] to remit the Boru tribute (then leviable off Leinster), until *luan*, by which the King unwarily understood Monday, but the more acute saint Doomsday, the word having both significations. Adamnan saw through the deception in a moment, and hastened to interrupt the plans of his brother saint.

"He sought therefore," says the Book of Leinster, "the place where [king] Finnachta was, and sent a clerk of his familia to summon him to a conference. Finnachta, at the instant, busied himself with a game of chess, and the cleric said, 'Come, speak with Adamnan.'

"'I will not,' he answered, 'until this game be ended.'

"The ecclesiastic returned to Adamnan and retailed him this answer. Then the saint said, 'Go and tell him that in the interval

[1] *See* above, p. 170.

[2] For Molling, *see* above, p. 209–10. The following translation is by Standish Hayes O'Grady, "Silva Gadelica," p. 422.

I shall chant fifty psalms, in which fifty is a single psalm that will deprive his children and grandchildren, and even any namesake of his, for ever of the kingdom.'[1]

"Again the clerk accosted Finnachta and told him this, but until his game was played the King never noticed him at all.

"'Come, speak with Adamnan,' repeated the clerk, 'and——'

"'I will not,' answered Finnachta, 'till this [fresh] game, too, shall be finished,' all which the cleric rendered to Adamnan, who said:

"'A second time begone to him, tell him that I will sing other fifty psalms, in which fifty is one that will confer on him shortness of life.'

"This, too, the clerk, when he was come back, proclaimed to Finnachta, but till the game was done, he never even perceived the messenger, who for the third time reiterated his speech.

"'Till this new game be played out I will not go,' said the King, and the cleric carried it to Adamnan.

"'Go to him,' the holy man said, 'tell him that in the meantime I will sing fifty psalms, and among them is one that will deprive him of attaining the Lord's peace.'

"This the clerk imparted to Finnachta, who, when he heard it, with speed and energy put from him the chess-board, and hastened to where Adamnan was.

"'Finnachta,' quoth the saint, 'what is thy reason for coming now, whereas at the first summons thou camest not?'

"'Soon said,' replied Finnachta. 'As for that which first thou didst threaten against me; that of my children, or even of my namesakes, not an individual ever should rule Ireland—I took it easily. The other matter which thou heldest out to me—shortness of life—that I esteemed but lightly, for Molling had promised me heaven. But the third thing which thou threatenedst me—to deprive me of the Lord's peace—that I endured not to hear without coming in obedience to thy voice.'

"Now the motive for which God wrought this was: that the gift which Molling had promised to the King for remission of the tribute He suffered not Adamnan to dock him of."

It would be easy to multiply such scenes from the writings of the ancient Irish. That they are not altogether eleventh or twelfth-century inventions, but either the embodiment of a

[1] For a description of the awful consequences of a saint's curse that make a timid lunatic out of a valliant warrior see O'Donovan's fragmentary "Annals," p. 233.

vivid tradition, or else, in some cases, the working-up of earlier documents, now lost, is, I think, certain, but we possess no criterion whereby we may winnow out the grains of truth from the chaff of myth, invention, or perhaps in some cases (where tribal honour is at stake) deliberate falsehood. The only thing we can say with perfect certainty is that this is the way in which the contemporaries of St. Lawrence O'Toole pictured for themselves the contemporaries of St. Columcille and St. Adamnan.

CHAPTER XIX

THE BARDIC SCHOOLS

We must now, leaving verifiable history behind us, attempt a cautious step backwards from the known into the doubtful, and see what in the way of literature *is said* to have been produced by the pagans. We know that side by side with the colleges of the clergy there flourished, perhaps in a more informal way, the purely Irish schools of the Brehons and the Bards. Unhappily however, while, thanks to the great number of the Lives of the Saints,[1] we know much about the Christian colleges, there is very little to be discovered about the bardic institutions. These were almost certainly a continuation of the schools of the druids, and represented something far more antique than even the very earliest schools of the Christians, but unlike them they were not centred in a fixed locality nor in a cluster of houses, but seem to have been peripatetic. The bardic scholars grouped themselves not round a locality but round a personality, and wherever it pleased their master to wander—and that was pretty much all

[1] O'Clery notices, in his Féilire na Naomh, the lives of thirty-one saints written in Irish, all extant in his time, not to speak of Latin ones. I fancy most of them still survive. Stokes printed nine from the Book of Lismore; Standish Hayes O'Grady four more from various sources.

round Ireland—there they followed, and the people seem to have willingly supported them.

There seems to be some confusion as to the forms into which what must have been originally the druidic school disintegrated itself in the fifth and succeeding centuries, but from it we can see emerging the poet, the Brehon, and the historian, not all at once, but gradually. In the earliest period the functions of all three were often, if not always, united in one single person, and all poets were *ipso facto* judges as well. We have a distinct account of the great occasion upon which the poet lost his privilege of acting as a judge merely because he was a poet. It appears that from the very earliest date the learned classes, especially the "files," had evolved a dialect of their own, which was perfectly dark and obscure to every one except themselves. This was the Béarla Féni, in which so much of the Brehon law and many poems are written, and which continued to be used, to some extent, by poets down to the very beginning of the eighteenth century. Owing to their predilection for this dialect, the first blow, according to Irish accounts, was struck at their judicial supremacy by the hands of laymen, during the reign of Conor mac Nessa, some time before the birth of Christ. This was the occasion when the sages Fercertné and Neidé contended for the office of arch-ollav of Erin, with its beautiful robe of feathers, the Tugen.[1] Their discourse, still extant in at least three MSS. under the title of the "Dialogue of the Two Sages,"[2] was so learned, and they contended with one another in terms so abstruse that, as the chronicler in the Book of Ballymote puts it :—

"Obscure to every one seemed the speech which the poets uttered in that discussion, and the legal decision which they delivered was not clear to the kings and to the other poets.

"'These men alone,' said the kings, 'have their judgment and

---

[1] *See* Cormac's glossary *sub voce.*

[2] *See* "Irische Texte," Dritte Serie, 1 Heft, pp. 187 and 204.

their skill, and their knowledge. In the first place we do not understand what they say.'

"'Well, then,' said Conor, 'every one shall have his share therein from to-day for ever.'"[1]

This was the occasion upon which Conor made the law that the office of poet should no longer carry with it, of necessity, the office of judge, for, says the ancient writer, "poets alone had judicature from the time that Amairgin Whiteknee delivered the first judgment in Erin" until then.

That the Bardic schools, which we know flourished as public institutions with scarcely a break from the Synod of Drumceat in 590 (where regular lands were set apart for their endowment) down to the seventeenth century, were really a continuation of the Druidic schools, and embodied much that was purely pagan in their curricula, is, I think, amply shown by the curious fragments of metrical text-books preserved in the Books of Leinster and Ballymote, in a MS. in Trinity College, and in a MS. in the Bodleian, all four of which have been recently admirably edited by Thurneysen as a continuous text.[2] He has not however ventured upon a translation, for the scholar would be indeed a bold one who in the present state of Celtic scholarship would attempt a complete interpretation of tracts so antique and difficult. That they date, partially at least, from pre-Christian times seems to me certain from their prescribing amongst other things for the poet's course in one of his years of study a knowledge of the magical incantations called *Tenmlaida*, *Imbas forosnai*,[3] and *Dichetal do chennaib na tuaithe*, and making him in another year learn a certain poem or incantation called *Cétnad*, of which the text says that—

"It is used for finding out a theft. One sings it, that is to say, through the right fist on the track of the stolen beast" [observe the antique assumption that the only kind of wealth to be stolen is cattle]

[1] Agallamh an da Suadh.

[2] "Irische Texte," Dritte serie, Heft i.

[3] *See* above, p. 84.

"or on the track of the thief, in case the beast is dead. And one sings it three times on the one [track] or the other. If, however, one does not find the track, one sings it through the right fist, and goes to sleep upon it, and in one's sleep the man who has brought it away is clearly shown and made known. Another virtue [of this lay]: one speaks it into the right palm and rubs with it the quarters of the horse before one mounts it, and the horse will not be overthrown, and the man will not be thrown off or wounded."

Another *Cétnad* to be learned by the poet, in which he desires length of life, is addressed to "the seven daughters ot the sea, who shape the thread of the long-lived children."

Another with which he had to make himself familiar was the *Glam dichinn*,[1] intended to satirise and punish the prince who refused to a poet the reward of his poem. The poet—

"was to fast upon the lands of the king for whom the poem was to be made, and the consent of thirty laymen, thirty bishops"—a Christian touch to make the passage pass muster—"and thirty poets should be had to compose the satire; *and it was a crime to them to prevent it when the reward of the poem was withheld*"—a pagan touch as a make-weight on the other side! "The poet then, in a company of seven, that is, six others and himself, upon whom six poetic degrees had been conferred, namely a *focloc, macfuirmedh, doss, cana, cli, anradh,* and *ollamh,* went at the rising of the sun to a hill which should be situated on the boundary of seven lands, and each of them was to turn his face to a different land, and the *ollamh's* (ollav's) face was to be turned to the land of the king, who was to be satirised, and their backs should be turned to a hawthorn which should be growing upon the top of a hill, and the wind should be blowing from the north, and each man was to hold a perforated stone and a thorn of the hawthorn in his hand, and each man was to sing a verse of this composition for the king—the *ollamh* or chief poet to take the lead with his own verse, and the others in concert after him with theirs; and each then should place his stone and his thorn under the stem of the hawthorn, and if it was they that were in the wrong in the case, the ground of the hill would swallow them, and if it was the king that was in the wrong, the ground would swallow him and his wife, and his son and his steed, and his robes and his hound. The satire of the *macfuirmedh* fell on the hound, the satire

---

[1] See O'Curry's "Manners and Customs," vol. ii. p. 217, and "Irische Texte," Dritte serie, Heft. i. pp. 96 and 125.

of the *focloc* on the robes, the satire of the *doss* on the arms, the satire of the *cana* on the wife, the satire of the *clí* on the son, the satire of the *anrad* on the steed,[1] the satire of the *ollamh* on the king."

These instances that I have mentioned occurring in the books of the poets' instruction, are evidently remains of magic incantations and terrifying magic ceremonies, taken over from the schools and times of the druids, and carried on into the Christian era, for nobody, I imagine, could contend that they had their origin after Ireland had been Christianised.[2] And the occurrence in the poets' text-books of such evidently pagan passages, side by side with allusions to Athairné the poet—a contemporary of Conor mac Nessa, a little before the birth of Christ, Caoilte, the Fenian poet of the third century, Cormac his contemporary, *Laidcend mac Bairchida* about the year 400, and others—seems to me to be fresh proof for the real objective existence of these characters. For if part of the poets' text-books can be thus shown to have preserved things taught in the pre-Christian times—to be in fact actually pre-Christian—why should we doubt the reality of the pre-Christian persons mixed up with them?

The first poem written in Ireland by a Milesian is said to be the curious rhapsody of Amergin, the brother of Eber, Ir, and Erimon, who on landing broke out in a strain of exultation :—

> "I am the wind which breathes upon the sea,
> I am the wave of the ocean,
> I am the murmur of the billows,
> I am the ox of the seven combats,
> I am the vulture upon the rock,
> I am a beam of the sun,

---

[1] It is curious to thus make the steed rank apparently next to the king himself, and above the wife and son, for the *anrad* who curses the steed ranks next to the *ollamh*.

[2] Thurneysen expresses some doubt about the antiquity of the last citation.

I am the fairest of plants,
I am a wild boar in valour,
I am a salmon in the water,
I am a lake in the plain,
I am a word of science,
I am the point of the lance of battle,
I am the god who creates in the head [*i.e.*, of man] the fire [*i.e.*, the thought]
Who is it who throws light into the meeting on the mountain ?
Who announces the ages of the moon [if not I] ?
Who teaches the place where couches the sea [if not I] ?"[1]

There are two more poems attributed to Amergin of much the same nature, very ancient and very strange. Irish tradition has always represented these poems as the first made by our ancestors in Ireland, and no doubt they do actually represent the oldest surviving lines in the vernacular of any country in Europe except Greece alone.

The other pre-Christian poets[2] of whom we hear most, and to whom certain surviving fragments are ascribed, are Feirceirtné, surnamed *filé*, or the poet, who is usually credited with the authorship of the well-known grammatical treatise called *Uraicept na n-Éigeas* or "Primer of the Learned."[3] It was he

[1] See Text I. paragraph 123 of Thurneysen's "Mittelirische Verslehren" for three versions of this curious poem, printed side by side from the Books of Leinster and Ballymote, and a MS. in the Bodleian. The old Irish tract for the instruction of poets gives it as an example of what it calls *Cetal do chendaib.* I have followed D'Arbois de Jubainville's interpretation of it. He sees in it a pantheistic spirit, but Dr. Sigerson has proved, I think quite conclusively, that it is liable to a different interpretation, a panegyric upon the bard's own prowess, couched in enigmatic metaphor. (*See* "Bards of the Gael and Gaul," p. 379.)

[2] A number of names are mentioned—chiefly in connection with law fragments—of kings and poets who lived centuries before the birth of Christ, including an elegy by Lughaidh, son of Ith (from whom the Ithians sprang), on his wife's death, Cimbaeth the founder of Emania, before whose reign Tighearnach the Annalist considered *omnia monumenta Scotorum* to be *incerta*, Roigne, the son of Hugony the Great, who lived nearly three hundred years before Christ, and some others.

[3] The "Uraicept" or "Uraiceacht" is sometimes ascribed to Forchern.

who contended with Neidé for the arch-poet's robe, causing King Conor to decide that no poet should in future be also of necessity a judge. The Uraicept begins with this preface or introduction: "The Book of Feirceirtné here. Its place Emania; its time the time of Conor mac Nessa; its person Feirceirtné the poet; its cause to bring ignorant people to knowledge." There is also a poem attributed to him on the death of Curoi mac Daire, the great southern chieftain, whom Cuchulain slew, and the Book of Invasions contains a valuable poem ascribed to him, recounting how Ollamh Fódla, a monarch who is said to have flourished many centuries before, established a college of professors at Tara.

There was a poet called Adhna, the father of that Neidé with whom Feirceirtné contended for the poet's robe, who also lived at the court of Conor mac Nessa, and his name is mentioned in connection with some fragments of laws.

Athairné, the overbearing insolent satirist from the Hill of Howth, who figures largely in Irish romance, was contemporaneous with these, though I do not know that any poem is attributed to him. But he and a poet called Forchern, with Feirceirtné and Neidé, are said to have compiled a code of laws, now embodied with others under the title of *Breithe Neimhidh* in the Brehon Law Books.

There was a poet Lughar at the Court of Oilioll and Mève in Connacht about the same time, and a poem on the descendants of Fergus mac Róigh [Roy] is ascribed to him, but as he was contemporaneous with that warrior he could not have written about his descendants.

It gives examples of the declensions of nouns and adjectives in Irish, distinguishing feminine nouns from masculine, etc. It gives rules of syntax, and exemplifies the declensions by quotations from ancient poets. A critical edition of it from the surviving manuscripts that contain it in whole or part is a *desideratum*.

There is a prose tract called Moran's Will,[1] ascribed to Moran, a well-known jurist who lived at the close of the first century.

Several other authors, either of short poems or law fragments, are mentioned in the second and third centuries, such as Feradach king of Ireland, Modan, Ciothruadh the poet, Fingin, Oilioll Olum himself, the great king of Munster, to whom are traced so many of the southern families. Fithil, a judge, and perhaps some others, none of whom need be particularised.

At the end of the third century we come upon three or four names of vast repute in Irish history, into whose mouths a quantity of pieces are put, most of which are evidently of later date. These are the great Cormac mac Art himself, the most striking king that ever reigned in pagan Ireland, he who built those palaces on Tara Hill whose ruins still remain; Finn mac Cúmhail his son-in-law and captain; Ossian, Finn's son; Fergus, Ossian's brother; and Caoilte [Cweeltya] mac Ronáin.

The poetry ascribed to Finn mac Cúmhail, Ossian, and the other Fenian singers we will not examine in this place, but we must not pass by one of the most remarkable prose tracts of ancient Ireland with which I am acquainted, the famous treatise ascribed to King Cormac, and well known in Irish literature as the "Teagasg ríogh," or Instruction of a Prince, which is written in a curious style, by way of question and answer. Cairbré, Cormac's son, he who afterwards fell out with and overthrew the Fenians, is supposed to be learning kingly wisdom at his father's feet, and that experienced monarch instructs him in the pagan morality of the time, and gives him all kinds of information and advice. The piece, which is heavily glossed in the Book of Ballymote, on account of the antiquity of the language, is of some length, and is far too interesting to pass by without quoting from it.

[1] Udacht Morain, H. 2, 7, T. C., D.

THE INSTRUCTION OF A PRINCE.

"'O grandson of Con, O Cormac,' said Cairbré, 'what is good for a king.'[1]

"'That is plain,' said Cormac, 'it is good for him to have patience and not to dispute, self-government without anger, affability without haughtiness, diligent attention to history, strict observance of covenants and agreements, strictness mitigated by mercy in the execution of laws. . . . It is good for him [to make] fertile land, to invite ships to import jewels of price across sea, to purchase and bestow raiment, [to keep] vigorous swordsmen for protecting his territories, [to make] war outside his own territories, to attend the sick, to discipline his soldiers . . . let him enforce fear, let him perfect peace, [let him] give much of metheglin and wine, let him pronounce just judgments of light, let him speak all truth, for it is through the truth of a king that God gives favourable seasons.'

"'O grandson of Con, O Cormac,' said Cairbré, 'what is good for the welfare of a country?'

"'That is plain,' said Cormac, 'frequent convocations of sapient and good men to investigate its affairs, to abolish each evil and retain each wholesome institution, to attend to the precepts of the elders; let every assembly be convened according to law, let the law be in the hands of the nobles, let the chieftains be upright and unwilling to oppress the poor,'" etc., etc.

A more interesting passage is the following:—

"'O grandson of Con, O Cormac, what are the duties of a prince at a banqueting-house?'

"'A Prince on Samhan's [now All Souls] Day, should light his lamps, and welcome his guests with clapping of hands, procure comfortable seats, the cupbearers should be respectable and active in the distribution of meat and drink. Let there be moderation of music, short stories, a welcoming countenance, a welcome for the learned, pleasant conversations, and the like, these are the duties of the prince, and the arrangement of the banqueting-house.'"

After this Cairbré puts an important question which was asked often enough during the period of the Brehon law, and

[1] In the original in the Book of Ballymote: "A ua Cuinn a Cormaic, ol coirbre cia is deach [*i.e.*, maith], do Ri. Nin ol cormac [*i.e.*, Ni doiligh liom sin]. As deach [*i.e.*, maith], do eimh ainmne [*i.e.*, foighde] gan deabha [*i.e.*, imreasoin] uallcadi fosdadh [*i.e.*, foasdadh] gan fearg. Soagallamha gan mordhacht," etc. The glosses in brackets are written *above* the words.

which for over a thousand years scarce ever received a different answer. He asks, "For what qualifications is a king elected over countries and tribes of people?"

Cormac in his answer embodies the views of every clan in Ireland in their practical choice of a leader.

"From the goodness of his shape and family, from his experience and wisdom, from his prudence and magnanimity, from his eloquence and bravery in battle, and from the number of his friends."

After this follows a long description of the qualifications of a prince, and Cairbré having heard it puts this question:—"O grandson of Con, what was *thy* deportment when a youth;" to which he receives the following striking answer:

"'I was cheerful at the Banquet of the Midh-chuarta [Mee-cuarta, "house of the circulation of mead"], fierce in battle, but vigilant and circumspect. I was kind to friends, a physician to the sick, merciful towards the weak, stern towards the headstrong. Although possessed of knowledge, I was inclined towards taciturnity.[1] Although strong I was not haughty. I mocked not the old although I was young. I was not vain although I was valiant. When I spoke of a person in his absence I praised, not defamed him, for it is by these customs that we are known to be courteous and civilised (*riaghalach*).'"

There is an extremely beautiful answer given later on by Cormac to the rather simple question of his son:

"'O grandson of Con, what is good for me?'

"'If thou attend to my command,' answers Cormac, 'thou wilt not

---

[1] Compare Henry IV.'s advice to his son, not to make himself too familiar but rather to stand aloof from his companions.

"Had I so lavish of my presence been,
So common-hackneyed in the eyes of men,
So stale and cheap to vulgar company—
Opinion, that did help me to the crown,
Had still kept loyal to possession," etc.

As for Richard his predecessor—

"The skipping king, he ambled up and down
With shallow jesters and rash bavin wits,
Soon kindled, and soon burned; carded his state;
Mingled his royalty with capering fools,' etc.
"Henry IV.," Part I., act iii., scene 2.

mock the old although thou art young, nor the poor although thou art well-clad, nor the lame although thou art agile, nor the blind although thou art clear-sighted, nor the feeble although thou art strong, nor the ignorant although thou art learned. Be not slothful, nor passionate, nor penurious, nor idle, nor jealous, for he who is so is an object of hatred to God as well as to man.' "

" 'O grandson of Con,' asks Cairbré, in another place, 'I would fain know how I am to conduct myself among the wise and among the foolish, among friends and among strangers, among the old and among the young,' and to this question his father gives this notable response.

" 'Be not too knowing nor too simple ; be not proud, be not inactive, be not too humble nor yet haughty ; be not talkative but be not too silent ; be not timid neither be severe. For if thou shouldest appear too knowing thou wouldst be satirised and abused ; if too simple thou wouldst be imposed upon ; if too proud thou wouldst be shunned ; if too humble thy dignity would suffer ; if talkative thou wouldst not be deemed learned ; if too severe thy character would be defamed ; if too timid thy rights would be encroached upon.' "

To the curious question, " O grandson of Con, what are the most lasting things in the world ? " the equally curious and to me unintelligible answer is returned, " Grass, copper, and yew."

Of women, King Cormac, like so many monarchs from Solomon down, has nothing good to say, perhaps his high position did not help him to judge them impartially. At least, to the question, " O grandson of Con, how shall I distinguish the characters of women ? " the following bitter answer is given :

" 'I know them, but I cannot describe them. Their counsel is foolish, they are forgetful of love, most headstrong in their desires, fond of folly, prone to enter rashly into engagements, given to swearing, proud to be asked in marriage, tenacious of enmity, cheerless at the banquet, rejectors of reconciliation, prone to strife, of much garrulity. Until evil be good, until hell be heaven, until the sun hide his light, until the stars of heaven fall, women will remain as we have stated. Woe to him, my son, who desires or serves a bad woman, woe to every one who has got a bad wife ' " !

This Christian allusion to heaven and hell, and some others of the same sort, show that despite a considerable pagan flavouring the tract cannot be entirely the work of King Cormac, though it may very well be the embodiment and extension of an ancient pagan discourse, for, as we have seen, after Christianity had succeeded in getting the upper hand over paganism, a kind of tacit compromise was arrived at, by means of which the bards and *fîlés* and other representatives of the old pagan learning, were allowed to continue to propagate their stories, tales, poems, and genealogies, at the price of incorporating with them a small share of Christian alloy, or, to use a different simile, just as the vessels of some feudatory nations are compelled to fly at the mast-head the flag of the suzerain power. But so badly has the dovetailing of the Christian and the pagan parts been managed in most of the older romances, that the pieces come away quite separate in the hands of even the least skilled analyser, and the pagan substratum stands forth entirely distinct from the Christian accretion.

CHAPTER XX

THE SUGGESTIVELY PAGAN ELEMENT IN IRISH LITERATURE

IT is this easy analysis of early Irish literature into its ante-Christian and its post-Christian elements, which lends to it its absorbing value and interest. For when all spurious accretions have been stripped off, we find in the most ancient Irish poems and sagas, a genuine picture of pagan life in Europe, such as we look for in vain elsewhere.

"The Church," writes Windisch, "adopted towards pagan sagas, the same position that it adopted towards pagan law. . . . I see no sufficient ground for doubting that really genuine pictures of a pre-Christian culture are preserved to us in the individual sagas, pictures which are of course in some places faded, and in others painted over by a later hand." [1]

Again in his notes on the story of Déirdre, he remarks—

"The saga originated in pagan, and was propagated in Christian times, and that too without its seeking fresh nutriment as a rule from Christian elements. But we must ascribe it to the influence of Christianity that what is specifically pagan in Irish saga is blurred

[1] "Ich sehe daher keinen genügenden Grund daran zu zweifeln dass uns in den Einzelsagen wirklich echte Bilder einer *vorchristlichen* Cultur erhalten sind, allerdings Bilder die an einigen Stellen verblasst, an andern von späterer Hand übermalt sind" ("Irische Texte," I., p. 253).

over and forced into the background. And yet there exist many whose contents are plainly mythological. The Christian monks were certainly *not the first* who reduced the ancient sagas to fixed form, but later on they copied them faithfully, and propagated them after Ireland had been converted to Christianity."

Zimmer too has come to the same conclusion.

"Nothing," he writes, "except a spurious criticism which takes for original and primitive the most palpable nonsense of which Middle-Irish writers from the twelfth to the sixteenth century are guilty with regard to their own antiquity, which is in many respects strange and foreign to them: nothing but such a criticism can, on the other hand, make the attempt to doubt of the historical character of the chief persons of the Saga cycles.[1] For we believe that Mève, Conor mac Nessa, Cuchulain, and Finn mac Cúmhail, are exactly as much historical personalities as Arminius, or Dietrich of Bern, or Etzel, and their date is just as well determined as that of the above-mentioned heroes and kings, who are glorified in song by the Germans, even though, in the case of Irish heroes and kings, external witnesses are wanting.'"

M. d'Arbois de Jubainville expresses himself in like terms. "We have no reason," he writes, "to doubt of the reality of the principal *rôle* in this [cycle of Cuchulain];"[2] and of the story of the Boru tribute which was imposed on Leinster about a century later; he writes, "Le récit a pour base des faits réels, quoique certains détails aient été créés par l'imagination;" and again, "Irish epic story, barbarous though it is, is, like Irish law, a monument of a civilisation far superior to that of the most ancient Germans; if the Roman idea of the state was wanting to that civilisation, and, if that defect in it was a radical flaw, still there is an intellectual culture to be found

[1] "Nur eine Afterkritik die den handgreiflichsten Unsinn durch den mittelirische Schreiber des 12–16 Jahrh. sich am eigenem Altherthum versündigen das ihnen in mancher Hinsicht fremd ist für urfängliche Weisheit hält, nun eine solche Kritik kann, umgekehrt den Versuch machen an dem historischen Character der Hauptperson beider Sagenkreise zu zweifeln," etc. ("Kelt-Studien," Heft. II., p. 189).

[2] "Introduction à l'étude de la littérature celtique," p. 217.

there, far more developed than amongst the primitive Germans.' "[1]

"Ireland, in fact," writes M. Darmesteter in his "English Studies," well summing up the legitimate conclusions from the works of the great Celtic scholars, "has the peculiar privilege of a history continuous from the earliest centuries of our era until the present day. She has preserved in the infinite wealth of her literature a complete and faithful picture of the ancient civilisation of the Celts. Irish literature is therefore the key which opens the Celtic world."

But the Celtic world means a large portion of Europe, and the key to unlock the door of its past history is in the Irish manuscripts of saga and poem. Without them the student would have to view the past history of Europe through the distorting glasses of the Greeks and Romans, to whom all outer nations were barbarians, into whose social life they had no motive for inquiring. He would have no other means of estimating what were the feelings, modes of life, manners, and habits, of those great races who possessed so large a part of the ancient world, Gaul, Belgium, North Italy, parts of Germany, Spain, Switzerland, and the British Isles ; who burned Rome, plundered Greece, and colonised Asia Minor. But in the Irish romances and historical sagas, he sees come to light another standard by which to measure. Through this early Irish peep-hole he gets a clear look at the life and manners of the race in one of its strongholds, from which he may conjecture and even assume a good deal with regard to the others.

That the pictures of social life and early society drawn in the Irish romances represent phases not common to the Irish alone, but to large portions of that Celtic race which once owned so much of Europe, may be surmised with some certainty from the way in which characteristics of the Celts barely mentioned by Greek and Roman writers re-appear amongst the Irish in all the intimate detail and fond expansion

[1] Preface to "L'Épopée Celtique en Irlande."

of romance. M. d'Arbois de Jubainville has drawn attention to many such instances.

Posidonius, who was a friend of Cicero, and wrote about a hundred years before Christ, mentions a custom which existed in Gaul in his time of fighting at a feast for the best bit which was to be given to the most valiant warrior. This custom, briefly noticed by Posidonius, might be passed by unnoticed by the ordinary reader, but the Irish one will remember the early romances of his race in which the *curadh-mir* or "heroes bit" so largely figures. He will remember that it is upon this custom that one of the greatest sagas of the Cuchulain cycle, the feast of Bricriu, hinges. Bricriu, the Thersites of the Red Branch, having built a new and magnificent house, determines to invite King Conor and the other chieftains to a feast, for the house was very magnificent.

"The dining hall was built like that of the High-king at Tara. From the hearth to the wall were nine beds, and each of the side walls was thirty-five feet high and covered with ornaments of gilt bronze. Against one of the side walls of that palace was reared a royal bed destined for Conor,[1] king of Ulster, which looked down upon all the others. It was ornamented with carbuncles and precious stones and other gems of great price. The gold and silver and all sorts of jewellery which covered that bed shone with such splendour that the night was as brilliant as the day."

He had prepared a magnificent *curadh-mir* for the feast, consisting of a seven-year old pig, and a seven-year old cow that had been fed on milk and corn and the finest food since their birth, a hundred cakes of corn cooked with honey—and every

[1] This name is written Concobar in the ancient texts, and Conchúbhair in the modern language, pronounced Cun-hoo-ar or Cun-hoor, whence the Anglicised form Conor. The "b" was in early times pronounced, but there are traces of its being dropped as early as the twelfth century, though with that orthographical conservatism which so distinguishes the Irish language, it has been preserved down to the present day. Zimmer says he found it spelt Conchor in the twelfth-century book the Liber Landavensis. From this the form Crochor ("cr" for "cn" as is usual in Connacht) followed, and the name is now pronounced either *Cun-a-char* or *Cruch-oor.*

four cakes took a sack of corn to make them—and a vat or wine large enough to hold three of the warriors of the Ultonians. This magnificent "heroes' bit" he secretly promises to each of three warriors in turn, Laeghaire [Leary], Conall Cearnach, and Cuchulain, hoping to excite a quarrel among them. On the result of his expedient the saga turns.[1]

Again, Cæsar tells us that when he invaded the Gauls they did not fight any longer in chariots, but it is recorded that they did so fight two hundred years before his time, even as the Persians fought against the Greeks, and as the Greeks themselves must have fought in a still earlier age commemorated by Homer. But in the Irish sagas we find this epic mode of warfare in full force. Every great man has his charioteer, they fight from their cars as in Homeric days, and much is told us of both steed, chariot and driver. In the above-mentioned saga of Bricriu's feast it is the charioteers of the three warriors who claim the heroes' bit for their masters, since they are apparently ashamed to make the first move themselves. The charioteer was more than a mere servant. Cuchulain sometimes calls his charioteer friend or master (popa), and on the occasion of his fight with Ferdiad desires him in case he (Cuchulain) should show signs of yielding, to "excite reproach and speak evil to me so that the ire of my rage and anger should grow the more on me, but if he give ground before me thou shalt laud me and praise me and speak good words to me that my courage may be the greater," and this command his friend and charioteer punctually executes.

The chariot itself is in many places graphically de-

[1] The reminiscence of the hero-bit appears to have lingered on in folk memory. A correspondent, Mr. Terence Kelly, from near Omagh, in the county Tyrone, tells me that he often heard a story told by an old shanachie and herb-doctor in that neighbourhood who spoke a half-Scotch dialect of English, in which the hero-bit figured, but it had fallen in magnificence, and was represented as bannocks and butter with some minor delicacies.

scribed. Here is how its approach is pourtrayed in the Táin—

"It was not long," says the chronicler, "until Ferdiad's charioteer heard the noise approaching, the clamour and the rattle, and the whistling, and the tramp, and the thunder, and the clatter and the roar, namely the shield-noise of the light shields, and the hissing of the spears, and the loud clangour of the swords, and the tinkling of the helmet, and the ringing of the armour, and the friction of the arms; the dangling of the missive weapons, the straining of the ropes, and the loud-clattering of the wheels, and the creaking of the chariot, and the trampling of the horses, and the triumphant advance of the champion and the warrior towards the ford approaching him."

In the romance called the "Intoxication of the Ultonians," it is mentioned that they drave so fast in the wake of Cuchulain, that "the iron wheels of the chariots cut the roots of the immense trees." Here is how the romancist describes the advance of such a body upon Tara-Luachra.

"Not long were they there, the two watchers and the two druids, until a full fierce rush of the first band broke hither past the glen. Such was the fury with which they advanced that there was not left a spear on a rack, nor a shield on a spike, nor a sword in an armoury in Tara-Luachra that did not fall down. From every house on which was thatch in Tara-Luachra it fell in immense flakes. One would think that it was the sea that had come over the walls and over the corners of the world upon them. The forms of countenances were changed, and there was chattering of teeth in Tara-Luachra within. The two druids fell in fits and in faintings and in paroxysms, one of them out over the wall and the other over the wall inside."

On another occasion the approach of Cuchulain's chariot is thus described—

"Like a mering were the two dykes which the iron wheels of Cuchulain's chariot made on that day of the sides of the road. Like flocks of dark birds pouring over a vast plain were the blocks and round sods and turves of the earth which the horses would cast away behind them against the . . . of the wind. Like a flock of swans pouring over a vast plain was the foam which they flung before them over the muzzles of their bridles. Like the smoke from a royal hostel was the dust and breath of the dense vapour, because of the vehemence of the driving which Liag, son of Riangabhra, on that day gave to the two steeds of Cuchulain."[1]

Elsewhere the chariot itself is described as "wythe-wickered, two bright bronze wheels, a white pole of bright silver with a veining of white bronze, a very high creaking body, having its firm sloping sides ornamented with *cred* (tin?), a back-arched rich golden yoke, two rich yellow-peaked *alls*, hardened sword-straight axle-spindles." Laeghaire's chariot is described in another piece as "a chariot wythe-wickered, two firm black wheels, two pliant beautiful reins, hardened sword-straight axle-spindles, a new fresh-polished body, a back-arched rich silver-mounted yoke, two rich-yellow peaked *alls* . . . a bird plume of the usual feathers over the body of the chariot."[2]

Descriptions like these are constantly occurring in the Irish tales, and enable us to realise better the heroic period of warfare and to fill up in our imagination many a long-regretted lacuna in our knowledge of primitive Europe.

"Those philosophers," says Diodorus Siculus, a Greek writer of the Augustan age, speaking of the Druids, "like the lyric poets called bards, have a great authority both in affairs of peace and war, friends and enemies listen to them. Also when the two armies are in presence of one another and swords drawn and spears couched, they throw themselves into the midst of the combatants and appease them as though they were charming wild beasts. Thus even amongst the most savage barbarians anger submits to the rule of wisdom, and the god of war pays homage to the Muses."

To show that the manners and customs of the Keltoi or Celts of whom Diodorus speaks were in this respect identical with those of their Irish cousins (or brothers), and to give another instance of the warm light shed by Irish literature upon the early customs of Western Europe I shall convert the abstract

[1] *See* "Revue Celtique," vol. xiv. p. 417, translated by Whitley Stokes.

[2] Leabhar na h-Uidhre, p. 122, col. 2, translated by Sullivan, "Manners and Customs," vol. i. p. ccccl xxviii.

into the concrete by a page or two from an Irish romance, not an old one,[1] but one which no doubt preserves many original traditionary traits. In this story Finn mac Cúmhail or Cool[2] at a great feast in his fort at Allen asks Goll about some tribute which he claimed, and is dissatisfied at the answer of Goll, who may be called the Ajax of the Fenians. After that there arose a quarrel at the feast, the rise of which is thus graphically pourtrayed—

"'Goll,' said Finn, 'you have acknowledged in that speech that you came from the city of Beirbhé to the battle of Cnoca, and that you slew my father there, and it is a bold and disobedient thing of you to tell me that,' said Finn.

"'By my hand, O Finn,' said Goll, 'if you were to dishonour me as your father did, I would give you the same payment that I gave Cool.'

"'Goll,' said Finn, 'I would be well able not to let that word pass with you, for I have a hundred valiant warriors in my following for every one that is in yours.'

"'Your father had that also,' said Goll, 'and yet I avenged my dishonour on him, and I would do the same to you if you were to deserve it of me.'

"White-skinned Carroll O Baoisgne[3] spake, and 't is what he said: 'O Goll,' said he, 'there is many a man,' said he, 'to silence you and your people in the household of Finn mac Cúmhail.'

"Bald cursing Conan mac Morna spake, and 't is what he said, 'I swear by my arms of valour,' said he, 'that Goll, the day he has least men, has a man and a hundred in his household, and not a man of them but would silence you.'

"'Are you one of those, perverse, bald-headed Conan?' said Carroll.

"'I am one of them, black-visaged, nail-torn, skin-scratched, little-strength Carroll,' says Conan, 'and I would soon prove it to you that Cúmhail was in the wrong.'

---

[1] In Irish Fionn mac Cúmhail, pronounced "Finn (or Fewn in Munster), mac Coo-wil" or "Cool."

[2] I translated this from manuscript in my possession made by one Patrick O'Pronty (an ancestor, I think, of Charlotte Brontë) in 1763. Mr. Standish Hayes O'Grady has since published a somewhat different text of it.

[3] Pronounced "Bweesg-na," the triphthong *aoi* is always pronounced like *ee* in Irish.

"It was then that Carroll arose, and he struck a daring fist, quick and ready, upon Conan, and there was no submission in Conan's answer, for he struck the second fist on Carroll in the middle of his face and his teeth."

Upon this the chronicler relates how first one joined in and then another, until at last all the adherents of Goll and Finn and even the captains themselves are hard at work. "After that," he adds, "bad was the place for a mild, smooth-fingered woman or a weak or infirm person, or an aged, long-lived elder." This terrific fight continued "from the beginning of the night till the rising of the sun in the morning," and was only stopped—just as Diodorus says battles were stopped—by the intervention of the bards.

"It was then," says the romancist, "that the prophesying poet of the pointed words, that guerdon-full good man of song, Fergus Finnbheóil, rose up, and all the Fenians' men of science along with him, and they sang their hymns and good poems, and their perfect lays to those heroes to silence and to soften them. It was then they ceased from their slaughtering and maiming, on hearing the music of the poets, and they let their weapons fall to earth, and the poets took up their weapons and they went between them, and grasped them with the grasp of reconciliation."

When the palace was cleared out it was found that 1,100 of Finn's people had been killed between men and women, and eleven men and fifty women of Goll's party.

Cæsar speaks of the numbers who frequented the schools of the druids in Gaul; "it is said," he adds, "that they learn there a great number of verses, and that is why some of those pupils spend twenty years in learning. It is not, according to the druids, permissible to entrust verses to writing although they use the Greek alphabet in all other affairs public and private." Of this prohibition to commit their verses to paper, we have no trace, so far as I know, in our literature, but the accounts of the early bardic schools entirely bear out the description here given of them by Cæsar, and again shows the solidarity of custom which seems to have existed between the various Celtic tribes. According to our early manuscripts it took from nine to twelve years for a student to take the highest degree at the bardic schools, and in many cases where the pupil failed to master sufficiently the subjects of the year, he had probably to spend two over it, so that it is quite possible that some might spend twenty years over their learning. And much of this learning was, as Cæsar notes, in verse. Many earlier law tracts appear to have been so, and even many of the earliest romances. There is a very interesting account extant called the "Proceedings of the Great Bardic Association," which leads up to the Epic of the Táin Bó Cuailnge, the greatest of the Irish romances, according to which this great tale was at one time lost, and the great Bardic Institution was commanded to hunt for and recover it. The fact of it being said that the perfect tale was lost for ever "and that only a fragmentary and broken form of it would go down to posterity" perhaps indicates, as has been pointed out by Sullivan, "that the filling up the gaps in the poem by prose narrative is meant." In point of fact the tale, as we have it now, consists half of verse and half of prose. Nor is this peculiar to the Táin. Most of the oldest and many of the modern tales are composed in this way. In most cases the verse is of a more archaic character and more difficult than the prose. In very many an expanded prose narrative of several pages is followed by a more condensed poem saying the same thing. So much did the Irish at last come to look upon it as a matter of course that every romance should be interspersed with poetry, that even writers of the seventeenth and eighteenth centuries who consciously invented their stories as a modern novelist invents his, have interspersed their pieces with passages, in verse, as did Comyn in his Turlough mac Stairn, as did the author of the Son of Ill-counsel, the author of the Parliament of Clan Lopus, the author of the Women's Parliament, and others. We may take it, then, that in the earliest days the romances were composed in verse and learned by heart by the students

—possibly before any alphabet was known at all; afterwards when lacunæ occurred through defective memory on the part of the reciter he filled up the gaps with prose. Those who committed to paper our earliest tales wrote down as much of the old poetry as they could recollect or had access to, and wrote the connecting narrative in prose. Hence it soon came to pass that if a story pretended to any antiquity it had to be interspersed with verses, and at last it happened that the Irish taste became so confirmed to this style of writing that authors adopted it, as I have said, even in the seventeenth and eighteenth centuries.

In spite of the mythological and phantastic elements which are undoubtedly mingled with the oldest sagas,

"the manners and customs in which the men of the time lived and moved, are depicted," writes Windisch,[1] "with a naïve realism which leaves no room for doubt as to the former actuality of the scenes depicted. In matter of costume and weapons, eating and drinking, building and arrangement of the banqueting-hall, manners observed at the feast, and much more, we find here the most valuable information." "I insist upon it," he says in another place, "that Irish saga is the only richly-flowing source of unbroken Celtism."

All the remaining linguistic monuments of Breton, Cornish, and Welsh, "would form," writes M. d'Arbois de Jubainville,

"un ensemble bien incomplet et bien obscur sans la lumière que la littérature irlandaise projette sur ces débris. C'est le vieil irlandais qui forme le trait d'union pour ainsi dire entre les dialectes neo-celtiques de la fin du moyen âge ou des temps modernes, et le Gaulois des inscriptions lapidaires, des monnaies, des noms propres conservés par la littérature grecque et la littérature romaine." [2]

It may, then, be finally acknowledged that those of the great nations of to-day, whose ancestors were mostly Celts, but whose language, literature, and traditions have completely disappeared, must, if they wish to study their own past, turn

[1] "Irische Texte," I., p. 252.

[2] "Études grammaticales sur les langues Celtiques," 1881, p. vii.

themselves first to Ireland. When we find so much of the brief and scanty information given us by the classics, not only borne out, but amply illustrated by old Irish literature, when we find the dry bones of Posidonius and Cæsar rise up again before us with a ruddy covering of flesh and blood, it is not too much to surmise that in other matters also the various Celtic races bore to each other a close resemblance.

Much more could be said upon this subject, as that the four Gallo-Roman inscriptions to Brigantia found in Great Britain are really to the Goddess Brigit;[1] that the Brennus who burned Rome 390 years before Christ and the Brennus who stormed Delphi 110 years later were only the god Brian, under whose tutelage the Gauls marched; and that Lugudunum, Lugh's Dún or fortress, is so-called from the god Lugh the Long-handed, to whom two Celtic inscriptions are found, one in Spain and one in Switzerland, as may be seen set forth at length in the volumes of Monsieur d'Arbois de Jubainville.

[1] *See* above pp. 53 and 161.

CHAPTER XXI

THE OLDEST BOOKS AND POEMS

THE books of saga, poetry, and annals that have come down to our day, though so vastly more ancient and numerous than anything that the rest of Western Europe has to show, are yet an almost inappreciable fragment of the literature that at one time existed in Ireland. The great native scholar O'Curry, who possessed a unique and unrivalled knowledge of Irish literature in all its forms, has drawn up a list of lost books which may be supposed to have contained our earliest literature.

We find the poet Senchan Torpéist—according to the account in the Book of Leinster, a manuscript which dates from about the year 1150—complaining that the only perfect record of the great Irish epic, the Táin Bó Cuailnge[1] or Cattle-spoil of Cooley, had been taken to the East with the Cuilmenn,[2] or Great Skin Book. Now Zimmer, who made a special and minute study of this story, considers that the earliest redaction of the Táin dates from the seventh century.

[1] Pronounced "Taun Bo Hoo-il-n'ya." The "a" in Táin is pronounced nearly like the "a" in the English word "Tarn."

[2] Cuilmenn—it has been remarked, I think, by Kuno Meyer—seems cognate with Colmméne, glossed *nervus*, and Welsh *cwlm*, "a knot or tie." It is found glossed *lebar*—*i.e.*, leabhar, or "book."

This legend about Senchan—a real historical poet whose eulogy in praise of Columcille, whether genuine or not, was widely popular—is probably equally old, and points to the early existence of a great skin book in which pagan tales were written, but which was then lost. The next great book is the celebrated Saltair of Tara, which is alluded to in a genuine poem of Cuan O'Lochain about the year 1000, in which he says that Cormac mac Art drew up the Saltair of Tara. Cormac, being a pagan, could not have called the book a Saltair or Psalterium, but it may have got the name in later times from its being in metre. All that this really proves, however, is that there then existed a book about the prerogatives of Tara and the provincial kings so old that Cuan O'Lochain—no doubt following tradition—was not afraid to ascribe it to Cormac mac Art who lived in the third century. The next lost book is called the Book of the Uacongbhail, upon which both the O'Clerys in their Book of Invasions and Keating in his history drew, and which, according to O'Curry, still existed at Kildare so late as 1626. The next book is called the Cin of Drom Snechta. It is quoted in the Leabhar na h-Uidhre, or "Book of the Dun Cow"—a MS. of about the year 1100—and often in the Book of Ballymote and by Keating, who in quoting it says, "And it was before the coming of Patrick to Ireland that that book existed,"[1] and the Book of Leinster ascribes it to the son of a king of Connacht who died either in 379 or 499. The next books of which we find mention were said to have belonged to St. Longarad, a contemporary of St. Columcille. The scribe who wrote the glosses on the Féilirè of Angus the Culdee, said that the books existed still in his day, but that nobody could read them; for which he accounts by the tale that Columcille once paid Longarad a visit in order to see his books, but that his host refused to show them, and that Columcille then said, "May your books be of no use after you, since

[1] For the authorship of this book see above, p. 71.

you have exercised inhospitality about them." On account of this the books became illegible after Longarad's death. Angus the Culdee lived about the year 800, but Stokes ascribes the Féilĭrè to the tenth century; a view, however, which Mr. Strachan's studies on the Irish deponent verb, which is of such frequent occurrence in the Féilĭrè, may perhaps modify. At what time the scholiast wrote his note on the text is uncertain, but it also is very old. It is plain, then, that at this time a number of illegible books—illegible no doubt from age—existed; and to account for this illegibility the story of Columcille's curse was invented. The Annals of Ulster quote another book at the year 527 under the name of the Book of St. Mochta, who was a disciple of St. Patrick. They also quote the Book of Cuana at the year 468 and repeatedly afterwards down to the year 610, while they record the death of Cuana, a scribe, at the year 738, after which no more quotations from Cuana's book occur.

The following volumes, almost all of which existed prior to the year 1100, are also alluded to in our old literature:—The Book of Dubhdaleithe; the Yellow Book of Slane; the original Leabhar na h-Uidhre, or "Book of the Dun Cow"; the Books of Eochaidh O'Flanagain; a certain volume known as the book eaten by the poor people in the desert; the Book of Inis an Dúin; the short Book of Monasterboice; the Books of Flann of Monasterboice; the Book of Flann of Dungiven; the Book of Downpatrick; the Book of Derry; the Book of Sábhal Patrick; the Black Book of St. Molaga; the Yellow Book of St. Molling; the Yellow Book of Mac Murrough; the Book of Armagh (not the one now so called); the Red Book of Mac Egan; the Long Book of Leithlin; the Books of O'Scoba of Clonmacnois; the "Duil" of Drom Ceat; the Book of Clonsost; the Book of Cluain Eidhneach (the ivy meadow) in Leix; and one of the most valuable and often quoted of all, Cormac's great Saltair of Cashel, compiled by Cormac mac Culinan, who was at once king of Munster and archbishop of Cashel,[1] and who fell in battle in 903, according to the chronology of the "Four Masters." The above are certainly only a few of the books in which a large early literature was contained, one that has now perished almost to a page. Michael O'Clery, in the Preface to his Book of Invasions written in 1631, mentions the books from which he and his four antiquarian friends compiled their work—mostly now perished!—and adds:—

"The histories and synchronisms of Erin were written and tested in the presence of those illustrious saints, as is manifest in the great books that are named after the saints themselves and from their great churches; for there was not an illustrious church in Erin that had not a great book of history named from it or from the saints who sanctified it. It would be easy, too, to know from the books which the saints wrote, and the songs of praise which they composed in Irish that they themselves and their churches were the centres of the true knowledge, and the archives and homes of the manuscripts of the authors of Erin in the elder times. But, alas! short was the time until dispersion and decay overtook the churches of the saints,

---

[1] "At what time this book was lost," says O'Curry, "we have no precise knowledge, but that it existed, though in a dilapidated state, in the year 1454 is evident from the fact that there is in the Bodleian Library at Oxford (Laud 610) a copy of such portions of it as could be deciphered at that time, made by Shawn O'Clery for Mac Richard Butler. From the contents of this copy and from the frequent references to the original for history and genealogies found in the Books of Ballymote, Lecan, and others, it must have been an historical and genealogical compilation of large size and great diversity."

A legible copy of the Saltair appears, however, to have existed at a much later date. I discovered a curious poem in an uncatalogued MS. in the Royal Irish Academy by one David Condon, written apparently at some time between the Cromwellian and Williamite wars, in which he says—

"Saltair Chaisill is dearbh gur léigheas-sa
Leabhar ghleanna-dá-locha gan gó ba léir dam,
Leabhar Buidhe Mhuigleann (?) obair aosta," &c.

I.e., "Surely I have read the Saltair of Cashel, and the Book of Glendaloch was certainly plain to me, and the Yellow Book of Mulling (?) (*see* above, p. 210), an ancient work, the Book of Molaga, and the lessons of Cionnfaola, and many more (books) along with them which are not (now) found in Ireland."

their relics, and their books; for there is not to be found of them now [1631] but a small remnant that has not been carried away into distant countries and foreign nations—carried away so that their fate is unknown from that time unto this."

As far as actual existing documents go, we have no specimens of Irish MSS. written in Irish before the eighth century. The chief remains of the old language that we have are mostly found on the Continent, whither the Irish carried their books in great numbers, and unfortunately they are not books of saga, but chiefly, with the exception of a few poems, glosses and explanations of books used evidently in the Irish ecclesiastical schools.[1] A list of the most remarkable is worth giving here, as it will help to show the extraordinary geographical diversity of the Irish settlements upon the Continent, and the keenness with which their relics have been studied by European scholars—French, German, and Italian. The most important are the glosses found in the Irish MSS. of Milan, published by Ascoli, Zeuss, Stokes, and Nigra; those in St. Gall—a monastery in Switzerland founded by St. Gall, an Irish friend of Columbanus, in the sixth century—published by Ascoli and Nigra; those in Wurtzburg, published by Zimmer and Zeuss; those in Carlsruhe, published by Zeuss; those in Turin, published by Zimmer, Nigra, and Stokes in his "Goidelica"; those in Vienna, published by Zimmer in his "Glossæ Hibernicæ" and Stokes in his "Goidelica"; those in Berne, those in Leyden, those in Nancy, and the glosses on the Cambrai Sermon, published by Zeuss.[2] Next in antiquity to these are the Irish parts of the Book of Armagh, the poems in the MSS. of St.

[1] Such, for example, is the fragment of a commentary on the Psalter published by Kuno Meyer in "Hibernica Minora," from Rawlinson, B. 512. The original is assigned by him, judging from its grammatical forms, to about the year 750. It is very ample and diffuse, and tells about the Shophetîm, or Sophtim, as the writer calls it, the Didne Haggamîm, etc., and is an excellent example of the kind of Irish commentaries used by the early ecclesiastics.

[2] "Gram. Celt.," p. 1004–7.

Gall and Milan,[1] and some of the pieces published by Windisch in his "Irische Texte." Next to this is probably the Martyrology of Angus the Culdee. And then come the great Middle-Irish books—the Leabhar na h-Uidhre, the Book of Leinster, and the rest.

From a palæographic point of view the oldest books in Ireland are probably the "Domhnach Airgid," a copy of the Four Gospels in a triple shrine of yew, silver-plated copper, and gold-plated silver, which St. Patrick was believed to have given to St. Carthainn when he told that saint with a shrewd wisdom, which in later days aroused the admiration of Mr. Matthew Arnold, to build himself a church "that should not be too near to himself for familiarity nor too far from himself for intercourse." It probably dates from the fifth or sixth century. The Cathach supposed to have been surreptitiously written by Columcille from Finnian's book[2]—a Latin copy of the Gospels in Trinity College, Dublin; the Book of Durrow, a beautiful illuminated copy of the same; the Book of Dimma, containing the Four Gospels, ritual, and prayers, probably a work of the seventh century; the Book of Molling, of probably about the same date; the Gospels of Mac Regol, the largest of the Old Irish Gospel books, highly but not elegantly coloured, with an interlinear Anglo-Saxon version in a late hand carried through its pages; the Book of Kells, the unapproachable glory of Irish illumination, and some other ecclesiastical books. After them come the Leabhar na h-Uidre and the great books of poems and saga.

Although the language of these sagas and poems is not that of the glosses, but what is called "Middle-Irish," still it does not in the least follow that the poems and sagas belong to the Middle-Irish period. "The old Middle-Irish manuscripts," says Zimmer, "contain for the most part only Old Irish texts re-written." [3] "Unfortunately," says Windisch, "every new

[1] Published by Zeuss in his "Grammatica Celtica."

[2] *See* above, p. 175. [3] "Keltische Studien," Heft i. p. 88.

copyist has given to the text more or less of the linguistic garb of his own day, so that as far as the language of Irish texts goes, it depends principally upon the age of the manuscript that contains them."[1] And again, in his preface to Adamnan's vision, he writes: "Since we know that Irish texts were rewritten by every fresh copyist more or less regularly in the speech of his own day, the real age or a prose text cannot possibly be determined by the linguistic forms of its language."[2] It is much easier to tell the age of poetry than prose, for the gradual modification of language, altering of words, shortening of inflexions, and so on, must interfere with the metre, so that when we find a poem in a twelfth-century manuscript written in Middle Irish and in a perfect metrical form, we may—no matter to what age it is *ascribed*—be pretty sure that it cannot be more than two or three centuries older than the manuscript that contains it. Yet even of the poems Dr. Atkinson writes: "The poem *may* be of the eighth century, but the forms are in the main of the twelfth."[3] Where poems that really are of ancient date have had their language modified in transcription so as to render them intelligible, the metre is bound to suffer, and this lends us a criterion whereby to gauge the age of verse, which is lacking to us when we come to deal with prose.

This modification of language is not uncommon in literature and takes place naturally, but I doubt if there ever was a literature in which it played the same important part as in Irish. Thus let us take the story of the Táin Bó Cuailnge, of which I shall have more to say later on. Zimmer, after long and careful study of the text as preserved to us in a manuscript of about the year 1100, came to the conclusion from the marks of Old Irish inflexion, and so forth, which still remain in the eleventh-century text, that there had been two recensions of

[1] Preface to Loinges Mac n-Usnig, "Irische Texte," i. 61.

[2] "Irische Texte," i. p. 167.

[3] Preface to the list of contents of the *facsimile* Book of Leinster.

the story, a pre-Danish, that is, say, a seventh-century one, and a post-Danish, that is a tenth- or eleventh-century one. Thus the epic may have been originally committed to paper in the seventh century, modified in the tenth, transcribed into the manuscripts in which we have it in the eleventh and twelfth, and propagated from that down to the eighteenth century, in copies every one of which underwent more or less alteration in order to render it more intelligible; and it was in fact in an eighteenth-century manuscript, yet one that differed, as I subsequently discovered, in few essentials from the copy in the Book of Leinster that I first read it. As the bards lived to please so they had to please to live. The popular mind only receives with pleasure and transmits with readiness popular poetry upon the condition that it is intelligible,[1] and hence granting that Finn mac Cool was a real historical personage, it is perfectly possible that some of his poetry was handed down from generation to generation amongst the conservative Gael, and slightly altered or modified from time to time to make it more intelligible, according as words died out and inflexions became obsolete. The Oriental philologist, Max Müller, in attempting to explain how myths arose (according to his theory) from a disease of language, thinks that during the transition period of which he speaks, there would be many words "understood perhaps by the grandfather, familiar to the father, but strange to the son, and misunderstood by the grandson." This is exactly what is taking place over half Ireland at this very moment, and it is what has always been at work amongst a people whose language and literature go back with certainty for nearly 1,500 years. Accordingly before the art of writing became common, ere yet expensive vellum MSS. and a highly-

[1] With the exception of the ancient Irish prayers like Mairinn Phádraig, preserved by tradition, which are for the most part not intelligible to the reciters, but which owe their preservation to the promise usually tacked on at the end that the reciters shall receive some miraculous or heavenly blessing. *See* my "Religious Songs of Connacht."

paid class of historians and schools of scribes to a certain extent stereotyped what they set down, it is altogether probable that people who trusted to the ear and to memory, modified and corrupted but still handed down, at least some famous poems, like those ascribed to Amergin or Finn mac Cool. That the Celtic memory for things unwritten is long I have often proved. I have heard from peasants stanzas composed by Donogha Mór O'Daly, of Boyle, in the thirteenth century; I have recovered from an illiterate peasant, in 1890 in Roscommon, verses which had been jotted down in phonetic spelling in Argyleshire by Macgregor, Dean of Lismore, in the year 1512, and which may have been sung for hundreds of years before it struck the fancy of the Highland divine to commit them to paper;[1] and I have again heard verses in which the measure and sense were preserved, but found on comparing them with MSS. that several obsolete words had been altered to others that rhymed with them and were intelligible.[2] For these reasons I should, in many cases, refuse absolutely to reject the authenticity of a poem simply because the language is more modern than that of the bard could have been to whom it is ascribed, and it seems to me equally uncritical either to accept or reject much of our earliest poetry, except what is in highly-developed metre, as a good deal of it may possibly be the actual (but linguistically modified) work of the supposed authors.

This modifying process is something akin to but very different in degree from Pope's rewriting of Donne's satires or Dryden's version of Chaucer, inasmuch as it was probably both unconscious and unintentional. To understand better how this modification may have taken place, let us examine a

[1] *See* my note on the Story of Oscar au fléau, in "Revue Celtique," vol. xiii. p. 425.

[2] Cf. my note on Bran's colour, at p. 277 of my "Beside the Fire."

few lines of the thirteenth-century English poem, the "Brut" of Layamon :—

"And swa ich habbe al niht
Of mine swevene swithe ithoht,
For ich what to iwisse
Agan is al my blisse."

These lines were, no doubt, intelligible to an ordinary Englishman at the time. Gradually they become a little modernised, thus :—

"And so I have all night
Of min-e sweeven swith ythought,
For I wat to ywiss
Agone is all my bliss."

Had these verses been preserved in folk-memory they must have undergone a still further modification as soon as the words sweeven (dream), swith (much), and ywiss (certainty) began to grow obsolete, and we should have the verse modified and mangled, perhaps something in this way :—

"And so I have all the night
Of my dream greatly thought,
For I wot and I wis
That gone is all my bliss."

The words "I wot and I wis," in the third line, represent just about as much archaism as the popular memory and taste will stand without rebelling. Some modification in the direction here hinted at may be found in, I should think, more than half the manuscripts in the Royal Irish Academy to-day, and just in the same sense as the lines,

"For I wot and I wis
That gone is my bliss,"

are Layamon's ; so we may suppose,

"Dubthach missi mac do Lugaid
Laidech lantrait

Mé ruc inmbreith etir Loegaire
Ocus Patraic," [1]

to be the fifth century O'Lugair's, or

" Leathaid folt fada fraich,
Forbrid canach fann finn," [2]

to be Finn mac Cúmhail's.

Of the many *poems*—as distinguished from sagas, which are a mixture of poetry and prose—said to have been produced from pagan times down to the eighth century, none can be properly called epics or even épopées. There are few continued efforts, and the majority of the pieces though interesting for a great many reasons to students, would hardly interest an English reader when translated. Unfortunately, such a great amount of our early literature being lost, we can only judge of what it was like through the shorter pieces which have been preserved, and even these short pieces read rather jejune and barren in English, partly because of the great condensation of the original, a condensation which was largely brought about by the necessity of versification in difficult metres. In order to see beauty in the most ancient Irish verse it is absolutely necessary to read it in the original so as to perceive and appreciate the alliteration and other *tours de force* which appear in every line. These verses, for instance, which Mève, daughter of Conan, is said to have pronounced over Cuchorb, her hus-

[1] In more modern Irish :—

" Dubhthach mise, mac do Lughaidh
Laoi-each lán-traith
Mé rug an bhreith idir Laoghaire
Agus Pádraig."

I.e., " I am Dubhthach, son of Lewy the lay-full, full-wise. It is I who delivered judgment between Leary and Patrick." *Traith* is the only obsolete word here.

[2] In modern Irish, " Leathnuighidh folt fada fraoch," *i.e.*, "Leathnuighidh fraoch folt fada, foirbridh (fásaidh) canach (ceannabhán) fann fionn," *i.e.*, " Spreads heath its long hair, flourishes the feeble, fair cotton-grass."

band, in the first century, appear bald enough in a literal translation :—

" Moghcorb's son whom fame conceals [covers]
Well sheds he blood by his spears,
A stone over his grave—'tis a pity—
Who carried battle over Cliú Máil.

My noble king, he spoke not falsehood,
His success was certain in every danger,
As black as a raven was his brow,
As sharp was his spear as a razor," etc.

One might read this kind of thing for ever in a translation without being struck by anything more than some occasional *curiosa felicitas* of phrase or picturesque expression, and one would never suspect that the original was so polished and complicated as it really is. Here are these two verses done into the exact versification of the original, in which interlinear vowel-rhymes, alliterations, and all the other requirements of the Irish are preserved and marked :—

" Mochorb's son of Fiercest FAME,
KNown his NAME for bloody toil,
To his Gory Grave is GONE,
He who SHONE o'er SHouting Moyle.

Kindly King, who Liked not LIES,
Rash to RISE to Fields of Fame,
Raven-Black his Brows of FEAR,
Razor-Sharp his SPEAR of flame," etc.[1]

This specimen of Irish metre may help to place much of our poetry in another light, for its beauty depends less upon the intrinsic substance of the thought than the external elegance

[1] Here is the first verse of this in the original. The Old Irish is nearly unintelligible to a modern. I have here modernised the spelling :—

" Mac Mogachoirb Cheileas CLÚ
Cun fearas CRÚ thar a gháibh
Ail uas a Ligi—budh LIACH—
Baslaide CHLIATH thar Cliú Máil."

The rhyming words do not make perfect rhyme as in English, but pretty nearly so—*clu cru, liath cliath, gáibh máil.*

of the framework. We must understand this in order to do justice to our versified literature, for the student must not imagine that he will find long-sustained epics or interesting narrative poems after the manner of the Iliad or Odyssey, or even the Nibelungenlied, or the "Song of Roland;" none such now exist: if they did exist they are lost. The early poems consist rather of eulogies, elegies, historical pieces, and lyrics, few of them of any great length, and still fewer capable of interesting an English reader in a translation. Occasionally we meet with touches of nature poetry of which the Gael has always been supremely fond. Here is a tentative translation made by O'Donovan of a part of the first poem which Finn mac Cúmhail is said to have composed after his eating of the salmon of knowledge:—

"May-Day, delightful time! How beautiful the colour; the blackbirds sing their full lay; would that Laighaig were here! The cuckoos sing in constant strains. How welcome is ever the noble brilliance of the seasons! On the margin of the branching woods the summer swallows skim the stream. The swift horses seek the pool. The heath spreads out its long hair, the weak, fair bog-down grows. Sudden consternation attacks the signs, the planets, in their courses running, exert an influence; the sea is lulled to rest, flowers cover the earth."

The language of this poem is so old as to be in parts unintelligible, and the broken metre points to the difficulties of transmission over a long period of time, yet he would be a bold man who would ascribe with certainty the authorship of it to Finn mac Cúmhail in the third century, or the elegy on Cuchorb to Mève, daughter of Conan, a contemporary of Virgil and Horace. And yet all the history of these people is known and recorded with much apparent plausibility and many collateral circumstances connecting them with the men of their time. How much of this is genuine historical tradition? How much is later invention? It is difficult to decide at present.

CHAPTER XXII

EARLY SAGA AND ROMANCE

During the golden period of the Greek and Roman genius no one ever wrote a romance. Epics they left behind them, and history, but the romance, the Danish saga, the Irish *sgeul* or *úrsgeul* was unknown. It was in time of decadence that a body of Greek prose romance appeared, and with the exception of Petronius' semi-prose "Satyricon," and Apuleius' "Golden Ass," the Latin language produced in this line little of a higher character than such works as the Gesta Romanorum. In Greece and Italy where the genial climate favoured all kinds of open-air representations, the great development of the drama took the place of novelistic literature, as it did for a long time amongst the English after the Elizabethan revival. In Ireland, on the other hand, the dramatic stage was never reached at all, but the development of the *úrsgeul*, romance, or novel, was quite abnormally great. I have seen it more than once asserted, if I mistake not, that the dramatic is an inevitable and an early development in the history of every literature, but this is to generalise from insufficient instances. The Irish literature which kept on developing—to some extent at least—for over a thousand years, and of which hundreds of volumes still exist, never evolved a drama, nor so much, as far as I know, as even a miracle play, although these are found in Welsh and even Cornish. What Ireland did produce, and produce nobly and well, was romance; from the first to the last, from the seventh to the seventeenth century, Irishmen, without distinction of class, alike delighted in the *úrsgeul.*

When this form of literature first came into vogue we have no means of ascertaining, but the narrative prose probably developed at a very early period as a supplement to defective narrative verse. Not that verse or prose were then and there committed to writing, for it is said that the business of the bards was to learn their stories by heart. I take it, however, that they did not actually do this, but merely learned the incidents of a story in their regular sequence, and that their training enabled them to fill these up and clothe them on the spur of the moment in the most effective garments, decking them out with passages of gaudy description, with rattling alliterative lines and "runs" and abundance of adjectival declamation. The bards, no matter from what quarter of the island, had all to know the same story or novel, provided it was a renowned one, but with each the sequence of incidents, and the incidents themselves were probably for a long time the same; but the language in which they were tricked out and the length to which they were spun depended probably upon the genius or bent of each particular bard. Of course in process of time divergences began to arise, and hence different versions of the same story. That, at least, is how I account for such passages as "but others say that it was not there he was killed, but in," etc., "but some of the books say that it was not on this wise it happened, but," and so on.

It is probable that very many novels were in existence before the coming of St. Patrick, but highly unlikely that they were at that time written down at full length. It was probably only after the country had become Christianised and full of schools and learning that the bards experienced the desire of writing down their sagas, with as much as they could recapture of the ancient poetry upon which they were built. In the Book of

Leinster, a manuscript of the twelfth century, we find an extraordinary list of no less than 187 of those romances with THREE HUNDRED AND FIFTY of which an ollamh had to be acquainted. The ollamh was the highest dignitary amongst the bards, and it took him from nine to twelve years' training to learn the two hundred and fifty prime stories and the one hundred secondary ones along with the other things which were required of him. The prime stories—combinations of epic and novel, prose and poetry—are divided in the manuscripts into the following romantic catalogue :—Destructions of fortified places, Cow spoils (*i.e.*, cattle-raiding expeditions), Courtships or wooings, Battles, Cave-stories, Navigations, Tragical deaths, Feasts, Sieges, Adventures, Elopements, Slaughters, Water-eruptions, Expeditions, Progresses, and Visions. "He is no poet," says the Book of Leinster, "who does not synchronise and harmonise all the stories." We possess, as I have said, the names of 187 such stories in the Book of Leinster, and the names of many more are given in the tenth- or eleventh-century tale of Mac Coisè ; and all the known ones, with the exception of one tale added later on, and one which, evidently through an error in transcription, refers to Arthur instead of Aithirne, are about events prior to the year 650 or thereabouts. We may take it, then, that this list was drawn up in the seventh century.

Now, who were the authors of these couple of hundred romances ? It is a natural question, but one which cannot be answered. There is not a trace of their authorship remaining, if authorship be the right word for what I suspect to have been the gradual growth of race, tribal, and family history, and of Celtic mythology, told and retold, and polished up, and added to ; some of them, especially such as are the descendants of a pagan mythology, must have been handed down for perhaps countless generations, others recounted historical, tribal, or family doings, magnified during the course of time, others again of more recent date, are perhaps fairly accurate accounts of actual events, but all PRIOR TO ABOUT THE YEAR 650. I take it that so soon as bardic schools and colleges began to be formed, there was no class of learning more popular than that which taught the great traditionary stories of the various tribes and families of the great Gaelic race, and the intercommunication between the bardic colleges propagated local tradition throughout all Ireland.

The very essence of the national life of Erin was embodied in these stories, but, unfortunately, few out of the enormous mass have survived to our day, and these mostly mutilated or in mere digests. Some, however, exist at nearly full length, quite sufficient to show us what the romances were like, and to cause us to regret the irreparable loss inflicted upon our race by the ravages of Danes, Normans, and English. Even as it is O'Curry asserts that the contents of the strictly historical tales known to him would be sufficient to fill up four thousand of the large pages of the "Four Masters." He computed that the tales about Finn, Ossian, and the Fenians alone would fill another three thousand pages. In addition to these we have a considerable number of imaginative stories, neither historical nor Fenian, such as the "Three Sorrows of Story-telling" and the like, sufficient to fill five thousand pages more, not to speak of the more recent novel-like productions of the later Irish.[1]

It is this very great fecundity of the very early Irish in the production of saga and romance, in poetry and prose, which best enables us to judge of their early-developed genius, and considerable primitive culture. The introduction of Christianity neither inspired these romances nor helped to produce them; they are nearly all anterior to it, and had they been preserved to us we should now have the most remarkable body of primitive myth and saga in the whole western world. It is probably this consideration which makes M. Darmesteter say

[1] O'Curry was no doubt accurate, as he ever is, in this computation, but there would probably be some repetition in the stories, with lists of names and openings common to more than one, and many late poor ones.

of Irish literature: "real historical documents we have none until the beginning of the decadence—a decadence so glorious, that we almost mistake it for a renaissance since the old epic sap dries up only to make place for a new budding and bourgeoning, a growth less original certainly, but scarcely less wonderful if we consider the condition of continental Europe at that date." The decadence that M. Darmesteter alludes to is the rise of the Christian schools of the fifth and sixth centuries, which put to some extent an end to the epic period by turning men's thoughts into a different channel.

It is this "decadence," however, which I have preferred to examine first, just because it does rest upon real historical documents, and can be proved. We may now, however, proceed to the mass of saga, the bulk of which in its earliest forms is pagan, and the spirit of which, even in the latest texts, has been seldom quite distorted by Christian influence. This saga centres around several periods and individuals: some of these, like Tuathal and the Boru tribute, Conairé the Great and his death, have only one or two stories pertaining to them. But there are three cycles which stand out pre-eminently, and have been celebrated in more stories and sagas than the rest, and of which more remains have been preserved to us than of any of the others. These are the Mythological Cycle concerning the Tuatha De Danann and the Pre-Milesians; the Heroic, Ultonian, or Red-Branch Cycle,[1] in which Cuchulain is the dominating figure; and the Cycle of Finn mac Cúmhail, Ossian, Oscar, and the High-kings of Ireland who were their contemporaries—this cycle may be denominated the Fenian or Ossianic.

[1] M. d'Arbois de Jubainville calls this the Ulster, and calls the Ossianic the Leinster Cycle.

CHAPTER XXIII

THE MYTHOLOGICAL CYCLE

THE cycle of the mythological stories which group themselves round the early invasions of Erin is sparsely represented in Irish manuscripts. Not only is their number less, but their substance is more confused than that of the other cycles. To the comparative mythologist and the folk-lorist, however, they are perhaps the most interesting of all, as throwing more light than any of the others upon the early religious ideas of the race. Most of the sagas connected with this pre-Milesian cycle are now to be found only in brief digests preserved in the Leabhar Gabhála,[1] or Book of Invasions of Ireland, of which large fragments exist in the Books of Leinster and Ballymote, and which Michael O'Clery (collecting from all the ancient sources which he could find in his day) rewrote about the year 1630.

This tells us all the early history of Ireland and of the races that inhabited it before our forefathers landed. It tells us of how first a man called Partholan made a settlement in Ireland, but how in time he and his people all died of the plague, leaving the land deserted; and how after that the Nemedians, or children of Nemed, colonised the island and multiplied in it,

[1] "L'yowar (rhyming to *hour*) gow-awla," the "book of the takings or holdings of Ireland."

until they began to be oppressed by the Fomorians, who are usually described as African sea-robbers, but the etymology of whose name seems to point to a mythological origin "men from under sea." [1] A number of battles took place between the rival hosts, and the Fomorians were defeated in three battles, but after the death of Nemed, who, like Partholan, died of a plague, the Fomorians oppressed his people again, and, led by a chief called Conaing, built a great tower upon Tory, *i.e.*, Tower Island, off the north-west coast of Donegal. On the eve of every Samhain [Sou-an, or All Hallow's] the wretched Nemedians had to deliver up to these masters two-thirds of their children, corn, and cattle. Driven to desperation by these exactions they rose in arms, stormed the tower, and slew Conaing, all which the Book of Invasions describes at length. The Fomorians being reinforced, the Nemedians fought them a second time in the same place, but in this battle most of them were killed or drowned, the tide having come in and washed over them and their foes alike. The crew of one ship, however, escaped, and these, after a further sojourn of seven years in Ireland, led out of it the surviving remnants of their race with the exception of a very few who remained behind subject to the Fomorians. Those who left Ireland divided into three bands: one sought refuge in Greece, where they again fell into slavery; the second went—some say—to the north of Europe; and the third, headed by a chief called Briton Mael—hence, say the Irish, the name of Great Britain—found refuge in Scotland, where their descendants remained until the Cruithni, or Picts, overcame them.

After a couple of hundred years the Nemedians who had fled to Greece came back again, calling themselves Fir-bolg,[2] *i.e.*, "sack" or "bag" men, and held Ireland for

[1] Keating derives it from *foghla*, "spoil," and *muir*, "sea," which is an impossible derivation, or from *fo muirib*, as if "along the seas," but it really means "under seas."

[2] Also Fir Domnan and Fir Galeóin, two tribes of the same race.

about thirty-five years in peace, when another tribe of invaders appeared upon the scene. These were no less than the celebrated Tuatha De Danann, who turned out to be, in fact, the descendants of the second band of Nemedians who had fled to the north of Europe, and who returned about thirty-six years later than their kinsmen, the Firbolg.

The Tuatha De Danann soon overcame the Firbolg, and drove them, after the Battle of North Moytura,[1] into the islands along the coast, to Aran, Islay, Rachlin, and the Hebrides,[2] after which they assumed the sovereignty of the island to themselves.

This sovereignty they maintained for about two hundred

[1] When the oldest list of current Irish sagas was drawn up, probably in the seventh century, only one battle of Moytura was mentioned ; this was evidently what is now known as the second battle. In the more recent list contained in the introduction to the Senchus Mór there is mention made of both battles. There is only a single copy of each of these sagas known to exist. Of most of the other sagas of this cycle even the last copy has perished.

[2] Long afterwards, at the time that Ireland was divided into five provinces, the Cruithnigh, or Picts, drove the Firbolg out of the islands again, and they were forced to come back to Cairbré Niafer, king of Leinster, who allotted them a territory, but placed such a rack-rent upon them that they were glad to fly into Connacht, where Oilioll and Mève—the king and queen who made the Táin Bo Chuailgne—gave them a free grant of land, and there Duald Mac Firbis, over two hundred and fifty years ago, found their descendants in plenty. According to some accounts, they were never driven wholly out of Connacht, and if they are a real race—as, despite their connection with the obviously mythical Tuatha De Danann, they appear to be—they probably still form the basis of population there. Máine Mór, the ancestor of the O'Kellys, is said to have wrested from them the territory of Ui Máiné (part of Roscommon and Galway) in the sixth century. Their name and that of their fellow tribe, the Fir Domnan, *appear* to be the same as the Belgæ, and the Damnonii of Gaul and Britain, who are said to have given its name to Devonshire. Despite their close connection in the Book of Invasions and early history of Ireland, the Firbolg stand on a completely different footing from the De Danann tribes. Their history is recorded consecutively from that day to this ; many families trace their pedigree to them, and they never wholly disappeared. No family traces its connection to the De Danann people ; they wholly disappear, and are in later times regarded as gods, or demons, or fairies.

years, until the ancestors of the present Irish, the Scots, or Gaels, or Milesians, as they are variously called, landed and beat the Tuatha De Danann, and reigned in their stead until they, too, in their turn were conquered by the English. The Book of Conquests is largely concerned with their landing and first settlements and their battles with the De Danann people whom they ended in completely overcoming, after which the Tuatha Dé assume a very obscure position. They appear to have for the most part retired off the surface of the country into the green hills and mounds, and lived in these, often appearing amongst the Milesian population, and sometimes giving their daughters in marriage to them. From this out they are confounded with the *Sidhe* [Shee], or spirits, now called fairies, and to this very day I have heard old men, when speaking of the fairies who inhabit ancient raths and interfere occasionally in mortal concerns either for good or evil, call them by the name of the Tuatha De Danann.

The first battle of Moytura was fought between the Tuatha De Danann and the Firbolg, who were utterly routed, but Nuada, the king of the Tuatha Dé, lost his hand in the battle. As he was thus suffering from a personal blemish, he could be no longer king, and the people accordingly decided to bestow the sovereignty on Breas [Bras],[1] whose mother was a De Danann, but whose father was a king of the Fomorians, a people who had apparently never lost sight of or wholly left Ireland since the time of their battles with the Nemedians over two hundred years before. The mother of Breas, Eiriu,[2] was a person of authority, and her son was elected to the sovereignty on the understanding that if his reign was found unsatisfactory he should resign. He gave seven pledges of his intention of doing so. At this time the Fomorians again

[1] Bress in the older form.

[2] When the Milesians landed they found a Tuatha De Danann queen, called Eiriu, the old form of Eire or Erin, from whom the island was believed to take its name. John Scotus is called in old authorities Eriugena, not Erigena.

smote Ireland heavily with their imposts and taxes, as they had done before when the Nemedians inhabited it. The unfortunate De Dannan people were reduced to a state of misery. Ogma[1] was obliged to carry wood, and the Dagda himself to build raths for their masters, and they were so far reduced as to be weak with hunger.

In the meantime the kingship of Breas was not successful. He was hard and niggardly. As the saga of the second battle of Moytura puts it—

> "The chiefs of the Tuatha De Danann were dissatisfied, for Breas did not grease their knives; in vain came they to visit Breas; their breaths did not smell of ale. Neither their poets, nor bards, nor druids, nor harpers, nor flute-players, nor musicians, nor jugglers, nor fools appeared before them, nor came into the palace to amuse them."

Matters reached a crisis when the poet Coirpné came to demand hospitality and was shown "into a little house, small, narrow, black, dark, where was neither fire nor furniture nor bed. He was given three little dry loaves on a little plate. When he rose in the morning he was not thankful." He gave vent then to the first satire ever uttered in Ireland, which is still preserved in eight lines which would be absolutely unintelligible except for the ancient glosses.

After this the people of the De Danann race demanded the abdication of Breas, which he had promised in case his reign did not please them. He acknowledged his obligation to them, but requested a delay of seven years, which they allowed him, on condition that he gave them guarantees to touch nothing belonging to them during that time, "neither our houses nor our lands, nor our gold, nor our silver, nor our cattle, nor anything eatable, we shall pay thee neither rent nor fine to the end of seven years." This was agreed to.

But the intention of Breas in demanding a delay of seven years was a treacherous one; he meant to approach his father's

[1] For him see above, pp. 113-15.

kindred the Fomorians, and move them to reinstate him at the point of the sword. He goes to his mother who tells him who his father is, for up to that time he had remained in ignorance of it; and she gives him a ring whereby his father Elatha, a king of the Fomorians, may recognise him. He departs to the Fomorians, discovers his father and appeals to him for succour. By his father he is sent to Balor, a king of the Fomorians of the Isles of Norway—a locality probably ascribed to the Fomorians after the invasions of the Northmen—and there gathered together an immense army to subdue the Tuatha De Danann and give the island to their relation Breas.

In the meantime Nuada, whose hand had been replaced by a silver one, reascends the throne and is joined by Lugh of the Long-hand, the "Ildana" or "man of various arts." This Lugh was a brother of the Dagda and of Ogma, and is perhaps the best-known figure among the De Danann personalities. Lugh and the Dagda and Ogma and Goibniu the smith and Diancécht the leech met secretly every day at a place in Meath for a whole year, and deliberated how best to shake off the yoke of the Fomorians. Then they held a general meeting of the Tuatha De and spoke with each one in secret.

"'How wilt thou show thy power?' said Lugh, to the sorcerer Mathgen.

"'By my art,' answered Mathgen, 'I shall throw down the mountains of Ireland upon the Fomorians, and they shall fall with their heads to the earth;' then told he to Lugh the names of the twelve principal mountains of Ireland which were ready to do the bidding of the goddess Dana[1] and to smite their enemies on every side.

---

[1] Jubainville translates Tuatha De Danann by "tribes of the goddess Dana." Danann is the genitive of Dana, and Dana is called the "mother of the gods," but she is not a mother of the bulk of the De Danann race, so that Jubainville's translation is a rather venturesome one, and the Old Irish themselves did not take the word in this meaning; they explained it as "the men of science who were as it were gods." "Tuatha dé Danann, *i.e.*, Dee in taes dána acus andé an taes trebtha," *i.e.*, "the men of science were (as it were) gods and the laymen no-gods."

"Lugh asked the cup-bearer: 'In what way wilt thou show thy power?'

"'I shall place,' answered the cup-bearer, 'the twelve principal lakes of Ireland under the eyes of the Fomorians, but they shall find no water in them, however great the thirst which they may feel;' and he enumerated the lakes, 'from the Fomorians the water shall hide itself, they shall not be able to take a drop of it; but the same lakes will furnish the Tuatha De Danann with water to drink during the whole war, though it should last seven years.'

"The Druid Figal, the son of Mamos, said, 'I shall make three rains of fire fall on the faces of the Fomorian warriors; I shall take from them two-thirds of their valour and courage, but so often as the warriors of the De Danann shall breathe out the air from their breasts, so often shall they feel their courage and valour and strength increase. Even though the war should last seven years it shall not fatigue them.'

"The Dagda answered, 'All the feats which you three, sorcerer, cup-bearer, druid, say you can do, I myself alone shall do them.'

"'It is you then are the Dagda,'[1] said those present, whence came the name of the Dagda which he afterwards bore."

Lugh then went in search of the three gods of Dana—Brian, Iuchar, and Iucharba (whom he afterwards put to death for slaying his father, as is recorded at length in the saga of the "Fate of the Children of Tuireann"[2]) and with these and his other allies he spent the next seven years in making preparations for the great struggle with the Fomorians.

This saga and the whole story of the Tuatha De Danann contending with the Fomorians, who are in one place in the saga actually called *sidhe*, or spirits, is all obviously mythological, and has usually been explained, by D'Arbois de Jubainville and others, as the struggle between the gods or good spirits and the evil deities.

[1] Whitley Stokes translates this by "good hand." It is explained as—*Dago-dêvo-s*, "the good god." The "Dagda, *i.e.*, daigh dé, *i.e.*, dea sainemail ag na geinntib é," *i.e.*, "Dagda ie ignis Dei," for "with the heathen he was a special god," MS. 16, Advocates' Library, Edinburgh.

[2] Paraphrased by me in English verse in the "Three Sorrows of Story-telling."

The following episode also shows the wild mythological character of the whole.

"Dagda," says the saga, "had a habitation at Glenn-Etin in the north. He had arranged to meet a woman at Glenn-Etin on the day of Samhan [November day] just a year, day for day, before the battle of Moytura. The Unius, a river of Connacht, flows close beside Glenn-Etin, to the south. Dagda saw the woman bathe herself in the Unius at [Kesh] Coran. One of the woman's feet in the water touched Allod Eche, that is to say Echumech to the south, the other foot also in the water touched Lescuin in the north. Nine tresses floated loose around her head. Dagda approached and accosted her. From thenceforth the place has been named the Couple's Bed. The woman was the goddess Mór-rígu"—

the goddess of war, of whom we shall hear more in connection with Cuchulain.

As for the Dagda himself, his character appears somewhat contradictory. Just as the most opposite accounts of Zeus are met with in Greek mythology, some glorifying him as throning in Olympus supreme over gods and men, others as playing low and indecent tricks disguised as a cuckoo or a bull; so we find the Dagda—his real name was Eochaidh the Ollamh—at one time a king of the De Danann race and organiser of victory, but at another in a less dignified but more clearly mythological position. He is sent by Lugh to the Fomorian camp to put them off with talk and cause them to lose time until the De Danann armaments should be more fully ready. The following account exhibits him, like Zeus at times, in a very unprepossessing character:—

"When the Dagda had come to the camp of the Fomorians he demanded a truce, and he obtained it. The Fomorians prepared a porridge for him; it was to ridicule him they did this, for he greatly loved porridge. They filled for him the king's cauldron which was five handbreadths in depth. They threw into it eighty pots of milk and a proportionate quantity of meal and fat, with goats and sheep and swine which they got cooked along with the rest. Then they poured the broth into a hole dug in the ground. 'Unless you eat all that's there,' said Indech to him, 'you shall be put to death; we do not want you to be reproaching us, and we must satisfy you.' The Dagda took the spoon; it was so great that in the hollow of it a man and a woman might be contained. The pieces that went into that spoon were halves of salted pigs and quarters of bacon. The Dagda said, 'Here is good eating, if the broth be as good as its odour,' and as he carried the spoonful to his mouth, he said, 'The proverb is true that good cooking is not spoiled by a bad pot.'[1]

"When he had finished he scraped the ground with his finger to the very bottom of the hole to take what remained of it, and after that he went to sleep to digest his soup. His stomach was greater than the greatest cauldrons in large houses, and the Fomorians mocked at him.

"He went away and came to the bank of the Eba. He did not walk with ease, so large was his stomach. He was dressed in very bad guise. He had a cape which scarcely reached below his shoulders. Beneath that cloak was seen a brown mantle which descended no lower than his hips. It was cut away above and very large in the breast. His two shoes were of horses' skin with the hair outside. He held a wheeled fork, which would have been heavy enough for eight men, and he let it trail behind him. It dug a furrow deep enough and large enough to become the frontier mearn between two provinces. Therefore is it called the 'track of the Dagda's club.'"

When the fighting began, after the skirmishing of the first days, the De Danann warriors owed their victory to their superior preparations. The great leech Diancecht cured the wounded, and the smith Goibniu and his assistants kept the warriors supplied with constant relays of fresh lances. The Fomorians could not understand it, and sent one of their warriors, apparently in disguise, to find out. He was Ruadan, a son of Breas by a daughter of Dagda.

"On his return he told the Fomorians what the smith, the carpenter, the worker in bronze, and the four leeches who were round the spring, did. They sent him back again with orders to kill the smith Goibniu. He asked a spear of Goibniu, rivets of Credné the bronze-worker, a shaft of Luchtainé the carpenter, and they gave him what he asked. There was a woman there busy in sharpening the

[1] Thus perilously translated by Jubainville; Stokes does not attempt it.

weapons. She was Cron, mother of Fianlug. She sharpened the spear for Ruadan. It was a chief who handed Ruadan the spear, and thence the name of chief-spear given to this day to the weaver's beam in Erin.

"When he had got the spear Ruadan turned on Goibniu and smote him with the weapon. But Goibniu drew the javelin from the wound and hurled it at Ruadan; who was pierced from side to side, and escaped to die among the Fomorians in presence of his father. Brig [his mother, the Dagda's daughter] came and bewailed her son. First she uttered a piercing cry, and thereafter she made moan. It was then that for the first time in Ireland were heard moans and cries of sorrow. It was that same Brig who invented the whistle used at night to give alarm signals"—

the mythological genesis of the saga is thus obviously marked by the first satire, first cry of sorrow, and first whistle being ascribed to the actors in it.

In the end the whole Fomorian army moved to battle in their solid battalions, "and it was to strike one's hand against a rock, or thrust one's hand into a nest of serpents, or put one's head into the fire, to attack the Fomorians that day." The battle is described at length. Nuada the king of the De Danann is killed by Balor. Lugh, whose counsel was considered so valuable by the De Danann people that they put an escort of nine round him to prevent him from taking part in the fighting, breaks away, and attacks Balor the Fomorian king.

"Balor had an evil eye, that eye only opened itself upon the plain of battle. Four men had to lift up the eyelid by placing under it an instrument. The warriors, whom Balor scanned with that eye once opened,[1] could not—no matter how numerous—resist their enemies."

When Lugh had met and exchanged some mystical and

[1] A legend well known to the old men of Galway and Roscommon, who have often related it to me, tells us that when Conan (Finn mac Cúmhail's Thersites) looked through his fingers at the enemy, they were always defeated. He himself did not know this, nor any one except Finn, who tried to make use of it without letting Conan know his own power.

unintelligible language with him, Balor said, "Raise my eyelid that I may see the braggart who speaks with me."

"His people raise Balor's eyelid. Lugh from his sling lets fly a stone at Balor which passes through his head, carrying with it the venomous eye. Balor's army looked on." The Mór-rígu, the goddess of war, arrives, and assists the Tuatha De Danann and encourages them. Ogma slays one of the Fomorian kings and is slain himself. The battle is broken at last on the Fomorians; they fly, and Breas is taken prisoner, but his life is spared.

"It was," says the saga, "at the battle of Moytura that Ogma, the strong man, found the sword of Tethra, the King of the Fomorians. Ogma drew that sword from the sheath and cleaned it. It was then that it related to him all the high deeds that it had accomplished, for at this time the custom was when swords were drawn from the sheath they used to recite the exploits[1] they had themselves been the cause of. And thence comes the right which swords have, to be cleaned when they are drawn from the sheath; thence also the magic power which swords have preserved ever since"—

to which curious piece of pagan superstition an evidently later Christian redactor adds, "weapons were the organs of the demon to speak to men. At that time men used to worship weapons, and they were a magic safeguard."

The saga ends in the episode of the recovery of the Dagda's harp, and in the cry of triumph uttered by the Mór-rígu and by Bodb, her fellow-goddess of war, as they visited the various heights of Ireland, the banks of streams, and the mouths of floods and great rivers, to proclaim aloud their triumph and the defeat of the Fomorians.

M. d'Arbois de Jubainville sees in the successive colonisations of Partholan, the Nemedians, and the Tuatha De Danann, an Irish version of the Greek legend of the three successive ages

[1] There is a somewhat similar passage ascribing sensation to swords in the Saga of Cuchulain's sickness.

of gold, silver, and brass. The Greek legend of the Chimæra, otherwise Bellerus, the monster slain by Bellerophon, he equates with the Irish Balor of the evil eye; the fire from the throat of Bellerus, and the evil beam shot from Balor's eye may originally have typified the lightning.[1]

[1] The First Battle of Moytura, the Second Battle of Moytura, and the Death of the Children of Tuireann are three sagas belonging to this cycle. Others, now preserved in the digest of the Book of Invasions, are, the Progress of Partholan to Erin, the Progress of Nemed to Erin, the Progress of the Firbolg, the Progress of the Tuatha De Danann, the Journey of Mile-son of Bile to Spain, the Journey of the Sons of Mile from Spain to Erin, the Progress of the Cruithnigh (Picts) from Thrace to Erin and thence into Alba.

CHAPTER XXIV

THE HEROIC OR RED BRANCH CYCLE—CUCHULAIN

THE mythological tales that we have been glancing at deal with the folk who are fabled as having first colonised Erin ; they treat of peoples, races, dynasties, the struggle between good and evil principles. The whole of their creations are thrown back, even by the Irish annalists themselves, into the dim cloud-land of an unplumbed past, ages before the dawn of the first Olympiad, or the birth of the wolf-suckled twins who founded Rome. There is over it all a shadowy sense of vagueness, vastness, uncertainty.

The Heroic Cycle, on the other hand, deals with the history of the Milesians themselves, the present Irish race, within a well-defined space of time, upon their own ground, and though it does not exactly fall within the historical period, yet it does not come so far short of it that it can be with any certainty rejected as pure work of imagination or poetic fiction. It is certainly the finest of the three greater saga-cycles, and the epics that belong to it are sharply drawn, numerous, clear cut, and ancient, and for the first time we *seem*, at least, to find ourselves upon historical ground, although a good deal of this seeming may turn out to be illusory. Yet the figures of Cuchulain, Conor mac Nessa, Naoise, and Déirdre, Mève,

Oilioll, and Conall Cearnach, have about them a great deal of the circumstantiality that is entirely lacking to the dim, mist-magnified, and distorted figures of the Dagda, Nuada, Lugh the Long-handed, and their fellows.

The gods come and go as in the Iliad, and according to some accounts leave their posterity behind them. Cuchulain himself, the incarnation of Irish ἀριστεία, is according to certain authorities the son of the god Lugh the Long-handed.[1] He himself, like another Anchises, is beloved of a goddess and descends into the Gaelic Elysium,[2] and the most important epic of the cycle is largely conditioned by an occurrence caused by the curse of a goddess, an occurrence wholly impossible and supernatural.[3] Yet these are for the most part excrescences no more affecting the conduct of the history than the actions of the gods affect the war round Troy. Events, upon the whole, are motivated upon fairly reasonable human grounds, and there is a certain air of probability about them. The characters who now make their appearance upon the scene are not long prior to, or are contemporaneous

[1] *See* "Compert Conculaind," by Windisch in "Irische Texte," t. i. p. 134, and Jubainville's "Epopée Celtique en Irlande," p. 22.

[2] *See* the story of Cuchulain's sick-bed, translated by O'Curry in the first volume of the "Atlantis," and by Mr. O'Looney in Sir J. Gilbert's "Facsimiles of the National MSS. of Ireland," and by Windisch in "Irische Texte," vol. i., pp. 195–234, and by M. de Jubainville in his "Epopée Celtique," p. 174, and lastly, Mr. Nutt's "Voyage of Bran," vol. ii., p. 38.

[3] This is the periodic curse which overtook the Ulstermen at certain periods, rendering them feeble as a woman in child-bed, in consequence of the malediction of the goddess Macha, who was, just before the birth of her children, inhumanly obliged by the Ultonians to run against the king's horses. The only people of the northern province free from this curse were the children born before the curse was uttered, the women, and the hero Cuchulain. It transmitted itself from father to son for nine generations, and is said to have lasted five nights and four days, or four nights and five days. But one would think from the Táin Bó Cuailnge, that it must have lasted much longer. For this curse *see* Jubainville's "Epopée Celtique," p. 320. I was, not long ago, told a story by a peasant in the county Galway not unlike it, only it was related of the mother of the celebrated boxer Donnelly.

with, the birth of Christ; and the wars of the Tuatha De Danann, Nemedians, and Fomorians, are left some seventeen hundred years behind.

This cycle, which I have called the "Heroic" or "Red Branch," might also be named the "Ultonian," because it deals chiefly with the heroes of the northern province. One saga relates the birth of Conor mac Nessa. His mother was Ness and his father was Fachtna Fathach, king of Ulster, but according to what is probably the oldest account, his father was Cathba the Druid. This saga relates how, through the stratagem of his mother Ness, Conor slipped into the kingship of Ulster, displacing Fergus mac Róigh [Roy], the former king, who is here represented as a good-natured giant, but who appears human enough in the other sagas.[1] Conor's palace is described with its three buildings; that of the Red Branch, where were kept the heads and arms of vanquished enemies; that of the Royal Branch, where the kings lodged; and that of the Speckled House, where were laid up the shields and spears and swords of the warriors of Ulster. It was called the Speckled or Variegated House from the gold and silver of the shields, and gleaming of the spears, and shining of the goblets, and all arms were kept in it, in order that at the banquet when quarrels arose the warriors might not have wherewith to slay each other.

Conor's palace at Emania contained, according to the Book of Leinster, one hundred and fifty rooms, each large enough for three couples to sleep in, constructed of red oak, and bordered with copper. Conor's own chamber was decorated with bronze and silver, and ornamented with golden birds, in whose eyes were precious stones, and was large enough for thirty

[1] Except in one place in the Táin Bó Cuailnge, where his sword is spoken of, which was like a thread in his hand, but which when he smote with it extended itself to the size of a rainbow, with three blows of which upon the ground he raised three hills. The description of Fergus in the Conor story preserved in the Book of Leinster, is simply and frankly that of a giant many times the size of an ordinary man.

warriors to drink together in it. Above the king's head hung his silver wand with three golden apples, and when he shook it silence reigned throughout the palace, so that even the fall of a pin might be heard. A large vat, always full of good drink, stood ever on the palace floor.

Another story tells of Cuchulain's mysterious parentage. His mother was a sister of King Conor ; consequently he was the king's nephew.

Another again relates the wooing of Cuchulain, and how he won Emer for his wife.

Another is called Cuchulain's "Up-bringing," or teaching, part of which, however, is found in the piece called the "Wooing of Emer." This saga relates how he, with two other of the Ultonians, went abroad to Alba to perfect their warlike accomplishments, and how they placed themselves under the tuition of different female-warriors,[1] who taught them various and extraordinary feats of arms. He traverses the plain of Misfortune by the aid of a wheel and of an apple given him by an unknown friend, and reaches the great female instructress Scathach, whose daughter falls in love with him.

An admirable example occurs to me here, of showing in the concrete that which I have elsewhere laid stress upon, namely, the great elaboration which in many instances we find in the modern versions of sagas, compared with the antique vellum texts. It does not at all follow that because a story is written down with brevity in ancient Irish, it was also told with brevity. The oldest form of the saga of Cuchulain's "Wooing of Emer" contains traces of a pre-Danish or seventh-century text, but the condensed and shortened relation of the saga found in the oldest manuscript of it, is almost certainly not the form in which the bards and ollavs related it. On the contrary, I believe that the stories now epitomised in ancient vellum texts were even then told, though not written down,

[1] The female warrior and war-teacher was not uncommon among the Celts, as the examples of Boadicea and of Mève of Connacht show.

at full length, and with many flourishes by the bards and professed story-tellers, and that the skeletons merely, or as Keating calls it, the "bones of the history,"[1] were in most instances all that was committed to the rare and expensive parchments. It is more than likely that the longer modern paper redactions, though some of the ancient pagan traits, especially those most incomprehensible to the moderns, may be missing, yet represent more nearly the *manner* of the original bardic telling, than the abridgments of twelfth or thirteenth-century vellums.

In this case the ancient recension,[2] founded on a pre-Danish text, merely mentions that Scathach's house, at which Cuchulain arrives, after leaving the plain of Misfortune,

> "was built upon a rock of appalling height. Cuchulain followed the road pointed out to him. He reached the castle of Scathach. He knocked at the door with the handle of his spear and entered. Uathach, the daughter of Scathach, meets him. She looked at him, but she spoke not, so much did the hero's beauty make her love him. She went to her mother and told her of the beauty of the man who had newly come. 'That man has pleased you,' said her mother. 'He shall come to my couch,' answered the girl, 'and I shall sleep at his side this night.' 'Thy intention displeases me not,' said her mother."

One can see at a glance how bald and brief is all this, because it is a précis, and vellum was scarce. I venture to say that no bard ever told it in this way. The scribes who first committed this to parchment, say in the seventh or eighth century, probably wrote down only the leading incidents as they remembered them. They may not have been themselves either bards, ollavs, or story-tellers. It is chiefly in the later centuries, after the introduction of paper, when the economising of space ceased to be a matter of importance, that we find our sagas told with all the redundancy of description, epithet, and incident with which I suspect the very earliest bards embellished all those sagas of which we have now only little more

[1] "Cnámha an tseanchusa." [2] Rawlinson, B. 512.

than the skeletons. Compare, for instance, the ancient version which I have just given, with the longer modern versions which have come down to us in several paper manuscripts, of which I here use one in my own possession, copied about the beginning of the century by a scribe named O'Mahon, upon one of the islands on the Shannon.

In the first place this version tells us that on his arrival at Scathach's mansion he finds a number of her scholars and other warriors engaged in hurling outside the door of her fortress. He joins in the game and defeats them—this is a true folk-lore introduction. He finds there Naoise, Ardan, and Ainnlè, the three sons of Usnach, celebrated in perhaps the most touching saga of this whole cycle, and another son of Erin with them. This is a literary touch, by one who knew his literature.[1] Learning that he is come from Erin, they ask news of their native country, and salute him with kisses. They then bring him to the Bridge of the Cliffs, and show him what their work is during the first year, which was learning to pass this bridge.

> "Wonderful," says the saga, "was the sight that bridge afforded when any one would leap upon it, for it narrowed until it became as narrow as the hair of one's head, and the second time it shortened until it became as short as an inch, and the third time it grew slippery until it was as slippery as an eel of the river, and the fourth time it rose up on high against you until it was as tall as the mast of a ship."

All the warriors and people on the lawn came down to see Cuchulain attempting to cross this bridge. In the meantime Scathach's *grianán* or sunny house is described: "It had seven great doors, and seven great windows between every two doors of them, and thrice fifty couches between every two windows of them, and thrice fifty handsome marriageable girls, in scarlet cloaks, and in beautiful and blue attire, attending and waiting upon Scathach."

[1] For Déirdre in her lament over the three does call them "three pupils of Scathach."

Then Scathach's lovely daughter, looking from the windows of the *grianán*, perceives the stranger attempting the feat of the bridge, and she falls in love with him upon the spot. Her emotions are thus described: "Her face and colour constantly changed, so that now she would be as white as a little white flowret, and again she would become scarlet," and in the work she was embroidering she put the gold thread where the silver thread should be, and the silver thread into the place where the gold thread should go; and when her mother notices it, she excuses herself by saying beautifully, "I would greatly grieve should he not return alive to his own people, in whatever part of the world they may be, for I know that there is some one to whom it would be anguish to know that he is thus."

This refined reflection of the girl we may with certainty ascribe to the growth of modern sentiment, and it is extremely instructive to compare it with the ancient, and no doubt really pagan version; but I strongly suspect that the bridge over the cliffs is no modern embellishment at all, but part of the original saga, though omitted from the pre-Norse text which only tells us that Scathach's house was on the top of a rock of appalling height.

It was during this sojourn of Cuchulain in foreign lands that he overcame the heroine Aoife,[1] and forced her into a marriage with himself. He returned home afterwards, having left instructions with her to keep the child she should bear him, if it were a daughter, "for with every mother goes the daughter," but if it were a son she was to rear him until he should be able to perform certain hero-feats, and until his finger should be large enough to fill a ring which Cuchulain left with her for him. Then she was to send him into Erin, and bid him tell no man who he was; also he desired

[1] Pronounced "Eefă." The triphthong *aoi* has always the sound of *ee* in English. The stepmother of the Children of Lir was also called Aoife.

her not to teach him the feat of the Gae-Bulg, "but, however," says the saga, "it was ill that command turned out, for it was of that it came to pass that Conlaoch [the son] fell by Cuchulain."[1]

I know of no prose saga of the touching story of the death of this son, slain by his own father, except the *résumé* given of it by Keating,[2] but there exists a poem or épopée upon the subject which was always a great favourite with the Irish scribes, and of which numerous but not ancient copies exist. This is the Irish Sohrab and Rustum, the Celtic Hildebrand and Hadubrand. The son comes into Ireland, but in consequence of his mother's command, refuses to tell his name. This is looked upon as indicating hostility, and many of the Ultonians fight with him, but he overcomes them all, even the great Conall Cearnach. Conor in despair sends for Cuchulain, who with difficulty slays him by the feat of the Gae-Bolg, and then finds out when too late that the dying champion is his own son. So familiar to the modern Irish scribes was this piece that in my copy, in the last verse, which ends with Cuchulain's lament over his son—

"I am the bark (buffeted) from wave to wave,
I am the ship after the losing of its rudder,

---

[1] I quote this from my paper version. The oldest text only says that "Cuchulain told her that she should bear him a son, and that upon a certain day in seven years' time that son should go to him; he told her what name she should give him, and then he went away."

[2] P. 279 of John O'Mahony's edition, translated also by M. de Jubainville in his "Épopée Celtique," who comparing the Irish story with its Germanic counterpart expresses himself strongly on their relative merits: "Tout est puissant, logique, primitif, dans la pièce irlandaise; sa concordance avec la pièce persanne atteste une haute antiquité. Elle peut remonter aux époques celtiques les plus anciennes, et avoir été du nombre des *carmina* chantés par les Gaulois à la bataille de Clusium en 295 av. J.—C. Le poème allemand dont on a une copie du huitième siècle est une imitation inintelligente et affaiblie du chant celtique qui a dû retentir sur les rives du Danube et du Mein mille ans plus tôt, et dont la rédaction germanique est l'œuvre de quelque naïf Macpherson, prédécesseur honnêtement inhabile de celui du dix-huitième siècle."

I am the apple upon the top of the tree
That little thought of its falling."[1]

instead of the text of the third line stands a rough picture of a tree with a large apple on the top!

Another saga[2] tells of Cuchulain's *geasa* [gassa] or restrictions. It was *geis* or tabu to him to narrate his genealogy to one champion, as it was also to his son Conlaoch, to refuse combat to any one man, to look upon the exposed bosom of a woman, to come into a company without a second invitation, to accept the hospitality of virgins, to boast to a woman, to let the sun rise before him in Emania, he must when there rise before it, etc. There is in this saga a graphic description of the pagan king's retinue journeying with him to be fed in the house of a retainer.

> "All the Ultonian nobles set out; a great train of provincials, sons of kings and chiefs, young lords and men-at-arms, the curled and rosy youth of the kingdom, and the maidens and fair ringleted ladies of Ulster. Handsome virgins, accomplished damsels, and splendid, fully-developed women were there. Satirists and scholars were there, and the companies of singers and musicians, poets who composed songs and reproofs, and praising-poems for the men of Ulster. There came also with them from Emania historians, judges, horse-riders, buffoons, tumblers, fools, and performers on horseback. They all went by the same way, behind the king."[3]

Dismissing Cuchulain for the present, we pass on now to another personality of the Red Branch saga — the Lady Déirdre.

[1] "Is mé an barc o thuinn go tuinn,
Is mé an long iar ndul d'á stiúr.
Is mé an t-ubhall i mbárr an chroinn
Is beag do shaoil a thuitim."

See Miss Brooke's "Reliques of Ancient Irish Poetry," 2nd ed. p. 393. See also Kuno Meyer's note at p. xv of his edition of *Cath Finntragha*, in which he bears further evidence to the antiquity and persistence of this story.

[2] See the Book of Leinster, 107–111, a MS. copied about the year 1150.

[3] Thus translated by my late lamented friend and accomplished scholar Father James Keegan of St. Louis.

CHAPTER XXV

DÉIRDRE

One of the key-stone stories of the Red Branch Cycle is Déirdre, or the Fate of the Children of Usnach. Cuchulain, though he appears in this saga, is not a prominent figure in it. This piece is perhaps the finest, most pathetic, and best-conceived of any in the whole range of our literature. But like much of that literature it exists in the most various recensions, and there are different accounts given of the death of all the principal characters.

This saga commences with the birth of Déirdre. King Conor and his Ultonians had gone to drink and feast in the house of Felim, Conor's chief story-teller, and during their stay there Felim's wife gives birth to a daughter. Cathba the Druid prophesies concerning the infant, and foretells that much woe and great calamities shall yet come upon Ulster because of her. He names her Déirdre.[1] The Ultonians are smitten with horror at his prophecies, and order her to be instantly put to death. The most ancient text, that of the twelfth-century Book of Leinster, tells the beginning of this saga exceedingly tersely.

[1] Pronounced "Dare-dră," said to mean "alarm." Jubainville translates it "Celle-qui-se-débat."

"'Let the girl be slain,' cried the warriors. 'Not so,' said King Conor, 'but bring ye her to me to-morrow; she shall be brought up as I shall order, and she shall be the woman whom I shall marry.' The Ultonians ventured not to contradict the King; they did as he commanded.

"Déirdre was brought up in Conor's house. She became the handsomest maiden in Ireland. She was reared in a house apart: no man was allowed to see her until she should become Conor's wife. No one was permitted to enter the house except her tutor, her nurse, and Lavarcam,[1] whom they ventured not to keep out, for she was a druidess magician whose incantations they feared.

"One winter day Déirdre's tutor slew a young tender calf upon the snow outside the house, which he was to cook for his pupil. She beheld a raven drinking the blood upon the snow. She said to Lavarcam, 'The only man I could love would be one who should have those three colours, hair black as the raven, cheeks red as the blood, body white as the snow.' 'Thou hast an opportunity,' answered Lavarcam, 'the man whom thou desirest is not far off, he is close to thee in the palace itself; he is Naesi, son of Usnach.' 'I shall not be happy,' answered Déirdre, 'until I have seen him.'"

This famous story "which is known," as Dr. Cameron puts it, "over all the lands of the Gaeḋ, both in Ireland and Scotland,"[2] has been more fortunate than any other in the whole range of Irish literature, for it has engaged the attention of, and been edited from different texts by, nearly every great Celtic scholar of this century.[3] Yet I luckily discovered last

[1] In the older form Leborcham. She is generally described as Conor's messenger; in one place she is called his *bean-cainte* or "talking-woman"; this is the only passage I know of in which she is credited with any higher powers. She is said elsewhere to have been the daughter of two slaves of Conor's household, Oa or Aué and Adarc.

[2] Yet when in Trinity College Dublin, a few years ago, the subject—the first Irish subject for twenty-seven years—set for the Vice-Chancellor's Prize in English verse was "Déirdre," it was found that the students did not know what that word meant, or what Déirdre was, whether animal, vegetable, or mineral. So true it is that, despite all the efforts of Davis and his fellows, there are yet two nations in Ireland. Trinity College might to some extent bridge the gap if she would, but she has carefully refrained from attempting it.

[3] O'Flanagan first printed two versions of it in the solitary volume which comprises the "Transactions of the Gaelic Society," as early as

year in the museum in Belfast by far the amplest and most graphic version of them all, bound up with some other pieces of different dates. It was copied at the end of the last or the beginning of the present century by a northern scribe, from a copy which must have been fairly old to judge from the language and from the glosses in the margin. I give here a literal translation of the opening of the story from this manuscript, and it is an admirable example of the later extension and embellishment of the ancient texts.

THE OPENING OF THE FATE OF THE SONS OF USNACH, FROM A MS. IN THE BELFAST MUSEUM.

"Once upon a time Conor, son of Fachtna, and the nobles of the Red Branch, went to a feast to the house of Feidhlim, the son of

---

1808. The older of these two versions agrees closely with that contained in "Egerton, 1782," of the British Museum, but neither of the MSS. which he used is now known to exist. Eugene O'Curry edited the story from the text in the Yellow Book of Lecan, with a translation in the "Atlantis," a long defunct Irish periodical. Windisch edited the oldest existing version, that of the Book of Leinster, in the first volume of "Irische Texte." None of these three versions differ appreciably. In the second volume of the same, Dr. Whitley Stokes edited a consecutive text from 56 and 53 of the MSS. in the Advocates' Library at Edinburgh, the latter of which is a vellum of the fifteenth century. Finally, the text of both these MSS. was published in full in vol. ii. of Dr. Cameron's "Reliquiæ Celticæ," where he also gives a translation of the first. Keating, too, in his history, retells the story at considerable length. Windisch's, O'Curry's, and O'Flanagan's texts were reprinted in 1883 in the "Gaelic Journal." In addition to all these Mr. Carmichael published in Gaelic in 1887 an admirable folk-lore version of the story from the Isles of Scotland in the thirteenth volume of the "Transactions of the Inverness Gaelic Society," and the tale is retold in English, chiefly from this version, by Mr. Jacobs in the first series of his "Celtic Fairy Tales." M. d'Arbois de Jubainville has given a French translation of the entire story from the Book of Leinster, the older Edinburgh MS., and the Highland Folktale, the latter two being translated by M. Georges Dottin. Macpherson made this story the foundation of his "Darthula." Dr. Dwyer Joyce published the story in America as an English poem. Sir Samuel Ferguson, Dr. Todhunter, and the present writer have all published adaptations of it in English verse, and Mr. Rolleston made it the subject of the Prize Cantata at the Féis Ceóil in Dublin in 1897. Hence I may print here this new and full opening of a piece so celebrated. For text see *Zeit. f. Celt. Phil.* II. 1, p. 142.

Doll, the king's principal story-teller ; and the King and people were merry and light hearted, eating that feast in the house of the principal story-teller, with gentle music of the musicians, and with the melody of the voices of the bards and the ollavs, with the delight of the speech and ancient tales of the sages, and of those who read the keenes (?) (written on) flags and books ; (listening) to the prognostications of the druids and of those who numbered the moon and stars. And at the time when the assembly were merry and pleasant in general it chanced that Feidhlim's wife bore a beautiful, well-shaped daughter, during the feast. Up rises expeditiously the gentle Cathfaidh, the Head-druid of Erin, who chanced to be present in the assembly at that time, and a bundle of his ancient . . . ? fairy books in his left hand with him, and out he goes on the border of the rath to minutely observe and closely scrutinise the clouds of the air, the position of the stars and the age of the moon, to gain a prognostication and a knowledge of the fate that was in store for the child who was born there. Cathfaidh then returns quickly to all in presence of the King and told them an omen and prophecy, that many hurts and losses should come to the province of Ulster on account of the girl that was born there. On the nobles of Ulster receiving this prophecy they resolved on the plan of destroying the infant, and the heroes of the Red Branch bade slay her without delay.

"'Let it not be so done,' says the King ; 'it is not laudable to fight against fate, and woe to him who would destroy an innocent infant, for agreeable is the appearance and the laugh of the child ; alas ! it were a pity to quench her (life). Observe, O ye Nobles of Ulster, and listen to me, O ye valiant heroes of the Red Branch, and understand that I still submit to the omen of the prophecies and foretellings of the seers, but yet I do not submit to, nor do I praise, the committing of a base deed, or a deed of treachery, in the hope of quenching the anger of the power of the elements. If it be a fate which it is not possible to avoid, give ye, each of you, death to himself, but do not shed the blood of the innocent infant, for it were not (our) due (to have) prosperity thereafter. I proclaim to you, moreover, O ye nobles of Emania, that I take the girl under my own protection from henceforth, and if I and she live and last, it may be that I shall have her as my one-wife and gentle consort. Therefore, I assure the men of Erin by the securities of the moon and sun, that any one who would venture to destroy her either now or again, shall neither live nor last, if I survive her.'

"The nobles of Ulster, and every one in general listened silent and mute, until Conall Cearnach, Fergus mac Roigh, and the heroes of the Red Branch rose up together, and 'twas what they said, 'O High-king of Ulster, right is thy judgment, and it is (our) due to observe it, and let it be thy will that is done.'

"As for the girl, Conor took her under his own protection, and placed her in a moat apart, to be brought up by his nurse, whose name was Lavarcam, in a fortress of the Red Branch, and Conor and Cathfaidh the druid gave her the name of Déirdre. Afterwards Déirdre was being generously nurtured under Lavarcam and (other) ladies, perfecting her in every science that was fitting for the daughter of a high prince, until she grew up a blossom-bearing sapling, and until her beauty was beyond every degree surpassing. Moreover, she was nurtured with excessive luxury of meat and drink that her stature and ripeness might be the greater for it, and that she might be the sooner marriageable. This is how Déirdre's abode was (situated, namely) in a fortress of the Branch, according to the King's command, every (aperture for) light closed in the front of the dún, and the windows of the back (ordered) to be open. A beautiful orchard full of fruit (lay) at the back of the fort, in which Déirdre might be walking for a while under the eye of her tutor at the beginning and the end of the day; under the shade of the fresh boughs and branches, and by the side of a running, meandering stream that was winding softly through the middle of the walled garden. A high, tremendous difficult wall, not easy to surmount, (was) surrounding that spacious habitation, and four savage man-hounds (sent) from Conor (were) on constant guard there, and his life were in peril for the man who would venture to approach it. For it was not permitted to any male to come next nor near Déirdre, nor even to look at her, but (only) to her tutor, whose name was Cailcin, and to King Conor himself. Prosperous was Conor's sway, and valiant was the fame (*i.e.*, famous was the valour) of the Red Branch, defending the province of Ulster against foreigners and against every other province in Erin in his time, and there were no three in the household of Emania or throughout all Banba [Ireland] more brilliant than the sons of Uisneach, nor heroes of higher fame than they, Naoise [Neeshă], Ainle, and Ardan.

"As for Déirdre, when she was fourteen years of age she was found marriageable and Conor designed to take her to his own royal couch. About this time a sadness and a heavy flood of melancholy lay upon the young queen, without gentle sleep, without sufficient food, without sprightliness—as had been her wont.

"Until it chanced of a day, while snow lay (on the ground), in the winter, that Cailcin, Déirdre's tutor, went to kill a calf to get ready food for her, and after shedding the blood of the calf out upon the snow, a raven stoops upon it to drink it, and as Déirdre perceives that, and she watching through a window of the fortress, she heaved a heavy sigh so that Cailcin heard her. 'Wherefore thy melancholy, girl?' said he. 'Alas that I have not yon thing as I see it,' said she. 'Thou shalt have that if it be possible,' said he, drawing his hand dexterously so that he gave an unerring cast of his knife at the raven, so that he cut one foot off it. And after that he takes up the bird and throws it over near Déirdre. The girl starts at once, and fell into a faint, until Lavarcam came up to help her. 'Why art thou as I see thee, dear girl,' said she, 'for thy countenance is pitiable ever since yesterday?' 'A desire that came to me,' said Déirdre. 'What is that desire?' said Lavarcam. 'Three colours that I saw,' said Déirdre, 'namely, the blackness of the raven, the redness of the blood, and the whiteness of the snow.' 'It is easy to get that for thee now,' said Lavarcam, and arose (and went) out without delay, and she gathered the full of a vessel of snow, and half the full of a cup of the calf's blood, and she pulls three feathers out of the wing of the raven. And she laid them down on the table before the girl. Déirdre began as though she were eating the snow and lazily tasting the blood with the top of the raven's feather, and her nurse closely scrutinising her, until Déirdre asked Lavarcam to leave her alone by herself for a while. Lavarcam departs, and again returns, and this is how she found Déirdre—shaping a ball of snow in the likeness of a man's head and mottling it with the top of the raven's feather out of the blood of the calf, and putting the small black plumage as hair upon it, and she never perceived her nurse examining her until she had finished. 'Whose likeness is that?' said Lavarcam. Déirdre starts and she said, 'It is a work easily destroyed.' 'That work is a great wonder to me, girl,' said Lavarcam, 'because it was not thy wont to draw pictures of a man, (and) it was not permitted to the women of Emania to teach thee any similitude but that of Conor only.' 'I saw a face in my dream,' said Déirdre, 'that was of brighter countenance than the King's face, or Cailcin's, and it was in it that I saw the three colours that pained me, namely, the whiteness of the snow on his skin, the blackness of the raven on his hair, and the redness of the blood upon his countenance, and oh woe! my life will not last, unless I get my desire.' 'Alas for thy desire, my darling,' said Lavarcam. 'My desire, O gentle nurse,' said Déirdre. 'Alas! 'tis a pity thy desire, it is difficult to get it,' said Lavarcam, 'for fast and close is the fortress of the Branch, and high and difficult is the enclosure round about, and [there is] the sharp watch of the fierce man-hounds in it.' 'The hounds are no danger to us,' said Déirdre. 'Where did you behold that face?' said Lavarcam. 'In a dream yesterday,' said Déirdre, and she weeping, after hiding her face in her nurse's bosom, and shedding tears plentifully. 'Rise up from me, dear pupil,' said Lavarcam, 'and restrain thy tears henceforth till thou eatest food and takest a drink, and after Cailcin's eating his meal we shall talk together about the dream.' Her nurse raises Déirdre's head, 'Take courage, daughter,' said she, 'and be patient, for I am certain that thou shalt get thy desire, for according to human age and life, Conor's time beside thee is not (to be) long or lasting.'

"After Lavarcam's departing from her, she [Lavarcam] perceived a green mantle hung in the front of a closed-up window on the head of a brass club and the point of a spear thrust through the wall of the mansion. Lavarcam puts her hand to it so that it readily came away with her, and stones and moss fell down after it, so that the light of day, and the grassy lawn, and the Champion's Plain in front of the mansion, and the heroes at their feats of activity became visible. 'I understand, now, my pupil,' said Lavarcam, 'that it was here you saw that dream.' But Déirdre did not answer her. Her nurse left food and ale on the table before Déirdre, and departed from her without speaking, for the boring-through of the window did not please Lavarcam, for fear of Conor or of Cailcin coming to the knowledge of it. As for Déirdre, she ate not her food, but she quenched her thirst out of a goblet of ale, and she takes with her the flesh of the calf, after covering it under a corner of her mantle, and she went to her tutor and asks leave of him to go out for a while (and walk) at the back of the mansion. 'The day is cold, and there is snow darkening in (the air) daughter,' said Cailcin, 'but you can walk for a while under the shelter of the walls of the mansion, but mind the house of the hounds.'

"Déirdre went out, and no stop was made by her until she passed down through the middle of the snow to where the den of the man-hounds was, and as soon as the hounds recognised her and the smell of the meat they did not touch her, and they made no barking till she divided her food amongst them, and she returns into the house afterwards. Thereupon came Lavarcam, and found Déirdre lying upon one side of her couch, and she sighing heavily and shedding tears. Her nurse stood silent for a while observing her, till her heart was softened to compassion and her anger departed from her. She stretched out her hand, and 'twas what she said, 'Rise up, modest daughter, that we may be talking about the dream, and tell me did you ever see that black hero before yesterday?' 'White hero, gentle nurse, hero of the pleasant crimson cheeks,' said Déirdre. 'Tell me without falsehood,' said Lavarcam, 'did you ever see that warrior before yesterday, or before you bored through the window-work with the head of a spear and with a brass club, and till you looked out through it on the warriors of the Branch when they were at their feats of activity on the Champion Plain, and till you saw all the dreams you spoke of?' Déirdre hides her head in her nurse's bosom, weeping, till she said, 'Oh, gentle mother and nurturer of my heart, do not tell that to my tutor; and I shall not conceal from thee that I saw him on the lawn of Emania, playing games with the boys, and learning feats of valour, and och! he had the beautiful countenance at that time, and very lovely was it yesterday (too).' 'Daughter,' said Lavarcam, 'you did not see the boys on the green of Emania from the time you were seven years of age, and that is seven years ago.' 'Seven bitter years,' said Déirdre, 'since I beheld the delight of the green and the playing of the boys, and surely, too, Naoise surpassed all the youths of Emania.' 'Naoise, the son of Uisneach?' said Lavarcam. 'Naoise is his name, as he told me,' said Déirdre, 'but I did not ask whose son he was.' 'As he told you!' said Lavarcam. 'As he told me,' said Déirdre, 'when he made a throw of a ball, by a miss-cast, backwards transversely over the heads of the band of maidens that were standing on the edge of the green, and I rose from amongst them all, till I lifted the ball, and I delivered it to him, and he pressed my hand joyously.' 'He pressed your hand, girl!' said Lavarcam. 'He pressed it lovingly, and said that he would see me again, but it was difficult for him, and I did not see him since until yesterday, and oh, gentle nurse, if you wish me to be alive take a message to him from me, and tell him to come to visit me and talk with me secretly to-night without the knowledge of Cailcin or any other person.' 'Oh, girl,' said Lavarcam, 'it is a very dangerous attempt to gain the quenching of thy desire [being in peril] from the anger of the King, and under the sharp watch of Cailcin, considering the fierceness of the savage man-hounds, and considering the difficulty of (scaling) the enclosure round about.' 'The hounds are no danger to us,' said Déirdre. 'Then, too,' said Lavarcam, 'great is Conor's love for the children of Uisneach, and there is not in the Red Branch a hero dearer to him than Naoise.' 'If he be the son of Uisneach,' said Déirdre, 'I heard the report of him from the women of Emania, and that great are his own territories in the West of Alba, outside of Conor's sway, and, gentle nurse, go to find Naoise, and you can tell him how I am, and how much greater my love for him is than for Conor.' 'Tell him that yourself if you can,' said Lavarcam, and she went out thereupon to seek Naoise till he was found, and till he came with her to Déirdre's dwelling in the beginning of the night, without Cailcin's knowledge. When Naoise beheld the splendour of the girl's countenance he is filled with a flood of love, and Déirdre beseeches him to take her and escape to Alba. But Naoise thought that too hazardous, for fear of Conor. But in the course (?) of the night Déirdre won him over, so that he consented to her, and they determined to depart on the night of the morrow.

"Déirdre escaped in the middle of the night without the knowledge of her tutor or her nurse, for Naoise came at that time and his two brothers along with him, so that he bored a gap at the back of the hounds den, for the dogs were dead already through poison from Déirdre.

"They lifted the girl over the walls, through every rough impediment, so that her mantle and the extremity of her dress were all tattered, and he set her upon the back of a steed, and no stop was made by them till (they reached) Sliabh Fuaid and Finn-charn of the watch, till they came to the harbour and went aboard a ship and were driven by a south wind across the ocean-waters and over the back-ridges of the deep sea to Loch n-Eathaigh in the west of Alba, and thrice fifty valiant champions [sailed] along with them, namely, fifty with each of the three brothers, Naoise, Ainle, and Ardan."

The three brothers and Déirdre lived for a long time happily in Scotland and rose to great favour and power with the King, until he discovered the existence of the beautiful Déirdre, whom they had carefully kept concealed lest he should desire her for his wife. This discovery drives them forth again, and they live by hunting in the highlands and islands.

It is only at this point that most of the modern copies, such as that published by O'Flanagan in 1808, begin, namely, with a feast of King Conor's, in which he asks his household and all the warriors of Ulster who are present, whether they are aware of anything lacking to his palace in Emania. They all reply that to them it seems perfect. "Not so to me," answers Conor, "I know of a great want which presseth upon you, namely, three renowned youths, the three luminaries of the valour of the Gaels, the three beautiful, noble sons of Usnach, to be wanting to you on account of any woman in the world." "Dared we say that," said they, "long since would we have said it."

Conor thereupon proposes to send ambassadors to them to solicit their return. He takes Conall Cearnach apart and asks him if he will go, and what would he do should the sons of

Usnach be slain while under his protection. Conall answers that he would slay without mercy any Ultonian who dared to touch one of them. So does Cuchulain. Fergus mac Róigh alone promises not to injure the King himself should he touch them, but any other Ultonian who should wrong them must die. Fergus and his two sons sailed to Alba, commissioned to proclaim peace to the sons of Usnach and bring them home. Having landed, Fergus gives forth the cry of a "mighty man of chace." Naoise and Déirdre were sitting together in their hunting booth playing at chess. Naoise heard the cry and said, "I hear the call of a man of Erin." "That was not the call of a man of Erin," said Déirdre, "but the call of a man of Alba." Twice again did Fergus shout, and twice did Déirdre insist that it was not the cry of a man of Erin. At last Naoise recognises the voice of Fergus, and sends his brother to meet him. Then Déirdre confesses that she had recognised the call of Fergus from the beginning. "Why didst thou conceal it then, my queen?" said Naoise. "A vision I had last night," said Déirdre, "for three birds came to us from Emania having three sups of honey in their beaks, and they left them with us, but they took with them three sups of our blood." "And how readest thou that, my queen," said Naoise. "It is," said Déirdre, "the coming of Fergus to us with a peaceful message from Conor, for honey is not more sweet than the peaceful message of the false man."

But all is of no avail. Fergus and his sons arrive and spend the night with the children of Usnach, and despite of all that Déirdre can do, she sees them slowly win her husband round to their side, and inspire him with a desire to return once more to Erin.

Next morning they embark. Déirdre weeps and utters lamentations; she sings her bitter regret at leaving the scenes where she had been so happy.

"Delightful land," she sang, "yon eastern land, Alba, with its wonders. I had never come hither out of it had I not come with Naoise. . . .

"The Vale of Laidh, Oh in the Vale of Laidh, I used to sleep under soft coverlet; fish and venison and the fat of the badger were my repast in the Vale of Laidh.

"The Vale of Masan, oh the Vale of Masan, high its harts-tongue, fair its stalks, we used to enjoy a rocking sleep above the grassy verge of Masan.[1]

"The vale of Eiti, oh the vale of Eiti! In it I raised my first house, lovely was its wood (when seen) on rising, the milking-house of the sun was the vale of Eiti.

"Glendarua, oh Glendarua! my love to every one who enjoys it; sweet the voice of the cuckoo upon bending bough upon the cliff above Glendarua.

"Dear is Droighin over the strong shore. Dear are its waters over pure sand; I would never have come from it had I not come with my love."

She ceased to sing, the vessel approached the shore, and the fugitives are landed once more in Erin. But dangers thicken round them. Through a strategy of King Conor's Fergus is placed under *geasa* or tabu by a man called Barach to stay and partake of a feast with him, and thus detached from the sons of Usnach, who are left alone with his two sons instead. Then Déirdre again uses all her influence with her husband and his brothers to sail to Rathlin and wait there until they can be rejoined by Fergus, but she does not prevail. After that she has a terrifying dream, and tells it to them, but Naoise answered lightly in verse—

"Thy mouth pronounceth not but evil,
O maiden, beautiful, incomparable;
The venom of thy delicate ruby mouth
Fall on the hateful furious foreigners."

Thereafter, as they advanced farther upon their way towards King Conor's palace at Emania, the omens of evil grow

[1] "Gleann Masáin, ón Gleann Masáin,
Árd a chneamh, geal a ghasáin,
Do ghnidhmís codladh corrach
Os inbhear mongach Masáin."

thicker still, and all Déirdre's terrors are re-awakened by the rising of a blood-red cloud.

"'O Naoise, view the cloud
That I see here on the sky,
I see over Emania green
A chilling cloud of blood-tinged red.

I have caught alarm from the cloud
I see here in the sky,
It is like a gore-clot of blood,
The cloud terrific very-thin.'"

And she urged them to turn aside to Cuchulain's palace at Dundalgan, and remain under that hero's safeguard till Fergus could rejoin them. But she cannot persuade the others that the treachery which she herself sees so clearly is really intended. Her last despairing attempt is made as they come in sight of the royal city; she tells them that if, when they arrrive, they are admitted into the mansion in which King Conor is feasting with the nobles of Ulster round him, they are safe, but if they are on any pretext quartered by the King in the House of the Red Branch, they may be certain of treachery. They *are* sent to the House of the Red Branch, and not admitted among the King's revellers, on the pretended grounds that the Red Branch is better prepared for strangers, and that its larder and its cellar are better provided with food and drink than the King's mansion. All now begin to feel that the net is closing over them. Late in the night King Conor, fired with drink and jealousy, called for some one to go for him and bring him word how Déirdre looked, "for if her own form live upon her, there is not in the world a woman more beautiful than she." Lavarcam, the nurse, undertakes to go. She, of course, discloses to Déirdre and Naoise the treachery that is being plotted against them, and returning to Conor she tells him that Déirdre has wholly lost her beauty, whereat, "much of his jealousy abated, and he continued to indulge in feasting and enjoyment a long while, until he thought of Déirdre a second time." This time he does not trust Lavarcam, but sends one of his retainers, first reminding him that his father and his three brothers had been slain by Naoise. But in the mean time the entrances and windows of the Red Branch had been shut and barred and the doors barricaded by the sons of Usnach. One small window, however, had been left open at the back and the spy climbed upon a ladder and looked through it and saw Naoise and Déirdre sitting together and playing at chess. Déirdre called Naoise's attention to the face looking at them, and Naoise, who was lifting a chessman off the board, hurled it at the head and broke the eye that looked at them. The man ran back and told the King that it was worth losing an eye to have beheld a woman so lovely. Then Conor, fired with fury and jealousy, led his troops to the assault, and all night long there is fighting and shouting round the Red Branch House, and Naoise's brothers, helped by the two sons of Fergus, pass the night in repelling attack, and in quenching the fires that break out all round the house. At length one of Fergus's sons is slain and the other is bought off by a bribe of land and a promise of power from King Conor, and now the morning begins to dawn, but the sons of Usnach are still living, and Déirdre is still untaken. At last Conor's druid, Cathba, consents to work a spell against them if Conor will plight his faithful word that having once taken Déirdre he will not touch or harm the sons of Usnach. Conor plights his word and troth, and the spell is set at work. The sons of Usnach had left the half-burnt house and were escaping in the morning light with Déirdre between them when they met, as they thought, a sea of thick viscid waves, and they cast down their weapons and spread abroad their arms and tried to swim, and Conor's soldiers came and took them without a blow. They were brought to Conor and he caused them to be at once beheaded. It was then the druid cursed Emania, for Conor had broken his plighted word, and that curse was fulfilled in the misery that fell upon the province during the wars with Mève. He cursed also the house of Conor, and prophesied that none of his descendants should possess Emania for ever, "and that," adds the saga, "has been verified, for neither Conor nor any of his race possessed Emania from that time to this." [1]

As for Déirdre, she was as one distracted; she fell upon the ground and drank their blood, she tore her hair and rent her dishevelled tresses, and the lament she broke forth into has long been a favourite of Irish scribes. She calls aloud upon the dead, "the three falcons of the mount of Culan, the three lions of wood of the cave, the three sons of the breast of the Ultonians, the three props of the battalion of Chuailgne, the three dragons of the fort of Monadh."

"The High King of Ulster, my first husband,
I forsook him for the love of Naoise.

. . . . . .

That I shall live after Naoise
Let no man on earth imagine.

. . . . . .

Their three shields and their three spears
Have often been my bed.

. . . . . .

I never was one day alone
Until the day of the making of the grave,
Although both I and ye
Were often in solitude.

My sight has gone from me
At seeing the grave of Naoise."

[1] We have seen that none of the race of Ir claim descent from Conor; all their great families O'Mores, O'Farrells, etc., descend from Fergus mac Róigh [Roy] or Conall Cearnach (*see* p. 69 note); yet Conor had twenty-one sons, all of whom, says Keating, died without issue except three—"Benna, from whom descended the Benntraidhe; Lamha, from whom came the Lamhraidhe; and Glasni, whose descendants were the Glasnaide; but even of these," adds Keating, "there is not at this day a single descendant alive in Ireland." *See* O'Mahony's translation, p. 278.

She remembers now in her own agony another woman who would lament with her could she but know that Naoise had died.

> "On a day that the nobles of Alba [Scotland] were feasting,
> And the sons of Usnach, deserving of love,
> To the daughter of the lord of Duntrone
> Naoise gave a secret kiss.
>
> He sent to her a frisking doe,
> A deer of the forest with a fawn at its foot,
> And he went aside to her on a visit
> While returning from the host of Inverness.
>
> But when I heard that
> My head filled full of jealousy,
> I launched my little skiff upon the waves,
> I did not care whether I died or lived.
>
> They followed me, swimming,
> Ainnlé and Ardan, who never uttered falsehood,
> And they turned me in to land again,
> Two who would subdue a hundred.
>
> Naoise pledged me his word of truth,
> And he swore in presence of his weapons three times,
> That he would never cloud my countenance again
> Till he should go from me to the army of the dead.
>
> Alas! if she were to hear this night
> That Naoise was under cover in the clay,
> She would weep most certainly,
> And I, I would weep with her sevenfold."[1]

After her lay of lamentation she falls into the grave where the three are being buried, and dies above them. "Their flag was raised over their tomb, and their names were written in Ogam, and their funeral games were celebrated. Thus far the tragedy of the sons of Usnach."

The oldest and briefest version of this fine saga, that preserved in the Book of Leinster, ends differently, and even more

[1] "Och! da gcluinfeadh sise anocht
Naoise bheith fá bhrat i gcré,
Do ghoilfeadh sise go beacht,
Acht do ghoilfinn-se fá seacht lé."

tragically. On the death of Naoise, who is slain the moment he appears on the lawn of Emania, Déirdre is taken, her hands are bound behind her back and she is given over to Conor.

"Déirdre was for a year in Conor's couch, and during that year she neither smiled nor laughed nor took sufficiency of food, drink, or sleep, nor did she raise her head from her knee. When they used to bring the musicians to her house she would utter rhapsody—

"'Lament ye the mighty warriors
Assassinated in Emania on coming,' etc.

When Conor would be endeavouring to sooth her, it was then she would utter this dirge—

"'That which was most beauteous to me beneath the sky,
And which was most lovely to me,
Thou hast taken from me—great the anguish—
I shall not get healed of it to my death,' etc.

"'What is it you see that you hate most?' said Conor.

"'Thou thyself and Eoghan [Owen] son of Duthrecht,'[1] said she.

"'Thou shalt be a year in Owen's couch then,' said Conor. Conor then gave her over to Owen.

"They drove the next day to the assembly at Muirtheimhne. She was behind Owen in a chariot. She looked towards the earth that she might not see her two gallants.

"'Well, Déirdre,' said Conor, 'it is the glance of a ewe between two rams you cast between me and Owen.'

"There was a large rock near. She hurled her head at the stone, so that she broke her skull and was dead.

"This is the exile of the sons of Usnach and the cause of the exile of Fergus and of the death of Déirdre."

It was in consequence of Conor's treachery in slaying the sons of Usnach while under Fergus's protection that this warrior turned against his king, burnt Emania, and then seceded into Connacht to Oilioll [Ulyul] and Mève, king and queen of that province, where he took service with about fifteen hundred Ultonians who, indignant at Conor, seceded along with him. "It was he," says Keating, summing up the substance of

[1] Who had slain Naoise at Conor's bidding, in the older version.

the sagas, "who carried off the great spoils from Ulster whence came so many wars and enmities between the people of Connacht and Ulster, so that the exiles who went from Ulster into banishment with Fergus continued seven, or as some say, ten years in Connacht, during which time they kept constantly spoiling, destroying and plundering the Ultonians, on account of the murder of the sons of Usnach. And the Ultonians in like manner wreaked vengeance upon them, and upon the people of Connacht, and made reprisals for the booty which Fergus had carried off, and for every other evil inflicted upon them by the exiles and by the Connacht men, insomuch that the losses and injuries sustained on both sides were so numerous that whole volumes have been written upon them, which would be too long to mention or take notice of at present."

It was with the assistance of Fergus and the other exiles that Mève undertook her famous expedition into Ulster, of which we must now speak.

CHAPTER XXVI

THE TÁIN BÓ CUAILNGE

THE greatest of the heroic sagas and the longest is that which is called the Táin Bó Cuailnge,[1] or "Cattle-Raid of Cooley," a district of Ulster contained in the present county of Louth, into which Oilioll and Méadhbh [Mève], the king and queen of Connacht, led an enormous army composed of men from the four other provinces, to carry off the celebrated Dun Bull of Cooley.

Although there is a great deal of verbiage and piling-up of rather barren names in this piece, nevertheless there are also several finely conceived and well-executed incidents. The saga which, according to Zimmer, was probably first committed to writing in the seventh or eighth century, is partially preserved in the Leabhar na h-Uidhre, a manuscript made about the year 1100, and there is a complete copy of it in the Book of Leinster made about fifty years later. I have chiefly translated from a more modern text in my own possession, which differs very slightly from the ancient ones.

The story opens with a conversation between Mève, queen of Connacht, and Oilioll her husband, which ends in a dispute as to which of them is the richest. There was no modern Married Women's Property Act in force, but Irish ladies

[1] Pronounced "Taun Bo Hooiln'ya."

seem to have been at all times much more sympathetically treated by the Celtic tribes than by the harder and more stern races of Teutonic and Northern blood, and Irish damsels seem to have been free to enjoy their own property and dowries.[1] The story, then, begins with this dispute as to which, husband or wife, is the richer in this world's goods, and the argument at last becomes so heated that the pair decide to have all their possessions brought together to compare them one with another and judge by actual observation which is the most valuable. They collected accordingly jewels, bracelets, metal, gold, silver, flocks, herds, ornaments, etc., and found that in point of wealth they were much the same, but that there was one great bull called Finn-bheannach or White-horned, who was really calved by one of Mève's cows, but being endowed with a certain amount of intelligence considered it disgraceful to be under a woman, and so had gone over to Oilioll's herds. With him Mève had nothing that could compare. She made inquiry, however, and found out from her chief courier that there was in the district of Cuailnge in Louth (Mève lived at Rathcroghan in Roscommon) a most celebrated bull called the Dun Bull of Cuailnge belonging to a chieftain of the name of Darè. To him accordingly she sends an embassy requesting the loan of the bull for one year, and promising fifty heifers in return. Darè was quite willing, and promised to lend the animal. He was in fact pleased, and treated the embassy generously, giving them good lodgings with plenty of food and drink—too much drink in fact. The fate of nations is said to often hang upon a thread. On this occasion that of Ulster and Connacht depended upon a drop more or less, absorbed by one of the ten men who constituted Mève's embassy. This man unfortunately passed the just limit, and Darè's steward coming in at the moment heard him say that it was small thanks to his

[1] Yet in the Brehon law a woman is valued at only the seventh part of a man, three cows instead of twenty-one ; but if she is young and handsome she has her additional "honour price."

master to give his bull "for if he hadn't given it we'd have taken it." That word decided the fate of provinces. The steward, indignant at such an outrage, ran and told his master, and Darè swore that now he would lend no bull, and what was more, but that the ten men were envoys he swore he would hang them. With indignity they were dismissed, and returned empty-handed to Mève's boundless indignation. She in her turn swore she would have the bull in spite of Darè. She immediately sent out to collect her armies, and invited Leinster and Munster to join her. She was in fact able to muster most of the three provinces to march against Ulster to take the bull from Darè, and in addition she had Fergus mac Roy and about fifteen hundred Ulster warriors who had never returned to their homes nor forgiven Conor for the murder of the sons of Usnach. She crossed the Shannon at Athlone, and marched on to Kells, within a few miles of Ulster, and there she pitched her standing camp. She was accompanied by her husband and her daughter who was the fairest among women. Her mother had secretly promised her hand to every leader in her army in order to nerve them to do their utmost.

At the very beginning Mève is forewarned by a mysterious female of the slaughter which is to come. She had driven round in her chariot to visit her druid and to inquire of him what would come of her expedition, and is returning somewhat reassured in her mind by the druid's promise which was—

"'Whosoever returneth or returneth not, thou shalt return,' and," says the saga, "as Mève returned again upon her track she beheld a thing which caused her to wonder, a single woman (riding) beside her, upon the pole of her chariot. And this is how that maiden was. She was weaving a border with a sword of bright bronze[1] in her right hand with its seven rings of red gold, and, about her, a spotted speckled mantle of green, and a fastening brooch in the

[1] "Findruini." See Book of Leinster, f. 42, for the old text of this, but I am here using a modern copy, not trusting myself to translate accurately from the old text.

mantle over her bosom. A bright red gentle generous countenance, a grey eye visible in her head, a thin red mouth, young pearly teeth she had. You would think that her teeth were a shower of white pearls flung into her head. Her mouth was like fresh coral? [*partaing*]. The melodious address of her voice and her speaking tones were sweeter than the strings of curved harp being played. Brighter than the snow of one night was the splendour of her skin showing through her garments, her feet long, fairy-like, with (well) turned nails. Fair yellow hair very golden on her. Three tresses of her hair round her head, one tress behind falling after her to the extremities of her ankles.

"Mève looks at her. 'What makest thou there, O maiden?' said Mève.

"'Foreseeing thy future for thee, and thy grief, thou who art gathering the four great provinces of Ireland with thee to the land of Ulster, to carry out the Táin Bó Cuailnge.'

"'And wherefore doest thou me this?" said Mève.

"'Great reason have I for it,' said the maiden. 'A handmaid of thy people (am I),' said she.

"'Who of my people art thou?' said Mève.

"'Féithlinn, fairy-prophetess of Rathcroghan, am I,' said she.

"'It is well, O Féithlinn, prophetess,' said Mève, 'and how seest thou our hosts?'

"'I see crimson over them, I see red,' said she.

"'Conor is in his sickness[1] in Emania,' said Mève, 'and messengers have reached me from him, and there is nothing that I dread from the Ultonians, but speak thou the truth, O Féithlinn, prophetess,' said Mève.

"'I see crimson, I see red,' said she.

"'Comhsgraidh Meann . . . is in Innis Comhsgraidh in his sickness, and my messengers have reached me, and there is nothing that I fear from the Ultonians, but speak me truth, O Féithlinn, prophetess, how seest thou our host?'

"'I see crimson, I see red.'

"'Celtchar, son of Uitheachar, is in his sickness,' said Mève, 'and there is nothing I dread from the Ultonians, but speak truth, O Féithlinn, prophetess.'

"'I see crimson, I see red,' said she.

"'. . . ?' said Mève, 'for since the men of Erin will be in one place there will be disputes and fightings and irruptions amongst them,

[1] This is the mysterious sickness which seizes upon all the Ultonians at intervals except Cuchulain. *See* p. 294, note 3.

about reaching the beginnings or endings of fords or rivers, and about the first woundings of boars and stags, of venison, or matter of venery, speak true, O Féithlinn, prophetess, how seest thou our host? said Mève.

"'I see crimson I see red,' said she."

After this follows a long poem, wherein "she foretold Cuchulain to the men of Erin."

The march of Mève's army is told with much apparent exactness. The names of fifty-nine places through which it passed are given; and many incidents are recorded, one of which shows the furious, jealous, and vindictive disposition of the amazon queen herself. She, who seems to have taken upon herself the entire charge of the hosting, had made in her chariot the full round of the army at their encamping for the night, to see that everything was in order. After that she returned to her own tent and sat beside her husband Olioill at their meal, and he asks her how fared the troops. Mève then said something laudatory about the Gaileóin,[1] or ancient Leinstermen, who were not of Gaelic race, but appear to have belonged to some early non-Gaelic tribe, cognate with the Firbolg.

"'What excellence perform they beyond all others that they be thus praised?' said Oilioll.

"'They give cause for praise,' said Mève, 'for while others were choosing their camping-ground, they had made their booths and shelters; and while others were making their booths and shelters, they had their feast of meat and ale laid out; and while others were laying out their feasts of bread and ale, these had finished their food and fare; and while others were finishing their food and fare, these were asleep. Even as their slaves and servants have excelled the slaves and servants of the men of Erin, so will their good heroes and youths excel the good heroes and youths of the men of Erin in this hosting.'

"'I am the better pleased at that,' said Oilioll, 'because it was with me they came, and they are my helpers.'[2]

[1] For more about the Gaileóin see p. 598 of Rhys's Hibbert Lectures, and O Curry, "M. and C.," vol. ii. p. 260.

[2] They were countrymen of Oilioll's.

"'They shall not march with thee, then,' said Mève, 'and it is not before me, nor to me, they shall be boasted of.'

"'Then let them remain in camp,' said Oilioll.

"'They shall not do that either,' said Mève.

"'What shall they do, then?' said Findabar, daughter of Oilioll and Mève, 'if they shall neither march nor yet remain in camp.'

"'My will is to inflict death and fate and destruction on them,' said Mève."

It is with the greatest difficulty that Fergus is enabled to calm the furious queen, and she is only satisfied when the three thousand Gaileóins have been broken up and scattered throughout the other battalions, so that no five men of them remained together.

Thereafter the army came to plains so thickly wooded, in the neighbourhood of the present Kells, that they were obliged to cut down the wood with their swords to make a way for their chariots, and the next night they suffered intolerably from a fall of snow.

"The snow that fell that night reached to men's legs and to the wheels of chariots, so that the snow made one plain of the five provinces of Erin, and the men of Ireland never suffered so much before in camp, none knew throughout the whole night whether it was his friend or his enemy who was next him, until the rise early on the morrow of the clear-shining sun, glancing on the snow that covered the country."

They are now on the borders of Ulster, and Cuchulain is hovering on their flank, but no one has yet seen him. He lops a gnarled tree, writes an Ogam on it, sticks upon it the heads of three warriors he had slain, and sets it up on the brink of a ford. That night Oilioll and Mève inquire from the Ultonians who were in her army more particulars about this new enemy, and nearly a sixth part of the whole Táin is taken up by the stories which are then and there related about Cuchulain's earliest history and exploits, first by Fergus, and, when he is done relating, by Cormac Conlingeas, and when he has finished, by Fiacha, another Ultonian. This long digression, which is one of the most interesting parts of the whole saga, being over, we return to the direct story.

Cuchulain, who knows every tree and every bush of the country, still hangs upon Mève's flank, and without showing himself during the day, he slays a hundred men with his sling [1] every night.

Mève, through an envoy, asks for a meeting with him, and is astonished to find him, as she thinks, a mere boy. She offers him great rewards in the hope of buying him off, but he will have none of her gold. The only conditions upon which he will cease his night-slaying is if Mève will promise to let him fight with some warrior every day at the ford, and will promise to keep her army in its camp while these single combats last, and this Mève consents to, since she says it is better to lose one warrior every day than one hundred every night.

A great number of single combats then take place, each of which is described at length. One curious incident is that of the war-goddess, whom he had previously offended, the Mór-rígu,[2] or "great queen," attacking him while fighting with the warrior Loich. She came against him, not in her own figure, but as a great black eel in the water, who wound itself around his legs, and as he stooped to disengage himself Loich wounded him severely in the breast. Again she came against him in the form of a great grey wolf-bitch, and as Cuchulain turned to drive her off he was again wounded. A third time she came against him as a heifer with fifty other heifers round her, but Cuchulain struck her and broke one of her eyes, just as Diomede in the Iliad wounds the goddess

[1] Crann-tábhail; it is doubtful what kind of missile weapon this really was. It was certainly of the nature of a sling, but was partly composed of wood.

[2] *See* above, p. 54 and 291. *Rigú* is the old form of *ríoghan*.

Cypris when she appears against him.[1] Cuchulain, thus embarrassed, only rids himself of Loich by having recourse to the mysterious feat of the Gae-Bolg, about which we shall hear more later on. His opponent, feeling himself mortally hurt, cries out—

"'By thy love of generosity I crave a boon.'

"'What boon is that?' said Cuchulain.

"'It is not to spare me I ask,' said Loich, 'but let me fall forwards to the east, and not backward to the west, that none of the men of Erin may say that I fell in panic or in flight before thee.'

"'I grant it,' said Cuchulain, 'for surely it is a warrior's request.'"

After this encounter Cuchulain grew terribly despondent, and urged his charioteer Laeg again to hasten the men of Ulster to his assistance, but their pains were still upon them, and he is left alone to bear the brunt of the attack as best he may. Mève also breaks her compact by sending six men against him, but them he overcomes, and in revenge begins again to slay at night.

Thereafter follows the episode known in Irish saga as the Great Breach of Moy Muirtheimhne. Cuchulain, driven to despair and enfeebled by wounds, fatigue, and watching, was in the act of ascending his chariot to advance alone against the men of the four provinces, moving to certain death, when the

[1] "ὁ δέ Κύπριν ἐπῴχετο νηλέι χαλκῷ,
Γιγνώσκων ὅτ' ἄναλκις ἔην θεός, οὐδὲ θεάων
Τάων αΐ τ' ἀνδρῶν πόλεμον κατα κοιρανέουσιν,
Οὔτ' ἄρ' 'Αθηναίη, οὔτε πτολίπορθος 'Ενυώ.
'Αλλ ὅτε δή ῥ' 'εκίχανε πολὺν καθ' ὅμιλον ὀπάζων,
'Ενθ' ἐπορεξάμενος, μεγαθύμου Τυδέος υἱὸς
"Ακρην οὔτασε χεῖρα, μετάλμενος ὀξέϊ δουρὶ
'Αβληχρήν. εἶθαρ δὲ δόρυ χροὸς ἀντετόρησεν,
'Αμβροσίου διὰ πέπλου, ὃν οἱ Χάριτες κάμον αὐταὶ,
Πρυμνὸν ὑπὲρ θέναρος· ῥέε δ' ἄμβροτον αἷμα θεοῖο
'Ιχώρ, οἷος πέρ τε ῥέει μακάρεσσι θεοῖσιν."
Iliad, v. 330.

A better instance except for the sex is where he afterwards wounds Ares. (*See* v. 855.)

eye of his charioteer is arrested by the figure of a tall stranger moving through the camp of the enemy, saluting none as he moved, and by none saluted.

"That man," said Cuchulain, "must be one of my supernatural friends of the shee[1] folk, and they salute him not because he is not seen."

The stranger approaches, and, addressing Cuchulain, desires him to sleep for three days and three nights, and instantly Cuchulain fell asleep, for he had been from before the feast of Samhain till after Féil Bhrighde[2] without sleep, "unless it were that he might sleep a little while beside his spear, in the middle of the day, his head on his hand, and his hand on his spear, and his spear on his knee, but all the while slaughtering, slaying, preying on, and destroying, the four great provinces."

It was after this long sleep of Cuchulain's that, awaking fresh and strong, the Berserk rage fell upon him. He hurled himself against the men of Erin, he drove round their flank, he "gave his chariot the heavy turn, so that the iron wheels of the chariot sank into the earth, so that the track of the iron wheels was (in itself) a sufficient fortification, for like a fortification the stones and pillars and flags and sands of the earth rose back high on every side round the wheels." All that day, refreshed by his three days' sleep, he slaughtered the men of Erin.

Other single combats take place after this, in one of which the druid Cailitin and his twenty sons would have slain him had he not been rescued by his countryman Fiacha, one of those Ultonians who with Fergus had turned against their king and country when the children of Usnach were slain.

It was only at the last that his own friend Ferdiad was despatched against him, through the wiles of Mève. Ferdiad

[1] In Irish, *sidh*. The stranger is really Cuchulain's divine father.

[2] This is incredible, for the sickness of the Ultonians could not have endured so long.

was not a Gael, but of the Firbolg or Firdomhnan race,[1] yet he proved very nearly a match for Cuchulain. Knowing what Mève wanted with him, he positively refused to come to her tent when sent for, and in the end he is only persuaded by her sending her druids and ollavs against him, who threatened "to criticise, satirise, and blemish him, so that they would raise three blisters[2] on his face unless he came with them." At last he went with them in despair, "because he thought it easier to fall by valour and championship and weapons than to fall by [druids'] wisdom and by reproach."

The fight with Ferdiad is perhaps the finest episode in the Táin. The following is a description of the conduct of the warriors after the first day's conflict.

THE FIGHT AT THE FORD.[3]

"They ceased fighting and threw their weapons away from them into the hands of their charioteers. Each of them approached the other forthwith and each put his hand round the other's neck and gave him three kisses. Their horses were in the same paddock that night, and their charioteers at the same fire; and their charioteers spread beds of green rushes for them with wounded men's pillows

[1] The prominence given to and the laudatory comments on the non-Gaelic or non-Milesian races, such as the Gaileóins and Firbolg in this saga is very remarkable. It seems to me a proof of antiquity, because in later times these races were not prominent.

[2] These are the three blisters mentioned in Cormac's Glossary under the word *gaire*. Nede satirises—wrongfully—his uncle Caier, king of Connacht; "Caier arose next morning early and went to the well. He put his hand over his countenance, he found on his face three blisters which the satire had caused, namely, Stain, Blemish, and Defect [*on, anim, eusbaidh*], to wit, red and green and white."

[3] I give here, for the most part, the translation given by Sullivan in his Addenda to O'Curry's "Manners and Customs," but it is an exceedingly faulty and defective one from a linguistic point of view. However, even though some words may be mistranslated or their sense mistaken, it is immaterial here. Windisch is said to have finished a complete translation of the Táin, but it has not as yet appeared anywhere. Max Netlau has studied the texts of the Ferdiad episode in vols. x. and xi. of the "Revue Celtique."

to them. The professors of healing and curing came to heal and cure them, and they applied herbs and plants of healing and curing to their stabs, and their cuts, and their gashes, and to all their wounds. Of every herb and of every healing and curing plant that was put to the stabs and cuts and gashes, and to all the wounds of Cuchulain, he would send an equal portion from him, westward over the ford to Ferdiad, so that the men of Erin might not be able to say, should Ferdiad fall by him, that it was by better means of cure that he was enabled to kill him.

"Of each kind of food and of palatable pleasant intoxicating drink that was sent by the men of Erin to Ferdiad, he would send a fair moiety over the ford northwards to Cuchulain, because the purveyors of Ferdiad were more numerous than the purveyors of Cuchulain. All the men of Erin were purveyors to Ferdiad for beating off Cuchulain from them, but the Bregians only were purveyors to Cuchulain, and they used to come to converse with him at dusk every night. They rested there that night."

The narrator goes on to describe the next day's fighting, which was carried on from their chariots "with their great broad spears," and which left them both in such evil plight that the professors of healing and curing "could do nothing more for them, because of the dangerous severity of their stabs and their cuts and their gashes and their numerous wounds, than to apply witchcraft and incantations and charms to them to staunch their blood and their bleeding and their gory wounds."

Their meeting on the next day follows thus :—

"They arose early the next morning and came forward to the ford of battle, and Cuchulain perceived an ill-visaged and a greatly lowering cloud on Ferdiad that day.

"'Badly dost thou appear to-day, O Ferdiad,' said Cuchulain, 'thy hair has become dark this day and thine eye has become drowsy, and thine own form and features and appearance have departed from thee.'

"'It is not from fear or terror of thee that I am so this day,' said Ferdiad, 'for there is not in Erin this day a champion that I could not subdue.'

"And Cuchulain was complaining and bemoaning and he spake these words, and Ferdiad answered :

CUCHULAIN.

Oh, Ferdiad, is it thou?
Wretched man thou art I trow,
By a guileful woman won
To hurt thine old companion.

FERDIAD.

O Cuchulain, fierce of fight,
Man of wounds and man of might,
Fate compelleth each to stir
Moving towards his sepulchre."[1]

The lay is then given, each of the heroes reciting a verse in turn, and it is very possibly upon these lays that the prose narrative is built up. The third day's fighting is then described in which the warriors use their "heavy hand-smiting swords," or rather swords that gave "blows of size."[2] The story then continues—

"They cast away their weapons from them into the hands of their charioteers, and though it had been the meeting pleasant and happy, griefless and spirited of two men that morning, it was the separation, mournful, sorrowful, dispirited, of the two men that night.

"Their horses were not in the same enclosure that night. Their charioteers were not at the same fire. They rested that night there.

"Then Ferdiad arose early next morning and went forwards alone to the ford of battle, for knew that that day would decide the battle and the fight, and he knew that one of them would fall on that day there or that they both would fall.

. . . .

"Ferdiad displayed many noble, wonderful, varied feats on high that day, which he never learned with any other person, neither with Scathach, nor with Uathach, nor with Aife, but which were invented by himself that day against Cuchulain.

"Cuchulain came to the ford and he saw the noble, varied, wonderful, numerous feats which Ferdiad displays on high.

[1] This is the metre of the original. The last lines are literally, "A man is constrained to come unto the sod where his final grave shall be." The metre of the last line is wrong in the Book of Leinster,

[2] Tortbullech = toirt-bhuilleach.

"'I perceive these, my friend, Laeg' [said Cuchulain to his charioteer], 'the noble, varied, wonderful, numerous feats which Ferdiad displays on high, and all these feats will be tried on me in succession, and, therefore, it is that if it be I who shall begin to yield this day thou art to excite, reproach, and speak evil to me, so that the ire of my rage and anger shall grow the more on me. If it be I who prevail, then thou shalt laud me, and praise me, and speak good words to me that my courage may be greater.'[1]

"'It shall so be done indeed, O Cuchulain,' said Laeg.

"And it was then Cuchulain put his battle-suit of conflict and of combat and of fight on him, and he displayed noble, varied, wonderful, numerous feats on high on that day, that he never learned from anybody else, neither with Scathach, nor with Uathach, nor with Aife. Ferdiad saw those feats and he knew they would be plied against him in succession.

"'What weapons shall we resort to, O Ferdiad?' said Cuchulain.

"'To thee belongs thy choice of weapons till night,' said Ferdiad.

"'Let us try the Ford Feat then,' said Cuchulain.

"'Let us indeed,' said Ferdiad. Although Ferdiad thus spoke his consent it was a cause of grief to him to speak so, because he knew that Cuchulain was used to destroy every hero and every champion who contended with him in the Feat of the Ford.

"Great was the deed, now, that was performed on that day at the ford—the two heroes, the two warriors, the two champions of Western Europe, the two gift and present and stipend bestowing hands of the north-west of the world; the two beloved pillars of the valour of the Gaels, and the two keys of the bravery of the Gaels to be brought to fight from afar through the instigation and intermeddling of Oilioll and Mève.

"Each of them began to shoot at other with their missive weapons from the dawn of early morning till the middle of midday. And when midday came the ire of the men waxed more furious, and each of them drew nearer to the other. And then it was that Cuchulain on one occasion sprang from the brink of the ford and came on the boss of the shield of Ferdiad, son of Daman, for the purpose of striking his head over the rim of his shield from above. And it was then that Ferdiad gave the shield a blow of his left elbow and cast

[1] A common trait even in the modern Gaelic tales, as in the story of Iollan, son of the king of Spain, whose sweetheart urges him to the battle by chanting his pedigree; and in Campbell's story of Conall Gulban, where the daughter of the King of Lochlann urges her bard to exhort her champion in the fight lest he may be defeated, and to give him "Brosnachadh file fir-ghlic," *i.e.*, the urging of a truly wise poet.

Cuchulain from him like a bird on the brink of the ford. Cuchulain sprang from the brink of the ford again till he came on the boss of the shield of Ferdiad, son of Daman, for the purpose of striking his head over the rim of the shield from above. Ferdiad gave the shield a stroke of his left knee and cast Cuchulain from him like a little child on the brink of the ford.

"Laeg [his charioteer] perceived that act. 'Alas, indeed,' said Laeg, 'the warrior who is against thee casts thee away as a lewd woman would cast her child. He throws thee as foam is thrown by the river. He grinds thee as a mill would grind fresh malt. He pierces thee as the felling axe would pierce the oak. He binds thee as the woodbine binds the tree. He darts on thee as the hawk darts on small birds, so that henceforth thou hast nor call nor right nor claim to valour or bravery to the end of time and life, thou little fairy phantom,' said Laeg.

"Then up sprang Cuchulain with the rapidity of the wind and with the readiness of the swallow, and with the fierceness of the dragon and the strength of the lion into the troubled clouds of the air the third time, and he alighted on the boss of the shield of Ferdiad, son of Daman to endeavour to strike his head over the rim of his shield from above. And then it was the warrior gave the shield a shake, and cast Cuchulain from him into the middle of the ford, the same as if he had never been cast off at all.

"And it was then that Cuchulain's first distortion came on, and he was filled with swelling and great fulness, like breath in a bladder, until he became a terrible, fearful, many-coloured, wonderful Tuaig, and he became as big as a Fomor, or a man of the sea, the great and valiant champion, in perfect height over Ferdiad.[1]

"So close was the fight they made now that their heads met above and their feet below and their arms in the middle over the rims and bosses of their shields. So close was the fight they made that they cleft and loosened their shields from their rims to their centres. So close was the fight which they made that they turned and bent and shivered their spears from their points to their hafts. Such was the closeness of the fight which they made that the Bocanachs and Bananachs, and wild people of the glens, and demons of the air screamed from the rims of their shields and from the hilts of their swords and from the hafts of their spears. Such was the closeness of the fight which they made that they cast the river out of its bed and out of its course, so that it might have been a reclining and reposing couch for a king or for a queen in the middle of the ford, so that

[1] Compare this with the Berserker rage of the Northmen.

there was not a drop of water[1] in it unless it dropped into it by the trampling and the hewing which the two champions and the two heroes made in the middle of the ford. Such was the intensity of the fight which they made that the stud of the Gaels darted away in fright and shyness, with fury and madness, breaking their chains and their yokes, their ropes and their traces, and that the women and youths, and small people, and camp followers, and non-combatants of the men of Erin broke out of the camp south-westwards.

"They were at the edge-feat of swords during the time. And it was then that Ferdiad found an unguarded moment upon Cuchulain, and he gave him a stroke of the straight-edged sword, and buried it in his body until his blood fell into his girdle, until the ford became reddened with the gore from the body of the battle-warrior. Cuchulain would not endure this, for Ferdiad continued his unguarded stout strokes, and his quick strokes and his tremendous great blows at him. And he asked Laeg, son of Riangabhra, for the Gae Bulg. The manner of that was this: it used to be set down the stream and cast from between the toes [*lit.* in the cleft of the foot], it made the wound of one spear in entering the body, but it had thirty barbs to open, and could not be drawn out of a person's body until it was cut open. And when Ferdiad heard the Gae Bulg mentioned he made a stroke of the shield down to protect his lower body. Cuchulain thrust the unerring thorny spear off the centre of his palm over the rim of the shield, and through the breast of the skin-protecting armour, so that its further half was visible after piercing his heart in his body. Ferdiad gave a stroke of his shield up to protect the upper part of his body, though it was 'the relief after the danger.' The servant set the Gae Bulg down the stream and Cuchulain caught it between the toes of his foot, and he threw an unerring cast of it at Ferdiad till it passed through the firm deep iron waistpiece of wrought iron and broke the great stone which was as large as a millstone in three, and passed through the protections of his body into him, so that every crevice and every cavity of him was filled with its barbs.

"'That is enough now, indeed,' said Ferdiad, 'I fall of that. Now indeed may I say that I am sickly after thee, and not by thy hand should I have fallen,' and he said [*here follow some verses*]. . . .

"Cuchulain ran towards him after that, and clasped his two arms about him and lifted him with his arms and his armour and his clothes across the ford northward, in order that the slain should lie

[1] *Cf.* the common Gaelic folk-lore formula, "they would make soft of the hard and hard of the soft, and bring cold springs of fresh water out of the hard rock with their wrestling."

by the ford on the north, and not by the ford on the west with the men of Erin.

"Cuchulain laid Ferdiad down there, and a trance and a faint and a weakness fell then on Cuchulain over Ferdiad.

"'Good, O Cuchulain,' said Laeg, 'rise up now for the men of Erin are coming upon us, and it is not single combat they will give thee since Ferdiad, son of Daman, son of Darè, has fallen by thee.'

"'Servant,' said he, 'what availeth me to arise after him that hath fallen by me.'"

Cuchulain is carried away swooning after this fight and is brought by the two sons of Géadh to the streams and rivers to be cured of his stabs and wounds, by plunging him in the waters and facing him against the currents, "for the Tuatha De Danann sent plants of grace and herbs of healing (floating) down the streams and rivers of Muirtheimhne, to comfort and help Cuchulain, so that the streams were speckled and green overhead with them." The Finglas, the Bush, the Douglas, and eighteen other rivers are mentioned as aiding to cure him.

During the period of Cuchulain's leeching many events were happening in Mève's camp, amongst others the tragic death of her beautiful daughter, Finnabra.[1] Isolated bands of the men of Ulster were now beginning to at last muster in front of Mève, and amongst them came a certain northern chief, who was, as her daughter secretly confessed to Mève, her own love and sweetheart beyond all the men of Erin.

The prudent Mève immediately desires her to go to him, if he is her lover, and do everything in her power to make him draw off his warriors. This design, however, got abroad, and came to the ears of the twelve Munster princes who led the forces of the southern province in Mève's army. These gradually make the discovery that the astute queen had secretly promised her daughter's hand to each one of the twelve, as an inducement to him to take part in her expedition. Infuriated at being thus trifled with and at Mève's treachery

[1] Or Findabar, the fair-eyebrowed one.

in now sending her daughter to the Ultonian, they fall with all their forces upon the queen's battalion and the whole camp becomes a scene of blood and confusion. The warrior Fergus at last succeeds in separating the combatants, not before seven hundred men have fallen. But when Finnabra saw the slaughter that was raging, of which she herself was cause, "a blood-torrent burst from her heart in her bosom through (mingled) shame and generosity," and she was taken up dead.

In the meantime Cuchulain is joined by another great Ultonian warrior, who is also being leeched. He had fallen upon the men of Erin single-handed, and received many wounds, one from Mève herself, who fought, like Boadicea, at the head of her troops. He describes the amazon who wounded him to Cuchulain—

"A largely-nurtured, white-faced, long-cheeked woman, with a yellow mane on the top of her two shoulders, with a shirt of royal silk over her white skin, and a speckled spear red-flaming in her hand; it was she who gave me this wound, and I gave her another small wound in exchange.

"'I know that woman,' said Cuchulain, 'that woman was Mève, and it had been glory and exultation to her had you fallen by her hand.'"

Afterwards Sualtach, father of Cuchulain, heard the groans of his son as he was being cured, and said, "Is it heaven that is bursting, or the sea that is retiring, or the land that is loosening, or is it the groan of my son in his extremity that I hear?" said he. Cuchulain despatches him to urge the Ultonians to his assistance. "Tell them how you found me," he said; "there is not the place of the point of a needle in me from head to foot without a wound, there is not a hair upon my body without a dew of crimson blood upon the top of every point, except my left hand alone that was holding my shield."

And now the Ultonians begin to rally and face the men of Erin. Troops are seen to pour in from every quarter of

Ulster, gathering upon the plains of Meath for the great battle that was impending. Mève sends out her trusted messenger to bring word of what is going on amongst the hostile bands. His first report is that the noise of the Ultonians hewing down the woods before their chariots with the edge of their swords was "like nothing but as it were the solid firmament falling upon the surface-face of the earth, or as it were the sky-blue sea pouring over the superficies of the plain, as it were the earth being rent asunder, or the forests falling [each tree] into the grasp and fork of the other."

Mac Roth, the chief messenger, is again sent out to observe the gathering of the hosts and to bring word of what bands are coming in to the hill where Conor, king of Ulster, has set up his standard. On his return at nightfall there follows a long, minute, and tedious account, something like the list of ships in the Iliad, only broken by the questions of Mève and Oilioll, and the answers of Fergus. It contains, however, some passages of interest. The scout describes the arrival of twenty-nine different armaments around their respective chiefs at the hill where King Conor is encamping. Incidentally he gives us descriptions of characters of interest in the Saga-cycle. As he ends his description of each band and its leaders, Oilioll turns to Fergus, and Fergus from Mac Roth's description recognises and tells him who the various leaders are. In this way we get a glimpse at Sencha, the wise man, the Nestor of the Red Branch, whose counsel was ever good. "That man," said Fergus, "is the speaker and peace-maker of the host of Ulster, and I pledge my word that it is no cowardly or unheroic counsel which that man will give to his lord this day, but counsel of vigour and valour and fight." We see the arrival of Feirceirtné, the arch-ollav of the Ultonians, or Cathbadh the Druid, he who had prophesied of Déirdre at her birth, who was supposed, according to the earliest accounts, to have been the real father of King Conor, he who weakened the children of Usnach by his spells; and we see also Aithirne, the infamous and overbearing poet of the Ultonians, about whom much is related in other tales. "The lakes and rivers," said Fergus, "recede before him when he satirises them, and rise up before him when he praises them." "There are not many men in life more handsome or more golden-locked than he," said Mac Roth, "he bears a gleaming ivory[-hilted] sword in his right hand." With this sword he amuses himself, something like the Norman trouvère Taillefer at the battle of Hastings, by casting it aloft and letting it fall almost on the heads of his companions but without hurting them. The arch-druid is described as having scattered whitish-grey hair, and wearing a purple-blue mantle with a large gleaming shield and bosses of red brass, and a long iron sword of foreign look. Conor's leech, Finghin, led a band of physicians to the field; "that man could tell," said Fergus, "what a person's sickness is by looking at the smoke of the house in which he is." Another hero whom we catch a glimpse of is the mighty Conall Cearnach, the greatest champion of the north, whose name was till lately a household word around Dunsevrick, he who afterwards so bloodily avenged Cuchulain's death, "the sea over seas, the bursting rock, the furious troubler of hosts," as Fergus calls him.

We also see the youth Erc, son of Cairbré Niafer the High-king, who comes from Tara to assist his grandfather King Conor. It is curious, however, that in this catalogue of the Ultonians quite as much space is given to the description of men whose names are now—so far, at least, as I know—unknown to us, as to those who often and prominently figure in our yet remaining stories.

At last the great battle of the Táin comes off, when the men of Ulster meet the men of Ireland fairly and face to face. Prodigies of valour are performed on both sides, and Fergus—who after Cuchulain is certainly the hero of the Táin—seconded by Oilioll, by Mève, by the Seven Mainès, and by the sons of Magach, drives the Ultonians back on his side of the battle three times. Conor, who is on the other flank, perceives that the men of his far wing are being broken, and loudly

"he shouts to the Household of the Red Branch, 'hold ye the place in the battle where I am, till I go find who it is who has thrice inclined the battle against us on the north.'

"'We take that upon ourselves,' said they, 'for heaven is over us, and earth is under us, and unless the firmament fall down upon the wave-face of the earth, or the ocean encircle us, or the ground give way under us, or the ridgy blue-bordered sea rise over the expanse[1] of life, we shall give not one inch of ground before the men of Erin till thou come to us again, or till we be slain.'"

Conor hastens northward and finds himself confronted by the man he had so bitterly wronged, whose hand had lain heavy on his province and himself, Fergus, who now comes face to face with him after so many years. Tremendous are the strokes of Fergus.

"He smote his three enemy blows upon Conor's shield 'Eochain' so that the shield screamed thrice upon him, and the three leading waves of Erin answered it.

"'Who,' cries Fergus, 'holds his shield against me in this battle?'[2]

"'O Fergus,' cried Conor, 'one who is greater and younger and handsomer, and more perfect than thyself is here, and whose father and whose mother were better than thine; one who slew the three great candles of the valour of the Gaels, the three prosperous sons of Usnach, in spite of thy guarantee and thy protection, the man who banished thee out of thy own land and country, the man who made of it a dwelling-place for the deer and the roe and the foxes, the man who never left thee as much as the breadth of thy foot of territory in Ulster, the man who drove thee to the entertainment of women,[3] and the man who will drive thee back this day in the presence of the men of Erin, [I] Conor, son of Fachtna Fathach, High-king of Ulster, and son of the High-king of Ireland."

Despite this boasting he would certainly have been slain by his great opponent had not one of his sons clasped his arms in

[1] "Tulmuing." *See* p. 7.

[2] I do not think this is rightly translated, but the passage is obscure to me.

[3] Alluding to Fergus serving with Queen Mève.

supplication around Fergus's knees and conjured him not to destroy Ulster, and Fergus, melted by these entreaties, consented to remain passive if Conor retired to the other wing of the battle, which he did.

In the meantime Mève had sent away the Dun Bull with fifty heifers round him and eight men, to drive him to her palace in Connacht, "so that whoever reached Cruachan alive, or did not reach it, the Dun Bull of Cuailnge should reach it as she had promised."

Cuchulain, who had joined the Ultonians, and whose arms had been taken from him, lest in his enfeebled condition he should injure himself by taking part in the fray, unable to bear any longer the look of the battle, the shouting and the war-cries, rushes into the fight with part of his broken chariot for a weapon, and performs mighty feats. At length he ceases to slay at Mève's solicitation, whose life he spares, and the shattered remnants of her host begin slowly to withdraw across the ford. "Oilioll draws his shield of protection behind the host [*i.e.*, covers the rear], Mève draws her shield of protection in her own place, Fergus draws his shield of protection, the Mainès draw their shield of protection, the sons of Magach draw their shield of protection behind the host; and in this manner they brought with them the men of Erin across the great ford westward," nor did they cease their retreat till Mève and her army found themselves at Cruachan in Connacht, whence they had set out.

The long saga ends with a decided anti-climax, the encounter between the Dun Bull, whom Mève had carried off, and her own bull, the White-Horned.[1] These bulls, according to one

[1] The Finnbheannach, pronounced "Fin-van-ach." Both the bulls were endowed with intelligence. One of the virtues of the Dun Bull was that neither Bocanachs nor Bananachs nor demons of the glens could come into one cantred to him. There emanated from him, too, when returning home every evening, a mysterious music, so that the men of the cantred where he was, required no other music. The war-goddess herself, the Mór-rigú, speaks to him.

of the most curious of the short auxiliary sagas to the Táin, were really rebirths of two men who hated each other during life, and now fought it out in the form of bulls. When they caught sight of each other they pawed the earth so furiously that they sent the sods flying across their shoulders, "they rolled the eyes in their heads like flames of fiery lightning." All day long they charged, and thrust, and struggled, and bellowed, while the men of Ireland looked on, "but when the night came they could do nothing but be listening to the noises and the sounds." The two bulls traversed much of Ireland during that night.[1] Next morning the people of Cruachan saw the Dun Bull coming with the remains of his enemy upon his horns. The men of Connacht would have intercepted him, but Fergus, ever generous, swore with a great oath that all that had been done in the pursuit of the Táin was nothing to what he would do if the Dun Bull were not allowed to return to his own country with his kill. The Dun made straight for his home at Cuailnge in Louth. He drank of the Shannon at Athlone, and as he stooped one of his enemy's loins fell off from his horn, hence Ath-luain, the Ford of the Loin. After that he rushed, mad with passion, towards his home, killing every one who crossed his way. Arrived there, he set his back to a hill and uttered wild bellowings of triumph, until "his heart in his breast burst, and he poured his heart in black mountains of brown blood out across his mouth."

Thus far the Táin Bó Cuailnge.

[1] Every place in Ireland, says the saga, that is called Cluain-na-dtarbh, Magh-na-dtarbh, Bearna-na-dtarbh, Druim-na-dtarbh, Loch-na-dtarbh, *i.e.*, the Bull's meadow, plain, gap, ridge, lake, etc., has its name from them!

CHAPTER XXVII

THE DEATH OF CUCHULAIN

ALTHOUGH Cuchulain won for himself in this war an imperishable fame, yet he was not destined to enjoy it long, for he perished before arriving at middle age.[1] The account of his death is preserved in the Book of Leinster, a manuscript of the middle of the twelfth century, which quotes incidentally from an Irish poet[2] of the seventh century, thus showing that Cuchulain was at this early age the hero of the poets. Unfortunately the opening of the story in the Book of Leinster is lost, but many modern extensions of the saga still exist, from one of which in my possession I shall supply what is missing.[3]

Cuchulain had three formidable enemies, who were bent upon his life, these were Lughaidh [Lewy] the son of the

[1] He died at the age of twenty-seven years, according to the Annals of Tighearnach, and also according to a note in the Book of Ballymote, which Charles O'Conor of Belinagare identifies as an extract from the Synchronisms of Flann of Monasterboice, who died in 1056. But an account in a MS. H. 3. 17, in Trinity College, Dublin, which was copied about the year 1460, asserts that Cuchulain died in his fifty-ninth year. (*See* O'Curry's MS. Mat., p. 507.)

[2] Cennfaelad, son of Ailill.

[3] This MS., which contains many of the Cuchulain sagas, was copied about a hundred years ago by a scribe named Seághain O'Mathghamhna on an island in the Shannon.

Momonian king Curigh,[1] whom Cuchulain had slain, Erc, the son of Cairbré Niafer king of all Ireland, who was slain in the battle of Rosnaree,[2] and the descendants of the wizard Calatin, who with his twenty sons and his son-in-law fell by Cuchulain in one of the combats at the Ford, during the raid of the Táin. His wife, however, brought into the world three posthumous children, daughters.[3] These unhappy creatures Mève mutilated by cutting off their right legs and left arms, so that they might be odious and horrible, and all the fitter for the dread profession she proposed for them—evil wizardry. She reared them carefully, and so soon as they were of a fitting age she sent them into the world to gain a knowledge of charms and spells, and druidism, and witchcraft, and incantations. In pursuit of this knowledge they roamed throughout the world, and at last returned to the queen as perfect adepts as might be.

Thereupon she convened a second muster of the men of the four provinces, and joined by Lewy the son of Curigh, and Erc the son of Cairbré Niafer, both of whose parents had fallen by Cuchulain, and having with her the odious but powerful children of Calatin, eager to avenge the death of their father and their family, she again marched upon Ulster

[1] The older form of this name is Curoi. A detailed account of this saga is given by Keating. *See* p. 282 of O'Mahony's edition. The saga is also told under the title of *Aided Conrui*, in Egerton 88, British Museum.

[2] The saga of the battle of Rosnaree has recently been published with a translation by Rev. Ed. Hogan, S.J.

[3] Some say six children—three daughters and three sons. The MS. H. i. 8, in Trinity College, which dates from about 1460, according to O'Curry, relates thus : "And the sons of Cailitin were eight years after the Táin before they went to pursue their learning, for they were but infants in cradles at the time their father was killed. Nine years for them after that pursuing their learning. Seven years after finishing their learning was spent in making their weapons, because there could be found but one day in the year to make their spears. And three years after that did the sons of Cailitin spend in assembling and marching the men of Erin to Belach Mic Uilc in Magh Muirtheimhne (Cuchulain's patrimony)."

during the sickness of their warriors, and began to plunder and to burn and to drive away a mighty prey. King Conor immediately surmised that it was against Cuchulain the expedition was prepared, and without a moment's delay he depatched Lavarcam his female messenger, to desire him instantly to leave his palace and his patrimony at Dundealgan[1] in the plain of Muirtheimhne, and come to himself at Emania, there to be under the King's immediate orders. This command he gave, thinking to rescue Cuchulain from the possible effects of his own valour and rashness, for there was scarcely a man of distinction in any of the four provinces of Erin some of whose relatives had not been slain by him.

Lavarcam found the hero upon the shore, between sea and land, intent upon the slaying of sea-fowl with his sling, but though birds many flew over him and past him, not one could he bring down—they all escaped him. And this was to him the first bad omen. Very reluctantly did he obey the call of Conor, and sorely loath was he to leave his patrimony. He accompanied Lavarcam, however, to Emania, and abode there in his own bright-lighted crystal *grianán*. Then Conor consulted with his druids as to how best to keep him there, and they sent the bright ladies of Emania, and his wife Emer, and the poets and the musicians, and the men of science, to surround and distract and amuse him, with conversation and music and banquets.

In the meantime, however, Mève's army had advanced upon and burned Dundealgan, and the children of Calatin had promised that within three days and three nights they would bring Cuchulain to his doom.

And now ensues what is to my mind one of the most powerful incidents in all this saga—the malignant ghoulish efforts of the children of Calatin to draw forth Cuchulain from his place of safety, and on the other side the anxiety of the druids and ladies, and the frenzied heart-sick efforts of his

[1] Now Dundalk in the County Louth.

wife, and his mistress, to detain him. The loathsome wizards flew through the air and stationed themselves upon the plain outside Emania—

"They smote the soil and beat and tore it up around them, so that they made of fuz-balls, and of stalks of *sanna*, and of the fine foliage of the oaks, as it were ordered battalions, and hosts, and multitudes of men, and the confused shoutings of the battalions and of the war-bands, and the battle array, were heard on all sides, as it were striking and attacking the fortress."

Geanan the druid, the son of old Cathbadh, was watching Cuchulain this day. As soon as the sounds of war and shouting reached him Cuchulain rose and "looked forth, and he saw the battalions smiting each other unsparingly," as he thought, and he burned at once with fury and shame; but the druid cast his two arms round him in time to prevent him from bursting forth to relieve the apparently foe-beleaguered town. Over and over again must the druid assure him that all he saw was blind-work and magic, and unreal phantoms, employed by the clan Calatin to lure him forth to his destruction.[1] It was impossible, however, to keep Cuchulain from at least looking, and, the next time he looked forth,

"he thought he beheld the battalions drawn up upon the plains, and the next time he looked after that he thought he saw Gradh son of Lir upon the plain, and it was a *geis* (tabu) to him to see that, and then he thought moreover that he heard the harp of the son of Mangur playing musically, ever-sweetly, and it was a *geis* to him to listen to those pleasing fairy sounds, and he recognised from these things that his virtue was indeed overcome, and that his *geasa* (tabus) were broken, and that the end of his career had arrived, and that his valour and prowess were destroyed by the children of Calatin."

After that one of the daughters of the wizard Calatin,

[1] "Ni bhfuil acht saobh-lucht siabhartha ann súd, sian-sgarrtha duaibhsiocha draoidheachta do dhealbhadar clann cuirpthe Chailitin go claonmhillteach fad' chómhair-se, dod' chealgadh, agus dod' chomh-bhuaidhreadh, a churaidh chalma chath-bhuadhaigh."

assuming the form of a crow, came flying over him and incited him with taunts to go and rescue his homestead and his patrimony from the hands of his enemies. And although Cuchulain now understood that these were enchantments that were working against him, yet was he none the less anxious to rush forth and oppose them, for he felt moved and troubled in himself at the shouting of the imaginary hosts, and his memory, and his senses, and his right mind were afflicted by the sounds of that ever-thrilling harp.

Then the druid used all his influence, explaining to him that if he would only remain for three days more in Emania the spells would have no power, and he would go forth again, "and the whole world would be full of his victories and his lasting renown," and thereafter the ladies of Emania and the musicians closed round him, and they sang sweet melodies, and they distracted his mind, and the day drew to a close:—the clan Calatin retired baffled, and Cuchulain was himself once more.

During that night the ladies and the druids took council together and determined to carry him away to a glen so remote and lonely that it was called the Deaf Valley, and to hide him there, preparing for him a splendid banquet, with music, and poets, and delights of every kind.

Next morning came the accursed wizards and inspected the city, and they marvelled that they saw not Cuchulain, and that he was neither beside his wife, nor yet amongst the other heroes of the Red Branch. Then they understood that he had been hidden away by Cathbadh the druid, "and they raised themselves aloft, lightly and airily, upon a blast of enchanted wind, which they created to lift them," and went soaring over the entire province of Ulster to discover his retreat. This they do by perceiving Cuchulain's grey steed, the Liath Macha, standing outside at the entrance to the glen. Then the three begin their wizardry anew, and made, as it were, battalions of warriors to appear round the glen, and they raised anew the sounds of arms and the shouts of war and conflict, as they had done at Emania.

The instant the ladies round Cuchulain heard it they also shouted, and the musicians struck up—but in vain ; Cuchulain had caught the sound. They succeeded, however, in calming his mind, and in inducing him to pay no heed to the false witcheries of the clan Calatin. These continued for a long time waiting and filling the air with their unreal battle tumult, but Cuchulain did not appear. Then they understood that the druids had been more powerful than they. Mad with impotent fury one of them enters the glen, and pushes her way right into the very fortress where Cuchulain was feasting. Once there she changes herself into the form of the beautiful Niamh [Nee-av], Cuchulain's love and sweetheart. First she stood at the door in the likeness of an attendant damsel, and beckoned to the lady to come to her outside. Niamh, thinking she has something to communicate, follows her through the door and out into the valley, and the other ladies follow Niamh. Instantly she raises an enchanted fog between them and the dún, so that they wander astray, and their minds are troubled. But she, assuming the form of the lady Niamh herself, slips back into the fortress, comes to Cuchulain, and cries to him : "Up, O Cuchulain, and meet the men of Erin, or thy fame shall be lost for ever, and the province shall be destroyed." At this speech Cuchulain is astounded, for Niamh had bound him by an oath that he would not go forth or take arms until she herself should give him leave, and this leave he never thought to receive of her until the fatal time was over. "I shall go," said Cuchulain, "and that is a pity, O Niamh," said he, "and after that it is difficult to trust to woman, for I had thought thou hadst not given me that leave for the gold of the world, but since it is thou who dost let me go to face the men of Erin, I shall go." After that he rose and left the dún. "I have no reason for preserving my life longer," said Cuchulain, "for the end of my time is come, and all my *geasa* (tabus) are lost, and Niamh has let me go to face the men of Erin ; and since she has let me, I shall go."

Afterwards the real Niamh overtakes him at the entrance to the glen, and assured him with torrents of tears, and wild sobs, that it was not she who had given him leave, but the vile enchantress who had assumed her form, and she conjured him with prayers and piteous entreaties to remain with her. But Cuchulain would not believe her, and urged Laeg to catch his steeds and yoke them, for he thought that he beheld—

"The great battle-battalions ranged upon the green of Emania, and the whole plain filled up and crowded with broad bands of hundreds of men, with champions, and steeds, and arms, and armour, and he thought he heard the awful shoutings, and [saw] the burnings extending, widely-let-loose through the buildings of Conor's city, and him-seemed that there was nor hill nor rising ground about Emania that was not full of spoils, and it appeared to him that Emer's sunny-house was overthrown and had fallen out over the ramparts of Emania, and that the House of the Red Branch was in one blaze, and that all Emania was one meeting-place of fire, and of black, dark, spacious, brown-red smoke."[1]

Then Cuchulain's brooch fell from his hand and pierced his foot, another omen of ill. Nor would his noble grey war-horse allow himself to be caught. It was only when Cuchulain addressed him with persuasive words of verse that he consented to let himself be harnessed to the chariot, and even then "he

[1] Up to this I have followed the version of my own modern manuscript. From this out, however, the version in the twelfth-century Book of Leinster is used. Monsieur d'Arbois de Jubainville, in his introduction to the fragment of the saga in the Book of Leinster, seems to think that Emania was really besieged, and women and children slaughtered round its walls by the men of Erin, whereas it would appear that the lost part of the saga refers to some such version as I have given from my manuscript, and that it was only the wizardry and sorcery of the children of Calatin, who raised these phantasms. This is the more evident because Cuchulain, when he issues forth, meets no enemy until he has arrived at the plain of Muirtheimhne. Jubainville's words are, "Cependant les cris de douleur des femmes et des enfants qu'on massacrait jusqu'au pied des remparts d'Emain macha [Emania] parvinrent à son oreille : on en verra un peu plus bas les conséquences, dont la dernière fut la mort du heros."

lets fall upon his fore feet, from his eyes, two large tears of blood." In vain did the ladies of Emania try to bar his passage, in vain did fifty queens uncover their bosoms before him in supplication. "He is the first," says the saga, "of whom it is recounted that women uncovered before him their bosoms." [1]

Thereafter another evil omen overtook him, for as he pursued the high road leading to the south,

"and had passed the plain of Mogna, he perceived something, three hags of the half-blind race,[2] who were on the track before him cooking a poisoned dog's flesh upon spits of holly. Now it was a *geis* (tabu) to Cuchulain to pass a cooking-fire without visiting it and accepting food. It was another *geis* to eat of his own name" [*i.e.*, a hound, he is Cu-Chulain or Culan's hound], "so he pauses not, but passes the three hags. Then one of them cries to him—

"'Come, visit us, Cuchulain.'

"'I shall not visit you,' said Cuchulain.

"'There is something to eat here,' replied the hag; 'we have a dog to offer thee. If our cooking-place were great,' said she, 'thou wouldst come, but because it is small thou comest not; a great man who despises the small, deserves no honour.'

"Cuchulain then moved over to the hag, and she with her left hand offered him half the dog. Cuchulain ate, and it was with his left hand he took the piece, and he placed part of it under his left thigh, and his left hand and his left thigh were cursed, and the curse reached all his left side, which from his head to his feet lost a great part of its power."

At last Cuchulain meets the enemy on his ancestral patrimony of Moy Muirtheimhne, drawn up in battle array, with shield to shield as though it were one solid plank that was around them. Cuchulain displays his feats from his chariot, especially "his three thunder-feats—the thunder of an hundred, the thunder of three hundred, the thunder of thrice nine men."

[1] It was *geis*, or tabu, to him to behold the exposed breast of a woman. See above, p. 301.

[2] These are in my version the three daughters of Calatin.

"He played equally with spear, shield, and sword, he performed all the feats of a warrior. As many as there are of grains of sand in the sea, of stars in the heaven, of dewdrops in May, of snowflakes in winter, of hailstones in a storm, of leaves in a forest, of ears of corn in the plains of Bregia, of sods beneath the feet of the steeds of Erin on a summer's day, so many halves of heads, and halves of shields, and halves of hands and halves of feet, so many red bones were scattered by him throughout the plain of Muirtheimhne, it became grey with the brains of his enemies, so fierce and furious was Cuchulain's onslaught."

The plan which Erc, son of the late High-king Cairbrè Niafer had adopted was to place two men pretending to fight with one another upon each flank of the army and a druid standing near who should first make Cuchulain separate the combatants, and should then demand from him his spear, since there ran a prophecy to the effect that Cuchulain's spear should kill a king, but if they could get the spear from him they at least would be safe from the prophecy; it would not be one of them who should be slain by it.

Cuchulain separates the fighters as the druid asks him, by killing each of them with a blow.

"'You have separated them,' said the druid, 'they shall do each other no more harm.'

"'They would not be so silenced,' said Cuchulain, 'hadst thou not prayed me to interfere between them.'

"'Give me thy spear, O Cuchulain,' said the druid.

"'I swear by the oath which my nation swears,' said Cuchulain, 'you have no greater need of the spear than I. All the warriors of Erin are come together against me, and I must defend myself.'

"'If thou refuse me,' said the druid, 'I shall solemnly utter against thee a magic curse.'

"'Up to this time,' replied Cuchulain, 'no curse has ever been levelled against me for any act of refusal on my part.'"

And with that he reversed his spear and threw it at the druid butt foremost, killing him and nine more. Lewy, the son of Curigh, immediately picked it up.

"'Whom,' said he to the children of Calatin, 'is this to overthrow?'

"'It is a king whom that spear shall slay,' said they.

Lewy hurled it at Cuchulain's chariot, and it pierced Laeg, his charioteer.

Cuchulain bade his charioteer farewell.

"'To-day,' said Cuchulain, 'I shall be both warrior and charioteer.'"

The same incident happens again. Cuchulain kills the second druid in the same way, and his spear is picked up by Erc.

"'Children of Calatin,' said Erc, 'what exploit shall this spear perform?'

"'It shall overthrow a king,' said they.

"'You said this spear would overthrow a king when Lewy hurled it some time ago,' said Erc.

"'Nor were we deceived,' said they, 'that spear has brought down the king of the charioteers of Ireland, Laeg, the son of Riangabhra, Cuchulain's charioteer.'"

Erc hurls the spear and it passes through the side of Cuchulain's noble steed, the Liath Macha. Cuchulain took a fond farewell of the animal who galloped with half the yoke around its neck to the lake from whence he had first taken it, on the mountain of Fuad in far-off Armagh.

The third time a druid demands his spear, and is killed by Cuchulain, who throws it to him handle foremost. The spear is picked up this time by Lewy son of Curigh.

"'What feat shall this spear perform, ye children of Calatin?' said Lewy.

"'It shall overthrow a king,' said they.

"'Ye said as much when Erc hurled it this morning,' answered Lewy.

"'Yes,' answered the children of Calatin, 'and our word was true. The spear which Erc hurled has wounded mortally the king of the steeds of Ireland, the Liath Macha.'

"'I swear then,' said Lewy, 'by the oath which my nation swears, that Erc's blow smote not the king which this spear is to slay.'"

Then Lewy hurls the spear, and this time pierces Cuchulain through the body, and Cuchulain's other steed burst the yoke and rushed off and never ceased till he, too, had plunged into the lake from which Cuchulain had taken him in far-off Munster.[1] Cuchulain remained behind, dying in his chariot. With difficulty and holding in his entrails with one hand, he advanced to a little lake hard by, and drank from it, and washed off his blood. Then he propped himself against a high stone a few yards from the lake, and tied himself to it with his girdle. "He did not wish to die either sitting or lying, it was standing," says the saga, "that he wished to meet death."

But his grey steed, the Liath Macha,[2] returned once more to defend his lord, and made three terrible charges, scattering with tooth and hoof all who would approach the stone where Cuchulain was dying. At last a bird was seen to alight upon his shoulder. "Yon pillar used not to be a settling place for birds," said Erc. They knew then that he was dead. Lewy, the son of Curigh, seized him by the back hair and severed his head from his body.

But Cuchulain was too important an epic hero to thus finish with him. Another very celebrated, but probably later épopée tells of how his friend Conall Cearnach pursued the retreating army and exacted vengeance for his death. A brief digest of Conall's revenge is contained in the Book of Leinster, but modern copies of much longer and more literary versions exist, and there was no more celebrated poem amongst the later Gael than that

[1] The belief in water-horses is quite common even still amongst the old people in all parts of Connacht, and, I think, over the most of Ireland.

[2] With the Liath Macha so renowned throughout the whole Cuchulain saga compare Areiōn, the celebrated steed of Adrastus, who saved his master at the rout of the Argeian chiefs round Thebes. The Liath Macha returns to the *water* from whence it came, and Areiōn, too, was believed to have been the offspring of Poseidōn. He is alluded to by Nestor in the Iliad xxiii. 346:

> *ὀυκ ἔσθ' ὅς κέ σ'ἕλῃσι μετάλμενος ὀυδὲ παρέλθῃ,*
> *οὐδ' εἴ κεν μετόπισθεν 'Αρείονα δῖον ἔλαυνοι,*
> *'Αδρήστου ταχὺν ἵππον ὃς ἐκ θεόφιν γένος ἦεν.*

He appears, however, to have been black not grey. Hesiod alludes to him as *μέγαν ἵππον Αρείονα κυανοχαίτην.*

called the Lay of the Heads in which Conall Cearnach returns to Emer, Cuchulain's wife, to Emania, with a large bundle of heads strung upon a gad, or withy-wand, thrust through their mouths from cheek to cheek, and there explains in a lay to Emer who they were.

In the ancient version in the Book of Leinster it is only Lewy who is slain by Conall. In my more modern recension he slays Erc and the children of Calatin as well, and recovers the head of Cuchulain, which he found being used as a football by two men near Tara. "If this city," said he of Tara, "were Erc's own lordship and patrimony I would burn it down, but since it is the very navel and meeting-point of the men of Ireland, I shall affront it no more."

Emer's joy and her grief on recovering her husband's head are touchingly described.

"She washed clean the head and she joined it on to its body, and she pressed it to her heart and her bosom, and fell to lamenting and heavily sorrowing over it, and began to suck in its blood and to drink it,[1] and she placed around the head a lovely satin cloth. 'Ochone!' said she, 'good was the beauty of this head, although it is low this day, and it is many of the kings and princes of the world would be keening it if they thought it was like this; and the men who demand gold and treasure, and ask petitions of the men of Erin and Alba [*i.e.*, the poets and druids] thou wast their one love and their one choice of the men of the earth, and woe for me that I remain behind this day; for there was not of the women of Erin, nor in the whole great world, a woman mated with a husband, or unmated, not a single one, who, until this day, was not envious of me; for many were the goods and jewels and rents and tributes from the countries of the world that thou broughtest to me, with the valour and strength of thy hand,' and she took his hand in hers and fell to making lamentations over it, and to telling of its fame and its exploits, and 't was what she said, 'Alas!' said she, 'it is many of the kings and of the chieftains and of the strong men of the world that fell by this hand, and it is

[1] "Do rinne an ceann do niamhghlanadh agus do chuir ar a chollain féin é, agus do dhruid re na h-ucht agus n-a h-urbhruinne é, agus do ghaibh ag tuirse agus ag trom-mhéala os a chionn, agus do ghaibh ag sughadh a choda fola agus ag a h-ól," etc. This was to express affection. Déirdre does the same when her husband is slain, she laps his blood.

many of the goods and treasures of this world that were scattered by it upon poets and men of knowledge,' and she spake the lay,

"'Ochone O head, Ochone O head,'" etc.

Afterwards Conall Cearnach arrives with his pile of heads and planted them carefully "all round about the wide grass-green lawn" upon pointed sticks, and relates to Emer who they were and how they fell.[1]

"Thereafter," says the saga, "Emer desired Conall to make a wide very deep tomb for Cuchulain," and she laid herself down in it along with her gentle mate, and she set her mouth to his mouth, and she spake—

"'Love of my soul,' she said, 'O friend, O gentle sweetheart, and O thou one choice of the men of the earth, many is the woman envied me thee until now, and I shall not live after thee;' and her soul departed out of her, and she herself and Cuchulain were laid in the one grave by Conall, and he raised their stone over their tomb, and he wrote their names in Ogam, and their funeral games were performed by him and by the Ultonians.

"THUS FAR THE RED ROUT OF CONALL CEARNACH."

[1] This is the celebrated Laoi na gceann, or Lay of the Heads, which begins by Emer asking—

"A Chonaill cia h-iad na cinn?
Is dearbh linn gar dheargais h-airm,
Na cinn o thárla ar an ngad
Slointear leat na fir d'ar baineadh."

It was popular in the Highlands also. There is a copy in the book of the Dean of Lismore, published by Cameron in his "Reliquiæ Celticæ," vol. i. p. 66. Also in the Edinburgh MSS. 36 and 38. See *ibid.* pp. 113 and 115. The piece consists of 116 lines. The oldest form of Emer's lament over Cuchulain, "Nuallguba Emire," is in the Book of Leinster, p. 123, *a.* 20. It is a kind of unrhymed chant. The lament I have given is from my own modern manuscript.

CHAPTER XXVIII

OTHER SAGAS OF THE RED BRANCH

Another saga belonging to this cycle affords so curious a picture of pagan customs that it is worth while to give here some extracts from it. This is the story of Mac Dáthó's Pig and Hound, which is contained in the Book of Leinster, a MS. copied about the year 1150. It was first published without a translation by Windisch in his "Irische Texte," from the Book of Leinster copy collated with two others. It has since been translated by Kuno Meyer from a fifteenth-century vellum.[1] The story runs as follows.

Mac Dáthó was a famous landholder in Leinster, and he possessed a hound so extraordinarily strong and swift that it could run round Leinster in a day. All Ireland was full of the fame of that hound, and every one desired to have it. It struck Mève and Oilioll, king and queen of Connacht, to send an embassy to Mac Dáthó to ask him for his hound, at the same time that the notion came to Conor, king of Ulster, that he also would like to possess it. Two embassies reach Mac Dáthó's house at the same time, the one from Connacht and the other from Ulster, and both ask for the hound for their respective masters. Mac Dáthó's house was one of those open

[1] "Hibernica Minora," p. 57, from Rawlinson B. 512, in the Bodleian Library. I have followed his excellent translation nearly verbatim.

hostelries[1] of which there were five at that time in Ireland.

"Seven doors," says the saga, "there were in each hostelry, seven roads through it, and seven fireplaces therein. Seven caldrons in the seven fireplaces. An ox and a salted pig would go into each of these caldrons, and the man that came along the road would (*i.e.*, any traveller who passed the way was entitled to) thrust the flesh fork into the caldron, and whatever he brought up with the first thrust, that he would eat, and if nothing were brought up with the first thrust there was no other for him."

The messengers are brought before Mac Dáthó to his bed, and questioned as to the cause of their coming.

"'To ask for the hound are we come,' said the messengers of Connacht, 'from Oilioll and from Mève, and in exchange for it there shall be given three score hundred milch cows at once, and a chariot with the two horses that are best in Connacht under it, and as much again at the end of the year besides all that.'

"'We, too, have come to ask for it,' said the messengers of Ulster, 'and Conor is no worse a friend than Oilioll and Mève, and the same amount shall be given from the north (*i.e.*, from the Ultonians) and be added to, and there will be good friendship from it continually.'

"Mac Dáthó fell into a great silence, and was three days and nights without sleeping, nor could he eat food for the greatness of his trouble, but was moving about from one side to another. It was then his wife addressed him and said, 'Long is the fast in which thou art,' said she; 'there is plenty of food by thee, though thou dost not eat it.'

"And then she said—

"Sleeplessness was brought
To Mac Dáthó into his house.
There was something on which he deliberated
Though he speaks to none.[2]

He turns away from me to the wall,
The Hero of the Féne of fierce valour,
His prudent wife observes
That her mate is without sleep."

A dialogue in verse follows. The wife advises her husband

[1] In Old Irish, Bruiden; in modern, Bruidhean (Bree-an).

[2] "Tucad turbaid chotulta / do Mac Dáthó co a thech.
Ros bói ni no chomairled / cen co labradar fri nech."

to promise the hound to both sets of messengers. In his perplexity he weakly decides to do this. After the messengers had stayed with him for three nights and days, feasting, he called to him first the envoys of Connacht and said to them—

"'I was in great doubt and perplexity, and this is what is grown out of it, that I have given the hound to Oilioll and Mève, and let them come for it splendidly and proudly, with as many warriors and nobles as they can get, and they shall have drink and food and many gifts besides, and shall take the hound and be welcome.'

"He also went with the messengers of Ulster and said to them, 'After much doubting I have given the hound to Conor, and let him and the flower of the province come for it proudly, and they shall have many other gifts and you shall be welcome.' But for one and the same day he made his tryst with them all."

Accordingly on the appointed day the warriors and men of each province arrive at his hostelry in great state and pomp.

"He himself went to meet them and bade them welcome. ''Tis welcome ye are, O warriors,' said he, 'come within into the close.'

"Then they went over, and into the hostelry; one half of the house for the men of Connacht and the other half for the men of Ulster. That house was not a small one. Seven doors in it and fifty beds between (every) two doors. Those were not faces of friends at a feast, the people who were in that house, for many of them had injured other. For three hundred years before the birth of Christ there had been war between them.[1]

"'Let the pig be killed for them,' said Mac Dáthó."

This celebrated pig had been fed for seven years on the milk of three score milch cows, and it was so huge that it took sixty men to draw it when slain. Its tail alone was a load for nine men.

"'The pig is good,'" said Conor, king of Ulster.

"'It is good,'" said Oilioll, king of Connacht.

Then there arose a difficulty about the dividing of the pig. As in the case of the "heroes bit" the best warrior was to

[1] But especially since Fergus mac Róigh or Roy had deserted Ulster and gone over to Connacht on the death of Déirdre.

divide it. King Oilioll asked King Conor what they should do about it, when suddenly the mischievous, ill-minded Bricriu spoke from a chamber overhead and asked, "How should it be divided except by a contest of arms seeing that all the valorous warriors of Connacht were there."

"'Let it be so,' said Oilioll.

"'We like it well,' said Conor, 'for we have lads in the house who have many a time gone round the border.'

"'There will be need of thy lads to-night, O Conor,' said a famous old warrior from Cruachna Conalath in the west. 'The roads of Luachra Dedad have often had their backs turned to them (as they fled). Many, too, the fat beeves they left with me.'

"''Twas a fat beef thou leftest with me,' said Munremar mac Gerrcind, 'even thine own brother, Cruithne mac Ruaidlinde from Cruachna Conalath of Connacht.'

"'He was no better,' said Lewy mac Conroi, 'than Irloth, son of Fergus, son of Leite, who was left dead by Echbél, son of Dedad, at Tara Luachra.'

"'What sort of man do ye think,' said Celtchair mac Uthechair, 'was Conganchnes, son of (that same) Dedad, who was slain by myself, and me to strike the head off him?'

"Each of them brought up his exploits in the face of the other, till at last it came to one man who beat every one, even Cet mac Mágach of Connacht.[1]

"He raised his prowess over the host, and took his knife in his hand, and sat down by the pig. 'Now let there be found,' said he, 'among the men of Ireland one man to abide contest with me, or let me divide the pig.'

"There was not at that time found a warrior of Ulster to stand up to him, and great silence fell upon them.

"'Stop that for me, O Laeghaire [Leary],' said Conor, [King of Ulster, *i.e.*, 'Delay, if you can, Cet's dividing the pig'].

---

[1] He is well known in the Ultonian saga. Keating describes him in his history as a "mighty warrior of the Connachtmen, and a fierce wolf of evil to the men of Ulster." It was he who gave King Conor the wound of which, after nine years, he died. He was eventually slain by Conall Cearnach as he was returning in a heavy fall of snow from a plundering excursion in Ulster, carrying three heads with him. See O'Mahony's Keating, p. 274, and Conall Cearnach was taken up for dead and brought away by the Connacht men after the fight, but recovered. This evidently formed the plot of another saga now I think lost.

"Said Leary, 'It shall not be—Cet to divide the pig before the face of us all!'

"'Wait a little, Leary,' said Cet, 'that thou mayest speak with me. For it is a custom with you men of Ulster that every youth among you who takes arms makes us his first goal.[1] Thou, too, didst come to the border, and thus leftest charioteer and chariot and horses with me, and thou didst then escape with a lance through thee. Thou shalt not get at the pig in that manner!'

"Leary sat down upon his couch.

"'It shall not be,' said a tall, fair warrior of Ulster, coming out of his chamber above, 'that Cet divide the pig.'

"'Who is this?' said Cet.

"'A better warrior than thou,' say all, 'even Angus, son of Hand-wail of Ulster.'

"'Why is his father called Hand-wail?' said Cet.

"'We know not indeed,' say all.

"'But I know,' said Cet; 'once I went eastward (*i.e.*, crossed the border into Ulster), an alarm-cry is raised around me, and Hand-wail came up with me, like every one else. He makes a cast of a large lance at me. I make a cast at him with the same lance, which struck off his hand, so that it was (*i.e.*, fell) on the field before him. What brings the son of that man to stand up to me?' said Cet.

"Then Angus goes to his couch.

"'Still keep up the contest,' said Cet, 'or let me divide the pig.'

"'It is not right that thou divide it, O Cet,' said another tall, fair warrior of Ulster.

"'Who is this?' said Cet.

"'Owen Mór, son of Durthacht,' say all, 'king of Fernmag.'[2]

"'I have seen him before,' said Cet.

"'Where hast thou seen me,' said Owen.

"'In front of thine own house when I took a drove of cattle from thee; the alarm cry was raised in the land around me, and thou didst meet me and didst cast a spear at me, so that it stood out of my shield. I cast the same spear at thee, which passed through thy

---

[1] This is what Cuchulain also does the day he assumes arms for the first time. The story of his doings on that day and his foray into Connacht as recited by Fergus to Oilioll and Mève forms one of the most interesting episodes of the Táin Bó Cùailnge. Every young Ultonian on assuming arms made a raid into Connacht.

[2] It was he who, in the oldest version of the Déirdre saga, slew Naoise, and it was to him Conor made Déirdre over at the end of a year. See above p. 317.

head and struck thine eye out of thy head, and the men of Ireland see thee with one eye ever since.'

"He sat down in his seat after that.

"'Still keep up the contest, men of Ulster,' said Cet, 'or let me divide the pig.'

"'Thou shalt not divide it,' said Munremar, son of Gerrcend.

"'Is that Munremar?' said Cet.

"'It is he,' say the men of Ireland.

"'It was I who last cleaned my hands in thee, O Munremar,' said Cet; 'it is not three days yet since out of thine own land I carried off three warriors' heads from thee, together with the head of thy first son.'

"Munremar sat down on his seat.

"'Still the contest,' said Cet, 'or I shall divide the pig.'

"'Verily thou shalt have it,' said a tall, grey, very terrible warrior of the men of Ulster.

"'Who is this?' said Cet.

"'That is Celtchair, son of Uithechar,' say all.

"'Wait a little, Celtchair,' said Cet, 'unless thou comest to strike me. I came, O Celtchair, to the front of thy house. The alarm was raised around me. Every one went after me. Thou comest like every one else, and going into a gap before me didst throw a spear at me. I threw another spear at thee, which went through thy loins, nor has either son or daughter been born to thee since."

"After that Celtchair sat down on his seat.

"'Still the contest,' said Cet, 'or I shall divide the pig.'

"'Thou shalt have it,' said Mend, son of Sword-heel.

"'Who is this?' said Cet.

"'Mend,' say all.

"'What! deem you,' said Cet, 'that the sons of churls with nicknames should come to contend with me? for it was I was the priest,[1] who christened thy father by that name, since it is I that cut off his heel, so that he carried but one heel away with him. What should bring the son of that man to contend with me?'

"Mend sat down in his seat.

"'Still the contest,' said Cet, 'or I shall divide the pig.'

"'Thou shalt have it,' said Cumscraidh, the stammerer of Macha, son of Conor.

"'Who is this?'

"'That is Cumscraidh,' say all.

"He is the makings of a king, so far as his figure goes. . . .

---

[1] This phrase, introduced by a Christian reciter or copyist, need not in the least take away from the genuine pagan character of the whole.

"'Well,' said Cet, 'thou madest thy first raid on us. We met on the border. Thou didst leave a third of thy people with me, and camest away with a spear through thy throat, so that no word comes rightly over thy lips, since the sinews of thy throat were wounded, so that Cumscraidh, the stammerer of Macha, is thy name ever since.'

"In that way he laid disgrace and a blow on the whole province.

"While he made ready with the pig and had his knife in his hand, they see Conall *Ceârnach* [the Victorious], coming towards them into the house. He sprang on to the floor of the house. The men of Ulster gave him great welcome. 'Twas then [King] Conor threw his helmet from his head and shook himself [for joy] in his own place. 'We are glad,' said Conall, 'that our portion is ready for us, and who divides for you?' said Conall.

"One man of the men of Ireland has obtained by contest the dividing of it, to wit, Cet mac Mágach.

"'Is that true, Cet?' said Conall, 'art thou dividing the pig?'

There follows here an obscure dialogue in verse between the warriors.

"'Get up from the pig, Cet,' said Conall.

"'What brings thee to it?' said Cet.

"'Truly [for you] to seek contest from me,' said Conall, 'and I shall give you contest; I swear what my people swear since I [first] took spear and weapons, I have never been a day without having slain a Connachtman, nor a night without plundering, nor have I ever slept without the head of a Connachtman under my knee.'

"'It is true,' said Cet, 'thou art even a better warrior than I, but if Anluan mac Mágach [my brother] were in the house,' said Cet, 'he would match thee contest for contest, and it is a pity that he is not in the house this night.'

"'Aye, is he, though,' said Conall, taking the head of Anluan from his belt and throwing it at Cet's chest, so that a gush of blood broke over his lips. After that Conall sat down by the pig and Cet went from it.

"'Now let them come to the contest,' said Conall.

"Truly there was not then found among the men of Connacht a warrior to stand up to him in contest, for they were loath to be slain on the spot. The men of Ulster made a cover around him with their shields, for there was an evil custom in the house, the people of one side throwing stones at the other side. Then Conall proceeded to divide the pig, and he took the end of the tail in his mouth until he had finished dividing the pig."

The men of Connacht, as might be expected, were not pleased with their share. The rest of the piece recounts the battle that ensued both in the hostelry, whence "seven streams of blood burst through its seven doors," and outside in the close or *liss* after the hosts had burst through the doors, the death of the hound, the flight of Oilioll and Mève into Connacht, and the curious adventures of their charioteer.

The Conception of Cuchulain,[1] the Conception of Conor,[2] the Wooing of Emer,[3] the Death of Conlaoch,[4] the Siege of Howth,[5] the Intoxication of the Ultonians,[6] Bricriu's Banquet,[7] Emer's Jealousy and Cuchulain's Pining,[8] the Battle of Rosnaree,[9] Bricriu's Feast and the Exile of the Sons of Dael Dermuit,[10] Macha's Curse on the

[1] Windisch's "Irische Texte," Erste Serie, 134, and D'Arbois de Jubainville's "L'épopée Celtique en Irlande," p. 22.

[2] D'Arbois de Jubainville's "Épopée Celtique," p. 3.

[3] Translated by Kuno Meyer in "Revue Celtique," vol. xi., and "The Archæological Review," vol. i., and Jubainvilles' "Épopée Celtique," p. 39.

[4] A poem published by Miss Brooke in her "Reliques of Irish Poetry," p. 393 of the 2nd Edition of 1816. There are fragmentary versions of it in the Edinburgh MSS. 65 and 62, published in Cameron's "Reliquiæ Celticæ," vol. i. pp. 112 and 161, and in the Sage Pope Collection from the recitation of a peasant about a hundred years ago, p. 393. The oldest form of the story is in the Yellow Book of Lecan, and it has been studied in Jubainville's "Épopée Celtique," p. 52.

[5] Edited and translated by Stokes in the "Revue Celtique," vol. viii. p. 49.

[6] Translated by Hennessy for Royal Irish Academy, Todd Lecture, Ser. I.

[7] The text published by Windisch, "Irische Texte," I. p. 235, and translated by Jubainville in "Épopée Celtique," p. 81.

[8] The text published by Windisch, "Irische Texte,' I. p. 197, and by O'Curry in "Atlantis," vol. i. p. 362, with translation, and by Gilbert and O'Looney in "Facsimiles of National MSS. of Ireland." Translated into French by MM. Dottin, and Jubainville in "Épopée Celtique en Irlande," p. 174.

[9] Translated and edited by Rev. Edward Hogan, S.J., for the Royal Irish Academy, Todd, Lecture Series, vol. iv.

[10] The text edited by Windisch, "Irische Texte, Serie II., i. Heft, p. 164, and translated by M. Maurice Grammont, in Jubainville's "Épopée Celtique en Irlande," p. 150.

Ultonians,[1] the Death of King Conor,[2] the Wooing of Ferb,[3] the Cattle Spoil of Dartaid,[4] the Cattle Spoil of Flidais,[4] the Cattle Spoil of Regamon,[4] the Táin bé Aingen, the Táin Bo Regamna,[4] the Conception of the two Swineherds,[5] the Deaths of Oilioll (King of Connacht) and Conall Cearnach,[6] the Demoniac Chariot of Cuchulain,[7] the Cattle Spoil of Fraich,[8] are some of the most available of the many remaining sagas belonging to this cycle.

[1] Translated and edited by Windisch, "Dans les comptes rendus de la classe de philosophie et d' histoire de l' Académie royale des sciences de Saxe," says M. d'Arbois de Jubainville, who gives a translation from Windisch's text at p. 320 of his "Épopée Celtique."

[2] Edited and translated by O'Curry in Lectures on the MS. Mat. p. 637, and again by D'Arbois de Jubainville.

[3] Edited and translated by Windisch in "Irische Texte," Dritte Serie, Heft II., p. 445.

[4] These are short introductory stories to the Táin Bo Chuailgne; they have been edited and translated by Windisch in "Irische Texte," Zweite Serie, Heft II., p. 185-255.

[5] Edited and translated by Windisch, "Irische Texte," Dritte Serie, Heft I., p. 230, and translated into English by Alfred Nutt, in his "Voyage of Bran," vol. ii, p. 58.

[6] Translated and edited by Kuno Meyer in the "Zeitschrift für Celtische Philologie," I Band, Heft I., p. 102.

[7] Edited by O'Beirne Crowe in the "Journal of the Royal Historical and Archæological Association of Ireland," Jan., 1870.

[8] Edited by O'Beirne Crowe in "Proceedings of the Royal Irish Academy," 1871.

CHAPTER XXIX

THE FENIAN CYCLE

CUCHULAIN'S life and love and death entranced the ears of the great for many centuries, and into hundreds of bright eyes tears of pity had for a thousand years been conjured up by the pathetic tones of bards reciting the fate of her who perished for the son of Usnach. The wars of Mève and of Conor mac Nessa were household words in the hall of Muirchertach of the leather cloaks, and in the palace at the head of the weir —Brian Boru's Kincora. Whosoever loved what was great in conception, and admired the broad sweep of the epic called upon his bards to recite the loves, the wars, the valour, and the deaths of the Red Branch knights.[1]

But there was yet another era consecrated in story-telling, another age of history peopled by other characters, in which the households of many chieftains and some even of the chiefs themselves delighted. These are pictured in the romances that were woven around Conn of the Hundred Battles, his son Art

[1] Moore's genius has stereotyped amongst us the term Red Branch knight, which, however, has too much flavour of the mediæval about it. The Irish is *curadh*, "hero." The Irish for "Knight" in the appellations White Knight, Knight of the Glen, etc., is Ridire (pronounced "Rĭd-ĭr-yă," in Connacht sometimes corruptly "Rud-ir-ya"), which is evidently the mediæval "Ritter," *i.e.*, Rider.

the Lonely, his grandson Cormac mac Art, and his great-grandson Cairbrè of the Liffey. This cycle of romance may be called the "Fenian" Cycle, as dealing to some extent with Finn mac Cúmhail and his Fenian[1] militia, or the "Ossianic" Cycle since Ossian, Finn's son, is supposed to have been the author of many of the poems which belong to it.

In point of time—as reckoned by the Irish annalists and historians—the men of the Fenian Cycle lived something over two hundred years later than those of the Cuchulain era[2] and in none of the romances do we see even the faintest confusion or sign of intermingling the characters belonging to the different cycles. One of the surest proofs—if proof were needed—that Macpherson's brilliant "Ossian" had no Gaelic

[1] Moore helped to bring this word into common use under the form of Finnian in his melody, "The wine-cup is circling in Alvin's hall." It is probable that he derived the word from Finn, and meant by it "followers of Finn mac Cool." The Irish word is Fiann (pronounced "Fee-an") and has nothing to do with Finn mac Cúmhail. In the genitive it is nà Féine (na Fayna). It is a noun of multitude, and means the Fenian body in general. The individual Fenian was called Féinnidhe, *i.e.*, a member of the Fenian force. The bands of militia were called Fianna [Fee-ăn-a], The word is declined *An Fhiann, na Féinne, do'n Fhéinn* [In Eean, nă Fayn-a, don Aen] and its resemblance to the proper name Finn is only accidental. The English translation of Keating made early in the last century, by Dermot O'Conor, does not use the term "Fenian" at all, but translates the word by "Irish Militia." Nor does O'Halloran, in 1778· when he published his history, seem to have known the term. The first person who appears to have used it is Miss Brooke, as early as 1796 : in her translation of some Ossianic pieces, I find the lines—

> "He cursed in rage the Fenian chief
> And all the Fenian race."

I have been told that Macpherson had already used the word, but I have looked carefully through his Ossian and have not been able to find it. Halliday in his edition of Keating, in 1808, talks in a foot-note of "Fenian heroes." It was John O'Mahony the head-centre of the Irish Republican Brotherhood, a brilliant Irish scholar and translator of Keating, who succeeded in perpetuating the ancient historic memory by christening the "men of '68" the "Fenians."

[2] Cormac mac Art came to the throne, A.D. 227, according to the "Four Masters"; A.D. 213, according to Keating.

original, is the way in which the men and events of the two separate cycles are jumbled together.

As the war between Ulster and Connacht, which followed the death of the children of Usnach, is the great historic event which serves as basis to so many of the Red Branch romances, so the principal thread of history round which many of the Fenian stories are woven, is the gradual and slowly increasing enmity which proclaimed itself between the High-kings of Erin and their Fenian cohorts, resulting at last in the battle of Gabhra, the fall of the High-king, and the destruction of the Fenians.

Thus in the battle of Cnucha is related how Cúmhail [1] [Cool], the father of Finn, made war upon Conn of the Hundred Battles because he had raised Criomhthan of the Yellow Hair to the throne of Leinster, and how he obtained the aid of the Munster princes in the war. At the battle of Cnucha or Castleknock, near Cool's rath—now Rathcoole some ten miles from Dublin—Cool was routed and slain by the celebrated Connacht champion Aedh mac Morna, who lost an eye in the battle and was thenceforth called Goll (or the blind)[2] mac Morna. Many of the Munster Fenians followed Cool in this battle, and we find here the broadening rift between the Fenians of Munster and of Connacht which ultimately tended to bring about the dissolution of the whole body.

Again we find in the fine tale called the Battle of Moy Muchruime how Finn, through spite at his father Cool being thus killed by Conn of the Hundred Battles, kept out of the way when Conn's son Art was fighting the great battle of Moy Muchruime and gave him no assistance.

And again it was partly because Finn kept out of the way on that occasion that Conn's great-grandson fought the battle

[1] See p. 258, note 1.

[2] The word is long obsolete. Goll is a stock character in Fenian folk-lore, a kind of Ajax.

of Gabhra against Finn's son Ossian and his grandson Oscar, a battle which put an end to Fenian power for ever.

Of many of these tales we find two redactions, that of the old vellum MSS. and that of the modern paper ones, the latter being as a rule much longer and more decorative. Here, for instance, is the later version of one passage out of many which is slurred over or disregarded in the old one[1]; it is the sailing of Cúmhail, Finn's father, to Ireland to take the throne of Leinster. I translate this from a modern manuscript of the battle of Cnucha, in my own possession, as a good instance of the decorative, and in places inflated style of the later redactions of many of the Fenian sagas.

THE SAILING OF CÚMHAIL.

"Now the place where Cúmhail chanced to be at that time was between the islands of Alba and the deserts of Fionn-Lochlan, for he was hunting and deer-stalking there. And the number of those who were with the over-throwing hero Cúmhail in that place, was thrice fifty champions of his own near men. And he heard at that time that his country was left without any good king to defend it, and that Cáthaoir Mór [king of Leinster] had fallen in the pen of battle, and that there was no hero to keep the country. Thereupon, those chieftains were of a mind to proceed unto the isolated green isle of Erin, there to maintain with valour and might the red-hand province of Leinster. And joyfully they proceeded straight forwards towards their ship.[2]

"And there they quickly and expeditiously launched the towering,

---

[1] Contained in the Leabhar na h-Uidhre, a volume copied about the year 1100, and printed in "Revue Celtique," vol. ii. p. 86.

[2] With this thunderous description, all sound and fury, and signifying very little, compare the Homeric description of a like scene, clear, accurate, cut like a gem :

τοῖσιν δ'ἴκμενον οὖρον ἵει ἑκάεργος 'Απόλλων,
οἱ δ'ἱστὸν στήσαντ', ἀνά θ' ἱστία λευκὰ πέτασσαν·
ἐν δ'άνεμος πρῆσεν μέσον ἱστίον, ἀμφὶ δὲ κῦμα
στείρῃ πορφύρεον μεγάλ' ἴαχε, νηὸς ἰούσης·
'η δ' ἔθεεν κατὰ κῦμα, διαπρήσσουσα κέλευθα.

ILIAD I., p. 480.

But the Irish passage, though quoted here to exemplify a common feature of the Fenian tales, really dates from a time of decadence.

wide-wombed, broad-sailed bark, the freighted full-wide, fair-broad, firm-roped vessel, and they grasped their shapely well-formed broad-bladed, well-prepared oars, and they made a powerful sea-great, dashing, dry-quick rowing over the broad hollow-deep, full-foamed, pools [of the sea], and over the vast-billowed, vehement, hollow-broken rollers, so that they shot their shapely ships under the penthouse of each fair rock in the shallows nigh to the rough-bordered margin of the Eastern lands, over the unsmooth, great-forming, lively-waved arms of the sea, so that each fierce, broad, constant-foaming, bright-spotted, white-broken drop that the heroes left upon the sea-pool with that rapid rowing, formed [themselves] like great torrents upon soft mountains.

"When that valiant powerful company perceived the moaning of the loud billow-waves and the breaking forth of the ocean from her barriers, and the swelling of the abyss from her places, and the loud convulsion of the sea from her smooth streams, it was then they hoisted the variegated, tough-cordaged, sharp-pointed mast with much speed. And when the great foundation-blasts of the angry wind touched the even upright-standing, sword-straight masts, and when the huge-flying, loud-voiced, broad-bordered sails swallowed the wind attacking them suddenly with sharp voice, that stout, strong, active, powerful crew rose up promptly and quickly, and every one went straight to his work with speed and promptitude, and they stretched forth their ready courageous, white-coloured, brown-nailed hands most valiantly to the tackling, till they let the wind in loud, sharp, fast, voice-bursts into the shrouds of the mast, so that the ship gave an eager, very quick, vigorous leap forward, right straight into the salt-ocean, till they arrived in the delightfully-clear, cold-pooled, querulously-whistling, joyfully-calling reaches of the sea, and the dark sea rose speedily around them in desperate-daring floodful *doisleana*, in hardly-separated ridges and in rough-grey, proud-tongued, gloomy-grim, blue-capacious valleys, and in impetuous shower-topped wombs [of water]; and the great merriment of the cold wind was answered by the chieftains, strong-workingly, stout-enduringly, truly-powerfully, and they proceeded to manage and attend the high-ocean, until at last the strong and powerful sea overcame the intention of the high wind, and the murmur and giddy voice of the deep was humbled by that great rowing, till the sea became restful, smooth, and very calm behind them, until they took port and harbour at Inver Cholpa, which is at this time called Drogheda."

The stories about Cormac mac Art, his grandfather Conn of the Hundred Battles, and his son Cairbrè of the Liffey, which are numerous, are mostly more or less connected with the Fenians, and may, as they deal with the same era and the same characters, be conveniently classed along with the Fenian sagas. One of the best known of these sagas is the Battle of Moy Léana[1] in which Conn of the Hundred Battles slew his rival Owen, who had forced from him half his kingdom. Owen had lived for six years in Spain, and had married a daughter of the Spanish king. At the end of this time he was seized with great home-sickness and he proposed to return to Ireland. When his father-in-law heard this, he said to him :—

"If that Erin of which you speak, Owen, were a thing easily moved, we would deem it easier to send the soldiers and warriors of Spain with you thither to cut it from its foundation and lay it on wheels and carry it after our ships and place it a one angle of Spain"—a grandiloquent speech which Owen did not relish ; "He did not receive it with satisfaction, and it was not sweet to him," says the saga.

The King perceived this however, and offered him just what he wanted, two thousand warriors to help him and his exiles in acquiring the kingdom. The account of their embarcation and voyage is perhaps as good a specimen of exaggerated verbosity and of the rhetoric of the professed story-teller as any other in these sagas, which abound with such things, and it is perhaps worth while to give it at length. It will be seen that the story-teller or prose-poet, passes everything through the prism of his imagination, and aided by an extraordinary exuberance of vocabulary and unbounded wealth ot alliterative adjectives, wraps the commonest objects in a hurricane of—to use his own phrase—"misty-dripping" epithet. The Battle of Moy Léana is recorded in the Annals of Ulster, by Flann in the eleventh century, and by the Book of Leinster, and no doubt the essence of the saga is very ancient, but the

[1] Published by Eugene O'Curry for the Celtic Society. I adhere to his admirable, and at the same time perfectly literal, translation.

dressing-up of it, and especially the passage I am about to quote, is, in its style—not to speak of the language which is modern—almost certainly post-Norman.

THE SAILING OF OWEN MÓR.

"Then that vindictive unmerciful host went forward to the harbours and ports where their vessels and their sailing ships awaited them; and they launched their terrible wonderful monsters; their black, dangerous, many-coloured ships; their smooth, proper-sided, steady, powerful scuds, and their cunningly-stitched *Laoidheangs* from their beds and from their capacious, full-smooth places, out of the cool clear-winding creeks of the coast, and from the calm, quiet, well-shaped, broad-headed harbours, and there were placed upon every swift-going ship of them free and accurately arranged tiers of fully-smoothed, long-bladed oars, and they made a harmonious, united, co-operating, thick-framed, eager-springing, unhesitating, constant-going rowing against currents and wild tempests, so that loud, haughty, proud-minded, were the responses of the stout, fierce-fronted, sportive-topped billows in conversing with the scuds and beautiful prows."

"The dark, impetuous, proud, ardent waters became as white-streaked, fierce-rolling, languid-fatigued *Leibhiona*, upon which to cast the white-flanked, slippery, thick, straight-swimming salmon, among the dark-prowling, foamy-tracked heads [of sea monsters] from off the brown oars.

"And upon that fleet, sweeping with sharp rapidity from the sides and borders of the territories, and from the shelter of the lands, and from the calm quiet of the shores, they could see nothing of the globe on their border near them, but the high, proud, tempestuous waves of the abyss, and the rough, roaring shore, shaking and quivering, and the very-quick, swift motion of the great wind coming upon them, and long-swelling, gross-springing, great billows rising over the swelling sides of the [sea] valleys, and the savage, dangerous, shower-crested sea, maintaining its strength against the rapid course of the vessels over the expanse, until at last it became exhausted, subdued, drizzling and misty, from the conflict of the waves and fierce winds.

"The labouring crews derived increased spirits from the bounding of the swift ships over the wide expanse, and the wind coming from the rear, directly fair for the brave men, they arose manfully and vigorously to their work, and lashed the tough, new masts to the brown, smooth, ample, commodious bulwarks, without weakness, without spraining, without overstraining. Those ardent, expert crews put their hands to the long linen [sails] without shrinking, without mistake, from *Eibhil* to *Achtuaim*, and the swift-going, long, capacious ships, passed from the hand-force of the warriors, and over the deep, wet, murmuring pools of the sea, and past the winding, bending, fierce-showery points of the harbours, and over the high-torrented, ever-great mountains of the brine, and over the heavy, listless walls of the great waves, and past the dark, misty-dripping hollows of the shores, and past the saucy, thick-flanked, spreading, white-crested currents of the streams, and over the spring-tide, contentions, furious, wet, overwhelming fragments of the cold ocean, until the sea became rocking like a soft, fragrant, proud-bearing plain, swelling and heaving to the force of the anger and fury of the cold winds.

"The upper elements quickly perceived the anger and fury of the sea growing and increasing. Woe indeed was it to have stood between those two powers, the sea and the great wind when mutually attacking each other, and contending at the sides of strong ships and stout-built vessels and beautiful scuds. So that the sea was in showery-tempestuous, growling, wet, fierce, loud, clamorous, dangerous stages after them, whilst the excitement of the murmuring dark-deeded wind continued in the face and in the sluices of the ocean from its bottom to its surface. And tremulous, listless, long-disjointed, quick-shattering, ship-breaking, was the effect of the disturbance, and treacherous the shivering of the winds and the rolling billows upon the swift barks, for the tempest did not leave them a plank unshaken, nor a hatch unstarted, nor a rope unsnapped, nor a nail unstrained, nor a bulwark unendangered, nor a bed unshattered, nor a lifting uncast-down, nor a mast unshivered, nor a yard untwisted, nor a sail untorn, nor a warrior unhurt, nor a soldier unterrified, nor a noble unstunned—excepting the ardour and sailorship of the brave men who attended to the attacks and howlings of the fierce wind.

"However, now, when the wind had exhausted its valour and had not received reverence nor honour from the sea, it went forward, stupid and crestfallen, to the uppermost regions of its residence; and the sea was fatigued from its roarings and drunken murmurings, and the wild billows ceased their motions, so that spirit returned to the nobles and strength to the hosts, and activity to the warriors, and strength to the champions. And they sailed onwards in that order without delay or accident until they reached the sheltered smooth harbour of Cealga and the shore of the island of Greagraidhe."

Who or what the Fenians were, has given rise to the greatest diversity of opinion. The school of Mr. Nutt and Professor

Rhys would, I fancy, recognise in them nothing but tribal deities, euhemerised or regarded as men.[1] Dr. Skene and Mr. Mac Ritchie believed that they were an altogether separate race of men from the Gaels, probably allied to, or identical with, the Picts of history; and the latter holds that they are the *sidhe* [shee] or fairy folk of the Gaels. The native Irish, on the other hand, who were perfectly acquainted with the Picts, and tell us much about them, have always regarded the Fenians as being nothing more or less than a body of janissaries or standing troops of Gaelic and Firbolg families, maintained during several reigns by the Irish kings, a body which tended to become hereditary. Nor is there in this account anything inherently impossible or improbable, especially as the Fenian régime synchronises with a time when the Irish were probably aggressively warlike. Keating, writing in Irish about the year 1630, gives the traditional account of them as he gathered it from ancient books and other authorities now lost, and this certainly preserves some ancient and unique traits. He begins

[1] Mr. Nutt seems to believe that the whole groundwork of the Fenian tales is mythical. His position with regard to them is fairly summed up in this extract from his note on Mac Innes' Gaelic stories. "Every Celtic tribe," he writes, "possessed traditions both mythical and historical, the former of substantially the same character, the latter necessarily varying. Myth and history acted and reacted upon each other, and produced heroic saga which may be defined as myth tinged and distorted by history. The largest element is as a rule suggested by myth, so that the varying heroic sagas of the various portions of a race, have always a great deal in common. These heroic sagas, together with the official or semi-official mythologies of the pre-Christian Irish are the subject-matter of the Annals. They were thrown into a purely artificial chronological shape by men familiar with biblical and classical history. A framework was thus created into which the entire mass of native legend was gradually fitted, whilst the genealogies of the race were modelled, or it may be remodelled in accord with it. In studying the Irish sagas we may banish entirely from our mind all questions as to the truth of the early portions of the Annals. The subject matter of the latter is mainly mythical, the mode in which it has been treated is literary. What residuum of historic truth may still survive can be but infinitesimal." (*See* Mr. Nutt's valuable essay on Ossianic or Fenian Saga in "Waifs and Strays of Celtic Tradition," vol. ii. p. 399.)

by rejecting the ridiculous stories told about them, such as the battle of Ventry and the like, as well as the remarks of Campion and of Buchanan, who in his history of Scotland had called Finn a giant.

"It is proved," writes Keating, "that their persons were of no extraordinary size compared with the men that lived in their own times, and moreover that they were nothing more than members of a body of *buanadha* or retained soldiers, maintained by the Irish kings for the purpose of guarding their territories and of upholding their authority therein. It is thus that captains and soldiers are at present maintained by all modern kings for the purpose of defending their rule and guarding their countries.

"The members of the Fenian Body lived in the following manner. They were quartered on the people from November Day till May Day, and their duty was to uphold justice and to put down injustice on the part of the kings and lords of Ireland, and also to guard the harbours of the country from the oppression of foreign invaders. After that, from May till November, they lived by hunting and the chase, and by performing the duties demanded of them by the kings of Ireland, such as preventing robberies, exacting fines and tributes, putting down public enemies, and every other kind of evil that might afflict the country. In performing these duties they received a certain fixed pay. . . .

"However, from May till November the Fenians had to content themselves with game, the product of their own hunting, as this [right to hunt] was their maintenance and pay from the kings of Ireland. That is, the warriors had the flesh of the wild animals for their food, and the skins for wages. During the whole day, from morning till night they used to eat but one meal, and of this it was their wont to partake towards evening. About noon they used to send whatever game they had killed in the morning by their attendants to some appointed hill where there were wood and moorland close by. There they used to light immense fires, into which they put a large quantity of round sandstones. They next dug two pits in the yellow clay of the moor, and having set part of the venison upon spits to be roasted before the fire they bound up the remainder with sugàns—ropes of straw or rushes—in bundles of sedge, and then placed them to be cooked in one of the pits they had previously dug. There they set the stones which they had before this heated in the fire, round about them, and kept heaping them upon the bundles of meat until they had made them seethe freely, and the meat had become thoroughly cooked. From the greatness of these fires it has resulted that their sites are still to be recognised in many parts of Ireland by their burnt blackness. It is they that are commonly called *Fualachta na bhFiann*, or the Fenians' cooking-spots.

"As to the warriors of the Fenians, when they were assembled at he place where their fires had been lighted, they used to gather round the second of those pits of which we have spoken above, and there every man stripped himself to his skin, tied his tunic round his waist, and then set to dressing his hair and cleansing his limbs, thus ridding himself of the sweat and soil of the day's hunt. Then they began to supple their thews and muscles by gentle exercise, loosening them by friction, until they had relieved themselves of all sense of stiffness and fatigue. When they had finished doing this they sat down and ate their meal. That being over, they set about constructing their *fiann-bhotha* or hunting-booths, and preparing their beds, and so put themselves in train for sleep. Of the following three materials did each man construct his bed, of the brushwood of the forest, of moss, and of fresh rushes. The brushwood was laid next the ground, over it was placed the moss, and lastly fresh rushes were spread over all. It is these three materials that are designated in our old romances as the *tri Cuilcedha na bhFiann*—the three Beddings of the Fenians."

Every man who entered the Fenian ranks had four *geasa* [gassa, *i.e.*, tabus] laid upon him,

"The first, never to receive a portion with a wife, but to choose her for good manners and virtues; the second, never to offer violence to any woman; the third, never to refuse any one for anything he might possess; the fourth, that no single warrior should ever flee before nine [*i.e.*, before less than ten] champions."

There was a curious condition attached to entrance into the brotherhood which rendered it necessary that

"Both his father and mother, his tribe, and his relatives should first give guarantees that they should never make any charge against any person for his death. This was in order that the duty of avenging his own blood [wounds] should rest with no man other than himself, and in order that his friends should have nothing to claim with respect to him however great the evils inflicted upon him."

All the Fenians were obliged to know the rules of poetry,[1]

[1] "Of all these," says, with true Celtic hyperbole, the fifteenth-century vellum in the British Museum, marked "Egerton, 1782," "not a man was

for no figure in Irish antiquity, layman or cleric, could ever arrive at the rank of a popular hero unless he could compose, or at least appreciate a poem.

The Fenian tales and poems are extraordinarily numerous, but their conception and characteristics are in general distinctly different from those relating to the Red Branch. They have not the same sweep, the same vastness and stature, the same weirdness, as the older cycle. The majority of them are more modern in conception and surroundings. There is little or no mention of the war chariot which is so important a factor in the older cycle. The Fenians fought on foot or horseback, and we meet, too, frequent mention of helmets and mail-coats, which are post-Danish touches. Things are on a smaller scale. Exaggeration does not run all through the stories, but is confined to small parts of them, and it is set off by much that is trivial or humorous.

The Fenian stories became in later times the distinctly popular ones. They were far more of the people and for the

taken until he was a prime poet versed in the twelve books of poetry. No man was taken till in the ground a large hole had been made such as to reach the fold of his belt, and he put into it with his shield and a forearm's length of a hazel stick. Then must nine warriors having nine spears, with a ten furrows' width between them and him, assail him, and in concert let fly at him. If he were then hurt past that guard of his, he was not received into the Fian-ship. Not a man of them was taken until his hair had been interwoven into braids on him, and he started at a run through Ireland's woods, while they seeking to wound him followed in his wake, there having been between him and them but one forest bough by way of interval at first. Should he be overtaken he was wounded and not received into the Fian-ship after. If his weapons had quivered in his hand he was not taken. Should a branch in the wood have disturbed anything of his hair out of its braiding he was not taken. If he had cracked a dry stick under his foot [as he ran] he was not accepted. Unless that [at full speed] he had both jumped a stick level with his brow, and stooped to pass under one on a level with his knee, he was not taken. Unless also without slackening his pace he could with his nail extract a thorn from his foot he was not taken into the Fian-ship. But if he performed all this he was of Finn's people." (*See* "Silva Gadelica," p. 100 of English vol.)

people than those of the Red Branch. They were most intimately bound up with the life and thought and feelings of the whole Gaelic race, high and low, both in Ireland and Scotland, and the development of Fenian saga, for a period of 1,200 or 1,500 years, is one of the most remarkable examples in the world of continuous literary evolution. I use the word evolution advisedly, for there was probably not a century from the seventh to the eighteenth in which new stories, poems, and redactions of sagas concerning Finn and the Fenians were not invented and put in circulation, while to this very day many stories never committed to manuscript are current about them amongst the Irish and Scotch Gaelic-speaking populations. We have found no such steady interest evinced by the people in the Red Branch romances, and in attempting to collect Irish folk-lore I have found next to nothing about Cuchulain and his contemporaries, but great quantities about Finn, Ossian, Oscar, Goll, and Conan. The one cycle, then, antique in tone, language, and surroundings, was, I suspect, that of the chiefs, the great men, and the bards; the other—at least in later times—more that of the un-bardic classes and of the people.

I do not mean to say that many of the Cuchulain stories were not copied into modern MSS. and circulated freely among the people all over Ireland during the eighteenth century and the beginning of this, especially Cuchulain's training, Conlaoch's (his son's) death, the Fight at the Ford, and others, but these appear never to have put out shoots and blossoms from themselves and to have generated new and yet again new stories as did the ever-youthful Fenian tales; nor do they appear to have equally entwined themselves at this day round the popular imagination.

A striking instance of how the Ossianic tale continued to develop down to the eighteenth century was supplied me the other day when examining the Reeves Collection.[1] I there

[1] These MSS. volumes, fifty-four in number, had most of them belonged to Mr. MacAdam, editor of the "Ulster Journal of Archæology," from

came upon a story in a Louth MS., written, I think, in the last century, which seemed to me to contain one of the latest developments of Ossianic saga. It is called "The Adventures of Dubh mac Deaghla," and tells us of how a prophet was born of the race of Eiremóin, "and all say," adds the writer, "that it was he was the druid who prophesied to Fiacha Sreabhtainne that he should fall in the battle of Dubh-Cumair by the three brothers, Cairioll, Muircath, and Aodh." He also "prophesied to the race of Tuathal that Cairbré of the Liffey was that far-branching tree which was to spread round about through the great circuit of Erin, around which smote the powerful wind from the south-west, overthrowing it wholly to the ground—which wind meant the Fenians, as had been announced by the smith's daughter."[1] The Fenians it seems heard that this Torna had prophesied about them and intended to kill him, and he and his family had to emigrate to Britain. From there he sends a letter in true epistolary style to an old friend of his, one Conor son of Dathach, beginning "Dear Friend"—an evident mark of seventeenth or possibly eighteenth century authorship, for there are no letters written in this style in the older literature, and this piece evidently follows a

whom Bishop Reeves bought them. On the lamented death of that great scholar they were put up to auction, when the Royal Irish Academy bought some thirty volumes, the rest unfortunately were allowed to be scattered again to the four winds of heaven. For his exertions and generosity in securing even so many of these MSS., especially those which at first sight looked least important, but which contained treasures of folk-lore and folk-song, the Hon. Treasurer, the Rev. Maxwell Close, has placed Irish-speaking Ireland under yet another debt of gratitude to him. It is not always that which is most ancient which is most valuable from a literary or a national point of view. The pity of it is that any Irish MS. that comes into the market should not be bought up for the nation with the money assigned by the Government and confided to the Royal Irish Academy for Irish studies, unless a special search should show *that the Academy already possesses a copy of each piece in it.* I am convinced that many hundreds or thousands of pieces have been through neglect to do this irreparably lost to the nation. Oh the pity of it!

[1] This is in allusion to the romance of Moy Muchruime, where we read of the prophecy and what followed. For Cairbré *see* above, p. 32.

Latin or a Spanish, or possibly an English model. However this may be, Torna's letter asks Conor for news of the situation, and in time receives the following answer :

"To Torna son of Dubh, our dear friend in Glen Fuinnse in Britain in Saxony.

"Thy affectionate missive was read by me as soon as it arrived, and it had been a cause of joy to me, were it not for the way we are in at Tara at this moment.

"For we never felt until the Munster Fenians came and encamped at the marsh of Old Raphoe and Treibhe to the south-west; the warriors of Leinster also and *Baoisgnidh*, together with Clan Ditribh and Clan Boirchne, were to the south of them, towards the bottom of the stream of Gabhra and on the west towards the old fort of Mève ; and that same evening the King having received an account of the encamping of the Fenians urges messengers secretly to Connacht to the Clan of Conal Cruachna that they might come, along with all the king's friends from the western border of Erin ; and other messengers he despatches to Scotland for the Clan of Garaidh Glúnmhar, desiring Oscar of the blue Javelin, Aodh, Argal, and Airtre to come from abroad without delay, and that secretly.

"On the early morning of the morrow, before the stars of the air retired, the King urged the druids of Tara against the Fenians to argue with them, and ask what was the cause of their rebelling in this guise, or who it was with whom they had now come to do battle, because they appeared not in habiliments of peace or friendship, but a flush of anger appeared in the face and countenance of every several man of them.

"'And there is another unlawful thing of which ye are guilty,' said the druids, 'which shows that ye have broken the vow of allegiance and obedience to your king, in that ye have come in array and garb of battle to the door of his fortress without receiving his leave or advice, without giving him notice or warning. To what point of the compass do ye travel, or on what have ye set your mind [that ye act not] as is the right and due of a prince's subjects, and as was always before this the habitude of the bands that came before ye ; and as shall last with honest people till the end of the world.'

"However, now the druids are a-preaching to them and casting at them bold storm-showers of reproofs by way of retarding them till the coming back of the messengers who went abroad, for Mac Cool is not amongst them to excite them against us, and we hope that they will remain thus until help come to us. For this is the eleventh day since the druids went from us, and our watchmen who observe what approaches and what goes, disclose all tidings to us, and they are ever a-listening to the loud argument of the druids and the captains against one another. Moreover, the desire of the Fenians to make a rapid assault upon Tara is the less from their having heard that Cairbré was gone on his royal round to Dun Sreabhtainne to visit Fiacha,[1] though he is really not gone there, but to a certain place under cover of night with his women and the royal jewels of Tara. And it was lucky for him that he did not go to Dun Sreabhtainne, for the Fenians had sent Cairioll and nine mighty men with him to plunder Dun Sreabhtainne. In that, however, they miscarried, for his tutor was gone off before that with Fiacha, by order of the King, to the same place where the women were. That, however, we shall pursue no further at present.

"But it is easy for you who are knowledgeable to form a judgment upon the state in which the inhabitants of a country must be, over which such a whelming calamity is about to fall. Let me leave off. And here we send our affectionate greeting to you, and to you all, with the hope of some time seeing you in full health, but I have small hope of it.

> "From your faithful friend till death, Conor, son of Dathach in Tara, the royal fortress of Erin. Written the 20th day of the month of March in the year of the age of the world . . . [The figures in the MS. are not legible].

The romance, which is a long one, is chiefly occupied with events relating to the family of Dubh mac Deaghla in Britain. But later on in the book the Conor who despatched this letter turns up and gives in person a most vivid description of the Battle of Gowra, and the events which followed his letter.

I have only instanced and quoted from this comparatively unimportant story, as showing one of the very latest developments of Fenian literature, and as proving how thoroughly even the seventeenth and eighteenth century Gaels were imbued

[1] Fiacha was the King's son, and succeeded him in the sovereignty. He was finally slain by his nephews, the celebrated Three Collas—they who afterwards burned Emania and caused the Ultonian dynasty and the Red Branch knights, after a duration of more than seven hundred years, to set in blood and flame, never to rise again.

with, and realised the spirit of, the Fenian Cycle, and also as a peculiar specimen of what rarely happens in literature, but is always of great interest when it does happen—a specimen of unconscious saga developing into semi-conscious romance.

There are comparatively few ancient texts belonging to the Finn saga, compared with the wealth of old vellum books that contain the Red Branch stories. There is, however, quite enough of documentary proof to show that so early as the seventh century Finn was looked on as a popular hero.

The actual data that we have to go upon in estimating the genesis and development of the Fenian tales have been lucidly collected by Mr. Nutt. They are, as far as is known at present, as follows. Gilla Caemhain, the poet who died in 1072, says that it was fifty-seven years after the battle of Moy Muchruime that Finn was treacherously killed "by the spear points of Urgriu's three sons."[1] This would make Finn's

[1] "There were many among the Fenians," says Keating, "who were more remarkable for their personal prowess, their valour, and their corporeal stature than Finn. The reason why he was made king of the Fiann, and set over the warriors, was simply because his father and grandfather had held that position before him. Another reason also why he had been made king of the Fiann was because he excelled his contemporaries in intellect and learning, in wisdom and in subtlety, and in experience and hardihood in battlefields. It was for these qualities that he was made king of the Fiann, and not for his personal prowess or for the great size or strength of his body."

"Warrior better than Finn," says an old vellum MS. in the British Museum, "never struck his hand into chiefs, inasmuch as for service he was a soldier, a hospitaller for hospitality, and in heroism a hero. In fighting functions he was a fighting man, and in strength a champion worthy of a king, so that ever since and from that until this, it is with Finn that every such is co-ordinated."

And in another place the same vellum says, "A good man verily was he who had those Fianna, for he was the seventh king ruling Ireland, that is to say, there were five kings of the provinces, and the King of Ireland, he being himself the seventh conjointly with the King of all Ireland."

In a MS. saga in my own possession, called "The Pursuit of Sadhbh (Sive)," there is an amusing account of the truculence of the Fenians about their exclusive right of hunting, and the way they terrorised the people they were quartered on, but I have not space for this extract.

death take place in 252, for Moy Muchruime was fought according to the "Four Masters" in A.D. 195. Tighearnach the Annalist, who died in 1088, writes that Finn was killed in A.D. 283, "by Aichleach, son of Duibhdrean, and the sons of Urgriu of the Luaighni of Tara, at Ath-Brea upon the Boyne." The poet Cinaeth O Hartagain, who died in A.D. 985, wrote: "By the Fiann of Luagne was the death of Finn at Ath-Brea upon the Boyne." All these men in the tenth and eleventh centuries certainly believed in Finn as implicitly as they did in King Cormac.

The two oldest miscellaneous Irish MSS. which we have, are the Leabhar na h-Uidhre and the Book of Leinster. The Leabhar na h-Uidhre was compiled from older MSS. towards the close of the eleventh century, and the Book of Leinster some fifty years later. The oldest of them contains a copy of the famous poem ascribed to Dallan Forgaill in praise of St. Columcille, which was so obscure in the middle of the eleventh century that it required to be glossed. In this gloss, made perhaps in the eleventh century, perhaps long before, there is an explanatory poem on winter, ascribed to Finn, grandson of Baoisgne, that is our Finn mac Cool, and in the same commentary we find an explanation of the words "diu"=long, and "derc"=eye, in proof of which this verse is quoted, "As Gráinne," says the commentator, "daughter of Cormac, said to Finn."

> "There lives a man
> On whom I would love to gaze long,
> For whom I would give the whole world,
> O Son of Mary! though a privation!"

This verse, quoted as containing two words which required explanation in or before the eleventh century, pre-supposes the story of Diarmuid and Gráinne. In addition to this we have the apparently historical story of the "Cause of the Battle of Cnucha." We have also the story of the Mongan, an Ulster king of the seventh century, according to the annalists who declared that he was not what men took him to be, the son of the mortal Fiachna, but of the god Mananán mac Lir, and a re-incarnation of the great Finn, and calls back from the grave the famous Fenian, Caoilte, who proves it. This account is strongly relied upon by Mr. Nutt to prove the wild mythological nature of the Finn story, but it is by no means unique in Irish literature, for we find the celebrated Tuan mac Cairrill had a second birth also, and the great Cuchulain too has his parentage ascribed to the god Lugh, not to Sualtach, his reputed father. Consequently, supposing Finn to have been a real historical character of the third century, there would be nothing absolutely extraordinary in the story arising in half pagan times that Mongan, also an historical character, was a re-incarnation of Finn.

In the second oldest miscellaneous manuscript, the Book of Leinster, the references to Finn and the Fenians are much more numerous, containing three poems ascribed to Ossian, Finn's son, five poems ascribed to Finn himself, two poems ascribed to Caoilte the Fenian poet, a poem ascribed to one of Finn's followers, allusions to Finn in poems by one Gilla in Chomded and another, passages from the Dinnsenchas or topographical tract about Finn, the account of the battle of Cnámhross, in which Finn helps the Leinstermen against King Cairbré, the genealogy of Finn, and the genealogy of Diarmuid O'Duibhne.

Again, in the Glossary ascribed, and probably truly, to Cormac, King-Bishop of Cashel, A.D. 837–903, there are two allusions to Finn, one of which refers to the unfaithfulness of his wife. This, indeed, is not contained in the oldest copy, but Whitley Stokes, than whom there can be no better authority, believes these allusions to belong to the older portion of the Glossary, a work which is probably much interpolated.

But there is yet another proof of the antiquity of the Finn stories which Mr. Nutt does not note, and in some respects it is the most important and conclusive of all. For if, as D'Arbois de Jubainville has, I think, proved, the list of 187 historic tales contained in the Book of Leinster was really drawn up at the end of the seventh or beginning of the eighth century, we find that even then Finn or his contemporaries were the subjects of, or figure in, several of them, as in the story of "The Courtship of Ailbhe, daughter of King Cormac mac Art, by Finn," "The Battle of Moy Muchruime," where King Art, Cormac's father, was slain; "The Cave of Bin Edair," where Diarmuid and Gráinne took shelter when pursued by Finn; "The Adventures of Finn in Derc Fearna (the cave of Dunmore)," a lost tale; "The Elopement of Gráinne with Diarmuid," and perhaps one or two more.

Thus Finn is sandwiched in as a real person along with his other contemporaries, not only in tenth and eleventh century annalists and poets, but is also made the hero of historic romance as early as the seventh or eighth century. Side by side in our list with the battle of Moy Muchruime we have the battle of Moy Rath. Copies of both, coloured with the same literary pigments, exist. The last we *know* to be historical, it can be proved; why should not the first be also? It is true that the one took place 438 years before the other, but the treatment of both is absolutely identical, and it is the merest accident that we happen to have external evidence for the latter and not for the former. I can see, then, no sufficiently cogent reasons for viewing Finn mac Cúmhail with different eyes from those with which we regard his king. Cormac mac Art is usually acknowledged to have been a real king of flesh and blood, whose buildings are yet seen on the site of Tara, after whose daughter Gráinne one of them is named, why should Finn, his chief captain, who married that Gráinne, be a deity euhemerised? I do not see any arguments sufficient to differentiate this case of Finn, to whom no particular supernatural qualities (except the knowledge he got when he chewed his thumb) are attributed, from that of Cormac and other kings and heroes who were the subjects of bardic stories, and whose deaths were recorded in the Annals, except the accident that the creative imagination of the later Gaels happened to seize upon him and make him and his contemporaries the nucleus of a vast literature instead of some earlier or later group of perhaps equally deserving champions. Finn has long since become to all ears a pan-Gaelic champion just as Arthur has become a Brythonic one.

Of the Fenian sagas the longest—though it is only fragmentary—is that known as the Dialogue or Colloquy of the Ancients, which is preserved in the Book of Lismore, and would fill about 250 of these pages. The plot of it is simple enough. Caoilte [Cweeltya] the poet and Ossian, almost sole survivors of the Fenians—who had lived on after the battle of Gabhra, where Cairbré, the High-king, broke their power for ever—meet in their very old age St. Patrick and the new preachers of the gospel. Patrick is most desirous of learning the past history of the island from them, and the legends connected with streams and hills and raths and so forth, and these are willingly recounted to him, and were all written[1] down by Brogan Patrick's scribe for posterity to read hereafter. The saga describes their wanderings along with the saint, the stories they relate to him, and the verses—over a couple of thousand—sung or repeated by them to the clerics and others.[2] Some of these pieces are exceedingly beautiful. Here is a specimen, the lament which Credé made over her husband who was drowned at the battle ot Ventry. Caoilte repeats the verses to Patrick :

"The haven roars, and O the haven roars, over the rushing race of *Rinn-da-bharc.* The drowning of the warrior of *Loch-da-chonn,* that

[1] *See* above, p. 116.

[2] This has been edited by Standish Hayes O'Grady in his "Silva Gadelica," from the Book of Lismore.

is what the wave impinging on the strand laments.[1] Melodious is the crane, and O melodious is the crane, in the marshlands of *Druim-dá-thrén.* 'Tis she who may not save her brood alive. The wild dog of two colours is intent upon her nestlings. A woful note, and O a woful note is that which the thrush in Drumqueen emits, but not more cheerful is the wail which the blackbird makes in Letterlee. A woful sound, and O a woful sound, is that the deer utters in Drumdaleish. Dead lies the doe of Drumsheelin,[2] the mighty stag bells after her. Sore suffering, and O suffering sore, is the hero's death, his death, who used to lie by me. . . . Sore suffering to me is Cael, and O Cael is a suffering sore, that by my side he is in dead man's form; that the wave should have swept over his white body, that is what hath distracted me, so great was his delightfulness. A dismal roar, and O a dismal roar, is that the shore's surf makes upon the strand. . . . A woful booming, and O a boom of woe, is that which the wave makes upon the northward beach, butting as it does against the polished rock, lamenting for Cael now that he is gone. A woful fight, and O a fight of woe, is that the wave wages with the southern

---

[1] "Géisid cuan, ón géisid cuan
Os buinne ruad rinn da bharc,
Badad laeich locha dhá chonn
Is ed cháinios tonn re trácht."

"Silva Gadelica," p. 113 of Gaelic volume, p. 122 of English volume. I have not altered Dr. O'Grady's beautiful translation.

[2] This passage and that about the crane are not explained in the "Colloquy," but curiously enough I find the same passage in the saga called the Battle of Ventry, which Kuno Meyer published in "Anecdota Oxoniensia" from a fifteenth-century vellum in the Bodleian. The lady is there called Gelges [white swan], and as she sought for Cael among the slain "she saw the crane of the meadow and her two birds and the wily beast yclept the fox a-watching of her birds, and when she covered one of the birds to save it he would make a rush at the other bird, so that the crane had to stretch herself out between them both, so that she would rather have found and suffered death by the wild beast than that her birds should be killed by him. And Gelges mused on this greatly and said, "I wonder not that I so love my fair sweetheart, since this little bird is in such distress about its birdlets. She heard, moreover, a wild stag on Drum Reelin above the harbour, and it was vehemently bewailing the hind from one pass to the other, for they had been nine years together and had dwelt in the wood that was at the foot of the harbour, the wood of Feedesh, and the hind had been killed by Finn, and the stag was nineteen days without tasting grass or water, mourning for the hind. "It is no shame for me," said Gelges, "to find death with grief for Cael, as the stag is shortening his life for grief of the hind," etc.

shore. A woful melody, and O a melody of woe, is that which the heavy surge of Tullacleish emits. As for me the calamity which has fallen upon me having shattered me, for me prosperity exists no more."

Perhaps the Fenian saga, next in length and certainly in merit, is the well-known "Pursuit of Diarmuid and Gráinne."[1] Diarmuid of the Love-spot unwittingly causes Gráinne, daughter of Cormac mac Art, the High-king, to fall in love with him, just on the eve of her marriage with his captain, Finn mac Cool. He is driven to elope with her, and is pursued round Ireland by the vengeful Finn, who succeeds after many years in compassing the death of the generous and handsome Diarmuid by a wild boar, and then winning back to himself the love of the fickle Gráinne.

The Enchanted Fort of the Quicken Tree, the Enchanted Fort of Céis Corann,[2] the Little Brawl at Allen,[2] the Enchanted Fort of Eochaidh Beag the Red,[3] the Pursuit of Sive, daughter of Owen Óg, the Pursuit of the Giolla Deacar,[2] the Death of the Great Youth the King of Spain's son,[4] The Feast in the House of Conan,[5] the Legend of Lomnochtan of Slieve Riffé,[6] the Legend of Ceadach the Great,[7] the Battle of

[1] Pronounced "Graan-ya." This story has been edited and translated in the third volume of the Ossianic Society by Standish H. O'Grady, and has been since reprinted from his text. Dr. Joyce also translated it into English in his Old Celtic romances, but omits the cynical but most characteristic conclusion. The story was only known to exist in quite modern MSS., but I find an excellent copy written about the year 1660 in the newly-acquired Reeves Collection in the Royal Irish Academy. This saga was in existence in the seventh century, for it is mentioned in the list in the Book of Leinster. It is the subject of a recent cantata by the Marquis of Lorne and Mr. Hamish Mac Cunn.

[2] Published by O'Grady in his "Silva Gadelica."

[3] The Irish text published without a translation by Patrick O'Brien in his *Bláithfleasg*.

[4] I published in a periodical a translation of this from a MS. in my own possession.

[5] Published in vol. ii. of Ossianic Society.

[6] Is being published in the "Gaelic Journal" by the editor.

[7] Mentioned by Standish H. O'Grady, but I have met no copies of it, though I have heard a story of this name told orally.

Tulach na n-each,[1] the Battle of Ventry,[2] the Battle of Cnucha, the Battle of Moy Muchruime,[3] the Battle of Moy Léana,[4] the youthful Exploits of Finn mac Cool,[5] the Battle of Gabhra,[6] the Birth of King Cormac,[7] the Battle of Crinna,[7] the Cause of the Battle of Cnucha,[8] the Invitation of Maol grandson of Manannán to the Fenians of Erin,[9] the Legend of the Clown in the Drab Coat,[10] the Lamentation of Oilioll after his children,[11] Cormac's Adventure in the Land of Promise,[12] the Decision about Cormac's Sword,[13] an ancient fragment about Finn and Gráinne,[14] an ancient fragment on the Death of Finn[15]—are some of the remaining prose sagas of this cycle.

[1] Mentioned by Standish H. O'Grady.

[2] Published from a fifteenth-century vellum in the Bodleian by Kuno Meyer in a volume of the "Anecdota Oxoniensia."

[3] Published by Standish H. O'Grady in "Silva Gadelica" from the Book of Leinster. I have a seventeenth-century paper copy of the same saga which is completely different.

[4] Published by O'Curry for the Celtic Society.

[5] Edited by O'Donovan for the Ossianic Society and by Mr. David Comyn with a translation into modern Irish for the Gaelic League.

[6] Edited by O'Kearney for the Ossianic Society, vol. i.

[7] Published in "Silva Gadelica."

[8] A brief tale in the Leabhar na h-Uidhre, published in "Revue Celtique," vol. ii.

[9] Mentioned by Standish H. O'Grady in his preface to Diarmuid and Gráinne, but unknown to me.

[10] Published without a translation by O'Daly of Anglesea Street in "Irish Self-taught," and with a translation in the "Silva Gadelica."

[11] Usually joined on to the modern version of the Battle of Mochruime.

[12] Published by Standish H. O'Grady for the Ossianic Society, vol. iii. p. 212, from a modern MS.; and by Whitley Stokes in "Irische Texte," iii. Serie, Heft. i. p. 203, from the Book of Ballymote and Yellow Book of Lecan.

[13] Published by Stokes in the same place as the last.

[14] "Zeitschrift für Celt. Phil.," Band I. Heft. 3, p. 458, translated by Kuno Meyer.

[15] *Ibid.*, and O'Grady, "Silva Gadelica."

CHAPTER XXX

MISCELLANEOUS ROMANCE

In addition to the stories that centre round Cuchulain and round Finn there are a number of miscellaneous ones dealing with episodes or characters in Irish history; some are in short groups or minor cycles, but others are completely independent tales. All are built upon lines similar to those which we have been considering, and they are composed for the most part in a mixture of both verse and prose. Some of these sagas deal with pre-Christian times, and others with the early mediæval period. Very few, if any, deal with post-Danish and still fewer with post-Norman subjects. The seventh century was the golden era of the Irish saga, and nothing that the race did in later times improved on it. Out of the hundred and eighty-seven stories whose names are preserved in the Book of Leinster, in a list which must have been, as D'Arbois de Jubainville points out, drawn up in the seventh century, about one hundred and twenty seem to have utterly perished. Of the others —many of which, however, are preserved only in the baldest and most condensed form—some four or five relate to the Fenian Cycle, some eighteen are Red Branch stories, and some eight or nine, mostly preserved in the colourless digests of the Book of Invasions, are mythological. About twenty-one of the others belong to minor groups, or are miscellaneous single tales. Some of them are of the highest interest and antiquity. Of these the storming of the Bruidhean [Bree-an] or Court of Dá Derga is, after the Táin Bó Cuailnge, probably the oldest and most important saga in the whole range of Irish literature.

These two stories substantially dating from the seventh century, and perhaps formed into shape long before that time, are preserved in the oldest miscellaneous MSS. which we possess, and throw more light upon pagan manners, customs, and institutions than perhaps any other.[1]

The period in which the Court-of-Dá-Derga story is laid is about coincident with that of the Red Branch Cycle, only it does not deal with Emania, and the Red Branch, but with Leinster, Tara, and the High-king of Erin, who was there resident. The High-king at this time was the celebrated Conairè the "Great," and rightly, if we may believe our Annals, was he so called, for he had been a just, magnanimous, and above all fortunate ruler of all Ireland for fifty years.[2] So just was he, and so strict, that he had sent into banishment a number of lawless and unworthy persons who troubled his

[1] There is an almost complete copy of this saga in the Leabhar na h-Uidhre. Like the Táin Bó Cuailnge, it has never been published in a translation. The language is much harder and more archaic than that of the Táin. I have principally drawn upon O'Curry's description of it, for I can only guess at the meaning of a great part of the original. Were all Europe searched the scholars who could give an adequate translation of it might be counted on the fingers of both hands—if not of one.

[2] According to the "Four Masters" he was slain in AM. 5161 [*i.e.*, 43 B.C.], after a reign of seventy years. "It was in the reign of Conairè," the "Four Masters" add, "that the Boyne annually cast its produce ashore at Inver Colpa. Great abundance of nuts were annually found upon the Boyne and the Buais. The cattle were without keeping in Ireland in his reign on account of the greatness of the peace and concord. His reign was not thunder-producing nor stormy. It was little but the trees bent under the greatness of their fruit." It is from Conairè the Ernaan tribes were descended. They were driven by the Rudricians, *i.e.*, the Ultonians of the Red Branch, into Munster, and from thence they were driven by the race of Eber [the Mac Carthys, etc. of Munster], into the western islands.

kingdom. Among these were his own five foster brothers whom he was reluctantly compelled to send into exile along with the others. These people all turned to piracy, and plundered the coasts of England, Scotland, and even Ireland, wherever they found an opportunity of making a successful raid upon the unarmed inhabitants.[1] It so happened that the son of the King of Britain, one Ingcel, also of Irish extraction, had been banished by his father for his crimes, and was now making his living in much the same way as the predatory Irishmen. These two parties having met, being drawn together by a fellow-feeling and their common lawlessness, struck up a friendship, and made a league with one another, thus doubling the strength of each. Soon after this the High-king found himself in Clare, called thither to settle, according to his wont, some dispute between rival chiefs. His business ended, he was leisurely taking his way with his retinue back to his royal seat at Tara, when on entering the borders of Meath he beheld the whole country in the direction of his city a sheet of flame and rolling smoke. Terrified at this, and divining that the banished pirates had made a descent on his capital during his absence, he turned aside and took the great road that, leading from Tara to Dublin, passed thence into the heart of Leinster. Pursuing this road the King crossed the Liffey in safety and made for the Bruighean [Bree-an] or Court of Dá Derg on the road close to the river Dothar or Dodder, called ever since Boher-na-breena,[2] the "road of the Court," close to Tallacht, not far from Dublin. This was one of the six great courts of universal hospitality[3] in Erin, and Dá Derg, its master, was delighted and honoured by the visit from the High-king.

[1] It appears to have been partly in order to check raids like this, that the High-kings maintained the Fenians a couple of centuries later, for their chief duty was "to watch the harbours."

[2] A constant rendezvous for pedestrians and bicyclists from Dublin, not one in ten thousand of whom knows the origin of the name or its history

[3] For a description of another of these courts *see* above p. 355.

The pirates having plundered Tara, took to their vessels, and having laden them with their spoils were now under a favourable breeze running along the sea coast towards the Hill of Howth, when they perceived from afar the King's company making in their chariots for Dublin along the great high road. One of his own foster brothers was the first to recognise that it was the High-king who was there. He was kept in view and seen at last to enter Dá Derg's great court of hospitality. The pirates ran their ships ashore to the south of the Liffey, and Ingcel the Briton set off as a spy to examine the court and the number of armed men about it; to see if it might not be possible to surprise and plunder it during the night. On his return he is questioned by his companions as to what he saw, and by this simple device—familiar to all poets from Homer down—we are introduced to the principal characters of his court, and are shown what the retinue of a High-king consisted of in the sixth or seventh century, about which time the saga probably took definite shape on parchment, or in the second or third century if we are to suppose the traits to be more archaic than the composition of the tale. We have here a minute account of the King and the court and the company, with their costumes, insignia, and appearance. We see the King and his sons, his nine pipers or wind-instrument players, his cupbearers, his chief druid-juggler, his three principal charioteers, their nine apprentice charioteers, his hostages the Saxon princes, his equerries and outriders, his three judges, his nine harpers, his three ordinary jugglers, his three cooks, his three poets, his nine guardsmen, and his two private table attendants. We see Dá Derg, the lord of the court, his three doorkeepers, the British outlaws, and the king's private drink-bearers. Here is the description of the King himself—

"'I saw there a couch,'[1] continued Ingcel, 'and its ornamentation was more beautiful than all the other couches of the Court, it is cur-

[1] Here is the original as given by O'Curry, "Manners and Customs," vol. iii. p. 141. This will show the exceeding difficulty of the language

tained round with silver cloth, and the couch itself is richly ornamented. I saw three persons on it. The outside two of them were fair both hair and eyebrows, and their skin whiter than snow. Upon the cheek of each was a beautiful ruddiness. Between them in the middle was a noble champion. He has in his visage the ardour and action of a sovereign, and the wisdom of an historian. The cloak which I saw upon him can be likened only to the mist of a May morning. A different colour and complexion are seen on it each moment, more splendid than the other is each hue. I saw in the cloak in front of him a wheel broach of gold, that reaches from his chin to his waist. Like unto the sheen of burnished gold is the colour of his hair. Of all the human forms of the world that I have seen his is the most splendid.[1] I saw his gold-hilted sword laid down near him. There was the breadth of a man's hand of the sword exposed out of the scabbard. From that hand's breadth the man who sits at the far end of the house could see even the smallest object by the light of that sword.[2] More melodious is the melodious sound of that sword than the melodious sounds of the golden pipes which play music in the royal house. . . . The noble warrior was asleep with his legs upon the lap of one of the men, and his head in the lap of the other. He awoke up afterwards out of his sleep and spake these words—

"'"I have dreamed of danger-crowding phantoms,
A host of creeping treacherous enemies,
A combat of men beside the Dodder,
And early and alone the King of Tara was killed."'"

This man whom Ingcel had seen was no other than the High-king.

The account of the juggler is also curious—

"'I saw there,' continued Ingcel, 'a large champion in the middle of the house. The blemish of baldness was upon him. Whiter than the cotton of the mountains is every hair that grows upon his head.

"Atcondarc and imdae acas bacáimiu acomthach oldáta imdada in tigi olchena. Seolbrat nairgdidi impe acas cumtaige isin dimdae. Atcondarc triar ninni," etc.

[1] Keating says that according to some Conairè reigned only 30 years.

[2] The allusion appears to be to a bright steel sword in an age of bronze. Perhaps the music referred to means the vibration of the steel when struck. The "Sword of light" is a common feature in Gaelic folk-lore. Of course iron was common in Ireland centuries before this time, but the primitive description of *Sword of light*, transmitted itself from age to age.

He had ear-clasps of gold in his ears and a speckled white cloak upon him. He had nine swords in his hand and nine silvery shields and nine balls of gold. He throws every one of them up into the air and not one falls to the ground, and there is but one of them at a time upon his palm, and like the buzzing of bees on a beautiful day was the motion of each passing the other.'

"'Yes,' said Ferrogain [the foster brother], 'I recognise him, he is Tulchinne, the Royal druid of the King of Tara; he is Conairè's juggler,[1] a man of great power is that man.'"

Dá Derg himself is thus described—

"'I saw another couch there and one man on it, with two pages in front of him, one fair, the other black-haired. The champion himself had red hair and had a red cloak near him. He had crimson cheeks and beautiful deep blue eyes, and had on him a green cloak. He wore also a white under-mantle and collar beautifully interwoven, and a sword with an ivory hilt was in his hand, and he supplies every couch in the Court with ale and food, and he is incessant in attending upon the whole company. Identify that man.'

"'I know that man,' said he, 'that is Da Derg himself. It was by him the Court was built, and since he has taken up residence in it, its doors have never been closed except on the side to which the wind blows; it is to that side only that a door is put. Since he has taken to house-keeping his boiler has never been taken off the fire, but continues ever to boil food for the men of Erin. And the two who are in front of him are two boys, foster sons of his, they are the two sons of the King of Leinster.'"

Not less interesting is the true Celtic hyperbole in Ingcel's description of the jesters: "I saw then three jesters at the fire. They wore three dark grey cloaks, and if all the men of Erin were in one place and though the body of the mother or the father of each man of them were lying dead before him, not one of them could refrain from laughing at them."

In the end the pirates decide on making their attack. They marched swiftly and silently across the Dublin mountains, surrounded and surprised the court, slew the High-king caught there, as in a trap, and butchered most of his attendants.

[1] "Cleasamhnach," from *cleas*, "a trick," a living word still.

After this tale of Dá Derg come a host of sagas, all calling for a recognition, which with our limited space it is impossible to grant them. Of these one of the most important, though neither the longest nor the most interesting, is the account of the Boromean or Boru tribute, a large fragment of which is preserved in the Book of Leinster, a MS. of about the year 1150.

When Tuathal or Toole, called Techtmhar, or the Possessor, was High-king of Ireland, at the close of the first century, he had two handsome daughters, and the King of Leinster asked one of them in marriage and took and brought home to his palace the elder as his wife. This was as it should be, for at that time it was not customary for the younger to be married "before the face of the elder." The Leinster men, however, said to their king that he had left behind the better girl of the two. Nettled at this the King went again to Tara and told Tuathal that his daughter was dead and asked for the other. The High-king then gave him his second daughter, with the courteous assurance "had I one and fifty daughters they were thine." When he brought back the second daughter to his palace in Leinster she, like another Philomela, discovered her sister alive and before her. Both died, one of shame the other of grief. When news of this reached Tara steps were taken to punish the King of Leinster. Connacht and Ulster led a great hosting with 12,000 men into Leinster to plunder it. The High-king too marched from Tara through Maynooth to Naas and encamped there. The Leinstermen were at first successful; they beat the Ultonians and killed their prince; but at last all the invading forces having combined defeated them and slew the bigamist king. They then levied the blood-tax, which was as follows:—Fifteen thousand cows, fifteen thousand swine, fifteen thousand wethers, the same number of mantles, silver chains, and copper cauldrons, together with one great copper reservoir to be set up in Tara's house itself, in which would fit twelve pigs and twelve kine. In addition to this they had to pay thirty red-eared cows with calves of the same colour, with halters and spancels of bronze and bosses of gold.

The consequences of this unfortunate tribute were to the last degree disastrous for Ireland. The High-kings of Ireland continued for ages to levy it off Leinster, and the Leinstermen continued to resist. The Fenians took part in the conflict, for they followed Finn mac Cúmhail in behalf of the men of Leinster against their own master the High-king. The tribute continued to be levied, off and on, during the reigns of forty kings, whenever Leinster seemed too weak to resist, or whenever the High-king deemed himself strong enough to raise it: until King Finnachta at last remitted it at the close of the seventh century, at the request of St. Molling.[1]

> "It is beyond the testimony of angels,
> It is beyond the word of recording saints,
> All the kings of the Gaels
> That make attack upon Leinster."[2]

Of course the unfortunate province, thus plundered during generations, lost in some measure its nationality, and no doubt it was partly owing to this that it seemed more ready than any other district to ally itself with the Danes. The great Brian is said to have gained his title of Borumha or Boru through his having reimposed the tribute on Leinster, but though he conquered that province and plundered it, I am aware of no good authority for his actually re-imposing the Boru tribute.

Some of the early saints' lives, too, may be considered as belonging almost as much to historico-romantic as to hagiological literature. From one of these, at least, we must give an extract, so that this voluminous side of Irish literature may not remain unrepresented. Here is a fragment of the life of St. Ceallach [Kal-lach] which is preserved in that ample repo-

[1] *Sec* above p. 236.

[2] Broccan's poem in the Book of Leinster translated by O'Neill Russell, in an American periodical.

sitory of ecclesiastical lore the Leabhar Breac, a great vellum manuscript written shortly after the year 1400. The story[1] deals with the dispute between Guairé [Goo-ăr-yă], a well-known king of Connacht, and St. Ceallach, the latter of whom had during his student life left St. Ciaran and his studies, and thus drawn down upon himself the prediction of that great saint that he would die by point of weapon.

Guairé having banished Ceallach, against whom his mind had been poisoned by lying tongues, the fugitive took refuge in an island in Loch Con, where he remained for a long time. Guairé, still excited against him through the lies of go-betweens, invited him to a feast with intent to kill him. He refuses however to go. The King's messengers then requested him to at least allow his four condisciples, the only ones who had remained with him in his solitude, to go with them to the feast, saying that they would bear the king's messages to him when they returned. "I will neither prevent them from going nor yet constrain them to go," answered Ceallach, the result of which was that the four condisciples returned along with the envoys, and the king was greatly pleased to see them come, and meat and drink, with good welcome, were provided for them. After this the saga proceeds.

DEATH OF CEALLACH.

"Then a banqueting-house apart was set in order for them, and thither for their use the fort's best liquor was conveyed. On Guairé's either side were set two of them, and—with an eye to win them that they might leave Ceallach—great gifts were promised to them; all the country of Tirawley, four unmarried women such as themselves should choose out of the province, and, with these, horses and kine, sufficient marriage dowry for their wives (such gifts by covenant to be secured to them), and an adequate equipment of arms to be furnished to each one.

"That night they abode there, but, at the morning's meal, with one accord they consented to kill Ceallach.

[1] Translated by Standish Hayes O'Grady in "Silva Gadelica," whose vigorous rendering I have closely followed.

"Thence they departed to Loch Con, and where they had left the boat they found it, and pulling off they reached Ceallach. They found him with his psalter spread out before him, as he said the psalms, nor did he speak to them. When he had made an end of his psalmody he looked at them, and marked their eyes unsteady in their heads, and clouded with the hue of parricide.

"'Young men,' said Ceallach, 'ye have an evil aspect, since ye went from me your natures ye have changed, and I perceive in you that for King Guairé's sake ye have agreed to murder me.'

"Never a tittle they denied, and he went on, 'An ill design it is, but follow now no longer your own detriment, and from me shall be had gifts, which far beyond all Guairé's promises shall profit you.'

"They rejoined, 'By no means shall we do as thou wouldst have us, Ceallach, seeing that if we acted so, not in all Ireland might we harbour anywhere.' And, even as they spoke, at Ceallach they drave with their spears in unison; yet he made shift to thrust his psalter in between him and his frock. They stowed him then in the boat amidships, two of themselves in the bow, and so gained a landing-place. Thence they carried him into the great forest and into the dark recesses of the wood.

"Ceallach said: 'This that ye would do I count a wicked work indeed, for in Clonmacnois [if ye spared me] ye might find shelter for ever, or should it please you to resort rather to Bláthmac and to Dermot, sons of Aedh Sláine, who is now King of Ireland [ye would be secure].'

[*Then Ceallach utters a poem of twenty-four lines.*]

"'To advise us further in the matter is but idle,' they retorted, 'we will not do it for thee.'

"'Well then,' he pleaded, 'this one night's respite grant to me for God's sake.'

"'Loath though we be to concede it, we will yield thee that,' they said. Then they raised their swords which in their clothes they carried hidden, and at the sight of them a mighty fear took Ceallach. They ransacked the wood until they found a hollow oak having one narrow entrance, and to this Ceallach was committed, they sitting at the hole to watch him till the morning. They were so to the hour of night's waning end, when drowsy longing came to them, and deep sleep fell on them then.

"Ceallach, in trouble for his violent death, slept not at all, at which time it was in his power to have fled had it so pleased him, but in his heart he said that it were misbelief in him to moot evasion of the living God's designs. Moreover, he reflected that even were he so to flee they must overtake him, he being but emaciated and feeble, after the Lent. Morning shone on them now, and he (for fear to see it and in terror of his death) shut to the door, yet he said: 'to shirk God's judgment is in me a lack of faith, Ciaran, my tutor, having promised me that I must meet this end, and as he spoke he flung open the tree's door. The Raven called then, and the Scallcrow, the Wren, and all the other birds. The Kite of Cluain-Eó's yew tree came, and the red Wolf of Drum-mic-dar, the deceiver whose lair was by the island's landing-place.

"'My dream of Wednesday's night last past was true,' said Ceallach, 'that four wild dogs rent me and dragged me through the bracken, and that down a precipice I then fell, nor evermore came up,' and he uttered this lay:—

"'HAIL to the Morning, that as a flame falls on the ground; hail to Him, too, that sends her, the Morning many-virtued, ever-new![1]

"'O Morning fair, so full of pride, O sister of the brilliant Sun, hail to the beauteous morning that lightest for me my little book!

"'Thou seest the guest in every dwelling, and shinest on every tribe and kin; hail O thou white-necked beautiful one, here with us now, golden-fair, wonderful!

"'My little book with chequered page tells me that my life has not been right. Maelcróin, 't is he whom I do well to fear; he it is who comes to smite me at the last.

"'O Scallcrow, and O Scallcrow, small grey-coated, sharp-beaked fowl, the intent of thy desire is apparent to me, no friend art thou to Ceallach.

"'O Raven that makest croaking, if hungry thou art now, O bird, depart not from this same homestead until thou eatest a surfeit of my flesh!

"'Fiercely the Kite of Cluain-Eó's yew tree will take part in the scramble, the full of his grey talons he will carry off, he will not part from me in kindness.

"'To the blow [that fells me] the fox that is in the darkling wood will make response at speed, he too in cold and trackless confines shall devour a portion of my flesh and blood.

"'The wolf that is in the rath upon the eastern side of Drum-mic-dar, he on a passing visit comes to me, that he may rank as chieftain of the meaner pack.

"'Upon Wednesday's night last past I beheld a dream, I saw the wild dogs dragging me together eastward and westward through the russet ferns.

---

[1] "Is mochean in maiten bán
No taed for lár, mar lasán,
Is mochean do'n té rusfói
In maiten buadach bithnói"

"'I beheld a dream, that into a green glen they took me, four there were that bore me thither, but methought, ne'er brought me out again.

"'I beheld a dream, that to their house my condisciples brought me, for me they poured out a drink, and to me did they a drink quaff.

"'O tiny Wren most scant of tail, dolefully hast thou piped prophetic lay, surely thou art come to betray me and to curtail my gift of life![1]

"'O Maelcróin and O Maelcróin, thou hast resolved upon an unrighteous deed, for ten hundred golden ingots Owen's son[2] had ne'er consented into thy death!

"'O Maelcróin and O Maelcróin, pelf it is that thou hast taken to betray me; for this world's sake thou hast accepted it, accepted it for the sake of hell!

"'All precious things that ever I had, all sleek-coated grey horses, on Maelcróin I would have bestowed them, that he should not do me this treason.

"'But Mary's great Son up above me, thus addresses speech to me, 'Thou must leave earth, thou shalt have heaven; welcome awaits thee, Ceallach.'"

The saint is then, as soon as the morning had fully risen, taken out of the tree by the four traitors, and put to death. The kite and the wolf and the scallcrow tear his flesh. The remainder of what is really a fine saga describes the hunt for the murderers and their final death at the hands of Ceallach's brother, who wrested for himself all the territory that Guairé had given them, marries Guairé's daughter, and is, like Ceallach his brother, finally himself put to death by Guairé's treachery.

It would be quite impossible within the limits of a volume like this to give any adequate study of the evolution of Irish saga. All Irish romances are compositions upon which more or less care had evidently been bestowed, in ancient times, as is evidenced by their being all shot through and through with verse. These verses amount to a considerable portion of the

[1] Compare the legend of the wren's having betrayed the Irish to the English, whence the universal pursuit of him made by boys on St. Stephen's day.

[2] Ceallach himself.

saga, often to nearly a quarter or even a third of the whole, and Irish versification is usually very elaborate, and not the work of any mere inventor or story-teller, but of a highly-trained technical poet. Very few pieces indeed, and these mostly of the more modern Fenian tales, are written in pure prose. It may be that the reciter of the ancient sagas actually *sang* these verses, or certainly gave them in a different tone from the prose narrative with which he filled up the gap between them. Whether the same man was both the composer of the verse and the framer of the prose narrative, in each particular story, is a difficult question to answer, but I should think that in most cases, at least in the older saga, incidents had been taken up by the bards and poets as themes for their verses, for perhaps ages before they were brought together by somebody and woven into one complete épopée with a prose intermixture. Dr. Sullivan thought that the Táin Bó Cuailnge was all originally written in verse, and has his own interpretation for the account given in the curious tale, the "Proceedings of the Great Bardic Institution," which tells us that the story was at one time lost, and that the Bardic Association was commanded to search for and recover it. This, according to him, meant that the verses had been lost, and that only a fragmentary form of it had been saved, the gaps being filled with prose. I do not quite know how far this is a probable suggestion, because it would appear to be reversing the processes which produce epic poetry in other literatures. The complete versified epic, the Iliad, the Odyssey, the Mahābhārata, are indeed "the hatch and brood of time," embodying not the first but the *last* results of a long series of national poetry. But to this last result, so close to them, so easily attainable, the Irish never arrived, and hence the various ballads that compose the books of their Red Branch Iliad, or Fenian Odyssey, remains separate to this day, and find their unity, if at all, only by means of a bridge of prose thrown across from poem to poem, by men who were not poets. Had the internal development of the Irish not been so rudely arrested by the Northmen towards the close of the eighth and the beginning of the ninth century, there is every reason to believe that both the Red Branch and the Fenian Cycle would have undergone a further development and appeared in poems of continuous verse.

The poems with which these sagas are intermixed are mostly of two kinds, one kind, speeches in the form of lays, placed in the mouths of the actors, prefaced by such words as "and he sang," "so that he spake the lay," or the like, and the other kind, which occurs less often, is as it were a *résumé* in verse of what had been just told in prose. In almost every case I should imagine that the narrative poems are the oldest, and of them the prose is not unfrequently, as it were, an explanation and an extension.

That the Irish had already made some approach to the construction of a great epic is evident from the way in which they attempted, from a very early date, to group a number of minor sagas, which were evidently independent in their origin, round their great saga the Táin Bó Cuailnge. There are twelve minor tales which the Irish called preface-stories to the Táin and which they worked into it by links, some of which, at least, were evidently forged long after the story which they were wanted to connect. Especially remarkable in this way is the story of the metempsychosis of the two swineherds, whose souls passed into the two bulls who occasioned the great war of the Táin,—a story which is of a distinctly independent origin, and which was forced to do duty as an outlying book, as it were, of the Táin Bó Cuailnge.

How very great the number of Irish sagas must have been can be conjectured from the fact that out of the list of one hundred and eighty-seven contained in the Book of Leinster, at least one hundred and twenty have completely disappeared, and of the majority of the remainder we have only brief digests, whilst very many of the ones still preserved, are not mentioned in the Book of Leinster at all, thus proving that the list given in that manuscript is an imperfect one. A perfect one would have contained at the very least two hundred and fifty prime stories and one hundred secondary ones, for this was the number which every ollamh or chief poet was obliged, by law, to know. The following are some of the best known and most accessible of the earlier sagas which we have not yet mentioned, and which do not belong to any of the greater cycles. This list is drawn up, not according to the age of the texts or the manuscripts which contain them, but according to the date of the events to which they refer, and round which they are constructed.

SIXTH CENTURY B.C.—The destruction of Dinn Righ, otherwise called the exile of Labhraidh [Lowry] the Mariner. This appears to have been one of a group of lost romances which centred round the children of Ugony the Great,[1] of some of which Keating has given a *résumé* in his history.[2]

SECOND CENTURY B.C.—The King of the Leprechanes' journey to Emania, and how the death of Fergus mac Léide, King of Ulster, was brought about.[3]

The triumphs of Congal Clàringneach, which deals with a revolution in the province of Ulster, the death of the King of Tara, and accession of Congal to the throne.[4]

The Courtship of Etain by Eochaidh Aireach, King of Ireland, who came to the throne 134 years B.C., according to the "Four Masters."

[1] For him, *see* above, p. 25.

[2] Some account of this saga is given in O'Curry's MS. Materials, p. 256, and by Keating, p. 253, of O'Mahony's translation. The entire saga is preserved in the Yellow Book of Lecan. My friend, the late Father James Keegan, made me a translation of another version, which he afterwards published in a St. Louis paper.

[3] Translated and edited by Standish Hayes O'Grady, p. 269 of his "Silva Gadelica."

[4] Only one copy of this tale was known to O'Curry in 205, Hodges and Smith, R. I. A.

[5] Edited without a translation by Windisch, in his "Irische Texte," i. p. 117, and referred to at length by O'Curry, "Manners and Customs," vol. ii. pp. 192-4; and summarised and examined by Alfred Nutt, in his "Voyage of Bran." *See* for this saga, p. 102, above.

FIRST CENTURY B.C.—The Courtship of Crunn's wife.[1] To this century belong the Red Branch tales.

FIRST CENTURY A.D.—The Battle of Ath Comair, fought by the three Finns, brothers of Mève, Queen of Connacht.[2]

The Destruction of the Bruidhean [Bree-an] Da Choga, in West Meath, where Cormac Conloingeas, the celebrated son of King Conor mac Nessa, was killed about the year 33.[3]

The Revolution of the Aitheach Tuatha, and the Death of Cairbrè Cinn-cait by the free clans of Ireland.[4]

SECOND CENTURY A.D.—The Death of Eochaidh [Yohy], son of Mairid.[5]

The progress of the Deisi from Tara.[6]

The Courtship of Moméra, by Owen Mór.[7] (The Fenian tales and tales of Conn of the Hundred Battles, and Cormac mac Art, relate to this and the following century.)

THIRD CENTURY.—The Adventures of Teig, son of Cian [Kee-an], son of Oilioll Olum.[8]

The Siege of Drom Damhgaire, where Cormac mac Art attempted to lay a double tribute on the two provinces of Munster.[9]

FOURTH CENTURY.—The History of the Sons of Eochaidh Muighmheadhon [Mwee-va-on] father of Niall of the Nine Hostages.[10]

Death of King Criomhthann [Criv-han or Criffan] and of Eochaidh Muighmheadhon's three sons.[11]

---

[1] This was Macha who pronounced the curse on the Ultonians. *See* above, p. 294 note 3. The story is preserved in the Harleian MS. 5280, British Museum.

[2] There is a long extract from this battle given by O'Curry in his "Manners and Customs," vol. ii. pp. 261–3.

[3] Preserved in the Leabhar na h-Uidhre. *See* O'Curry, "Manners and Customs," vol. iii. p. 254. There is a full copy in H. 3. 18, T. C., D.

[4] In H. 3. 18, T. C., D. *See* above, p. 27.

[5] Edited from the Leabhar na h-Uidhre by O'Beirne Crowe, in the "Journal of the Royal Irish Historical and Archæological Association, 1870," and by Standish Hayes O'Grady, "Silva Gadelica," p. 265.

[6] *See* O'Curry, "Manners and Customs," vol. ii. p. 205. I think Kuno Meyer has translated this saga somewhere. *See* p. 40.

[7] Published by O'Curry for the Celtic Society as an appendage to the Battle of Moy Léana. *See* above, p. 368.

[8] Translated by O'Grady, "Silva Gadelica," p. 385, and studied at length by Alfred Nutt, in his "Voyage of Bran," vol. i. p. 201.

[9] *See* O'Curry's "Manners and Customs," vol. ii. p. 212, and MS. Materials p. 271. This saga is contained at length in the Book of Lismore.

[10] Translated in O'Grady's "Silva Gadelica," p. 368.

[11] *Ibid.*, p. 373.

FIFTH CENTURY.—The Expedition or Hosting of Dáithi, the last pagan king of Ireland, who was killed by lightning at the foot of the Alps.[1]

SIXTH CENTURY.—Death of Aedh Baclamh.[2]

Death of King Diarmuid—he who was cursed by St. Ruadhan.[3]

The birth of Aedh [Ae] Sláine,[4] the son of Diarmuid, who came to the throne in 595, according to the "Four Masters."

The Wooing of Becfola, in the reign of Aedh Sláine's son.[5]

The Voyage of the Sons of Ua Corra.[6]

SEVENTH CENTURY.—The Proceedings of the Great Bardic Institution.[7]

The Battle of Moyrath.[8]

Suibhne's Madness, a sequel to the last.[9]

The Feast of Dún na ngedh,[8] a preface tale to the Battle of Moyrath.

The Voyage of Snedgus and Mac Riaghla.[10]

The Love of Dubhlacha for Mongan.[11]

The Death of Maelfathartaigh, son of Ronán,[12] who was King of Leinster about the year 610.

---

[1] This is one of the tales in the Book of Leinster list. Modern versions are common.

[2] *See* above, p. 228, note, translated in "Silva Gadelica," p. 70.

[3] *Ibid.*, p. 76. [4] *Ibid.*, p. 88.

[5] A short tale, translated in "Silva Gadelica," p. 91.

[6] Translated in the "Revue Celtique."

[7] Published by Professor Connellan for the Ossianic Society in 1860, vol. v.

[8] Published by O'Donovan in 1842 for the Irish Archæological Society.

[9] MS. 60, Hodges and Smith, R. I. A.

[10] Edited, with English translation, by Whitley Stokes, in "Revue Celtique," vol. ix., and translated into modern Irish by Father O'Growney in the "Gaelic Journal," vol. iv. p. 85, from the Yellow Book of Lecan.

[11] Edited by Kuno Meyer in "Voyage of Bran," vol. i. p. 58, from the Book of Fermoy. This version seems to have escaped the notice of D'Arbois de Jubainville, who says in his "Essai d'un Catalogue," "Cette pièce parait perdue." I have in my own possession a copy in a MS. written by a scribe named O'Mahon in the last century, which is at least twice as long as that published by Kuno Meyer.

[12] The story of an Irish Hippolytus, whose death at his father's hands is compassed by his step-mother, *spretæ injuria formæ*. O'Curry mentions this tale, MS. Materials, p. 277. It is one of the stories in the catalogue of the Book of Leinster, under the head of Tragedies. Another Hippolytus story is that of the death of Comgan, son of the King of the Decies, quoted by O'Curry, "Manners and Customs," vol. ii. p. 204, but I do not know from what MS.

EIGHTH CENTURY.—The Voyage of Maelduin.[1]

There are very few sagas, indeed, which deal with events posterior to the eighth century, and among those which do (like the stories about Callaghan of Cashel and the Danes, or the Leeching of Cian's leg, which relates to the reign of Brian Boru, or O'Donnell's Kerne, which seems as late as the sixteenth century) there are not many whose literary merits stand high. It is evident from this, that, apart from the poets, almost all the genuine literary activity of Ireland centred around the days of her freedom, and embraced a vast range of time, from the mythical De Danann period down to the birth of Christ, and from that to the eighth century, and that after this period and the invasions of the Northmen and Normans, Irish national history produced few subjects stimulating to the national muse; so that the literary production which still continued, though in narrower channels and in feebler volume, looked for inspiration not to contemporaneous history, but to the glories of Tara, the exploits of Finn mac Cúmhail, and the past ages of Irish greatness.

The number of sagas still surviving, though many of them are mere skeletons, may be conjectured from the fact that O'Curry, in his manuscript lectures on Irish history, quotes from or alludes to ninety different tales, all of considerable antiquity, whilst M. d'Arbois de Jubainville, in his "Essai d'un Catalogue de la littérature épique de l'Irlande," gives the names of no less than about 540 different pieces.

[1] Translated, but not very literally, by Joyce in his "Early Celtic Romances," and by M. Lot in D'Arbois de Jubainville's "Épopée Celtique," critically edited by Whitley Stokes in the "Revue Celtique," t. ix. p. 446, and x. pp. 50–95.

CHAPTER XXXI

PRE-DANISH POETS

THE sagas and historic tales, and the poetry that is mingled with them, are of far greater importance from a purely literary point of view than any of the other known productions during the pre-Norman period. Although in almost every instance, I may say, their authorship is unknown, they are or infinitely greater interest than those pieces whose authorship has been carefully preserved. One of the first poets of renown after St. Patrick's time was Eochaidh [Yohy], better known as Dallán Forgaill. It is to him the celebrated "Amra," or elegy on Columcille, whose contemporary he was, is ascribed,[1] and this poem in the Béarla Feni, or Fenian dialect, has come down to us so heavily annotated that the text preserved is the oldest miscellaneous manuscript we have, the Leabhar na h-Uidhre, is almost smothered in glosses and explanations, and indeed would be perfectly unintelligible without them. The gloss and commentary is really far more interesting than the poem, which indeed, considering the fame of Dallán,

[1] Mr. Strachan, however, has lately cast doubts upon its genuineness and ascribes it in its present form to a later date.

is very disappointing; but no doubt it derived half its importance from being in the Fenian dialect, and hence incomprehensible to the ordinary reader. "He wrote," says the learned Colgan, who published at Louvain the lives of the saints which O'Clery collected for him at the beginning of the seventeenth century, "in the native speech, and in ancient style, several little works which cannot in later ages be easily penetrated by many otherwise well versed in the old native idiom and antiquity, and hence they are illustrated by our more learned antiquaries with scattered commentaries, and as rare monuments of our ancient language and antiquity it is customary to lecture on them and expound them in the schools of antiquaries of our nation. Among these is one panegyric or poem always held in great esteem on the praises of St. Colomb, and entitled 'Amra Choluim cille,'" etc. Colgan adds in a note, "I have in my possession one copy of this work, but putting aside a few scattered commentaries which it contains, it is penetrable to-day to only a few, and these the most learned."

This obscure poem is not, so far as I can see, composed in any metre or rhythm. It, with its gloss, is divided into seven chapters and an introduction. Here is the comment on the first words *Dia*, *Dia*, which will show better than anything that could be written, the very high state of independent development which the Irish poets had early attained in the technique of their art. We must remember that the manuscript in which we find this was copied about the year 1100, and the commentary may be much older. Irish is indeed the only vernacular language of western Europe where poetic technique had reached so high a perfection in the eleventh century. Fully to see the significance of this one must remember that the English language had not at this time even begun to emerge. Compare this highly-developed critical commentary with anything of the same age that Germany, France, or Italy has to show.

"*Dia, Dia,*[1] God, God, etc.," says the commentator, "it is why he doubles the first word on account of the rapidity[2] and avidity of the praising, as *Deus, Deus meus,* etc. But the name of that with the Gael is 'Return-to-a-usual-sound,' for there be three similar standards of expression with the poets of the Gaels, that is *re-return to a usual sound,* and *renarration mode* and *reduplication,* and this is the mark of each of them. The *return* indeed is a doubling of one word in one place in the round, without adhering to it from that forth. The *renarration* mode again is renarrating from a like mode; that means the one word—to say it frequently in the round, with an intervention of other words between them, as this—

'Came the foam which the plain filters,[3]
Came the ox through fifty warriors;
So came the keen active lad
Whom brown Cu Dinisc left.'

But 'reduplication' is, namely 'refolding,' that is 'bi-geminating,' as this—

"I fear fear / after long long /
Pains strong strong / without peace peace /
Like each each / until doom doom /
For gloom gloom / will not cease cease."[4]

[1] I follow here O'Beirne Crowe's imperfect rendering. If he translates some words of this difficult piece inaccurately it does not much matter for my purpose.

[2] *Ar abela no ar lainni an molta.* This word *Abél* for "quick," "rapid," though neither in O'Reilly's nor Windisch's nor the Scotch Gaelic dictionaries, is a common one in the spoken language of West Connacht. It occurs twice in the "Three Shafts of Death," where it is mistranslated by "awful," but it must be carefully distinguished from M. I. *Abdul,* Keating's *Adhbhal.* The word is not known in Waterford, and my friend the late Mr. Fleming, who was the chief authority in the Royal Irish Academy on the spoken language, and who hailed from that county, was, I believe, unacquainted with it.

[3] This translation is evident nonsense, but I cannot better it. The original is "Ric in sithbe sitlas mag."

[4] Is é immoro adíabul, *i.e.,* afhillind, *i.e.,* doemnad, ut est hoc, *i.e.,*

"Águr águr iar céin chéin
Bith i péin, phein ni síth síth,
Amail cách cách, co bráth bráth,
In cech tráth tráth, cid scíth scíth."

My translation is in the exact metre of the original, and conveys in English the manner in which the heptasyllabic Irish lines were pronounced, in which, despite of what some continental scholars have

"There are two divisions of these in this fore-speech [to the Amra]; that is, we have the 'Return-to-a-usual-sound' and the 'renarration-mode,' but in the body of the hymn we have the 'renarration-mode' only."

Here is another passage which will show the difficulty that was found so early as the eleventh century in explaining this Fenian dialect.

"IT IS A HARP WITHOUT A *ceis*, IT IS A CHURCH WITHOUT AN ABBOT—*i.e.*, *ceis* is a name for a small harp which is used as an accompaniment to a large harp in co-playing; or it is a name for the small pin which holds the cord in the wood of the harp; or for the tacklings, or for the heavy cord. Or the *ceis* in the harp is what holds the side part with its chords in it, as the poet said—it was Ros [1] mac Find who sang it, or Ferceirtné [2] the poet,

> The base-chord concealed not music from the harp of Crabtene,
> Until it dropped sleep-deaths upon hosts.
>
> . . . . . .
>
> Sweeter than any music, the harp
> Which delighted Labhraidh [Lowry] Lorc the Mariner,
> Though sullen about his secrets was the King,
> The *ceis*, or base-chord of Craftiné concealed it not."

This poem is an allusion to the sagas which grouped themselves round the sons of Ugony the great and Lowry the Mariner, who reigned about 530 years B.C.

In another place he quotes a poem of Finn mac Cúmhail's.

"'AND SEA-COURSE'—*i.e.*, he was skilful in the art of *renis* [3] that is 'of the sea,' or it may be *rian* that would be right in it, as Finn, grandson of Baoisgne [Bweesgna] said—

> "'A tale I have for you. Ox murmurs,
> Winter roars, summer is gone.
> Wind high cold, sun low,
> Cry is attacking, sea resounding.

---

advanced, there is, I believe, *no alternation of beat or stress at all*, and neither trochee nor iambus. O'Beirne Crowe mistranslates *águr* by "I ask."

[1] Ros was chief poet of Erin in the time of St. Patrick, and is said to have helped him in redacting the Brehon Law.

[2] Ferceirtné was the poet at Conor mac Nessa's Court in the first century B.C., who contended in the "Dialogue of the Two Sages," *see* above p. 240.

[3] See above for *réin* being used for sea, p. 10.

Very red raying has concealed form.
Voice of geese [Barnacles] has become usual,
Cold has caught the wings of birds,
Ice-frost time; wretched, very wretched.[1]
A tale I have for you.'"

Another verse quoted alludes to the chess-board of Crimhthann Nianáir, who came to the throne eleven years before the birth of Christ.[2]

"FECHT AFOR NIA NEM—*i.e.*, the time when the champion would come, that is Columcille, for *nia* means a champion, as is said—

"'The chessboard of Crimhthann, brave champion,
A small child carries it not on his arm (?)
Half of its chessmen are of yellow gold.
The other half of white bronze.
One man of its chessmen alone
Would purchase six married couples.'"

The ancient commentator quotes, thirty-five times in all, from various poems, in explanation of his text, including poems ascribed to Columcille himself, and to Gráinne, the daughter of Cormac mac Art, who eloped from Finn mac Cúmhail. He quotes the satire made on Breas in the time of the Tuatha De Danann, and a verse of St. Patrick (some of whose Irish poetry is also quoted by the "Four Masters"), and a poet called Colman mac Lenene, who was first a poet, but afterwards became a saint, and founded the great school of Cloyne.

[1] The translation is doubtful. Dr. Sigerson has well versified it in his "Bards of the Gael and Gaul," p. 116. The original has a curious metrical effect not unlike that other piece attributed to Finn, quoted above p. 275. It might be printed thus—

Scél lém duib
Dordaid dam
Snigid gaim
Rofaith sam.
Gaeth ard huar,
Isel grian
Gair arrith
Ruthach rían.

Roruad rath
Rocleth cruth,
Rogab gnath
Giugrand guth.
Rogab uacht
Ete én,
Aigre ré
E, mosclé.

[2] *See* above p. 27 for Crimhthann's chess-board.

Dallán wrote two other Amras, one on Senan of Innis Cathaigh, "which," remarks Colgan, "on account of antiqueness of style and gracefulness is amongst those fond of antiquity, always held in great esteem," and another in praise of Conall of Inskeel in Donegal, in one grave with whom he was buried. There has also come down to us in the same inscrutable Fenian dialect a poem of his consisting of eighty-four lines on the shield of Hugh, King of Oriel, which, unlike his Amra, is in perfect rhyme and metre.[1]

It was he who headed the bardic body when they were so nearly banished from the kingdom, and were only saved by the intervention of St. Columcille at the Synod of Drom Ceat [Cat], of which more hereafter. There is a curious specimen of his overbearing truculence in a story preserved in the same manuscript (of about the year 1100) that has preserved his Amra; it is headed "A Story from which it is inferred that Mongan was Finn mac Cúmhail." The poet was stopping with Mongan, King of Ulster.

[1] Published by Professor Connellan, but without a translation, at p. 258 of Vol. V. of Ossianic Society's publications. It, too, is in the Féni dialect. The first verse, in honour of Dubh-Giolla, "the Black Attendant," which was the name of the King's shield will show its abstruseness.

"Dub gilla dub, arm naise,
Eo Rosa raon slegh snaise,
Adeardius daib diupla gainde
d'Aodh do cinn lainne glaise."

It would appear that Dallán could write Irish as well as Béarla Féni from this verse, which is ascribed to him by the "Four Masters." "Dallán Forgaill," they say, "dixit hoc do bhás Choluim Cille."

"Is leigheas legha gan lés
Is dedhail smeara re smuais
Is abhran re cruit gan chéis
Sinne déis ar nargain uais."

It is the healing of a leech without light [*i.e.*, in the dark]; it is a dividing of the marrow from the bone; it is the song of a harp without a base-string that we are, after being deprived of our noble." This verse does not occur in the Amra, though the expression a "harp without a base-string" does.

"Every night the poet would recite a story to Mongan. So great was his lore that they were thus from Halloweve till May-day. He had gifts and food from Mongan. One day Mongan asked his poet what was the death of Fothad Airgdech. Forgoll said he was slain at Duffry in Leinster. Mongan said it was false. The poet [on hearing that] said he would satirise him with his lampoons, and he would satirise his father and his mother and his grandfather, and he would sing [spells] upon their waters, so that fish should not be caught in their river-mouths. He would sing upon their woods so that they should not give fruit, upon their plains so that they should be barren for ever of any produce.

"Mongan [thereupon] promised him his fill of precious things, so far as [the value of] seven bondmaids, or twice seven bondmaids, or three times seven. At last he offers him one-third, or one-half of his land, or his whole land; at last [everything] save only his own liberty with that of his wife Breóthigernd, unless he were redeemed before the end of three days.

"The poet refused all except as regards his wife. For the sake of his honour Mongan consented. Thereat his wife was sorrowful, the tear was not taken from her cheek. Mongan told her not to be sorrowful, help would certainly come to them."

Eventually the poet is very dramatically shown to be in the wrong.[1]

Dallán Forgaill was succeeded in the Head Ollamhship of all the Irish bards by his pupil Senchan Torpeist, who was equally overbearing, and whose intolerable insolence is admirably satirised in the story called the "Proceedings of the Great Bardic Association." Only two poems of his have come down to us, one being his elegy on the death of his master Dallán Forgaill.

[1] *See* the whole story, carefully edited by Kuno Meyer, in "The Voyage of Bran," p. 45, where the poet is called Forgoll, but this is evidently the same as our Dallán Forgaill, though Kuno Meyer appears not to think so, for he has the following note: "Forgoll seems to have been an overbearing and exacting *filé* of the type of Athirne and Dallán Forgaill." But as the story synchronises with the life of Dallán Forgaill, and there is, so far as I know, no second poet known as Forgoll, it is evidently the same person. The "Dallán," *i.e.*, the "blind man" (for he lost his eyesight through overstudy), being prefixed to Forgaill appears to inflect it in the genitive case, as An Tighearna easbuig, "the Lord Bishop," *i.e.*, the lord of a bishop, "the blind man of a Forgall."

The next great lay poet of importance seems to have been Cennfaeladh, who died in 678, whose verses are constantly cited by the "Four Masters." He was originally an Ulster warrior who was wounded in the battle of Moyrath, which was fought when Adamnan, Columcille's biographer, was eleven years old, and he was brought to be cured to the house of one Brian in Tuaim Drecain, where there were three schools, one of classics,[1] one of law, and one of poetry. He used to áttend—apparently during his convalescence—these various schools, and what he heard in the day he would repeat to himself at night, so that "his brain of forgetfulness was extracted from his head after its having been cloven in the battle of Moyrath." "And he put a clear thread of poetry through them, and wrote them on flags and on tables, and he put them into a vellum book." Hence he became a great lawyer as well as a poet, and a considerable part of the celebrated Brehon Law Book, called the Book of Acaill, is ascribed to him.[2]

Angus Céile Dé[3] [Kail-a Day], or the Culdee, is the next poet of note who claims our attention. He flourished about the year 800, and is the author of the well-known Féilirè, or Calendar. In this work one stanza in *rinn áird* metre is

[1] Scoil "legind."

[2] *See* one of the poems ascribed to him printed by Professor Connellan from the Book of Ballymote, Ossianic Society, vol. v. p. 268. If it is Cennfealadh's it has been greatly altered during the course of transcription.

[3] Céile Dé, or Culdee, *i.e.*, "Servus Dei," was a phrase used with much latitude, and in general denoted an ascetic, but occasionally also a missionary, monk. We find the Dominicans of Sligo called Culdees in a MS. of the year 1600. They seem to have arisen in the seventh or early eighth century. The Scottish Culdees, becoming lax in later times, married and established a spurious hereditary order. There is, of course, no truth in the fable that they were the pre-Patrician or early Scottish Christians, a notion which Campbell has propagated in his fine poem "Reulura," *i.e.*, "réull-úr":—

"Peace to their souls, the pure Culdees
Were Albyn's earliest priests of God,
Ere yet an island of her seas
By foot of Saxon monk was trod!"

devoted to each day of the year, in connection with the name of some saint—an Irish one wherever possible. The Féilìrè is followed by a poem of five or six hundred lines, which with its glosses and commentaries is probably the most extensive piece of Old Irish poetry that we have. Whitley Stokes, who edited it with great care, considers it to be of the tenth rather than the late eighth or early ninth century. If so, this would leave its authorship doubtful, but it has been shown, I think by Kuno Meyer, that the number of deponental forms contained in it might point to a higher antiquity than that which Whitley Stokes allows. It has certainly been always hitherto accepted as the work of Angus, and as it cannot well, in any case, be more than a century or so later, we may let it stand here, as it has always done, under his name. In the ancient and curious Irish notes and commentary on the Féilìrè we find a great number of verses quoted from the poet-saints, and these include St. Patrick, St. Ciaran the elder, St. Comgall with St. Columcille his friend, St. Ité the virgin, St. Kevin of Glendaloch, St. Ciaran of Clonmacnois, St. Molaise [Moleesha] of Devenish (who sent Columcille to banishment), St. Mochuda of Lismore, St. Molling, St. Fechin of Fore, St. Aireran of Clonard, Maelruan of Tallaght, Adamnan (Columcille's biographer), and Angus the Culdee himself, a goodly company of priests and poets; but no one seems to have been anything esteemed in ancient Erin unless he either was or was reputed to be a poet! Of true poetic spirit it contains not much, but it is a wonderful example of technical difficulties overcome. The metre is one of the most difficult, a six-syllable one, with dissyllabic endings. The first stanzas, translated into the metre of the original, run as follows:—

"Bless, O Christ, my speaking,
King of heavens seven,
Strength and wealth and POWER
In this HOUR be *given.*

Given,[1] O thou brightest,
Destined chains to sever,
King of Angels GLORIOUS,
And victORIOUS *ever*.

Ever o'er us shining,
Light to mortals given,
Beaming daily, NIGHTLY,
BRIGHTLY out of heaven."

The Saltair na Rann has also been usually ascribed to Angus, but it can hardly be, as Dr. Whitley Stokes has shown, earlier than the year 1000,[2] for it mentions apparently as contemporaries Brian king of Munster, and Dub-da-lethe archbishop of Armagh, appointed in 988. It is a collection of one hundred and sixty-two poems in early Middle Irish containing between eight and nine thousand lines, mostly composed in Deibhidh [D'yevvee] metre. These poems are all of a more or less religious cast, and most of them are based (like the Saxon Caedmon's) on Old Testament history, but they also contain a prodigious deal of curious matter. The opening poem begins—

"Mo rí-se rí nime náir."[3]
("My king is the King of noble Heaven.")

---

[1] This *tour de force*, which consists of laying stress in the beginning of each succeeding stanza upon the word which ended the last, is common in Irish and is called *conachlonn*. It is much used by Angus. It seems to be self-evolved in Irish, whose prosody is full of original terms unborrowed from the Latin, which, to my mind, tells strongly in favour of pre-Christian culture. It is curious that Horace who falls into *conachlonn* in his second ode, never returned to a form so well adapted to lyric purposes :—

"Dextera sacras jaculatus arces
Terruit urbem.
Terruit gentes," etc.

[2] He has edited the text without a translation from the only MS. that contains it—Rawlinson, B 502, in the Bodleian, in the "Anecdota Oxoniensia" Series. Oxford deserves splendidly of Celtic scholars. If only Dublin would follow her example!

[3] "Mo rí-se rí nime náir
Cen huabur cen immarbáig,
Dorósat domun dualach,
Mo rí bith-beo bith-buadach."

It tells of the creation of the world, of the sun, of heaven and earth, light and darkness, day and night, of how the earth separated from the primal material, and was surrounded by the firmament, the world being "like an apple, goodly and round"; then the king created the mists, the current of the cold watery air, the four chief winds, and the eight sub-winds, with their colours, "the white, the clear purple, the blue, the great green, the yellow, the red truly-bold, . . . the black, the grey, the speckled (?), the dark (?), the dull-black, the dun-coloured."[1] The poet then discusses the distance from the earth to the firmament, the seven planets, the distance from the earth to the moon, from moon to sun, the windless ethereal heaven, the distance between the firmament and the sun, the motionless Olympus or third heaven, the distance from the firmament to heaven and from the earth to the depths of hell, the five zones, the firmament round the earth, like its shell round an egg, the seventy-two windows of the firmament, with a shutter on each, the seventh heaven revolving like a wheel, with the seven planets from the creation, the signs of the zodiac,[2] the time (30 days 10½ hours) that the sun is in each, the day of the month on which it enters each, the month in which it is in each, the division of the firmament into twelve

[1] "In gel in corcarda glan,
In glass ind uaine allmar,
In buidi in derg, derb dána,
Nisgaib fergg frisodála,
In dub, ind liath ind alad,
In t-emen in chiar chálad,
Ind odar doirchi datha
Nidat soirchi sogabtha."

The hundred and fifty-second poem, which is a beautiful one, again asks what are the colours of the winds. Line 7,948.

[2] A good example of how Irish assimilates foreign words by cutting off their endings :—

"Aquair, Pisc, Ariet, Tauir, Treb,
Geimin choir, ocus Cancer,
Leo Uirgo, Libru, Scoirp scrus,
Sagitair, Capricornus."

Leo is pronounced *L'yo* as a monosyllable.

parts, and the five things which every intelligent man should know—the day of the month, age of the moon, height of the tide, day of the week, and saints' festivals![1]

The attribution of colours to the winds in this poem is curious and appears to be Irish. I have met traces of this fancy even amongst the modern peasantry. There is a strange entry in the Great Brehon Law Book, the Seanchas Mór, which quotes the colours of the winds in the same order.

"The colour of each," says this strange passage, "differs from the other, namely, the white and the crimson, the blue[2] and the green, the yellow and the red, the black and the grey, the speckled and the dark, the *ciar* (dull black) and the grisly. From the east comes the crimson wind, from the south the white, from the north the black, from the west the dun. The red and the yellow winds are produced between the white and the crimson, the green and the grey between the grisly and the white, the grey and the *ciar* between the grisly and the jet-black, the dark and the mottled between the black and the crimson. And those are all the sub-winds contained in each and all the cardinal winds."

After thus describing the creation of the world in the first poem, we are introduced in subsequent ones to heaven and the angels, who are named for us, and then shown hell and Lucifer's abode, the description of which, except that it is in verse, reminds us of that given by St. Brendan. Next we are introduced to Adam and Eve, and it is stated that Adam had spent a thousand years in the Garden of Eden. The jealousy of Lucifer is described, and his temptation of Eve, whom he persuades to open the door and let him into the garden. Then he makes her eat the apple, and Adam takes half from

[1] *See* Whitley Stokes' introduction for the analysis of the 1st, the 11th, and the 12th poem.

[2] "Glas" must be here translated "blue." It is a colour used by the Irish with great latitude, and apparently means yellowish, or light blue, or greenish grey. To this day a *grey* eye is *súil ghlas* and *green* grass is *feur glas*, yet the colour of grass is not that of a grey or even of a grey-green eye. We want a study on colours and their shades as at present used by the Irish and the Scotch Highlanders.

her and eats also. The eleventh poem describes the evil result, and is quite Miltonic and imaginative. It tells us how for a week, after being driven out, Adam and his wife remain without fire, house, drink, food, or clothing. He then begins to lament to Eve over all his lost blessings and admits that he has done wrong. Thereupon Eve asks Adam to kill her, so that God may pity him the more. Adam refuses. He goes forth in his starvation to seek food, and finds nothing but herbs, the food of the lawless beasts. He proposes then to Eve to do penance and adore God in silence, Eve in the Tigris for thirty days, and Adam in the Jordan for forty-seven days, a flagstone under their feet and the water up to their necks. Eve's hair fell dishevelled round her and her eyes were directed to heaven in silent prayer for forgiveness. Then Adam prays the river Jordan "to fast with him against God, with all its many beasts, that pardon may be granted to him." Then the stream ceased to flow, and gathered together every living creature that was in it, and they all supplicate the angelic host to join with them in beseeching God to forgive Adam. They obtain their request, and forgiveness is granted to Adam and to all his seed except the unrighteous. When the devil, however, hears this, he, "like a man in the shape of a white angel," goes to Eve as she stands in the Tigris, and gets her to leave her penance, saying that he had been sent by God. They then go to Adam, who at once recognises the devil, and shows Eve how she has been deceived. Eve falls half dead to the ground and reproaches Lucifer. He, however, defends himself, and repeats to them at length the story of his expulsion from heaven for refusing to worship Adam. He concludes by threatening vengeance on him and his descendants. Adam and his wife then live alone for a year on grass, without fire, house, music, or raiment, drinking water from their palms, and eating green herbs in the shadows of trees and in caverns. Eve brings forth a beautiful boy, who at once proceeds to cut grass for his father, who calls him Cain. God at last pities Adam and sends Michael to him with various seeds, and Michael teaches him husbandry and the use of animals. Seven years afterwards Eve brings forth Abel. In a vision she sees Cain drinking the blood of Abel.

In this manner, with a free play of the imagination, the writer runs through both Old and New Testaments, down to the denial of Peter and the death of Christ, in 150 poems, to which are appended twelve more, eleven of them in a different and more melodious metre, "rannaigheacht mhór," on the resurrection.

There were a number of other pre-Danish poets, but only occasional pieces of theirs have been preserved. Their obits are often mentioned by the annalists, but the few longer pieces of theirs that have survived to our day being mostly historical or genealogical, and as such devoid of much literary interest, we may neglect them.

CHAPTER XXXII

THE DANISH PERIOD

THE first onfall of the Danes seems to have been made about the year 795, and for considerably over two centuries Erin was shaken from shore to shore with ever-recurring alarms, and for many years every centre of population lived in a state of terror, not knowing what a day might bring forth. Monasteries and colleges were burnt again and again, and built again and again, only to be reburnt. Numbers of invaluable books were destroyed, gold and silver work was carried off in quantities, and a state of unrest produced, which must have made learning in many parts of the island well-nigh impossible.

Strange to say, despite the troubled condition of Ireland during these two or three centuries, she produced a large number of poets and scholars, the impulse given by the enthusiasm of the sixth and seventh centuries being still strong upon her. Unquestionably the greatest name amongst her men of learning during this period is that of the statesman, ecclesiastic, poet and scholar, Cormac mac Culinan, who was at once king and bishop of Cashel,[1] and one of the most

[1] It was not he, however, who built Cormac's Chapel at Cashel, but Cormac Mac Carthy, in the twelfth century. I am not sure whether Cashel had been formed into an archiepiscopal see at this time, but he is certainly called bishop of Cashel.

striking figures in both the literary and political history of these centuries.

To him we owe that valuable compilation, so often quoted already under the title of "Cormac's Glossary," which is by far the oldest attempt at a comparative vernacular dictionary made in any language of modern Europe.[1] Of course it has been enlarged by subsequent writers, but the idea and much of the matter remains Cormac's. In its original conception, it was meant to explain and interpret words and phrases which in the ninth century had become obscure to Irish scholars, and as might be expected, it throws light on many pagan customs, on history, law, romance, and mythology. Cormac's other literary effort was the compilation of the Saltair of Cashel, now most unhappily lost, but it appears to have been a great work. In it was contained the Book of Rights,[2] drawn up for the readjustment of the relations existing between princes and tribes, and still preserved. St. Benignus was said to have originally composed in verse a complete statement of the various rights, privileges, and duties of the High-king, the provincial kings, and the local chieftains. This, like so much of ancient and primitive law, was drawn up in verse so as to be thus stereotyped for the future, and easily remembered at a time when books were scarce. Cormac seems to have enlarged, modified, and brought it up to date to suit the changing times, and it was subsequently redacted again in Brian Boru's day in a sense favourable to Munster.[3] The king-bishop was a most remarkable man and an excellent scholar. He appears to have known Latin, Greek, Hebrew, and Danish, and to have been one of the finest Old Gaelic scholars of his day, and withal an accomplished poet, though his verses are now lost. He was slain in battle in the year

[1] The celebrated Vocabularius S. Galli was, according to Zimmer, the work of an Irish monk.

[2] Leabhar na gCeart.

[3] It has been most carefully edited and translated in a large volume by O'Donovan for the Celtic Society, in 1847

908,[1] under circumstances so curiously described in the fragmentary annals edited by O'Donovan that it may be worth repeating here. He was, as we know from other sources, betrothed to the Princess Gormfhlaith or Gormly, daughter of Flann Sionna [Shinna], king of Meath and High-king of Ireland, but determining to enter the Church he returned her with her dowry to her father without consummating the marriage; after this he took orders, and rose in time to be archbishop of Cashel as well as king of Munster. Gormly, however, was married against her will to Cearbhall [Caroll], king of Leinster. It was in the year 908 that Flann, the High-king, with Caroll king of Leinster, now his son-in-law, prepared to meet Munster and to assert by arms his right to the presentation of the ancient church of Monasterevan, but it seems probable that he also bore the king-archbishop a grudge for his treatment of his daughter Gormly. Here is the annalistic account of the sequel:—

DEATH OF CORMAC MAC CULINAN.[2]

"The great host of Munster was assembled by the same two, that is, Flaherty,[3] [abbot of Scattery Island, in the Shannon], and Cormac [mac Culinan], to demand hostages of Leinster and Ossory, and all the men of Munster were in the same camp. . . . And noble ambassadors came from Leinster from Caroll, son of Muirigan [king of that province], to Cormac first, and they delivered a message of peace from the Leinstermen, *i.e.*, one peace to be in all Erin until May following (it being then the second week in autumn), and to give hostages into the keeping of Maenach, a holy, wise, and pious man, and of other pious men, and to give jewels and much property to Cormac and Flaherty.

"Cormac was much rejoiced at being offered this peace, and he afterward went to tell it to Flaherty and how he was offered it from

[1] 903 according to the "Four Masters."

[2] From the fragment copied by Duald Mac Firbis in 1643 from a vellum MS. of Mac Egan of Ormond, a chief professor of the old Brehon Law, a MS. which was so worn as to be in places illegible at the time Mac Firbis copied it; published by O'Donovan for the Archæological Society. I have altered O'Donovan's translation very slightly.

[3] In Irish, "Flaithbheartach."

Leinster. When Flaherty heard this he was greatly horrified, and 't was what he said, 'This shows,' said he, 'the littleness of thy mind and the feebleness of thy nature, for thou art the son of a plebeian,' and he said many other bitter and insulting words, which it would be too long to repeat.

"The answer which Cormac made him was, 'I am certain,' Cormac said, 'of what the result of this [obstinacy of yours] will be, a battle will be fought, O holy man,' said he, 'and [I] Cormac shall be under a curse for it, and it is likely that it will be the cause of death to thee [also].' And when he had said this he came into his own tent, afflicted and sorrowful. And when he sat down he took a basketful of apples and proceeded to divide them amongst his people and said, 'My dear people,' he said, 'I shall never give you apples again from this out for ever.' 'Is it so, O dear earthly lord?' said his people; 'why art thou sorrowful and melancholy with us; it is often thou hast boded evil for us?' 'It is,' [said Cormac,] 'as I say, and yet, dear people, what melancholy thing have I said, for though I should not distribute apples to you with my own hand, yet there shall be some one of you in my place who will.' He afterwards ordered a watch to be set, and he called to him the holy, pious, and wise man, Maenach, son of Siadhal [Shiel], the chief co-arb or successor of Comhghall, and he made his confession and will in his presence, and he took the body of Christ from his hand, and he resigned the world in the presence of Maenach, for he knew that he would be killed in battle, but he did not wish that many others should know it. He also ordered that his body should be brought to Cloyne if convenient, but if not to convey it to the cemetery of Diarmuid, [grand] son of Aedh Roin, where he had studied for a long time. He was very desirous, however, of being interred at Cloyne of Mac Lenin. Maenach, however, was better pleased to have him interred at Disert Diarmada, for that was one of [Saint] Comhghall's towns, and Maenach was Comhghall's successor. This Maenach, son of Shiel, was the wisest man of his time, and he now exerted himself much to make peace, if it were possible, between the men of Leinster and Munster.

"Many of the forces of Munster deserted unrestrained. There was great noise, too, and dissension in the camp of the men of Munster at this time, for they heard that Flann, son of Malachy [High-king of Ireland], was in the camp of the Leinster men [helping them] with great forces of foot and horse. It was then Maenach said, 'Good men of Munster,' said he, 'you ought to accept of the good hostages I have offered you to be placed in the custody of pious men till May next, namely, the son of Caroll, king of Leinster, and the son of the king of Ossory.' All the men of Munster were saying that it was Flaherty [the abbot], son of Inmainên alone who compelled them to go [to fight] into Leinster.

"After this great complaint which they made, they came over Slieve Mairgé from the west to Leithglinn Bridge. But Tibraidé, successor of Ailbhé [of Emly], and many of the clergy along with him tarried at Leithglinn, and also the servants of the army and the horses which carried the provisions.

"After this trumpets were blown and signals for battle were given by the men of Munster, and they went forward till they came to Moy-Ailbhé.[1] Here they remained with their back to a thick wood awaiting their enemies. The men of Munster divided themselves into three equally large battalions, Flaherty, son of Inmainên, and Ceallach, son of Caroll, king of Ossory, over the first division; Cormac mac Culinan, king of Munster, over the middle division; Cormac, son of Mothla, King of the Deisi, and the King of Kerry, and the kings of many other tribes of West Munster, over the third division. They afterwards came on in this order to Moy-Ailbhe. They were querulous on account of the numbers of the enemy and their own fewness. Those who were knowledgable, that is those who were amongst themselves, state that the Leinstermen and their forces amounted to three times or four times the number of the men of Munster or more. Unsteady was the order in which the men of Munster came to the battle. Very pitiful was the wailing which was in the battle—as the learned who were in the battle relate—the shrieks of the one host in the act of being slaughtered and the shouts of the other host exulting over that slaughter. There were two causes for which the men of Munster suffered so sudden a defeat; for Céileachar, the brother of Cingégan, suddenly mounted his horse and said, 'Nobles of Munster,' said he, 'fly suddenly from this abominable battle, and leave it between the clergy themselves who could not be quiet without coming to battle,' and afterwards he suddenly fled accompanied by great hosts. The other cause of the defeat was: When Ceallach, son of Caroll, saw the battalion in which were the chieftains of the King of Erin cutting down his own battalion he mounted his horse and said to his own people, 'Mount your horses and drive the enemy before you.' And though he said this, it was not to really fight he said so but to fly. Howsoever it resulted from these causes that the Munster battalion fled together. Alas! pitiful and great was the slaughter throughout Moy-Ailbhe afterwards. A cleric was not spared more than a layman, there

[1] The plain where this battle of Bealach Múghna or Ballaghmoon was fought is in the very south of the county Kildare, about 2½ miles to the north of the town of Carlow.

they were all equally killed. When a layman or a clergyman was spared it was not out of mercy, it was done but out of covetousness, to obtain a ransom from them, or to bring them into servitude. King Cormac, however, escaped in the van of the first battalion, but the horse leaped into a trench and he fell off it. When a party of his people who were flying perceived this, they came to the King and put him up on his horse again. It was then he saw a foster son of his own, a noble of the Eoghanachts, Aedh by name, who was an adept in wisdom and jurisprudence and history and Latin; and the King said to him, 'Beloved son,' said he, 'do not cling by me, but take thyself out of it as well as thou canst; I told thee that I should be killed in this battle.' A few remained along with Cormac, and he came forward along the way on horseback, and the way was besmeared throughout with much blood of men and horses. The hind feet of his horse slipped on the slippery way in the track of blood, and the horse fell right back and [Cormac's] back and neck were both broken, and he said, when falling, 'In manus tuas, Domine, commendo spiritum meum,' and he gave up the ghost; and the impious sons of malediction came and thrust spears through his body, and cut off his head.

"Although much was the slaying on Moy-Ailbhe to the east of the Barrow, yet the prowess of Leinster was not satiated with it, but they followed up the rout westwards across Slieve Mairgé, and slew many noblemen in that pursuit.

"In the very beginning of the battle Ceallach, son of Caroll, king of Ossory, and his son were killed at once. Dispersedly, however, others were killed from that out, both laity and clergy. There were many good clergymen killed in this battle, as were also many kings and chieftains. In it was slain Fogartach, son of Suibhne [Sweeny], an adept in philosophy and divinity, King of Kerry, and Ailell, son of Owen, the distinguished young sage and high-born nobleman, and Colman, Abbot of Cenn-Etigh, Chief Ollav of the judicature of Erin, and hosts of others also, quos longum est scribere. . . .

"Then a party came up to Flann, having the head of Cormac with them, and 't was what they said to Flann, 'Life and health, O powerful victorious king, and Cormac's head to thee from us; and as is customary with kings raise thy thigh and put this head under it and press it with thy thigh.' Howsoever Flann spoke evil to them, it was not thanks he gave them. 'It was an enormous act,' said he, 'to have taken off the head of the holy bishop, but, however, I shall honour it instead of crushing it.' Flann took the head into his hand and kissed it, and carried thrice round him the consecrated head of the holy bishop and martyr. The head was afterwards honourably carried away from him to the body where Meaenach, son of Shiel, successor of Comhghall, was, and he carried the body of Cormac to Castledermot, where it was honourably interred, and where it performs signs and miracles.

"Why should not the heart repine and the mind sicken at this enormous deed; the killing and the mangling with horrid arms of this holy man, the most learned of all who came or shall come of the men of Erin for ever? The complete master in Gaedhlic and Latin, the archbishop most pious, most pure, miraculous in chastity and prayer, a proficient in law and in every wisdom, knowledge, and science, a paragon of poetry and learning, a head of charity and every virtue, a sage of education, and head-king of the whole of the two Munster provinces in his time!"

Gormly, the betrothed, but afterwards repudiated wife of Cormac, was also a poet, and there are many pieces ascribed to her. She was, as I mentioned, married to Caroll king of Leinster, who was severely wounded in this battle. He was carried home to be cured in his palace at Naas, and Gormly the queen was constant in her attendance on him. One day, however, as Caroll was becoming convalescent he fell to exulting over the mutilation of Cormac at which he had been present. The queen, who was sitting at the foot of his bed, rebuked him for it, and said that the body of a good man had been most unworthily desecrated. At this Caroll, who was still confined to bed, became angry and kicked her over with his foot in the presence of all her attendants and ladies.

As her father, the High-king, would do nothing for her when she besought him to wipe out the insult, and procure her separation from so unworthy a husband, her young kinsman Niall Glún-dubh, or the Black-Kneed, took up her cause, and obtained for her a separation from her husband and restoration of her dowry. When her husband was killed, the year after this, by the Danes, she married Niall, who in time succeeded to the throne as High-king of all Ireland, and who was one of the noblest of her monarchs. He was slain in the end by the Danes, and the monarchy passed away from the houses both of her father and her husband, and she, the daughter of one High-king, the wife of another, bewails in her old age the poverty and neglect into which she had fallen. She dreamt one night that King Niall stood beside her, and she made a leap forwards to clasp him in her arms, but struck herself against the bed-post, and received a wound from which she never recovered.[1] Many of her poems are lamentations on her kinsman and husband Niall. They seem to have been current amongst the Highland as well as the Irish Gaels, for here is a specimen jotted down in phonetic spelling by the Scotch Dean Macgregor about the year 1512:

"Take, grey monk, thy foot away,
  Lift it off the grave of Neill!
Too long thou heapest up the clay
  On him who cannot feel.[2]

Monk, why must thou pile the earth
  O'er the couch of noble Neill?
Above my friend of gentle birth
  Thou strik'st a churlish heel.

Let him be, at least to-night,
  Mournful monk of croaking voice,
Beneath thee lies my heart's delight,
  Who made me to rejoice.

[1] So it is stated in Mac Echagain's Annals of Clonmacnois, but O'Curry thinks this is a mistake and that she did recover.

[2] The first verse runs thus in modern Gaelic:

"Beir a mhanaigh leat do chos
  Tóg anois i de thaoibh Néill
Is ró mhór chuiris de chré
  Ar an té le' luidhinn féin."

See p. 75 of the Gaelic part of the book of the Dean of Lismore.

Literally: "Monk, remove thy foot, lift it off the grave of Niall, too long heapest thou the earth on him by whom I fain would lie!

"Too long dost thou, O monk there, heap the earth on noble Niall. Go gently, brown friend, press not the earth with thy sole.

"Do not firmly close the grave; sorrowful, cleric, is thy office; lift [thy foot] off the bright Niall Black-knee; monk, remove thy foot!

"The son of the descendant of Niall of the white gold, 'tis not of my will that he is bound [in the grave]; let his grave and stone be left: monk, remove thy foot!

"I am Gormly, who compose the verse; daughter of hardy Flann. Stand not upon his grave! Monk, remove thy foot!"

Monk, remove thy foot, I say!
Tread not on the sacred ground
Where he is shut from me away,
In cold and narrow bound!

I am Gormly—king of men
Was my father, Flann the brave.
I charge thee, stand thou not again,
Bald monk, upon his grave."

Another poet of the ninth century was Flanagan, son of Ceallacħ, king of Bregia. He is quoted by the "Four Masters."[1] One poem of his, of 112 lines, on the deaths of the kings of Ireland, is preserved in the Yellow Book of Lecan.

Mailmura, of Fahan, whom the "Four Masters" call a great poet, was a contemporary of his, and wrote a poem on the Milesian Migrations.[2]

Several other poets lived in the ninth century, the chief of whom was probably Flann mac Lonáin, for the "Four Masters" in recording his death style him "the Virgil of the Scottic race, the chief ollamh of all the Gaels, the best poet that was in Ireland in his time." Eight of his poems, containing about one thousand lines, have survived. He was from the neighbourhood of Slieve Echtgé, or Aughty, in South Connacht. One of his poems records how Ilbrechtach the harper was travelling over these barren

[1] One of his pieces, quoted by the "Four Masters," shows he was a true poet. It is on the death of the king, Aedh Finnliath, who died in 877, and runs thus:—

"Long is the wintry night,
With fierce gusts of wind,
Under pressing grief we have to encounter it,
Since the red-speared king of the noble house lives no longer.

It is awful to observe
The waves from the bottom heaving,
To these may be compared
All those who with us lament him."

See O'Curry's "Manners and Customs," vol. ii. p. 96, and "Four Masters" *sub anno.*

[2] Published by the Irish Archæological Society in the "Irish Nennius," in 1847.

mountains along with the celebrated poet Mac Liag, and, as they paused to rest on Croghan Head, Mac Liag surveyed the prospect beneath him, and said, "Many a hill and lake and fastness is in this range; it were a great topographical knowledge to know them all." "If Mac Lonáin were here," said the harper, "he could name them all, and give the origin of their names as well." "Let this fellow be taken and hanged," said Mac Liag. The harper begged respite till next day, and in the meantime Mac Lonáin comes up and recites a poem of one hundred and thirty-two lines beginning—*Aoibhinn aoibhinn Echtgé árd*.

Amongst other things, he relates that he met a Dalcassian —*i.e.*, one of Brian Boru's people from Clare—at Moy Finé in Galway, who had just finished serving twelve months with a man in that place, from whom he had received a cow and a cloak for payment. On his way home to the Dalcassians with his cloak and his cow he met the poet, and said to him—

"'Sing to me the history of my country,
It is sweet to my soul to hear it.

Thereupon I sang for him the poem,
Nor did he show himself the least loath:
All that he had earned—not mean nor meagre—
To me he gave it without deduction.

The upright Dalcassians heard of this,
They received him with honour in their assembly;
They gave to him—the noble race—
Ten cows for every quarter of his own cow.'"

Mac Lonáin was the contemporary of Cormac mac Culinan, whom he eulogises.

Some other poets of great note flourished during the Danish period, such as Cormac "an Eigeas," who composed the celebrated poem to Muircheartach, or Murtagh of the Leather Cloaks,[1] son of the Niall so bitterly lamented by Gormly, on the occasion of his marching round Ireland, when he set out

[1] Na gcochal croicinn.

from his palace at ancient Aileach near Derry, and returned to it again after levying tribute and receiving hostages from every king and sub-king in Ireland. This great O'Neill well deserved a poet's praise, for having taken Sitric, the Danish lord of Dublin, Ceallachan of Munster, the king of Leinster, and the royal heir of Connacht as hostages, he, understanding well that in the interests of Ireland the High-kingship should be upheld, positively refused to follow the advice of his own clan and march on Tara, as they urged, to take hostages from Donagh the High-king. On the contrary, he actually sent of his own accord all those that had been given him during his circuit to this Donagh as supreme governor of Ireland. Donagh, on his part, not to be out-done in magnanimity, returned them again to Murtagh with the message that he, into whose hands they had been delivered, was the proper person to keep them. It was to commemorate this that Cormac wrote his poem of two hundred and fifty-six lines :—

> *"A Mhuircheartaigh Mheic Néill náir*
> *Ro ghabhais giallu Inse-Fáil."* [1]

But the names of the poets Cinaeth or Kenneth O'Hartigan, and Eochaidh O'Flynn, are the most celebrated amongst those of the tenth century. Allusions to and quotations from the first, who died in 975, are frequent, and nine or ten of his poems, containing some eight hundred lines, have been preserved perfect for us. Of O'Flynn's pieces, fourteen are enumerated by O'Reilly, containing in the aggregate between seventeen and eighteen hundred lines. In them we find in verse the whole early and mythical history of Ireland. We have, for instance, one poem on the invasion of Partholan ; one on the invasion of the Fomorians ; another on the division of Ireland between the sons of Partholan ; another on the destruction of the tower of Conaing and the battles between

[1] "O Muircheartach, son of noble Niall,
Thou hast taken hostages of Inisfail."

the Fomorians and the Nemedians; another on the journey of the Nemedians from Scithia and how some emigrated to Greece and others to Britain after the destruction of Conairé's tower; another on the invasion of the sons of Milesius; another on the history of Emania built by Cimbaeth some three hundred years before Christ, up to its destruction by the Three Collas in the year 331. This poet in especial may be said to have crystallised into verse the mythic history of Ireland with the names and reigns of the Irish kings, and to have thrown them into the form of real history. O'Clery, in his celebrated Book of Invasions, has drawn upon him very largely, quoting, often at full length, no less than twelve of his poems. Hence many people believe that he was one of the first to collect the floating tribe-legends of very early Irish kings, and the race-myths of the Tuatha De Danann and their contemporaries, and that he cast them into that historical shape in which the later annalists record them, by fitting them into a complete scheme of genealogical history like that of the Old Testament. But whether all these things had taken solid shape and form before he versified them anew we cannot now decide. According to O'Reilly and O'Curry this poet died in 984, nine years after O'Hartigan; but M. d'Arbois de Jubainville remarks that he has been unable to find out any evidence for fixing upon this date.

A little later lived Mac Liag, whom Brian Boru elevated to the rank of Arch-Ollamh of Erin, and who lived at his court at Kincora in the closest relationship to him and his sons. He has been credited—erroneously according to O'Curry—with the authorship of a Life of Brian Boru, which unfortunately has perished, only a single ancient leaf, in the hand-writing of the great antiquary Mac Firbis, surviving. Several of his poems, however, are preserved,[1] containing

[1] The "Four Masters" thought so highly of Mac Liag's poetry that they actually go out of their way to record both the first verse he ever composed and the last. An extraordinary compliment!

between twelve and thirteen hundred lines in all, and are of the highest value as throwing light both on the social state and the policy of Ireland under Brian. One of his poems gives a graphic description of the tribute of Ireland being driven to Brian at his palace in Kincora in the present county of Clare. The poet went out from the court to have a look at the flocks and herds, and when he returned he said to the King, "Here comes Erin's tribute of cows to thee, many a fat cow and fat hog on the plain before thee." "Be they ever so many," said the King, "they shall be all thine, thou noble poet." Amongst the other part of the tribute which the poet describes as coming in to Brian were one hundred and fifty butts of wine from the Danes of Dublin, and a tun of wine for every day in the year from the Danes of Limerick. He describes Brian as sitting at the head of the great hall of Kincora,[1] the king of Connacht sat on his right hand and the king of Ulster on his left; the king of Tir-Eóghain [Tyrone] sat opposite to him. At the door-post nearest to Brian sat the king of Leinster, and at the other post of the open door sat Donough, son of Brian, and Malachy,[2] king of Meath. Murrough, the king's eldest son who died so valiantly at Clontarf, sat in front of his father with his back turned to him, with Angus, a prince of Meath, and the king of Tirconnell on his left. One of his poems ends with two complimentary stanzas to Brian Boru, his son Murrough, his nephew Conaing, and Tadhg [Teig] O'Kelly, the king of Ui Máine—all four of whom a short time afterwards were left stiff and stark upon the field of Clontarf.

The shadow of the bloody tragedy there enacted hangs heavily over all Mac Liag's later poems and those of his contemporaries, and there are few more pathetic pieces in the language than his wail over Kincora left desolate by the death

[1] Or Kancora, in Irish *Ceann Coradh—i.e.*, "the head of the weir."

[2] In Irish "Maelsheachlainn," often contracted into the sound of "M'louglinn," and now always Anglicised Malachy.

of almost every chieftain who had gone forth from it to meet the Danes.

> "Oh where, Kincora, is Brian the great!
> Oh, where is the beauty that once was thine!
> Oh, where are the princes and nobles that sate
> At the feast in thy halls, and drank the red wine.[1]
> Where, oh, Kincora?
>
> . . . . .
>
> And where is the youth of majestic height,
> The faith-keeping prince of the Scots? Even he
> As wide as his fame was, as great as his might,
> Was tributary, oh, Kincora, to me!
> Me, oh, Kincora.
>
> They are gone, those heroes of royal birth,
> Who plundered no churches, who broke no trust;
> 'Tis weary for me to be living on earth
> When they, oh, Kincora, lie low in the dust!
> Low, oh, Kincora.[2]

In the same strain does Mac Gilla Keefe,[3] another contemporary poet, lament, in a piece which, according to a manuscript quoted by Hardiman, called the "Leabhar Oiris,"

[1] Thus Mangan; in the original—

> "A Chinn-Choradh, caidhi Brian,
> No caidhi an sciamh do bhi ort;
> Caidhi maithe no meic righ
> Ga n-ibhmís fín ad port?"

[2] Literally: "O Kincora, where is Brian? or where is the splendour that was upon thee? Where are the nobles and the sons of kings with whom we used to drink wine in thy halls. . . . Where is the man most striking of size, the son of the king of Alba who never forsook us? Although great were his valour and his deeds, he used to pay tribute to me (the poet), O Kincora. . . . They have gone, side by side, the sons of kings who never plundered church; there shall never be their like in the world again, so in my wisdom I testify, O Kincora."

See Hardiman's "Irish Minstrelsy," vol. ii. p. 196, where the text of this poem is published, with a fearful metrical translation which, under the influence of Macpherson, calls the Dalcassian princes "the flower of Temora"! which, however, is advantageously used to rhyme with Kincora!

[3] In Irish: "Mac Giolla Caoimh."

he composed when in the north of Greece, whither he had travelled in the itinerant Milesian manner on his way to try if he could find the site of Paradise. The poem begins :—

"Mournful night! and mournful WE!
Men we BE who know no peace.
We no GOLD for STRAINS of PRIDE
HOLD this SIDE the PLAINS of Greece."[1]

"'I remember my setting my face to pay a visit to Brian (Boru) and he at that time feasting with Cian, the son of Mulloy,[2] and he thought it long my being absent from him.'

"'God welcome you back to us,' cried Cian, 'O learned one, who comest [back from the north] from the House of O'Neill. Poet, your wife is saying that you have almost altogether forsaken your own house.'

"'You have been away for three quarters of year, except from yesterday to to-day.' 'Why that,' said Murrough, son of Brian, 'is the message of the raven from the ark!'

"'[Come now] tell us all the wealth you have brought from the north,' said Brian, the High-king of the host of Carn i Neid, 'tell the nobles of the men of Innisfail, and swear by my hand that you tell no lie.'

"'By the King who is above me,' [said I], 'this is what I brought from the north, twenty steeds, ten ounces of gold, and ten score cows of cattle.'

"'[Why] we, the two of us, shall give him more steeds and more cattle [than that] without speaking of what Brian will give,' said Cian, the son of Mulloy.

"'[And] by the King of Heaven who has brought me into silence this night, and who has darkened my brightness, I got ten times as much as that at the banquet before Brian lay down.

---

[1] This verse is an imitation of the original, which runs—

"Uathmhar [i] an oidhche *anocht*
A chuideacht [fhíor-]*bhocht* gan bhréig,
Crodh ni SA[o]ILTÍ dh[ao]ibh air DHUAN
Air an TTAOIBHSI THUAIDH do'n nGréig."

See Hardiman's "Irish Minstrelsy," vol. ii. p. 202, where a poetical version of this lyric is given in the metre of Campbell's "Exile of Erin"! He does not say from what MS. he has taken this poem. O'Curry is silent on Mac Gilla Keefe, but O'Reilly mentions another poem of his on the provinces of Munster.

[2] In Irish, "Maolmhuadh."

"'I got seven town-lands, Oh, King of the Kings, who hast sent me from the west, and a half town-land [besides] near every palace in which Brian used to be.'

"Said Murrough, good son of Brian, 'To-morrow'—and it was scarce sensible for him—'as much as you have got last night you shall get from me myself, and get it with my love.'"[1]

Mag Liag was not at Clontarf himself, but his friend and fellow-poet, Errard mac Coisé [Cŭsha] was in the train of Malachy, king of Meath, to whom he was then attached. This poet gave Mac Liag a minute account of the battle, and Mac Liag himself visited the spot before the slain had been interred, as we see from another of his poems. In a kind of dialogue between him and Mac Coisé he makes the latter relate to him the names of the fallen, and describe the positions in which their dead bodies were found upon the battle-field. It is exceedingly probable that it was Mac Liag, perhaps with Mac Coisé's aid, who compiled that most valuable chronicle called the "Wars of the Gael with the Gaill," *i.e.*, of the Irish with the Northmen.[2] This narrative bears both external and internal evidence of its antiquity, for there is a portion of it preserved in the Book of Leinster, a MS of about the year 1150. "The author," says Dr. Todd, who has edited it,[3] "was either

[1] I am not sure that I have translated this correctly.

"Do rádh Murchadh deagh-mhac Bhriain
Air na mhárach, 's níor chiall uaidh
Uiriod a bhfuairís aréir
Geabhair uaim féin 's ni air th-fhuath."

[2] Charles O'Conor ascribes it to him, but neither Keating, the "Four Masters," nor Colgan, who all make use of it, mention a word about the author.

[3] In the "Master of the Rolls" Series, in 1867. "That the work was compiled from contemporary materials," says Dr. Todd, "may be proved by curious incidental evidence. It is stated in the account given of the Battle of Clontarf that the full tide in Dublin Bay on the day of the battle (23rd April, 1014) coincided with sunrise, and that the returning tide at evening aided considerably in the defeat of the enemy. It occurred to the editor, on considering this passage, that a criterion might be derived from it to test the truth of the narrative and of the date assigned by the Irish Annals to the Battle of Clontarf. He therefore proposed to the Rev. Samuel Haughton, M.D., Fellow of Trinity College, and Professor of Geology in

himself an eye-witness of the battle of Clontarf, or else compiled his narrative from the testimony of eye-witnesses." It is edited in 121 chapters, and is sufficiently long to fill over a hundred of these pages. Beginning with the earliest Danish invasion at the close of the eighth century, it traces the progress of the Northmen in forty chapters up to the time when Mathgamhain [Mahon] and Brian were ruling over the Dalcassians. After that the book concerns itself chiefly with the history of Brian, describing the deaths of his brother Mahon, and the revenge he took, and his gradual but irregular attainment of the High-kingship, he being the first of the race of Eber who had reached this dignity for hundreds of years. The distress suffered by the Irish at the hands of the white foreigners (the Norwegians) and the black foreigners (the Danes)—who, by the way, were bitter enemies and often fought with each other, even on Irish soil—is graphically described. The Northmen put, says the writer,

"a king [of their own] over every territory, and a chief over every chieftaincy, and an abbot over every church, and a steward over every village, and a soldier in every house, so that none of the men of Erin had power to give even the milk of his cow, or as much as the clutch

---

the University of Dublin, to solve for him this problem : 'What was the hour of high water at the shore of Clontarf in Dublin Bay on the 23rd of April, 1014.' The editor did not make known to Dr. Haughton the object he had in view in this question, and the coincidence of the result obtained with the ancient narrative is therefore the more valuable and curious."

Dr. Haughton read a paper on the mathematics of this complex and difficult question before the Royal Irish Academy, in May, 1861, in which he proved that the tide—a neap tide—was full along the Clontarf shore at about 5h. 30m. a.m., and that the evening tide was full in about 5h. 55m. p.m. "The truth of the narrative," says Dr. Todd, "is thus most strikingly established. In the month of April the sun rises at from 5h. 30m. to 4h. 30m. The full tide in the morning therefore coincided nearly with sunrise ; a fact which holds a most important place in the history of the battle, and proves that our author if not himself an eye-witness, must have derived his information from those who were. 'None others,' as Dr. Haughton observes, 'would have invented the fact that the battle began at sunrise and that the tide was then full in. The importance of the time of tide became evident at the close of the day, when the returned tide prevented the escape of the Danes from the Clontarf shore to the north bank of the Liffey."

of eggs of one hen in succour or in kindness to an aged man or to a friend, but was forced to preserve them for this foreign steward or bailiff or soldier. And though there were but one milk-giving cow in the house, she durst not be milked for an infant of one night, nor for a sick person, but must be kept for the steward or bailiff or soldier of the foreigners. And however long he might be absent from the house his share or his supply durst not be lessened : although there were in the house but one cow, it must be killed for the meal of one night, if the means of supply could not be otherwise procured. . . .

"In a word," continues the writer in a strain of characteristic hyperbole, "although there were an hundred sharp, ready, cool, never-resting, brazen tongues in each head, and a hundred garrulous, loud-unceasing voices from each tongue, they could not recount nor narrate, nor enumerate, nor tell, what all the Gael suffered in common, both men and women, laity and clergy, old and young, noble and ignoble, of hardship and of injury, and of oppression in every house, from these valiant, wrathful, foreign, purely-pagan people.

"And though numerous were the oft-victorious clans of the many-familied Erin," yet could they do nothing against the "untamed, implacable hordes by whom that oppression was inflicted, because of the excellence of their polished, ample, treble-heavy, trusty, glittering corslets, and their hard, strong, valiant swords, and well-rivetted long spears, and ready brilliant arms of valour, besides ; and because of the greatness of their achievements and of their deeds, their bravery, their valour, their strength, their venom, and their ferocity, and because of the excess of their thirst and their hunger for the brave, fruitful, nobly-inhabited, smooth-plained, sweet-grassy land of Erin, full of cataracts, rivers, bays."

The book ends with the battle of Clontarf and the "return from Fingall," *i.e.*, the march of the Dalcassians to their homes in Munster. The death of Brian in this great battle fought on Good Friday, the 23rd of April,[1] 1014, is thus described :—

[1] An ancient Irish missal preserved in the Bodleian contains this petition for the Irish king and his army, in its Litany for *Easter Eve* : "Ut regem Hibernensium et exercitum ejus conservare digneris—ut eis vitam et sanctitatem atque victoriam dones." If this missal is posterior to 1014 it must have been the reminiscence of Clontarf which inspired the prayer for the day following the battle. If the missal is older than the battle, then the coincidence is curious. The prayer was just a day late. The same missal mentions in its Litanies the names Patrick, Brendan, Brigit, Columba, Finnian, Ciaran, and St. Fursa, and contains collect, secret and post communion pro rege [for the Irish king].

DEATH OF BRIAN BORUMHA AT CLONTARF.

"As for Brian, son of Cenneidigh [Kennedy], when the battalions joined arms in the battle, his skin was spread for him, and he opened his psalter and joined his hands, and began to pray after the battle had commenced, and there was no one with him but his own attendant, whose name was Latean (from whom are the O'Lateans still in Munster.)[1] Brian said to the attendant, 'Look thou at the battalions and the combat whilst I sing the psalms.' He sang fifty psalms and fifty prayers and fifty paternosters, and after that he asked the attendant how were the battalions. And the attendant answered, 'Mixed and closely confronted are the battalions, and each of them has come within the grasp of the other, and not louder on my ears would be the echo of blows from Tomar's wood if seven battalions were cutting it down, than the thud-blows on heads and bones and sculls between them.' And he asked how was Murchadh's [Murrough's son's] standard, and the attendant said, 'It stands, and many of the banners of the Dál Cais [North Munster, *i.e.*, Brian's own men] around it, and many heads thrown to it, and a multitude of trophies and spoils with heads of foreigners are along with it.' 'That is good news indeed,' said Brian.

"His skin cushion was readjusted beneath him, and he sang the psalms and the prayers and the paters as before, and he again asked the attendant how the battalions were, and the attendant answered and said, 'There is not living on earth the man who could distinguish one from the other, for the greater part of the hosts on each side are fallen, and those who are alive are so covered with spatterings of crimson blood and armour, that a man could not know his own son—they are so intermingled.' He then asked how was Murchadh's standard. The attendant said it was far from him, and that it passed through the battalions westward, and was still standing. Brian said, 'The men of Erin will be well,' said he, 'so long as that standard stands, for their courage and valour shall remain in them all, so long as they can see that standard."

"His cushion was readjusted under Brian, and he sang fifty psalms and fifty prayers and fifty paters, and all that time the fighting continued. After that he again asked the attendant how went the battalions, and the attendant answered, 'It is like as if Tomar's wood were after burning its undergrowth and young trees, and that seven battalions had been for six weeks cutting them down, and it with its stately trees and huge oaks still standing, just so are the battalions on both sides, after the greater part of them have fallen leaving but a few valiant heroes and great chieftains still standing. So are

[1] Evidently the interpolation of a copyist.

the battalions on both sides pierced and wounded and scattered, and they are disorganised all round like the grindings of a mill turning the wrong way; and the foreigners are now defeated, and Murchadh's standard is fallen.' 'That is piteous news,' said Brian; 'by my word, said he, 'the generosity and valour of Erin fell when that standard fell; and truly Erin has fallen of that, for there shall never come after him a champion like him. And what the better were I though I should escape this, and though it were the sovereignty of the world I should attain, after the fall of Murchadh and Conaing and the other nobles of the Dál Cais.'

"'Woe is me,' said the attendant, 'if thou wouldst take my advice thou wouldst get thee to thy horse, and we would go to the camp and remain there amongst the gillies, and every one who comes out of the battle will come to us, and round us they will rally, for the battalions are now mixed in confusion, and a party of the foreigners have rejected the idea of retreating to the sea, and we know not who shall come to us where we now are.'

"'Oh God; boy,' said Brian, 'flight becomes me not, and I myself know that I shall not go from here alive, and what should it profit me though I did, for Aoibheall [Eevil][1] of Craig Liath [Lee-a], came to me last night,' said he, 'and she told me that the first of my sons whom I should see this day would be he who should succeed me in the sovereignty, and that is Donough,[2] and go thou OLatean,' said he, 'and take these steeds with thee, and receive my blessing and carry out my will after me, that is to say, my body and soul to God and to St. Patrick, and that I am to be carried to Armagh, and my blessing to Donough for discharging my last bequests after me, that is to say, twelve score cows to be given to the co-arb of Patrick and the Society of Armagh, and their own proper dues to Killaloe and the Churches of Munster, and he knows that I have not wealth of gold or silver, but he is to pay them in return for my blessing and for his succeeding me. Go this night to Sord [Swords] and desire them to come to-morrow early for my body, and to convey it thence to Damhliag of Cianan, and then let them carry it to Lughmhagh [Loo-wā, *i.e.*, Louth], and let Maelmuiré mac Eochadha, the co-arb of Patrick and the Society of Armagh come to meet me at Lughmhagh.'

"While they were engaged in this conversation the attendant perceived a party of the foreigners approaching them. The Earl Brodar was there and two warriors along with him.

"'There are people coming towards us here,' said the attendant.

---

[1] The family *banshee* of the Royal house of Munster.

[2] In Irish, Donnchadh, pronounced "Dunnăχa," as Murchadh is pronounced "Murrăχa," in English Murrough

"'What kind of people?' said Brian.

"'Blue stark-naked people,' said the attendant.

"'My woe,' said Brian, 'they are the foreigners of the armour, and it is not for good they come.'

"While he was saying this he arose and stepped off his cushion and unsheathed his sword. Brodar passed him by and noticed him not. One of the three who were there and who had been in Brian's service said '*Cing, Cing*!' said he, that is, 'This is the king.' '*No, no! but prist prist*,' says Brodar, 'not he,' said he, 'but a noble priest.' 'By no means,' said the soldier, 'but it is the great king Brian.' Brodar then turned round and appeared with a bright gleaming battle-axe in his hand, with the handle set in the middle [of the head]. When Brian saw him he looked intently at him, and gave him a sword-blow that cut off the left leg at the knee and the right leg at the foot. The foreigner gave Brian a stroke which crushed his head utterly, and Brian killed the second man that was with Brodar, and they fell mutually by each other.

"There was not done in Erin, since Christianity—except the beheading of Cormac mac Culinan—any greater deed than this. He was, in sooth, one of the three best that ever were born in Erin, and one of the three men who most caused Erin to prosper, namely, Lugh the Long-handed, and Finn mac Cúmhail [Cool], and Brian, son of Kennedy; for it was he that released the men of Erin and its women from the bondage and iniquity of the foreigners and the pirates. It was he that gained five-and-twenty battles over the foreigners, and who killed them and banished them. . . In short, Erin fell by the death of Brian."

The "War of the Gael with the Gaill" appears to me to be a book which throws a strong light upon the genesis and value of the historical saga of Ireland. Here is a real historical narrative of unquestionable authority, and of the very highest value for the history of these countries, which is contemporaneous,[1] or almost so, with the events which it relates. Its accuracy on matters of fact have been abundantly proved from Danish as well as from Irish sources. And yet the whole

[1] It is edited from the Book of Leinster, a MS. which was copied about 1150, which contains the first 28 chapters, from a vellum of about two centuries later, which wants five chapters at the beginning and eight at the end, and from a perfect transcript made by the indefatigable Brother Michael O'Clery in 1635 "out of the book of Cuconnacht O'Daly," who died according to the "Four Masters," in 1139.

account is dressed up and bedizened in that peculiarly Irish garb which had become stereotyped as the dress of Irish history. It contains the exaggeration, the necessary touch of the marvellous, and above all the poetry, without which no Irish composition could hope for a welcome.

First as to the exaggeration: the whole piece is full of it. A good example is the description of the armies meeting on Clontarf:—

"It will be one of the wonders of the day of judgment to relate the description of this tremendous onset. There arose a wild, impetuous, precipitate, furious, dark, frightful, voracious, merciless, combative, contentious vulture, screaming and fluttering over their heads. There arose also the Bocanachs and the Bananachs and the wild people of the glens, and the witches and the goblins and the ancient birds, and the destroying demons of the air and firmament, and the feeble demoniac phantom host, and they were screaming and comparing the valour and combat of both parties."

The reader expected some traditional flourish such as this, and the essential truth of the narrative is no whit impaired by it.

Nor does the miraculous episode of Dunlang O'Hartigan, fresh from the embraces of the fairy queen, foretelling to Murrough that he must fall, detract from the truth that he does fall. Dunlang had promised Murrough not to abandon him, and he appears beside him on the very eve of the battle. Murrough gently reproaches him and says:—

"'Great must be the love and attachment of some woman for thee which has induced thee to abandon me.' 'Alas, O King,' answered Dunlang, 'the delight which I have abandoned for thee is greater, if thou didst but know it, namely, life without death,[1] without cold,

[1] *I.e.*, Beside his fairy lover. This incident is greatly expanded in the modern MS. story of the Battle of Clontarf, of which there exist numerous copies; in these the gliding of history into romance is very apparent. In the modern version the fairy Aoibheall is introduced begging O'Hartigan not to fight and promising him life and happiness for two hundred years if he will put off fighting for only one day.

"A Dhunlaing seachain an cath
Gus an mhaidin amárach.
Geobhair da chéad bliadhan de ré
Agus seachain cath aon-laé."

without thirst, without hunger, without decay, beyond any delight of the delights of the earth to me, until the judgment, and heaven after the judgment, and if I had not pledged my word to thee I would not have come here, and, moreover, it is fated for me to die on the day that thou shalt die.'

"'Shall I receive death this day then?' said Murrough.

"'Thou shalt, indeed,' said Dunlang, 'and Brian and Conaing shall receive it, and almost all the nobles of Erin, and Turlough thy son.'

"'That is no good encouragement to fight,' said Murrough, 'and if we had had such news we would not have told it to *thee*, and moreover,' said Murrough, 'often was I offered in hills, and in fairy mansions, this world and these gifts, but I never abandoned for one night my country nor mine inheritance for them.'"

Some such touch as this, of the weird and the miraculous, the reader also expected.

As for poetry, the whole piece is full of it. It contains over five hundred lines of verse, in poems attributed to Brian Boru himself and his brother Mahon, to Maelmhuadh or Molloy, who so treacherously slew Mahon, to the sister of Aedh Finnliath [Finleea], king of Ireland in 869;[1] to Cormac mac Culinan, the king-bishop; to Cuan O'Lochain, a great poet who died in 1024; to Beg mac Dé the prophet, and to Columcille, his contemporary; to Colman mac Lenin, the poet-saint; to Gilla Mududa O'Cassidy, a poet contemporaneous with Mac Liag; to Mac Liag himself; to Gilla Comgaill O'Slevin, inciting O'Neill against Brian; to a poet called Mahon's blind man; to St. Bercan the prophet; to an unnamed cleric, and to at least six anonymous poets.

I have dwelt at some length upon these peculiarities of composition, because I wish to lay stress on the fact that the narrative form and the romantic dress in which the early history of Ireland is preserved (through the medium of sagas) need not

[1] This is genuine, and is also quoted by the "Four Masters" and O'Clery in his Book of Invasions. Probably all the poems are genuine except the prophecies and the pieces put into the mouths of the actors, that is of Brian, Mahon, Molloy, and the cleric. These were probably composed by the writer of the history.

detract from its substantial veracity. We can prove the minute accuracy of the Clontarf story and there seems scarcely more reason to doubt that of the battle of Moyrath, fought in Adamnan's time, or possibly the *substantial* accuracy of the battles of Cnoca, or of Moy Léana; we must, however, remember that with each fresh redaction, fresh miraculous agencies, and fresh verbiage were added.

The battle of Clontarf put an end to the dream of a Danish kingdom in Ireland, and though numerous bodies of the Northmen remained in their sea-coast settlements, and continued for many years after this to give much trouble, yet it put a stop to all further invasion from their mother country, and once more the centres of Irish learning and civilisation could breathe freely.

CHAPTER XXXIII

FROM CLONTARF TO THE NORMAN CONQUEST

BRIAN, semi-usurper though he was, was in every sense a great statesman as well as a great warrior. He found almost every seat of learning in ruins, and every town and palace in Ireland a shattered wreck. Before he died he had gone far towards restoring them. He rebuilt the monasteries, re-erected the churches, refounded the schools. "He sent professors and masters to teach wisdom and knowledge," says the history from which we have been quoting; but the schools had been hopelessly broken up, the scribes had perished, the books—"the countless hosts of the illuminated books of the men of Erin"—had been burned and "drowned." Hence he found himself obliged to despatch his emissaries and the few men of learning who had survived that awful time, "to buy books beyond the sea and the great ocean, because," says the history,

"their writings and their books in every church and in every sanctuary where they were, were burnt and thrown into water by the plunderers from beginning to end [of their invasions], and Brian himself gave the price of learning, and the price of books, to every one separately who went on this service." "By him were erected also noble churches and sanctuaries in Erin . . . many works also, and repairs were made by him. By him were erected the church of Cell Dálua[1] and the church of Inis Cealtra, and the round tower

[1] Killaloe, Inniscaltra, and Tomgraney.

of Tuam Gréine, and many other works in like manner. By him were made bridges and causeways and high roads. By him were strengthened also the dúns and fortresses and islands and celebrated royal forts of Munster. . . . The peace of Erin was proclaimed by him, both of churches and people, so that peace throughout all Erin was made in his time. He fined and imprisoned the perpetrators of murders, trespass, robbery, and war. He hanged and killed and destroyed the robbers and thieves and plunderers of Erin. . . . After the banishment of the foreigners out of all Erin and after Erin was reduced to a state of peace, a single woman came from Torach in the north of Erin to Clíodhna in the south of Erin, carrying a ring of gold on a horse-rod, and she was neither robbed nor insulted."[1]

The bardic schools began to revive again, for the bards too had felt the full pressure of the invasion, their colleges had been broken up, and many of themselves been slain. One aim of the Norsemen was to destroy all learning. "It was not allowed," writes Keating, "to give instruction in letters." . . . "No scholars, no clerics, no books, no holy relics, were left in church or monastery through dread of them. *Neither bard nor philosopher nor musician pursued his wonted profession in the land.*"

The eleventh and twelfth centuries, however, witnessed a great revival of art and learning. Indeed, from the reign of Brian until the coming of the Normans, Irish metal-work, architecture, and letters flourished wonderfully. It is from this brief period of comparative rest that the three most important relics of Celtic literature now in the world date, the Leabhar na h-Uidhre, the Book of Leinster, and the Book of Hymns. The eleventh and twelfth centuries produced also many men of literature, including the annalist Tighearnach who was Abbot of Clonmacnois and died in

[1] On this episode Moore wrote his melody, "Rich and rare were the gems she wore." An Irish poet contemporaneous with this event celebrated it less poetically—

"O Thoraigh co Clíodna cais
Is fail óir aice re a h-ais
I ré Bhriain taoibh-ghil nár thim
Do thimchil aoin-bhen Eirinn."

1088; and Dubdaléithe, Archbishop of Armagh, who died in 1065, who wrote Annals of Ireland which are now lost, but which are quoted both in the Annals of Ulster and in the "Four Masters." The greatest scholar, chronologist, and poet of this period is unquestionably Flann, the *fear-léighinn* or head-teacher of the school of Monasterboice, who died in 1056. Though he is called Flann *Mainstreach*, or Flann of the Monastery, he was really a layman — one proof out of many, that the schools and colleges which grew up round religious institutions were as much secular as theological. He composed a valuable series of synchronisms, in which he synchronised the kings of the Assyrians, Medes, Persians, Greeks, and the Roman emperors, with the kings of Ireland, in parallel columns century by century, and sums up the most important portions of his teaching in a poem of some twelve hundred lines intended evidently as a class-book for his pupils. A piece of more value is one which synchronises the reigns of the Irish monarchs with those of the Irish provincial kings and the kings of Scotland, from the time of King Laeghaire who received St. Patrick, down to the death of Murtough O'Brien in 1119, these later years having been completed by some other hand.

No fewer than two thousand lines of Flann's poetry were copied into the Book of Leinster less than a hundred years after his own death, and there are nearly as many more in other manuscripts. They are, however, though composed in elaborate metres, anything but creative and imaginative poems. The most of them consist of annals or history versified, evidently with the intention of being committed to memory, because the great ollamhs like Flann were really rather historians and philosophers than what we call poets, and they used their metrical art, very often though not always, to enshrine their knowledge. There is, however—except to the historian—nothing particularly inspiriting in a poem of 204 lines on the monarchs of Erin and kings of Meath who are descended from

Niall of the Nine Hostages, giving the names, length of reign, and manner of death of each, despite the undoubted skill with which the technical difficulties of a thorny metre are overcome.[1] Some of his pieces, however, are of more living interest, as his poem on the history of Oileach or Ailech, the palace of the O'Neills near Derry, in which he takes us to the time of the Tuatha De Danann, and in his poem on the battles fought by the Kinel Owen. Indeed as O'Curry well puts it,

"Many a name lying dead in our genealogical tracts and which has found its way into our evidently condensed chronicles and annals, will be found in these poems connected with the death or associated with the brilliant deeds of some hero whose story we would not willingly lose; while, on the other hand, many an obscure historical allusion will be illustrated and many an historical spot as yet unknown to the topographer will be identified, when a proper investigation of these and other great historical poems preserved in the Book of Leinster, shall be undertaken as part of the serious study of the history and antiquities of our country."[2]

This summing-up of O'Curry's as to the poems of Flann, is one which may be also applied to several of his contemporaries and successors, such as Coleman O'Seasnan who died in 1050, one of whose poems on the kings of Emania and of Ulster contains 328 lines; Giolla Caomhghin [Gilla Keevin], who died in 1072, some thirteen or fourteen hundred lines of whose poetry has been preserved; Tanaidhe O'Mulconry, who died in 1136; Giolla Moduda O'Cassidy, who died in 1143, and whose poems, still extant, amount to nearly nine hundred lines; and

[1] Compare the first verse in *Deibhidh* metre—

"Midhe Maigen Chlainne Cuind,
Cáin-fhorod Clainne Neill Neart-luind,
Cride [Cain] Banba Bricce,
Mide Magh na Mór-chipe."

I.e., "Meath, the place of the children of Conn, beautiful house of the children of Niall, strength-renowned. The heart of celebrated Erin, Meath, the place of the great battalions."

[2] O'Curry's "Manners and Customs," vol. ii. p. 156.

Giolla-na-naomh O'Dunn who died in 1160, and of whom we still possess fourteen hundred verses.[1]

The compositions of two rather earlier poets, Erard mac Coisé [Cŭsha] and Cuan O'Lochain possess more interest. They died in 1023 and 1024 respectively. Mac Coisé's four surviving poems and his prose allegory are all of great interest. As for Cuan O'Lochain, he was chief poet of Erin in his day, and according to Mac Echagain's "Annals of Clonmacnois" and an entry in the Book of Leinster, he and a cleric named Corcran were elected to govern Ireland during the interregnum which succeeded the death of King Malachy, who quietly reassumed, after the death of Brian Boru, the High-kingship of which that monarch had deprived him. This is a convincing proof of the honour attached to the office of "ollamh of all Ireland."

One of O'Lochain's pieces is of special value, because it describes and names every chief building, monument, rath, and remarkable spot in and around Tara, both those erected in Cormac mac Art's time and those added afterwards; both those which were in ruins when the poet wrote, and those which had been described by former authors from the time of Cormac till his own.[2] Another poem of his is on the *geasa* [gassa] or tabus of the king of Ireland, and on his prerogatives. It was tabu for him to let the sun rise on him when in bed in the plains of Tara, or for him to alight on a Wednesday on the plain of Bregia, or to traverse the plain of Cuillenn after sunset, or to launch his ship on the first Monday after May Day, etc. Another is a beautiful poem on the origin of the river Shannon, called from a lady Sinann, who ventured near Connla's well, a thing tabu to a female—to steal the nuts of knowledge. There grew nine splendid mystical hazel trees

[1] There are a great number of other poets of whom only one or two poems survive, and others are mentioned as great poets by the annalists, of whom not a line has come down to us.

[2] This piece has been published at full length in Petrie's "History and Antiquities of Tara."

around this well, and they produced the most beautiful nuts of rich crimson colour, and as these lovely nuts, filled full with all that was loveliest and most refined in literature, poetry, and art, dropped off their branches into the well, they raised a succession of red shining bubbles. The salmon at the sound of the falling nuts darted forward to eat them and afterwards made their way down the river, their lower side covered with beautiful crimson spots from the effect of the crimson nuts. Whoever could catch and eat these salmon were in their turn filled with the knowledge of literature and art, for the power of the nuts had to some extent passed into the fish that eat them. These were the celebrated "eó feasa" [yo fassa], or salmon of knowledge, so frequently alluded to by the poets. To approach this well was tabu to a woman, but Sinann attempted it, when the well rose up and drowned her, and carried her body down in a torrent of water to the river which was after her called Shannon.

Altogether about 1,200 lines of Cuan O'Lochain's poetry have been preserved.[1] It would be useless for our purpose to go more minutely into the history of those pre-Norman poets. It is not the known poetry of early Irish poets which, as a rule, is of most interest to the purely literary student, but rather the unknown and the traditional.

We must now take a glance at the Irish of this later period upon the Continent.

Those brilliant names in the history of European scholarship who distinguished themselves under Charlemagne, his son, and his grandsons, Clemens, Dicuil, and Scotus Erigena, who all taught in the Court schools, Dungal who taught in Pavia, Sedulius who worked in Lüttich, Fergal, or Virgil who ruled in Salzburg, and Moengal, the teacher of St. Gall, were

[1] There are two different etymologies of the name in a poem on the river Shannon of several hundred verses, made by a native of the county Roscommon in the eventful year 1798. There is also a different version of the origin of the river in a folk tale which I recovered this year from a native of the same county.

not altogether without successors. It is true that Ireland's great mission of instruction and conversion came to a close with the eleventh century, yet for two centuries more, driven by that innate instinct for travel and adventure which was so strong within them, that it resembled a second nature, we find Irish monks creating new foundations on the Continent, especially in Germany. One of the most noteworthy of these was a monk from the present Donegal, Muiredach mac Robertaigh, who assumed the Latin name of Marianus Scotus, or Marian the Irishman. In 1076 he had succeeded in establishing an Irish monastery at Ratisbon, or, as the Germans call it, Regensburg, the fame of which rapidly spread, and attracted to it many of his countrymen from Ulster, so many, that the parent monastery failed to accommodate them; and a branch house, that of St. Jacob, was completed in 1111. From these points Irish monks penetrated in all directions. Frederick Barbarossa, in 1189, on his way from the Crusades, founded even at Skribentium, in what is now Bulgaria, a monastery with an Irish abbot. About the same time the Irish abbots of Ratisbon are found writing to King Wratislaw of Bohemia to facilitate the passage of their emissaries into Poland. Under the influence of these two Irish houses, St. James of Ratisbon and St. Jacob, quite a number of other Irish monasteries were founded, that of Würzburg in 1134, Nürnberg in 1140, Constanz in 1142, St. George in Vienna in 1155, Eichstädt in 1183, St. Maria in Vienna in 1200.

These Irish monks who, in the eleventh, twelfth, and thirteenth centuries left the north of Ireland and thus planted themselves in Germany, were, says Zimmer, worthy successors of those apostles and scholars who laboured from the seventh to the tenth century in France, Switzerland, and Burgundy, "full of religious zeal, piety, sobriety, and a genuine love of learning."[1] A chronicle of the monastery of Ratisbon,

[1] "Sie waren noch würdige Epigonen jener Glaubensboten und Gelehrten des 7-10 Jahrhunderts, die wir im Frankreich kennen lernten;

written in 1185, states that the greater part of all the existing documents belonging to the different Irish monasteries which sprang from it had been written by Marianus Scotus himself. A specimen, writes Zimmer, of his beautiful script and the remarkable rapidity of his work may be seen at the Court Library of Vienna, where is preserved a copy of St. Paul's Epistles in 160 sheets, written by him in 1079, between March 23rd and May 17th. Very many of the monks—Malachias, Patricius, Maclan, Finnian, and others—who came to these monasteries from Ireland brought books with them which they presented to the German monasteries. The century which succeeded the Battle of Clontarf was the most flourishing period of the Irish monks in Germany. In the thirteenth century their influence visibly declines. Once the English had commenced the conquest of Ireland the monasteries ceased to be recruited by men of sanctity and learning, but were resorted to by men who sought rather material comfort and a life of worldly freedom.[1] The result was that towards the end of the thirteenth and the beginning of the fourteenth century most of the Irish establishments in Germany came to an end, being either made over to Germans, like of those of Vienna and Würzburg, or else altogether losing their monastic character like that of Nuremberg.

As for the parent monastery, that of St. James of Ratisbon, its fate was most extraordinary, and deserves to be told at greater length. It had, of course, always been from its foundation inhabited by Irish monks alone, and was known as the Monasterium Scotorum, or Monastery of the Irishmen. But when in process of time the word Scotus became ambiguous, or, rather, had come to be almost exclusively

voll Glaubenseifer, Frömmigkeit, Enthaltsamkeit und Sinn für Studien" ("Preussisches Jahrbuch," January, 1887).

[1] "Propter abundantiam et propter liberam voluntatem vivendi," quotes Zimmer.

applied to what we now call Scotchmen,[1] the Scotch prudently took advantage of it, and claimed that they, and not the Irish, were the real founders of Ratisbon and its kindred institutions, and that the designation *monasterium Scotorum* proved it, but that the Irish had gradually and unlawfully intruded themselves into all these institutions which did not belong to them. Accordingly it came to pass by the very irony of fate—analogous to that which made English writers of the last century claim Irish books and Irish script as Anglo-Saxon—that the great parent monastery of St. James of Ratisbon was actually given up to the Scotch by Leo X. in 1515, and all the unfortunate Irish monks there living were driven out! The Scotch, however, do not seem to have made much of their new abode, for though the monastery contained some able men during the first century of its occupation by them—

"It exercised," says Zimmer, "no influence worth mentioning upon the general cultivation of the German people of that region, and may be considered but a small contributor towards mediæval culture in general, for the only share the Scotch monks can really claim in a monument like that of the Church of St. James of Ratisbon, is the fact of their having collected the gold for its erection from the pockets of the Germans, In comparison with these how noble appear to us those apostles from Ireland, of whom we find so many traces in different parts of the kingdom, of the monks from the beginning of the seventh to the end of the tenth century"!

This monastery was finally secularised in 1860.

[1] F. F. Warren, quoted by Miss Stokes in her "Six Months in the Appenines," gives a list of twenty-nine Irish monasteries in France, and eighteen in Germany and Switzerland, with many more in the Netherlands and in Italy. Numberless others founded by the Irish passed into foreign hands.

CHAPTER XXXIV

SUDDEN ARREST OF IRISH DEVELOPMENT

THE semi-usurpation of Brian Boru, which broke through the old prescriptional usage (according to which the High-kings of Ireland had, for the preceding five hundred years, been elected only from amongst the northern or southern Ui Neill, that is, from the descendants of Niall of the Nine Hostages), produced no evil effects, but much good so long as Brian himself lived; yet his action was destined to have the worst possible influence upon the future of Ireland, an evil influence comparable only to that caused by the desertion of Tara four centuries and a half before. The High-kingship being thus thrown open, as it were, to any Irish chief sufficiently powerful to wrest it from the others, became an object of constant dispute and warfare, the O'Neills kings of Ulster, the O'Conors of Connacht, the O'Briens of Munster, and the princes of Leinster, all contended for it, so that from the death of Malachy, Brian Boru's successor, there was scarcely a single High-king who was not, as the Irish annalists call it, "a king with opposition."[1] Hence despite the immediate

[1] After Malachy reigned Donough O'Brien, son of Brian Boru; after him Diarmuid of Leinster, of the race of Cáthaoir Mór; after him two

revival of art and literature which followed the defeat of the Northmen, the country was in many ways politically weakened, the inherent defects of the clan system accentuated, and the land, already much exhausted by the Danish wars,[1] was left open to the invasion of the Normans.

It was in May, 1169, that the first force of these new invaders landed, and, aided by the incompetence of a particularly feeble High-king, they had so thoroughly established themselves in Ireland by the close of the century, that they succeeded in putting an end to the Irish High-kingship, under which Ireland had subsisted for over a thousand years. Then began that permanent war—very different, indeed, from what the Irish tribes waged among themselves—which, almost from its very commencement, *thoroughly arrested Irish development, and disintegrated Irish life.*

It is not too much to say that for three centuries after the Norman Conquest Ireland produced nothing in art, literature, or scholarship, even faintly comparable to what she had achieved before. With the Normans came collapse;

"Red ruin and the breaking up of laws,"

and all the horrors of chronic and remorseless warfare.

We must now examine the history of Irish art, as displayed in metal-work, buildings, and illuminated manuscripts.

That peculiar class of design which Irish artists developed so successfully in "the countless hosts of the illuminated books of the men of Erin," is not really of Irish origin at

other O'Briens, then an O'Lochlainn king of Ulster, then O'Conor of Connacht, then another O'Lochlainn, and then another O'Conor, King Roderick, in whose time the Normans landed.

[1] Although the backbone of the Danish power was broken at Clontarf, desultory warfare with them did not cease for long after. Even so late as 1021 they were able to penetrate into the city of Armagh for the seventeenth time during two hundred years, and burnt the whole city to the ground, with its churches and books. Within two years of the battle of Clontarf they burned Glendalough and Clonard.

all. It is not even Celtic. The late researches of M. Solomon Reinach and others into the genuine remains of the Celts of Gaul and the Continent have discovered in their ornamentation scarcely a trace at all of the so-called Irish patterns. They are in truth not Irish, but Eastern. They seem to have started from Byzantium, spread over Dalmatia and North Italy, and finally found their way into Ireland. The early forms of pre-Christian Irish art show no trace whatsoever of those peculiar interlaced patterns and convoluted figures which are usually associated with the name of Celtic design. The engraved patterns on the tumulus of New Grange, dating from probably about 800[1] years before the Christian era, and the similar scribings upon sepulchral chambers at Louchcrew, Telltown, and other places, do not show a particle of interlaced work, but consist for the most part of circles with rays, arrangements of concentric circles, patterns of double and triple spirals, and lozenges. Indeed, it is the spiral, in countless forms and applications, which seems to have been really indigenous to the earliest inhabitants of Ireland, and with it the interlaced and convoluted figures of non-Irish post-Christian art became blended, gradually driving it out. These in their turn perished, degraded and abased by admixture with Gothic forms introduced by the Normans, whose invasion soon put an end to the development of all art in Ireland save that of architecture.

The so-called Celtic design of Ireland, with its interlaced bands, its convolutions, its knots, its triquetras, is really a survival of what once, starting from the East, spread over a large portion of western and northern Europe, but which soon died out there overwhelmed by Gothic and other influences; whilst in Ireland, where it was applied with far truer artistic feeling and far finer elaboration than elsewhere, it has been preserved in countless works of stone,

[1] This is the minimum date assigned them by Mr. George Coffey in his admirable monograph upon the subject.

bronze, and parchment. A scrutiny of early Scandinavian art and of the architectural styles of Italy known as the Latino-Barbaro and Italo-Bizantino, with portions of the art of other countries, have revealed traces of the so-called Celtic designs in places and under circumstances which prove that they cannot be—as used to be generally supposed—the work of exiled Irishmen. Nevertheless, there is a certain individuality in the working out of these designs when brought to perfection by Irish hands, which sufficiently distinguishes Irish art from that of other countries. For in Ireland the interlaced decoration was grafted on to the more archaic and pre-Christian style.

"The peculiar spirals found on these bronzes of that [pre-Christian] time," says Miss Stokes,[1] "the trumpet pattern, the even more archaic single-line spirals, zigzags, lozenges, circles, dots, are all woven in with interlaced designs, with marvellous skill and sense of beauty and charm of varied surface, added to which is an unsurpassed feeling for colour where the style admits of colour, as in enamels and illumination. Besides all this, the interlacings, taken by themselves, gradually undergo a change in character under the hand of an Irish artist. They become more inextricable, more involved, more infinitely varied in their twistings and knottings, and more exquisitely precise and delicate in execution than they are ever seen to be on continental work, so far as my experience goes."

The original pre-Christian art of the Irish Celts, that known to Cuchulain and Conor mac Nessa and the heroes of the Red Branch, survives only upon a few bronzes and upon the stones of a few sepulchral mounds. The tracings upon the sepulchral mounds are rude—though we find in some instances evidences of designs deliberately worked out to cover a given surface—and they mostly consist of recognisable symbols of Sun and Fire worship. The bronze sword-sheaths of Lisnacroghera, which are magnificent specimens of early Irish art, are a development of these patterns, but bear no trace of that interlaced work which was introduced with Christianity. There are several other bronze ornaments, evidently pre-Christian,

[1] "Six Months in the Apennines," Introductory Letter.

which exhibit the same kind of designs, notably what appear to be two horns of a radiated crown exquisitely decorated by spiral lines in relief, and which, said Mr. Kemble, "for beauty of design and execution may challenge comparison with any specimen of cast bronze-work that it has ever been my fortune to see." Miss Stokes, however, has shown that these pieces were not cast, but repoussé, and consequently, she writes—

"If not the finest pieces of casting ever seen, yet as specimens of design and workmanship they are perhaps unsurpassed. The surface is here overspread with no vague lawlessness, but the ornament is treated with fine reserve, and the design carried out with the precision and delicacy of a master's touch. The ornament on the cone flows round and upwards in lines gradual and harmonious as the curves in ocean surf, meeting and parting only to meet again in lovelier forms of flowing motion. In the centre of the circular plate below—just at the point or hollow whence all these lines flow round and upwards, at the very heart, as it might seem, of the whole work—a crimson drop of clear enamel may be seen."

These beautiful fragments are almost certainly pre-Christian, and may even have been worn by Conairé the Great or Conor mac Nessa. They represent a variety of design which stands midway between the stone engravings and the art of the early Christians. It is a remarkable fact, amply proven and universally acknowledged, that the bronze-work of the pre-Christian Irish was never surpassed by their post-Christian metal-work. Indeed, while the pagan Irish are proved to have attained great skill in the art of design, in working of metals, and especially in the art of enamelling by various processes, the specimens of the earliest Christian metal-work, such as St. Patrick's bell, are exceedingly rude and barbarous—possibly because the skilled pagan workmen did not turn their hands to such business, and the Christian converts had themselves to do the best they could.

Many of the monks, however, appear to have given themselves up to metal-work, and reached a very high pitch of excellence in it, as may be seen at a glance by the inspection of such master works as the two-handed Ardagh chalice, the cross of Cong, and numerous shrines, cúmhdachs [coodachs], or book-cases, and croziers. The ornamental designs upon the later Christian metal-work reached their highest perfection in the tenth and eleventh centuries, and the work of this period exhibits about forty different varieties of design, in which animal forms are only sparingly used, and in which there is no trace of foliate pattern. Indeed, these are not found in Irish metal-work before the period of decadence in the thirteenth century. Although the best specimens of Christian art in metal-work belong to the tenth and eleventh centuries, we are not to assume from this that the metal-work of the earlier Christian artists did not keep pace with the work of the early Christian scribes, who produced such magnificent specimens of penmanship and colour in the seventh and eighth centuries. They may have done so, but no relics of their work are left. According to Dr. Petrie, few, if any, of the more distinguished churches of Ireland were destitute of beautiful metal-work in the shape of costly shrines at the coming of the Norseman, as the frequent allusions in the Irish annals show; but scarcely one of these escaped their destructive raids, and hence the finest surviving specimens are of a much later date than the finest surviving manuscripts,[1] which were only destroyed whenever met with, but were not, like the costly metal-work, an object of eager and unremitting pursuit.

In sculpture the Irish never produced anything finer than their tall, shapely, richly but not over-richly ornamented

[1] The earliest surviving book-shrine, that of Molaise's Gospels, was made between the year 1001 and 1025; the earliest dated crozier is 967; the earliest bell-shrine may be assigned to 954. The Cross of Cong dates from about 1123. That the earlier Christian craftsmen must have made good work, if only it had survived, may be inferred from the fine silver chalice of Kremsmünster, in Lower Austria, dating from between the years 757 and 781.

Celtic crosses. The Ogam-inscribed stones, of which over a couple of hundred remain, are perfectly plain and undecorative. Some of the later inscribed tombstones (of which some two hundred and fifty remain), contain, it is true, fine chisel-work, but the numerous high Celtic crosses, covered many of them with elaborate sculpture in relief, with undercutting, and ornamented with the divergent and interlaced spiral pattern, show the finest artistic instinct. Most of these beautiful works of art are later than the year 900, but hardly one is posterior to the Norman invasion, which soon put a stop to such artistic luxuries.

The Irish were not a nation of builders. Most of the early Irish houses, even at Tara, were, as we have seen, of wood. The ordinary dwelling-house was either a cylindrical hut of wickerwork with a cup-shaped roof, plastered with clay and thatched with reeds, or else a quadrilateral house built of logs or of clay. The so-called city of Royal Tara was, in fact, a vast enclosure, containing quite a number of different raths, and houses inside the raths. The buildings seem to have been constructed of the timbers of lofty trees planted side by side, probably carved into fantastic shapes upon the outside, while the inside walls were closely interwoven with slender rods, over which a putty or plaster of loam was smoothly spread, which, when even and dry, was painted in bright colours, chiefly red, yellow, and blue. The roofs were formed of smooth joists and cross-beams, and probably thatched with rods and rushes, much in the same manner as the houses of the peasantry to-day. The floors appear to have been of earth, carefully hardened and beaten down, and then covered with a coat of some kind of hard and shiny mortar. No doubt some very fine barbaric effects were realised in these buildings, some of which, as is evidenced by the description of Cormac's Teach Midhchuarta, must have been immense. There were as many as seven dúns, or raths, round Tara, each containing within it many houses, and each surrounded by a mound, or vallum, planted with a stockade like a Maori pah.[1] The finest house of all, painted in the gayest colours, planted in the sunniest spot, and provided overhead with a balcony, was reserved for the ladies of the place, and was called the grianán [greeanawn], or sunny house.

Stone, however, was used in places, at a very early date, long before the first century, as may be seen from the stone forts of western and south-western Ireland, huge structures of which one of the best known is Dún-Angus, in the Isle of Arran, but there was no knowledge of mortar. Masonry was also used occasionally by the early monks in constructing their little clocháns, or beehive cells, and their oratories, with rounded roofs, built without a vestige of an arch, the whole surrounded by an uncemented stone wall, or cashel.

The Irish do not seem to have done much in stone-work until the Danish invasions forced them to construct the round towers in which to take shelter when the enemy was upon them, saving thus their jewels, books, and shrines. The Danes, who made rapid marches across the country, could not burn these towers nor throw them down, nor could they spend the time necessary to reduce them by famine, lest the country should be roused behind them, and their retreat to their ships cut off. The idea and form of the round tower the Irish almost certainly derived from the East. In Lord Dunraven's "Notes on Irish Architecture" the path of these buildings from Ravenna across Europe and into Ireland is distinctly shown; but while only about a score of examples survive in the rest of Europe, Ireland alone possesses a hundred and eighteen of these curious structures. There are three well-marked styles of towers. The doors and windows of the earlier ones are primitive and horizontal, but in the later ones the rude entablature of the earlier towers has given way

[1] This was the case with most of those earthen circumvallations, called in different parts of Ireland *raths* and *lisses*, and in Hibernian English *forts* or *forths*. The houses were inside the embankment, which was in most cases protected by a wall of stakes planted round its summit.

to the decorated Romanesque arch, and the beauty and number of the arched windows is greatly increased.

The transition from the horizontal to the round-arched style is shown in the Church of Iniscaltra, erected two years after the battle of Clontarf, and many years before the true Romanesque appeared in England. From that time till the coming of the Normans, Irish ecclesiastical architecture—the only kind practised, for the Irish did not live in or build castles—progressed enormously, and several fine specimens belonging to the twelfth century still survive.

"The remains," writes Miss Stokes, "of a great number of monuments belonging to the period between the fifth and twelfth centuries of the Christian era, have survived untouched by the hand either of the restorer or of the destroyer, and in them, when arranged in consecutive series, we can trace the development from an early and rude beginning to a very beautiful result, and watch the dovetailing, as it were, of one style into another, till an Irish form of Romanesque architecture grew into perfection. The form of the Irish Church points to an original type which has almost disappeared elsewhere—that of the Shrine or Ark, not of the Basilica."

The Norman invasion, however, put a complete stop to the natural development of Irish Romanesque, and changed the building of churches into that of castles, in which the Irish only copied, so far as they built at all, the pattern of the invader.

The art, however, in which the Irish earliest excelled, and in which they have really no rivals in Europe, was in that of writing and illuminating manuscripts. The most recent authority on the subject, Johan Adolf Brunn in his "Inquiry into the Art of Illuminated MSS. of the Middle Ages," acknowledges that the fame of the Celtic school, "dating from the darker centuries of the Middle Ages, excels that of any of its rivals." Westwood, the great British authority, declares that were it not for Irishmen these islands would contain no primitive works of art worth mentioning, and asserts that the Book of Kells is "unquestionably the most elaborately executed manuscript of so early a date, now in existence." Even Giraldus Cambrensis, who came in with the early Normans, was struck dumb with admiration of the exquisite book shown him at Kildare, which of all the miracles with which Kildare was credited was to him the greatest. Here, he writes, "you may see the visage of majesty divinely impressed, on one side the mystic forms of the evangelists having now six, now four, now two wings, on one side the eagle, on another the calf, on one side the face of a man, on the other of a lion, and an almost infinite quantity of other figures. . . . A careless glance at the whole," he goes on to say, "reveals no particular excellence, but if, looking closer at it, the spectator examined the work in detail he would see how extraordinarily subtle and delicate were the knots and lines, how bright and fresh the colours remained, how interlaced and bound together was the whole, so that we would feel inclined to believe that it could hardly be a human composition but the works of angels. In fact," writes Cambrensis, "the oftener and closer I inspect it,[1] the more certain I am to be struck with something new, with something ever more and more wonderful." Indeed, the story ran, that such figures and such colouring were due to no mere mortal invention, but that an

[1] The whole passage is worth transcribing in the original. "Inter numerosa Kildariæ miracula nihil mihi miraculosius occurrit quam liber ille mirandus, tempore Virginis [he means St. Brigit] ut aiunt, angelo dictante, consumptus. Hic Majestatis vultum videas divinitus impressum, hinc mysticas Evangelistarum formas, nunc senas, nunc quaternas, nunc binas alas habentes: hinc aquilam, inde vitulum, hinc hominis faciem, inde leonis, aliasque figuras fere infinitas. Quas si superficialiter et usuali more minus acute conspexeris, litura potius videbitur quam ligatura, nec ullam prorsus attendes subtilitatem. Sin autem ad perspicacius intuendum oculorum aciem invitaveris, et longe penitius ad artis arcana et transpenetraveris, tam delicatas et subtiles tam arctas et artitas, tam nodosas et vinculatim colligatas, tam que recentibus adhuc coloribus illustratas, notare poteris intricaturas, ut veré hæc omnia potius angelica quam humana diligentia jam asseveraveris esse composita. Hæc equidem quanto frequentius et diligentius intueor semper quasi novis obstupeo semper magis ac magis admiranda conspicio." Master of the Rolls series, vol. v., p. 123.

angel had appeared to the scribe in his sleep and taught him how to make these wondrous drawings, "and thus," adds Cambrensis, "through the revelation of the angel, the prayer of Brigit, and the imitation of the scribe, that book was written."

Now Giraldus Cambrensis, as Johan Adolf Brunn observes, "knew to perfection the master-achievements of the non-Celtic schools of art of contemporary date," and "although referring to a particular work of especial merit," says Brunn, "the testimony of this mediæval writer may well be placed at the head of an inquiry into the art in general of the Celtic illuminated manuscripts, emphasising as it does the salient characteristics of the style followed by this distinguished school of illumination, its minute and delicate drawing, its brilliancy of colouring, and, above all, that amazing amount of devoted and patient labour, which underlies its intricate composition, and creates the despair of any one who tries to copy them."

Between six and seven centuries later Westwood expresses himself in terms not unlike those of Cambrensis, of the now scanty remains of ancient Irish illumination—

"Especially deserving of notice," he writes, "is the extreme delicacy and wonderful precision, united with an extraordinary minuteness of detail with which many of these ancient manuscripts were ornamented. I have examined with a magnifying glass the pages of the Gospel of Lindisfarne, and the Book of Kells, for hours together, without ever detecting a false line or an irregular interlacement; and when it is considered that many of these details consist of spiral lines, and are so minute as to be impossible to have been executed without a pair of compasses, it really seems a problem not only with what eyes but also with what instruments they could have been executed. . . . I counted in a small space, measuring scarcely three quarters of an inch by less than half an inch in width, in the Book of Armagh, not fewer than one hundred and fifty-eight interlacements of a slender ribbon pattern formed in white lines edged with black ones upon a black ground."[1]

The Book of Armagh, as we have seen, was written in 807, or perhaps, as the "Four Masters" antedate at this period, in 812,

[1] "The Miniatures and Ornaments of Anglo-Saxon and Irish MSS."

while the Book of Kells is ascribed, according to the best judges, to the close of the seventh century.

The seventh and eight centuries, before the island was disturbed by the Danes, were the most flourishing period of the Irish illuminator and scribe. But their schools continued to turn out very fine work as late as the twelfth century, and Gilbert, in his "Facsimiles of the National Manuscripts of Ireland," states that there are perhaps no finer specimens of minute old writing extant than those in the margins and interlineations of a copy of the Gospels written by Maelbrigte Ua Maelruanaigh [Mulroony], in Armagh, in 1138, that is, seventeen years after that city had for the last time been burnt and plundered by the Danes.

Like all the other arts of civilised life, that of the illuminator and decorative scribe was brought to a standstill by the Norman warriors, nor do the Irish appear after this period to have produced a single page worth the reproduction of the artistic palæographer. The reason of this, no doubt, was that the Irish artist in former days could—no matter how septs fell out or warring tribes harried one another—count upon the sympathy of his fellow countrymen even when they were hostile. Under the new conditions caused by the Norman settlements in each of the four provinces, he could count on nothing, not even on his own life. All confidence was shaken, all peace of mind was gone, the very name of so-called government produced a universal terror, and Ireland became, to use a graphic expression of the Four Masters, a "trembling sod." "No words," writes Mrs. Sophie Bryant, with perfect truth, "could describe that arrest of development so eloquently or so lucidly as the facts of Irish art-history." "Since then" [*i.e.*, since the Norman invasion], writes Miss Stokes, one of the highest living authorities upon this subject, "the native character of Ireland has best found expression in her music. No work of purely Celtic art, whether in illumination of the sacred writings, or in gold, or bronze, or stone, was wrought by Irish hands after that century ;" and as we shall now see this decay of Irish art is reflected in the falling off of Irish literature, which continued languishing until the great revival which took place about the year 1600.

CHAPTER XXXV

FOUR CENTURIES OF DECAY

FOR four centuries after the Anglo-Norman, or more properly the Cambro-Norman invasion, the literature of Ireland seems to have been chiefly confined to the schools of the bards, and the bards themselves seem to have continued on the rather cut-and-dry lines of tribal genealogy, religious meditations, personal eulogium, clan history, and elegies for the dead. There reigns during this period a lack of imagination and of initiative in literature; no new ground is broken, no fresh paths entered on, no new saga-stuff unearthed, no new metres discovered. There is great technical skill exhibited, but little robust originality; great cleverness of execution, but little boldness of conception. How closely the bards ran in the groove of their predecessors is evident from the number of poems of doubtful authorship, ascribed by some authorities to bards of the pre-Norman or even Danish period, and by others to poets of the thirteenth, fourteenth, or even fifteenth centuries, the work of the later period being so very often both in style and language scarcely distinguishable from the earlier which it imitates.

Another characteristic of these four centuries is the number of hereditary bards of the same name and family which we find generation after generation, each one imitating his predecessor, and producing his inauguration odes, his eulogies, and his elegies, for each succeeding race of chiefs and patrons.

This period is the post-epic, post-saga period. Probably not one of the Red Branch stories was even materially altered during it. Stories of the Fenian cycle, however, continued to be propagated and improved upon, and no doubt many new ones were invented. But there is little or no trace of the composition of fresh miscellaneous saga, and the only poetry that seems to have flourished beside the classic metres of the bards is the so-called "Ossianic," a good deal of which may, perhaps, have assumed something of its present form during this period.

Some attempt there was at the careful keeping of annals, but scarcely any at writing regular history, though the fifteenth century produced McCraith's "Exploits of Torlough," to be noticed further on. We shall now briefly glance at this period age by age.

The thirteenth century, that succeeding the coming of the Normans, is far more barren in literature than the one which preceded them. Only five or six poets are mentioned as belonging to it, and their surviving poems amount to only a few hundred lines, with the exception of those of the great religious bard Donogha Mór O'Daly, who died in 1244 "a poet," record the "Four Masters," "who never was and never shall be surpassed." All his poems extant are of a religious character. He was buried in the abbey of Boyle, in the county of Roscommon, in which county I have heard, up to a few years ago, verses ascribed to him repeated by more than one old peasant. It is usually believed that he was a cleric and abbot of the beautiful monastery of Boyle, but there is no evidence for this, and he may have been in fact a layman. Thirty-one poems of his, containing in all some four thousand two hundred lines, have been preserved, and for their great smoothness have earned for their author the not very happy title of the Ovid of Ireland. Here is a specimen of one of his shorter pieces, written on his unexpectedly finding himself unable to shed a tear after his arriving at Loch Derg on a pilgrimage :

"Alas, for my journey to Loch Derg, O King of the churches and the bells ; 'I have come' to weep thy bruises and thy wound, and yet from my eye there cometh not a tear.[1]

"With an eye that moistens not its pupil, after doing every evil, no matter how great, with a heart that seeketh only (its own) peace, alas ! O king, what shall I do ?

"Without sorrowfulness of heart, without softening, without contrition, or weeping for my faults,—Patrick head of the clergy, he never thought that he could gain God in this way.

"The one son of Calphurn, since we are speaking of him, 'alas ! O Virgin, sad my state !' he was never seen whilst alive without the trace of tears in his eye.

"In (this) hard, narrow stone-walled (cell), after all the evil I have done, all the pride I have felt. Alas ! my pity ! that I find no tear, and I buried alive in the grave.

"O one-Son, by whom all were created, and who didst not shun the death of the three thorns, with a heart than which stone is not more hard, 'tis pity my journey to Loch Derg."

Here is another specimen, a good deal of which I once heard from a poor beggarman in the County Mayo, but it is also preserved in numerous manuscripts :

"My son, remember what I *say*,
That on the *Day* of Judgment's shock,
When men go stumbling down the *Mount*,
The sheep may *count* thee of their flock.[2]

And narrow though thou find the path
To Heaven's high rath, and hard to gain,
I warn thee shun yon broad white road
That leads to the abode of pain.

---

[1] "Truagh mo thuras ar Loch Dearg
A righ na gceall a's na gclog,
Do chaoineadh do chneadh 's do chréacht
'S nach dtig déar thar mo rosg."

See "Gaelic Journal," vol. iv. p. 190.

[2] "Ná tréig mo theagasg a mhic
Cidh baogh'lach lá an chirt do chách
Ag sgaoileadh dhóib ó an tsliabh
Rachaidh tu le Dia na ngrás."

See my "Religious Songs of Connacht," p. 28.

For us is many a snare designed,
  To fill our mind with doubts and fears.
Far from the land where lurks no sin,
  We dwell within our Vale of Tears.

Not on the world thy love bestow,
  Passing as flowers that blow and die ;
Follow not thou the specious track
  That turns the back on God most high.

But oh ! let faith, let hope, let love,
  Soar far above this cold world's way,
Patience, humility, and awe—
  Make them thy law from day to day.

And love thy neighbour as thyself,
  (Not for his pelf thy love should be),
But a greater love than every love
  Give God above who loveth thee.

. . .

The seven shafts wherewith the Unjust
  Shoots hard to thrust us from our home,
Canst thou avoid their fiery path,
  Dread not the wrath that is to come.

Shun sloth, shun greed, shun sensual fires,
  (Eager desires of men enslaved)
Anger and pride and hatred shun,
  Till heaven be won, till man be saved.

To Him, our King, to Mary's son
  Who did not shun the evil death,
Since He our hope is, He alone,
  Commit thy body, soul, and breath.

Since Hell each man pursues each day,
  Cleric and lay, till life be done,
Be not deceived as others may,
  Remember what I say, my son." [1]

[1] Literally : "Do not forsake my teaching, my son, and although dangerous be the Day of Right for all, on their scattering from the Mount, thou shalt go with God of the graces.

"The road to heaven of the saints though to thee it seem narrow, slender, hard, yet shun the road of the house of the pains, many a one has journeyed to it away from us.

"Against us was treachery designed, to bring us down from the artificer

The fourteenth century possesses exactly the same characteristics as the thirteenth, only the poets are more numerous. O'Reilly mentions over a score of them whose verses amount to nearly seven thousand lines. Of these the best known is probably John Mór O'Dúgan of whom about 2,600 lines survive—important rather for the information they convey than for their poetry. His greatest, or at least his most valuable piece, is about the tribes and territories of the various districts in Meath, Ulster, and Connacht, on the arrival of the Normans, and the names of the chiefs who ruled them.[1] In this poem he devotes 152 lines to Meath, 354 to Ulster, 328 to Connacht, and only 56 to Leinster, death having apparently carried him off (in the year 1372) before he had finished his researches into the tribes and territories of that district. But luckily for us his younger contemporary—Gilla-na-naomh O'Huidhrin [Heerin]—took it up and completed it,[2] so that the two poems, usually copied together, form a single piece of 1,660 lines in *deibhidh* [d'yĕvee] metre, which has thrown

of the elements, in banishment from the land of the living in a Valley of Tears art thou.

"To the world give not love, is it not transient the blossom of the branches? do not follow the track of those who are journeying to hell from God of the Saints.

"Hope, faith, and love, let thee have in God forever, humility, and patience without anger, truth without deception in thy walk," etc.

[1] It begins—

"Triallam timchioll na Fódhla,
Gluaisid fir ar furfhógra,
As na fóidibh a bhfuileam
Na Cóigeadha cuartuigheam."

The whole has been most ably edited by Dr. O'Donovan for the Irish Archæological Society.

[2] His poem in continuation begins—

"Tuille feasa ar Erinn óigh,
Ni maith seanchaidh nach seanóir,
Seanchas cóir uaim don feadhain
Na slóigh ó'n Boinn báinealaigh."

"More knowledge on virgin Ireland, not good is an historian unless he be an elder, proper history from me to the tribe, the hosts from Boyne of the white cattle."

more light upon names and territories than perhaps any other of the same extent. It is, despite the difficult and recondite verse, a work mainly of research and not of poetry. The same may be said of nearly all O'Dugan's poems, another of which called the "Forus Focal," is really a vocabulary in verse of obsolete words, which though of similar orthography have different or even contrary meanings. It was in this century the great miscellaneous collection called the Book of Ballymote was compiled.

The fifteenth century differs very little in character from the preceding one. We find about the same number of poets with about the same amount of verses—between six and seven thousand lines, according to O'Reilly—still surviving, or as O'Reilly underrates the number, probably about ten thousand lines. The poets were now beginning to feel the rude weight of the prosaic Saxon, and Fergal O'Daly chief poet of Corcamroe, Maurice O'Daly a poet of Breffny, Dermot O'Daly of Meath, Hugh Óg Mac Curtin, and Dubhthach [Duffach] son of Eochaidh [Yohee] "the learned," with several more, are mentioned as having been cruelly plundered and oppressed by Lord Furnival and the English. It was in this century that those most valuable annals usually called the Annals of Ulster were compiled from ancient books now lost, by Cathal Maguire who was born in 1438. The great collection called the Book of Lecan was copied at the beginning of this century, and another most important work the "Caithréim, or warlike exploits of Turlough O'Brien," was written about the year 1459 by John Mac Craith, chief historian of North Munster. This though composed in a far more exaggerated and inflated style than even the "War of the Gael with the Gaill," which it resembles, yet gives the most accurate account we have of the struggles of the Irish against the English in Munster from the landing of Henry II. till the death of Lord de Clare in 1318. It was at the very beginning of this century the hagiographical collection called the Leabhar Breac was made.

The sixteenth century cannot properly be said to mark a transition period in Irish literature, as it does in the literature of so many other European countries. It has, indeed, left far more numerous documents behind it than the preceding one, but this is mainly due to the fact that less time has elapsed during which they could be lost. Their style and general contents differ little, until the very close of the century, from those of their predecessors. O'Reilly chronicles the names of about forty poets whose surviving pieces amount to over ten thousand lines. But so many MSS. which were in O'Reilly's time in private hands, or which, like the Stowe MSS., were unapproachable by students, have since been deposited in public libraries or become otherwise accessible, that it would, I think, be safe to add at least half as much again to O'Reilly's computation. I have even in my own possession poems by nearly a dozen writers belonging to the sixteenth and seventeenth centuries whose names are not mentioned at all by O'Reilly; and the O'Conor Don has shown me a manuscript copied at Ostend, in Belgium, in 1631, for one Captain Alexander Mac Donnell, from which O'Curry transcribed a thousand pages of poems "of which with a very few exceptions," he writes, "no copies are known to me elsewhere in Ireland." A considerable number of these poems, nearly all of them unknown to O'Reilly, were composed in the fourteenth, fifteenth, and sixteenth centuries, so that this one manuscript alone would largely swell O'Reilly's estimate for this period.

Enormous quantities of books however, belonging to the sixteenth and seventeenth centuries, have been lost, and are still being lost every day. It is an accident that Friar O'Gara's[1] and the O'Conor Don's collection--both compiled abroad—have escaped. If, during the middle of the sixteenth

[1] Made in the Low Countries by an exiled friar of the County Galway, a great collection of poetry in the classical metres. See "Transactions of the Gaelic Society," 1808, p. 29.

century, a collector of poetry had gone round transcribing the classical poems of that age, he would have found large collections preserved in the houses of almost every scion of the old Gaelic nobility, with scarcely an exception. On the break-up of the houses of the Irish chiefs the archives of their families and their manuscript libraries were lost or carried abroad. An excellent example of what may be called tribal poetry, such as every great Gaelic house possessed, is contained in a manuscript in Trinity College, which a Fellow of the last century, called O'Sullivan, luckily got transcribed for himself, and which is now in the college library.[1] The collection thus made, from about 1570 to 1615, goes under the title of the "Book of the O'Byrnes," and contains sixty or seventy poems made by their own family bards and by several of the leading bards of Ireland, for the various members of the O'Byrnes of Ranelagh near Dublin, and of the O'Byrnes of Wicklow, who for three generations maintained their struggle with the English, only succumbing in the beginning of the seventeenth century.

Other family records of this nature, which were once possessed in every county by the bardic families and by the chiefs, have perished by the score. A glance at a few typical poems belonging to the O'Byrnes will give a good idea of the functions of the sixteenth-century bards, and the nature of their poems. They are composed on all kinds of subjects

[1] H. I. 14, in Trinity College. It is copied unfortunately by one of the most incompetent of scribes, and is full of mistakes of all kinds. The poets who wrote for the O'Byrnes were Rory Mac Craith, Owen O'Coffey, Mahon O'Higinn, Donal Mac Keogh, Niall O'Rooney, Angus O'Daly, John O'Higinn, Eochaidh O'Hussey, Maoileachlainn O'Coffey, T. O'Mulconry, Donogha Mac Keogh, and others. A copy of the "Book of the O'Byrnes" was in possession of the O'Byrnes of Cabinteely, near Dublin, in the beginning of the century. Hardiman and O'Reilly each had a copy, but as I have seen the scribe employed by the Royal Irish Academy engaged for days in writing out of the wretched copy in Trinity College, it is to be presumed that the Council of that body has assured itself that these copies have since perished.

connected with the wars, genealogy, and history of the tribe and its chiefs. Many are eulogiums, some warnings, some political poems, some elegies. Here are two or three specimens; the first a poem of fifty-six lines, by Angus O'Daly, on the head of one of the chiefs of the clan spiked on the battlements of Dublin.

"O body which I see without a head,
It is the sight of thee which has withered up my strength,
Divided and impaled in Ath-cliath [Dublin],
The learned of Banba [Ireland] will feel its loss."[1]

"Who will relieve the wants of the poor?
Who will bestow cattle on the learned?
O body, since thou art without a head
It is not life which we care to choose after thee."

Another poem, by John O'Higinn asks who[2] will buy nine verses from him. By his hand he swears, though high the fame of the men of Leinster, they are all cowed now. The O'Tooles of the once heavy gifts have consented to the peace of the English, and till they revoke it they will not give one white groat for twenty-marks-worth of a poem. The Cavanaghs are as bad, the Fitzgeralds and the O'Mores, too, are afraid of the foreigners to buy a poem. One man alone is not obedient to foreign English custom, Aodh [O'Byrne] son of John, the true sweetheart of the bardic schools of the race of the plain of Conn. Except him, the grandson of Redmond alone, the poet sees not one who

[1] "A cholann do chím gun ceann
Sibh d' fhaicsin, do shearg mo bhrigh,
Rannta ar sparra a n-Athcliath,
D'éigsi Bhanba bhias a dhith."
(H. 1. 14, T. C., D., fol. 84 a.)

[2] "Cia cheannchas ádhmad naoi rann,
Dá bhfághadh connra ar súd?
Ar Laighnibh cidh 'r b'ard a dteisd
Do m' aithne is cruaidh an cheisd úd.

will buy his nine stanzas—or if such exist, he knows them not.[1]

Another poem of 180 lines by Eochaidh [Yohee] O'Hussey is on the extreme winsomeness and beauty of a certain lady of the O'Byrnes, Rose by name, probably the famous wife of Fiach O'Byrne, who, poor thing, was afterwards captured by the English in 1595 and by them burned alive in the yard of Dublin Castle. The English statesmen who record this piece of work in the State Papers, did not in the least understand the civilisation or customs of Lady Rose, her bards and her clan, and it is only at the present day that it is possible for the scholar through the medium of the State Papers on one side and native Irish documents on the other, to put himself *en rapport* with both parties; it is a process both absorbing and painful. "What is troubling the ladies of the Gael?" asks the poet, "is it want of gold or lack of jewels, wherefore is the dear troop downcast? Why are the queens of princely race disquieted? Why rise they up heavy at heart? Why lie they down discomfited? Why are their spirits troubled? It is because one lady so excels them all, she is the troubler of the hosts of the men of Inisfail, the one cause of the sorrow of our ladies. Let me," adds the poet gallantly, "have the singing of her."[2]

Another is by Maoilsheachlainn [Malachy in English] O'Coffey, on seeing one of the O'Byrnes' strongholds, probably Ballinacor, occupied by a stranger.[3] Another by one

[1] "Acht ua Réamainn thuilleas bládh,
Ni h-aithne dham shoir no shiar,
Neach le ceannach [mo] naoi rann,
Ma tá ann, ni fheadar c' iad."

[2] "Creud ag buaidhreadh ban ngaoidheal
An dith óir no iol-mhaoineadh,
Cuis aith-mheillte an diorma díl,
Ríoghna flaith-fréimhe fuinnidh."
(H. I. 14, T. C., D., fol. 126 a.)

[3] "Ni bhfuair mé 'na n-áitibh ann,
Acht lucht gan aithne orom [orm],
Mo chreach geur, mo chrádh croidhe,
An sgeul fá ttáim troithlidhe."

of the O'Mulconrys warns Fiach O'Byrne, that whether he likes to hear it or not, the axe of the English is raised above his head to strike him down.[1] The poet points to the Leinster septs who had been exterminated or escaped destruction by making submission, and how is Fiach to escape, and especially how to escape treachery?

Another poem composed by Donough Mac Eochaidh, or Keogh, with high political intent, is intended to bring about a closer feeling of friendship between the sons of Fiach O'Byrne and John son of Redmond O'Byrne, who had been alienated, designedly, as he intimates, by a lying story propagated by a foreigner, whereas the O'Byrnes of Ranelagh ever sought to avoid giving offence, and no evil story calculated to increase enmity should be believed about one by the other.[2]

Another poet of the Mac Eochaidhs, the household bards of the O'Byrnes, sings the generosity of Torlagh, son of Fiacha, "their fame is the wealth of the tribe of Ranelagh, that is the saying of every one who knows them,[3] the bestowal of their jewels, that is the treasure of the tribe of Ranelagh, of the numerous incursions." "Small is their desire to amass treasures, nobler is the thing for which they conceive

[1] "Fuath gach fir fuighioll a thuaidhe,
Tuig a Fhiacha, duit is dual,
Má tá nach binn libh mo labhra,
Os cionn do chinn do thárla an tuath."

O'Donovan, in his manuscript catalogue, quotes the last two lines of the verse in note 3, and translates them, "My bitter woe my heart's oppression is the news for which I grieve." Afterwards he erased the words "for which I grieve" and wrote instead "it wastes my vigour," thus showing that he did not understand the original, for one translation is as bad as the other. The difficult word *troithlidhe* which perplexed him, is a common one in Roscommon, I have frequently heard it in the sense of "chilly." The translation is, "the news which chills me."

[2] "Fréamh Raghnaill ni rabhadar
Acht ag seachnadh inbhéime
Sgeul meuduighthe faltanais
Doibh nior chreidte ar a chéile."

[3] "A gclu is ionmhus d'fhuil Raghnaill
Rádh gach eólaigh is é sin."

a wish ; every single man of the blood of Fiach O'Bryne has taken upon himself to distribute his riches for Fiach !"[1]

Another poem is a splendid war-song by Angus O'Daly on a victory of the O'Byrnes over the English. "I rejoice that not one was left of the remnant of the slaughter but the captive who is in hand in bondage :"[2] "the blaze of the burning country makes day out of midnight for them."

A remarkable poet of the end of this century was another Angus O'Daly, the Red Bard, or Angus of the Satires, as he was called. He seems to have been employed by the English statesmen, Lord Mountjoy and Sir George Carew, for the deliberate purpose of satirising all the Gaelic families in the kingdom, and those Anglo-Normans who sympathised with them. Angus travelled the island up and down on this sinister mission. It was indeed an evil time. The awful massacres of Rathlin and Clanaboy in Ulster, the hideous treachery of Mullaghmast in Leinster, the revolting deeds of Bingham in the west, and the unspeakable horrors that followed on the Geraldines rebellion in the south, had reduced the Irish nobles to a condition of the direst poverty. This poverty and the inhospitality which he connected with it—points on which the Irish were particularly sore—were the mark at which Angus aimed his arrows. He usually polished off each house or clan in a single rann or quatrain. His Irish rhymes are peculiarly happy. Here are some specimens of his satire. He says of Thomas Fitzgerald, Knight of Glynn, that he looked so grudgingly at him as he ate his supper that the piece half-chewed

[1] "Beag a ndúil a ndéanamh ionmhais
Uaisle an nidh dá dtabhraid toil,
Do ghabh gach aon-fhear d'fhuil Fhiacha
Sgaoileadh a chruidh d'Fiacha, air."

[2] "Thug gárda láidir mhic Aodha mhic Sheáin
Dochur ar barda (?) a n-aoil-chaisleán,
'S báidh liom nár fágadh neach d'fhuighioll an áir
Acht an bráighe atá fá dhaoirse a[r] láimh."

The second line of this is quite incomprehensible, and runs in the MS. *do chur ar ar barda.*

stuck in his throat at the very sight of the other's eyes. Of Limerick he says the only thing he was thankful for was the bad roads which would prevent him from ever seeing it again. Of the Fitzmaurices he says that he will neither praise them nor satirise them, for they are just poor gentlemen—admirable satire, and it cannot be doubted that they keenly felt the point of it! Often, however, Angus is only abusive —thus of Maguire of Enniskillen he says that "he is a badger for roughness and greyness, an ape for stature and ugliness, a lobster for the sharpness of his two eyes, a fox for the foulness of his breath,"[1] a verse in which the happiness of the Irish rhyming carries off the poverty of the sentiment. He harps on the blindness of the Mac Ternans,[2] the misanthropy of the Mac Gillycuddy, the inborn evil of the Fitzgibbons,[3] the poverty of the O'Callaghans, the bad wines of the O'Sullivans, the decrepitude of the O'Reillys, and so on.

The Red Bard went on with his satires on the men of the four provinces, with none to say him nay, until he came to Tipperary, where he was misguided enough to satirise the chief of the O'Meaghers, whose servant, stung out of all control, forgot that the person of a bard was sacred, and instantly thrust a knife into his throat, thus putting an end to him and his satires. Angus, however, even as he died, uttered one rann in which, for the good of his soul, he revoked all his former

[1] "Broc ar ghairbhe 's ar ghlaise,
Apa ar mhéad 's ar mhio-mhaise,
Gliomach ar ghéire a dhá shúil,
Sionnach ar bhréine, an Bárún."

[2] "Caoch an inghean, caoch an mháthair,
Caoch an t-athair, caoch an mac,
Caoch an capall bhíos fá 'n tsráthair,
Leath-chaoch an cú, caoch an cat."

[3] "Ni fhuil fearg nach dtéid ar gcúl
Acht fearg Chriost le cloinn Ghiobun
Beag an t-iongnadh a mbeith mar tá
Ag fás i n-olc gach aon lá."

This rann was often quoted in after days about Fitzgibbon, Lord Clare, who passed the Union.

verses: "All the false judgments I have passed upon the men of Munster I recant them; the meagre servant of the grey Meagher has passed as much of a false judgment upon me."

So greatly had the literary production of Ireland passed into the hands of the bards during the period we are now considering, that it will be well to study the evolution of the bardic body down to the close of the sixteenth century, in a separate chapter.

CHAPTER XXXVI

DEVELOPMENT OF IRISH POETRY

SOME of the very earliest Irish poems—of which we have specimens in the verses attributed to Amergin, son of Milesius, and in the first satire ever uttered in Ireland, and in many more pieces of a like character [1]—appear to have been unrhymed, and to have depended for their effect partly upon rapidity of utterance, partly on a tendency towards alliteration,

[1] This is a kind of rhetoric ; some of these unrhymed outbursts were called *rosg* by the Irish. Irish literature is full of such pieces. Some of the Brehon Law though printed in prose seems to have been composed in it. Other examples are the cry of the Mór-rígan, or war-goddess, in the end of the Battle of Moytura.

" Peace to heav'n Heav'n to earth Earth neath heav'n Strength in each," etc.	" Sith go neim Neamh go domhan, Domhan fá neim Neart i gcách," etc.

or the description of the Dun Bull of Cuailnge in the Táin Bo, or part of the first poem attributed to Finn mac Cool, or the well-known eulogy on Goll the Fenian, or Mac Mhurighs incitement at the battle of Harlaw, or some of the verses in the preface to the Amra. About the last specimen of unrhymed poetry, in a species of Droighneach metre, I find in the Annals of Loch Cé on the death of Mac Dermot as late as 1568.

" Gég iothmar fhineamhna na n-éigeas ocus na n-ollaman,
Craobh cumra cnuais na gcliar ocus na gcerbach,
Dóss díona na ndámh ocus na ndeóraidh
Bile buadha buan fhoscaidh na mbrughaidh ocus na mbiattach."

and in some cases on a strongly-marked leaning towards dissyllabic words.

Soon after the time of St. Patrick and the first Christian missionaries, the Irish are found for certain using rhyme—how far they had evolved it before the coming of the Latin missionaries is a moot question. The Book of Hymns has preserved genuine specimens of the Latin verses of Columcille and other early saints, which either rhyme, or have a strong *tendency* towards rhyme, though few of these early verses are found wholly chiming on the accented syllables.[1] It is a tremendous claim to make for the Celt that he taught Europe to rhyme; it is a claim in comparison with which, if it could be substantiated, everything else that he has done in literature pales into insignificance. Yet it has been made for him by some of the foremost European scholars. The great Zeuss himself is emphatic on the point; "the form of Celtic poetry,"[2] he writes, "to judge both from the older and the more recent examples adduced, appears to be more ornate than the poetic form of any other nation, and even more ornate in the older poems than in the modern ones; from the fact of which greater ornateness it undoubtedly came to pass that at the very time the Roman Empire was hastening to its ruin, the Celtic poems—at first entire, afterwards in part—passed over not only into the song of the Latins, but also into those of other nations and remained

[1] Thus the nearest approach that Columcille makes to Latin rhyme is in the final unaccented syllable. See his "Altus" beginning

"Altus prosator vetustus
Dierum et ingenitus
Erat absque origine
Primordii et crepidine.

Sed et erit in sæcula
Sæculorum infinita
Cui est unigenitus
Christus et sanctus spiritus," etc.

[2] "Formam poesis celticæ, exemplis allatis, tam vetustioribus quam recentioribus vel hodiernis, magis ornatum esse apparet quam ullius gentis formam poeticam, ac magis ornatam in vetustioribus carminibus ipsis, quam in recentioribus. Quo majore ornatu, haud dubie effectum est, ut jam inde ab illis temporibus quibus ad interitum ruebat Romanum imperium, celtica forma, primum integra, deinde ex parte, non solum in latina sed etiam (aliarum) linguarum carmina transferretur atque in iis permanserit" ("Grammatica Celtica," Ebel's edition, p. 977).

in them." In another place he remarks the advance towards rhyme made in the *Latin* poetry of the Anglo-Saxons, and unhesitatingly ascribes it to Irish influence. "We must believe," he writes, "that this form was introduced among them by the Irish, as were the arts of writing and of painting and of ornamenting manuscripts, since they themselves in common with the other Germanic nations made use in their poetry of nothing but alliteration."[1] Constantine Nigra expresses himself even more strongly in his edition of the glosses in the Codex Taurinensis. He says—

"The idea that rhyme originated amongst the Arabs must be absolutely rejected as fabulous. . . . Rhyme, too, could not in any possible way have evolved itself from the natural progress of the Latin language. Amongst the Latins neither the thing nor the name existed. We first meet with final assonance or rhyme at the close of the fourth or beginning of the fifth century in the Latin hymns of the Milanese Church, which are attributed to St. Ambrose and St. Augustine. The first certain examples of rhyme, then, are found on Celtic soil and amongst Celtic nations, in songs made by poets who are either of Celtic origin themselves or had long resided amongst Celtic races. It is most probable that these hymns of Middle Latin were composed according to the form of Celtic poetry which was then flourishing, and which exhibits final assonance in all the ancient remains of it hitherto discovered. It is true that the more ancient Irish and British poems which have come down to us do not appear to be of older date than the seventh or eighth century [Nigra means, in their present form], but it must not be rashly inferred that the Celtic races, who were always tenacious of the manners and customs

[1] "Magis progressa consonantia, cum frequentiore allitteratione, amplior finalis sæpius trissyllaba invenitur in Anglo-Saxorum carminibus latinis; ad quos, cum ipsi principio cum ceteris Germanis non usi sint nizi allitteratione, ab Hibernis hanc formam esse transgressam putandum est, ut transiit scriptura atque ars pingendi codices et ornandi" (Ibid., p. 946).

In another passage he expresses himself even more strongly; for of rhyme he says: "Hanc formam orationis poeticæ quis credat esse ortam primum apud poetas Christianos finientis imperii Romani et transisse ad bardos Cambrorum et in carmina gentilia Scandinavorum" (Editio Ebel, p. 948).

of their ancestors, had not employed the same poetic forms already, long before, say in the earliest centuries of our era." [1]

After arguing that the Irish rule of "Slender-with-Slender and Broad-with-Broad," a rule which was peculiar to the Celts alone of all the Aryan races, contained in itself the germ of rhyme, he sums up his argument thus positively: "We must conclude, then, that this late Latin [Romanic] verse, made up of accent, and of an equal number of syllables, may have arisen in a twofold way, first by the natural evolution of the Latin language itself; or secondly, by the equally efficacious example of neighbouring Celtic peoples, but we conclude that *final assonance, or rhyme, can have been derived only from the laws of Celtic phonology.*" [2]

Thurneysen, on the other hand, who has done such good service for the study of Irish metric by his publication of the text of the fragmentary Irish poets' books,[3] is of opinion that the Irish derived their regular metres with a given number of

[1] "Origo enim rîmæ arabica inter fabulas omnino rejicienda est. . . . Porro rîma ex solo naturali processu latinæ linguæ explicari nullo modo potest. Apud Latinos nec res extitit nec nomen. . . . Assonantia finalis vel rîma, sæculo quarto abeunte et quinto incipiente vulgaris ævi, primus occurrit in hymnis latinis ecclesiæ mediolanensis qui sancto Ambrosio et Sancto Augustino tribuuntur. Prima itaque rîmæ certa exempla inveniuntur in solo celtico, apud celticas gentes, in carminibus conditis a poetis, qui vel celticæ originis sunt, vel apud celticas gentes diu commoraverunt. Verosimile ut hosce hymnos mediæ latinitatis constructos esse juxta formam celticæ poesis quæ tunc vigebat, et quæ jam assonantiam finalem præbet in antiquis ejus reliquiis huc-usque detectis. Profecto carmina hibernica et brittanica vetustiora quæ ad nos pervenerunt sæculum octavum vel septimum superare non videntur. Sed temere non est affirmare celticas gentes quæ moris consuetudinisque majorum tenaces semper fuerunt, jam multo antea, primis nempe vulgaris ævi sæculis, eamdem poeticam formam adhibuisse" ("Glossæ Hibernicæ Veteres Codicis Taurinensis." Lutetiæ. 1869. p. xxxi.).

[2] "Concludendum est igitur versum romanicum, accentu legatum et pari syllabarum numero, oriri potuisse ex duplicis causæ concursu, nempe à naturali explicatione latinæ linguæ, et ab exemplo pariter efficaci affinium celticorum populorum; sed rîmam seu assonantiam finalem, a solis celticæ phonologiæ legibus derivatam esse" (Ibid., p. xxxii.).

[3] "Mittelirische Verslehren," "Irische Texte," iii. p. 1.

syllables in each line, from the Latins;[1] and Windisch agrees with him in saying that the Irish verse-forms were influenced by Latin,[2] though he thinks that Thurneysen presses his theory too far. The latter, in opposition to Zimmer,[3] will not for instance allow the genuineness of St. Fiacc's metrical life of St. Patrick because it is in a rhymed and fairly regular metre, a thing which, according to him, the Irish had not developed at that early period. It seems necessary to me, however, to take into account the peculiar prosody of the Irish, especially the *tour de force* called *áird-rinn* used in *Deibhidh* [d'yevvee] metre, which we find firmly established in their oldest poems,[4] and which makes the rhyming word ending the second line contain a syllable more than the rhyming word which ends the first, while if the accent fall in the first line on the ultimate syllable it mostly falls in the second line on the penultimate, if it falls on the penultimate in the first line it generally falls on the antepenultimate in the second, as—

> "Though men owe respect to them,
> Presage of woe—a poem.
>
> The slender free palms of her
> Than gull on sea are whiter.

[1] *See* his article in "Revue Celtique," vi., p. 336.

[2] "Dass die irische Versform von der lateinischen Versform beeinflusst worden ist, scheint mir zweifellos zu sein. Es fragt sich nur was die irischen Barden schon hatten als dieser Einfluss begann. Das was Thurneysen ihnen zugestehen will ist mir etwas zu wenig" ("Irische Texte," iii. 2, p. 448).

[3] "Wir haben," says Zimmer, of this hymn, "ein altes einfaches und ehrwürdiges Monument vor uns, an das eine jüngere Zeit mit verändertem Geschmack, passend und unpassend, an—und eingebaut hat."

[4] *Deibhidh*, in Old Irish *Debide*, a neuter word, which Thurneysen translates "cut in two," is not really a rhyme but a generic name for a metre, containing twenty-four species. The essence of the principal *Deibhidh*, however, is the peculiar manner of rhyming with words of a different length, so that this system has sometimes been loosely called *Deibhidh* rhyme. In the oldest poetry a trisyllable instead of a dissyllable rhyme could be used as the end word of the second line when the first line ended with a monosyllable, but in the strictness of later times this was disallowed.

A far greater than ány
Man has killed my Cómpany." [1]

This peculiarly Irish feature was not borrowed from the Latins, but is purely indigenous. The oldest books of glosses on the Continent contain verses formed on this model.[2] According to Thurneysen's theory the Irish learned how to write rhymed verse with lines of equal syllables sometime between, say, the year 500 and 700, but the *Deibhidh* metre with *áird-rinn* is found in their oldest verses, bound up with rhyme in their accurate seven-syllable lines. Why should two of these ingredients, the rhyme and the stated number of verses have come fróm the Romans when the *Deibhidh áird-rinn* (which apparently implies rhyme) did not? Besides is it credible, on the supposition that the pre-Christian Irish neither counted their syllables nor rhymed, that within less than a couple of hundred years after coming in contact

[1] "Tús onóra cidh dual dí,
Tuar anshógha an eigsi.

Glac bárr-lag mar chúbhair tonn
Do sháraigh dath na bhfaoilionn.

Gníomh follus fáth na h-eachtra
Fá'r ciorrbadh mo chuideachta."

These specimens are taken from unedited manuscripts in my own possession, copied by O'Curry from I know not what originals.

[2] Thus in the Codex St. Pauli we find these verses :—

" Messe ocus Pangur ban
Cechtar náthar fria saindán
Bith a menma-sunn fri seilgg
Mu menma céin im sain-ceirdd.

Caraim-se fos ferr gach clu
Oc mo lebran leir ingnu
Ni foirmtech frimm Pangur ban
Caraid sesin a macc-dán."

with the rude Latin verse of Augustin and Ambrose, they had brought rhyming verses to such a pitch of perfection as we see, in, say, the "Voyage of Bran," which according to both Kuno Meyer and Professor Zimmer, was written in the seventh century, the very first verse of which runs—

"Crôib dind *abaill* a h-Emain
Dofed *samaill* do *gnáthaib*
Gésci findarggait *fora*
Abrait *glano* co *m-bláthaib*"?

The whole of this poem, too, is shot through with verses of *Deibhidh*, and the rhymes are extraordinarily perfect.[1] This at least is clear, that already in the seventh century the Irish not only rhymed but made intricate *Deibhidh* and other rhyming metres,[2] when for many centuries after this period

[1] The end rhyming words in verses 6–10 for example are as follows—fóe nóe, *bátha* hil*blátha*, bláthaib thráthaib, gnáth tráth, *datho* moith*gretho*, *chéul* Arggut*néul*, *mrath* etar*gnath*, cruais clúais, *bás* ind*gás*, n-*Emne* com*amre*.

[2] Compare, too, the verses that the monk wrote in the margin of the St. Gall MS. which he was copying, on hearing the blackbird sing—

"Dom farcai fidbaidae *fál*
Fomchain lóid lain luad nad cél
Huas mo lebrán ind*línech*
Fomchain *trírech* inna nén;"

the language of which is so ancient as to be nearly unintelligible to a modern, though the metre is common from that day to this. "A thicket of bushes surrounds me, a lively blackbird sings to me his lay, I shall not conceal it, above my many-lined book he sings to me the trill of the birds," etc. Commenting on these verses Nigra says feelingly, "Mentre traduco questi versi amo figurarmi il povero monaco che, or fá più di mille anni, stava copiando il manoscritto, e distratto un istante dal canto dei merli contemplava dalla finestra della sua cella la verde corona di boscaglie che circondava il suo monastero nell Ulster o nel Connaught, e dopo avere ascoltato l'agile trillo degli uccelli, recitava questi strofe, e rapigliava poi più allegro l'interrotto lavoro."

It has often been alleged that the word rhyme is derived from the Irish *rím*, "number," *rímaire*, "a reckoner," and *rimim*, "I count;" but in Anglo-Saxon *rím* has the same meaning, so that unless the Anglo-Saxons borrowed the word, as they certainly did the thing, from the Irish, this is inconclusive.

In fol. 8a of the "Liber Hymnorum" we read in the preface to the very ancient hymn "In Trinitate spes mea," the following note: "Incertum

the Germanic nations could only alliterate—a thing which though sometimes used in Irish verse is in no way fundamental to it. In England so late as the beginning of the fifteenth century, the virile author of the book of Piers Ploughman used alliteration in preference to rhyme, and, indeed, down to the first half of the sixteenth century English poets, for the most part, exhibit a disregard for fineness of execution and technique of which not the meanest Irish bard attached to the pettiest chief could have been guilty. After the seventh century the Irish brought their rhyming system to a pitch of perfection undreamt of, even at this day, by other nations. Perhaps by no people in the globe, at any period of the world's history, was poetry so cultivated and, better still, so remunerated, as in Ireland. The elaborateness of the system they evolved, the prodigious complexity of the rules, the subtlety and intricacy of their poetical code are astounding.

The real poet of the early Gaels was the *filé* [fillă]. The bard was nothing thought of in comparison with him, and the legal price of his poems was quite small compared with the remuneration of the *filé*. It was the bard who seems to have been most affected by Latin influence, and the metres which he used seem to have been of relatively new importation. Where the *filé* received his three milch cows for a poem the bard only bore away a calf. The bards were divided into two classes, the Saor and Daor bards, or the patrician and

est hautem in quo tempore factus est, Trerithim dana doronadh ocus xi. caiptell déac ann, ocus dalíni in cech caiptiull, ocus se sillaba déc cechai. Is foi is rithim doreir in ómine dobit ann., *i.e.*, "in rhyme it was made and eleven chapters thereon and two lines in every chapter, and sixteen syllables in each. It is on *i* the *rhyme* is because of the 'omine' that is in it." In the preface to the hymn, "Christus in nostra insula," the scholiast writes, "Trerithim dana dorigned," which Whitley Stokes translates by "in *rhythm* moreover it was made," but *rithim* evidently means the same in both passages, namely, *rhyme* not rhythm, at least if the first passage is rightly translated by Dr. Stokes himself. I doubt, however, if *rím* or *rithim* ever meant "rhyme" in Irish.

plebeian.[1] There were eight grades in each class, one of the many examples of the love of the Irish for minute classification, a quality with which they are not usually credited, at least, not in modern times. Each of these sixteen classes of bard has his own peculiar metre or framework for his verses, and the lower bard was not allowed to encroach on the metres sacred to the bard next in rank.[2]

The fīlés [fillăs] were, as we have said, the highest class of poets. There were seven grades of Filé,[3] the most exalted

[1] The various Saor bands were called the *Anshruth-bairdne* (great stream of poetry ?), the *Sruth di aill* (stream down two cliffs ?), the *Tighearn-bhard* (lord bard), the *Adhmhall*, the *Tuath-bhard* (lay bard), the *bo-bhard* (cow-bard) and the *Bard áine*. The highest of the Daor bards was called the *cúl-bhard* (back bard), and after him came the *Sruth-bhard* (stream-bard), the *Drisiuc*, the *cromluatha*, the *Sirti-uí*, the *Rindhaidh*, the *Long-bhard*, and the *bard Loirrge*.

[2] Thus the head of the patrician bards was entitled to make use of the metres called *nath*, metres in which the end of each line makes a vowel rhyme or an alliteration with the beginning of the next, the number of syllables in the line and of lines in the verse being irregular. There were six kinds of *náth* metres, called *Deachna*. All these the first bard practised with two honourable metres besides, called the great and little *Séadna*. The ANSHRUTH used the two kinds of metres called *Ollbhairdne*, the SRUTH DI AILL used *Casbhairdne*, the TIGHEARN-BHARD used *Duan-bhairdne*, a generic metre of which there were six species called *Duan faidesin*, *duan cendálach*, *fordhuan*, *taebh-chasadh*, *tul-chasadh*, and *sreth-bhairdne*. All the metres which these five employed were honourable ones, and went under the generic name of *príomhfódhla*. Then came the ADHMHALL with seven measures for himself, *bairdne faidessin*, *blogh-bhairdne*, *brac-bhairdne*, *snedh-bhairdne*, *sem-bhairdne*, *imard-bhairdne*, and *rathnuall*. The TUATH-BHARD had all the *Rannaigheacht* metres and the BO-BARD all the *Deibhidh* metres, and these two, Rannaigheacht and Deibhidh, though thus lowly thought of in early—probably pre-Danish—days, were destined in later times, like the cuckoo birds, to oust their fellows and reign in the forefront for many hundred years. The Tuath-bhard had also two other metres *Seaghdha* and *Treochair*, and the Bo-bhard in addition to Deibhidh had long and short *deachnbhaidh*.

The classification of the Daor bards and their metres is just as minute.

[3] The lowest grade of *filé* was called the *fuclue* (word maker ?). In his first year he had to learn fifty ogams and straight ogams amongst them. He had to learn the grammar called *Uraicept na n-éigsine*, and the preface to it, and that part of the book called *réimeanna*, or courses,

being called an ollamh [ollav], a name that has frequently occurred throughout this book. They were so highly esteemed that the annalists give the obituaries of the head-ollamhs as if they were so many princes. The course of study was originally perhaps one of seven years. Afterwards it lasted for twelve years or more.[1] When a poet had worked his way up after at least twelve but perhaps sometimes twenty years of study, through all the lower degrees, and had at last attained the rank of ollamh, he knew, in addition to all his other knowledge, over three hundred and fifty different kinds of versification, and was able to recite two hundred and fifty prime stories and one hundred secondary ones. The ancient and fragmentary manuscripts from which these details are taken, not only give the names of the metres but have actually preserved examples of between two and three hundred of them taken from different ancient poems, almost all of which have perished to a line, but they give a hint of what once existed. Nearly all the text books used in the career of the poet during his twelve years' course are lost, and with them have gone the particulars of a civilisation probably the most unique and interesting in Europe.

The bardic schools were at no time an unmixed blessing to Ireland. They were non-productive in an economic sense, and as early as the seventh century the working classes felt that these idle multitudes constituted an intolerable drain upon the nation's resources. Keating in his history says that at this time the bardic order contained a third of the men of Ireland, by which he means a third of the free clans or patricians. These quartered themselves from November to May upon the chiefs and farmers. They had also reached an intolerable pitch of insolence. According to the account in the Leabhar

with twenty *dréachts* (stories ?), six metres and other things. The six metres were the six *dians* called *air-sheang*, *midh-sheang*, *iar-sheang*, *air-throm*, *midh-throm*, and *iar-throm*.

[1] Each of the twelve years had its own course of the same nature as the above.

Breac they went about the country in bands carrying with them a silver pot, which the populace named the "pot of avarice," which was attached by nine chains of bronze hung on golden hooks, and which was suspended on the spears of nine poets, thrust through the links at the end of the chains. They then selected some unfortunate victim, and approached in state his homestead, having carefully composed a poem in his laudation. The head poet entering chanted the first verse, and the last poet took it up, until each of the nine had recited his part, whilst all the time the nine best musicians played their sweetest music in unison with the verses, round the pot, into which the unfortunate listener was obliged to throw an ample guerdon of gold and silver. Woe to him indeed, if he refused; a scathing satire would be the result, and sooner than endure the disgrace of this, every one parted to them with a share of his wealth. Aedh mac Ainmirech, the High-king of Ireland, who reigned at the end of the seventh century—the same who afterwards lost his life in the battle of Bolgdún in raising the thrice cursed Boru tribute—"considering them," as Keating puts it, "to be too heavy a burden upon the land of Ireland," determined to banish the whole profession. This was the third attempt to put down the poets, who had always before found a refuge in the northern province when expelled from the others. But now King Aedh [Ae] summoned a great convention of all Ireland at Drum Ceat [Cat] near Limavaddy in the north of Ireland, to deliberate upon several matters of national interest, of which the expulsion of the bards was not the least important. The fate of the Bardic Institution was trembling in the balance, when Columcille, an accomplished bard himself as we have seen, crossed over from Iona with a retinue of 140 clerics, and by his eloquence and great influence succeeded in checking the fury of the exasperated chieftains: the issue of the great convention which lasted for a year and one month, was—so far as the bards were concerned—that their numbers were indeed reduced, but it was agreed that the High-king should retain in his service one chief ollamh, and that the kings of the five provinces, the chiefs of each territory, and the lords of each sub-district should all retain an ollamh of theii own. No other poets except those especially sanctioned were to pursue the poetic calling.

If the bards lost severely in numbers and prestige on this occasion they were in the long run amply compensated for it by their acquiring a new and recognised status in the state. Their unchartered freedom and licentious wanderings were indeed checked, but, on the other hand, they became for the first time the possessors of fixed property and of local stability. Distinct public estates in land were set apart for their maintenance,[1] and they were obliged in return to give public instruction to all comers in the learning of the day, after the manner of university professors. Rathkenry in Meath, and Masree in Cavan are particularly mentioned as bardic colleges then founded, where any of the youth of Ireland could acquire a knowledge of history and of the sciences.[2] The High-king, the provincial kings, and the sub-kings were all obliged by law to set apart a certain portion of land for the poet of the territory, to be held by him and his successors free of rent, and a law was passed making the persons and the property of poets sacred, and giving them right of sanctuary in their own land from all the men of Ireland. At the same time the amount of reward which they were allowed to receive for their poems was legally settled. From this time forward for nearly a thousand years the bardic colleges, as distinct from the ecclesiastical ones, taught poetry, law, and history, and it was they who educated the lawyers, judges, and poets of Ireland.

As far as we can judge the bards continued to flourish in equal power and position with the dignitaries of the Church,

[1] I have seen it stated, but I do not know on what authority, that their income derived from land, in what is the present county of Donegal, was equal to £2,000 a year.

[2] *Scc* Keating's "Forus Feasa" under the reign of Aedh mac Ainmireach.

and their colleges must have been nearly as important institutions as the foundations of the religious orders, until the onslaught of the Northmen reduced the country to such a state that "neither bard, nor philosopher, nor musician," as Keating says, "pursued their wonted profession in the land." It was probably at this time that the carefully observed distinction between the bard and the *filé* broke down, for in later times the words seem to have been regarded as synonymous.

For some time after the Norman conquest the bardic colleges seem to have again suffered eclipse; and, as we have seen, the century that succeeded that invasion appears to have produced fewer poets than any other. But the great Anglo-Norman houses soon became Irishised and adopted Irish bards of their own. There are many incidents recorded in the Irish annals and many stories gathered from other sources which go to show that the importance of the bards as individuals could not have been much diminished during the Anglo-Norman régime. One of them is worth recording. In the beginning of the thirteenth century the steward of the O'Donnell went to Lisadill,[1] near Sligo, to collect rents, and some words passed between him and the great poet Murrough O'Daly, who, unaccustomed to be thwarted in anything, clove the head of the steward with an axe. Then, fearing O'Donnell's vengeance, he fled to Clanrickard and the Norman De Bourgos, and at once addressed a poem to Richard De Burgo, son of William Fitzadelm, in which he states that he, the bard, was used to visit the courts of the English, and to drink wine at the hands of kings and knights, and bishops and abbots. He tells De Bourgo that he has now a chance of making himself illustrious by protecting him, O'Daly of Meath, who now throws himself on his generosity and whose poems demand attention. As for O'Donnell, he had given him small offence.

[1] Lios-an-doill *i.e.*, the "blind man's fort." *See* the preface to O'Donovan's "Satires of Angus," for this story.

"Trifling our quarrel with the man,
A clown to be abusing me,
Me to kill the churl,
Dear God! Is this a cause for enmity?"

De Bourgo accordingly received and protected him, until O'Donnell, coming in furious pursuit, laid waste his country with fire and sword. Fitzadelm submitted, but passed on the poet to the O'Briens of North Munster. But O'Donnell again pursuing with fury, these also submitted, and secretly dispatched the poet to the people of Limerick who received him. O'Donnell hurried on and laid siege to the city, and its inhabitants in terror expelled the poet once more, who was passed on from hand to hand until he came to Dublin. But the people of Dublin, terrified at O'Donnell's threats, sent him away; and he crossed over into Scotland where his fame rose higher than before, and where his poems remained so popular that when the Dean of Lismore in Argyle jotted down nearly four hundred years ago in phonetic spelling a number of poems just as he heard them, they included a disproportionately large number of this O'Daly's,[1] who was afterward known as Murrough the Scotchman. At last in return for some fine laudatory verses upon O'Donnell he was graciously pardoned by that chieftain and returned to his native country.

The Anglo-Normans not only kept bards of their own, but some of themselves also became poets. The story of Silken Thomas and his bard whose verses urged him on to rebellion, is well known. It is curious, too, to find one of the Norman Nugents of Delvin in the sixteenth century making the most perfect classical Irish verses, lamenting his exile from Ireland, the home of *his* ancestors, the Land of Fintan, the old Plain of Ir, the country of Inisfail.

"Loth to Leave, my *fain* eyes swim,
I Part in *Pain* from Erinn.

[1] He preserved eight pieces of O'Daly, who is called Muireach Albanach, and in one place Muireach Lessin Dall (*i.e.*, Lios-an-Doill) O'Daly.

Land of the L*oud* sea-rollers,
PR*ide of* PR*oud* steed-controllers."[1]

After a few generations the Anglo-Normans had completely forgotten Norman-French, and as they never, with few exceptions, learned English, they identified themselves completely with the Irish past, so that amongst the Irish poets we find numbers of Nugents, Englishes, Condons, Cusacks, Keatings, Comyns, and other foreign names.

It was only after the Anglo-Norman government had developed into an English one that the bards began to feel its weight. The slaying of the Welsh bards by Edward is now generally regarded as a political fiction. There is no fiction, however, about the treatment meted out to the Irish ones. The severest acts were passed against them over and over again. The nobles were forbidden to entertain them, in the hope that they might die out or starve, and the Act of Elizabeth alleges one of the usual lying excuses of the Elizabethan period: "Item," it says, "for that those rhymours by their ditties and rhymes made to divers lords and gentlemen in Ireland to the commendation and high praise of extortion, rebellion, rape, ravin, and other injustice, encourage those lords and gentlemen rather to follow those vices than to leave them, and for making of the said rhymes rewards are given by the said lords and gentlemen, (let) for abolishing of so heinous an abuse, orders be taken." Orders were taken, and taken so thoroughly that O'Brien, Earl of Thomond, obliged to enforce them against the bards, hanged three distinguished poets, "for which abominable, treacherous act," say the "Four Masters," "the earl was satirised and denounced." I find a northern bard about this time, the close of the sixteenth

[1] "Diombuaidh *Triall*, o Thulchaibh Fáil
Diombuaidh *Iath* Eireann d'fhágbháil,
Iath mhilis na *MBeann* MBeachach,
Inis na *N-Eang* N-Óig-eachach."

Deibhidh metre. *See* Hardiman, vol. ii. p. 226.

century, thus lamenting the absence of his patron, Aedh [Ae] Mac Aonghasa :—

> "If a **S***age* of **S**ong should be
> In the *wage* of ***C****ourt* or **K**ing.
> HA ! the **G**allows **G**uards the **WAY.**
> AH ! since **AE** from *port* took wing." [1]

Spenser the poet was not slow in finding out what a power his Irish rivals were in the land, and he at once set himself to malign and blacken them. "There are," he writes, "amongst the Irish a certain kind of people called bards, which are to them instead of poets,"—the insinuation is that the bards are not real poets !—"the which are had in so high regard and estimation among them, that none dare displease them for fear to run into reproach through their offence, and to be made infamous in the mouths of all men." On which, Eudoxus, his friend, is made to remark innocently that he had always thought that poets were to be rather encouraged than put down. "Yes," answers Spenser, "they should be encouraged when they desire honour and virtue, but," he goes on, "these Irish bards are for the most part of another mind, and so far from instructing young men in moral discipline, that whomsoever they find to be most licentious of life, most bold and lawlesse in his doings, most dangerous and desperate in all parts of disobedience and rebellious disposition, him they set up and glorify in their rhythmes, him they praise to the people and to young men make an example to follow."

The allegation that the bards praised what was licentious is an untruth on the part of the great poet. Few English Elizabethans, once they passed over into Ireland, seem to have been able to either keep faith or tell truth ; there was never

[1] "Dá *ndimghiodh duine* re dán
Fá *chiniodh* don *chuire* ríogh
Do bhiadh *croch roimhe* ar gach *raon*
Och! gan *Aodh Doire* dar ndíon."

Rannaigheacht Mór metre. From a MS. poem.

such a thoroughly dishonourable race, or one so utterly devoid of all moral sense, as the Irish "statesmen" of that period. The real reason why Spenser, as an undertaker, blackens the character of the Irish poets is not because their poems were licentious—which they were not—but because, as he confesses later on, they are "tending for the most part to the hurt of the English or [the] maintenance of their owne lewde libertie, they being most desirous thereof."

Spenser's ignorant and self-contradictory criticism on the merits of the Irish bards has often been quoted as if it constituted a kind of hall-mark for them! "Tell me, I pray you," said his friend, "have they any art in their compositions, or be they anything wittie or wellmannered as poems should be?"

"Yea, truly," says Spenser, "I have caused divers of them to be translated unto me, that I might understand them, and surely they savoured of sweet art and good invention, but skilled not in the goodly ornaments of poesie, yet were they sprinkled with some pretty flowers of their natural device, which gave good grace and comeliness unto them; the which it is a great pity to see abused to the gracing of wickedness and vice, which with good usage would serve to adorn and beautify virtue."

The gentle poet is here almost copying the words of the Act, which perhaps he himself helped to inspire, according to which the bardic poems are in praise of "extortion, rebellion, rape, ravin, and other injustice." I have, however, read hundreds of the poems of the sixteenth and seventeenth centuries, but have never come across a single syllable in laudation of either "extortion, rape, ravin, or other injustice," but numerous poems inciting to what the Act calls "rebellion," and what Spenser terms "the hurt of the English and the maintenance of their owne lewde libertie."

It would be difficult to overrate the importance of the colleges of the hereditary bards and the influence they exercised in the life of the sixteenth century. They fairly reflected public opinion, and they also helped to make it what it was. There is a great difference between their poems and the *memoria technicha* verses of the ancient ollamhs, whose historical and genealogical poems, which they composed in their official capacity, are crowded with inorganic phrases and "chevilles" of all kinds. The sixteenth-century poet was a man of wit and learning, and frequently a better and more clear-seeing statesman than his chief, who was in matters of policy frequently directed by his bard's advice. They certainly had more national feeling than any other class in Ireland, and were less the slaves of circumstances or of mere local accidents, for they traversed the island from end to end, were equally welcome north, south, east, and west, and had unrivalled opportunities for becoming acquainted with the trend of public affairs, and with political movements.

Most people, owing to their comparative neglect of Irish history, seem to be of opinion that the bards were harpers, or at least musicians of some sort. But they were nothing of the kind. The popular conception of the bard with the long white beard and the big harp is grotesquely wrong. The bards were verse-makers, pure and simple, and they were no more musicians than the poet laureate of England. Their business was to construct their poems after the wonderful and complex models of the schools, and when—as only sometimes happened—they wrote a eulogy or panegyric on a patron, and brought it to him, they introduced along with themselves a harper and possibly a singer to whom they had taught their poem, and in the presence of their patron to the sound of the harp, the only instrument allowed to be touched on such occasions, the poem was solemnly recited or sung. The real name of the musician was not *bard*—the bard was a verse-maker—but *oirfideadh* [errh-fid-yă], and the musicians, though a numerous and honourable class, were absolutely distinct from the bards and *filés*. It was only after the complete break-up of the Gaelic polity, after the wars of Cromwell and of William, that the verse-maker merges in the musician, and the harper and the bard become fused in one, as was the case with Carolan, commonly called the last of the bards, but whom his patron, O'Conor of Belanagare, calls in his obituary of him, not a *bard*, but an *oirfideadh*.

Down to the close of the sixteenth century and during the greater part of the seventeenth, verse, with few exceptions, continued to be made in the classical metres of Ireland, by specially trained poets, who did not go outside these metres. In the ensuing century the classical metres began to be discarded and a wonderful and far-reaching change took place, which shall be made the subject of a future chapter. We must now proceed to examine a species of popular poetry which flourished during all this period side by side with the bardic schools, although no trace remains to-day of its origin or its authors. This is the so-called Ossianic poetry.

CHAPTER XXXVII

THE OSSIANIC POEMS

SIDE by side with the numerous prose sagas which fall under the title of "Fenian," and which we have already examined in Chapter XXIX., there exists an enormous mass of poems, chiefly narrative, of a minor epic type, or else semi-dramatic épopées, usually introduced by a dialogue between St. Patrick and the poet Ossian. Ossian[1] was the son of Finn mac Cúmhail, vulgarly "Cool," and he was fabled to have lived in Tír na n-óg [T'yeer na nogue], the country of the ever-young, the Irish Elysium, for three hundred years, thus surviving all his Fenian contemporaries, and living to hold colloquy with St. Patrick. The so-called Ossianic poems are extraordinarily numerous, and were they all collected would probably (between those preserved in Scotch-Gaelic and in Irish) amount to some 80,000 lines. My friend, the late Father James Keegan, of St. Louis, once estimated them at 100,000. The most of them, in the form in which they have come down to us at the present day, seem to have been composed in rather loose metres, chiefly imitations of Deibhidh and Rannaigheacht mór, and they were

[1] In Irish Oisín, pronounced "Esheen," or "Ussheen." However, the Scotch Gaelic form has, thanks to the genius of Macpherson, so overshadowed the Irish one that it may be allowed to remain.

even down to our fathers' time exceedingly popular both in Ireland and the Scotch Highlands, in which latter country Iain Campbell, the great folk-lorist, made the huge collection which he called Leabhar na Féinne, or the Book of the Fenians.

Some of the Ossianic poems relate the exploits of the Fenians, others describe conflicts between members of that body and worms, wild beasts and dragons, others fights with monsters and with strangers come from across the sea; others detail how Finn and his companions suffered from the enchantments of wizards and the efforts made to release them, one enumerates the Fenians who fell at Cnoc-an-áir, another gives the names of about three hundred of the Fenian hounds, another gives Ossian's account of his three hundred years in the Land of the Young and his return, many more consist largely of semi-humorous dialogues between the saint and the old warrior; another is called Ossian's madness; another is Ossian's account of the battle of Gabhra, which made an end of the Fenians, and so on.[1]

The Lochlannachs, or Norsemen, figure very largely in these poems, and it is quite evident that most of them—at least in the modern form in which we now have them—are post-Norse productions. The fact that the language in which they have for the most part come down to us is popular and modern, does not prove much one way or the other, for these small epics which, more than any other part of Irish literature, were handed down from father to son and propagated orally, have had their language unconsciously adjusted from age to age, so as to leave them intelligible to their hearers. As a consequence the metres have in many places also suffered, and the old Irish system, which required a certain number of

[1] Standish Hayes O'Grady, in the third vol. of the Ossianic Society, gives the names of thirty-five of these poems, amounting to nearly 11,000 lines. The Ossianic Society printed about 6,000 lines. The Franciscans have shown me a MS. with over 10,000 lines, none of which has been printed.

syllables in each line, has shown signs of fusing gradually with the new Irish system, which only requires so many accented syllables.

It is, however, perfectly possible—as has been supposed by, I think, Mr. Nutt and others—that after the terrible shock given to the island by the Northmen, this people usurped in our ballads the place of some older mythical race; and Professor Rhys was, I believe, at one time of opinion that Lochlann, as spoken of in these ballads, originally meant merely the country of lochs and seas, and that the Lochlanners were a submarine mythical people, like the Fomorians.

The spirit of banter with which St. Patrick and the Church are treated, and in which the fun just stops short of irreverence, is a mediæval, not a primitive, trait, more characteristic, thinks Mr. Nutt, of the twelfth than of any succeeding century. We may remember the inimitable felicity with which that great English-speaking Gael, Sir Walter Scott, has caught this Ossianic tone in the lines which Hector McIntyre repeats for Oldbuck—

> "Patrick the psalm-singer,
> Since you will not listen to one of my stories,
> Though you have never heard it before,
> I am sorry to tell you
> You are little better than an ass;"

to which the saint, to the infinite contempt of the unbelieving antiquary, is made to respond—

> "Upon my word, son of Fingal,
> While I am warbling the psalms,
> The clamour of your old woman's tales
> Disturbs my devotional exercises."

Whereat the heated Ossian replies—

> "Dare you compare your psalms
> To the tales of the bare-armed Fenians,
> I shall think it no great harm
> To wring your bald head from your shoulders."

Here, however, is a real specimen from the Irish, which will give some idea of the style of dialogue between the pair. St. Patrick, with exaggerated episcopal severity, having Ossian three-quarters starved, blind, and wholly at his mercy, desires him to speak no more of Finn or of the Fenians.

"OSSIAN.

"Alas, O Patrick, I did think that God would not be angered thereat; I think long, and it is a great woe to me, not to speak of the way of Finn of the Deeds.

"PATRICK.

"Speak not of Finn nor of the Fenians, for the Son of God will be angry with thee for it, he would never let thee into his court and he would not send thee the bread of each day.

"OSSIAN.

"Were I to speak of Finn and of the Fenians, between us two, O Patrick the new, but only not to speak loud, he would never hear us mentioning him.

"PATRICK.

"Let nothing whatever be mentioned by thee excepting the offering of God, or if thou talkest continually of others, thou, indeed, shalt not go to the house of the saints.

"OSSIAN.

"I will, O Patrick, do His will. Of Finn or of the Fenians I will not talk, for fear of bringing anger upon them, O Cleric, if it is God's wont to be angry."

In another poem St. Patrick denounces with all the rigour of a new reformer.

"PATRICK.

"Finn is in hell in bonds, 'the pleasant man who used to bestow gold,' in penalty of his disobedience to God, he is now in the house of pain in sorrow. . . .

"Because of the amusement [he had with] the hounds and for attending the (bardic) schools each day, and because he took no heed of God, Finn of the Fenians is in bonds. . . .

"Misery attend thee, old man, who speakest words of madness; God is better for one hour than all the Fenians of Erin.

"OSSIAN.

"O Patrick of the crooked crozier, who makest me that impertinent answer, thy crozier would be in atoms were Oscar present.

"Were my son Oscar and God hand to hand on Knock-na-veen, if I saw my son down it is then I would say that God was a strong man.

"How could it be that God and his clerics could be better men than Finn, the chief King of the Fenians, the generous one who was without blemish?

"All the qualities that you and your clerics say are according to the rule of the King of the Stars, Finn's Fenians had them all, and they must be now stoutly seated in God's heaven.

"Were there a place above or below better than heaven, 'tis there Finn would go, and all the Fenians he had. . . .

"Patrick, inquire of God whether he recollects when the Fenians were alive, or hath he seen east or west, men their equal in the time of fight.

"Or hath he seen in his own country, though high it be above our heads, in conflict, in battle, or in might, a man who was equal to Finn?

"PATRICK.

(*Exhausted with controversy and curious for Ossian's story.*)

"Ossian sweet to me thy voice,
Now blessings choice on the soul of Finn!
But tell to us how many deer
Were slain at Slieve-na-man finn.

"OSSIAN.

"We the Fenians never used to tell untruth, a lie was never attributed to us; by truth and the strength of our hands we used to come safe out of every danger.

"There never sat cleric in church, though melodiously ye may think they chant psalms, more true to his word than the Fenians, the men who shrank never from fierce conflicts.

. . . . . .

"O Patrick, where was thy God the day the two came across the sea who carried off the queen of the King of Lochlann in ships, by whom many fell here in conflict.

"Or when Tailc mac Treoin arrived, the man who put great slaughter on the Fenians; 'twas not by God the hero fell, but by Oscar in the presence of all.

"Many a battle victory and contest were celebrated by the Fenians of Innisfail. I never heard that any feat was performed by the king of saints, or that *he* reddened his hand.

"PATRICK.

"Let us cease disputing on both sides, thou withered old man who art devoid of sense; understand that God dwells in heaven of the orders, and Finn and his hosts are all in pain.

"OSSIAN.

"Great, then, would be the shame for God not to release Finn from the shackles of pain; for if God Himself were in bonds my chief would fight on his behalf.

"Finn never suffered in his day any one to be in pain or difficulty without redeeming him by silver or gold or by battle and fight, until he was victorious.

"It is a good claim I have against your God, me to be amongst these clerics as I am, without food, without clothing or music, without bestowing gold on bards,

"Without battling, without hunting, without Finn, without courting generous women, without sport, without sitting in my place as was my due, without learning feats of agility and conflict, etc."

Many of these poems contain lyrical passages of great beauty. Here, as a specimen, is Ossian's description of the things in which Finn used to take delight. It is a truly lyrical passage, in the very best style, rhyme, rhythm and assonance are all combined with a most rich vocabulary of words expressive of sounds nearly impossible to translate into English. It might be thus attempted in verse, though not quite in the metre of the original. Finn's pursuits as depicted here by Ossian show him to have been a lover of nature, and are quite in keeping with his poem on Spring; his are the tastes of one of Matthew Arnold's "Barbarians" glorified.

"FINN'S PASTIMES.

"Oh, croaking Patrick, I curse your tale.
Is the King of the Fenians in hell this night?
The heart that never was seen to quail,
That feared no danger and felt no spite.[1]

[1] In the original Ossian asks—

"An éagcóir nár mhaith le Dia
Ór a's biadh do thabhairt do neach?
'Nior dhiultaigh Fionn treun ná truagh
Ifrionn fuar má 's é a theach."

What kind of a God can be yours, to grudge
  Bestowing of food on him, giving of gold?
Finn never refused either prince or drudge;
  Can his doom be in hell in the house of cold.[1]

The desire of my hero who feared no foe
  Was to listen all day to Drumderrig's sound,
To sleep by the roar of the Assaroe,
  And to follow the dun deer round and round.

The warbling of blackbirds in Letter Lee,
  The strand where the billows of Ruree fall,
The bellowing ox upon wild Moy-mee,
  The lowing of calves upon Glen-da-vaul.

The blast of a horn around Slieve Grot,
  The bleat of a fawn upon Cua's plain,
The sea-birds scream in a lonely spot,
  The croak of the raven above the slain,

The wash of the waves on his bark afar,
  The yelp of the pack as they round Drumliss,
The baying of Bran upon Knock-in-ar,
  The murmur of fountains below Slieve Mis.

The call of Oscar upon the chase,[2]
  The tongue of the hounds on the Fenians' plain,
Then a seat with the men of the bardic race,
  —Of these delights was my hero fain.

But generous Oscar's supreme desire,
  Was the maddening clashing of shield on shield,

[1] Irish writers always describe Hell as cold, not hot. This is so even in Keating. The "cold flag of hell."

[2] In the original—

"Glaodh Oscair ag dul do sheilg
  Gotha gadhar ar leirg na bh Fiann
Bheith 'na shuidhe ameasg na ndámh
  Ba h-é sin de ghnáth a mhian.

Mian de mhianaibh Oscair fhéil
  Bheith ag éisteacht re béim sgiath,
Bheith i gcath ag cosgar cnámh
  Ba h-é sin de ghnáth a mhian."

And the hewing of bones in the battle ire,
And the crash and the joy of the stricken field."[1]

In entire accordance with this enthusiastic love of nature is Ossian's delightful address to the blackbird of Derrycarn, a piece which was a great favourite with the scribes of the last century.[2] Interpenetrated with the same almost sensuous

[1] Literally: "O Patrick, woful is the tale that the Fenian king should be in bonds, a heart devoid of spite or hatred, a heart stern in maintaining battles.

"Is it an injustice at which God is not pleased to bestow gold and food on any one? Finn never refused either the strong or the wretched, although cold Hell is his house.

"It was the desire of the son of Cúmhal of the noble mien to listen to the sound of Drumderg, to sleep by the stream of the Assaroe, and to chase the deer of Galway of the bays.

"The warbling of the blackbird of Letter Lee, the wave of Ruree [Dundrum Bay in the County Down] lashing the shore, the bellowing of the ox of Moy Meen, the lowing of the calf of Glendavaul.

"The cry of the hunting of Slieve Grot, the noise of the fawns around Slieve Cua, the scream of the seagulls over yonder Irris, the cry of the ravens over the host.

"The tossing of the hulls of the barks by the waves, the yell of the hounds at Drumlish, the voice of Bran at Knockinar, the murmur of the streams around Slieve Mis.

"The call of Oscar, going to the chase, the cry of the hounds at Lerg-na-veen—(then) to be sitting amongst the bards: that was his desire constantly.

"A desire of the desires of generous Oscar, was to be listening to the crashing of shields, to be in the battle at the hewing of bones: that was ever *his* desire." (*See* Ossianic Society, vol. iv. The Colloquy between Ossian and Patrick.)

[2] Printed by O'Flanagan in the "Transactions of the Gaelic Society," 1808, and translated by Dr. Sigerson in his "Bards of the Gael and Gall." I cannot refrain from the pleasure of quoting the following verses from his beautiful translation:—

"The tuneful tumult of that bird,
The belling deer on ferny steep:
This welcome in the dawn he heard,
These soothed at eve his sleep.

Dear to him the wind-loved heath,
The whirr of wings, the rustling brake;
Dear the murmuring glens beneath,
And sob of Droma's lake.

The cry of hounds at early morn,
The pattering deer, the pebbly creek,
The cuckoo's call, the sounding horn,
The swooping eagle's shriek."

delight at the sights and sounds of nature, are the following verses which the Scotsman, Dean Macgregor, wrote down—probably from the recitation of a wandering harper or poet—some three hundred and eighty years ago.

"Sweet is the voice in the land of gold,[1]
And sweeter the music of birds that soar,
When the cry of the heron is heard on the wold,
And the waves break softly on Bundatrore.

Down floats on the murmuring of the breeze
The call of the cuckoo from Cossahun,
The blackbird is warbling amongst the trees,
And soft is the kiss of the warming sun.

The cry of the eagle at Assaroe
O'er the court of Mac Morne to me is sweet;
And sweet is the cry of the bird below,
Where the wave and the wind and the tall cliff meet.

Finn mac Cool is the father of me,
Whom seven battalions of Fenians fear,
When he launches his hounds on the open lea,
Grand is their cry as they rouse the deer."

Caoilte [Cweeltya] too, the third great Fenian poet, was as impressionable to the moods of nature as his friends Ossian and Finn. Compare with the foregoing poems his lay on the Isle of Arran, in Scotland.[2]

THE ISLE OF ARRAN.

"Arran of the many stags, the sea inpinges upon her very shoulders! An isle in which whole companies were fed, and with ridges among which blue spears are reddened.

"Skittish deer are on her pinnacles, soft blackberries on her

---

[1] *See* p. 59 of the Gaelic part of the book of the Dean of Lismore. The first verse runs thus in modern Gaelic:—

"Binn guth duine i dtir an óir,
Binn an glór chanaid na h-eóin,
Binn an nuallan a gnidh an chorr,
Binn an tonn i mBun-da-treóir."

[2] *See* "Silva Gadelica," p. 109 of the English, p. 102 of the Irish volume. I retain Mr. O'Grady's beautiful translation of this and the following piece.

waving heather; cool water there is in her rivers, and musk upon her russet oaks.[1]

"Greyhounds there were in her and beagles, blackberries and sloes of the dark blackthorn, dwellings with their backs set close against her woods, while the deer fed scattered by her oaken thickets.

"A crimson crop grew on her rocks, in all her glades a faultless grass; over her crags affording friendly refuge leaping went on, and fawns were skipping.

"Smooth were her level spots, fat her wild swine, cheerful her fields. . . . her nuts hung on the boughs of her forest hazels, and there was sailing of long galleys past her.

"Right pleasant their condition, all, when the fair weather set in. Under her river-banks trouts lie; the seagulls wheeling round her grand cliff answer one the other—at every fitting time delectable is Arran!"

In another poem that Caoilte is fabled to have made after he met and consorted with St. Patrick is a vivid description of a freezing night as it appeared to a hunter. A great frost and heavy snow had fallen upon the whole country, so that the russet branches of the forest were twisted together, and men could no longer travel. "A fitting time it is now," said Caoilte, "for wild stags and for does to seek the topmost points of hills and rocks; a timely season for salmons to betake them into cavities of the banks," and he uttered a lay.

"Cold the winter is, the wind is risen, the high-couraged unquelled stag is on foot, bitter cold to-night the whole mountain is, yet for all that the ungovernable stag is belling.[2]

---

[1] "Oighe *baetha* ar a bennaib
Monainn *maetha* ar a mongaib,
Uisce fuar ina *h-aibhnib*,
Mes ar a *dairghib* donnaib."

Note the exquisite metre of this poem of which the above verse is a specimen.

[2] This, like most of the couple of thousand verses scattered throughout the "Colloquy of the Ancients," is in *Deibhidh* metre, which would thus run in English :—

"Cold the Winter, cold the Wind,
The Raging stag is Ravin'd,
Though in one Flag the Floodgates cling,
The Steaming Stag is belling."

"The deer of Slievecarn of the gatherings commits not his side to the ground; no less than he, the stag of frigid Echtgé's summit who catches the chorus of the wolves.

"I, Caoilte, with Brown Diarmuid,[1] and with keen, light-footed Oscar; we too in the nipping nights' waning end, would listen to the music of the [wolf] pack.

"But well the red deer sleeps that with his hide to the bulging rock lies stretched, hidden as though beneath the country's surface, all in the latter end of chilly night.

"To-day I am an aged ancient, and but a scant few men I know; once on time, though, on a cold and icebound morning I used to vibrate a sharp javelin hardily.

"To Heaven's King I offer thanks, to Mary Virgin's Son as well; often and often I imposed silence on [daunted] a whole host, whose plight to-night is very cold [*i.e.*, who are all dead now]."

It is curious that in the more modern Ossianic pieces, such as the scribes of the seventeenth and eighteenth centuries delighted in transcribing, there is little mention made of Caoilte, and the complaints about surviving the Fenians and being vexed by the clerics are more usually put into the mouth of Ossian.

Here is one of the moans of Ossian in his old age, when fallen on evil times, and thwarted at every turn by St. Patrick and his monks.

"Long was last night in cold Elphin,[2]
More long is to-night on its weary way,
Though yesterday seemed to me long and ill,
Yet longer still was this dreary day.

[1] This was Diarmuid of the Love-spot, who eloped with Gráinne, and was killed by the wild boar, from whom the Campbells of Scotland claim descent, as is alluded to in Flora Mac Ivor's song in "Waverley":—

"Ye sons of Brown Diarmuid who slew the wild boar."

[2] "Is fada anocht i n-Ailfinn,
Is fada linn an oidhche aréir,
An lá andhiu cidh fada dham,
Ba leór-fhad an lá andé.

See p. 208 of my "Religious Songs of Connacht" for the original of this poem, which I copied from a MS. in the Belfast Museum. The Dean of Lismore in Argyle jotted this poem down in phonetic spelling nearly

And long for me is each hour new born,
  Stricken, forlorn, and smit with grief
For the hunting lands and the Fenian bands,
  And the long-haired, generous, Fenian chief.

I hear no music, I find no feast,
  I slay no beast from a bounding steed,
I bestow no gold, I am poor and old,
  I am sick and cold, without wine or mead.

I court no more, and I hunt no more,
  These were before my strong delight,
I cannot slay, and I take no prey:
  Weary the day and long the night.

No heroes come in their war array,
  No game I play, there is nought to win;
I swim no stream with my men of might,
  Long is the night in cold Elphin.

Ask, O Patrick, thy God of grace,
  To tell me the place he will place me in,
And save my soul from the Ill One's might,
  For long is to-night in cold Elphin."

There is a considerable thread of narrative running through these poems and connecting them in a kind of series, so that several of them might be divided into the various books of a Gaelic epic of the Odyssic type, containing instead of the wanderings and final restoration of Ulysses, the adventures and final destruction of the Fenians, except that the books would be rather more disjointed. There is, moreover, splendid

four hundred years ago, but the name of Elphin, being strange to him, he took the words to be *na neulla fúm*, "the clouds round me," *ni nelli fiym* he spells it. Elphin is an episcopal seat in the county Roscommon, where St. Patrick abode for a while when in Connacht. I often heard in that county the story of Ossian meeting St. Patrick when drawing stones in Elphin, but always thought that the people of Roscommon localised the legend in their own county. But the discovery of the Belfast copy—and I believe there is another one in the British Museum—shows that this was not so, and the Dean of Lismore's book proves the antiquity of the legend. That Ailfinn (Elphin) was the original word is proved by rhyming to *linn*, *sinn* and *Finn*, which *Fiym* (= fúm) could not do.

material for an ample epic in the division between the Fenians of Munster and Connacht and the gradual estrangement of the High-king, leading up to the fatal battle of Gabhra; but the material for this last exists chiefly in prose texts, not in the Ossianic lays. It is very strange and very unfortunate that notwithstanding the literary activity of Gaelic Ireland before and during the penal times, no Keating, or Comyn, or Curtin ever attempted to redact the Ossianic poems and throw them into that epic form into which they would so easily and naturally have fitted. These pieces appear to me of even greater value than the Red Branch sagas, as elucidating the natural growth and genesis of an epic, for the Irish progressed just up to the point of possessing a large quantity of stray material, minor episodes versified by anonymous long-forgotten folk-poets; but they never produced a mind critical enough to reduce this mass to order, coherence, and stability, and at the same time creative enough to itself supply the necessary lacunæ. Were it not that so much light has by this time been thrown upon the natural genesis of ancient national epics, one might be inclined to lay down the theory that the Irish had evolved a scheme of their own, peculiar to themselves, and different altogether from the epic, a scheme in which the same characters figure in a group of allied poems and romances, each of which, like one of Tennyson's idylls, is perfect in itself, and not dependent upon the rest, a system which might be taken to be a natural result of the impatient Celtic temperament which could not brook the restraints of an epic.

The Ossianic lays are almost the only narrative poems which exist in the language, for although lyrical, elegiac, and didactic poetry abounds, the Irish never produced, except in the case of the Ossianic épopées, anything of importance in a narrative and ballad form, anything, for instance, of the nature of the glorious ballad poetry of the Scotch Lowlands.

The Ossianic metres, too, are the eminently epic ones of Ireland. It was a great pity, and to my thinking a great mistake, for Archbishop Mac Hale not to have used them in his translation of Homer, instead of attempting it in the metre of Pope's Iliad—one utterly unknown to native Ireland.

I have already observed that great producers of literature as the Irish always were—until this century—they never developed a drama. The nearest approach to such a thing is in these Ossianic poems. The dialogue between St. Patrick and Ossian—of which there is, in most of the poems, either more or less—is quite dramatic in its form. Even the reciters of the present day appear to feel this, and I have heard the censorious self-satisfied tone of Patrick, and the querulous vindictive whine of the half-starved old man, reproduced with considerable humour by a reciter. But I think it nearly certain—though I cannot prove it [1]—that in former days there was real acting and a dialogue between two persons, one representing the saint and the other the old pagan. It was from a less promising beginning than this that the drama of Æschylus developed. But nothing could develope in later Ireland. Everything, time after time, was arrested in its growth. Again and again the tree of Irish literature put forth fresh blossoms, and before they could fully expand they were nipped off. The conception of bringing the spirit of Paganism and of Christianity together in the persons of the last great poet and warrior of the one, and the first great saint of the other, was truly dramatic in its conception, and the spirit and humour with which it has been carried out in the pieces which have come down to us are a strong presumption that under happier circumstances something great would have developed from it. If any one is still found to repeat Macaulay's hackneyed taunt about the Irish race never having produced a great poem, let him ask himself if it is likely that a country, where, for a hundred years after Aughrim and the Boyne, teachers who for long before that

[1] I once saw a letter in an Irish-American paper by some one whose name I forget, in which he alleged that in his youth he had actually seen the Ossianic lays thus acted.

had been in danger, were systematically knocked on the head, or sent to a jail for teaching; where children were seen learning their letters with chalk on their father's tombstones—other means being denied them; where the possession of a manuscript might lead to the owner's death or imprisonment, so that many valuable books were buried in the ground, or hidden to rot in walls[1]—whether such a country were a soil on which an epic or anything else could flourish. How, in the face of all this, the men of the seventeenth and eighteenth centuries preserved in manuscript so much of the Ossianic poetry as they did, and even rewrote or redacted portions of it, as Michael Comyn is said to have done to "Ossian in the Land of the Ever-Young," is to me nothing short of amazing.

Of the authorship of the Ossianic poems nothing is known. In the Book of Leinster are three short pieces ascribed to Ossian himself, and five to Finn, and other old MSS. contain poems ascribed to Caoilte, Ossian's companion and fellow survivor, and to Fergus, another son of Finn; but of the great mass of the many thousand lines which we have in seventeenth and eighteenth century MSS. there is not much which is placed in Ossian's mouth as first hand, the pieces as I have said generally beginning with a dialogue, from which Ossian proceeds to recount his tale. But this dramatic form of the lay shows that no pretence was kept up of Ossian's being the singer of his own exploits.[2] From the paucity of the pieces attributed to him in the oldest MSS. it is probable that the Gaelic race only gradually singled him out as their typical pagan poet, instead of Fergus or Caoilte or any other of his

[1] Like the Book of Lismore and others. *See* Sullivan's preface to O'Curry's "Manners and Customs."

[2] "Ich vermuthe," says Windisch ("Irische Texte," I. i. p. 63), "dass Ossin (Ossian) auf dieser Wege zu einer Dichtergestalt geworden ist. Die Gedichte die ihm in der Sage in den Mund gelegt werden, galten als sein Werk und wurden allmählig zum Typus einer ganzen Literaturgattung." But the same should hold equally true of Caoilte, in whose mouth an equal number of poems are placed.

alleged contemporaries, just as they singled out his father Finn, as the typical pagan leader of their race; and it is likely that a large part of our Ossianic lay and literature is post-Danish, while the great mass of the Red Branch saga is in its birth many centuries anterior to the Norsemen's invasion.[1]

[1] The following Ossianic poems have been published in the "Transactions of the Ossianic Society." In vol. iii., 1857, "The Lamentation of Ossian after the Fenians," 852 lines. In vol. iv., 1859, "The Dialogue between Ossian and Patrick," 684 lines; "The Battle of Cnoc an Áir," 336 lines; "The Lay of Meargach," 904 lines; "The Lay of Meargach's Wife," 388 lines; "The names of those fallen at Cnoc an Áir," 76 lines; "The Chase of Loch Léin," 328 lines; "The Lay of Ossian in the Land of the Ever-Young," 636 lines; and some smaller pieces. Vol. vi., 1861, contains: "The Chase of Slieve Guilleann," 228 lines; "The Chase of Slieve Fuaid," 788 lines; "The Chase of Glennasmóil," 364 lines; "The Hunt of the Fenians on Sleive Truim," 316 lines; "The Chase of Slieve-na-mon," 64 lines; "The Chase of the Enchanted Pigs of Angus of the Boyne" [son of the Dagda], 280 lines; "The Hunt on the borders of Loch Derg," 80 lines; "The Adventures of the Great Fool" [which, however, is not an Ossianic poem], 632 lines.

I have in my own possession copies of several other Ossianic poems, one of which, "The Lay of Dearg," in Deibhidh metre, consisting of 300 lines, is ascribed to Fergus, Finn's poet, not to Ossian.

"Is mé Feargus, file Fhinn
De gnáith-fhéinn Fhinn mhic Cúmhail,
O thásg na bhfear sin nár lag
Trian a ngaisge ni inneósad."

In the library of the Franciscans' Convent in Dublin there is a seventeenth-century collection of Ossianic poems, all in regular classical metres, containing, as I have computed, not less than 10,000 lines. Not one of these poems has been, so far as I know, ever published. The poems printed by the Ossianic Society are not in the classical metres, though I suspect many of them were originally so composed, but they have become corrupted passing from mouth to mouth.

CHAPTER XXXVIII

THE LAST OF THE CLASSIC POETS

THE first half of the seventeenth century saw an extraordinary re-awakening of the Irish literary spirit. This was the more curious because it was precisely at this period that the old Gaelic polity with its tribal system, brehon law, hereditary bards, and all its other supports, was being upheaved by main force and already beginning to totter to its ruin. This was the period when to aggravate what was already to the last degree bitter—the struggle for the soil and racial feuds—a third disastrous ingredient, polemics, stept in, and inflamed the minds of the opposing parties, with the additional fanaticism of religious hatred. Yet whether it is that their works have been better preserved to us than those of any other century, or whether the very nearness of the end inspired them to double exertions, certain it is that the seventeenth century, and especially the first half of it, produced amongst the Irish a number of most gifted men of letters. Of these the so-called Four Masters, Seathrún or Geoffrey Keating, Father Francis O'Mulloy, Lughaidh [Lewy] O'Clery, and Duald Mac Firbis were the most important of the purely Irish prose writers, whilst Phillip O'Sullivan Beare, Father Ward, and Father Colgan, John Lynch (Bishop of Killala), Luke Wadding, and Peter Lombard (Archbishop of Armagh), reflected credit upon their native country by their scholarship, and elucidated its history chiefly through the medium of Latin, as did Ussher and Sir James Ware, two great scholars of the same period produced by the Pale.

The century opened with an outburst of unexpected vigour on the part of the old school of Irish classical bards, over whose head the sword was then suspended, and whose utter destruction, though they knew it not, was now rapidly approaching. This outburst was occasioned by Teig mac Dairé,[1] the ollamh or chief poet of Donough O'Brien, fourth Earl of Thomond, (whose star, thanks to English influence, was at that time in the ascendant), making little of and disparaging in elaborate verse the line of Eremon,[2] and the reigning families of Meath, Connacht, Leinster, and Ulster, whilst exalting the kings of the line of Eber, of whom the O'Briens were at that time the greatest family. The form this poem took was an attack upon the poems of Torna Eigeas, a poet who flourished soon after the year 400, and who was tutor to Niall of the Nine Hostages, but whose alleged poems I have not noticed, not believing those attributed to him to be genuine, as they contain distinct Christian allusions, and as the language does not seem particularly antique. The bards, however, accepted these pieces as the real work of Torna, and Teig mac Dairé now attacks him on account of his partiality for the Eremonian Niall one thousand two hundred years before, and argues that he had done wrong, and that Eber, as the elder son of Milesius, should have had the precedency over Ir and Eremon, the younger children, and that consequently the princes of Munster, who were Eberians, should take precedency of the O'Nialls, O'Conors, and other Eremonians of the Northern provinces, and of Leinster. Teig asserts that it

[1] His real name was Mac Brodin, "Daré" or Dairé being his father's name.

[2] *See* above, p. 64.

was Eber or Heber, son of Milesius, from whom Ireland was called Hiber-nia. This poem, which contained about one hundred and fifty lines, began with the words *Olc do thagrais a Thorna*, "Ill hast thou argued, O Torna," and was immediately taken up and answered by Lughaidh [Lewy] O'Clery, the ollamh of the O'Donnells, in a poem containing three hundred and forty lines, beginning "O Teig, revile not Torna." To this Teig replied in a piece of six hundred and eighty-eight lines, beginning *Eist-se a Lughaidh rem' labhradh*, "Listen to my speech, O Lewy," and was again immediately answered in a poem of about a thousand lines by O'Clery, beginning, *Do chuala ar thagrais a Thaidhg*, "I have heard all that thou hast argued, O Teig." In this poem O'Clery collects such facts as he can find in history and in ancient authors, to prove that the Eremonians had always been considered superior to the Eberians in past ages. This called forth another rejoinder from his opponent of one hundred and twenty-four lines, beginning *A Lughaidh labhram go séimh*, "Let us speak courteously, O Lewy," which was in its turn answered by O'Clery in a poem beginning *Ná broisd mise a Mhic Dhaire*, "Provoke me not, O son of Dairé."

By this time the attention of the whole Irish literary world had been centred upon this curious dispute, and on the attacks and rejoinders of these leading poets representing the two great races of Northern and Southern Ireland respectively. Soon the hereditary poets of the other great Gaelic houses joined in, as their own descent or inclination prompted. Fearfeasa O'Cainte, Torlough O'Brien, and Art Og O'Keefe were the principal supporters of Teig mac Daire and the Southern Eberians, while Hugh O'Donnell, Robert Mac Arthur, Baoghalach ruadh Mac Egan, Anluan Mac Egan, John O'Clery, and Mac Dermot of Moylurg, defended Lewy and the Northern Eremonians. For many years the conflict raged, and the verses of both parties collected into a volume of about seven thousand lines, is known to this day as "The Contention of the Poets."

There is something highly pathetic in this last flickering up of the spirit of the hereditary classical bards, who conducted this dispute in precisely the same metre, language, tone, and style, as their forefathers of hundreds of years before would have done it, and who chose for the subject-matter of dispute an hereditary quarrel of twelve hundred years' standing. Just as the ancient history of the Irish began with the distinction between the descendants of the sons of Milesius, of which we read so much at the beginning of this volume, so on the self-same subject does the literary spirit of the ancient time which had lasted with little alteration from the days of St. Patrick, flare up into light for a brief moment at the opening of the seventeenth century, ere it expired for ever under the sword of Cromwell and of William.

It is altogether probable, however, that under the appearance of literary zeal and genealogical fury, the bards who took part in this contest were really actuated by the less apparent motive of rousing the ardour of their respective chiefs, their pride of blood, and their hatred of the intruder. If this, as I strongly suspect, were the underlying cause of the "Contention," their expiring effort to effect the impossible by the force of poetry—the only force at their command—is none the less pathetic, than would have been on the very brink of universal ruin, their quarrelling, in the face of their common enemy, upon the foolish old genealogies of a powerless past.

We know a good deal, however, about this Teig, son of Dairé, the ollamh of the O'Briens, of whose poetry, all written in elaborate and highly-wrought classical metres, we have still about three thousand four hundred lines. He possessed down even to the middle of the seventeenth century a fine estate and the castle of Dunogan with its appurtenances, which belonged to him by right of his office, as the hereditary *ollamh* of Thomond. He was hurled over a cliff in his old age by a soldier of Cromwell, who is said to have yelled after him with savage exultation as he fell, "Say your rann now, little man."[1]

[1] See O'Flanagan's "Transactions of the Gaelic Society, 1808," p. 29.

A beautiful inauguration ode to the English-bred Donogh O'Brien, fourth Earl of Thomond, proclaims him a bard of no ordinary good sense and merit.

"Bring thy case before Him (God) every day, beseech diligently Him from whom nothing may be concealed, concerning everything of which thou art in care, Him from whom thou shalt receive relief.

"Run not according to thine own desire, O Prince of the Boru tribute, let the cause of the people be thy anxiety, and that is not the anxiety of an idle man.

"Be not thou negligent in the concerns of each : since it is thy due to decide between the people, O smooth countenance, be easy of access, and diligent in thine own interests.

"Give not thyself up to play nor wine nor feast nor the delight of music nor the caresses of maidens ; measure thou the ill-deeds of each with their due reward, without listening to the intervention of thy council.

"For love, for terror, for hatred, do not pass (be thou a not-hasty judge) a judgment misbecoming thee, O Donough—no not for bribes of gold and silver." [1]

In another poem, Mac Dairé warns the O'Briens to be advised by him, and not plunge the province into war, and to take care how they draw down upon themselves his animosity. Here are a few of these verses, translated into the exact equivalent of the Deibhidh metre in which they are written. They will give a fair idea of a poet's arrogance.

"'Tis not War we Want to Wage
With THomond THinned by outrage.

SLIGHT not Poets' Poignant spur
Of RIGHT ye Owe it hOnour.

Can there Cope a Man with Me
In Burning hearts Bitterly,

---

[1] "Ar ghrádh ar uamhan, ná ar fhuath
Ná beir (bi ad' bhreitheamh neamh-luath)
Breith nár *chóir*, a *Dhonchadh*, dhuit,
Ar *chomhthaibh óir* ná arguit."

This fine poem, containing in all 220 lines, was published by O'Flanagan in 1808.

At my **BL**ows men **BLUSH** I wis,
Bright **FLUSH** their **F**urious **F**aces.[1]

Store of blister-**R**aising **R**anns
These are my **W**eighty **W**eapons,
Poisoned, **ST**riking **STRONG** through men,
They **L**ive not **LONG** so stricken.

SHelter from my **SH**afts or rest
Is not in **F**urthest **F**orest,
Far they **FALL**, words **S**oft as **S**now,
No **WALL** can **W**ard my arrow.[2]

. . . . .

To **QU**ench in **QU**arrels good deeds,
To **R**aise up **WR**ongs in hundreds,
To **NAIL** a **NAME** on a man,
I **FAIL** not—**FAME** my weapon."

The men who most distinguished themselves in the extraordinary outburst of classical poetry that characterised the early seventeenth century were Teig Dall O'Hĭginn, a poet of the county Sligo, brother to the Archbishop of Tuam, and Eochaidh [Yohy] O'Hussey, the chief bard of the Maguire of Fermanagh. Teig Dall O'Hĭginn has left behind him at least three thousand lines, all in polished classical metres, and

[1] "Tig díom da ndearntaoi m'fioghal
Gríosadh bhur ngruadh lasamhail,
Fios bhur gníomh a's gníomh bhur sean
Tig a sgrios díom no a ndídean."

From a MS. of my own ; this poem contains a hundred lines.

[2] "Ni bhi díon i ndiamhraibh gleann
Ná i bhfíodh dhlúith uaignach fhairseang,
Ná i múr caomh *cneas-aolta* cuir,
Ag fear m'*easaonta* ó'm armuibh.

Múchadh deigh-ghníomh, deargadh gruadh,
Toirmeasg ratha re diombuan,
Cur anma a's *eachta* ar fhear
Creachta ár n-airm-ne re n-áireamh."

O'Hussey nearly four thousand. Teig Dall was the author of the celebrated poem addressed to Brian O'Rorke, urging him to take up arms against Elizabeth on the principle "si vis pacem para bellum:" it begins *D'fhior cogaidh comhailtear síothchain* "to a man of war peace is assured," and it had the desired effect. The verses of these bards throw a great deal of light upon the manners customs and politics of the age. There is a curious poem extant by this Teig Dall, in which he gives a graphic account of a night he spent in the house of Maolmordha Mac Sweeny, a night which the poet says he will remember for ever.[1] He met on that memorable night in that hospitable house Brian mac Angus Mac Namee, the poet in chief to Torlogh Luineach O'Neill, Brian mac Owen O'Donnellan, the poet of Mac William of Clanrickard, and Conor O'Hĭginn, the bard of Mac William-Burke. Not only did the chieftain himself, Mac Sweeny, pay him homage, but he received presents—acknowledgment evidently of his admitted genius—from the poets as well. Mac Sweeny gave to him a dappled horse, one of the best steeds in Ireland, Brian mac Angus gave him a wolf-dog that might be matched against any; while from Brian mac Owen he received a book —"a full well of the true stream of knowledge,"—in which were writ "the cattle-spoils, courtships, and sieges of the world, an explanation of their battles and progress, it was the flower of the King-books of Erin."[2] Where, he asks, are all those chiefs gone now? Alas! "the like of the men I found before me in that perfect rath of glistening splendour, ranged along the coloured sides of the purple-hung mansion, no eye

[1] "Tánac oidhche go h-Eas-Caoile
Budh cuimhin liom go lá an bhráith,
Mairfidh *choidhche* ár *ndol* do'n *dún-sa*
Cor na *h-oidhche* a's *cúrsa* cháich."
Metre Séadna.

[2] "Tána, Tochmairc, Toghla an bheatha,
Do bhi 'san aiscidh fuair mé,
Mincaċhadh a *gċath*, 's a *gcéimeann*
Sġath rí-leabhar Eireann é."

ever saw before,"[1] but they are scattered and gone, and the death of four of them in especial seemed a loss from which Banba [Ireland] thought she could never recover. This great poet, in my opinion by far the finest of his contemporaries, came to a tragical end. Six of the O'Haras of Sligo calling at his house, ate up his provisions, and in return he issued against them a special satire. This satire, consisting of twelve ranns in Deibhidh [D'yevvee] metre,[2] stung them to such a pitch that they returned and cut out the tongue that could inflict such exquisite pain, and poor O'Hĭginn died of their barbarous ill-treatment some time prior to the year 1617. None of the bardic race had ever thought that such an end could overtake the great poet at the hands of the Gael themselves. It was only a short time before that, when some bard envying him his position at Coolavin in the west, far from the inroads of the murdering foreigner, had sung :—

" Would I Were in Cool-O-vinn
Where Haunteth Teig O Higinn

[1] " Samhail na bhfear fuaireas rómham
'San ráth foirththe do b'úr niamh
Ar sleasaibh *datha* an *dúin chorcra*
Ni *fhaca súil rompa* riamh."

See Catalogue of Irish MSS. in British Museum.

[2] It commences :—

" Sluagh seisir tháinig do m' thigh,
Béarfad uaim iúl an tseisir,
Tearc do lacht mé ar na mhárach
O thart na ré selánach (*i.e.*, bitheamhnach) ;'

and the last verse runs :—

" Guidhim Dia do dhóirt a fhuil
O sé a mbás bheith na mbeathaidh,
(Ni mhairid gar marthain sin !)
Nár marbhthar an sluagh seisir."

I.e., " I pray to God who poured his blood, since it is their death to be in life,—they do not live whose living is that of theirs !—may that crew of six be never slain " ! This last poem of the unfortunate Teig Dall is preserved in H. 1. 17 T.C.D. f. 116, 6, whence I copied it, but it has lately been printed in the brilliantly descriptive Catalogue of the Irish MSS. in the British Museum.

There my **LEASE** of **LIFE** were free
From **STRIFE** in **PEACE** and Plenty." [1]

We find the poet O'Gnive, the author of the well-known poem, "The Stepping-down of the Gael," [2] bitterly lamenting in Deibhidh metre, the death of O'Higinn, and that breaking-up of the Bardic schools which was even then beginning.

"Fallen the **LAND** of Learned men,
The Bardic **BAND** is fallen;
None now **LEARN** true **SONG** to Sing,
How **LONG** our **FERN** is Fading!

Fearful your Fates O'Higinn,
And Yohy Mac Melaughlinn,
Dark was the **DAY** through **FEUD** Fell
The **GOOD**, the **GAY**, the **GENTLE**. [3]

---

[1] I found this poem in a MS. in Trinity College, Dublin, written by one of the Maguires about the year 1700, but I forget its numbering. I quote the verse from memory :—

"Och gan mé i g Cúl O fhFinn
Mar a bhfuil Tadhg O h-Uiginn,
Dfheudſainn suan go seasgar ann
Gan uamhain easgair orom."

[2] *See* Hardiman's "Irish Minstrelsy," vol. ii. p. 102. But it may not have been the same O'Gneev or O'Gnive, who laments Teig Dall, or if it was, he must have been a very old man, seeing he accompanied Shane O'Neill to London in 1562. His poem on the "Stepping-down of the Gael" has been spiritedly translated by Sir Samuel Ferguson, beginning—

"My heart is in woe,
And my soul is in trouble,
For the mighty are low,
And abased are the noble."

But the metre is the favourite and dignified Deibhidh.

[3] "Oighidh Thaidhg dhuan-sgagtha Dhoill,
Eag Eochaigh mhic Mhaoilsheachlainn,
Tug draoithe Eireann fá oil,
Géibheann maoithe fa mhenmoin."

From a manuscript of my own. *i.e.*, "The tragic-fate of Teig Dall, the Strainer-of-lays, the death of Eochaidh Mac Melaughlin has brought the druids (*i.e.*, learned poets) of Ireland under reproach, and fetters of weakness on [their] spirits."

Ye were Masters Made to please
O'Higinnses, O'Dalys;
GLOOMY ROCKS have WRought your fates,
Ye PLUMY FLOCKS of Poets."

O'Hussey, probably the greatest contemporary rival of Teig Dall, is best known through Mangan's translation of his noble ode to Cuchonnacht Maguire, lord of Fermanagh,[1] who was caught by the elements on some warlike expedition and in danger of being frozen and drowned.

"Where is my chief, my master, this black night? movrone!
Oh, cold, cold, miserably cold is this black night for Hugh,
Its showery, arrowy, speary sleet pierceth one through and through,
Pierceth one to the very bone.

. . . .

An awful, a tremendous night is this, meseems,
The floodgates of the rivers of heaven I think have been burst wide,
Down from the overcharged clouds, like unto headlong ocean's tide,
Descends grey rain in roaring streams.

Though he were even a wolf ranging the round green woods,
Though he were even a pleasant salmon in the unchainable sea,
Though he were a wild mountain eagle, he could scarce bear, he,
This sharp sore sleet, these howling floods." [2]

---

[1] This prince had also been eulogised by Teig Dall O'Higinn in a poem of 164 lines, beginning *Mairg fheuchas ar Inis Ceithlind*, "Alas for him who beholds Enniskillen."

[2] In the original—

"Fuar liom an oidhche-se d'Aodh!
Cúis tuirse troime a cith-bhraon!
Mo thruaighe sin d'ár seise [*i.e.*, caraid!]
Nimh fuaire na h-oidhche-se.

Anocht is nimh lem' chridhe,
Fearthar frasa teinntidhe,
I gcómhdháil na gclá seacta
Mar tá is orgráin aigeanta."

The literal meaning of this last verse, which may be profitably compared with Mangan's translation, is, "This night it is venom to my heart how the fiery showers are rained down, in the company of the frozen

When it is remembered that O'Hussey composed this poem in that most difficult and artificial of metres, the Deibhidh, of which we have just given specimens, it will be seen how much Mangan has gained by his free and untrammelled metre, and what technical difficulties fettered O'Hussey's art, and lent glory to his triumph over them.

Both these great poets and their contemporaries had been reared in the bardic colleges, which continued to exist, though with gradually diminishing prestige, until near the close of the seventeenth century. I doubt if a single college survived into the eighteenth, to come under the cruel law which made it penal for a Catholic to teach a school. In the seventeenth century, however, several famous colleges of poetry are still found. They are frequently alluded to by the poets of that century, both in Ireland and Scotland, and always under the generic name of "the schools," by which they mean the bardic institutions. Few or none of those persons who did not themselves come of a bardic tribe were admitted into them, which accounts for the prevalence of the same surnames among the poets for several centuries, O'Dalys, O'Hĭginnses, O'Coffeys, Macgraiths, Conmees, Wards, O'Mulconrys,[1] etc. None of the students were allowed to come from the neighbourhood of the college, but only from far-away parts of Ireland, so as not to be distracted by the propinquity of friends and relations.

spikes; how it is, is a horror to the mind." The next verse is also worth giving.

> "Do h-osgladh as ochtuibh neóil
> Doirse uisgidhe an aidheóir,
> Tug sé minlinnte ann a muir,
> Do sgeith an firmimint a hurbhuidh."

"There has been thrown open, out of the bosom of the clouds, the doors of the waters of the air. It has made of little linns a sea; the firmament has belched forth her destructiveness." The metre of the last line in this verse is wrong, for it contains nine not seven syllables.

[1] O'Reilly mentions eight Mac-an-bháirds or Wards, eleven O'Clerys, seven O'Coffeys, eight O'Hĭginnses, nine O'Mulconrys and no less than twenty-eight O'Dalys, who were by far the most numerous and perhaps the ablest bardic tribe in all Ireland.

This produced a certain unity of feeling among the bardic race, and to a great extent broke down all class prejudice, so much so, that the bards were almost the only people in later Ireland who belonged to their country rather than to their lord, or tribe, or territory. It may very well be, however, that the bardic race was not in the long run an advantage to Ireland, and that the elaborate system of pedigrees which they preserved, and their eulogies upon their particular patrons tended to keep the clan spirit alive to the detriment of the idea of a unified nationality, and to the exclusion of new political modes of thought.

However this may be, it is absolutely necessary to study the poets of the sixteenth and seventeenth centuries if one would come to a right understanding of the great transformation scene then being enacted. The feelings, aspirations, and politics of the Irish themselves are faithfully reflected in them, and though no Irish historian, except perhaps O'Halloran, has ever read them, yet no historian can afford to utterly neglect them. It has become common of late years to deny that there was any real national struggle of Ireland against England in the seventeenth century, and my friend Mr. Standish O'Grady, in particular, from a perusal of the English State Papers and other documents, has striven with eloquence and brilliancy to prove that the fight was a social and an economic one, a conflict between the smaller gentry and the great upper lords. But such a view of the case is flatly contradicted, indeed absolutely disproved, by a study of the Irish bards. The names of Erin, Banba, Fódhla, the Plain of Conn, the Land of the Children of Ir and Eber, are in their mouths at every moment, and to the very last they persisted in their efforts to combine the Gael against the Gall. Here, for instance, is a poem, one specimen out of scores, by an unknown poet of the sixteenth century, exhorting the Irish of all the provinces to resistance, and it would be impossible to tell to what tribe or even to what province the poet belonged. I translate the poem here into a modification of the Irish metre, and one which, it seems to me, could be very well taken over, and adapted with a fairly good effect into English.[1]

" Fooboon upon you, ye hosts of the Gael,
For your own Innisfail has been taken,
And the Gall is dividing the emerald lands
By your treacherous bands forsaken.[2]

Clan Carthy of Munster from first unto last
Have forsaken the past of their sires,
And they honour no longer the men that are gone,
Or the song of the God-sent lyres.

The O'Briens of Banba whom Murrough led on,
They are gone with the Saxon aggressor,

---

[1] The metre of the original is hepta-syllabic, each line ending in a dissyllable, and there is no regular beat or accentuation in the verse, which, though printed as a four-line stanza, would really run some way thus—

" Foobon on ye,
Cringe *cowards*,
Are your *powers*
Departed ?

Galls your country
Are *tearing*,
Over*bearing*,
Flint-hearted."

The Irish themselves, either through the influence of English verse or through the natural evolution of the Irish language, changed this metre in the next century into one not unlike my English verses above.

[2] This piece is taken from a manuscript of my own ; I have never met this fine poem elsewhere. The word *fooboon*, upon which the changes are so rung, is new to me, and is not contained in any Irish or Scotch-Gaelic dictionary, the nearest approach to it is O'Reilly's *fúbta*, "humiliation" ; but I find the words *fubub fubub* in the sense of "shame," "fy," in the Turner MS., "Reliquiæ Celticæ," vol. ii. p. 325. The metre of this poem is Little Rannaigheacht, and the first verse runs thus—

" Fúbún fúibh a shluagh *Gaoidheal*
Ni mhair *aoin-neach* agaibh
Goill ag comh-roinn bhur *gcríche*
Re sluagh *sithe* mar [*i.e.* bhur] samhail."

Literally : " Fooboon to you, O host of the Gaels, not a man of you is alive : the Galls are together-dividing your lands, while ye are [unsubstantial] like a fairy host. The Clan Carthy of Leath Mogha [*i.e.*, Southern Ireland], and to call them out down to one man, there is not—and sad is the disgrace—one person of them imitating the [old] Gaels," etc.

They have bartered the heirloom of ages away
  And forgotten to slay the oppressor.

The old race of Brian mac Yohy[1] the stern,
  With gallowglass kerne and bonnacht,[2]
They are down on their knees, they are cringing to-day,
  'Tis the way through the province of Connacht.

In the valleys of Leinster the valorous band
  Who lightened the land with their daring,
In Erin's dark hour now shift for themselves,
  The wolves are upon them and tearing.

And O'Neill, who is throned in Emania afar,
  And gave kings unto Tara for ages,
For the earldom of Ulster has bartered, through fear,
  The kingdom of heroes and sages.[3]

Alas for the sight! the O'Carrolls of Birr
  Swear homage in terror, sore fearing,
Not a man one may know for a man, can be found
  On the emerald ground of Erin.

And O'Donnell[4] the chieftain, the lion in fight,
  Who defended the right of Tirconnell,
(Ah! now may green Erin indeed go and droop!)
  He stoops with them—Manus O'Donnell!

---

[1] Yohy is the pronunciation of the Irish Eochaidh, genitive Eochach, or even Eathach. The Eochaidh here alluded to is Eochaidh Muigh-mheadhon [Mwee-va-on], father of Niall of the Nine Hostages. He came to the throne in 356, and from his son Brian the O'Conors, O'Rorkes, O'Reillys, MacDermots, etc., of Connacht are descended, who all went under the generic name of the Ui Briain, as the families descended from his other son, Niall of the Nine Hostages are the Ui Neill. *See* above, pp. 33 and 34.

[2] Bonnacht is a "mercenary soldier."

[3] "O Néill Oiligh a's *Eamhna*
    Ri *Teamhrach* agus Tailltean,
  Tugsad ar *iarlacht* Uladh
    Rioghacht go h-úmhal aimhghlic."

I.e., "O'Neill of Aileach and of Emania, King of Tara and of Tailtinn, they have given away for the earldom of Ulster, a kingdom submissively unwisely."

[4] Manus O'Donnell died in 1563, so that this poem must have been composed somewhat earlier.

Fooboon for the court where no English was spoke,
  Fooboon for the yoke of the stranger,
Fooboon for the gun in the foreigner's train,
  Fooboon for the chain of danger.

Ye faltering madmen, God pity your case !
  In the flame of disgrace ye are singeing.
Fooboon is the word of the bard and the saint,
  Fooboon for the faint and cringing."

The session of the bardic schools began about Michaelmas,[1] and the youthful aspirants to bardic glory came trooping, about that season, from all quarters of the four provinces to offer with trembling hearts their gifts to the ollamh of the bardic college, and to take possession of their new quarters. Very extraordinary these quarters were ; for the college usually consisted of a long low group of whitewashed buildings, excessively warmly thatched, and lying in the hollow of some secluded valley, or shut in by a sheltering wood, far removed from noise of human traffic and from the bustle of the great world. But what most struck the curious beholder was the entire absence of windows or partitions over the greater portion of the house.

According as each student arrived he was assigned a windowless room to himself, with no other furniture in it than a couple of chairs, a clothes rail, and a bed. When all the students had arrived, a general examination of them was held by the professors and ollamhs, and all who could not read and write Irish well, or who appeared to have an indifferent memory, were usually sent away. The others were divided into classes, and the mode of procedure was as follows : The students were called together into the great hall or sitting-room, amply illuminated by candles and bog-torches, and we may imagine the head ollamh, perhaps the venerable and patriotic O'Gnive himself, addressing them upon their chosen profession, and finally proposing some

[1] This account of the later bardic schools is chiefly derived from a curious book, the "Memoirs of Clanrickard," printed in London in 1722.

burning topic such as O'Neill's abrogation of the title of O'Neill, for the higher class to compose a poem on, in perhaps the Great or Little Rannaigheacht [Ran-ee-ăcht] metre, while for the second class he sets one more commonplace, to be done into Deibhidh [D'yevvee] or Séadna [Shayna], or some other classic measure, and any student who does not know all about the syllabification, quartans, concord, correspondence, termination, and union, which go to the various metres, is turned over to an inferior professor.

The students retired after their breakfasts, to their own warm but perfectly dark compartments, to throw themselves each upon his bed,[1] and there think and compose till supper-hour, when a servant came round to all the rooms with candles, for each to write down what he had composed. They were then called together into the great hall, and handed in their written compositions to the professors, after which they chatted and amused themselves till bed-time.

On every Saturday and the eve of every holiday the schools broke up, and the students dispersed themselves over the country. They were always gladly received by the landowners of the neighbourhood, and treated hospitably until their return on Monday morning. The people of the district never failed to send in, each in turn, large supplies to the college, so that, what between this and the presents brought by the students at the beginning of the year, the professors are said to have been fairly rich.

The schools always broke up on the 25th of March, and the holidays lasted for six months, it not being considered judicious to spend the warm half of the year in the close college, from which all light and air-draughts had been so carefully excluded.

I can hardly believe, however, that the students of law, history, and classics—all the educated classes could speak

[1] Hence the bardic expression, "luidhe i leabaibh sgol," *i.e.*, "to lie in the beds of the schools," equivalent to becoming a poet.

Latin, which was their means of communication with the English[1]—were treated as here described, or enjoyed such long holidays. It was probably only a special class of candidates for bardic degrees who were thus dealt with, and the account above given may be somewhat exaggerated; the students probably composed in their dark compartments only on certain days.

In the seventeenth century we find that the three or four hundred metres taught in the schools of the tenth century had been practically restricted to a couple of dozen, and these nearly all heptasyllabic. It is quite probable, as Thurneysen asserts, that the metres of the early Roman hymns — themselves probably largely affected by Celtic models—exercised in their turn a reflex influence upon Irish poetry, and especially on that of the bards, in contradistinction to that of the *filés*. Indeed, it is pretty certain that if the Roman metres had not before existed in Irish the bards would have made no scruple about copying them; and they may thus have come by these octosyllabic and heptasyllabic lines about which they were in after times so particular. Of the metres chiefly in vogue in the schools of the later centuries, the most popular was the Deibhidh, of which I have already given so many examples.[2] It was, as it were, the official metre—the hexameter of the Gael. All the seven thousand and odd lines of the "Contention of the Bards," for instance, are written in it. Great Rannaigheacht[3] [Ran-ee-ăcht] was another prime heptasyllabic favourite. It ran thus—

[1] Campion, who wrote in 1574, says of the Irish of his day: "They speake Latine like a vulgar language learned in their schooles of Leachcraft and law, whereat they begin children and holde on sixteene or twentie yeares." After the Battle of the Curlew Mountains, MacDermot, anxious to let the Governor know where the body of Sir Conyers Clifford lay, wrote a note to him in Latin.

[2] *See* above, pp. 518–523.

[3] Of Little Rannaigheacht I gave an example a few pages back in the

"To Hear Handsome Women WEEP,
In DEEP distress Sobbing Sore,
Or Gangs of Geese scream for FAR,
They sweeter ARE than ARTS snore."[1]

I may observe here that there has been on the part of

poem "Fooboon." Séadna [Shayna] was another great favourite, built on the model of the following verse, with or without alliteration—

"Teig of herds the Gallant Giver,
Right receiver of our love,
Teig thy Name shall KNow no *ending*,
Branch un-B*ending*, Erin's glove."

This verse runs rhythmically, but that it does so is only an accident. The Irish could always have got their Séadna verses, at least, of eight and seven syllables, to run smoothly if they had wished, but they did not. Here is a more Irish-like stanza in the same metre—

"Of / lowliness / came a / daughter,
And / he who / brought her / was / God,
Noble / her / son and / stately,
Ennobling / greatly / this / sod."

Great Séadna is the same metre as this, except that every verse ends with a word of three syllables. In Middle Séadna the first and third lines end in trisyllables, the second and fourth in dissyllables. Ae-fri-Slighe is like Middle Séadna, except that instead of the first and third lines being octosyllabic, they all have seven syllables, as—

"Ye who bring to slavery
Men of mind and reading,
God bring down your bravery,
Leave you vexed and bleeding."

Little Deachna is a pretty metre with five syllables to each line, as—

"God gives me three *things*,
Them he *brings* all three
When the soul is *born*
Like a *corn* in me."

Great Deachna contained eight and six syllables, each line ending in dissyllables—

"I believe this *wafer* holy,
Which is *safer* surely,
Flesh, blood, *Godhead* strangely mingled,
In bread *bodied* purely."

The above metres are a few of the most favourite.

[1] "Mná módhach' go ngoimh ag gul,
Gan árach ar sgur d'á mbrón,
Caoi chadhain an oidhche fhuar
Is binne 'ná fuaim do shrón."

From a manuscript of my own, a comic poem by an anonymous bard, on a snoring companion.

Irish Continental scholars an extraordinary amount of discordant theories as to the scansion of the Irish classical metres. None of them seem to be agreed as to how to scan them. Zimmer insists that the word-accent and the metrical accent in Irish are identical, which, as Kuno Meyer has shown, is plainly not the case. He would probably scan—

"Or wíld geese thát scream fróm fàr,"

while Kuno Meyer again would insist on reading—

"Ór wild geése that scréam from fár,"

because, as he says, all heptasyllabic lines are to be read as trochaic, a theory which may apply very well to some lines, as to the above, but which is almost certain to break down after a line or two, as in the very next line of this verse which I have taken for a model—

"Théy sweet / ér are / thán Arts / snóre,"

a scansion which does extraordinary violence to the natural pronunciation of the words. I, for my part, do not believe that there was ever any real metrical accent, that is, any real alternation of stressed and unstressed syllables in the classical Irish metres.[1] The one thing certain about them is the fixed number of syllables and the rhyme, but each verse was, as it were, separately scanned, if one may use such a term, on its

[1] Windisch appears to me to have come closest to the truth : "If we suppose," he says, "that the accented syllable coincides with the natural accent of the word, if we consider that polysyllabic words, besides having an accented syllable, can also have a semi-accented one (neben den Hauptton auch einen Nebenton haben können), finally, if we take it for granted that the syllables in which rhyme or alliteration appear must also bear the accent or up-beat of the voice (in der Hebung stehen mussen), we then at once come to the conclusion that each half-verse contains a specified number of accented syllables, without, however, any *regular* interchange of up and down beats of accented and unaccented syllables." —*See* "Irische Texte," I. i. p. 157.

own merits. Thus the verse just quoted would be read some way thus—

> "To hear handsome
>   Women *weep*
> In *deep* distress,
>   Sobbing sore,
> Or gangs of geese
>   Scream from *far*,
> They sweeter *are*
>   Than Arts snore."

I have frequently heard preserved in ranns or proverbs, even to this day, isolated quatrains in these classic metres pronounced by the people,[1] and they never dream of pronouncing them otherwise than according to the natural stress of the voice upon the words themselves, as if they were talking prose, —they never attempt to transform the seven-syllable lines into trochees, as Kuno Meyer would, nor the eight-syllable lines into iambics. Of this old Gaelic prosody there appears to be a

[1] Thus when O'Carolan, in the last century, made the extempore response to the butler who prohibited his entering the cellar

> "Mo chreach a Dhiarmuid Ui Fhloinn
> Gan tu ar dorus ifrinn,
> 'S tu nach leigfeadh neach ad' chó'r
> 'San áit bheitheá do dhoirseóir."

He spoke (perhaps unwittingly) an excellent Deibhidh stanza, but he never scanned it,

> "Mó chreach / á Dhiar / múid Ui / Fhloínn
> Gan tu / ár dor / us if / rinn."

He said,

> "Mo chreách / a Dhíarmuid / Uí / Fhloínn
> Gan tú / ar dórus / ifrinn."

So, too, in a rann I heard from a friend in the county Mayo, and printed in my "Religious Songs of Connacht," p. 232 :—

> "Ni meisge is miste liom
> Acht leisg a feicsint orom [orm],
> Gan digh meisge 's miste an greann
> Acht ni gnáth meisge gan mi-greann,

which is not spoken as—

> "Ní meis / gé is / míste liom,"

but as—

> "Ni / méisge / is míste / liom."

distinct reminiscence in Burns. Take this verse of his for example—

" Blythe, blythe, and merry was she,
  Blythe was she but and ben,
Blythe by the banks of Ern,
  And blythe in Glenturit glen."

This, supplying, say the syllable "and," in the second and third lines makes a good Rannaigheacht mór quatrain, which the poet evidently pronounced exactly as an old Irish bard would have done.

" Blythe, blythe,
  And merry was she,
And blythe was she
  But and ben,
Blythe by
  The banks of Ern,
And blythe in
  Glenturit glen."

Bonaventura O'Hussey was another fine classical poet of the beginning of the seventeenth century. He was educated for a bard, but afterwards became a Franciscan in Louvain, where he wrote and published an Irish work on Christian Doctrine in 1608, which was reprinted in Antwerp three years later. The Irish, having no press of their own in Ireland (though they had some outside it), were obliged to print and set up all their books abroad, chiefly at Louvain, Antwerp, Rome, and Paris. Any attempt to introduce founts of Irish type in the teeth of the English Government would, I think, have been futile, so that except for the works she was able to print in Irish type abroad, and afterwards to smuggle in, Ireland during the seventeenth century was thrown nearly a couple of hundred years out of the world's course, by having to use manuscripts instead of printed books. It is curious to find O'Hussey compressing the Christian doctrine into two hundred and forty lines of the most accurate Deibhidh metre. When leaving for his foreign home he bade farewell to Erin in a poem of great beauty.

"*Slowly* pass my Aching Eye,
Her H*oly* Hills of beauty
Neath me TOSSING TO and fro,
Hoarse CRies the CROSSING billow.'[1]

In another poem he laments sorely at leaving the poets and the schools "to try another trade," that of a cleric, which he says he does, not because he thinks less of poetry, or because the glory that was once to be had from it was departing amongst the people of Erin, but from religious motives alone.

"Now I *stand* to Try a Trade
Mid Bardic B*and* less famèd
Than the P*art* of Poet is
Hacked is my H*eart* in pieces.

'Tis not that I Veer from Verse
So Followed by my Fathers,
Lest the *fame* it Once did Win
In *vain* be Asked in Erin."[2]

Fearfeasa O'Cainti was another well-known poet of this period who attempted to rouse the Irish to action. Here are a few of his verses to the O'Driscoll—

"Many a Mulct—requite their sin—
Fetch from them heir of Finnin;

---

[1] "Do chuadar as rinn mo ruisg
Do tholcha is áluinn éaguisg,
Is *tuar orcra* dá n-éisi
Dromla fhuar na h-aibheisi.'
From a manuscript of my own.

[2] "Ni fuath d'ealadhain m' *aithreach*
Thug fúm *aigneadh* aithrigheach,
No an *ghlóir* do *gheibhthí* dá chionn
Ar *neimhnidh* ó *phór* Eirionn."

From a manuscript of my own. This poem appears not to have been known to O'Reilly.

SPARE not to SPURN the brute Gall
To BURN the BEAR and jackal.[1]

Ruthless Rapine leads them on
Slaying CHief CHild CHampion!
BLood they BLINDLY *spilt*, no law
BINDING their *guilt* in Banba.

Pour their BLood to BLEND with blood,
Conor HAND of Hardihood,
CALL for ransom not my King;
Slay ALL, be Untransacting.

Lies they Lie! their Love is one
With TReachery and TReason,
Nay! thou Needest NOT my spur;
Revenge is HOT, Remember!"

The quantity of verse composed in these classic metres all through the seventeenth century was enormous, and amounts to at least twenty thousand lines of the known poets not to speak of the anonymous ones. Not more than a dozen of them have ever been published,[2] and yet no one can pretend

[1] "Iomdha eiric nach í sin
Agad a oighre Fhinghin,
Gan *séana* ar *garbh-amhsaibh* Gall
Méala an *t-amhgar-soin* d'fhulang."

I.e., "Many an eric that is not that, [be] to thee, O heir of Finneen, without refusing [to inflict loss] on the coarse-monsters of Galls: a grief to endure that affliction!" From a manuscript of my own. This poem was also unknown to O'Reilly. It consists of 180 lines, and begins *Leó féin cuirid clann Iotha*, *i.e.*, "By themselves go the children of the Ithians," of whom the O'Driscolls were the chief tribe. For an account of the little band of Ithians, the fourth division of the Gaelic family see above, p. 67.

[2] Since writing the above a German Celticist, Ludwig Christian Stern, has written a most interesting account of a collection of bardic poems, chiefly of the fifteenth and sixteenth centuries, now preserved in the Royal Library at Copenhagen. This interesting collection is chiefly dedicated to the praises of the Maguires of Fermanagh, and is the work of a number of accomplished poets, most of whom are unknown to O'Reilly, even by

to understand the inner history of Ireland at that period without a reference to them. Their chief characteristic is an intense compression which produces an air of weighty sententiousness. This was necessitated by the .laws of their composition, which required at the end of every second line a break or suspension of the sense (such as in English would be usually expressed by a semi-colon or colon), and which absolutely forbade any carrying over of the sense from one stanza into another. Hence the thought of the poet had with each fresh quatrain to be concentrated into twenty-eight syllables (thirty syllables in Séadna metre), with a break or pause at the end of the fourteenth (or fifteenth). Accordingly O'Gnive calls the poets the "schoolmen of condensed speech," [1] and the Scotch bard Mac Muirich in the Red Book of Clanranald speaks of Teig Dall O'Higinn as putting into less than a half-rann what others would take a whole crooked stanza to express.[2] The classical metres went, in Irish, under the generic name of *Dán Díreach*, or "straight verse;" and O'Molloy, who wrote an Irish prosody in Latin in the seventeenth century, carried away by a contemplation of its difficulties, exclaims that it is "Omnium quæ unquam vidi vel audivi, ausim dicere quæ sub sole reperiuntur, difficilimum."

name. The whole collection contains 5,576 lines, of which Herr Julius Stern has printed about a thousand, thus having the honour of being the first to render accessible a fair specimen of the work of the current poetry of the schools in the sixteenth century. The characteristics of this poetry he appraises, very justly as I think, in the following words, "The language is choice and difficult, the poetry is of the traditional type, poor in facts, but elevated, stately, learned, and *very artistic*." See for this interesting article the "Zeitschrift für Celtische Philologie," II. Band, 2 Heft., pp. 323–373, "Eine Sammlung irischer Gedichte in Kopenhagen."

[1] "Ni mhair sgoluidhe sgéil teinn
D'uibh nDálaigh ná d'uibh n-Uiginn."
From a manuscript of my own.

[2] "Reliquiæ Celticæ," vol. ii. p. 297. Last stanza.

It was during the seventeenth century that the greatest change in the whole poetical system of the Irish and Scotch Gaels was accomplished, and that a new school of versification arose with new ideals, new principles, and new methods, which we shall briefly glance at in the following chapter.

CHAPTER XXXIX

RISE OF A NEW SCHOOL

IN poetry the external form, or framework, or setting of the poetic thought—the word-building in which the thought is enshrined—has varied vastly from age to age and from nation to nation. There is the system of the Greeks and Romans, according to which every syllable of every word is, as it were, hall-marked with its own "quantity," counted, that is, (often almost independently of the pronunciation) to be in itself either short or long, and their verse was made by special collocations of these short or long syllables—a form highly artistic and beautiful.

Then there is the principle of the Anglo-Saxon, Icelandic, and Teutonic peoples, which prevailed in England even down to the time of Chaucer, in which verse is marked only by accent and staff-rhyme, in other words is alliterative as in the "Book of Piers Ploughman."

Lastly, there is the rhymed poetry of the later Middle Ages, of which outside of Wales and Ireland there probably exists no example in a European vernacular language older than the ninth century. This system, apparently invented by the Celts, assumed in Ireland a most extraordinary and artificial form of its own, the essence of which was that they divided the consonants into *groups*,[1] and any consonant belonging to a particular group was allowed to rhyme with any other consonant belonging to the same. Thus a word ending in *t* could rhyme with a word ending in *p* or *c*, but with no other ; a word ending in *b* could rhyme with one ending in *g* or *d*, but with no other, and so on. Thus "rap" would have been considered by the Irish to make perfect rhyme with "sat" or "mac" but not with "rag" ; and "rag" to make perfect rhyme with "slab" or "mad," but not with "cap," "sat" or "mac."

This classification of the consonants which was taught in the Irish schools for very many hundred years, and which forms the basis of the classical poetry which we spoke of in the last chapter, is to a considerable extent—I do not quite know how far—founded upon really sound phonological principles,[2] and the ear of the Irishman was so finely attuned to it that no mistake was ever made, for while such rhymes as "Flann" and "ram" fell agreeably on his ear, any Irish poet for a thousand years would have shuddered to hear "Flann" rhymed with "raff." This accurate ear for the classification of consonants is now almost a lost sense, but even still traces of it may be found in the barbarous English rhymes of the Irish peasantry, as in such rude verses as this from the County Cavan—

"By loving of a maiD,
One Catherine Mac CaBe,
My life it was betrayeD,
She's a dear maid on me."

[1] Their classification was as follows :—
S stood by itself because of the peculiar phonetic laws which it obeys.
P.C.T. called soft consonants [really hard not soft].
B.G.D. called hard consonants [these are in fact rather soft than hard].
F. CH. TH. called rough consonants.
LL. M. NN. NG. RR. called strong consonants.
Bh. Dh. Ch. Mh. L.N.R. called light consonants.

[2] "Diese Klasseneinteilung bekundet einen feinen Sinn für das Wesen der Laute," says Herr Stern, in the article I have just quoted from. See also the prosody in O'Donovan's grammar.

Or this—

> "I courted lovely *Mary* at the *age* of sixteeN·
> Slender was her *waist* and her carriage genteeL."

Or this from the County Dublin—

> "When you were an acorn on the tree toP
> Then was I an aigle[1] coCK,
> Now that you are a withered ould bloCK
> Still am I an aigle cock."

Or this from the County Cork—

> "Sir Henry kissed behind the bush
> Sir Henry kissed the QuaKer;
> Well and what if he did
> Sure he didn't aTe her!"

Upon the whole, however, that keen perception for the nuances of sound, and that fine ear which insisted upon a liquid rhyming only with a fellow liquid, and so on of the other classes, may be considered as almost wholly lost.

We now come to the great breaking up and total disruption of the Irish prosody as employed for a thousand years by thousands of poets in the bardic schools and colleges. The principles of this great change may be summed up in two sentences; first, *the adoption of vowel rhyme in place of consonantal rhyme*; second, *the adoption of a certain number of accents in each line in place of a certain number of syllables*. These were two of the most far-reaching changes that could overtake the poetry of any country, and they completely metamorphosed that of Ireland.

It was only on the destruction of the great Milesian and Norman families in the seventeenth century, that the rules of poetry, so long and so carefully guarded in the bardic schools, ceased to be taught; and it was the break up of these schools which rendered the success of the new principles

[1] "Eagle." This English rann dramatically denotes the longevity of that bird, as does also a well-known Irish one.

possible. A brilliant success they had. Almost in the twinkling of an eye Irish poetry completely changed its form and complexion, and from being, as it were, so bound up and swathed around with rules that none who had not spent years over its technicalities could move about in it with vigour, its spirit suddenly burst forth in all the freedom of the elements, and clothed itself, so to speak, in the colours of the rainbow. Now indeed for the first time poetry became the handmaid of the many, not the mistress of the few; and through every nook and corner of the island the populace, neglecting all bardic training, burst forth into the most passionate song. Now, too, the remnant of the bards—the great houses being fallen—turned instinctively to the general public, and threw behind them the intricate metres of the schools, and dropped too, at a stroke, several thousand words, which no one except the great chiefs and those trained by the poets understood, whilst they broke out into beautiful, and at the same time intelligible verse, which no Gael of Ireland and Scotland who has ever heard or learned it is likely ever to forget. This is to my mind perhaps the sweetest creation of all Irish literature, the real glory of the modern Irish nation, and of the Scottish Highlands, this is the truest note of the enchanting Celtic siren, and he who has once heard it and remains deaf to its charm can have little heart for song or soul for music. The Gaelic poetry of the last two centuries both in Ireland and in the Highlands is probably the most sensuous attempt to convey music in words, ever made by man. It is absolutely impossible to convey the lusciousness of sound, richness of rhythm, and perfection of harmony, in another language. Scores upon scores of new and brilliant metres made their appearance, and the common Irish of the four provinces deprived of almost everything else, clung all the closer to the Muse. Of it indeed they might have said in the words of Moore—

"Through grief and through danger thy smile has cheered my way
Till hope seemed to bud from each thorn that round about me lay."

It is impossible to convey any idea of this new outburst of Irish melody in another language. Suffice it to say that the principle of it was a wonderful arrangement of vowel sounds, so placed that in every accented syllable, first one vowel and then another fell upon the ear in all possible kinds of harmonious modifications. Some verses are made wholly on the Á sound, others on the Ó, Ú, É, or Í sounds, but the majority on a wonderful and fascinating intermixture of two, three, or more. The consonants which played so very prominent a part under the old bardic system were utterly neglected now, and vowel sounds alone were sought for.

The Scottish Gaels, if I am not mistaken, led the way in this great change, which metamorphosed the poetry of an entire people in both islands. The bardic system, outside of the kingdom of the Lord of the Isles, had apparently scarcely taken the same hold upon the nobles, in Scotland as in Ireland, and the first modern Scotch Gaelic poet to start upon the new system seems to have been Mary, daughter of Alaster Rua MacLeod, who was born in Harris in 1569, and who appears to have possessed no higher social standing than that of a kind of lady nurse in the chief's family. If the nine poems in free vowel metres, which are attributed to her by Mackenzie in his great collection,[1] be genuine, then I should consider her as the

[1] See for her poems "Sár-obair na mbárd Gaelach," by Mackenzie, p. 22. Unfortunately he gives us no full account of where the poems were collected, all he says is, "We have the authority of several persons of high respectability, and on whose testimony we can rely, that Mary McLeod was the veritable authoress of the poems attributed to her in this work." This is, in an important matter of the kind, very unsatisfactory, but Mary's poem, "*An talla 'm bu ghná le MacLeód*," seems to bear internal evidence of its own antiquity in its allusions to the chief's bow—

"Si do lámh nach robh tuisleach,
Dol a chaitheadh a chuspair
Led' bhogha cruaidh ruiteach deagh-neóil,"

to which she alludes again in the line—

"Nuair leumadh an tsaighead ó do mheoir."

("When the arrow would leap from your fingers.")

pioneer of the new school. Certainly no Irishman nor Irishwoman of the sixteenth century has left anything like Mary's metres behind them, and indeed I have not met more than one or two of them used in Ireland during that century.[1] No one, for instance, would have dreamt of vowel-rhyming thus, as she does over the drowning of Mac'Illachallun:

"My *grief* my *pain*,
Rel*ief* was *vain*
The *seething wave*
Did *leap* and *rave*,
And *reeve* in *twain*,
Both *sheet* and *sail*,
And *leave* us *bare*
And FOUNDERING.

Alas, *indeed*,
For her you *leave*
Your brothers *grief*
To them will *cleave*.
It was on *Eas*ter
Monday's *feast*
The branch of *peace*
Went DOWN WITH YOU."

The earliest intimations of the new school in Ireland which I have been able to come across, occur towards the very close of the sixteenth century, one being a war ode on a victory of the O'Byrnes,[2] and the other being an abhran or

[1] There are some poems in the Book of Ballymote in almost the same metre as the well-known "Seaghan O'Duibhir an Ghleanna." This metre was technically called, "Ocht-foclach Corranach beag." O'Curry gives a specimen in "Manners and Customs," vol. iii. p. 393, from the Book of Ballymote which has an astonishingly modern air, and may well give pause to those who claim that Irish accentual poetry is derived from an English source.

[2] This poem, which like O'Daly's war-song, is entirely accentual and vowel-rhyming, begins thus—

"A *Bhratach* ar a *bhfaicim-se* in *gruaim* ag fás
Dob' *annamh* leat in *caglais* do *bhuan*-choimheád,

song addressed by a bard unknown to me, one John Mac Céibhfinn to O'Conor Sligo, apparently on his being blockaded by Red Hugh in the country of the Clan Donogh in 1599.

As for the classical metres of the schools they were already completely lost by the middle of the eighteenth century, and the last specimen which I have found composed in Connacht is one by Father Patrick O'Curneen,[1] to the house of the O'Conors, of Belanagare, in 1734, which is in perfect Deibhidh metre.

> "She who RUles the RAce is one
> SPrung from the SParring Ternon,
> MARY MILD of MIEN O'Rorke,
> Our FAIRY CHILD QUEEN bulwark.[2]

> Da *mairfeadh* [sin] fear-*seasta* na *gcruadh*-throdán
> Feadh t'*amhairc* do bhiadh *agat* do'n *tuaith* 'na h-áit.

"O Flag, upon whom I see the melancholy growing,
Seldom was it thy lot to constantly guard the church (shut up there);
If there lived the man-who-withstood the hard conflicts
Far-as-thy-eye-could-see thou wouldst have of the country in place of it" [*i.e.*, the church.]

(*See* Catalogue of the MSS. in the British Museum.)

[1] The O'Curneens were, according to Mac Firbis's great Book of Genealogies, the hereditary poets and ollamhs of the O'Rorkes, with whom the O'Conors were closely related. The O'Conors' ollamh was O'Mulchonry.

[2] This poem begins—

> "Togha teaghlaigh tar gach tír
> Beul átha na gcárr gclaidh-mhín
> Múr is fáilteach re file
> An dún dáilteach deigh-inigh."

I.e., "A choice hearth beyond every country, is the mouth of the ford of the cars [Belanagare], the smooth-ditched. A fortress welcome-giving to poet, the bestowing homestead of good generosity." The accented system had now been in vogue for nearly a century and a half, and if O'Curneen had wished to preserve an even rise and fall of accent in his verses (which he does do in his first line) he might have done so. That he did not do so, and that none of the straight-verse or classical poets attempted it, long

Let me PRAY the PUISSANT one
To MARK them in their MANSION,
Guard from FEAR their FAME and wed
Each YEAR their NAME and homestead."

In Munster I find the poet Andrew Mac Curtin some time between the year 1718 and 1743,[1] complaining to James Mac Donnell, of Kilkee, that he had to frame "a left-handed awkward ditty of a thing," meaning a poem of the new school; "but I have had to do it," he says, "to fit myself in with the evil fashion that was never practised in Erin before, since it is a thing that I see, that greater is the respect and honour every dry scant-educated boor, or every clumsy *baogaire* of little learning, who has no clear view of either alliteration or poetry,[2] gets from the noblemen of the country, than the courteous very-educated shanachy or man of song, if he compose a well-made lay or poem." Nevertheless, he insists that he will make a true poem, "although wealthy men of herds, or people of riches think that I am a fool if I compose a lay or poem in good taste, that is not my belief. Although rich men of herds, merchants, or people who put out money to grow, think that great is the blindness and want of sense to

after they had become acquainted with the other system, seems to me a strong proof that they did not intend it, and that they really possessed no system of "metrical accent" at all.

It is noticeable that O'Curneen wrote this poem in the difficult bardic dialect, so that Charles O'Conor of Belanagare, whose native language was Irish, was obliged in his copy to gloss over twenty words of it with more familiar ones of his own. These uncommon bardic terms were wholly thrown aside by the new school.

[1] His poem with its prose Irish preface is addressed to Sorley Mac Donnell, and Isabel, his wife, who was an O'Brien. They were married in 1718, and Mac Donnell died in 1743. See a collection of poems written by the Clare bards in honour of the Mac Donnells of Kilkee and Killone, in the County of Clare, collected and edited by Brian O'Looney for Major Mac Donnell, for private circulation in 1863.

[2] "Nach léir dó *uaim* no aisde."

compose a *duan* or a poem, they being well satisfied if only they can speak the Saxon dialect, and are able to have stock of bullocks or sheep, and to put redness [*i.e.*, of cultivation] on hills—nevertheless, it is by me understood that they are very greatly deceived, because their herds and their heavy riches shall go by like a summer fog, but the scientific work shall be there to be seen for ever," etc. The poem which he composed on that occasion was, perhaps, the last in Deibhidh metre composed in the province of Munster.[1]

In Scotland the Deibhidh was not forgotten until after Sheriffmuir, in 1715. There is an admirable elegy of 220 lines in the Book of Clanranald on Allan of Clanranald, who was there slain.[2] It is in no way distinguishable from an Irish poem of the same period. There are other poems in this book in perfect classical metres, for in the kingdom of the Lord of the Isles the bards and their schools may be said to have almost found a last asylum. Indeed, up to this period, so far as I can see,—whatever may have been the case with the spoken language—the written language of the two countries was absolutely identical, and Irish bards and harpers found a second home in North Scotland and the Isles, where such poems as those of Gerald, fourth Earl of Desmond, appear to have been as popular as they were in Munster. We may, then, place the generation that lived between Sheriffmuir and Culloden as that which witnessed the end of the classical metres in both countries, over all Ireland and Gaelic-speaking Scotland, from Sutherland in the North, to the County Kerry in the South, so that, from that day to this, vowel-rhyming accented metres which had been making their way in both

[1] I have since, however, found a poem by Micheál óg O'Longain, written as late as 1800, which goes somewhat close to real Deibhidh. It begins—

> "Tagraim libh a Chlann Éibhir,
> Leath bhur lúith nach lán léir libh
> Méala dhaoibh thar aoin eile
> A dul d'éag do'n gaoidheilge."

[2] Cameron's "Reliquiæ Celticæ," vol. ii. p. 248.

countries from a little before the year 1600, have reigned without any rival.

Wonderful metres these were. Here is an example of one made on the vowels é [æ] and ó, but while the arrangement in the first half of the verse is o/é, é/o, é/o, o; the arrangement in the second half is o é, o é, o é, é. I have translated it in such a way as to mark the vowel rhymes, and this will show better than anything else the plan of Irish poetry during the last 250 years. To understand the scheme thoroughly the vowels must not be slurred over, but be dwelt upon and accentuated as they are in Irish.

"The pOets with lAys are uprAising their nOtes
  In amÁze, and they knOw how their tOnes will delight,
For the gOlden-hair lAdy so grAceful, so pOseful,
  So gAElic, so glOrious enthrOned in our sight.
Unfolding a tAle, how the sOul of a fAy must
  Be clOthed in the frAme of a lAdy so bright,
UntOld are her grAces, a rOse in her fAce is
  And nO man so stAid is but fAints at her sight."[1]

Here is another verse of a different character, in which three words follow each other in each line, all making a different vowel-rhyme.

"O *swan* BRIGHTLY GLEAMING o'er *ponds* WHITELY BEAMING,
  Swim *on* LIGHTLY CLEAVING and *flashing* through sea,
The *wan* NIGHT is LEAVING my *fond* SPRITE in GRIEVING
  Be*yond* SIGHT, or SEEING thou'rt *passing* from me."

[1] This is a poem by the Cork bard, Tadhg Gaolach O'Sullivan, who died in 1800. He wrote this poem in his youth, before his muse gave itself up, as it did in later days, to wholly religious subjects. In the original the rhymes are on é and ú.

"Taid Éigse 'gus úghdair go trúpach ag plÉireacht
  So súgach, go sglÉipeach 's a ndrÉachta dá snígheam
Ar SpÉir-bhruinnioll mhúinte do phlúr-sgoth na h-Éireann
  Do úr-chriostal gAolach a's rÉiltion na righeacht;
Ta fiúnn-lil ag plÉireacht mar dhúbha ar an Éclips,
  Go clúdaighthe ag PhoÉbus, le Aon-ghile gnaoi,
'Sgur'na gnúis mhilis lÉightear do thúirling Cupid caÉmh-ghlic
  Ag múchadh 'sag milleadh lAochra le trEan-neart a shaoighid."

Here is another typical verse of a metre in which many poems were made to the air of Moreen ni [nee] Cullenáin. It is made on the sounds of o, ee, ar—o, ar—o, repeated in the same order four times in every verse, the second and third o's being dissyllables. It is a beautiful and intricate metre.

"AlOne with mE a bARd rOving
On guARd gOing ere the dawn,
Was bOld to sEE afAR rOaming
The stAR MOreen ni Cullenaun.
The Only shE the ARch-gOing
The dARk-flOwing fairy fawn,
With sOulful glEE the lARks sOaring
Like spARks O'er her lit the lawn." [1]

Here is another metre from a beautiful Scotch Gaelic poem. The Scotch Gaels, like the Irish, produced about the same time a wonderful outburst of lyric poetry worthy to take a place in the national literature beside the spirited ballads of the Lowlands. Unlike the Lowlands, however, neither they nor the Irish can be said to have at all succeeded with the ballad.

"To a fAR mountain hARbour
Prince ChARlie came flYing,
The wInds from the HIghlands
Wailed wIld in the air,
On his breast was no stAR,
And no guARd was besIde him,
But a girl by him glIding
Who guIded him there.

---

[1] "*D' easgadh* an *pheacaidh*, *fóríor*,
Do *sheól sinn* faoi dhlighthibh námhad,
Gan *flathas Airt*, ag *pór Gaoidheal*,
Gan *seóid puinn*, gan cion gan áird,
'Sgach *bathlach bracach beól-bhuidhe*
De'n *chóip chríon* do rith thar sáil
I *gceannas flaith 's* i *gcóimh-thigheas*
Le *Móirin* ni Chuillionáin."

This is a verse from the same poem, but not the one above translated.

Like a rAy went the mAiden
Still fAithful, but mOurning,
For ChARlie was pARting
From heARts that adOred him,
And sIghing besIde him
She spIed over Ocean
The Oarsmen befOre them
Approaching their lair." [1]

These beautiful and recondite measures were meant apparently to imitate music, and many of them are wedded to well-known airs. They did not all come into vogue at the same time, but reached their highest pitch of perfection and melody—melody at times exaggerated, too luscious, almost cloying—about the middle of the eighteenth century, at a time when the Irish, deprived by the Penal laws of all possibility of bettering their condition or of educating themselves, could do nothing but sing, which they did in every county of Ireland, with all the sweetness of the dying swan.

Dr. Geoffrey Keating, the historian, himself said to have been a casual habitué of the schools of the bards, and a close friend of many of the bardic professors, was nevertheless one

[1] *See* "Eachtraidh a' Phrionnsa le Iain Mac Coinnich," p. 270. The poem is by D. B. Mac Leóid. It looks like a later production, but will exemplify a not uncommon metre.

Gu cladach a' *chuain*
Ri *fuar*-ghaoth an Anmoich
Thriall TeArlach gan deAllradh
Air Allaban 's e sgìth,
Gun reull air a bhroIlleach
No freIceadan a fAlbh leis
Ach ainnir nan gòrm-shul
Bu dealbhaiche lìth.
Mar *dhaoimean* 'san *oidhche*
Bha(n) *mhaighdean* fu *thùrsa*
Si *cràiteach* mu *Thearlach*
Bhi *fàgail* a *dhùthcha* ;
Bu trom air a *h-osna*,
S bu *ghoirl* deòir a *sùilean*
Nuair chonnaic i 'n *iùbhrach*
A ' *dlùthadh* re tìr."

of the first to wring himself free from the fetters of the classical metres, and to adopt an accented instead of a syllabic standard of verse. We must now go back and give some account of this remarkable man, and of some of his contemporaries of the seventeenth century.

CHAPTER XL

PROSE WRITERS OF THE SEVENTEENTH CENTURY

DURING the first half of the seventeeth century, the Irish, heavily handicapped as they were, and deprived of the power of printing, nevertheless made tremendous efforts to keep abreast of the rest of Europe in science and literature. It was indeed an age of national scholarship which has never since been equalled. It was this half century that produced in rapid succession Geoffrey Keating, the Four Masters, and Duald Mac Firbis, men of whom any age or country might be proud, men who amid the war, rapine, and conflagration, that rolled through the country at the heels of the English soldiers, still strove to save from the general wreck those records of their country which to-day make the name of Ireland honourable for her antiquities, traditions, and history, in the eyes of the scholars of Europe.

Of these men, Keating, as a prose writer, was the greatest. He was a man of literature, a poet, professor, theologian, and historian, in one. He brought the art of writing limpid Irish to its highest perfection, and ever since the publication of his history of Ireland some two hundred and fifty years ago, the modern language may be said to have been stereotyped.

Born in Tipperary, not of a native Irish, but of an ancient

Norman family, as he takes care to inform us, he was at an early age sent to the Continent to be educated for the priesthood. There in the cloisters of some foreign seminary his young heart was early rent with accounts of robbery, plunder, and confiscation, as chieftain after chieftain was driven from his home and patrimony, and compelled to seek asylum and shelter from the magnanimous Spaniard. "The same to me," cries, in the hexameter of the Gael, some unhappy wanderer contemporaneous with Keating, driven to find refuge where he could, "the same to me are mountain or ocean, Ireland or the West of Spain, I have shut and made fast the gates of sorrow over my heart."[1] And there was scarcely a noble family in any corner of the island whose members might not have repeated the same. At this particular period there were few priests of note who had not received a foreign education, and few of the great houses who had not the most intimate relations with France and Spain: indeed in the succeeding century these two countries, especially France, stood to the Irish Celts in nearly the same familiar relation as England does at present.

After his return from Spain, Keating, now a doctor of divinity, was appointed to a church in Tipperary, where his fame as a preacher soon drew crowds together. Amongst these arrived one day—unluckily for Keating, but luckily for Ireland—a damsel whose relations with the English Lord President of Munster were said not to bear the strictest investigation, and it so chanced that the preacher's subject that day was the very one which, for good reasons, least commended itself to the lady. All eyes were directed against her, and she, returning aggrieved and furious, instigated Carew to at once put the anti-Popery laws in execution against Keating.

[1] "Ionann dam sliabh a's sáile
Eire a's iarthar Easpáine,
Do chuireas dúnta go deas
Geata dlúth ris an doilgheas."

Copied from a MS. in Trinity College. I forget its number.

The difficulties which the learned men of Ireland had to fight their way through, even from the first quarter of the seventeenth century, have scarcely been sufficiently understood or appreciated, but they are well illustrated in the case of Keating. It is usually assumed that the Penal laws did not begin to operate to the intellectual ruin of the Irish until the eighteenth century. But, in truth, the paths of learning and progress were largely barred by them after the first quarter of the seventeenth century. Already, as early as 1615, King James had issued a commission to inquire into the state of education in Ireland, and the celebrated Ussher, then Chancellor of St. Patrick's, was placed at the head ot it. Ussher was far and away the greatest scholar of the Pale in the seventeenth century, and his efforts in the cause of Irish antiquities have received deserved recognition from all native writers, and yet even Ussher appears to have shut up remorselessly the native schools wherever he found them, on the ground that the teachers did not conform to the established religion. Here is how he acted towards the father of the celebrated John Lynch, the learned antiquarian and author of the "Cambrensis Eversus,"[1] who was at the head of a native college in Galway.

"We found," says Ussher, "at Galway a publique schoolmaster, named Lynch, placed there by the cittizens, who had great numbers of schollers not only out of the province [of Connacht] but (even) out of the 'Pale' and other partes resorting to him. Wee had proofe during our continuance in that citty, how his schollers proffitted under him by the verses and orations which they presented us. Wee sent for that schoolemaster before us, and seriously advised him to conform to the religion established ; and not prevailing with our advices, *we enjoyned him to forbear teaching* ; and I, the Chancellour, did take recognizance of him and some others of his relatives in that citty, in the sum of 400 *li* sterling [at that time, fully equal to £2,000] to his Majesty's use, that from thenceforth he

[1] Published by the Celtic Society in 1848, in 3 vols., with a translation and copious notes.

should forbeare to teach any more, without the speciall license of the Lord Deputy."[1]

Twelve years later we find this enlightened and really great scholar lending all his authority to a pronouncement headed : "The judgment of divers of the Archbishops and Bishops of Ireland concerning toleration of Religion," in which he thus delivers himself :—

"The religion of the Papists is superstitious and idolatrous, their faith and doctrine erroneous and heretical ; their church in respect of both apostatical. To give them therefore a toleration is to consent that they may freely exercise their religion and profess their faith and doctrine, and is a grievous sin, and that in two respects :

"1. It is to make ourselves accessory not only to their superstitious idolatries and heresies, and in a word to all the abominations of Popery, but also (which is a consequent of the former) to the perdition of the seduced people which perish in the deluge of the Catholick apostacy.

"2. To grant them toleration in respect of any money to be given or contribution to be made by them, is to set religion at sale, and with it the souls of the people whom Christ our Saviour hath redeemed with His most precious blood," etc.

This document was signed by James Ussher, of Armagh, Primate, with eleven other bishops, and promulgated on the 23rd of April, 1627.[2]

It may have been in consequence of the fresh fillip thus given to a policy which had till then been largely in abeyance—for fear of provoking physical resistance—that Carew, already incited against Keating by his lady friend, sent out a force

[1] Regal Visitation Book, A.D. 1622, MS. in Marsh's Library, Dublin, quoted by D'Arcy McGee in his "Irish Writers of the Seventeenth Century," p. 85 ; but Hardiman, in his "West Connaught," no doubt rightly gives the date of this visitation as 1615. A writer in the "Dublin Penny Journal," identified this schoolmaster with the author of the "Cambrensis Eversus," but Hardiman shows that it must have been his father. *See* "West Connaught," p. 420 note.

[2] Elrington's great edition of Ussher's works in 17 vols., but I have not noted volume or page.

of soldiers to seize him and bring him a prisoner into Cork. Keating, however, received information of the design, and fled into the famous Glen of Aherlow, where he remained for some years effectually hidden. It was at this time, that finding himself unable to continue his priestly labours, he conceived the ambitious design of writing a history of Ireland from the earliest times down to the Norman Conquest. In pursuance of this intention he is said to have travelled in disguise up and down through the island to consult the ancient vellum books, at that time still preserved in the families of the hereditary brehons or in the neighbourhood of the ancient monasteries, which are said to have been everywhere gladly shown to him except in the province of Connacht and parts of Ulster, where some of the old families refused to allow him to inspect their books because he was a Norman by race and not a Gael!

"I conceive," says Keating, in his preface, "that my testimony ought the more readily to be admitted from the fact that I treat therein more particularly of the Gaels, and if any man deem that I give them too much credit, let him not imagine that I do so through partiality, praising them more than is just through love of my own kindred, for I belong, according to my own extraction, to the Old Galls or the Anglo-Norman race. I have seen that the natives of Ireland are maligned by every modern Englishman who speaks of the country. For this reason, being much grieved at the unfairness those writers have shown to Irishmen, I have felt urged to write a history of Ireland myself."

The value of Keating's history is very great to the student of Irish antiquity, not because of any critical faculty on the part of Keating himself, for (perhaps luckily) this was a gift he was not endowed with, but on account of the very lack of it. What Keating found in the old vellums of the monasteries and the brehons, as they existed about the year 1630—they have, many of them, perished since—he rewrote and redacted in his own language like another Herodotus. He invents nothing, embroiders little. What he does not find before him, he does not relate, *οὐδε γαρ οὐν λέγεται*, as is the formula of Herodotus. He composed his history in the south of Ireland, at nearly the same time that the Four Masters in the north of Ireland were collecting the materials for their annals, and though he wrote *currente calamo*, and is in matters of fact less accurate than they are, yet his history is an independent compilation made from the same class of ancient vellums, often from the very same books from which they also derived their information, and it must ever remain a co-ordinate authority to be consulted by historians along with them and the other annalists.[1]

The opening words of his history may serve as a specimen of his style. It begins thus—

"Whoever sets before him the task of inquiring into and investigating the history and antiquity of any country, ought to adopt the mode that most clearly explains its true state, and gives the most correct account of its inhabitants. And because I have undertaken to write and publish a history of Ireland, I deem myself obliged to complain of some of the wrongs and acts of injustice practised towards its inhabitants, as well towards the Old Galls [Anglo-Normans], who have been in possession of the country for more than four centuries since the English invasion, as towards the Gaels themselves, who have owned it for three thousand years. For there is no historian who has written upon Ireland since the English invasion, who does not strive to vilify and calumniate both Anglo-Irish colonists and the Gaelic natives. We have proofs of this in the accounts of the country given by Cambrensis, Spenser, Stanihurst,

[1] The books of ancient authority which Keating quotes as still existing in his own day, are the Psalter of Cashel, compiled by Cormac mac Culinan; the Book of Armagh, apparently a different book from that now so-called; the Book of Cluain-Aidnech-Fintan in Leix, the Book of Glendaloch, the Book of Rights, the [now fragmentary] Leabhar na h-Uidhre, the Yellow Book of Moling, the Black Book of Molaga. He also mentions the Book of Conquests, the Book of the Provinces [a book of the genealogies of the Gaelic tribes of each province], the Book of Reigns [said to have been written by Gilla Kevin, a bard of the eleventh century], the Book of Epochs, the Book of Synchronisms [by Flann of the Monastery], the Dinnseanchus [a book of the etymologies, and history of names and places, published from various MSS. by Whitley Stokes, in the "Folklore Review"], the Book of the Pedigrees of Women, and a number of others.

Hanmer, Camden, Barclay, Morrison, Davis, Campion, and all the writers of the New Galls [*i.e.*, later English settlers] who have treated of this country. So much so that when they speak of the Irish one would imagine that these men were actuated by the instinct of the beetle[1]; for it is the nature of this animal, when it raises its head in the summer to flutter about without stooping to the fair flowers of the meadow or to the blossoms of the garden—not though they be all roses and lilies—but it bustles hurriedly around until it meets with some disgusting ordure, and it buries itself therein. So it is with the above-named writers. They never allude to the virtues and the good customs of the old Anglo-Irish and Gaelic nobility who dwelt in Ireland in their time. They write not of their piety or their valour, or of what monasteries they founded, what lands and endowments they gave to the Church, what immunities they granted to the ollamhs, their bounty to the ecclesiastics and prelates of the Church, the relief they afforded to orphans and to the poor, their munificence to men of learning, and their hospitality to strangers, which was so great that it may be said, in truth, that they were not at any time surpassed by any nation of Europe in generosity and hospitality, in proportion to the abilities they possessed. Witness the meetings of the learned which they used to convene, a custom unheard of amongst other nations of Europe. And yet nothing of all this can be found in the English writers of the time, but they dwell upon the customs of the vulgar, and upon the stories of ignorant old women, neglecting the illustrious action of the nobility, and all that relates to the ancient Gaels that inhabited this island before the invasion of the Anglo-Normans."

Keating's history[2] was perhaps the most popular book ever written in Irish, and, as it could not be printed, it was propa-

[1] "Innus gur ab é nós, beagnach, an phrimpolláin do ghníd, ag scríobhadh ar Eirionchaibh."

[2] The first volume of Keating's History was published in Dublin by Halliday, in 1811, but that brilliant young scholar did not live to complete it. John O'Mahoney, the Fenian Head Centre, published a splendid translation of the whole work from the best MSS. which in his exile he was able to procure, in New York in 1866, but its introduction into the United Kingdom was prohibited on the grounds that it infringed copyright. Dr. Todd remarks on this translation, "notwithstanding the extravagant and very mischievous political opinions avowed by Mr. O'Mahoney, his translation of Keating is a great improvement upon the ignorant and dishonest one published by Mr. Dermod O'Connor more than a century ago,"—a foolish remark of Dr. Todd's, who must have

gated by hundreds of manuscript copies all over the island. He is the author of two other voluminous books of a theological and moral nature, called the "Key to the Shield of the Mass," and the "Three Shafts of Death." Keating was witty, and very fond of a good story. Here is a specimen which I translate from his latter work. Pirates were a familiar feature in the life of Keating's day, and he tells the following amusing tale of one engaged in this trade, probably an O'Driscoll. Talking of the fruit of this world Keating remarks that though it tastes sweet it ends bitterly.

THE STORY OF MAC RAICIN.

"I think it happens to many a one in this world as it did to the wild and ignorant Kerne from the west of Munster who went aboard a warship to seek spoils on the ocean. And he put ashore in England, and at the first town that they met on land the townspeople came to welcome them and bring them to their houses to entertain them, for the people of the town were mostly innkeepers. And the Kerne wondered at their inviting himself, considering that he did not know any of them. But he himself and some of the people who were with him went to the house of one of them, to the inn, and the people of the house were very kind to them for a week, so that what between the cleanliness of the abode, and the excellence of his bed, food, and drink, the Kerne thought his position a delightful one.

"However, when he and his company were taking their leave the innkeeper called the accountant he had, saying, '*make reckoning*,' that means in Irish, 'pay your bill,' and with that the accountant came, and he commenced to strip the people so that they were obliged to give full payment for everything they had had in the house while there, and they were left bare when they went away.

---

understood that most readers of Keating are to be found amongst men to whom his own political opinions thus unnecessarily vented, were equally "mischievous." Dr. Robert Atkinson published the Text of the "Three Shafts of Death" without a translation, but with a most carefully-compiled and admirable glossary in 1890. Keating's third work has never been published, but I printed some extracts from a good MS. of it lent me by the O'Conor Don in an American paper. My friend Mr. John Mac Neill has pointed me out what is apparently a fourth work of Keating's on the Blessed Virgin.

And, moreover, the Kerne wondered what was the cause of himself and the others being plundered like that, for before this he had never known food to be bought or sold.

"And when he came to Erin his friends began asking him to give an account of England. He began to tell them, and said that he never did see a land that was better off for food and drink, fire and bedding, or more pleasant people, and I don't know a single fault about it, says he, except that when strangers are taking leave of the people who entertain them, there comes down on them an infernal horrid wretch that they call Mac Rakeen[1] (make reckoning) who handles strangers rudely, and strips and spoils them."

Keating then draws the moral in his own way, "that land of England is the world; the innkeepers, the world, the flesh, and the devil; the Kerne, people in general; and Mac Rakeen the Death."

During the time when Keating was in hiding he is said to have visited Cork and to have transcribed manuscripts which he required for the purposes of his history almost under the very eyes of the Lord President himself, and to have visited Dublin in the same manner. After the departure of Carew he reappeared, and seems to have died quietly as parish priest of Tubrid in Tipperary about the year 1650.

Almost every native scholar produced by Ireland during the seventeenth century seems to have been hampered by persecution in the same way as Keating, and loud and bitter were the complaints of the Irish at the policy of the English Government in cutting them off from education. Peter Lombard, the Catholic Archbishop of Armagh, who died in 1625, and who wrote in Latin and published—of course abroad, he would not well do it at home—a "Commentary on the Kingdom of Ireland," assures his countrymen and all Europe that it had been the steady plan of the English Government to cut off education from the Irish, and to prevent them having a university of their own, despite the

[1] From the Kerne's, who was of course utterly ignorant of English, mistaking "make" for the Irish "Mac," it is plain that the ancient pronunciation of this word (Anglo-Saxon *macian*) had not then been lost.

keen longing which his countrymen had for liberal studies, and the way in which they had always hitherto distinguished themselves in them. Even, he asserts, whilst England was still Catholic, her policy had been the same, and when the question of an Irish university was being debated in the English Council it had no bitterer enemy than a celebrated Catholic bishop. When some one afterwards remonstrated with this dignitary for opposing a work at once so holy and so salutary as the establishment of a Catholic university in Ireland, the answer made him was that it was not as a Catholic bishop he opposed it, but as an English senator.[1] "Well for him," remarks Lombard grimly, "if in the council of God and his saints, when the severe sentence of the Deity is passed upon the bishop, the senator by a like display of nimble wit may escape it."

When the university, so long and so anxiously sought for, was actually founded, "most capacious, most splendid," as Lombard puts it, *at their expense*, in the shape of Trinity College, Dublin, and they found themselves excluded from its benefits, their indignation, as expressed by Lombard and others, knew no bounds.[2] But their indignation was of little use,

[1] "Cum Hiberni et bene sint affecti, et insigniter idonei ad studia literarum et liberalium artium, utpote ingeniis bonis et acutis passim præditi, non potuit hactenus obtineri unquam à præfectis Anglis ut in Hibernia Universitas studiorum erigeretur. Imò dum aliquando de eâ re etiam, Catholico tempore, in Concilio Angliæ propositio fieret, obstitit acerrimé unus e primariis Senatoribus, et ipse quidem celebris episcopus, quem cum postea alius quidam admoneret, mirari se quod is utpote episcopus Catholicus tam sanctum atque salutare opus impediret. Respondit ille se non ut Episcopum Catholicæ Ecclesiæ sed ut Senatorem regni Angliæ sententiam istam in concilio protulisse, quâ opus istud impediretur.

"Quod bene forte se haberet si in Concilio Dei et Sanctorum ejus quando de Episcopo severior daretur sententia, ab eâ, pari posset acumine Senator liberari" ("De Hibernia Commentarius." Louvain, 1632).

[2] "Toties requisita studiorum Universitas ante annos aliquot erectum fuit decreto Reginæ (tametsi sumptibus Indigenarum) juxta civitatem Dubliniensem, capacissimum et splendidissimum collegium, in quo ordinatum est ut disciplinæ omnes liberales traderentur, sed ab hæreticis magistris, quales cùm Hibernia nequaquam subministraret ex Anglia

because they could not back it by their arms, and when they did so, they were beaten by Cromwell, and their last state rendered twenty times worse than their first.

Mac Firbis was another native Irish author of great learning who wrote in Irish contemporaneously with Keating. He was himself descended from Dathi, the last pagan monarch of Ireland, and his family had been for time out of mind the hereditary historians of North Connacht. The great Book of Lecan was compiled by one of his ancestors. His own greatest surviving work is his Book of Genealogies which contains enough to fill thirteen hundred pages of O'Donovan's edition of the "Four Masters." This he compiled during the horrors of the Cromwellian war, simply as a labour of love, and in the hope that at least the names and genealogies of the nation might be saved to posterity out of what then seemed the ruin of all things. Another book of his was a catalogue of Irish writers.[1] Mac Firbis mentions that even in his own day he had known Irish chieftains who governed their clans according to the "words of Fithal and the Royal Precepts," that is, according to the books of the Brehon law. He also compiled or wrote out the "Chronicon Scotorum," apparently from old manuscripts preserved in his family. He compiled, too, a glossary of the ancients laws, of which only a fragment exists, and made copies of five other ancient glossaries and law tracts. He says himself, in his Book of Genealogies, that he had compiled a dictionary of the Brehon laws in which he had given

submissi sunt. Qui pro sua etiam propaganda et confirmanda religione, insuper acceperunt, et munus prædicandi doctrinam suam Evangelicam in civitate Dublinensi et mandatum exigendi juramentum, supremæ potestatis Reginæ in rebus ecclesiasticis, ab adolescentibus quos in literis instituebant," etc.

These extracts show the light in which the native Irish regarded the foundation of Trinity College.

[1] The late Mr. Hennessy I believe discovered and made a transcript of a portion of this book, which is in the Royal Irish Academy, but I have been unable to lay my hands on it.

extensive explanations of them. His genealogical volume is divided into nine books. The first treats of Partholan, the second of the Nemedians, the third of the Firbolg, the fourth of the Tuatha De Danann, the fifth of the Milesians, chiefly the Eremonians, the sixth of the Irians and the Eremonian tribes that went under the generic name of the Dal Fiatach, the seventh of the Eberians and of the Ithians of Munster, the eighth of the Saints of Ireland, and the ninth and last treats ot the families descended from the Fomorians, Danes, Saxons, and Anglo-Normans.

"Here," says Mac Firbis, "is the distinction which the profound historians draw between the three different races which are in Erin. Every one who is white of skin, brown of hair, bold, honourable, daring, prosperous, bountiful in the bestowal of property wealth and rings, and who is not afraid of battle or combats, they are the descendants of the sons of Milesius in Erin.

"Every one who is fair-haired, vengeful, large, and every plunderer, every musical person, the professors of musical and entertaining performances, who are adepts in all druidical and magical arts, they are the descendants of the Tuatha De Danann in Erin.[1]

"Every one who is black-haired, who is a tattler, guileful, tale-telling, noisy, contemptible, every wretched, mean, strolling, unsteady, harsh, and inhospitable person, every slave, every mean thief, every churl, every one who loves not to listen to music and entertainment, the disturbers of every council and every assembly, and the promoters of discord among people, these are of the descendants of the Firbolg, of the Gailiuns,[2] of Liogairné, and of the Fir Domhnann in Erin. But, however, the descendants of the Firbolg are the most numerous of all these.

"This is taken from an old book. And, indeed, that it is possible to identify a race by their personal appearance and dispositions I do not take upon myself positively to say, for it may have been true in the ancient times, until the race became repeatedly intermixed. For we daily see even in our own time, and we often hear it from our old men, that there is a similitude of people, a similitude of form, character, and names in some families of Erin compared with others."

[1] It must be observed that no Irish family is traced to a Tuatha De Danann ancestry.

[2] O'Curry. MS. Mat. p. 224. For a very different estimate of the Gailiuns or Gaileóins, *see* above p. 323.

Mac Firbis's book, which is an enlarged continuation down to the year 1650 or so, of the genealogical trees contained in the Books of Leinster, Ballymote, and Lecan, is as O'Curry remarks, perhaps the greatest national genealogical compilation in the world, and it is sad to think that almost every tribe and family of the many thousands mentioned in this great work has either been utterly rooted out and exterminated, or else been dispersed to the four winds of heaven, and the entire genealogical system and tribal polity, kept with such care for fifteen hundred years, has disappeared off the face of the earth with the men who kept it.

Lughaidh [Lewy] O'Clery, the great northern poet, ollamh and historian of the O'Donnells, who, in the "Contention of the Bards" opposed Mac Dairé, lived somewhat earlier than Keating and Mac Firbis. He has left behind him, written in the difficult archaic Irish of the professional ollamhs, an interesting life of Red Hugh O'Donnell, giving the history of the time from 1586 to 1602,[1] with a full account of his hero's birth, his treacherous capture and confinement in Dublin Castle, his escape and recapture, his second escape, and the hardships he underwent in returning to his people in Donegal, his inauguration as the O'Donnell, and his "crowded hour of glorious life," until his death at Simancas in 1608, poisoned as we now know almost to a certainty, from the publication of the State Papers, by an emissary of Mountjoy the Lord Deputy, and Carew the President of Munster. Of this, however, Lughaidh O'Clery had no suspicion, he only tells of the sudden and un-

[1] It is a mere accident that this valuable work has survived. The only known copy of it is in the handwriting of Lughaidh's son Cucogry, and the book was unknown to O'Reilly when he compiled his "Irish Writers." It was handed down in the O'Clery family until it came to Patrick O'Clery who lent it to O'Reilly, the lexicographer, some time after 1817, and, O'Reilly dying, the book was sold at his auction in spite of the protests of poor O'Clery. It is now in the Royal Irish Academy and has been edited by the late Father Denis Murphy, S.J., in 1893, whose translation I have for the most part followed. The text of this biography would fill about 150 pages of this book.

expected sickness which overtook O'Donnell and killed him after sixteen days, to the utter ruin of the cause of Ireland. Here is his account, which I give as a specimen of his style, of O'Donnell's preparations before the Battle of the Curlews:

"The occupation of O'Donnell's forces during the time that he was in this monastery was exercising themselves and preparing for the fight and for the encounter which they were called to engage in. They were cleaning and getting ready their guns, and drying and exposing to the sun their grain powder, and filling their pouches, and casting their leaden bullets and heavy spherical balls, sharpening their strong-handled spears and their war-pikes, polishing their long broadswords and their bright-shining axes, and preparing their arms and armour and implements of war."

O'Donnell's address to his soldiers is quite differently recorded from the way in which O'Sullivan Beare relates it; it is much less ornate and eloquent, but is probably far more nearly correct, for Lughaidh O'Clery may very well have heard it delivered himself, and it had not passed with him through the disfiguring medium of the Latin language.

"We, though a small number," said O'Donnell, "are on the side of the right as it seems to us, and the English whose number is large are on the side of robbery, in order to rob you of your native land and your means of living, and it is far easier for you to make a brave, stout, strong fight for your native land and your lives whilst you are your own masters and your weapons are in your hands, then when you are put into prison and in chains after being despoiled of your weapons, and when your limbs are bound with hard, tough cords of hemp, after being broken and torn, some of you half dead, after you are chained and taken in crowds on waggons and carts through the streets of the English towns through contempt and mockery of you. My blessing upon you, true men. Bear in your minds the firm resolution that you had when such insults and violence were offered to you (as was done to many of your race) that this day is the day of battle which you have needed to make a vigorous fight in defence of your liberty by the strength of your arms and by the courage of your hearts, while you have your bodies under your own control and your weapons in your hands. Have no dread nor fear of the great numbers of the soldiers of London, nor of the strangeness of their weapons and arms, but put your hope and confidence in the God of glory. I am certain if ye take to heart what I say the foreigner must be defeated and ye victorious."

O'Clery's summing up of the effects of the fatal battle of Kinsale, almost the only battle in which the Irish were defeated throughout the whole war, is pathetic.

"Though there fell," he writes, "but so small a number of the Irish in that battle of Kinsale, that they would not perceive their absence after a time, and, moreover, that they did not perceive it themselves then, yet there was not lost in one battle fought in the latter times in Ireland so much as was lost then.

"There was lost there, first, that one island which was the richest and most productive, the heat and cold of which were more temperate than in the greater part of Europe, in which there was much honey and corn and fish, many rivers, cataracts, and waterfalls, in which were calm productive harbours, qualities which the first man of the race of Gaedhal Glas, son of Niall, who came to Ireland beheld in it. . . There were lost, too, those who escaped from it of the free, generous, noble-born descendants of the sons of Milesius and of the prosperous, impetuous chiefs, of the lords of territories and tribes, and of the chieftains of districts and cantreds, for it is absolutely certain that there were never in Erin at any time together men who were better and more famous than the chiefs who were then, and who died afterwards in other countries one after the other, after their being robbed of their fatherland and their noble possessions which they left to their enemies on that battle-field. Then were lost besides, nobility and honour, generosity and great deeds, hospitality and goodness, courtesy and noble birth, polish and bravery, strength and courage, valour and constancy, the authority and the sovereignty of the Irish of Erin to the end of time."

An interesting prose work, evidently written by an eyewitness, exists of the wanderings of O'Neill and O'Donnell upon the Continent after they had fled from Ireland in 1607. It describes how they were driven by a storm past Sligo harbour and past the Arran islands, where they were unable to land for fear of the king's shipping then in Galway bay. For thirteen days they were hurried along by a tremendous storm. The narrator notes a curious incident which took place during the rough weather at open sea : two merlin falcons descended and alit upon the ship, which were caught by the sailors who kept and fed them ; they were ultimately given by O'Neill to the governor of a French town. After long buffeting by the storm and after hopelessly losing their way they fell in with three Danish ships who informed them that they were in Flemish waters. They were afterwards nearly wrecked on the coast of Guernsey, and finally, after twenty-one days at sea, they managed with the utmost difficulty to put in at "Harboure de Grace," on the French coast, just as their provisions had run out. Their reception by the French king, the machinations of the English ambassador against them, and their journey into Spain [1] are minutely described, evidently by some one who had been in their own company, probably a Franciscan friar. Their life and adventures in Spain are minutely recounted down to the period of O'Donnell's death, who was treacherously poisoned by an emissary from Carew, the President of Munster, with the sanction of Mountjoy, the Lord Deputy. It is noticeable that the Irish biographer entertained no suspicion of this foul crime, which has, as we have said, only come to light through the publication of the State Papers during the last few years.[2]

Another curious piece of historical narrative by a religious is the account given of the Irish wars from

[1] This interesting work, though drawn on by Father Meehan, seems to be unknown to Irish scholars. It contains 135 closely written pages. It was discovered in Colgan's cell at Louvain after his death, and is now amongst the uncatalogued manuscripts in the Franciscan's Monastery in Dublin, where it escaped the research of the late Sir John Gilbert, who catalogued their books for the Government, and of M. de Jubainville, who also spent some days in examining their MSS. I owe its discovery to the courtesy of the learned librarian, Father O'Reilly, who has permitted me to make a transcript of it for future publication.

[2] Here is a specimen of the language of this book : "Do rala ambasadoir rig Saxan sa gcath*raigh* in tan sin. Bui ag dénomh a landithill aidhmhillte *ocus* urchoide do na maithip dia madh eidir leiss. Teid sin a ndimhaoineass *ocus* a mitharbha, oir ni thug in Ri audiens no eisteacht go *feadh tri* lá do *acht* ag dhol dfiadhach gach laithe."

November, 1641, to January, 1647, by a northern friar called O'Mellon, who was an eye-witness of much of what he relates.[1]

Of a somewhat similar nature is the interesting account of Montrose's wars in the Book of Clanranald, a manuscript written in pure Irish and in Irish characters, by a Gael from the Islands, Niall Mac Vurich, the hereditary bard and historian of the Clanranald.[2] The Mac Vurichs, who are descended from a celebrated bard, Muireach O'Daly,[3] who fled into Scotland from O'Donnell about the year 1200, enjoyed the farm of Stailgarry and the "four pennies of Drimsdale, in South Uist, down to the middle of the last century, by virtue of their hereditary office." The object of Mac Vurich in writing the history of Montrose's campaign is to vindicate and extol the career of Alaster Mac Donald and the Gael. "Nothing," says the writer, "is here written except of the people whom I have seen myself and with a part of whose deeds I am acquainted from my own recollection." He gives detailed accounts of several of Montrose's battles in which the Gael, Irish and Scottish, were engaged. His account of the fight of Auldearn is an interesting specimen of his style. He tells us how Alaster Mac Donald, son of Coll Ciotach, son of Gillespie,[4] commanded on the right of the army that day, and was in the act of marshalling his foot when

---

[1] Here is a specimen of the language of this work which is much shorter than the account of O'Neill's and O'Donnell's wanderings; there is a fine copy of it made by O'Curry from the original in the Royal Irish Academy, which fills one hundred pages: "Fagbadh na croidheachta [what the English called *creaghts*] bochta, rugadar leo a ttoil féin diobh, an chuid do imthigh dona croidheachtaibh sios suas sair siar. Ann do marbhadh Cormac Ua Hagan mac Eoghain, oc oc as bocht! S do bhi Sior Feidhlinn a Cill Cainnigh an tan so. Do cuaidh cuid dinn don Breifni, cuid dinn go Conndae Arda Macha, co Conndae Tir Eoghain, co condae Luth," etc.

[2] Published in "Reliquiæ Celticæ," vol ii. p. 149, with an interesting introduction, but a most inaccurate translation.

[3] *See* pp 491–2 for an account of this O'Daly.

[4] These are the names alluded to by Milton in his famous sonnet, on

"a gentleman from Lord Gordon came with a message to him and spoke in this manner: 'Mac Donald, we have heard that there was an agreement and a friendship between our ancestors, and that they did not strike a blow against one another, whatever strife might have been between the other Scots and them; neither was the fame of any other tribe for valour greater than theirs; therefore, by way of renewing the agreement, I would wish to receive a favour from you, namely, an exchange of foot on the first day of my service to my earthly king, that is, you taking my foot forces and you sending me your own.

"That (arrangement) was promptly carried out by Alaster, son of Colla. He sent four score and ten of the veteran soldiers who had often been tested in great dangers in many places; and there came in their stead three hundred foot of the men of the Bog of Gight, Strathbogey, and the Braes,[1] who were not accustomed to skirmishing, hard conflict, or the loud, harsh noise of battle. Although that was a bad exchange for Alaster it was good for his men, for they were never in any battle or skirmish from which they came safer—it seemed to them that the cavalry of the Gordons had no duty to perform but to defend the foot from every danger!

"Alaster drew up his men in a garden which they had come to, and he found that there remained with him of his own men but two score and ten of his gentlemen. He put five and twenty of these in the first rank, and five and twenty of them in the rear rank, and drew up his three hundred foot of the Gordons in their midst and marched before them. The men who opposed him were the regiment of the laird of Lawers, well-trained men, and the gentlemen of Lewis along with them. The clamour of the fight began as is usual in every field of battle, which the foot who were behind Alaster son of Colla, could not well endure, for some of them would not hear the sough of an arrow or the whistling of a ball without ducking their heads or starting aside. Alaster's defence was to go backwards,

---

his *Tetrachordon*, which name, he says, the public could not understand.

> "Cries the stall-reader, 'Bless us! what a word on
> A title-page is this!' and some in file
> Stand spelling false while one might walk to Mile-
> End Green. Why it is harder, sirs, than *Gordon*,
> *Colkitto* or *Macdonnel* or *Galasp!*"

"Colkitto" is for Colla Ciotach, "left-handed Coll or Colla," and "Galasp" is Giolla-easpuig, now Gillespie. Alaster Mac Donald was killed at the battle of Cnoc na ndos by the renegade Murough O'Brien in 1647.

[1] "Do mhuinntir bhug na gaoithe, agus srathabhalgaidh agus bhraighe an mhachuire."

beckoning to his party with his hand to be of good courage and march on quickly while his gentlemen were entirely engaged in keeping their companies in order, but they failed to do it; and I knew men who killed some of the Gordons' foot in order to prevent them from flying. And when the enemy perceived this they prepared to attack them and charge. Alaster ordered his men then to gain the garden which they had forsaken before, but they were attacked with pikes and arrows and many of them were slain on every side of the garden before the party got into it. Alaster's sword broke, and he got another sword into his hand, and he did not himself remember who gave it to him, but some persons supposed it was his brother-in-law, Mac Cáidh [Davidson] of Ardnacross, who gave him his own sword. Davidson [himself], Feardorcha Mackay, and other good gentlemen fell at that time at the entrance of the garden who were waiting to have Alaster in before them."

Mac Vurich goes on to describe what happened to one of Alaster's gentlemen, Ranald Mac Ceanain of Múll, who found himself assailed by numbers of the enemy on the outside of this garden.

"He turned his face to his enemy, his sword was round his neck, his shield on his left arm, and a hand-gun in his right hand. He pointed the gun at them, and a party of pikemen who were after him halted. There happened to be a narrow passage before them, and on that account there was not one of his own party that had been after him but went before him. There was a great slaughter made of the Gordons' foot by the bowmen.[1] It happened at that moment that a bowman was running past Ranald, and he shooting at the Gordons. The bowman looked over his shoulder and saw the halt to which Ranald had brought the pikemen, and he turned his hand from the man that was before him, and aimed his arrow at Ranald, which struck him on the cheek, and he sent a handbreadth of it through the other cheek. Then Ranald fired the shot, but not at the bowman. He threw the gun away and put the hand to his sword, whilst his shield-arm was stretched far out from him in front, to defend himself against the pikes. He made an effort to get the sword, but it would not draw, for the belt turned round, and the sword did not

[1] "Do bhi marbhadh tiugh ag lucht bóghadh ga dhénamh ar na coisidhibh Gordonac[ha]." Readers of the "Legend of Montrose" will recollect the surprise and scorn with which Major Dugald Dalgetty learns that some of the Highlanders carried bows, but here we see the execution they wrought even in the hands of the Covenanters."

come out. He tried it the second time by laying the shield-hand under his [other] armpit against the scabbard of the sword, and he drew it out, but five pikes were driven into him between the breast and chin on his thus exposing (?) himself. However, not one of the wounds they gave him was an inch deep. He was for a while at this work, cutting at the pikes, and at all that were stuck in the boss of the shield. He set his back against the garden to defend himself, and was with difficulty working his way towards the door. The pikemen were getting daunted by all that were being cut, except one man who was striking at him desperately and fiercely. That man thought that he would keep his pike from being cut, and that his opponent would fall by him. Ranald was listening all the time to Alaster (inside the wall) rating the Gordons for the bad efforts they were making to relieve himself from the position where he was, and he was all the time step by step making for the door of the garden. At last when he thought that he was near the door he gave a high ready spring away from the pikeman, turning his back to him and his face to the door, stooping his head. The pikeman followed him and stooped his own head under the door, but Alaster was watching them and he gave the pikeman a blow, so that though he turned quickly to get back, his head struck against Ranald's thigh, from the blow Alaster gave him, and his body falls in the doorway and his head in the garden, and when Ranald straightened his back and looked behind him to the door, it was thus he beheld his adversary. The arrow that was stuck in Ranald was cut, and it was taken out of him, and he got it drawn away, and he found the use of his tongue all right, and power of speech—a thing he never thought to get again."

This book, which is in pure Irish, was meant to be read not only by the Highland Gaels, but by Irishmen as well, and indeed the Black Book of Clanranald was picked up on a second-hand bookstall in Dublin.

There were several other prose writers during the seventeenth century, whose books, unlike those of Keating, Mac Firbis, O'Clery, and others we have mentioned, had the good fortune to be printed, but their works are mostly religious. Florence Conry published in 1626 at Louvain a book called "the Mirror of the Pious"[1]; Hugh Mac Cathmhaoil, Archbishop of Armagh, published in 1618, also at Louvain, a book called "the Mirror of the Sacrament of Penance"[2]; Theobald Stapleton published

[1] "Sgathán an chrábhaidh." [2] "Sgathán Sacrameinte na h-Aithrighe."

at Brussels in 1639, a "Book of Christian Doctrine," one side Latin and the other Irish; Anthony Gernon published at Louvain in 1645, a book called "The Paradise of the Soul"[1]; Richard Mac Gilla Cody printed in 1667, a book on Miracles in Irish and English; Father Francis O'Mulloy published a long book called "The Lamp of the Faithful"[2] in Irish at Louvain in 1676, and in the following year his rare and valuable Irish Grammar in Latin and Irish, one half of which is dedicated to the subject of prosody, and is the fullest, most competent, and most interesting account which we have of the Irish classical metres as practised in the later schools, by one who was fully acquainted both with them and their methods.

Several minor romantic stories, mostly fabulous creations unconnected with Irish history, seem to have been written during this century, and many more were translated from French, Spanish, Latin, and possibly English.[3] Of the more important works of Michael O'Clery, we shall speak in the next chapter.

[1] "Párrthas an Anma." [2] "Lóchran na gcreidhmheach."

[3] In the MS. marked H. 2. 7. in Trinity College there is a story of Sir Guy, Earl of Warwick and Bocigam [Buckingham], and p. 348 of the same MS. another about Bibus, son of Sir Guy of Hamtuir. These must have been taken from English sources. Of the same nature, but of different dates, are Irish redactions of Marco Polo's travels, the Adventures of Hercules, the Quest of the Holy Grail, Maundeville's Travels, the Adventures of the Bald Dog, Teglach an bhuird Chruinn, *i.e.*, the Household of the Round Table, the Chanson de geste of Fierabras, Barlaam and Josaphat, the History of Octavian, Orlando and Melora, Meralino Maligno, Richard and Lisarda, the Story of the Theban War, Turpin's Chronicle, the Triumphs of Charlemagne, the History of King Arthur, the Adventures of Menalippa and Alchimenes, and probably many others.

CHAPTER XLI

THE IRISH ANNALS

WE have already at the beginning of this book had occasion to discuss the reliability of the Irish annals,[1] and have seen that from the fifth century onward they record with great accuracy the few events for which we happen to have external evidence, drawn either from astronomical discovery or from the works of foreign authors. We shall here enumerate the most important of these works, for though the documents from which they are taken were evidently of great antiquity, yet they themselves are only comparatively modern compilations mostly made from the now lost sources of the ancient vellum chronicles which the early Christian monks kept in their religious houses, probably from the very first introduction of Christianity and the use of Roman letters.

The greatest—though almost the youngest—of them all is the much-renowned "Annals of the Four Masters." This mighty work is chiefly due to the herculean labours of the learned Franciscan Brother, Michael O'Clery, a native of Donegal, born about the year 1580, who was himself descended from a long line of scholars.[2] He and another scion of

[1] *See* above pp. 38–43.

[2] For an account of how these O'Clerys came to Donegal see the interesting preface to Father Murphy's edition of the "Life of Red Hugh O'Donnell."

Donegal, Aedh Mac an Bháird, then guardian of St. Anthony's in Louvain, contemplated the compilation and publication of a great collection of the lives of the Irish saints.

In furtherance of this idea Michael O'Clery, with the leave and approbation of his superiors, set out from Louvain, and, coming to Ireland, travelled through the whole length and breadth of it, from abbey to abbey and priory to priory. Up and down, high and low, he hunted for the ancient vellum books and time-stained manuscripts whose safety was even then threatened by the ever-thickening political shocks and spasms of that most destructive age. These, whenever he found, he copied in an accurate and beautiful handwriting, and transmitted safely to Louvain to his friend Mac an Bháird, or "Ward" as the name is now in English. Ward unfortunately died before he could make use of the material thus collected by O'Clery, but it was taken up by another great Franciscan, Father John Colgan, who utilised the work of his friend O'Clery by producing, in 1645, the two enormous Latin quartos, to which we have already frequently alluded, the first called the "Trias Thaumaturga," containing the lives of Saints Patrick, Brigit, and Columcille; the second containing all the lives which could be found of all the Irish saints whose festivals fell between the first of January and the last of March. Several of the works thus collected by O'Clery and Colgan still happily survive.[1] On the break-up of the

[1] Copies of the lives of the following saints are still preserved in the Burgundian Library at Brussels, copied by Michael O'Clery, no doubt from vellum MSS. preserved at that time in Ireland. The Life of *Mochua* of Balla, the Life of St. Baithin (fragmentary), the Life of St. Donatus (fragmentary), the Life of St. *Finchua* of Bri Gabhan, the Life of St. Finnbharr of Cork, the Life of St. Creunata the Virgin, the Life of *St. Moling* (see above p. 210), the Life of *St. Finian* (see p. 196), the Life of St. Ailbhe, the Life of St Abbanus, the Life of St. Carthach (p. 211), the Life of St. Fursa (see above p. 198), the Life of St. Ruadhan (who cursed Tara, see p. 229), the Life of *St. Ceallach* (see p. 395), the Life of St. Maodhog or Mogue, the Life of St. Colman, the Life of *St. Senanus* (see p. 213), the Miracles of St. Senanus after his death, the Life of St. Caimin (see p. 214) in verse, the Life of St.

Convent of Louvain, they were transferred to St. Isidore's, in Rome, and in 1872 were restored to Ireland and are now in the Convent of the Franciscans, on Merchant's Quay, Dublin, a restoration which prompted the fine lines of the late poet John Francis O'Donnell.

> From Ireland of the four bright seas
> In troublous days these treasures came,
> Through clouds, through fires, through darknesses,
> To Rome of immemorial name,
> Rome of immeasurable fame :
> The reddened hands of foes would rive
> Each lovely growth of cloister—crypt—
> Dim folio, yellow manuscript,
> Where yet the glowing pigments live ;
> But a clear voice cried from Louvain
> " Give them to me for they are mine,"
> And so they sped across the main
> The saints their guard, the ship their shrine.

Before O'Clery ever entered the Franciscan Order he had been by profession an historian or antiquary, and now in his eager quest for ecclesiastical writings and the lives of saints, his trained eye fell upon many other documents which he could not neglect. These were the ancient books and secular annals of the nation, and the historical poems of the ancient

Kevin in prose, another Life of St. Kevin in verse, a third and different Life of St Kevin, the Life of St. Mochaomhog, the Life of *St. Caillin*, his poems and prophecies, the Poems of St. Senanus, *St. Brendan*, St. Columcille, and others, the Life of St. Brigid, the Life of St. Adamnan, the Life of St. Berchan, the Life of St. Grellan, the Life of St. Molaise, who banished St. Columcille (see above, p. 177), the Life of St. Lassara the Virgin, the Life of St. Uanlus, the Life of St. Ciaran of Clonmacnois and of St. Ciaran of Saighir, the Life of St. Declan, the Life of St. Benin, the Life of St. Aileran (see p. 197) the Life of *St. Brendan*. The lives of those saints which I have printed in italics are preserved on vellum elsewhere. Many more lives of saints doubtless exist. The father of the present Mac Dermot, the Prince of Coolavin, who was a good and fluent Irish speaker, had a voluminous Life of St. Atracta, or Athracht, and I believe of other saints' lives, on vellum, but on inquiring for it recently at Coolavin, I found it had been lent and lost. Many other old vellums have doubtless shared its fate.

bards. He indulged himself to the full in this unique opportunity to become acquainted with so much valuable material, and the results of his labours were two voluminous books, first the "Réim Rioghraidhe," or Succession of Kings in Ireland, which gives the name, succession, and genealogy of the kings of Ireland from the earliest times down to the death of Malachy the Great in 1022, and which gives at the same time the genealogies of the early saints of Ireland down to the eighth century, and secondly the "Leabhar Gabhála," or Book of Invasions,[1] which contains an ample account of the successive colonisations of Ireland which were made by Partholan, the Nemedians, and the Tuatha De Danann, down to the death of Malachy, all drawn from ancient books—for the most part now lost—digested and put together by the friar.

It was probably while engaged on this work that the great scheme of compiling the annals of Ireland occurred to him. He found a patron and protector in Fergal O'Gara, lord of Moy Gara and Coolavin, and with the assistance of five or six other antiquaries, he set about his task in the secluded convent of Donegal, at that time governed by his own brother, on the 22nd of January, 1632, and finished it on the 10th of August, 1636, having had, during all this time, his expenses and the expenses of his fellow-labourers defrayed by the patriotic lord of Moy Gara.

It was Father Colgan, at Louvain, who first gave this great work the title under which it is now always spoken of, that is, "The Annals of the Four Masters." Father Colgan in the preface to his "Acta Sanctorum Hiberniæ,"[2] after recounting

[1] There are several large fragments of other "Books of Invasions" in the Book of Leinster and other old vellum MSS., but when the Book of Invasions is now referred to, O'Clery's compilation is the one usually meant. It contains (1) the invasion of Ceasair before the flood; (2) the invasion of Partholan after it; (3) the invasion of Nemedh; (4) the invasion of the Firbolg; (5) that of the Tuatha De Danann; (6) that of the Milesians and the history of the Milesian race down to the reign of Malachy Mór.

[2] This great work was not the only one of the indefatigable Colgan. At his death, which occurred at the convent of his order in Louvain in 1658,

O'Clery's labours and his previous books goes on to give an account of this last one also, and adds :

"As in the three works before mentioned so in this fourth one, three [helpers of his] are eminently to be praised, namely, Farfassa O'Mulchonry, Perigrine[1] O'Clery, and Peregrine O'Duigenan, men of consummate learning in the antiquities of the country and of approved faith. And to these was subsequently added the co-operation of other distinguished antiquarians, as Maurice O'Mulconry who for one month, and Conary O'Clery who for many months, laboured in its promotion. But since those annals which we shall very frequently have occasion to quote in this volume and in the others following, have been collected and compiled by the assistance and separate study of so many authors, neither the desire of brevity would permit us always to quote them individually, nor would justice permit us to attribute the labour of many to one, hence it sometimes seemed best to call them the Annals of Donegal, for in our convent of Donegal they were commenced and concluded. But afterwards for other reasons, chiefly for the sake of the compilers themselves who were four most eminent masters in antiquarian lore, we have been led to call them the ANNALS OF THE FOUR MASTERS. Yet we said just now that more than four assisted in their preparation; however, as their meeting was irregular, and but two of them during a short time laboured in the unimportant and later part of the work, while the other four were engaged on the entire production, at least up to the year 1267 (from which the first part and the most necessary one for us is closed), we quote it under their name."

---

he left behind him the materials of three great unpublished works which are described by Harris. The first was "De apostulatu Hibernorum inter exteras gentes, cum indice alphabetico de exteris sanctis," consisting of 852 pages of manuscript. The next was "De Sanctis in Anglia in Britannia, Aremorica, in reliqua Gallia, in Belgio," and contained 1,068 pages. The last was "De Sanctis in Lotharingià et Burgundia, in Germania ad sinistrum et dextrum Rheni, in Italia," and contained 920 pages. None of these with the exception of a page or two have found their way back to the Franciscans' establishment in Dublin, nor are they—where many of the books used by Colgan lie—in the Burgundian Library in Brussels. It is to be feared that they have perished.

[1] In Irish Cucoigcriche, which, meaning a "stranger," has been latinised Peregrinus by Ward. I remember one of the l'Estrange family telling me how one of the O'Cucoigrys had once come to her father and asked him if he had any objection to his translating his name for the future into l'Estrange, both names being identical in meaning!

Michael O'Clery writes in his dedication to Fergal O'Gara, after explaining the scope of the work—

"I explained to you that I thought I could get the assistance of the chroniclers for whom I had most esteem in writing a book of annals in which these matters might be put on record, and that should the writing of them be neglected at present they would not again be bound to be put on record or commemorated even to the end of the world. All the best and most copious books of annals that I could find throughout all Ireland were collected by me—though it was difficult for me to collect them into one place—to write this book in your name and to your honour, for it was you who gave the reward of their labour to the chroniclers by whom it was written, and it was the friars of Donegal who supplied them with food and attendance."

The book is also provided with a kind of testimonium from the Franciscan fathers of the monastery where it was written, stating who the compilers were, and how long they had worked under their own eyes, and what old books they had seen with them, etc. In addition to this, Michael O'Clery carried it to the two historians of greatest eminence in the south of Ireland, Flann Mac Egan, of Ballymacegan, in the Co. Tipperary, and Conor mac Brody of the Co. Clare, and obtained their written approbation and signature, as well as those of the Primate of Ireland and some others, and thus provided he launched his book upon the world.

It has been published, at least in part, three times; first down to the year 1171—the year of the Norman Invasion—by the Rev. Charles O'Conor, grandson of Charles O'Conor, of Belanagare, Carolan's patron, with a Latin translation, and secondly in English by Owen Connellan from the year 1171 to the end. But the third publication of it—that by O'Donovan—was the greatest work that any modern Irish scholar ever accomplished. In it the Irish text with accurate English translation, and an enormous quantity of notes, topographical, genealogical, and historical, are given, and the whole is contained in seven great quarto volumes—a work of which any age or country might be proud. So long as Irish history exists, the "Annals of the Four Masters" will be read in O'Donovan's translation, and the name of O'Donovan be inseparably connected with that of the O'Clerys.

As to the contents of these annals, suffice it to say that like so many other compilations of the same kind, they begin with *the Deluge:* they end in the year 1616. They give, from the old books, the reigns, deaths, genealogies, etc., not only of the high-kings but also of the provincial kings, chiefs, and heads of distinguished families, men of science and poets, with their respective dates, going as near to them as they can go. They record the deaths and successions of saints, abbots, bishops, and ecclesiastical dignitaries. They tell of the foundation and occasionally of the overthrow of countless churches, castles, abbeys, convents, and religious institutions. They give meagre details of battles and political changes, and not unfrequently quote ancient verses in proof of facts, but none prior to the second century.[1] Towards the end the dry summary of events become more garnished, and in parts elaborate detail takes the place of meagre facts. There is no event of Irish history from the birth of Christ to the beginning of the seventeenth century that the first inquiry of the student will not be, "What do the 'Four Masters' say about it?" for the great value of the work consists in this, that we have here in condensed form the pith and substance of the old books of

[1] It is noteworthy that no poem is quoted previous to the reign of Tuathal Teachtmhar in the second century. After that onward we find verses quoted at the year 226 on the Ferguses, A.D. 284 on the death of Finn, A.D. 432 a poem by Flann on St. Patrick, at 448 another poem on Patrick, at 458 a poem on the death of King Laoghaire, in 465 a poem on the death of the son of Niall of the Nine Hostages, at 478 on the Battle of Ocha, which gave for five hundred years their supremacy to the House of Niall, and then more verses under the years 489, 493, 501, 503, 504, 506, 507, and so on. The poet-saint Beg mac Dé [*see* p. 232] is frequently quoted, as is Cennfaeladh, [p. 412] but the usual formula used in introducing verses is "of which the poet said," or "of which the rann was spoken," or "as this verse tells."

Ireland which were then in existence but which—as the Four Masters foresaw—have long since perished. The facts and dates of the Four Masters are not their own facts and dates. From confused masses of very ancient matter, they, with labour and much sifting, drew forth their dates and synchronisms and harmonised their facts.

As if to emphasise the truth that they were only redacting the Annals of Ireland from the most ancient sources at their command, the Masters wrote in an ancient bardic dialect full at once of such idioms and words as were unintelligible even to the men of their own day unless they had received a bardic training. In fact, they were learned men writing for the learned, and this work was one of the last efforts of the *esprit de corps* of the school-bred shanachy which always prompted him to keep bardic and historical learning a close monopoly amongst his own class. Keating was Michael O'Clery's contemporary, but he wrote—and I consider him the first Irish historian and trained scholar who did so—for the masses not the classes, and he had his reward in the thousands of copies of his popular History made and read throughout all Ireland, while the copies made of the Annals were quite few in comparison, and after the end of the seventeenth century little read.

The valuable but meagre *Annals of Tighearnach*, published by the Rev. Charles O'Conor with a rather inaccurate Latin translation, and now in process of publication by Dr. Whitley Stokes, were compiled in the eleventh century. Clonmacnois of which Tighearnach was abbot was founded in 544, and the Annals had probably for their basis, as M. d'Arbois de Jubainville remarks, some book in which from the very foundation of the monastery the monks briefly noted remarkable events from year to year. Tighearnach declares that all Irish history prior to the founding of Emania is uncertain.[1] Tighearnach himself died in 1088.

[1] See above, p. 42.

Another valuable book of Annals is the *Chronicon Scotorum*, of uncertain origin, edited for the Master of the Rolls in one volume by the late Mr. Hennessy, from a manuscript in the handwriting of the celebrated Duald Mac Firbis. It begins briefly with the legended Fenius Farsa, who is said to have composed the Gaelic language, "out of seventy-two languages." It then jumps to the year 353 A.D., merely remarking "I pass to another time and he who is will bless it, in this year 353 Patrick was born." At the year 432 we meet the curious record, "a morte Concculaind [Cuchulain] herois usque ad hunc annum 431, a morte Concupair [Conor] mic Nessa 412 anni sunt." Columcille's prayer at the battle of Cul Dremhne is given under the year 561, and consists of three poetic ranns. Cennfaeladh is another poet frequently quoted, and as in the "Four Masters," we meet with numerous scraps of poems given as authorities. On the murder of Bran Dubh, king of Leinster, which took place in 605, two verses are quoted curiously attributed to "an old woman of Leinster," "de quo anus Laighen locutus rand."

The *Annals of Ulster* cover the period from the year 431 to 1540. Three large volumes of these have been published for the Master of the Rolls, the first by Mr. Hennessy, the second and third by Dr. Mac Carthy. Some verses, but not many, are quoted as authorities in these annals also, from the beginning of the sixth century onward.

The *Annals of Loch Cé* begin at 1014 and end in 1590, though they contain a few later entries. They also are edited for the Master of the Rolls in two volumes by Mr. Hennessy. They contain scarcely more than half a dozen poetic quotations.

The *Annals of Boyle* contained in a thirteenth-century manuscript, begin with the Creation and are continued down to 1253. The fragmentary Annals of Boyle contain the period from 1224 to 1562.

The *Annals of Innisfallen* were compiled about the year

1215, but according to O'Curry were commenced at least two centuries before that period.

The *Annals of Clonmacnois* were a valuable compilation continued down to the year 1408. The original of these annals is lost, but an English translation of them made by one Connla Mac Echagan, or Mageoghegan, of West Meath, for his friend and kinsman Torlough Mac Cochlan, lord of Delvin, in 1627, still exists, and was recently edited by the late Father Denis Murphy, S.J.

These form the principal books of the annals of Ireland, and though of completely different and independent origin they agree marvellously with each other in matters of fact, and contain the materials for a complete, though not an exhaustive, history of Ireland as derived from internal sources.

It is very much to be regretted that no Irish writer before Keating ever attempted, with these and the many lost books of annals before him, to throw their contents into a regular and continuous history. But this was never done, and the comparatively dry chronicles remain still the sources from which must be drawn the hard facts of the nation's past, with the exception of those brief periods which have engaged the pens of particular writers, such as the history of the wars of Thomond, compiled about 1459 by Rory Mac Craith, or the Life of Red Hugh written a century and a half later by Lughaidh O'Clery, and the many historical sagas and "lives" dealing with particular periods, which are really history romanticised.

CHAPTER XLII

THE BREHON LAWS

ALTHOUGH treatises on law are not literature in the true sense of the word, yet those of Ireland are too numerous and valuable not to claim at least some short notice. When it was determined by the Government, in 1852, to appoint a Royal Commission to publish the Ancient Laws and Institutions of Ireland, those great native scholars O'Donovan and O'Curry (the only men who had arisen since the death of Mac Firbis who were competent to undertake the task) set about transcribing such volumes of the Irish law code as had escaped the vicissitudes of time, and before they died—which they did, unhappily, not long after they had begun this work—O'Donovan had transcribed 2,491 pages of text, of which he had accomplished a preliminary translation in twelve manuscript volumes, while his fellow labourer O'Curry had transcribed 2,906 pages more, and had accomplished a tentative translation of them which filled thirteen volumes. Four large volumes of these laws have been already published, and two more have been these very many years in preparation, but have not as yet seen the light.

The first two of the published volumes[1] contain the

[1] Published in 1865 and 1869.

Seanchus Mór [Shanăχus more], which includes a preface to the text, in which we are told how and where it was put together and purified, and the law of Athgabhail or Distress. The second volume contains the law of hostage-sureties, of fosterage, of Saer-stock tenure and Daer-stock tenure, and the law of social connexions. The third volume contains the so-called Book of Acaill, which is chiefly concerned with the law relating to torts and injuries. It professes to be a compilation of the dicta and opinions of King Cormac mac Art, who lived in the third century, and of Cennfaeladh, who lived in the seventh.[1] The fourth volume of the Brehon law consists of isolated law-tracts such as that on "Taking possession," that containing judgments on co-tenancy, right of water, divisions of land, and the celebrated *Crith Gabhlach* which treats of social ranks and organisation.

The text itself of the Seanchus Mór, which is comprised in the first two published volumes, is comparatively brief, but what swells it to such a size is the great amount of commentary in small print written upon the brief text, and the great amount of additional annotations upon this commentary itself. Whatever may have been the date of the original laws, the bulk of the text is much later, for it consists of the commentaries added by repeated generations of early Irish lawyers piled up as it were one upon the other.

Most of the Brehon law tracts derive their titles not from individuals who promulgated them, but either from the subjects treated of or else from some particular locality connected with the composition of the work. They are essentially digests rather than codes, compilations, in fact, of learned lawyers. The essential idea of modern law is entirely absent from them, if by law is understood a command given by some one possessing authority to do or to forbear doing, under pains and penalties. There appears to be, in fact, no sanction laid down in the Brehon law against those who violated its maxims, nor

[1] For him see above p. 412.

did the State provide any such. This was in truth the great inherent weakness of Irish jurisprudence, and it was one inseparable from a tribal organisation, which lacked the controlling hand of a strong central government, and in which the idea of the State as distinguished from the tribe had scarcely emerged. If a litigant chose to disregard the brehon's ruling there was no machinery of the law set in motion to force him to accept it. The only executive authority in ancient Ireland which lay behind the decision of the judge was the traditional obedience and good sense of the people, and it does not appear that, with the full force of public opinion behind them, the brehons had any trouble in getting their decisions accepted by the common people. Not that this was any part of their duty. On the contrary, their business was over so soon as they had pronounced their decision, and given judgment between the contending parties. If one of these parties refused to abide by this decision, it was no affair of the brehon's, it was the concern of the public, and the public appear to have seen to it that the brehon's decision was always carried out. This seems to have been indeed the very essence of democratic government with no executive authority behind it but the will of the people, and it appears to have trained a law-abiding and intelligent public, for the Elizabethan statesman, Sir John Davies, confesses frankly in his admirable essay on the true causes why Ireland was never subdued, that "there is no nation or people under the sunne that doth love equall and indifferent justice better than the Irish ; or will rest better satisfied with the execution thereof although it be against themselves, so that they may have the protection and benefit of the law, when uppon just cause they do desire it."

The Irish appear to have had professional advocates, a court of appeal, and regular methods of procedure for carrying the case before it, and if a brehon could be shown to have delivered a false or unjust judgment he himself was liable to damages. The brehonship was not elective ; it seems indeed in later times to have been almost hereditary, but the brehon had to pass through a long and tedious course before he was permitted to practise; he was obliged to be "qualified in every department of legal science," says the text; and the Brehon law was remarkable for its copiousness, furnishing, as Sir Samuel Ferguson remarks, "a striking example of the length to which moral and metaphysical refinements may be carried under rude social conditions." As a makeweight against the privileges which are always the concomitant of riches, the penalties for misdeeds and omissions of all kinds were carefully graduated in the interests of the poor, and crime or breach of contract might reduce a man from the highest to the lowest grade.

There is little intimation in the laws as to their own origin. Like the Common Law of England, to which they bear a certain resemblance, they appear to have been in great part handed down from time immemorial, probably without undergoing any substantial change. It is curious to observe how some of the typical test-cases carry us back as far as the second century. Thus the very first paragraph in the Law of Distress—one of the most important institutions among the Irish, for Distress was the procedure by which most civil claims were made good—runs thus:[1]

"Three white cows were taken by Asal from Mogh, son of Nuada, by an immediate seizure. And they lay down a night at Lerta on the Boyne. They escaped from him and they left their calves, and their white milk flowed upon the ground. He went in pursuit of them, and seized six milch cows at the house at daybreak. Pledges were given for them afterwards by Cairpre Gnathchoir for the seizure, for the distress, for the acknowledgment, for triple acknowledgment, for acknowledgment by one chief, for double acknowledgment."

But these things are supposed to have happened in the days

[1] This passage was already so old in the time of Cormac mac Cuilennáin or Culinan, who died in 907, that it required a gloss, for Cormac in his Glossary refers to the gloss on the passage.

of Conn of the Hundred Battles, yet the case remained a leading one till the sixteenth century.

The Brehon laws probably embody a large share of primitive Aryan custom. Thus it is curious to meet the Indian practice of sitting "dharna" or fasting on a debtor in full force amongst the Irish as one of the legal forms by which a creditor should proceed to recover his debt.[1] "Notice," says the text of the Irish law,

> "precedes every distress in the case of inferior grades, except it be by persons of distinction or upon persons of distinction; *fasting* precedes distress in their case. He who does not give a pledge to fasting is an evader of all. He who disregards all things shall not be paid by God or man. He who refuses to cede what should be accorded to fasting, the judgment upon him according to the Feini [brehon] is that he pay double the thing for which he was fasted upon, [but] he who fasts notwithstanding the offer of what should be accorded to him, forfeits his legal right to anything according to the decision of the Feini."

There were, according to Irish history, four periods at which special laws were enacted by legislative authority, first during the reign of Cormac mac Art in the third century, secondly when St. Patrick came, thirdly by Cormac mac Culinan the king-bishop of Cashel, who died in 903, and lastly by Brian Boru about a century later. But the great mass of the Brehon Code appears to have been traditionary, or to have grown with the slow growth of custom. None of the Brehon Law books so far as they have as yet been given to the public, shows any attempt to grapple with the nature of law in the abstract, or to deal with the general fundamental principles which underlie the conception of jurisprudence. A great number of the cases, too, which are raised for discussion in the law-books, appear to be rather possible than real, rather problematical cases proposed by a teacher to his students to be argued upon according to general principles, than as actual serious subjects for legal dis-

[1] See p. 229 for a case of fasting on a person.

cussion. This is particularly the case with a great part of the Book of Acaill.

The part of the Brehon Law called the Seanchus Mór was redacted in the year 438, according to the Four Masters, "the age of Christ 438, the tenth year of Laeghaire, the Seanchus and Feineachus of Ireland were purified and written." Here is how the book itself treats of its own origin:

"The Seanchus of the men of Erin—what has preserved it? The joint memory of two seniors; the tradition from one ear to another; the composition of poets; the addition from the law of the letter; strength from the law of nature; for these are the three rocks by which the judgments of the world are supported."

The commentary says that the Seanchus was preserved by Ross, a doctor of the Béarla Feini or Legal dialect, by Dubhthach [Duffach], a doctor of literature, and by Fergus, a doctor of poetry.

"Whoever the poet was that connected it by a thread of poetry before Patrick, it lived until it was exhibited to Patrick. The preserving shrine is the poetry, and the Seanchus is what is preserved therein." [1]

Dubhthach exhibited to Patrick—

"The judgments and all the poetry of Erin, and every law which prevailed among the men of Erin through the law of nature and the law of the seers, and in the judgments of the island of Erin and in the poets. . . . The judgments of true nature,' it tells us, 'which the Holy Ghost had spoken through the mouths of the brehons and just poets of the men of Erin from the first occupation of this island down to the reception of the faith, were all exhibited by Dubhthach to Patrick. What did not clash with the Word of God in the written law and in the New Testament and with the consensus of the believers, was confirmed in the laws of the brehons by Patrick and by the ecclesiastics and the chieftains of Erin; for the law of nature had been quite right, except the faith and its obligations, and the harmony of the church and the people—and this is the Seanchus Mór."

[1] Vol. i. p. 31.

M. d'Arbois de Jubainville,[1] however, has shown that the Seanchus Mór is really made up of treatises belonging to different periods, of which that upon Immediate Seizure is the oldest. While some of the other treatises must be of much later date, this tract, he has proved, cannot in its present form be later than the close of the sixth century, because it contains no trace of the right of succession accorded to women by an Irish council of about the year 600, while at the same time it cannot be anterior to the introduction of Christianity, because it contains mention of altar furniture amongst things seizable, and contains two Latin words, *altoir* (altar) and *cîs* (cinsus= census).[2] This, however, does not wholly discredit the tradition that St. Patrick had a hand in the final redaction of at least a part of the Seanchus Mór, for altars were certainly known in Ireland before Patrick, and the insertion of the clause about altar furniture may even have been due to the apostle himself. How far certain parts of the law may have reached back into antiquity and become stereotyped by custom before they became stereotyped by writing there is no means of saying. But, as M. d'Arbois de Jubainville has pointed out, the Seanchus Mór is closely related to the Cycle of Conor and Cuchulain, as the various allusions to King Conor, and to his arch-brehon Sencha, and to Morann the Judge, and to Ailill, and to the custom of the Heroes' Bit, show, while the cycle of Finn and Ossian is passed over.

There are many allusions to the Seanchus Mór in Cormac's Glossary, always referring to the glossed text, which must have been in existence before the year 900.[3] Again the text of the Seanchus Mór relies upon *judgments* delivered by ancient brehons

[1] "Cours de Littérature celtique," tome vii. "Études sur le droit Celtique," II. partie, chap. 2.

[2] Modern *cíos*, "rent." "Census," according to M d'Arbois de Jubainville, was pronounced "kêsus," and had a variant *cinsus* in Low Latin pronounced "cîsus," whence Irish *cîs* and German *Zins*.

[3] *See* under the words Athgabail, Flaith, Ferb, Ness, as Jubainville has pointed out.

such as Sencha, in the time of King Conor mac Nessa, but there is no allusion in its *text* to books or treatises. The gloss, on the other hand, is full of such allusions, and it is evident that in early times the names of the Irish Law Books were legion. Fourteen different books of civil law are alluded to by name in the glosses on the Seanchus, and Cormac in his Glossary gives quotations from five such books. It is remarkable that only one of the five quoted by Cormac is among the fourteen mentioned in the glosses on the Seanchus Mór, and this alone goes to show the number of books upon law which were in use amongst the ancient Irish, most of which have long since perished.

CHAPTER XLIII

THE EIGHTEENTH CENTURY

THE Irish of the eighteenth century being almost wholly deprived by law of all possibilities of bettering their condition, and having the necessary means of education rigidly denied them, turned for solace to poetry, and in it they vented their wrongs and bitter grief. I have met nothing more painful in literature than the constant, the almost unvarying cry of agony sent out by every one of the Irish writers during the latter half of the seventeenth and the first half of the eighteenth century.

There seems to have been very great literary activity amongst the natives in almost every county of Ireland during this period, and the poets it produced were countless; during this period, too, the Irish appear to have translated many religious books from French and Latin into Irish. In one way the work of the eighteenth century is of even more value to us than that of any earlier age, because it gives us the thoughts and feelings of men who, being less removed from ourselves in point of time, have probably more fully transmitted their own nature to their descendants—the Irish of the present day. Unhappily, however, though many volumes of the work of the eighteenth century have survived, yet countless others have been lost during the last fifty years, and the only body in Ireland competent to secure Irish manuscripts by purchase, takes unfortunately not the slightest heed of any modern Irish writings, which are daily perishing in numbers.

Of the poets of what I have called the New School, towards the end of the seventeenth century, the most noted was certainly David O'Bruadar, or Broder, whose extant poems would fill a volume. They are in the most various forms of the new metres, but their vocabulary and word-forms are rather those of the more ancient bards, which renders his poetry by no means easy of translation. He appears to have been the bard *par excellence* of the Williamite wars, and bitter is his cry of woe after the Boyne and Aughrim.

"One single foot of land there is not left to us, even as alms from the State; no, not what one may make his bed upon, but the State will accord us the grace—strange! of letting us go safe to Spain to seek adventures!

"They [the English] will be in our places, thick-hipped, mocking, after beating us from the flower of our towns, full of pewter, brass, plates, packages—English-speaking, shaven, cosy, tasteful.[1]

"There will be a beaver cape on each of their hags, and a silk gown from crown to foot; bands of churls will have our fortresses, full of Archys (?), cheeses and pottage.

"These are the people—though it is painful to relate it—who are living in our white moats, 'Goody Hook' and 'Mother Hammer,' 'Robin,' 'Saul,' and 'Father Salome'!

"The men of the breeches a-selling the salt,[2] 'Gammer,' 'Ruth,' and 'Goodman Cabbage,' 'Mistress Capon,' 'Kate and Anna,' 'Russell Rank,' and 'Master Gadder'!

"[They are now] where Déirdre, that fair bright scion used to roam, where Emer [3] and the Liath Macha [4] used to be, where Eevil [5]

---

[1] "Béidhid féin 'n ár n-áit go másach magaidh
D'éis ár sáruighthe, i mbláth ár mbailteadh,
Go péatrach, prásach, plátach, pacach,
Go béarla, beárrtha, bádhach (?) blasta."

[2] *I.e.*, Refusing hospitality except for payment.

[3] Cuchulain's wife.

[4] Cuchulain's grey steed. See p. 351, note.

[5] Aoibhioll [Eevil] of the Grey Crag, a queen of the Munster fairies. See p. 438, note, and p. 440, note.

used to be beside the Crag, and the elegant ladies of the Tuatha De Danann.

"Where the poet-schools, the bards, and the damsels were, with sporting, dance, wine and feasts, with pastime of kings and active champions."

For a moment, after the accession of James II. and during the viceroyalty of Tyrconnel, courage and hope returned to the natives. Their poetry, wherever preserved, is a veritable mirror wherein to read their transitions of feeling.

"Thanks be to *God*, this *sod* of misery
Is changed as *though* by a *blow* of wizardry;
James can *pass* to *Mass* in livery,
With priests in *white* and *knights* and chivalry."[1]

"Where goes John [*i.e.*, John Bull], he has no red coat on him [now], and no 'who goes there' beside the gate, seeking a way [to enrich himself], contentiously, in the teeth of law, putting me under rent in the night of misfortune.[2]

"Where goes Ralph and his cursed bodyguard, devilish prentices, the rulers of the city, who tore down on every side the blessed chapels, banishing and plundering the clergy of God.

"They do not venture [now] to say to us, 'You Popish rogue;' but our watchword is, 'Cromwellian Dog.'

"The cheese-eating clowns are sorrowful, returning every greasy lout of them to their trades, without gun, or sword, or arm exercise; their strength is gone, their hearts are beating. . . .

"After transplanting us, and every conceivable treachery, after transporting us over-sea to the country of Jamaica, after all whom they scattered to France and Spain.

"All who did not submit to their demands, how they placed their heads and hearts on stakes! and all of our race who were valiant in spirit, how they put them to death, foully, disgustingly!

"After all belonging to our church that the Plot hanged, and after the hundreds that have died in fetters from it, and all whom they

---

[1] This is the metre of the poem, a very common one among the New School. The poet is one Diarmuid Mac Carthy. I forget whence I transcribed his poem.

[2] "Cá ngabhann Seón ? ní'l cóta dearg air,
Ná " who goes there " re taebh an gheata 'ge,
Ag iarraidh slighe anaghaidh dlighe go spairneach,
Dom' chur fá chíos i n-oidhche an acarainn."

had deep down in the jail of every town, and all who were bound in the tower of London.

"After all their disregard for right, full of might and injustice, without a word [for us] in the law, who would not even write your name, but ever said of us 'Teigs and Diarmuids,' disrespectfully.

"There is many a Diarmuid *now*, both sensible and powerful! and many a Teig, too, both merry and jubilant! in the county of Eber, who is strong on the battlefield—the foreigners all everlastingly hated that name. . . .

"Friends of my heart, after all the thousands we lost, I cry impetuously to God in the heavens, giving thanks every day without forgetting, that it is in the time of this king[1] we have lived. . . .

"Having the fear of God, be ye full of almsgiving and friendliness, and forgetting nothing do ye according to the commandments; shun ye drunkenness and oaths and cursing, and do not say till death 'God damn' from your mouths," etc.

But Aughrim and the Boyne put an end to the dream that the Irish would ever again bear sway in their own land, and the carefully-devised Penal laws proceeded to crush all remaining independence of spirit out of them, and to grind away their very life-blood. Once more their poets fell back into lamentations over the past and impotent prophecies of the return of the Stuarts and the resurrection of Erin. Despite their sentimental affection for the paltry Stuarts, who ever used them as their tools, many of the poets were perfectly clear-sighted about them.

"It is the coming of King James that took Ireland from us,
With his one shoe English and his one shoe Irish.
He would neither strike a blow nor would he come to terms,
And that has left, so long as they shall exist, misfortune upon the Gaels."[2]

"Our case," says another poet, "is like the plague of Egypt; whoever chooses to break your lease, breaks it, and there is no good for you to go arguing your right."

---

[1] James II.

[2] "'Sé tigheacht Righ Séamas do bhain dínn Éire
Le n-a leath-bhróig gallda 's a leath-bhróig gaedhealach.
Ni thiubhradh sé buille uaidh ná réidhteacht
'S d'fág sin, fhad's mairid, an donas ar Ghaedhealaibh."

"King's rent, country's rent, clergy's rent, rent for your nose, rent for your back, rent for warming yourself, head-money at the head of every festival, hearth money, and money for readying roads![1]

"His goods are not taken from any one all at once, at one time; he must pay for being allowed to keep them first and be forced to sell them afterwards.

"If you happen to be alive, then you are the 'Irish rogue,' if you happen to be dead, then there's no more about you, except that your soul is [of course] in the fetters of pain, like the bird-flock that is among the clouds.

"It is the King of Kings—and King James, the Pope, the friars, and the fasting, and King Louis, who put Christendom under a settlement, that sent this ban upon the children of Milesius."

Every poet describes the condition of the native Irish in almost the same strains.

"Their warriors are no better off than their clergy; they are being cut down and plundered by them [the English] every day. See all that are without a bed except the furze of the mountains, the bent of the curragh, and the bog-myrtle beneath their bodies.

"Under frost, under snow, under rain, under blasts of wind, without a morsel to eat but watercress, green grass, sorrel of the mountain, or clover of the hills. Och! my pity to see their nobles forsaken!

"Their estates were estimated for, and are now in the hands of robbers, their towns are under the control of English-speaking bastards, their title deeds which were firm for a while, are now in the hands of foreigners, whose qualities are not mild.

"Their forts are under the sway of tradespeople; none of their fortresses is to be seen remaining for them, but black prisons and the houses of the fetters, and some of their heads parted from their tender bodies.

"And some of them in the clutch of famine so that they die, and some of them hunted to Connacht of the slaughter, [shut in], under the lock of the Shannon, not easy to open, and without provision to feed their mouths there—their warm dwellings under the control of the perjurers."

The feelings of the native Irish, smarting under the

[1] "Cíos righ, cíos tire, cíos cléire,
Cíos srôna, cíos tóna, cios teighte
Airgiod ceann i gceann gach féile
Airgiod teallaigh as bealaigh do réightiughadh."

I forget whence I copied this, but such pieces are innumerable

cowardice, selfishness, and incompetence of James II., were but moderately excited by the rather feeble attempt of his son to regain his father's kingdom by the sword. One or two stray bards, however, saluted his undertaking with poems:

> "Long in misery were we,
> No man free from English gall,
> Now our James is on the sea
> We shall see revenge for all.[1]
>
> Flowering branch of royal blood,
> Soon his bud shall burst to flame,
> James our friend is on the flood,
> Learned and good and first in fame.
>
> Luther's louts, and Calvin's clan,
> Every man who loved to lie,
> Boar-hounds of the bloody fang
> We shall see them hang on high.

But this and its fellows were only spasmodic rhapsodies. The Irish kept their real enthusiasm for the gallant attempt of Charles Edward, and the Jacobite poems of Ireland would, if collected, fill a large-sized volume.[2] So popular did Jacobite poetry become that it gave rise to a conventional form of its own,[3] which became almost stereotyped, and which seems to have been adopted as a test subject in bardic contests, and by all new aspirants to the title of poet. This form introduces the poet as wandering in a wood or by the banks of a river,

[1] "Fada sinn i ngalar buan
Faoi smacht cruaidh measg na nGall
O tá Séamas óg ar cuan
Bhéarfaid uatha díol d'á cheann," etc.

From a manuscript of my own.

[2] Hardiman printed about fifteen Jacobite poems in the second volume of his "Irish Minstrelsy," and O'Daly about twenty-five more in his "Irish Jacobite Poetry," 2nd edition.

[3] Or rather to the resurrection of an ancient theme long lost, for as Dr. Sigerson has shown, one of the Monks of St. Gall had already treated it in Latin nine hundred years before. See Constantine Nigra's "Reliquiæ Celticæ," and Dr. Sigerson's "Bards of the Gael and Gall," p. 413.

where he is astonished to perceive a beautiful lady approaching him. He addresses her, and she answers. The charms of her voice, mien, and bearing are portrayed by the poet. He inquires who and whence she is, and how comes she to be thus wandering. She replies that she is Erin, who is flying from the insults of foreign suitors and in search of her real mate. Upon this theme the changes are rung in every conceivable metre and with every conceivable variation, by the poets of the eighteenth century. Some of the best of these allegorical pieces are distinctly poetic, but they soon degenerated into conventionalism, so much so that I verily believe they continued to be written even after the death of the last Stuart. The possibility of a Jacobite rebellion gave rise to some fine war-songs also, calling upon the Irish to break their slumbers, but they were too exhausted and too thoroughly broken to stir, even in the eventful '45.

One of the earliest writers of Jacobite poetry, and perhaps the most voluminous man of letters of his day amongst the native Irish, was JOHN O'NEAGHTAN of the county Meath, who was still alive in 1715. One of his early poems was written immediately after the battle of the Boyne, when the English soldiery stripped him of everything he possessed in the world, except one small Irish book. Between forty and fifty of his pieces are enumerated by O'Reilly, and I have seen others in a manuscript in private hands.[1] These included a poem in imitation of those called "Ossianic," of 1296 lines, and a tale written about 1717 in imitation of the so-called Fenian tales, an amusing allegoric story called the "Adventures of Edmund O'Clery," and a curious but extravagant tale called the "Strong-armed Wrestler." Hardiman had in his possession a closely-written Irish treatise by O'Neaghtan of five hundred pages on general geography, containing many interesting particulars concerning Ireland, and a volume of Annals of Ireland from

[1] Bought by my friend Mr. David Comyn at the sale of the late Bishop Reeves's MSS.

1167 to about 1700.[1] He also translated a great many church hymns and, I believe, prose books from Latin. His elegy on Mary D'Este, widow of James II., is one of the most musical pieces I have ever seen, even in Irish—

> "**SLOW cause** of my fear
> **NO pause** to my tear.
> The brIghtest and whItest
> **LOW** lIes on her bier.
>
> **FAIR** Islets of green,
> **RARE** sIghts to be seen,
> Both hIghlands and Islands
> **THERE** sIgh for the Queen."

Torlough O'Carolan, born in 1670, and usually called "the last of the bards," was one of the best known poets of the first half of the eighteenth century. He was really a musician, not a bard, and his advent marked the complete break-down of the old Gaelic polity, according to which bard and harper were different persons. Carolan was born in Meath, but usually resided in Connacht, and having become blind from small-pox in his twenty-second[2] year he was educated as a harper, and achieved in his day an enormous renown. He composed over two hundred airs, many of them very lively, and usually addressed to his patrons, chiefly to those of the old Irish families. He composed his own words to suit his music, and these have given him the reputation of a poet. They are full of curious turns and twists of metre to suit his airs, to which they are admirably wed, and very few are in regular stanzas. They are mostly of a Pindaric nature, addressed to patrons or to fair ladies; there are some exceptions, however,

[1] In a MS. note by Hardiman in my copy of O'Reilly, he attributes to him a piece called "Jacobidis and Carina," and the "Battle of the Gap of the Cross of Brigit," which are unknown to me.

[2] In his fifteenth year, according to O'Reilly; his eighteenth, according to Hardiman's "Irish Minstrelsy," but Hardiman seems to have changed his opinion, for I have a note in his handwriting in which he states that Carolan was twenty-two years old when he became blind.

such as his celebrated ode to whiskey, one of the finest bacchanalian songs in any language, and his much more famed but immeasurably inferior "Receipt for Drinking." Very many of his airs and nearly all his poetry with the exception of about thirty pieces are lost.[1] He died in 1737 at Alderford, the house of the Mac Dermot Roe.

"When his death was known," says Hardiman, "it is related that upwards of sixty clergymen of different denominations, a number of gentlemen from the surrounding counties, and a vast concourse of country people, assembled to pay the last mark of respect to their favourite bard. All the houses in Ballyfarnon[2] were occupied by the former, and the people erected tents in the fields round Alderford House. The harp was heard in every direction. The wake lasted four days. On each side of the hall was placed a keg of whiskey, which was replenished as often as emptied. Old Mrs. Mac Dermot herself joined the female mourners who attended, 'to weep,' as she expressed herself, 'over her poor gentleman, the head of all Irish music.' On the fifth day his remains were brought forth, and the funeral was one of the greatest that for many years had taken place in Connacht."

Another good poet was TEIG O'NAGHTEN, who lived in Dublin, and is well known for a voluminous manuscript Irish-English dictionary, at which he worked from 1734 to 1749. Some twenty or thirty of his poems remain. Another learned poet and lexicographer was HUGH MAC CURTIN of the County Clare. With the assistance of his friend, a priest called Conor O'Begley, he produced a great English-Irish dictionary in Paris in 1732. He had previously published a grammar at Louvain in small octavo in 1728. This was no work to commend him to the powers that were, and he

[1] Hardiman has printed twenty-four of his poems in his "Ancient Irish Minstrelsy," and I printed about twelve more, mostly from manuscripts in my own possession. The late bookseller, John O'Daly, of Anglesea Street, had, I believe, a number of poems of Carolan in his possession, but the Royal Irish Academy did not buy them—or indeed any other of his unique stock of manuscripts—at his sale, and I fear they are now hopelessly lost.

[2] A small village on the border of the County Sligo.

appears to have been cast into prison, for in a touching note at p. 64 of the last edition of his grammar he asks the reader's pardon for confounding an example of the imperative with the potential mood, which he was caused to do "by the great bother of the brawling company that is round about me in this prison."[1] What became of him eventually I do not know.

Contemporaneous with him lived O'GALLAGHER, bishop of Raphoe, who had the unique distinction of publishing a book —a volume of Irish sermons—which went through over twenty editions. He, also, pursued letters in the midst of difficulties, at one time escaping from the English soldiers who were sent out to take him by the start of only a few minutes, the parish priest O'Hegarty of Killygarvan being captured in his stead, and promptly shot dead by the officer in command so soon as a rescue was attempted. His Irish is remarkable for its simplicity and its careless use of English and foreign words, carefully eschewed by men like Mac Curtin and O'Neaghtan.

Amongst the Southerns JOHN "CLÁRACH" MAC DONNELL was perhaps the finest poet of the first half of the eighteenth century, but his pieces have never been collected. It was in his house, near Charleville in the County Cork, that the poets of the south used to meet in bardic session to exercise their genius in public. He wrote part of a history of Ireland in Irish and translated a portion of Homer into Irish verse, but these are probably lost. He, too, cultivated letters under difficulty, and had, according to Hardiman, "on more occasions than one to save his life by hasty retreats from his enemies the bard-hunters." Some of his poems give dreadful

[1] O'Curtin's note runs—"As tré shiothbhuaireadh na cuideachtan cullóidighe atá timchioll orm annsa gcarcairse, do chuir mé an sompla déigheanach so do bheanas ris an Modh gcomhachtach so ionar ndiaigh, annso, san Modh foláirimh." This note was pointed out to me by my friend, Father Ed. Hogan, S.J., who has also been unable to trace the cause of Curtin's imprisonment, or his subsequent fate.

descriptions of the state of the Irish and the savage cruelty of their new masters. Here is how he describes one of them :—

"Plentiful is his costly living in the high-gabled lighted-up mansion of Brian, but tight-closed is his door, and his churlishness shut up inside with him, in Aherlow of the fawns, in an opening between two mountains, until famine cleaves to the people, putting them under its sway.

"His gate he never opens to the moan of the unhappy wretches, he never answers their groans nor provides food for their bodies; if they were to take so much as a little faggot or a scollop or a crooked rod, he would beat streams of blood out of their shoulders.

"The laws of the world, he used to tear them constantly to pieces, the ravening, stubborn, shameless hound, ever putting in fast fetters the church of God, and Oh! may heaven of the saints be a red-wilderness for James Dawson!" [1]

It would be impossible to enumerate here all the admirable and melodious poets produced—chiefly by the province of Munster—during the latter half of the eighteenth century and the beginning of this. A few of them, however, I must notice.

MICHAEL COMYN, of the County Clare, was the author of the prose story called "The Adventures of Torlogh, son of Starn, and the Adventures of his Three Sons,"[2] and he revived the Ossianic muse by his exquisite version—evidently based upon traditional matter—of "Ossian in the Land of the Young." [3]

BRIAN MAC GIOLLA MEIDHRE, or Merriman, whose poem of the "Midnight Court," contains about a thousand lines with four rhymes in each line, was another native of the County Clare. This amusing and witty poem, one certainly

[1] I printed the whole of this ferocious poem in the *Cork Archæological Journal*.

[2] Recently printed without a translation by Patrick O'Brien, of 46, Cuffe Street, Dublin.

[3] First printed nearly forty years ago by the Ossianic Society, and since then by my friend Mr. David Comyn, with a prose translation and glossary, and recently by my friend Mr. O'Flannghaoile, with translations in verse and prose.

not intended "virginibus puerisque," is a vision of Aoibhill [Eevil], queen of the Fairies of Munster, holding a court, where, when the poet sees it, a handsome girl is in the act of complaining to the queen that in spite of her beauty and fine figure and accomplishments she is in danger of dying unwed, and asking for relief. She is opposed by an old man, who argues against her. She answers him again, and the court finally pronounces judgment. Standish Hayes O'Grady once characterised this poem as being "with all its defects, perhaps the most tasteful piece in the language,"[1] and it is certainly a wonderful example of sustained rhythm and vowel-rhyme. It was written in 1781.

TADHG [TEIG] GAOLACH O'SULLIVAN, of the County Cork, was another of the most popular poets in his day. His earlier poems contained certain indiscretions for which, in later life, he made ample amends by devoting himself solely to religious poetry, and attempting to turn the force of public opinion against vice in every shape, especially drunkenness and immorality. A small volume of his religious poems, probably the best of the kind produced by any of the New School, was printed during his own lifetime in Limerick, and repeatedly afterwards, at Cappoquin, and I believe elsewhere, in Roman letters, and finally by O'Daly, of Anglesea Street, in Dublin, 1868. His poems are very musical and mellifluous, but abound in "Munsterisms," which make them difficult to readers from other provinces. He died in 1800.

Another fine poet of the County Clare was DONOUGH MAC

[1] *See* Ossianic Society, vol. iii. p. 36. It was printed with the following curious title-page, "Mediæ noctis consilium, auctore Briano Mac-Gilla-Meidhre, de comitatu Clarensi, in Momonia, A.D. MDCCLXXX. Poema heroico-comicum, quo nihil aut magis gracile aut poeticum aut magis abundans in hodierno Hiberniæ idiomati exolescit. Curtha a gclódh le Tomás mhic Lopuis ag Loch an chonblaigh Oghair, MDCCC." But both place and date are fictitious. It was almost certainly printed by O'Daly of Anglesea Street, for after his death I found amongst some papers of his the proof-sheets corrected with his own hand! My friend, Mr. Patrick O'Brien, of Cuffe Street, has since printed another edition with a brief vocabulary.

CONMARA, or Macnamara, as he is usually called in English. He was educated at Rome for the priesthood, but being of a wild disposition he was expelled from the ecclesiastical college there, and returning to Ireland, made his way to a famous school in the county Waterford at Slieve Gua, in the neighbourhood of which the people of the surrounding districts had for over a hundred years been accustomed to support "poor scholars" free of charge. He himself also opened a successful school, but a young woman of the neighbourhood, whom he had satirised, put a coal in the thatch and burnt him out. He led a rambling existence after that. He went to America and spent two summers and a winter in Newfoundland, which was then largely planted by the Irish. He appears to have also wandered a good deal about the Continent. The longest of his poems is a kind of mock Aeneid, describing his voyage to America and how the ship was chased by a French cruiser. Eevil, the fairy queen of Munster, brings him away in a dream to Elysium, where instead of Charon he finds "bald cursing Conan" the Fenian acting as ferryman. But he is best known by his beautiful lyric, "The Fair Hills of Holy Ireland," which he composed apparently when on the Continent. He led a ranting, roving, wild life, changed his religion a couple of times with unparalleled effrontery, but becoming blind in his old age, he repented of his sins and his misspent life, and died some time about the beginning of this century.[1] He was, like all these poets, a good scholar, as a Latin epitaph of fourteen verses, which he wrote over the pious Teig Gaolach proves—

> "Plangite Pierides, vester decessit alumnus,
> Eochades[2] non est, cuncta-que rura silent."

[1] His "Eachtra Giolla an Amarain" was published in 1853 by "S. Hayes," and recently with a number of his other poems translated into English, and republished with the late John Fleming's Irish life of the poet, by my friend Tomás O'Flannghaoile.

[2] *I.e.*, the descendant of Eochaidh Muighmheadhoin, father of Niall of the Nine Hostages. *See* above, p. 33.

Perhaps the best known at the present day of all the Munster poets is the witty, wicked OWEN ROE O'SULLIVAN from Slieve Luachra, in Kerry, whose sayings and songs have been proverbial for three generations, and whose fame has penetrated into many counties besides his own. All the poets I have mentioned hitherto, except perhaps the pious Teig Gaolach, were almost professional wits, but Owen Roe, to judge from the number of his *bons mots* that are still preserved, must have surpassed them all. All the poets I have mentioned were also Jacobite poets, but in elaboration of the usual Jacobite theme of the Lady Erin, Owen Roe is easily first. His denunciations of the foreigner were incessant. He was originally a working man, and laboured hard with plough and spade. His poem called the "Mower" is well known. His explanation of a Greek passage, which puzzled his employer's son fresh from a French college,[1] first brought him into repute, and he opened a school in the neighbourhood of Charleville as a teacher of Latin and Greek. As was the case with very many of the Munster bards, his passion for the frail sex was the undoing of him. He was denounced from the altar, and his school was given up. He died, still young, about the year 1784.

WILLIAM DALL O'HEFFERNAN, JOHN O'TOOMY "the Gay," ANDREW MAC GRATH (surnamed the Mangairè Súgach, or Merry Merchant, the frailest and wildest of all the bards), EGAN O'RAHILLY, of Slieve Luachra in Kerry, OWEN O'KEEFE, parish priest of Doneraile, and JOHN MURPHY, of Rathaoineach, are a few of the names that instantly suggest themselves to all readers of the Irish manuscripts of Munster.[2]

The north of Ireland produced a great number of poets also

[1] All the Irish of the eighteenth century had, when not *secretly* educated at home, to go abroad in pursuit of knowledge.

[2] Specimens of their poetry may be found in O'Daly's two excellent volumes, "The Poetry of Munster," and in his "Jacobite Relics" and in Walsh's "Popular Songs," but most of them are still in manuscript.

during the eighteenth century, of whom PATRICK LINDON and ART MAC CÚMHAIDH, both of the County Armagh, PHILLIP BRADY, of the County Cavan, and JAMES MAC CUAIRT, of the County Louth, a friend of Carolan's, were some of the best known, but owing to the fatal loss of Irish manuscripts, chiefly those of the northern half of Ireland, and the apparent determination of the Royal Irish Academy not to use any of the funds (granted by Government for the prosecution of Irish studies) in the preservation of any modern texts, it is to be feared that a great portion of their works and of those of at least a hundred other writers of the eighteenth century is now lost for ever.

It would be interesting to take a retrospect of the splendid lyrical outburst produced by our brothers of the Scotch Highlands contemporaneously with that of the poets I have just mentioned, but it would extend the scope of this work too much. There seems to me to be perhaps more substance and more simplicity and straightforward diction in the poems of the Scotch Gaels, and more melody and word play, purchased at the expense of a good deal of nebulousness and unmeaning sound, in those of the Irish Gaels; both, though they utterly fail in the ballad, have brought the lyric to a very high pitch of perfection.

In Connacht during the eighteenth century the conditions of life were less favourable to poetry, the people were much poorer, and there was no influential class of native schoolmasters and scribes to perpetuate and copy Irish manuscripts, as there was all over Munster, consequently the greater part of the minstrelsy of that province is hopelessly lost, and even the very names of its poets with the exception of CAROLAN, NETTERVILLE, MAC CABE, MAC GOVERN, and a few more of the last century, and MAC SWEENY, BARRETT, and RAFTERY of this century, have been lost. That there existed, however, amongst the natives of the province a most widespread love of song and poetry, even though most of their manuscripts have perished, is certain, for I have collected among them, not to speak of Ossianic lays and other things, a volume of love poems and two volumes of religious poems,[1] almost wholly taken from the mouths of the peasantry. This love of poetry and passion for song, which seems to be the indigenous birthright of every one born in an Irish-speaking district promises to soon be a thing of the past, thanks, perhaps partly, to the apathy of the clergy, who in Connacht almost always preach in English, and partly to the dislike of the gentry to hear Irish spoken, but chiefly owing to the far-reaching and deliberate efforts of the National Board of Education to extirpate the national language.

Upon the present century I need not touch. Its early years, during which Irish was the general language of the nation, witnessed little or no attempts at its literary cultivation, except amongst the people themselves, who, too poor to call the press to their aid, kept on copying and re-copying their beautiful manuscripts with a religious zeal, and producing poetry—but of no very high order—over the greater part of the country. Then came the famine, and with it collapse. In the *sauve-qui-peut* that followed, everything went by the board, thousands of manuscripts were lost, and the old literary life of Ireland may be said to have come to a close amidst the horrors of famine, fever, and emigration.

The advent of Eugene O'Curry and John O'Donovan, however, gave a great impetus to the work begun by O'Reilly and Hardiman, and men arose like Petrie and Todd to take a *literary* interest in the nation's past, and in the language that enshrined it. Meanwhile that language was fast dying as a living tongue without one effort being made to save it. It is only the last few years that have seen a real re-awakening of

[1] These are my "Religious Songs of Connacht," quoted more than once in this book as though published. They were meant to have been published simultaneously with it, but unfortunately the plates of both volumes were melted down, while I was revising these proofs, in the great fire at Sealy, Bryers and Walker's, Dublin.

interest amongst the people in their hereditary language, and the establishment of a monthly and a weekly paper, chiefly written in Irish.[1] The question whether the national language is to become wholly extinct like the Cornish, is one which must be decided within the next ten years. There are probably a hundred and fifty thousand households in Ireland at this moment where the parents speak Irish amongst themselves, and the children answer them in English. If a current of popular feeling can be aroused amongst these, the great cause—for great it appears even now to foreigners, and greater it will appear to the future generations of the Irish themselves—of the preservation of the oldest and most cultured vernacular in Europe, except Greek alone, is assured of success, and Irish literature, the production of which—though long dribbling in a narrow channel—has never actually ceased, may again, as it is even now promising to do, burst forth into life and vigour, and once more give that expression which in English seems impossible, to the best thoughts and aspirations of the Gaelic race.

[1] Conducted by the Gaelic League.

CHAPTER XLIV

THE HISTORY OF IRISH AS A SPOKEN LANGUAGE

WE must now follow the fortunes of the Irish language as a spoken tongue, "questo linguaggio difficile e davvero stupendo," as Ascoli calls it,[1] which after imposing itself upon both Dane and Norman, was brought face to face as early as the fourteenth century with its great competitor English, before which, despite its early victory in the contest, it has at last nearly but not quite gone down, after an unremitting struggle of nearly five centuries.

As early as the year 1360, the English appear to have taken the alarm at the inroads which the Irish language—at that time a much more highly-cultured form of speech than their own—had made upon the colonists, and we find King Edward issuing orders to the Sheriff of the Cross and Seneschal of the Liberty of Kilkenny in these terms[2]—

"As many of the English nation in the Marches and elsewhere have again become like Irishmen, and refuse to obey our laws and

[1] Preface to "Glossarium Palaeo-Hibernicum."

[2] Red Book in Archives of Diocese of Ossory. The statute is in the barbarous law-French of the period, "et si nul Engleys ou Irroies conversant entre Engleys use la lang Irroies entre eux-mesmes encontre cest ordinance, et de ceo soit attient, soint sez terrez," etc.

customs, and hold parliaments after the Irish fashion, and learn to speak the Irish tongue, and send their children among the Irish to be nursed and taught the Irish tongue, so that the people of English race have for the greater part become Irish; now we order (1) that no Englishman of any state or condition shall ... [under forfeiture of life, limbs, and everything else] follow these Irish customs, laws, and parliaments; (2) that any one of English race shall forfeit English liberty, if after the next feast of St. John the Baptist he shall speak Irish with other Englishmen and meantime *every Englishman must learn English* and must not have his children at nurse amongst the Irish."

In 1367, the last year of the administration of the Duke of Clarence, third son of Edward III, a parliament held at Kilkenny passed the famous act that inter-marriage with the Irish should be punished as high treason, and that any man of English race using the Irish language should forfeit all his land and tenements to the Crown, and forbidding also the entertainment of bards, ministrels, and rhymers.

These first attacks upon the language cannot possibly have produced much effect, for we find the English power within a hundred years after their passing, reduced to the lowest point, and there was scarcely an English or Norman noble in Ireland who had not adopted an Irish name, Irish speech, and Irish manners. The De Bourgo had became Mac William, and minor branches of the same stem had become Mac Philpins, Mac Gibbons, and Mac Raymonds; the Birminghams had became Mac Feóiris, the Stauntons Mac Aveeleys, the Nangles Mac Costellos, the Prendergasts Mac Maurices, the De Courcys Mac Patricks, the Bissetts of Antrim Mac Keons, etc.

A hundred years after the Statute of Kilkenny, the English, driven back into the Pale, which then consisted of less than four counties, passed a law in 1465, enjoining all men of Irish names within the Pale to take an English name, "of one towne as Sutton, Chester, Trym, Skryne, Corke, Kinsale; or colour as White, Black, Brown; or art or science as Cooke, Butler," and he and his issue were ordered to use these names or forfeit all their goods. This, however, the parliament was unable to carry through, none of the great Irish names within or alongside the Pale, Mac Murroughs, O'Tooles, O'Byrnes, O'Mores, O'Ryans, O'Conor Falys, O'Kellys, etc., seem to have been in the least influenced by it.

Next an attempt was made to maintain English in at least the seaports and borough towns, for we find an enactment of the year 1492–93 amongst the Archives of the Urbs Intacta, commanding that in Waterford, "no manner of man, freeman or foreign, of the city or suburb's dwellers, shall emplead nor defend in Irish tongue against any man in the court, but all they that any matters shall have in court to be administered, shall have a man that can speak English to declare his matter, except one party be of the country [*i.e.*, of Irish race] then every such dweller shall be at liberty to speak Irish."[1] Galway followed suit in 1520, and enacted that "no Irish judge or lawyer shall plead in no man's cause nor matter within this our court, for it agreeth not with the king's laws."[2]

How far these petty attempts were successful may be judged from the fact that Captain Ap Harry, a Welsh officer, describing in October, 1535, Lord Butler's march for the recovery of Dungarvan Castle, says, "We were met by his lordship's brother-in-law, Gerald Mac Shane, (Fitzgerald) Lord of the Decies, who, though a very strong man in his country, could speak never a word of English, but made the troops good cheer after the gentilest fashion that could be. All this journey from Dungarvan forth there is none alive that can remember that English man of war was ever in these parts." Still more striking is the statement that in the Dublin parliament of 1541, all the peers except Mac Gillapatric were of Norman or English descent, and yet not one except the Earl of Ormond could understand English.[3] A letter to the English Privy

[1] Municipal Archives of Waterford. Hist. MSS. Commission, 10th report. Appendix v. p. 323.

[2] Galway Archives. [3] "Ulster Journal of Archæology."

Council, written in 1569, by Dominicke Linche, of Galway, confirms this. "Even they of the best houses," he writes, "the brothers of the Erle of Clanrickarde, yea and one of his uncles, and he a bysshop, can neither speak nor understand in manner any thinge of their Prince's language, which language by the old Statutes of Galway, every man ought to learn and must speak before he can be admitted to any office within the Corporation."[1]

Nor had the extirpating policy succeeded even in the Pale, for we read in the State Papers that in the county of Kildare in 1534, "there is not one husbandman in effect that speaketh English nor useth any English sort nor manner, and their gentlemen be after the same sort." [2]

The great Earl of Kildare had nearly as many volumes of Irish as he had of English in his library. A catalogue of his books was drawn up in 1518. Amongst the Irish manuscripts were St. Berachán's book,[3] the Speech of Oyncheaghis (?) Cuchuland's Acts, the History of Clone Lyre, etc. Murchadh O'Brien, king of Thomond, promised Henry VIII. as early as 1547, when in London, that he and his heirs should use the English habit and manner, and to their knowledge the English language, and to their power bring up their children in the same.[4] And indeed that family seems to have been always the greatest prop of the English power in the South of Ireland. Thomas Moore, settling in Ireland in 1575, got his lands in King's County on the condition that his sons and servants "should use for the most the English tongue, habit, and government," and make no appeals to the Brehon law. Three years after this, in 1578, we find Lord Chancellor Gerard affirming that all the English, and the most part with delight,

[1] *See* "Journal of the Royal Society of Antiquaries of Ireland," 1897, p. 192.

[2] State Papers, part iii. vol. ii. p. 502.

[3] One of the four prophets of Ireland, *see* p. 210, note.

[4] Archdale ii, 27.

even in Dublin speak Irish, and greatly are spotted in manners, habit, and conditions with Irish stains.[1]

In the Vatican Library my friend Father Hogan found a MS. of about the year 1580 with a memorandum concerning certain Franciscan friars, three of whom spoke Irish only, including the Provincial who *preached all over Ireland*, five more knew Irish better than English, while five are entered as knowing English better than Irish, none are entered as knowing English only.

In 1585 the Irish chieftains of Hy Many, the O'Kellys country, agreed that "Teige mac William O'Kelly and Conor Oge O'Kelly shall henceforth behave themselves like good subjects and shall bring up their children after the English fashions and in the use of the English tongue."[3] Of course such enforced promises had no effect. We find in the State Papers that at St. Douay in 1600 were sixty young gentlemen, eldest sons of the principal gentlemen of the Pale, and that they all spoke Irish.[4]

In 1608 it was found that the superior of the Irish Jesuits, apparently a Pales-man, Father Christopher Holywood or Artane, near Dublin, could speak no Irish, and a document was sent at once to the General of the Jesuits, pointing out how this destroyed his usefulness in the Irish mission. Care was taken that the same mistake should not be made in appointing his successor, Robert Nugent.[5]

In 1609 we find Richard Conway, a Jesuit, writing that the English in Ireland took care that all [their own] children are taught English and chastise them if they speak their own native tongue[6] *(sic)*. Five or six years later Father Stephen

[1] Cal. of State Papers, p. 130.

[3] "Tribes of Hy Many," p. 20.

[4] State Papers, Dom. Eliz. an. 1600, p. 496.

[5] This was that Father Nugent who improved and developed the powers of the Irish harp. A letter in Irish to him from Maelbrighte O'Hussey is printed by Father Hogan, S.J., in "Ibernia Ignatiana," p. 167.

[6] Father Hogan's "Distinguished Irishmen of the Sixteenth Century," p. 38.

White writes, "Scarcely one in a thousand of the old Irish know even three words of any tongue except Irish, the modern Irish learn to speak Irish and English."[1]

Nevertheless the cause of the English language cannot have much progressed during the next fifty years, for we find in 1657 a petition presented to the Municipal Council of Dublin to the effect that "whereas by the laws all persons ought to speak and use the English tongue and habit,—contrary whereunto and in open contempt thereof, there is Irish commonly and usually spoken and the Irish habit worn not only in the streets and by such as live in the country and come to this city on market days, but also by and in several families in this city, to the scandalising of the inhabitants and magistrates of this city. And whereas there is much of swearing and cursing used and practised (as in the English tongue too much, so also in the Irish tongue)," etc. Irish, indeed, seems to have been the commonest language in Dublin at this time. James Howel in a letter written August 9, in 1630, says:

> "Some curious in the comparisons of tongues, say Irish is a dialect of the ancient British, and the learnedest of that nation in a private discourse I happened to have with him seemed to incline to this opinion, but I can assure your Lordship I found a great multitude of their radical words the same with the Welsh, both for sense and sound. The tone also of both nations is consonant, for when I first walked up and down the Dublin markets methought I was in Wales when I listened to their speech. I found the Irish tone a little more querulous and whining than the British, which I conjecture proceeded from their often being subjugated by the English."

During the Cromwellian wars most of the members of the Confederation of Kilkenny who took the side of the Nuncio Rinuccini knew little if anything of the English language, "qui," says Rinuccini in his MSS., "boni publici zelo flagrarent, plerique linguam quidem Ibernicam quia vernaculam,

[1] MS. in Royal Library of Brussels of Stephen White's "Vindiciæ," fo. 62. Consulted by Father Hogan, S.J.

bene, sed Anglicam male vel nullo modo callerent." When an order was issued by the Supreme Council for the new oath of association to be translated from English into Irish by each bishop for his diocese, it was found upon inquiry that some of the bishops did not understand a word of English. The Nuncio appears to have been very much impressed by the sweetness of the Irish language, but he had not leisure to devote himself to the study of it. Some of the Italian members of his household, however, became complete masters of it. Numbers of the poor people who had been plundered by the soldiery came to complain to him of their losses, and he notes in his diäry that their wail and lamentation in Irish was far more plaintive and expressive than any music of the great masters which he had ever heard among the more favoured nations of the Continent.[1]

Irish was at this time the usual "vehicle of business and of negociation with the natives, even amongst the learned," as we see in Carte's life of the Duke of Ormond, who was born in England in 1607 and educated as a Protestant by the Archbishop of Canterbury.

"The Duke," says Carte, "when about twenty or twenty-four years of age learned the Irish language by conversing with such Irish gentlemen as spoke it in London; he understood it perfectly well and could express himself well enough in familiar conversation, but considered himself not so well qualified as to discourse about serious matters; he afterwards on many occasions found himself at a great loss, as he had to negociate business of national importance with gentlemen who were far less intelligent in the English language than he was in the Irish. On such occasions he would use the same methods which he took with the titular bishop of Clogher, the great favourite of Owen O'Neil, and successor to that general in the command of the Ulster forces. This bishop he brought over to the king's interest, and gained his entire confidence by a conversation carried on between both parties in private. The Duke always spoke in English and the bishop in Irish, as neither understood the language

[1] "Transactions of the Ossory Arch. Society,' vol. ii. p. 350.

of the other so as to venture upon communicating his sentiments in it with any degree of accuracy or precision."[1]

The Irish themselves never neglected literature, and whenever their political star was in the ascendant the fortunes of their bards and learned men rose with it. Thus we find Rory O'More, the close friend of Owen Roe O'Neill, and the chief of the O'Mores of Leix, engaged in 1642 in an attempt to re-establish Irish schools and learning, and writing on the 20th of September, 1642, to Father Hugh de Bourgo at Brussels, "If we may, before Flan Mac Egan dies, we will see an Irish school opened, and therefore would wish heartily that these learned and religious fathers in Louvain would come over in haste with their monuments (?) and an Irish and Latin press." The Mac Egan here alluded to was the eminent Brehon and Irish antiquarian who lived at Bally-mac-Egan in the county Tipperary in Lower Ormond, whose imprimatur was considered so valuable that the Four Masters procured for their work his written approbation.[2] Seven years after this letter, the town of Wexford, from which O'More wrote in the interests of humanity and learning, sank in fire and ruin and its inhabitants both men and women were put to the sword in one universal massacre.

There were in the year 1650, forty-seven Jesuit priests in Ireland, according to a memorandum given me by Father Hogan, S.J., of these two—one from Meath the other from Kerry—spoke Irish only: and four from Dublin, all of course of English extraction, spoke English only, while the remaining forty-one spoke both languages. Seven of these bi-linguists were from Dublin and ten from Meath.

[1] Preface to Halliday's edition of Keating's "Forus Feasa," p. xi. The fine poet, David Bruadar (p. 592), wrote a satiric poem on the haste the Irish made to speak English when the Duke of Ormond was in power, two lines of which I quote from memory:

> "*Is mairg atá gan Bérla binn*
> *Ar dteacht an Iarla go h-Eirinn.*

[2] *See* above p. 578.

These instances show that Irish was the usual spoken language of the country, even in Dublin, but there are indications that the ardour with which it had been cultivated and the respect with which its professors had been regarded was dying out. Even as early as 1627 we find one Connla Mac Echagan of West Meath, translating the "Annals of Clonmacnois" into English,[1] and in his dedication to his friend and kinsman Torlogh Mac Cochlan, lord of Delvin, he says that formerly many septs lived in Ireland whose profession it was to chronicle and keep in memory the state of the kingdom, but, he adds, "now as they cannot enjoy that respect and gain by their profession, as heretofore they and their ancestors received, they set nought by the said knowledge, neglect their books, and choose rather to put their children to learn English than their own native language, insomuch that some of them suffer tailors to cut the leaves of the said books (which their ancestors held in great account) and sew them in long pieces to make their measures of, [so] that the posterities are like to fall into more ignorance of many things which happened before their time."

A little later, in 1639, Father Stapleton, in his "Doctrina Christiana," published in Irish and Latin—the first Irish book ever printed in Roman characters—throws the blame for the neglect of Irish literature first upon the Irish antiquarians "who have placed it under difficulties and hard words,[2] writing it in mysterious ways, and in dark difficult language," and secondly upon the upper classes "who bring their native natural language (which is powerful, perfect, honourable, learned, and sharply-exact in itself) into contempt and disrespect, and spend their time cultivating and learning other foreign tongues." [3]

[1] Published by the late Father Denis Murphy, S.J., for the Irish Antiquarian Society.

[2] I fear many of our moderns are also more or less open to this reproach.

[3] "Ar an adhbhar sin as cóir agus as iommochuibhe dúinne na Herenaig bheith ceanamhail gradhach onórach an ar dteangain ndúchais nádurtha

Peter Lombard, Archbishop of Armagh, in his book printed at Louvain in 1632, says that Irish is the language of the whole of Hibernia, but there were some differences of pronunciation in the various provinces, and between the learned and the common people, the universal opinion being that the people of Connacht spoke it best, they having both power of expression and propriety of phrase, while the men of Munster had the power of expression without the propriety, and the people of Ulster the propriety without the power of expression. The people of Leinster were considered deficient in both.[1]

O'Molloy in his "Lochrann na gCreidmheach," published in 1675, says that "no language is well understood by the common people of the island except Irish alone."[2] The students of the Irish College at Rome were at this time bound by rule to speak Irish, and an Irish book was to be read in the

féin, an ghaoilag, noch atá chomhfuelethach chomhmúchta soin, nach mór na deacha si as coimhne na nduine; a mhileán so as féidir a chur ar an aois ealathain noch as udair don teangain, do chuir i fá fórdhoreatheacht agus cruos focal, da scribha a modaibh agus fhocalaibh deamhaire doracha, dothuicseanta, agus ni fhoilid saor mórán d'ár nduinibh uaisle dobheir a tteanga dhuchais nadurtha (noch ata fortill fuirithe onórach fólamtha géarchuiseach inti féin) a ttarcuisne agus a neamhchionn, agus chaitheas a n-aimsir á saorthudh agus á foghlaim teangtha coimhtheach ele" (pp. 10 and 11, preface).

[1] "Tertio notandum quod hoc ipsum idioma sit vernaculum toti in primis Hiberniæ, tamsetsi cum aliquo discrimine tum quoad dialectum nonnihil variantem inter diversas provincias, tum quoad artificii observationem inter doctos et vulgares. . . . Et dialecti quidem variatio ita se habere passim æstimatur, ut cum sint quatuor Hiberniæ provinciæ Momonia Ultonia Lagenia Conactia, penes Conactes sit et potestas rectæ pronunciationis et phraseos vera proprietas, penes Momonienses potestas sine proprietate, penes Ultones proprietas sine potestate, penes Lagenos nec potestas pronunciationis nec phraseos proprietas."—"De Hibernia Commentarius," p. 7. Louvain, 1632. This shows the antiquity of the Irish saying, "tá ceart gan blas ag an Ulltach, ta blas gan ceart ag an Muimhneach, ni'l blas ná ceart ag an Laighneach, tá blas agus ceart ag an gConnachtach."

[2] "Ní maith tuigthear leis an bpobal gcoitcheann éinteangadh acht an ghaoidhealg amháin" (see p. 11). *See* also a mandate of the "Sacra Congregatio Visitationis."

refectory during dinner and supper,[1] and all candidates for the priesthood were directed by the Synod of Tuam, in 1660, to learn to read and write Irish well.

Sir William Petty, writing in 1672, has an interesting passage on the people of Wexford and of Fingal: "The language of Ireland is like that of the North of Scotland, in many things like the Welsh and Manques, but in Ireland the Fingallians" [the dwellers along the coast some miles north of Dublin] "speak neither English, Irish, nor Welsh, and the people about Wexford, though they speak in a language differing from English, Welsh, and Irish, yet it is not the same with that of the Fingallians near Dublin. Both these sorts of people are honest and laborious members of the kingdom." Petty's strictures upon the Irish language, of which he was utterly ignorant, and which he ludicrously asserts "to have few words," need not here be noticed. He appears to show, however, that the Irish had already begun to borrow some words from English, and expressed many of the "names of artificial things" in "the language of their conquerors by altering the termination and language only."

It need hardly be said that once the English Government got the upper hand in the seventeenth century, and placed bishops and clergy of its own in the sees and dioceses throughout Ireland, they made it a kind of understood bargain with their nominees that they should have no dealings and make no terms with the national Irish language. Bedell, who was an Englishman and had been created an Irish bishop, neglected this unwritten compact far enough to learn Irish himself and to translate, with the help of a couple of Irishmen, the Bible into Irish, and he also circulated a catechism in

[1] "Quando aderit Rector Hibernicus val alius linguæ peritus, legantur ad mensam ter in hebdomada, libri spirituales, in idiomati Hibernico compositi, ne alumni ejus obliviscantur."—Extracted from the "Archiv. Coll. Hib. Romæ," lib. xxiii., by Father Hogan, S.J.

English and Irish amongst the natives. He reaped his reward in the undying gratitude of the Irish and the equally bitter animosity of his own colleagues. Ussher, then primate, in answer to a pathetic letter of Bedell's asking what were the charges against him, said in his reply, "the course which you took with the Papists was generally cried out against, neither do I remember in all my life that anything was done here by any of us, at which the professors of the gospel did take more offense, or by which the adversaries were more confirmed in their superstitions and idolatry, whereas I wish you had advised with your brethren before you would aventure to pull down that which they have been so long a building,"[1] meaning the discrediting and destruction of the Irish language. The Irish, however, did not forget the efforts Bedell had made in behalf of their tongue, for, having taken him prisoner in the war of 1648, they treated him with every courtesy in their power, and when he died their troops fired a volley over his grave, crying out, *Requiescat ultimus Anglorum*, while a priest who was present was heard to exclaim with fervour, "*Sit anima mea cum Bedello.*"

Indeed, the attitude adopted by the Government and the bishops who were its loyal henchmen, placed the defenders of the Established Church in a very awkward and embarrassing position. They wanted to make Protestants of the people, but they could not talk to them nor preach to them. The only possible course for the bishops to pursue, supposing them to have been in earnest, and to have been ecclesiastics and not Government place-men, would have been to appoint Irish-speaking clergy under them, a thing which with scarcely an exception they utterly and obstinately refused to do. So that for a hundred and fifty years the native inhabitants of Ireland were obliged to pay a tenth of their produce to a foreign clergy whom they could not understand and who never troubled themselves to understand them. How gentlemen

[1] Elrington's "Life and Writings of Ussher."

and scholars like Ussher could take up the position they did, is marvellous. He declares with one breath that "the religion of the Papists is superstitious and idolatrous, their faith and doctrines erroneous and heretical, their church in respect of both apostatical, to give them therefore a toleration, or to consent that they may freely exercise their religion and profess their faith and doctrine is a grievous sin,"[1] and with the next breath he tells Bedell when he circulated books in the Irish language meant to convert these same Papists, that nothing was ever done "at which the professors of the gospel did take more offense." This can only be accounted for, so far as I can see, by strong social prejudice and race hatred. The desire to see the Irish and their language crushed and *in extremis* was stronger than the desire to make Protestants of them, and this feeling continued for at least a hundred and fifty years.[2] Even so late as the latter half of the eighteenth century we find Dr. Woodward, Protestant bishop of Cloyne, stating that "the difference of language is a very general (and where it obtains an *insurmountable*) object to any intercourse with the people," on the part of the Protestant clergy, but, he adds coolly, "if it be asked why the clergy do not learn the Irish language, I answer that it should be the object of Government rather to take measures to bring it into entire disuse,"[3] one of the most cynical avowals I can remember on the part of an Irish prelate as to what he was there for—not for the spiritual good of the people who paid him tithes,

[1] *See* above, p. 555.

[2] It was not, I think, until the tithe war took place, that the established clergy began to see anything irrational in their attitude. In 1834, however, the Hon. Power Trench, Archbishop of Tuam, wrote to Phillip Barron, of Waterford, editor of *Ancient Ireland*, a weekly magazine for the cultivation of the Irish language, regretting that in the whole of his diocese (where probably not one in twenty at that period understood a word of English) he had not outside of his own brother, a single clergyman who had "acquired a proficiency in the Irish language."

[3] "Present State of the Irish Church," seventh edition, 1787, p. 43, quoted by Anderson, in his "Native Irish."

but as the official tool of the Government to crush their nationality.

Even Dean Swift, so clear-sighted a politician where Ireland's financial wrongs were concerned, was in his policy towards the people's language quite at one with men like Ussher and Woodward. Yet he knew perfectly well that over three-fourths of the island he and his *confrères* were, so far as polemical arguments or conversion went, powerless either for good or evil. He was, like the other Protestant dignitaries of his day, a declared enemy of the Gaelic speech, which he considered prevented "the Irish from being tamed," and at one time he said he had a scheme by which their language "might *easily* be abolished and become a dead one in half an age, with little expense and less trouble." In another place he says, "it would be a noble achievement to abolish the Irish language in the kingdom, so far at least as to oblige all the natives to speak only English on every occasion of business, in shops, markets, fairs, and other places of dealing: yet I am wholly deceived if this might not be effectually done in less than half an age and at a very trifling expense; for such I look upon a tax to be, of only six thousand pounds to accomplish so great a work." Whatever the Dean's plan was, he did not further enlighten the public upon it, and the scheme appears to have died with him.

The absorbing power of Irish nationality continued so strong all through the seventeenth century that according to Prendergast many of the children of Oliver Cromwell's soldiers who had settled in Ireland could not speak a word of English.[1] It was the same all over the country. In 1760 Irish was so universally spoken in the regiments of the Irish Brigade that Dick Hennessy, Edmund Burke's cousin, learnt

[1] Robert Molesworth's "True Way to Make Ireland Happy," printed in 1697, is also quoted as an authority for this statement, but I have not been able to discover a copy of this book even in the Library of Trinity College.

it on foreign service.[1] Still later, during the Peninsular War, the English officers in one of the Highland regiments attempted to abolish the speaking of Gaelic at the mess table, but the Gaelic-speaking officers completely outvoted them. Irish was spoken at this time by *all the Milesian families of high rank*, except when they wished to deliberately Anglicise themselves. Michael Kelly, the musical composer and vocalist, who was born in Dublin in 1764, tells us in his "Reminiscences:"[2]—

"I procured an audience of the Emperor of Germany at Schoenbrunn, and found him with a half-dozen of general officers, among whom were Generals O'Donnell and Kavanagh, my gallant countrymen. The latter [he was from Borris in the Queen's County] said something to me in Irish which I did not understand, consequently made him no answer. The Emperor turned quickly on me and said, 'What! O'Kelly, don't you speak the language of your own country'? I replied, 'Please, your Majesty, none but the lower orders of the Irish people speak Irish.' The Emperor laughed loudly. The impropriety of the remark made before two Milesian Generals flashed into my mind in an instant, and I could have bitten off my tongue. They luckily did not, or pretended not to hear."

It is from the middle of the eighteenth century onward that the Irish language begins to die out. I doubt whether before that period any Milesian family either in Ireland or the Scotch Highlands spoke English in its own home or to its own children.

I have been at much pains to trace the decay of the language, and the extent to which it has been spoken at various periods from that day to this, and have consulted all the volumes of travellers and statisticians upon which I have been able to lay hands. The result, however, has not been very satisfactory so far as information goes. It is simply amazing that most Irish and many English writers, who have had to deal with Ireland from that day to this, have in their sketchy and

[1] Roche's "Memoirs of an Octogenarian."

[2] Vol. i. p. 263.

generally unreliable accounts of the island, its people, and its social conditions, simply ignored the fact that any other language than English was spoken in it at all. Perhaps the most trustworthy accounts of the anomalous condition of the Irish-speaking race in their own island are by foreigners who have recorded what they saw without prejudice one way or the other, whereas one cannot help thinking that English and Irish writers who, while going over the same ground, have yet absolutely ignored [1] all allusion to the question of language, did so because they found it a difficult and awkward question to deal with.

The first authorities I know of who speak of Irish as dying out are Dr. Samuel Madden, who, writing in 1738, states that not one in twenty was ignorant of English, and Harris, who, in his description of the county Down six years later, says that Irish prevailed only amongst the poorer Catholics. Both these statements, however, are preposterously exaggerated. In the very year that Madden wrote died O'Neill of Clanaboy, one of the best-known and most influential men of the county Down, and I found in the Belfast Museum the Irish manuscript of the funeral oration pronounced over his body,[2] and any O'Neill would probably at that period have turned in his grave had his funeral discourse been spoken in English.

Madden's statement that in 1738 nineteenth-twentieths of the population knew English is an incredible one and so utterly disproved by all the other evidence, that it is astonishing that so sound and careful a historian as Mr. Lecky should have accepted it as substantially true. The evidence upon the other side is overwhelming. Forty-seven years after Madden wrote this the German, Küttner, travelling through Ireland, wrote

[1] Thus on referring to a recent history of the County Sligo in two volumes by a distinguished author to see how far Irish prevailed in a certain barony, I find the fact that any other language than English either was or is spoken in Sligo, so far as I could see, quietly ignored. It is the same with most authors of local and county histories.

[2] I published this with a translation in the "Journal of Ulster Archæology."

a series of letters in which he distinctly says that he found the common people either did not understand English at all or understood it imperfectly.[1]

More than two generations had passed away after Madden's statement that nineteen-twentieths of the population knew English, when we find a Scotchman, Daniel Dewar, in a book entitled "Observations on the Character, Customs and Superstitions of the Irish," writing thus in 1812:—

"The number of people who speak this language [Irish] is much greater than is generally supposed. It is spoken throughout the province of Connaught by all the lower orders, a great part of whom scarcely understand any English, and some of those who do, understand it only so as to conduct business. They are incapable of receiving moral or religious instruction through its medium. The Irish is spoken very generally through the other three provinces except amongst the descendants of the Scotch in the north. It cannot be supposed that calculations on this subject should be perfectly accurate, but it has been concluded on good grounds that there are about two millions of people in Ireland [out of about six millions] who are incapable of understanding a continued discourse in English."

"I have always found," says Dewar, with much shrewdness, "that in places where gentlemen hostile to this tongue assured me there was not a word of it spoken, in these very districts I heard very little English." He gives an amusing account of the various contradictory objections that he found at that time urged against it.

"Some of the Anglo-Hibernians at that time (1808) strongly maintained that this dialect is so barbarous that it cannot answer the purpose of instruction, others that it would awaken the enthusiasm of the *Wild Irish* (as they call them) to make any attempt of this kind, and consequently that it might prove dangerous to the Government, and others, that they had no desire to be taught in Irish, and that it would be useless to send teachers among them for this purpose."

---

[1] "Das Englische wird vom gemeinen Volke entweder gar nicht oder sehr unvolkommen erlernt" ("Briefe Aus Irland," Leipzig, 1785, p. 214).

Dutton, in his statistical history of the county Clare, published in 1808, says that almost all the gentlemen of that county spoke Irish with the country people, but he adds, "scarcely one of their sons is able to hold a conversation in this language. The children of almost all those who cannot speak English are proud of being spoken to in English and answering in the same, even although you may question them in Irish. No Irish is spoken in any of the schools, and the peasants are anxious to send their children to them to learn English." This apparently does not refer to the hedge schools of the natives, but to the charter and other English schools. "I think the diversity of language and not the diversity of religion," writes Grattan, in 1811, "constitutes a diversity of people. I should be very sorry that the Irish language should be forgotten, but glad that the English language should be generally understood."[1] This seems to have been also the position taken up by his great rival Flood, who, when dying, left some £50,000 to Trinity College for the cultivation of the Irish language. Trinity College, however, never secured the money, and its so-called Irish professorship, lately established, in the fifties, is only an adjunct of its Divinity School, and paid and practically controlled, not by the college, nor by people in the least interested in the cultivation of Celtic literature, but by a society for the conversion of Irish Papists through the medium of their own language.

In 1825, that is eighty-seven years after Madden's statement that nineteen-twentieths of the population knew English, the Commissioners of Education in Ireland, in their first report laid before Parliament, state "it has been estimated that the number of Irish who employ the ancient language of the country exclusively is not less than 500,000, and that at least a million more, although they have some understanding of English and can employ it for the ordinary purposes of traffic, make use

[1] Grattan's "Miscellaneous Works," p. 321, edition of 1822.

of their [own] tongue on all other occasions as the natural vehicle of their thoughts."

Lappenberg, a German who travelled in Ireland, reckoned that out of a population of seven millions of inhabitants in 1835, four millions spoke Irish "als ihre Muttersprache."

In 1842 Mac Comber's "Christian Remembrancer," discussing the possibility of "converting" the Irish, says, "there are about 3,000,000 of Irish who still speak the Irish language and love it as their mother tongue," and "that part of the Irish population which still speaks and understands little else than Irish" is "nearly a third of the entire population of Ireland."

A German, J. C. Kohl, who travelled extensively in Ireland in 1843, shortly before the famine, says that in Clare the "children would run by the side of the car crying, 'Burnocks[1] halfpenny,' burnocks being an appellation applied to every stranger, and 'halfpenny' the only English that the little rogues seemed to know." The neglect of the use of Irish in the churches, which had even then set in, largely owing to the teaching and wishes of O'Connell and his parliamentarians, struck the German spectator as something astonishing, for apparently he could not understand how an ancient nation with whose fame all Europe had recently been filled owing to the exertions of O'Connell, should be casting away its national birthright. "The great city of Cork," he notes, "which lies in a district where much Irish is still spoken, contains only two churches where sermons are preached in Irish. A short time ago the Irish prisoners in Cork gaol petitioned the chaplain that he would preach his Sunday sermon to them in Irish."

This acute foreign observer gives a very interesting account of the state of the Irish language round Drogheda, a coast town some twenty miles north of Dublin, which is worth quoting

[1] "Burnocks" does not look like a real word. I have no idea what it means or it is meant for.

here since it accurately describes the condition of affairs over the greater part of Leinster sixty years ago, but which is now so absolutely extinct that few modern Irishmen could believe it except on the most unimpeachable testimony. "Drogheda," he writes, "is the last genuine Irish town, the suburbs of Drogheda are genuine Irish suburbs . . . and a great many people are to be found in the neighbourhood who speak the old Irish tongue more fluently and more frequently than the English." Kohl was hospitably entertained by a priest in Drogheda—whose name unfortunately he does not mention, but who appears to have been a man of superior intelligence. His house had several harps in it, and he was delighted by a young blind harper who first played Brian Boru's march for him, and then an air called the Fairy Queen. At Kohl's request the priest also sent for a reciter of Irish poetry, who asked what he would wish recited. "If you were to repeat all you know," said the priest, "we should have to listen all night, I suppose, and many other nights as well."

"The man," says Kohl, "began to recite and went on uninterruptedly for a quarter of an hour. His story, of which I, of course, understood not a word, but which my friendly host afterwards explained to me, treated of a Scottish enchantress named Aithura,[1] who forsaken by her Irish lover, Cuchullin, laid a cruel spell upon his son Konnell which compelled him by an irresistible enchantment, and entirely against his will, to follow, to persecute, to fight, and at last to destroy his father, Cuchullin. At the last moment, after stabbing his father to the heart in spite of the efforts by which he struggled to resist the horrible impulse of his destiny, his own heart broke in the struggle, and he and his father died together, while the revengeful spirit of the cruel enchantress hovered in exultation over the dying, repeating to her

[1] This is a singular distortion of the story of Aoife [Eefy] and the coming of her and Cuchulain's son, Conlaoch to Erin. *See* above p. 300.

treacherous lover the story of his inconstancy and her revenge." "I was glad," adds Kohl, "of assuring myself by oral demonstration of the actual existence of Ossianic poetry like this, at the present day. The reciter was, as I have said, a simple and ignorant man, with a good deal of the clown about him, and his recitation was as simple, unadorned, and undeclamatory as himself. Sometimes, however, when carried away by the interest of his story his manner and voice were animated and moving. At such times he fixed his eyes on his hearers as if demanding their sympathy and admiration for himself and his poem. Sometimes I noticed that the metre completely changed, and I was told that this was the case with all Irish poems, for that the metre was always made to suit the subject.[1] I also heard that the most beautiful part of this ballad was the dialogue of father and son upon the battlefield, but that a prose translation would give me no idea at all of its beauty."

The priest told him that "Ossianic poetry was very abundant in the neighbourhood of Drogheda." "This," he says, "I had heard before, and from all I heard in Ireland I am much inclined to believe—which indeed many have also conjectured—that Macpherson obtained the materials for his version of Ossian's poems from popular tradition and ballads of the North of Ireland. The whole Irish nation both in the south and north, is certainly much more imbued with the spirit of this poetry and still possesses many more traces of it than the Scottish people, whether of the Highlands or Lowlands." [2]

[1] This of course is a misapprehension.

[2] It is curious to observe that Kohl found the race of harpers by no means extinct in Ireland, and his testimony appears quite disinterested and trustworthy. "I afterwards heard," he says, "that piece (The Fairy Queen) on the pianoforte, but it did not sound half so soft and sweet as from the instrument of this blind young harper. . . . We were very much delighted with our harper who was certainly an accomplished artist, yet

Another very acute German traveller, Rodenberg, describes the people of Kerry as always speaking Irish among themselves in 1860, while their English was so bad that he could hardly understand it. He notices, however, that several words of corrupted English were interwoven with their Irish conversation, which so disgusted him that he remarks, "everything about these people is patchwork, their clothing, their dwellings, their language."[1] He reports at full length a most interesting conversation which he had with a priest near Limerick, who assured him that they had to pull down in order to build up, that is, pull down the edifice of the Irish language in which the people were denied education in order to build up a new education in the English language. "Nor is it," said the priest, "the first time that the Irishman has had to turn his hand

Ireland contains many of still greater ability and celebrity. The most celebrated of all, however, is a man named Byrne, blind also if I do not mistake. When, therefore, Moore sings—

"'The harp that once through Tara's hall
The soul of music shed
Now hangs as mute on Tara's wall
As if the soul were fled,'

his lamentation must not be literally understood." He also mentions that when he was in Drogheda "a concert was in preparation to be given next week at which seven harpers, mostly blind, were to play together."

An English tourist, C. R. Wild ["Vacations in Ireland," London, 1857], mentions meeting a harper at Leenane in Connemara in 1857, who requested permission to play to him during his meal. He describes him as "an ancient man bearing a small Irish harp such as were common in olden days; . . . the music produced was, for the most part, plaintive and slow, and the tones particularly soft and melodious." The priest who entertained Kohl had a number of harps in his house, but, unfortunately, the German says nothing of their size or shape. From these instances it would appear that the race of Irish harpers did not quite die out with those who assembled at Belfast at the close of the last century when Bunting secured so many of their airs, but that some lingered on till after the famine. How far these latter harpers could be regarded as the genuine descendants of the old race is doubtful.

[1] "Wenn sie unter sich sind so sprechen sie immer das naturale Irisch, aber auch das nicht mehr rein sondern mit corrumpirtem English durch-

against his most sacred things. Red Hugh of Donegal destroyed the house of his forefathers that the enemy might not make of it a fortress against his own people, but he wept while he destroyed it."[1]

In the Galway fish market Rodenberg could not hear a single word of English spoken. The population of Connacht was at this time a little under a million, and the census of 1861 showed that about one-tenth of the whole population were ignorant of English. The population of the city of Galway in this year was 23,787, of whom 3,511 were ignorant of English.

According to the census of 1891 something over three-quarters of a million people in Ireland were bi-linguists, and 66,140 could speak Irish only, thus showing that in thirty years Irish was killed off so rapidly *that the whole island contained fewer speakers in* 1891 *than the small province of Connacht alone did thirty years before.*

This extinguishing of the Irish language has not been the result of a natural process of decay, but has been chiefly caused by the definite policy of the Board of "National Education," as it is called, backed by the expenditure every year of many hundreds of thousands of pounds. This Board, evidently actuated by a false sense of Imperialism, and by an overmastering desire to centralise, and being itself appointed by Government chiefly from a class of Irishmen who have been steadily hostile to the natives, and being perfectly ignorant of the language and literature of the Irish, have pursued from the first with unvarying pertinacity the great aim of utterly exterminating this fine Aryan language.

The amount of horrible suffering entailed by this policy, and

woben. Alles an diesem Volke ist Fetzenwerk, ihre Kleidung, ihre Wohnung, ihre Sprache" ("Insel der Heiligen," vol. i. p. 185. Berlin, 1860).

[1] See Vol. ii. p. 9 for this interesting conversation in which the attitude of the typical Catholic priest towards his national language is shown.

the amount of hopeless ignorance stereotyped in hundreds of thousands of children, and the ruination of the life-prospects of hundreds of thousands more, by insisting upon their growing up unable to read or write, sooner than teach them to read and write the only language they knew, has counted for nothing with the Board of National Education, compared with their great object of the extermination of the Irish language, and the attainment of one Anglified uniformity. In vain have their own inspectors time after time testified to the ill results of denying the Irish-speakers education in their own language, in vain have disinterested visitors opened wide eyes of astonishment at schoolmasters who knew no Irish being appointed to teach pupils[1] who know no English. In vain have the schoolmasters themselves petitioned to be allowed to change the system, in vain did Sir Patrick Keenan (afterwards himself Chief Commissioner of National Education) address the Board saying, "the shrewdest people in the world are those who are bi-lingual, borderers have always been remarkable in this respect, but *the most stupid children I have ever met with* are those who were learning English while endeavouring to forget Irish. The real policy of the educationist would in my opinion be to teach Irish grammatically and soundly to the Irish-speaking people, *and then* to teach them English through the medium of their native language."[2] All in vain! Against the steady,

[1] In spite of the well-known opposition of the National Board the National Schoolmasters themselves as early as 1874 in their Congress unanimously passed the following resolution :—"The peasants in Irish-speaking districts have not English enough to convey their ideas, except such as relate to the mechanical business of their occupation. Hence they are not able in any degree to cultivate or impress the minds of their children (though often very intelligent themselves), who consequently grow up dull and stupid if they have been suffered to lose the Irish language or to drop out of the constant practice of it." This is *exactly* what I and every other spectator have found, and it means that the Board of National Education is engaged in replacing an intelligent generation of men by an utterly stupid and unintelligent one.

[2] Sir Patrick Keenan, C.B., K.C.M.G., who was for a time head of the Educational system in Ireland, and was employed by the Government to

unwavering, unrelenting determination to stamp out the Irish language which has been paramount in the Board ever since the days of Archbishop Whately, every representation passed unheeded, and it would appear that in another generation the Board—at the cost of unparalleled suffering—will have attained its object.

This is not the place to discuss the bearings of this question still less to drag in the names of individuals, but the reader who has followed the history of Irish literature to this will be perhaps anxious to have it continued up to date, and so I may as well here place on record what I and many others have seen with our own eyes over and over again.

An Irish-speaking family, endowed with all the usual intelligence of the Irish-speaking population, with a gift for song, poetry, Ossianic lays, traditional history, and story, send their children to school. A rational education, such as any self-governing country in Europe would give them, would teach them to read and write the language that they spoke, and that

report upon the plan of teaching the people of Malta in Maltese, reported to Parliament that the attempt to substitute English or Italian for Maltese in the schools was a fatal one. "Such a course wouid simply mean that the people are to get no chance, much less choice, of acquiring a knowledge either of their own or any other language." This is exactly true of spots in Ireland, and after his experiences in Donegal, Sir Patrick Keenan drew up the following memorial:—"1. That the Irish-speaking people ought to be taught the Irish language grammatically, and that school books in Irish should be prepared for the purpose. 2. That English should be taught to all Irish-speaking children through the medium of the Irish. 3. That if this system be pursued the people will be very soon better educated than they are now, or possibly can be *for many generations* upon the present system. And 4. That the English language will in a short time be more generally and purely spoken than it can be by the present system for many generations." When he became head of the National System of Education, Sir Patrick found himself unable to carry out his own recommendations without personal inconvenience, being probably afraid to offend his colleagues, and nothing has been since done to remove the scandal.

their fathers had read and spoken for fifteen hundred years before them. The exigencies of life in the United Kingdom would then make it necessary to teach them a second language—English. The basis of knowledge upon which they started, and which they had acquired as naturally as the breath of life, would in any fair system of education be kept as a basis, and their education would be built up upon it. They would be taught to *read* the Ossianics lays which they knew by heart before, they would be given books containing more of the same sort, they would be taught to read the poems, and they would have put into their hands books of prose and poetry of a kindred nature. They had picked up many items of information about the history of Ireland from their fathers and mothers, they would be given a simple history of Ireland to read. All this they would assimilate naturally and quickly because it would be the natural continuation of what they already in part possessed. But the exigencies of life in the United Kingdom makes it necessary to read English poems and English books, and to know something of English history also, this they would learn after the other.

Will it be believed, the Board of National Education insists upon the Irish-speaking child starting out from the first moment *to learn to read a language it does not speak.*[1] It is forbidden to be taught one syllable of Irish, easy sentences, poems, or anything else. It is forbidden to be taught one word of Irish history. Advantage is taken of *nothing* that the child knew before or that came natural to it, and the result is appalling.

Bright-eyed intelligent children, second in intelligence, I should think, to none in Europe, with all the traditional traits of a people cultured for fifteen hundred years, children endowed with a vocabulary in every-day use of about three thousand

[1] For many years the schoolmaster was not even allowed to explain anything in Irish to a child who knew no English! This rule, however, has been abrogated.

words [1] (while the ordinary English peasant has often not more than five hundred) enter the schools of the Chief Commissioner, to come out at the end with all their natural vivacity gone, their intelligence almost completely sapped, their splendid command of their native language lost for ever, and a vocabulary of five or six hundred English words, badly pronounced and barbarously employed, substituted for it, and this they in their turn will transmit to their children, while everything that they knew on entering the school, story, lay, poem, song, aphorism, proverb, and the unique stock-in-trade of an Irish speaker's mind, is gone for ever, *and replaced by nothing*.

I have long looked and inquired in vain, on all hands, for any possible justification of this system, and the more I have looked and inquired the more convinced I am that none such exists unless it be an unacknowledged political one. Its results at all events are only too obvious. The children are taught, if nothing else, to be ashamed of their own parents, ashamed of their own nationality, ashamed of their own names. The only idea of education they now have is connected not with the literary past of their own nation, but with the new board-trained schoolmaster and his school, which to them represent the only possible form of knowledge. They have no idea of anything outside of, or beyond, this. Hence they allow their beautiful Irish manuscripts to rot[2]—because

[1] Dr. Pedersen, a Dane, who recently resided for three months in the Arran Islands to learn the language that is there banned—at the present moment the only inhabitant in one of these islands, not counting coast-guards, who does not speak Irish is the schoolmaster!—took down about 2,500 words. I have written down a vocabulary of 3,000 words from people in Roscommon who could neither read nor write, and I am sure I fell 1,000 short of what they actually used. I should think the average in Munster, especially in Kerry, would be between 5,000 and 6,000. It is well known that many of the English peasants use only 300 words, or from that to 500.

[2] A friend of mine travelling in the County Clare sent me three Irish MSS. the other day, which he found the children tearing to pieces on the floor. One of these, about one hundred years old, contained a saga called the "Love of Dubhlacha for Mongan," which M. d'Arbois de Jubain-

the schoolmaster does not read Irish. They never sing an Irish song or repeat an Irish poem—the schoolmaster does not; they forget all about their own country that their parents told them—the schoolmaster *is not allowed to teach Irish history;* they translate their names into English—probably the schoolmaster has done the same; and what is the use of having an Irish name now that they are not allowed to speak Irish! Worst of all they have not only dropped their Irish Christian names, but they are becoming ashamed of the patron saints of their own people, the names even of Patrick

ville had searched the libraries of Europe for in vain. It is true that another copy of it has since been discovered, and printed and annotated with all the learning and critical acumen of two such world-renowned scholars as Professor Kuno Meyer and Mr. Alfred Nutt, both of whom considered it of the highest value as elucidating the psychology of the ancient Irish. The copy thus recovered and sent to me is twice as long as that printed by Kuno Meyer, and had the copy from which he printed been lost it would be unique. These things are happening every day. A man living at the very doors of the Chief Commissioner of National Education writes to me thus: "I could read many of irish Fenian tales and poems, that was in my father's manuscripts, he had a large collection of them. I was often sorry for letting them go to loss, but I could not copy the $\frac{1}{20}$th of them. . . . The writing got defaced, the books got damp and torn while I was away, I burned lots of them twice that I came to this country. . . . I was learning to write the old irish at that time; I could read a fair share of it and write a little." That man should have been taught to read and write his native language, and not practically encouraged to burn the old books, every one of which probably contained some piece or other not to be found elsewhere.

Even where the people had no manuscripts in common use amongst them, their minds were well-stored with poems and lays. A friend wrote to me from America the other day to interview a man who lived in the County Galway, who he thought had manuscripts. Not finding it convenient to do this, I wrote to him, and this is his reply: "Dear sir, about twenty years since I was able to tell about two Dozen of Ossian's Irish poems and some of Raftery's, and more Rymes composed by others, but since that time no one asked me since to tell one Irish story at a wake or by the fireside sine the old people died. Therefore when I had no practice I forgot all the storys that ever I had. I am old. Your most Humble Servant, Michael B."

Another writes: "I have no written manuscript. I had three poems about the dareg more [Dearg Mór] the first when he came to Ireland in search of his wife that shewed (?) him, when Gaul [Goll] faught him and

and of Brigit.[1] It is a remarkable system of education, and one well worth the minutest study that can be paid it, which

tied him he come to Ireland, a few years after, when he got older and stronger, and faught Gaul for 9 days in succession the ninth day Gaul killed him then in 18 years after his son called Cun [Conn] came to Ireland to have revenge and faught Gaul, and after eleven days fighting he was killed by Gaul. I had a poem called Lee na mna mora [Laoi na mná móire] or the poem of the big woman who faught Gaul for five days, but Osker [Oscar] kills her. I had the baptism of Ossian by St. Patrick the best of all and many others of Ossians' to numerous to mention now, I also had some poemes of Cucullan the death and the lady in English and in Irish I had the beetle in English and Irish and when fin [Finn] went to denmark in English and Irish and many other rymes of modern times. I seen some address in the Irish times last year where to write to some place in Dublin where Ossians poems Could be got but I forget the Number. The people that is living Now a days could not understand the old Irish which made me drop it altogether their parents is striving to learn their children English what themselves never learned so the boys and girls has neither good english or good Irish. Hoping your friends and well wishers are well, fare well old stock. M . . . ."

[1] This is the direct result of the system pursued by the National Board, which refuses to teach the children anything about Patrick and Brigid, but which is never tired of putting second-hand English models before them. Archbishop Whately, that able and unconventional Englishman, who had so much to do with moulding the system, despite his undoubted sense of humour, saw nothing humorous in making the children learn to repeat such verses as—

"I thank the goodness and the grace
Which on my birth have smiled,
And made me in these Christian days
A happy English child!"

and the tone of the Board may be gathered from this passage, I believe, which occurred in one of their elementary books: "On the east of Ireland is England, where the Queen lives. Many people who live in Ireland were born in England, *and we speak the same language, and are called one nation.*" The result of this teaching is apparent to every one who lives in Ireland, and does not shut his eyes. "God forbid I should handicap my daughter in life by calling her Brigid," said a woman to me once. "It was with the greatest difficulty I could make any of the Irish christen their children Patrick," said Father O'Reilly of Louisburgh to me, talking of his Australian mission. For the wholesale translation of names, such as O'Gara into Love, O'Lavin into Hand, Mac Rury into Rogers, and so on, which is still going on with unabated vigour, see an article by me in "Three Irish Essays," published by Fisher Unwin.

is able to produce these effects, but with even the smallest philological regard for the meaning of words, it cannot be called "education."

Ar n-a críochnughadh ag Ráth-Treagh anaice le Dúngar, i bparráiste Tigh-Baoithin i gcondae Roscomáin, an ficheadh lá Lúghnasa, le Dúbhglas de h-Íde, d'á ngoirthear go coitchionn an Craoibhín Aoibhinn, de phór na nGall-Ghaedhal i n-Eirinn.

Buidheachas le Dia !

CRÍOCH.

INDEX

[N.B. The introduction to this edition is not indexed.]

A

L

M